PROCEDURAL LAW OF THE EUROPEAN UNION

By

KOEN LENAERTS
Professor of European Law, Katholieke Universiteit Leuven (Belgium)
Judge in the Court of First Instance of the European Communities

And

DIRK ARTS
Advocaat, Member of the Brussels Bar

ROBERT BRAY, EDITOR
Legal Service of the European Parliament, Brussels

LONDON
SWEET & MAXWELL
1999

Published in 1999 by
Sweet & Maxwell
100 Avenue Road
Swiss Cottage
London NW3 3PF
(http://www.smlawpub.co.uk)

Computerset by LBJ Typesetting Ltd
of Kingsclere

Printed in England
by Clays Ltd, St Ives plc, St Ives

ISBN 0–421–65170–9

FOREWORD

There are already some very good books on European Union procedural law which give clear guidance to practitioners on the application of the basic rules.

This book is different in the sense that it really sets out to examine the principles on which such rules are based and to give a detailed exposition of the way in which the Court applies the rules. It will prove to be a valuable book from which to teach a course on litigation before the European Court and the Court of First Instance. Students will find it readable and stimulating—not here, to use Lord Wilberforce's famous phrase, mere "tabulated legalism" but a serious analysis of "how?" and "why?".

At the same time it is not only an "academic" book. It will give practitioners and judges a real understanding of the way things work not only at the Court itself but in the dialogue between national courts and the European Court through the reference procedure. There is, for example, a helpful discussion as to how the decision to refer should be taken and how the provisions of paragraph 3 of Article 234 of the Treaty (Final Courts) should be applied. (In the latter case the authors are generous about the judgment in *CILFIT*). The Court's jurisprudence dealing with the need for national remedies to be adapted so as effectively to protect Community law rights has developed considerably and sometimes controversially; at the time of *Francovich* it was plain (at any rate to me) that it was only the beginning of the story and that a lot of matters would have to be worked out in subsequent cases. The book deals valuably with such questions as these and the analysis of the cases, *e.g.* on what is a sufficiently serious breach to justify an order for compensation against the state in national courts is of considerably contemporary concern. There is still a long way to go in working out the parameters of this remedy and the chapter dealing with the subject will provide for practitioners and the courts a very useful starting point.

The actions for ingringement of Treaty obligations by a Member State and for annulment of Community Acts are dealt with in depth and, of particular relevance to practising lawyers, is the analysis of the right of individual challenge to the lawfulness of Community acts.

The concept of the scope of the "exception d'illégalité" ("objection of illegality") in Article 241 (ex 184) of the Treaty may be understood by civil lawyers but I have always found the subject difficult for a common lawyer. There is a helpful though brief analysis of this. Availability of interim measures, in many ways different from our interim forms of relief, the limits of appeals from the CFI and the detailed procedure before both the Court and the CFI are covered extensively.

The structure of the various sections follows a common pattern—contents of the form of action, the parties, procedural rules and the consequences of the judgment—which is helpful both to practitioners and students.

This is an excellent book which with its companion volume on the "constitutional law of the European Union" will be seen as one of the outstanding statements of European Union law and practice.

Slynn of Hadley

PREFACE

When this work was first published in Dutch as *Europees Procesrecht*, we stressed the importance of European law in the day-to-day life of the law. The continuing development of European law since then—especially in view of the entry into force of the Amsterdam Treaty—makes it even more vital for lawyers and students to know how to enforce European law and to be aware of the mechanisms affording protection against unlawful action on the part of Community institutions. Hence, it seemed to us that there was a need for an affordable book on European procedural law, which is what this entirely revised version, edited by Robert Bray, sets out to be.

In this work, considerable importance has been given to the primary role played by the national courts in their dialogue with the Court of Justice under the preliminary ruling procedure, for it is only too easy to overlook their role as courts of Community law, as well as to the various direct actions which can be brought in the Court of Justice and the Court of First Instance.

The preliminary ruling procedure, in fact, permeates three parts of the book. Part I, which introduces the judicial machinery of the European Union, sets out the basic features of the reference for a preliminary ruling and reviews the influence of Community law on national procedural rules, the aim being to give an overall picture of this key mechanism for collaboration between the national courts and the Court of Justice.

Part II—enforcement of Community law—deals with actions for infringement of Community law by a Member State together with preliminary rulings on the interpretation of Community law, in view of the fact that national courts often use that procedure to test the compatibility of national legal provisions with Community law.

Part III—protection against unlawful action by the Community institutions—discusses preliminary references as a means of raising in the Court of Justice the question of the validity of acts of the institutions where the applicant cannot bring a direct action. This part also deals with actions for annulment and failure to act and with claims for damages.

Part IV sets out a number of special forms of procedure, including a discussion of the jurisdiction of the Community Court in connection with intellectual property rights, conventions concluded by the Member States and police and judicial co-operation in criminal matters.

Part V considers procedure before the Court of Justice and the Court of First Instance. The appendices set out the Statute of the Court of Justice and the Rules of Procedure of the two tiers of the European Court.

Finally, for the reader's convenience all actions are described as far as possible on the same pattern: the subject-matter of the application, the identity of the parties, the special characteristics of the action and the effects of a judicial decision are dealt with in that order. Moreover, copious references are given to text books and learned articles as pointers to further reading.

This work is the companion volume to Koen Lenaerts and Piet Van Nuffel and Robert Bray (ed.), *Constitutional Law of the European Union*, Sweet and Maxwell, 1999, which sets out to provide an overview of the institutional and substantive law of the European Union. It reflects the state of the law on July 1, 1999.

It only remains to state that the views expressed in this book are our own and cannot be ascribed to the institutions to which we belong.

Koen Lenaerts
Dirk Arts
Robert Bray (editor)
Luxembourg and Brussels, July 1, 1999

CONTENTS

PART IV: SPECIAL FORMS OF PROCEDURE

NUMERICAL TABLE OF CASES

41/72 Getreide-Import v. Einfuhr-und Vorratsstelle Getreide [1973] E.C.R. 1; [1973] C.M.L.R. 465 10–016
43/72 Merkur v. Commission [1973] E.C.R. 1055 ..... 7–046, 11–027, 11–040
48/72 Brasserie de Haecht v. Wilkin-Janssen [1973] E.C.R. 77; [1973] C.M.L.R. 287 7–020
56/72 Goeth v. Commission [1973] E.C.R. 181 7–013
57/72 Westzucker v. Einfuhr-und Vorratsstelle Zucker [1973] E.C.R. 321 7–112
62/72 Bollmann v. Hauptzollamt Hamburg-Waltershof [1973] E.C.R. 269 23–015
63–69/72 Werhahn v. Council [1973] E.C.R. 1229 .... 11–012, 11–040, 11–045
70/72 Commission v. Germany [1973] E.C.R. 813; [1973] C.M.L.R. 741 .... 5–016, 5–042, 5–061
75/72R Perinciolo v. Council [1972] E.C.R. 1201 13–016
81/72 Commission v. Council [1973] E.C.R. 575; [1973] C.M.L.R. 639 .. 7–134
4/73 Nold Kohlen- und Baustoffgrosshandlung v. Commission [1974] E.C.R. 491; [1974] 2 C.M.L.R. 338 7–119
6 & 7/73 Commercial Solvents v. Commission [1974] E.C.R. 223; [1974] 1 C.M.L.R. 309 .... 14–005, 14–006
9/73 Schlüter v. Hauptzollamt Lörrach [1973] E.C.R. 1135 ...... 6–007, 7–014
15–33, 52–53, 57–109, 116–117, 123, 132, 135–137/73 Schots-Kortner v. Council, Commission and European Parliament [1974] E.C.R. 177 .... 7–006, 9–018
34/73 Variola v. Amministrazione Italiana delle Finanze [1973] E.C.R. 981 5–013
36/73 Nederlandse Spoorwegen v. Minister Verkeer en Waterstaat [1973] E.C.R. 1299; [1974] 2 C.M.L.R. 148 2–009
40–48, 50, 54–56, 111, 113, 114/73 Suiker Unie and Others v. Commission [1975] E.C.R. 1663; [1976] 1 C.M.L.R. 295 22–118
41, 43–48, 50, 111, 113–114/73 Générale Sucrière v. Commission [1973] E.C.R. 1465; [1974] 1 C.M.L.R. 215 22–092
41, 43, 44/73 Générale Sucrière v. Commission [1977] E.C.R. 445 22–163
112, 144 & 145/73 Campogrande and Others v. Commission [1974] E.C.R. 957 22–081
120/73 Lorenz v. Germany [1973] E.C.R. 1471 .... 5–017, 7–023
127/73 BRT v. SABAM [1974] E.C.R. 51 2–026
130/73 Vandeweghe v. Berufsgenossenschaft Chemische Industrie [1973] E.C.R. 1329; [1974] 1 C.M.L.R. 449 6–022
134/73 Holtz v. Council [1974] E.C.R. 1 8–014
146/73 Rheinmühlen-Düsseldorf v. Einfuhr- und Vorratsstelle Getreide und Futtermittel [1974] E.C.R. 139; [1974] 1 C.M.L.R. 523 .... 2–001, 2–005, 2–018, 2–027
153/73 Holtz and Willemsen v. Council and Commission [1974] E.C.R. 675; [1975] 1 C.M.L.R. 91 .... 11–005, 11–027, 11–030
166/73 Rheinmühlen-Düsseldorf v. Einfuhr- und Vorratsstelle Getreide und Futtermittel [1974] E.C.R. 33; [1974] 1 C.M.L.R. 523 .. 2–001, 2–005, 2–018
167/73 Commission v. France [1974] E.C.R. 359; [1974] 2 C.M.L.R. 216 .... 5–011, 5–022
169/73 Compagnie Continentale v. Council [1975] E.C.R. 117; [1975] 1 C.M.L.R. 578 .... 11–036, 11–041, 11–070
173/73 Italy v. Commission [1974] E.C.R. 709; [1974] 2 C.M.L.R. 593 .. 5–017
175/73 Union Syndicale, Massa and Kortner v. Council [1974] E.C.R. 917; [1975] 1 C.M.L.R. 131 .... 7–037, 16–011
181/73 Haegeman v. Belgium [1974] E.C.R. 449; [1975] 1 C.M.L.R. 515 6–018
185/73 Hauptzollamt Bielefeld v. König [1974] E.C.R. 607 ...... 7–116, 7–126

60/81 IBM v. Commission [1981] E.C.R. 2639; [1981] 3 C.M.L.R. 635 ...... 7–009, 7–011, 7–016, 7–017
60 and 190/81R IBM v. Commission [1981] E.C.R. 1857 13–009
65/81 Reina v. Landeskreditbank Baden-Württemberg [1982] E.C.R. 33; [1982] 1 C.M.L.R. 744 2–026
94/81 Commission v. Italy [1982] E.C.R. 739 5–031
96/81 Commission v. Netherlands [1982] E.C.R. 1791 ... 5–001, 5–054, 5–055, 22–066
97/81 Commission v. Netherlands [1982] E.C.R. 1819 ... 5–001, 5–055, 22–066
102/81 Nordsee v. Reederei Mond [1982] E.C.R. 1095 2–011
104/81 Hauptzollamt Mainz v. Kupferberg [1982] E.C.R. 3641; [19843] 1 C.M.L.R. 1 ...... 5–006, 6–018
106/81 Julius Kind v. EEC [1982] E.C.R. 2885 ...... 11–012, 11–045, 11–046, 11–048
108/81 Amylum v. Council [1982] E.C.R. 3107 22–017
109/81 Porta v. Commission [1982] E.C.R. 2469 17–007
110/81 SA Roquette Frères v. Council [1982] E.C.R. 3159 22–051
114/81 Tunnel Refineries v. Council [1982] E.C.R. 3189 7–107
115–116/81 Adoui and Cornuaille v. Belgium [1982] E.C.R. 1665; [1982] 3 C.M.L.R. 63 6–027
124/81 Commission v. United Kingdom [1983] E.C.R. 203; [1983] 2 C.M.L.R. 1 ...... 5–038, 22–019
132/81 Rijksdienst voor Werknemerspensioenen v. Vlaeminck [1982] E.C.R. 2953; [1983] 3 C.M.L.R. 559 2–033
135/81 Groupement des Agences de Voyage v. Commission [1982] E.C.R. 3799 ...... 7–037, 7–073
141–143/81 Holdijk [1982] E.C.R. 1299; [1983] 2 C.M.L.R. 3819 ...... 2–022, 6–027, 6–036
206/81R Alvarez v. European Parliament [1981] E.C.R. 2187 13–009
206/81A Alvarez v. European Parliament [1983] E.C.R. 2865 .. 22–152, 22–158
207/81 Ditterich v. Commission [1983] E.C.R. 1359 ...... 7–105, 11–054
210/81 Demo-Studio Schmidt v. Commission [1983] E.C.R. 3045; [1984] 1 C.M.L.R. 63 ...... 7–022, 7–071
211/81 Commission v. Denmark [1982] E.C.R. 4547; [1984] 1 C.M.L.R. 278 ...... 5–037, 5–045
213–215/81 Norddeutsches Vieh- und Fleischkontor v. Balm [1982] E.C.R. 3583 7–099
217/81 Interagra v. Commission [1982] E.C.R. 2233 11–022
230/81 Luxembourg v. European Parliament [1983] E.C.R. 255 7–031
232/81 Agricola Commerciale Olio v. Commission [1984] E.C.R. 3881 ... 7–073
232/81R Agricola Commerciale Olio v. Commission [1981] E.C.R. 2193 13–024
242/81 SA Roquette Frères v. Council [1982] E.C.R. 3213 ...... 7–040, 7–058
244/81 Klöckner-Werke v. Commission [1983] E.C.R. 1451 7–112
246/81 Lord Bethell v. Commission [1982] E.C.R. 2277; [1982] 3 C.M.L.R. 300 8–014
249/81 Commission v. Ireland [1982] E.C.R. 4005; [1983] 2 C.M.L.R. 104 ...... 5–012, 5–033
256/81 Pauls Agriculture v. Council and Commission [1983] E.C.R. 1707; [1983] 3 C.M.L.R. 176 ...... 11–059, 11–060
261/81 Walter Rau v. De Smedt PrbA [1982] E.C.R. 3961; [1983] 2 C.M.L.R. 496 ...... 2–039, 23–011
263/81 List v. Commission [1983] E.C.R. 103 22–120
266/81 Siot v. Ministero delle Finance [1983] E.C.R. 731 6–027
267–269/81 Amministrazione delle Finanze dello Stato v. SPI and SAMI [1983] E.C.R. 801; [1984] 1 C.M.L.R. 354 6–019

205/87 Nuova Ceam v. Commission [1987] E.C.R. 4427 7–069
209/87R EISA v. Commission [1987] E.C.R. 3453 13–016
214/87R Cockerill Sambre v. Commission [1987] E.C.R. 3463 13–016
223/87R ASSIDER v. Commission [1987] E.C.R. 3473 .... 13–016, 13–026
224/87 Koutchoumoff v. Commission [1989] E.C.R. 99 16–018
226/87 Commission v. Greece [1988] E.C.R. 3611 .... 5–020, 5–058, 9–005
229/87 Commission v. Greece [1988] E.C.R. 6347; [1990] 1 C.M.L.R. 797 .... 5–036, 5–037
240/87 Deville v. Administration des Impôts [1988] E.C.R. 3513; [1989] 3 C.M.L.R. 611 3–007
247/87 Star Fruit v. Commission [1989] E.C.R. 291; [1990] 1 C.M.L.R. 733 .... 5–025, 7–003, 8–014
265/87 Schräder v. Hauptzollamt Gronau [1989] E.C.R. 2237 6–006
275/87 Commission v. Council [1989] E.C.R. 259 7–134
C–287/87 Commission v. Greece [1990] E.C.R. I–125 5–064
290/87 Commission v. Netherlands [1989] E.C.R. 3083 .... 5–045, 5–054
C–301/87 France v. Commission [1990] E.C.R. I–307 5–017
302/87 European Parliament v. Council [1988] E.C.R. 5615 ..... 8–005, 8–020, 11–012
C–308/87 Grifoni v. Commission [1990] E.C.R. I–1203 11–070
C–343/87 Culin v. Commission [1990] E.C.R. I–225 .... 7–093, 7–114, 11–054
C–346/87 Bossi v. Commission [1989] E.C.R. 303 7–017
352/87 Farzoo v. Commission [1988] E.C.R. 2281 7–128
C–354/87 Weddel v. Commission [1990] E.C.R. I–3847 7–040
359/87 Pinna v. Caisse d'Allocations Familiales de la Savoie [1989] E.C.R. 585; [1990] 2 C.M.L.R. 561 10–022
361 & 362/87 Caturla-Poch and de la Fuente Pascual v. European Parliament [1989] E.C.R. 2471 7–123
371/87 Progoulis v. Commission [1988] E.C.R. 3081 16–015
374/87 Orkem v. Commission [1989] E.C.R. 3283 7–021
376/87R Distrivet v. Council [1988] E.C.R. 209 13–016
377/87 European Parliament v. Council [1988] E.C.R. 4017 ..... 8–001, 8–003, 8–006, 8–022, 22–170
378/87 Top Hit Holzvertrieb v. Commission [1989] E.C.R. 1359; [1991] 1 C.M.L.R. 261 7–131
383/87 Commission v. Council [1988] E.C.R. 4051 .... 8–001, 8–003
5/88 Wachauf v. Bundesamt für Ernährung und Forstwirtschaft [1989] E.C.R. 2609; [1991] 1 C.M.L.R. 328 3–022
14/88 Italy v. Commission [1989] E.C.R. 3677 7–112
16/88 Commission v. Council [1989] E.C.R. 3457 7–100
20/88 SA Roquette Frères v. Commission [1989] E.C.R. 1553; [1991] 2 C.M.L.R. 6 .... 11–026, 11–047, 11–077
22/88 Vreugdenhil and Others v. Minister van Landbouw en Visserij [1989] E.C.R. 2049; [1991] 2 C.M.L.R. 461 7–100
30/88 Greece v. Commission [1989] E.C.R. 3711 .... 6–020, 7–119
33/88 Allué and Others v. Università degli Studi di Venezia [1989] E.C.R. 1591; [1991] 1 C.M.L.R. 283 6–026
35/88 Commission v. Greece [1990] E.C.R. I–3125; [1991] 2 C.M.L.R. 876 5–016
62/88 Greece v. Council [1990] E.C.R. I–1527 7–118
68/88 Commission v. Greece [1989] E.C.R. 2965; [1989] 1 C.M.L.R. 31 .... 3–021, 3–025
C–70/88 European Parliament v. Council [1990] E.C.R. I–2041; [1992] 1 C.M.L.R. 91 .... 7–032, 12–005, 22–105
76/88 La Terza v. Court of Justice [1988] E.C.R. 1741 13–002

C–290/89 Commission v. Belgium [1991] E.C.R. I–2851 5–010
C–291/89 Interhotel v. Commission [1991] E.C.R. I–2257; [1993] 2 C.M.L.R. 202 . . . . 7–092, 10–016
C–298/89 Gibraltar v. Council [1993] E.C.R. I–3605; [1994] 4 C.M.L.R. 425 . . . . 7–031, 7–044, 7–058
C–304/89 Oliveira v. Commission [1991] E.C.R. I–2283; [1993] 2 C.M.L.R. 774 . . . . 7–092, 10–016
C–309/89 Codorniu v. Council [1994] E.C.R. I–1853; [1995] 2 C.M.L.R. 561 7–043
C–313/89 Commission v. Spain [1991] I–5231; [1994] 1 C.M.L.R. 256 . . 7–030
C–340/89 Vlassopoulou v. Ministerium für Justiz, Bundes-und Europaangelegenheiten Baden-Württemberg [1991] E.C.R. I–2357 3–011
C–354/89 Schiocchet v. Commission [1991] E.C.R. I–1775; [1994] 2 C.M.L.R. 189 7–120
C–355/89 Barr and Montrose Holdings [1991] E.C.R. I–3479 2–012
C–358/89 Extramet Industrie v. Council [1991] E.C.R. I–2501 . . . 7–043, 7–069
C–368/89 Crispoltoni v. Fattoria Autonoma Tabacchi [1991] E.C.R. I–3695 2–032
C–370/89 SGEEM and Etroy v. European Investment Bank [1992] E.C.R. I–6211; [1993] E.C.R. I–2583 . . . . 7–026, 11–013, 11–020
C–371/89 Emrich v. Commission [1990] E.C.R. I–1555 . . . . 5–025, 8–013
C–384/89 Ministère Public v. Tomatis and Fulchiron [1991] E.C.R. I–127 6–023
T–1/89 Rhône-Poulenc v. Commission [1991] E.C.R. II–867; [1991] E.C.R. II–637 . . . . 7–120, 22–081
T–4/89 BASF v. Commission [1991] E.C.R. II–1523; [1992] E.C.R. II–1591 7–120
T–4/89Rev. BASF v. Commission [1992] E.C.R. II–1591 . . . . . . 22–141, 22–143
T–7/89 Hercules Chemicals v. Commission [1991] E.C.R. II–1711; [1992] 4 C.M.L.R. 84 7–108
T–8/89 DSM v. Commission [1991] E.C.R. II–1833; [1992] E.C.R. II–2399 . . . . 7–112, 22–141
T–9/89 Hüls v. Commission [1992] E.C.R. II–499 . . . . . . 7–112, 7–120, 14–004, 22–063
T–10/89 Hoechst v. Commission [1992] E.C.R. II–629 . . . . 14–004, 22–063
T–11/89 Shell v. Commission [1992] E.C.R. II–757 . . . . 14–004, 22–063
T–12/89 Solvay v. Commission [1992] E.C.R. II–907 . . . . 14–004, 22–063
T–13/89 ICI v. Commission [1992] E.C.R. II–1021 . . . . 14–005, 22–063
T–14/89 Montedipe v. Commission [1992] E.C.R. II–1155; [1992] E.C.R. II–2409 . . . . 14–004, 22–063
T–15/89 Chemie Linz v. Commission [1992] E.C.R. II–1275 . . . 14–004, 22–063
T–18 & 24/89 Tagaras v. Court of Justice [1992] E.C.R. II–153; [1992] E.C.R. II–53 22–116
T–20/89RV Moritz v. Commission [1993] E.C.R. II–1423 . . . . . 15–018, 16–006
T–30/89 Hilti v. Commission [1990] E.C.R. II–163; [1992] 4 C.M.L.R. 16 . . . . 22–086, 22–103
T–33 & 74/89 Blackman v. European Parliament [1993] E.C.R. II–249 . . 7–128, 22–116
T–35/89T01 Zubizarreta v. Albani [1992] E.C.R. II–1599 . . . . . 22–094, 22–131
T–37/89 Hanning v. European Parliament [1990] E.C.R. II–463 . . . . 7–114, 7–115, 7–137, 11–054, 16–021, 22–018
T–38/89 Hochbaum v. Commission [1990] E.C.R. II–43 7–121
T–42/89 OPPO European Parliament v. W. Graf Yorck von Wartenburg [1990] E.C.R. II–299 22–035
T–42/89 W. Graf Yorck von Wartenburg v. European Parliament [1990] E.C.R. II–31 22–033

C–320/92 Finsider SpA v. Commission [1994] E.C.R. I–5697 .. 14–005, 15–016
C–332, C–333 and 335/92 Eurico Italia and Others v. Ente Nazionale Risi [1994] E.C.R. I–711; [1994] 2 C.M.L.R. 580 .... 2–026, 2–032
C–345/92 Commission v. Germany [1993] E.C.R. I–1115 5–065
C–354/92P Eppe v. Commission [1993] E.C.R. I–7027 .... 15–006, 15–007, 24–007
C–360/92 Publishers Association v. Commission [1995] E.C.R. I–23; [1995] 5 C.M.L.R. 33 7–113
C–382/92 Commission v. United Kingdom [1994] E.C.R. I–2435; [1995] 1 C.M.L.R. 345 .... 3–021, 5–054
C–383/92 Commission v. United Kingdom [1994] E.C.R. I–2479; [1995] 1 C.M.L.R. 345 3–021
C–386/92 Monin Automobiles [1993] E.C.R. I–2049 2–023
C–387/92 Banco Exterior de España v. Ayuntamiento de Valencia [1994] E.C.R. I–877; [1994] 3 C.M.L.R. 473 7–023
C–388/92 European Parliament v. Council [1994] E.C.R. I–2067 7–107
C–393/92 Almelo [1994] E.C.R. I–1477 2–011
C–398/92 Mund and Fester v. Hatrex [1994] E.C.R. I–467 ..... 5–007, 19–002
C–399/92, C–409/92, C–425/92, C–34/93, C–50–93 and C–78/93 Helmig and Others [1994] E.C.R. I–5727 2–028
C–404/92P X. v. Commission [1994] E.C.R. I–4737 15–018
C–410/92 Johnson v. Chief Adjudication Officer [1994] E.C.R. I–5483; [1994] 1 C.M.L.R. 725 .... 3–005, 3–013
C–412/92 P European Parliament v. Meskens [1994] E.C.R. I–3757 7–137
C–422/92 Commission v. Germany [1995] E.C.R. I–1097; [1996] 1 C.M.L.R. 383 5–022
C–424/92 Ladbroke Racing v. Commission [1993] E.C.R. I–2213 1–029
C–432/92 R. v. The Minister of Agriculture, Fisheries and Food, ex p. Anastasiou and Others [1994] E.C.R. I–3087; [1995] 1 C.M.L.R. 569 6–018
T–4/92 Vardakas v. Commission [1993] E.C.R. II–357 16–018
T–6, 52/92 Reinarz v. Commission [1993] E.C.R. II–1047 9–002
T–7/92 Asia Motor France v. Commission [1993] E.C.R. II–669; [1994] 4 C.M.L.R. 30 .... 7–112, 7–120, 8–020
T–10–12 & T–15/92 Cimenteries CBR and Others v. Commission [1992] E.C.R. II–2667; [1993] 4 C.M.L.R. 259 ..... 7–012, 7–018, 7–021, 7–108, 13–016
T–13/92 Moat v. Commission [1993] E.C.R. II–287 .... 11–054, 22–118
T–19/92 Leclerc v. Commission [1996] E.C.R. II–1851 .... 7–071, 22–090
T–22/92 Weissenfels v. European Parliament [1993] E.C.R. II–1095 .... 22–017, 22–051
T–24 & 28/92R Langnese-Iglo and Schöller Lebensmittel v. Commission [1992] E.C.R. II–1839; [1992] E.C.R. II–1713 .... 13–003, 13–029
T–25/92 Vela Palacios v. ESC [1993] E.C.R. II–201 7–114
T–29/92R SPO and Others v. Commission [1992] E.C.R. II–2161 .... 13–003, 13–029
T–35/92 John Deere Ltd v. Commission [1994] E.C.R. II–957 22–014
T–36/92 SFEI and Others v. Commission [1992] E.C.R. II–2479 7–022
T–37/92 BEUC and NCC v. Commission [1994] E.C.R. II–285; [1995] 4 C.M.L.R. 167 .... 7–022, 7–071
T–39–40/92 CB and Europay v. Commission [1994] E.C.R. II–49 .... 7–120, 14–006
T–43/92 Dunlop Slazenger v. Commission [1994] E.C.R. II–441 14–006

C–428/93 Monin Automobiles-Maison du Deux-Roues [1994] E.C.R. I–1707 2–032
C–431/93 Van Schijndel and Van Veen v. Stichting Pensioen fonds voor Fysiotherapeuten [1995] E.C.R. I–4705 3–014
C–433/93 Commission v. Germany [1995] E.C.R. I–2303 5–056
C–445/93 European Parliament v. Commission (not reported in the E.C.R.) 8–006
C–446/93 SEIM v. Subdirector-General das Alfândegas [1996] E.C.R. I–73 2–017
C–448/93P Commission v. Noonan [1995] E.C.R. I–2321 15–012
C–458/93 Saddik [1995] E.C.R. I–511; [1995] 3 C.M.L.R. 318 2–023
C–465/93 Atlanta Fruchthandelsgesellschaft and Others v. Bundesamt für Ernährung und Forstwirtschaft [1995] E.C.R. I–3761; [1996] 1 C.M.L.R. 575 .... 3–017, 13–006
C–472/93 Spano and Others v. Fiat Geotech SpA [1995] E.C.R. I–4321 .. 2–026
C–473/93 Commission v. Luxembourg [1996] E.C.R. I–3207; [1996] 3 C.M.L.R. 981 .... 5–039, 5–061
C–476/93P Nutral v. Commission [1995] E.C.R. I–4125 7–011
C–480/93P Zunis Holding and Others v. Commission [1996] E.C.R. I–1; [1996] 5 C.M.L.R. 219 .... 7–013, 15–016
C–485–486/93 Simitzi v. Municipality of Kos [1995] E.C.R. I–2655 6–039
T–2/93 Air France v. Commission [1994] E.C.R. II–323; [1994] E.C.R. II–533 .... 7–071, 22–122
T–3/93 Air France v. Commission [1994] E.C.R. II–121 7–008
T–4/93 André v. Commission [1994] E.C.R.–S.C. II–471 16–015
T–12/93 CCE Vittel and Others v. Commission [1995] E.C.R. II–1247 .... 7–071, 7–074
T–12/93R CCE Vittel and CE Pierval v. Commission [1993] E.C.R. II–449 .... 13–008, 13–016, 13–029
T–13/93 Cordier v. Commission [1993] E.C.R. II–1215 5–004
T–17/93 Matra Hachette v. Commission [1994] E.C.R. II–595 7–113
T–18/93 Marcato v. Commission [1994] E.C.R.-S.C. II–681 11–054
T–21/93 Peixoto v. Commission [1993] E.C.R. II–463 13–024
T–24/93R CMBT v. Commission [1993] E.C.R. II–543 .... 13–011, 13–016, 13–027, 22–103
T–29/93 Calvo Alonso-Cortés v. Commission [1993] E.C.R. II–1389 .... 5–025, 22–044
T–32/93 Ladbroke Racing Ltd v. Commission [1994] E.C.R. II–1015 .... 8–003, 8–014
T–35/93 Cucchiara and Others v. Commission [1994] E.C.R.-S.C. II–413 .... 22–016, 22–018
T–37/93 Stagakis v. European Parliament [1994] E.C.R.-S.C. I–A–137 ... 16–005
T–44/93 Saby v. Commission [1995] E.C.R.-S.C. II–541 16–015
T–46/93 Michäel-Chiou v. Commission [1994] E.C.R.-S.C. II–929 7–123
T–124/93 Werner v. Commission [1995] E.C.R. II–91 22–116
T–244 & 486/93 TWD Textilwerke Deggendorf GmbH v. Commission [1995] E.C.R. II–2265; [1996] 1 C.M.L.R. 332 .... 22–097, 22–116
T–246/93 Bühring v. Council and Commission [1998] E.C.R. II–171 ... 11–012, 11–079
T–432–434/93 Socurte v. Commission [1995] E.C.R. II–503 7–131
T–435/93 ASPEC and Others v. Commission [1995] E.C.R. II–1281 7–072
T–443/93 Casillo Grani v. Commission [1995] E.C.R. II–1375 7–075
T–447, T–448 and T–449/93 AITEC and Others v. Commission [1995] E.C.R. II–1971 .... 7–072, 7–074, 22–090, 22–116
T–450/93 Lisrestal v. Commission [1994] E.C.R. II–1177 7–104

C–94, 95/95 Bonifaci and Others and Berto and Others v. Italy [1997] E.C.R. I–3969 3–023
C–104/95 Kontogeorgas v. Kartonpak AE [1996] E.C.R. I–6643 2–032
C–107/95P Bundesverband der Bilanzbuchhalter v. Commission [1997] E.C.R. I–947 5–024
C–114–115/95 Texaco [1997] E.C.R. I–4263 3–013
C–122/95 Germany v. Council [1998] E.C.R. I–973 7–126
C–127/95 Norbrook Laboratories Ltd and Ministry of Agriculture, Fisheries and Food [1998] E.C.R. I–1531 3–023
C–130/95 Giloy [1997] E.C.R. I–4291 6–021
C–137/95P SPO and Others v. Commission [1996] E.C.R. I–1611 15–016
C–138/95P Campo Ebro and Others v. Council [1997] E.C.R. I–2027 .. 15–006
C–143/95P Commission v. Socurte and Others [1997] E.C.R. I–1 .... 7–128, 15–010
C–144/95 Maurin [1996] E.C.R. I–2909 6–006
C–147/95 Dimossia Epicheirissi Ilectrismou v. Evrenopoulos [1997] I–2057 6–004
C–149/95P Commission v. Atlantic Container Line and Others [1995] E.C.R. I–2165; [1995] All E.R. 853 .... 13–024, 15–003, 24–003
C–166/95P–R Commission v. Daffix [1997] E.C.R. I–983 .... 7–092, 7–105, 7–115, 15–010, 15–015
C–171/95 Tetik v. Land Berlin [1997] E.C.R. I–329 6–020
C–178/95 Wiljo v. Belgium [1997] E.C.R. I–585; [1997] 1 C.M.L.R. 627; [1997] All E.R. (E.C.) 226 .... 2–020, 2–022, 10–010
C–180/95 Draehmpaehl v. Urania Immobilienservice [1997] E.C.R. I–2195 3–005
C–181/95 Biogen v. Smithkline Beecham Biologicals [1996] E.C.R. I–717; [1997] 1 C.M.L.R. 704 .... 22–091, 22–096
C–184/95 Mercedes Lores Guillín (not reported in the E.C.R.) 2–026
C–188/95 Fantask and Others [1997] E.C.R. I–6783 3–013
C–191/95 Commission v. Germany [1998] E.C.R. I–5449 5–022
C–192–218/95 Société Comateb and Others v. Directeur Général des Douanes et Droits Indirects [1997] 165 3–007
C–219/95P Ferriere Nord v. Commission [1997] E.C.R. I–4411 15–005
C–235/95 AGS Assedic Pas-de-Calais v. Dumon and Froment [1998] E.C.R. I–4531 2–025
C–241/95 R. v. Intervention Board for Agriculture Produce, ex p. Accrington Beef Co. Ltd [1996] E.C.R. I–6699; [1997] 1 C.M.L.R. 675 10–010
C–242/95 GT-Link [1997] E.C.R. I–4449 3–007
C–245/95P Commission v. NTN and Koyo Seiko [1998] E.C.R. I–401 .. 22–090, 22–094, 22–179
C–246/95 Coen v. Belgian State [1997] E.C.R. I–403 16–019
C–253/95 Commission v. Germany [1996] E.C.R. I–2423 5–056
C–254/95P European Parliament v. Innamorati [1995] E.C.R. I–2707 .. 15–016, 15–018
C–257/95 Bresle v. Préfet de la Région Auvergne and Préfet du Puy-de-Dôme [1996] E.C.R. I–233 2–023
C–259/95 European Parliament v. Council [1997] E.C.R. I–5303 7–033
C–261/95 Palmisani [1997] E.C.R. I–4025 .... 2–018, 2–032, 3–007, 3–023, 6–007
C–263/95 Germany v. Commission [1998] E.C.R. I–441 7–110
C–265/95 Commission v. France [1997] E.C.R. I–6959 5–010

ALPHABETICAL TABLE OF CASES

Aannemersbedrijf PK Kraaijeveld and Others v. Gedeputeerde Staten van Zuid-Holland (C–72/95) 3–104
Abbott Trust v. Council and Commission (T–554/93 R) 13–008
Abello and Others v. Commission (C–30/96) 15–006
Abertal and Others v. Commission (C–213/91) 7–040, 7–058
Abertal and Others v. Council (C–264/91) 7–040, 7–043
AC-ATEL Electronics v. Hauptzollamt München-Mitte (C–30/93) 2–025
Acciaieria é Tubificio di Brescia v. High Authority (31/59) 13–025, 13–027
Acciaierie e Ferriere Pugliese v. High Authority (8/65) 7–113
Acciaierie Fonderie Ferriere di Modena and Others v. High Authority (55–59 & 61–63/63) 7–088
ACF Chemiefarma v. Commission (41/69) 7–107, 14–006
Adam v. Commission (828/79) 7–017
Adams v. Commission (145/83) 7–109, 11–036, 11–070, 11–076
Adia Interim v. Commission (T–19/95) 22–017
Administration des douanes et droits indirects v. Legros 6–039
Adoui and Cornuaille v. Belgium (115–116/81) 6–027
AEFMA v. Commission (C–107/93R) 13–016
AERPO and Others v. Commission (119/88) .. 11–027, 11–039, 11–045, 11–046
Affaires Maritimes á Bayonne v. Dorca Marine (50–581/82) 10–014
Affatato v. Commission (T–157/96) 22–125
Agence Européenne d'Intérims SA v. Commission (56/77) 22–062
Agricola Commerciale Olio v. Commission (232/81) 7–073, 13–024
AGS Assedic Pas-de-Calais v. Dumon and Froment (C–235/95) 2–025
Ahlström Osakeyhtiö v. Commission (C–89, 104, 114, 116–117, 125–129/85) 7–021, 7–098, 7–119
Ainsworth v. Commission (159 & 267/84; 12 & 264/85) 7–140
Air France v. Commission (T–2/93) 7–071, 22–122
—— v. —— (T–3/93) 7–008
—— v. —— (T–358/94) 7–072
AITEC v. Commission (T–447, 448, 449/93) 7–072, 7–074, 22–090, 22–116
—— v. —— (T–277/94) 5–025, 7–011, 8–004
AIUFFASS and AKT v. Commission (T–380/94) 7–072, 7–131
—— v. —— (C–55/97) 15–010
Ajinomoto and Nutrasweet v. Council (T–160/94) 7–024
A.J. Van Eick v. Commission (35/67) 7–104
AKZO Chemie BV and AKZO Chemie UK Ltd v. Commission (5/85) 7–103, 22–017
AKZO Chemie BV v. Commission (53/85) 7–004, 7–011, 7–021, 7–077, 7–109, 7–137
—— v. —— (62/86) 13–009
ALA and ALFER v. Commission (220–221/78) 7–128, 22–005
Alaimo v. Préfet du Rhône (68/74) 6–035
Albatros v. Sopéco (20/64) 2–039, 6–024
Albini v. Council and Commission (33/80) 9–001

Leur-Bloem (C–28/95) 6–021
Leussink-Brummelhuis v. Commission (169/83 & 136/84) 11–054, 11–069
Ley v. Commission (12 & 29/64) 7–018, 13–012, 22–051
Lilly Industries v. Commission (T–120/96) 22–095
Lisrestal v. Commission (T–450/93) 7–104
List v. Commission (263/81) 22–120
Lopes v. Court of Auditors (C–174/96) 22–185
Lord Bethell v. Commission (246/81) 8–014
Lorenz v. Germany (120/73) 5–017, 7–023
Lourenço Dias v. Director da Alfândega do Porto (C–343/90) 2–035, 6–026
Ludwigshafener Walzmühle v. Council and Commission (197–200, 243, 245 & 247/80) 11–005, 11–067, 22–068, 22–102
Luhleich v. Commission of the EAEC (68/63) 11–065
Luisi and Carbone v. Ministero de Tesoro (286/82 & 26/83) 3–022, 6–029
Lütticke v. Commission (48/65) 5–024, 8–008
—— v. Commission (4/69) 5–026, 11–001, 11–004, 11–067, 22–016
Lux v. Court of Auditors (69/83) 7–123
Luxembourg v. European Parliament (230/81) 7–031
—— v. —— (108/83) 7–015
—— v. —— (C–213/88 & 39/89) 7–015, 13–006

M. v. Commission (155/78) 22–073
MAAS v. Commission (T–121/96 & T–151/96) 7–013
Macchiorlati Dalmas v. Commission (21/64) 7–105, 9–005
Macevicius v. European Parliament (31/76) 7–129
Mackprang v. Commission (15/71) 8–014
Magorrian and Cunningham (C–246/96) 3–007, 3–013
Maindiaux v. ESC (146 & 431/85) 22–153
Maiseries de Beauce v. ONIC (109/79) 10–025
Maizena v. Council (139/79) 7–061, 7–080, 7–105, 7–106, 22–093
Mancini v. Commission (T–508/93) 22–017
—— v. —— (T–113/95) 16–015
Mandelli v. Commission (56/70R) 22–142
Manzoni v. Fonds National de Retraite des Ouvriers Mineurs (112/76) ... 2–057, 6–036, 6–037
Marcato v. Commission (44/71) 16–014
—— v. —— (T–64/91) 16–015
—— v. —— (T–18/93) 11–054
Marleasing v. La Comercial Internacional de Alimentación SA (C–106/89) 6–007
Marshall v. Southampton and South West Hampshire Area Health Authority (C–271/91) 3–022, 3–023
Martin Weber v. Commission (T–482/93) 7–058, 22–009
Marx Esser and Del Amo Martinez v. European Parliament (182/94) 7–092
Maso and Others (C–373/95) 2–032, 6–007
Matra v. Commission (C–225/91) 7–072, 7–120, 22–090
Matra Hachette v. Commission (T–17/93) 7–113
Mattheus v. Doego (93/78) 2–018
Maurin (C–144/95) 6–006
Maurissen and European Public Service Union v. Court of Auditors (193 & 194/87) 7–013, 16–011
—— v. Court of Auditors (T–23/91) 7–123
Maurissen and European Public Service Union v. Court of Auditors (T–192/94) 16–016

TABLE OF NATIONAL CASES

TABLE OF EUROPEAN UNION AND COMMUNITY TREATIES

TABLE OF EUROPEAN UNION AND COMMUNITY ACTS

TABLE OF EUROPEAN UNION AND COMMUNITY CONVENTIONS AND AGREEMENTS

Conventions

Agreements

TABLE OF REGULATIONS

Regulations

TABLE OF RULES OF PROCEDURE

TABLE OF NATIONAL LEGISLATION

National Legislation

Table of Statutory Instruments

ABBREVIATIONS

A.J.D.A.	L'actualité juridique – droit administratif
Anglo-Am.L.R.	Anglo-American Law Review
Cambridge L.J.	Cambridge Law Journal
C.D.E.	Cahiers de droit européen
C.M.L.R.	Common Market Law Reports
C.M.L.Rev.	Common Market Law Review
D.P.C.I.	Droit et pratique du commerce international
E.C. Bull.	Bulletin of the European Community
E.Comp.L.Rev.	European Competition Law Review
E.C.R.	European Court Reports
E.U. Bull.	Bulletin of the European Union
Eu.Gr.Z.	Europäische Grundrechte Zeitschrift
E.I.P.R.	European Intellectual Property Review
E.L.Rev.	European Law Review
Eu.R.	Europarecht
Eu.Z.W.	Europäische Zeitschrift für Wirtschaftsrecht
G.U.R.I.	Gazetta Ufficiale della Repubblica Italiana
Fordham I.L.J.	Fordham International Law Journal
I.C.L.Q.	International and Comparative Law Quarterly
Ir.J.E.L.	Irish Journal of European Law
J.B.L.	The Journal of Business Law
J.C.D.I.	Juris-Classeur Droit international
J.C.P.	Juris-Classeur Périodique
J.D.I.	Journal du droit international
J.T.	Journal des Tribunaux
J.T.D.E.	Journal des Tribunaux – Droit européen
J.Z.	Juristen–Zeitung
L.I.E.I.	Legal Issues of European Integration
Mich.L.Rev.	Michigan Law Review
M.L.R.	Modern Law Review
N.I.L.R.	Netherlands International Law Review
N.J.B.	Nederlands Juristenblad
N.J.W.	Neue Juristische Wochenschrift
N.T.B.	Nederlands Tijdschrift voor bestuursrecht
O.J.	Official Journal of the European Communities
P.L.	Public Law
Rec. Dalloz	Recueil Dalloz Sirey

Rev. dr. ULB	Revue de droit de l'ULB
R.G.D.I.P.	Revue générale de droit international public
Riv. dir. eur.	Rivista di diritto europeo
R.M.C.	Revue du Marché Commun
R.M.C.U.E.	Revue du Marché Commun et de l'Union européenne
R.M.U.E.	Revue du Marché Unique européen
R.S.C.D.P.C.	Revue de science criminelle et de droit pénal comparé
R.T.D.E.	Revue trimestrielle de droit européen
R.W.	Rechtskundig Weekblad
S.E.W.	Sociaal-economische wetgeving. Tijdschrift voor Europees en economisch recht
S.I.	Statutory Instrument
Texas I.L.J.	Texas International Law Journal
T.B.P.	Tijdschrift voor bestuurswetenschappen en publiekrecht
T.P.R.	Tijdschrift voor privaatrecht
Y.E.L.	Yearbook of European Law

ABBREVIATED FORMS FOR TREATIES AND ACTS

The following abbreviated forms for Treaties and legislative measures are used in this work:

Brussels Convention	Convention on Jurisdiction and the Enforcement of Judgments in Civil and Commercial Matters.
CFI Decision	Council Decision of October 24, 1988, establishing a Court of First Instance of the European Communities (88/591/ECSC, EEC, Euratom), [1988] O.J. L319/1, as amended by Council Decision of June 8, 1993 (93/350/ Euratom, ECSC, EEC) amending Decision 88/591/ECSC, EEC, Euratom establishing a Court of First Instance of the European Communities, [1993] O.J. L144/21, by Council Decision of March 7, 1994 (94/129/Euratom, ECSC, EC) amending Decision 93/350/Euratom, ECSC, EEC amending Decision 88/591/ECSC. EEC, Euratom establishing a Court of First Instance of the European Communities, [1994] O.J. L66/29 and by Council Decision of April 26, 1999 (1999/291/E.C., ECSC, Euratom) amending Decision 88/591/ECSC/Euratom establishing a Court of First Instance of the European Communities to enable it to give decisions in cases when constituted by a single judge, [1999] O.J. L114/52.
CFI Rules of Procedure	Rules of Procedure of the Court of First Instance of the European Communities of May 2, 1991 ([1991] O.J. L136/1, and L137/34), as amended on September 15, 1994 ([1994] O.J. L249/17), on February 17, 1995 ([1995] O.J. L44/64), on July 6, 1995 ([1995] O.J. L172/3), on March 12, 1997 ([1997] O.J. L103/6, and [1997] O.J. L351/72) and on May 17, 1999 ([1999] O.J. L135/92).

EAEC Treaty	Treaty establishing the European Atomic Energy Community.
ECJ Rules of Procedure	Rules of Procedure of the Court of Justice of the European Communities of June 19, 1991 ([1991] O.J. L176/7, and L383) as amended on February 21, 1995 ([1995] O.J. L44/61) and on March 11, 1997 ([1997] O.J. L103/1).
ECSC Treaty	Treaty establishing the European Coal and Steel Community.
E.C. Statute	Protocol on the Statute of the Court of Justice, signed at Brussels on April 17, 1957, as amended on October 24, 1988 ([1988] O.J. L319/1, and [1989] O.J. L241), on June 24, 1994 ([1994] O.J. C241/25), on December 22, 1994 ([1994] O.J. L379/1) and on June 6, 1995 ([1995] O.J. L131/33).
E.C. Treaty	Treaty establishing the European Community.
EEA Agreement	Agreement on the European Economic Area.
EEC Treaty	Treaty establishing the European Economic Community.
E.U. Treaty	Treaty on European Union.
Regulation No. 17	Council Regulation No. 17/62 ([1959–1962] O.J. Spec. Ed. 87), First Regulation implementing Articles 85 and 86 of the Treaty, as amended and supplemented by Regulation No. 59 ([1959–1962] O.J. Spec. Ed. 249), Regulation No. 118/63/EEC ([1963–1964] O.J. Spec. Ed. 55) and Regulation No. 2822/71/EEC ([1971] III O.J. Spec. Ed. 1035).
Rome Convention	Convention on the law applicable to contractual obligations ([1980] O.J. L266/1).

References made in this work to the Advocate General apply in the case of the Court of First Instance only where a judge has been designated to act as such.

TEXTBOOKS REFERRED TO THROUGHOUT

R. Barents, *Procedures en procesvoering voor het Hof van Justitie en het Gerecht van eerste aanleg van de EG*, Deventer, Kluwer, 1996, 525 pp.:
Barents, *Procedures*

M. Brealey and M. Hoskins, *Remedies in E.C. Law*, London, Sweet & Maxwell, 1998 (2nd ed.), 632 pp.
Brealey and Hoskins, *Remedies in E.C. Law*

R. Joliet, *Le droit institutionnel des Communautés européennes—Le contentieux*, Liège, Faculté de Droit, d'Economie et de Sciences sociales de Liège, 1981, 302 pp.:
Joliet, *Le contentieux*

K. Lenaerts and P. Van Nuffel, R. Bray (ed.), *Constitutional Law of the European Union*, London, Sweet & Maxwell, 1999, 700 pp.:
Lenaerts and Van Nuffel, *Constitutional Law of the European Union*

J. Rideau and F. Picod, *Code de procédures communautaires*, Paris, Litec, 1994, 1075 pp.:
Rideau and Picod, *Code de procédures communautaires*

H.G. Schermers and D. Waelbroeck, *Judicial Protection in the European Communities*, Deventer, Kluwer, 1992, 585 pp.:
Schermers and Waelbroeck, *Judicial Protection*

G. Vandersanden and A. Barav, *Contentieux communautaire*, Brussels, Bruylant, 1977, 722 pp.:
Vandersanden and Barav, *Contentieux communautaire*

D. Vaughan and P. Lasok, *Butterworths European Court Practice*, London, Butterworths, 1993, 581 pp.:
Vaughan and Lasok, *European Court Practice*

M. Waelbroeck, D. Waelbroeck and G. Vandersanden, *La Cour de Justice*, in M. Waelbroeck, J.-V. Louis, D. Vignes, J.-L. Dewost, G. Vandersanden, Commentaire Mégret, Vol. 10, Brussels, Editions de l'Université de Bruxelles, 1993, 666 pp.:
Commentaire Mégret

Part I
THE JUDICIAL ORGANISATION OF THE EUROPEAN UNION

Chapter 1

THE EUROPEAN COURTS

I. National Courts

National courts and tribunals are under an obligation to apply Community law in all cases between national authorities and natural or legal persons or between such persons[1] and to safeguard the rights conferred by Community law.[2] **1–001**

The primary role played by national courts in applying Community law is connected with the peculiar nature of that law. The Community treaties created a new legal order, directed at the Member States and their nationals. The relationship between the Community legal order and the national legal systems is characterised by the primacy of Community law and the direct effect of a whole series of provisions of Community law.[3] The question arises as to how individuals may assert the rights which they derive from those provisions. **1–002**

The system of legal protection formulated in the treaties does not provide for the creation of "Community courts" in the different Member States. It starts from the premise that the national courts are the bodies to which individuals may turn whenever action or failure to act on the part of national authorities or other individuals infringes rights conferred on them by Community law.[4] The national court is therefore the normal Community court to hear and determine all cases which do not fall within the jurisdiction of the Court of Justice or the Court of First Instance. Within the legal system of the individual's Member State, the national courts are the bridgehead of the Community legal order and secure the enforcement of Community law through dialogue with the Court of Justice.[5]

---

1 See para. 3–014, below, with regard to whether the national court is under a duty to raise a question of Community law of its own motion.

2 Case 106/77 *Amministrazione delle Finanze dello Stato v. Simmenthal* [1978] E.C.R. 629 at 644, para. 21, ECJ.

3 Opinion 1/91 *Draft agreement between the Community, on the one hand, and the countries of the European Free Trade Association, on the other, relating to the creation of the European Economic Area* [1991] E.C.R. I–6079 at I–6102, para. 21, ECJ. See Lenaerts and Van Nuffel, *Constitutional Law of the European Union*, paras 14–002—14–035.

4 Case 26/62 *Van Gend & Loos v. Nederlandse Administratie der Belastingen* [1963] E.C.R. 1 at 12, third para., ECJ.

5 Slynn, "What is a European Community Law Judge?" (1993) C.L.J. 234–244; Kapteyn, "Europe's Expectations of its Judges", in Jansen, Koster and Van Zutphen (eds), *European Ambitions of the National Judiciary*, The Hague, London, Boston, Kluwer Law International, 1997, at 181–189.

The Court of Justice has defined the task of national courts in its case law on the operation of the preliminary ruling procedure[6] and on the application of the principle of co-operation enshrined in Article 10 *(ex Article 5)* of the E.C. Treaty to national courts.[7]

II. The Court of Justice

1–003 The institution known as the "Court of Justice" consists of two courts, the Court of Justice and the Court of First Instance,[8] which, within their respective spheres of jurisdiction, ensure that in the interpretation and application of the treaties the law is observed.

A. Composition

1–004 The Court of Justice consists of 15 judges,[9] assisted by eight advocates general.[10] Should the Court so request, the Council may, acting unanimously, increase the number of judges[11] or advocates general.[12] Judges and advocates general are appointed for a term of six years by common accord of the governments of the Member States. They are chosen from persons whose independence is beyond doubt and who possess the qualifications required for appointment to the highest judicial offices in their respective countries or who are jurisconsults of recognised competence. Every three years there is a partial replacement of judges and advocates general. Eight and seven judges are replaced alternately and four advocates general. Retiring judges and advocates general may be reappointed.[13] The Treaty does not distribute the number of judges and advocates general among the

---

[6] See Chap. 2, below.

[7] See Chap. 3, below.

[8] E.C. Treaty, Art. 225 (*ex Art. 168a*), provides that a Court of First Instance is "attached" to the Court of Justice (see paras 1–016—1–029, below).

[9] E.C. Treaty, Art. 221 (*ex Art. 165*), para. 1.

[10] E.C. Treaty, Art. 222 (*ex Art. 166)*, para. 1. As the Court is at present composed, however, it has a ninth advocate general, A.M. La Pergola, who was the 13th judge before the accession of Austria, Finland and Sweden and agreed to serve the remainder of his term of office as an advocate general in order to ensure that the Court had an uneven number of judges: Art. 4 of the Decision of the Representatives of the Governments of the Member States of the European Communities of January 1, 1995 ([1995] O.J. L1/223) and Art. 11 of the Council Decision of January 1, 1995, adjusting the instruments concerning the accession of the new Member States to the European Union ([1995] O.J. L1/4), which amends Art. 20 of the relevant Act of Accession accordingly.

[11] E.C. Treaty, Art. 221 (*ex Art. 165*), para. 4.

[12] E.C. Treaty, Art. 222 (*ex Art. 166*), para. 3. For the part played by Advocates General, see Tridimas, "The Role of the Advocate General in the Development of Community Law: Some Reflections" (1997) C.M.L. Rev. 1349–1387 and Brealey and Hoskins, *Remedies in E.C. Law*, London, Sweet and Maxwell, 1998 (2nd ed.), p. 20, as regards the "persuasive value" of opinions of advocates general for national courts.

[13] The appointment requirements are set out in the E.C. Treaty, Art. 223 (*ex Art. 167*), paras. 1–4.

Member States or even provide that they must be nationals of Member States.[14] In practice, there is one judge from each Member State. The Court must always consist of an uneven number of judges when it takes its decisions,[15] which is why it has always had an uneven number of judges.[16] As far as advocates general are concerned, there is one for each of the five largest Member States[17]; the three remaining advocates general come alternately from the other 10 Member States.[18] If a judge's or advocate general's office falls vacant before the expiry of its term, a successor is appointed for the remainder of the normal term of office.[19]

Before taking up their duties, judges and advocates general take an oath, in open court, to perform their duties impartially and conscientiously and to preserve the secrecy of the deliberations of the Court.[20] Judges and advocates general are immune from legal proceedings, and they continue to enjoy immunity after they have ceased to hold office in respect of acts performed by them in their official capacity, including words spoken or written. Their immunity may be waived only by the Court sitting in plenary session. Where immunity has been waived and criminal proceedings are instituted against a judge or an advocate general, the member concerned may be tried only by the court competent to judge the members of the highest national judiciary.[21] **1–005**

---

[14] *Cf.* the Commission, of which only nationals of Member States may be members (E.C. Treaty, Art. 213 (*ex Art. 157*), para. 3) and which must include at least one national of each Member State, but may not include more than two members having the nationality of the same state (E.C. Treaty, Art. 213, para. 4). See also Barents, *Procedures*, at p. 19.

[15] E.C. Statute, Art. 15.

[16] Accordingly, the accession of new states in 1973 was to have increased the original number of judges from seven to 11 (Art. 17 of the 1972 Act of Accession, O.J., English Special Edition 1972 (March, 27)), but their number was reduced to nine on account of Norway's decision not to join the Community (Art. 4 of the Council Decision of January 1, [1973] O.J. L2). Following the accession of Greece, the Court had only 10 judges (Art. 16 of the 1979 Act of Accession, [1979] O.J. L291 and Council Decision of December 22, 1980, [1980] O.J. L380/6, after which the Council raised the number to 11 by Decision of March 31, 1981 ([1981] O.J. L100/20). The present number was laid down by Art. 10 of the Council Decision of January 1, 1995 adjusting the instruments concerning the accession of the new Member States to the European Union ([1995] O.J. L1/4), which amended Art. 17 of the 1985 Act of Accession ([1985] O.J. L302).

[17] France, Germany, Italy, Spain and the United Kingdom.

[18] When new Member States joined the Community in 1973, the original number of advocates general was increased from two to four (Art. 1 of the Decision of January 1, 1973, [1973] O.J. L2/29), which were to be shared among the four "large" Member States. After the accession of Greece, a fifth was added (Council Decision of March 30, 1981, [1981] O.J. L100/21) for a smaller Member State and, following the accession of Spain and Portugal, a sixth (Art. 18 of the 1985 Act of Accession, [1985] O.J. L302). The accession of further Member States has raised the number of advocates general to eight, and temporarily to nine (Art. 11 of the Council Decision of January 1, 1995 amending Art. 20 of the 1994 Act of Accession, [1995] O.J. L1/1): the five "large" Member States each put forward one person for appointment as advocate general, whilst the other Member States share out in turn the remaining three posts. See the Joint Declaration on Art. 31 of the Decision adjusting the instruments concerning the accession of the new Member States to the European Union, [1995] O.J. L1/221).

[19] E.C. Statute, Art. 7.

[20] E.C. Statute, Art. 2. By virtue of the E.C. Statute, Art. 8, the provisions of the Statute relating to judges (Arts. 2–7) also apply to advocates general.

[21] E.C. Statute, Art. 3.

Judges and advocates general may not hold any political or administrative office or engage in any occupation unless exemption is granted by the Council. After their term of office, they must act with integrity and discretion as regards the acceptance of certain appointments or benefits.[22] A judge or advocate general may only be deprived of his or her office or of his or her right to a pension or other benefits in its stead if, in the unanimous opinion of the other judges and advocates general, he or she no longer fulfils the requisite conditions or meets the obligations arising from his or her office.[23]

1–006 Immediately after their partial replacement, the judges elect one of their number as President of the Court for a term of three years, and he or she may be re-elected.[24] The rule that if an office falls vacant before the normal expiry date of its term, a successor is to be elected for the remainder of the term, also applies to the President.[25]

1–007 An election procedure is also used to appoint the Court Registrar for a term of six years,[26] and he or she may be reappointed.[27] If the office of Registrar falls vacant before the normal expiry date, a new Registrar is to be appointed for six years.[28] The Registrar takes the same oath before the Court as the judges and advocates general.[29]

B. Internal organisation

1–008 In principle the Court of Justice sits in plenary session, but the "exception" whereby it forms itself into chambers, each consisting of three, five or seven judges,[30] has in the meantime got the upper hand in terms of the number of cases decided by chambers as compared with the full Court. The Court has formed four three-judge chambers, whilst two chambers have four judges assigned to them (the judges other than the president of chamber take it in turn not to sit). In addition, there are two seven-judge chambers, with the result that each judge also belongs to one of those chambers. The President of the Court does not sit in any chamber. Each chamber is presided over by a president of chamber, who is appointed by the Court for one year.[31] The composition of the chambers and appointments of presidents of chambers are published in the *Official Journal of the European Communities*.[32]

1–009 When the Court sits in chambers, there is a quorum of three judges in the case of three- or five-judge chambers and of five judges in the case of

---

[22] E.C. Statute, Art. 4.
[23] E.C. Statute, Art. 6.
[24] E.C. Treaty, Art. 223 (*ex Art. 167*), para. 5; ECJ Rules of Procedure, Art. 7(1).
[25] ECJ Rules of Procedure, Art. 7(2).
[26] E.C. Treaty, Art. 224 (*ex Art. 168*); ECJ Rules of Procedure, Art. 12.
[27] ECJ Rules of Procedure, Art. 12(3).
[28] ECJ Rules of Procedure, Art. 12(7).
[29] E.C. Statute, Art. 9.
[30] E.C. Treaty, Art. 221 (*ex Art. 165*], para. 2.
[31] ECJ Rules of Procedure, Art. 10(1), subpara. 1. *E.g.* for the 1997–1998 judicial year, see the Decision of the Court of Justice of October 7, 1997, [1997] O.J. C331/1.
[32] ECJ Rules of Procedure, Art. 10(1), subpara. 3.

seven-judge chambers. Decisions of the full Court are valid if nine judges are sitting.[33]

At the end of the written procedure, the Court may at an administrative meeting assign any case to a chamber, upon consideration of the Judge-Rapporteur's preliminary report and after the advocate general has been heard, unless a Member State or a Community institution that is a party to the proceedings has objected.[34] A Member State or an institution which is a party to or an intervener in proceedings or which has submitted written observations in preliminary ruling proceedings is regarded as being a "party to the proceedings".[35] Apart from this, the Court itself lays down the criteria by which, as a rule, cases are assigned to chambers.[36] A chamber may, however, refer a case back to the Court at any stage in the proceedings.[37] Parties are not entitled to require that a judge of a particular nationality sit or not sit.[38] The Court therefore constitutes a genuinely "supranational" court *vis-à-vis* the Member States and specifically national procedural interests. **1–010**

The primary responsibility for decision-making within the Court lies with the Judge-Rapporteur, who is designated for each case by the President immediately after proceedings have been brought.[39] At the same time, the First Advocate General[40] assigns an advocate general to the case.[41] The Judge-Rapporteur and the advocate general follow the procedural progress of the case with particular heed. The Judge-Rapporteur is responsible for drawing up the preliminary report[42] and the report for the hearing.[43] Lastly, it falls to the Judge-Rapporteur to draw up the draft judgment and subsequently to revise it so that it reflects the consensus of the Court or the chamber (or the majority of the bench).[44] **1–011**

The advocate general, acting with complete impartiality and independence, makes, in open court, reasoned submissions ("the Advocate Gen-

---

33 E.C. Statute, Art. 15. It falls within the Court's power of internal organisation to assign the judges from a chamber which are to adjudicate a particular case (see Case C–7/94 *Landesamt für Ausbildungsförderung Nordrhein-Westfalen v. Lubor Gaal* [1995] E.C.R. I–1031 at I–1045, para. 13, ECJ, in which the German Government argued that the criteria determining the composition of the chamber adjudicating a case consisting of five judges from a chamber to which six judges had been appointed had not been published in the *Official Journal of the European Communities*). As far as the Court of First Instance is concerned, the CFI Rules of Procedure, Art. 32(4), provides that if in a chamber of three or five judges the number of judges assigned to that chamber is higher than three or five respectively, the president of the chamber is to decide which of the judges will be called upon to take part in the judgment of the case.

34 E.C. Treaty, Art. 221 (*ex Art. 165*), para. 3; ECJ Rules of Procedure, Art. 95(2).

35 ECJ Rules of Procedure, Art. 95(2), subpara. 2.

36 ECJ Rules of Procedure, Art. 9(3).

37 ECJ Rules of Procedure, Art. 95(3).

38 E.C. Statute, Art. 16, para. 4.

39 ECJ Rules of Procedure, Art. 9(2).

40 The First Advocate General is appointed for one year by the Court and has the rank of a president of chamber. He is *primus inter pares* among the advocates general (ECJ Rules of Procedure, Art. 10(1)).

41 E.C.J Rules of Procedure, Art. 10(2).

42 See para. 22–054, below.

43 See paras. 22–057, 22–058, below.

44 See paras. 22–105, 22–106, below.

eral's Opinion") on each case assigned to him or her in order to assist the Court in the performance of its task.[45]

1–012 The President directs the judicial business and the administration of the Court; he or she presides at hearings and deliberations.[46]

1–013 In performing its duties the Court has a variety of departments at its disposal. There is an interpreting service, a translation service, a research and documentation department, which also manages the Court's library, and internal administrative machinery (including personnel, finance and technical services departments). The Registry staff assist the Registrar in the performance of his or her judicial duties and as far as his or her administrative tasks are concerned, the Registrar can have recourse to the various departments of the Court. The judges and advocates general are each served by three law clerks, known as *référendaires* or legal secretaries, who carry out the preparatory work for the judges and advocates general, and three secretarial staff members.

C. Basic function

1–014 The Court of Justice plays the role of the Community's constitutional court, that is to say, as the guardian of the objectives and rules of law laid down in the Treaties.[47] The Court rules on applications by Member States or Community institutions in cases in which constitutional issues come to the fore,[48] such as the legality of Community secondary legislation, the preservation of institutional equilibrium, the demarcation of Community and national spheres of competence and the development of protection of fundamental rights.[49]

---

[45] E.C. Treaty, Art. 222 (*ex Art. 166*), para. 2. For an account of the office of Advocate General, see Borgsmidt, "The Advocate General at the European Court of Justice: A Comparative Study" (1988) E.L.Rev. 106–119.

[46] ECJ Rules of Procedure, Art. 8.

[47] Donner, "The Constitutional Powers of the Court of Justice of the European Communities" (1974) C.M.L.Rev. 127–140, and "The Court of Justice as a Constitutional Court of the Communities", in *Tussen het echte en het gemaakte*, Zwolle, Tjeenk Willink, 1986, 343–361; Due, "A Constitutional Court for the European Communities", in *Constitutional Adjudication in European Community and National Law. Essays for the Hon. Mr. Justice T.F. O'Higgins*, Dublin, Butterworths (Ireland), 1992, 3 at 4–9; Jacobs, "Is the Court of Justice of the European Communities a Constitutional Court?", *ibid.*, 25–32; Kapteyn, "The Role of the Court of Justice in the Development of the Community Legal Order", in *Il ruolo del giudice internazionale nell'evoluzione del diritto internazionale e comunitario*, Milan, CEDAM, 1995, at 157–173; Lenaerts, "Some Thoughts about the Interaction between Judges and Politicians" (1992) Y.E.L. 1–34; Mischo, "Un rôle nouveau pour la Cour de Justice?", (1990) R.M.C. 681–686; Pescatore, "Die Gemeinschaftsverträge als Verfassungsrecht—ein Kapitel Verfassungsgeschichte in der Perspektive des europäischen Gerichtshofs, systematisch geordnet", in *Festschrift Kutscher*, Baden-Baden, Nomos, 1981, at 319–338.

[48] The constitutional dimension is clearly recognisable in the Court's case law: see Lenaerts, *Le juge et la constitution aux Etats-Unis d'Amérique et dans l'ordre juridique européen*, Brussels, Bruylant, 1988. See also Weiler, "The Court of Justice on Trial. Review Essay of Hjalte Rasmussen: On Law and Policy in the European Court of Justice" (1987) C.M.L.Rev. 555–589.

[49] Rodríguez Iglesias, "Der Gerichtshof der Europäischen Gemeinschaften als Verfassungsgericht" (1992) *EuR.* 225–245. For the Court's jurisdiction to rule on the "constitutionality" of national law, see Rinze, "The Role of the European Court of Justice as a Federal Constitutional Court" (1993) P.L. 426–443.

Alongside this, the Court plays the role of a supreme court where—on a request from a national court for a preliminary ruling—it ensures the uniform application of Community law. In a certain sense, there is also a constitutional aspect to that function performed by the Court inasmuch as disparate application of Community law in the Member States would run counter to achievement of the objectives laid down in the Treaties.

It is self-evident that constitutional issues of Community law may also arise in cases brought before national courts or the Court of First Instance. Consequently, the Court of Justice is not the sole guardian of the Community legal order. But national courts may (and, in some cases, must) still bring the constitutional issue before the Court by requesting a preliminary ruling.[50] Likewise, it is possible to appeal against decisions of the Court of First Instance, which means that here again the Court of Justice can have the last word in determining legal questions with constitutional implications.[51] **1–015**

III. The Court of First Instance

A. Composition

The Court of First Instance consists of 15 judges.[52] They are appointed for a term of six years by common accord of the governments of the Member States.[53] They are chosen from persons whose independence is beyond doubt and who possess the ability required for appointment to judicial office. Membership of the Court is partially renewed every three years, although retiring judges are eligible for reappointment.[54] As in the case of the Court of Justice, there is no nationality requirement, but in practice there is one judge from each Member State. If a vacancy occurs during the term of office, the new judge is appointed for the remainder of his predecessor's normal term.[55] **1–016**

No separate advocates general are attached to the Court of First Instance, on the ground that not all cases brought before it require the assistance of an advocate general. However, a judge may be called upon to perform the task of advocate general in a given case.[56] In such case, he or **1–017**

---

[50] Chap. 2, below.

[51] para. 1–028, below.

[52] CFI Decision, Art. 2(1).

[53] E.C. Treaty, Art. 225 (*ex Art. 168a*) (3).

[54] E.C. Treaty, Art. 225(3).

[55] E.C. Statute, Art. 7, applicable by virtue of the E.C. Statute, Art. 44.

[56] CFI Decision, Art. 2(3). This rule is a "compromise" between the view that the advocate general's role principally consists of assisting the Court of Justice in its task of ensuring uniform interpretation of Community law and that therefore there is no need for an advocate general in the Court of First Instance, and the view that the advocate general's role is an essential safeguard for the legal protection of individuals and that therefore it is important for there to be an advocate general in the first-instance court. See Christianos, "Le Tribunal de première instance et la nouvelle organisation judiciaire des Communautés européennes", in *Le Tribunal de première instance des Communautés européennes*, Maastricht, European Institute for Public Administration, 1990, 17 at 23; Vandersanden, "Une naissance désirée: le Tribunal de première instance des Communautés européennes" (1988) J.T. 545 at 546.

she performs the same function as an advocate general in the Court of Justice and may not take part in the judgment of the case.[57] The decision to designate an advocate general in a particular case is taken at an administrative meeting of the Court of First Instance at the request of the chamber dealing with the case or to which the case is assigned.[58] Under Articles 17 and 18 of the CFI Rules of Procedure, the Court is to be assisted by an Advocate General when it sits in plenary session[59] and when a chamber considers that the legal difficulty or the factual complexity of the case requires the appointment of an advocate general. The President of the Court of First Instance then designates the judge called upon to perform the function of an advocate general.[60] The consequence is that references to the advocate general in the Rules of Procedure of the Court of First Instance apply only where a judge has been designated so to act (CFI Rules of Procedure, Article 2(2)).

1–018 Before taking up his or her duties, each judge takes an oath before the Court of Justice (CFI Rules of Procedure, Article 4(1)). Judges of the Court of First Instance have the same status as judges and advocates general of the Court of Justice[61] and are subject to the same constraints and obligations as regards taking up political or administrative offices and engaging in other occupations.[62]

A judge may be removed from his or her office only by the Court of Justice, after seeking the opinion of the Court of First Instance.[63] Before that opinion—which must be reasoned—is given, the judge concerned may make representations to the Court of First Instance in closed session.[64]

1–019 Immediately after their partial replacement, the judges elect a President from among their number for a term of three years,[65] and he or she may be re-elected. If the President gives up his or her office before the expiry of its term, a successor is to be elected only for the outstanding portion of the term.

---

[57] *Cf.* the E.C. Treaty, Art. 222 (*ex Art. 166*), para. 2, in conjunction with the CFI Decision, Art. 2(3) subpara. 2.

[58] CFI Rules of Procedure, Art. 19, para. 1; CFI Decision, Art. 2(3), subpara. 3, provides that the criteria for selecting such cases, as well as the procedures for designating the advocates general, are to be laid down in the CFI Rules of Procedure.

[59] Where, following the designation of an advocate general pursuant to the CFI Rules of Procedure, Art. 17, there is an even number of judges in the Court of First Instance sitting in plenary session, the President is to designate, before the hearing and in accordance with a rota established in advance by the Court and published in the *Official Journal of the European Communities*, the judge who will not take part in the judgment of the case (CFI Rules of Procedure, Art. 32(1), subpara. 2).

[60] CFI Rules of Procedure, Art. 19, para. 2.

[61] E.C. Treaty, Art. 225 (*ex Art. 168a*) (2); See also CFI Decision, Art. 2(5), by virtue of which Art. 21 of the Protocol on Privileges and Immunities of the European Communities is applicable to judges of the Court of First Instance and its Registrar, and E.C. Statute, Art. 44, which provides in particular that Arts 2–8 are applicable to the Court of First Instance and its members.

[62] See para. 1–005, above.

[63] E.C. Statute, Art. 44; CFI Rules of Procedure, Art. 5.

[64] For further particulars, see CFI Rules of Procedure, Art. 5.

[65] CFI Decision, Art. 2(2).

The Court appoints its Registrar.[66] The provisions relating to the status of the Registrar of the Court of Justice apply *mutatis mutandis* to the Registrar of the Court of First Instance.[67] **1–020**

B. Internal organisation

Unlike the Court of Justice, the Court of First Instance sits as a rule in chambers and only "exceptionally" in plenary session or constituted by a single Judge.[68] Pursuant to Article 2(4) of the CFI Decision and Article 10(1) of its Rules of Procedure, the Court of First Instance has formed five chambers, composed of three judges, each of which may be extended to form a new chamber (a chamber in extended composition) of five judges.[69] Under Article 12 of the CFI Rules of Procedure, the Court is to lay down criteria by which cases are to be allocated among the chambers.[70] As soon as the application initiating proceedings has been lodged, the President assigns the case to a chamber[71] on the basis of the criteria laid down by the Court—also pursuant to Article 12 of the CFI Rules of Procedure—for the purposes of allocating cases among the chambers with an equal number of judges.[72] Each chamber has a president appointed for one year.[73] The composition of the chambers and appointments of presidents of chambers are published in the *Official Journal of the European Communities*.[74] **1–021**

Whenever the legal difficulty or the importance of the case or special circumstances so justify, a case may be referred to the Court of First Instance sitting in plenary session or to a chamber consisting of a different

[66] E.C. Statute, Art. 45.

[67] *ibid.*

[68] CFI Decision, Art. 2(4); CFI Rules of Procedure, Art. 11(1). On April 26, 1999, the Council adopted a Decision, pursuant to E.C. Treaty, Article 225 (*ex Article 168a*), amending the CFI Decision so as to enable the Court of First Instance to give decisions when constituted by a single Judge ([1999] O.J. L114/52). The principle according to which the Court of First Instance normally sits in chambers composed of three or five judges remains unchanged. As where a case is referred to the Court sitting in plenary session, reference of a case to a single Judge is optional only and confined to situations determined in the CFI Rules of Procedure (amended to that effect by [1999] O.J. L135/92; see especially Art. 14(2)).

[69] See, *e.g.*, for the 1997–98 judicial year, the Decision of the Court of First Instance of July 2, 1997, [1998] O.J. C327/17.

[70] CFI Rules of Procedure, Art. 12, as amended on September 15, 1994 ([1994] O.J. L249/17). The Court has laid down the following criteria: actions concerning the implementation of the rules concerning state aid and the rules on trade protection measures are to be assigned, with effect from the lodging of the application and without prejudice to any subsequent application of Arts. 14 and 51, to chambers with an extended composition of five judges; all other cases are to be assigned with effect from the lodging of the application and without prejudice to subsequent application of arts. 14 and 51, to chambers of three judges. See Criteria for allocating cases to the chambers set out in Decision 98/C 327/31 of the Court of First Instance [1998] O.J. C327/17.

[71] CFI Rules of Procedure, Art. 13(1): *Cf.* ECJ Rules of Procedure, Art. 9(2) (case assigned to a chamber only for any preparatory inquiries) and Art. 95(2).

[72] For the period September 21, 1998 to September 30, 1999, see [1998] O.J. C327/17.

[73] CFI Rules of Procedure, Art. 15, para. 1.

[74] CFI Rules of Procedure, Art. 15, para. 3.

number of judges.[75] At any stage of the proceedings, the chamber hearing the case may, on its own initiative or at the request of the parties, make a proposal to this effect to the Court sitting in plenary session. The full Court then decides, after hearing the parties and the advocate general, whether or not to refer the case.[76]

A bench of the Court of First Instance can decide validly only when an uneven number of judges is sitting in the deliberations.

A quorum consists of three judges in the case of chambers and nine judges where the Court sits in plenary session.[77]

1–022 The procedure before the Court of First Instance largely parallels that before the Court of Justice (see Part V, below).

1–023 The tasks of the President and the Registrar of the Court of First Instance are, to the extent of their powers, similar to those of their counterparts in the Court of Justice.

1–024 As far as the personnel of the Court of First Instance is concerned, the following provision was inserted into the Statute of the Court of Justice by Council Decision:

> "The President of the Court of Justice and the President of the Court of First Instance shall determine, by common accord, the conditions under which officials and other servants attached to the Court of Justice shall render their services to the Court of First Instance to enable it to function. Certain officials or other servants shall be responsible to the Registrar of the Court of First Instance under the authority of the President of the Court of First Instance."[78]

The last sentence of that passage applies, of course, to the staff of the Registry and *cabinets* of the judges of the Court of First Instance (judges are assisted by, among others, two legal secretaries or *référendaires*, who perform the same duties as the legal secretaries of the judges and advocates general of the Court of Justice, and two secretarial staff members). The aim is to bring the staff of the Court of First Instance who are directly and exclusively concerned with the performance of its judicial function under the President and the Registrar, which constitutes a guarantee of independence from the other court.

C. Basic function

1–025 The Court of First Instance is the administrative court of the Community. Its essential function is to provide protection for natural or legal persons

[75] CFI Rules of Procedure, Art. 14, para. 1.
[76] CFI Rules of Procedure, Art. 51.
[77] E.C. Statute, Art. 15, applicable by virtue of the E.C. Statute, Art. 44. See also CFI Rules of Procedure, Art. 32(2), (3).
[78] E.C. Statute, Art. 45, para. 2.

against any unlawful act or omission of a Community institution.[79] Formerly, that function was carried out wholly by the Court of Justice.[80]

The purpose of establishing the Court of First Instance was to maintain and improve the quality and effectiveness of judicial protection in the Community legal order. In 1988 a steadily rising tide of cases had caused proceedings before the Court to become unacceptably protracted.[81] Furthermore, in cases requiring an appraisal of complex facts,[82] the Court of Justice could no longer provide the high quality of judicial protection which it was called upon to do.[83] The transfer in stages to the Court of First Instance of jurisdiction in all cases brought by natural or legal persons helped to allay those shortcomings.[84] At the same time, a two-tier court **1–026**

---

[79] Scherer and Zuleeg, "Verwaltungsgerichtsbarkeit", in Schweitzer (ed.), *Europäisches Verwaltungsrecht*, Vienna, Verlag der österreichischen Akademie der Wissenschaften, 1991, at 197–240.

[80] Natural or legal persons may still obtain indirect protection from the Court of Justice through the examination of the validity of Community measures in a reference for a preliminary ruling; See Chap. 10, below.

[81] The average duration of a direct action increased from 8.5 months in 1970 to 24 months. The average time taken to complete proceedings in a reference for a preliminary ruling was 17.5 months.

[82] Principally, competition and anti-dumping cases.

[83] For commentaries, see Van Ginderachter, "Le Tribunal de première instance des Communautés européennes. Un nouveau-né prodige?" (1989) C.D.E. 63–105; Millett, *The Court of First Instance of the European Communities*, London–Edinburgh, Butterworths, 1990; Biancarelli, "La création du Tribunal de première instance des Communautés européennes: un luxe ou une nécessité?" (1990) R.T.D.E. 1–25; da Cruz Vilaça, "The Court of First Instance of the European Communities: A Significant Step towards the Consolidation of the European Community as a Community governed by the Rule of Law" (1990) Y.E.L. 1–56; Lenaerts, "Le Tribunal de première instance des Communautés européennes: genèse et premiers pas" (1990) J.T. 409–415, and "The Development of the Judicial Process in the European Community after the Establishment of the Court of First Instance", in *Collected Courses of the Academy of European Law*, Vol. I, Book 1, Florence/Dordrecht, European University Institute, Martinus Nijhoff, 1991, at 53–113; Jung, "Das Gericht erster Instanz der Europäischen Gemeinschaften" (1992) EuR. 246–264; Van der Woude, "Le Tribunal de première instance 'Les trois premières années'" (1992) R.M.U.E. 113–157; Vesterdorf, "The Court of First Instance of the European Communities after Two Full Years of Operation" (1992) C.M.L.Rev. 897–915; Biancarelli, "Présentation générale du Tribunal de première instance des Communautés europénnes" (1995) R.M.C.U.E. 564–567; Neville Brown, "The First Five Years of the Court of First Instance and Appeals to the Court of Justice: Assessment and Statistics" (1995) C.M.L.Rev. 743–761; Palacio González, *El Sistema Judicial Comunitario*, Bilboa, Universidad de Deusto, 1996, at 87–94; Kirschner and Klüpfel, *Das Gericht erster Instanz der Europäischen Gemeinschaften*, Cologne/Berlin/Bonn/Munich, Carl Heymans Verlag KG, 1998.

[84] See the preamble to the CFI Decision. For a survey of the heads of jurisdiction transferred, see Gautron, "Les compétences du Tribunal de première instance" (1995) R.M.C.U.E. 568–575. On December 14, 1998, the Court of Justice sent to the Council a draft Council decision amending the CFI Decision and designed to enlarge the jurisdiction of the Court of First Instance by conferring on it, in particular, jurisdiction to hear and determine, within certain defined fields, actions for annulment brought by Member States. The proposed transfer of jurisdiction is designed to ensure a better administration of justice, in particular by limiting to the greatest possible extent the situations in which actions in which the same relief is sought must be brought simultaneously before the Court of Justice and the Court of First Instance. The actions for annulment covered by the proposed transfer of jurisdiction are those concerning (a) decisions of the Commission relating to the clearance of the accounts of the Member States with respect to the expenditure financed by the European Agricultural Guidance and Guarantee Fund, "Guarantee" Section; (b) decisions adopted

system was created for such cases, which could only improve the quality of legal protection.

1–027 By Article 225 (*ex Article 168a*) (1) of the E.C. Treaty, only preliminary references are excluded from the potential jurisdiction of the Court of First Instance. In contrast, all direct actions may be brought within its purview (in accordance with the decision-making procedure defined in Article 225(2)). At present, only direct actions (actions for annulment or for failure to act, actions for damages and actions pursuant to an arbitration clause) brought by a natural or legal person, irrespective of the applicable substantive Community law, come within the jurisdiction of the Court of First Instance. The Court also has jurisdiction in disputes between the Communities and their servants (staff cases).[85]

1–028 An appeal, on points of law only, may lie from the Court of First Instance to the Court of Justice. The Court of First Instance has sole jurisdiction to find the facts.[86]

1–029 Lastly, mention should be made of Article 47 of the Statute of the Court of Justice of the E.C.,[87] which deals with three complications regarding the allocation of jurisdiction as between the Court of Justice and the Court of First Instance. First, there is *formal mistake*: if an application or other procedural document addressed to the Court of First Instance is lodged by mistake with the Registrar of the Court of Justice, or *vice versa*, it is to be transmitted immediately from one Registrar to the other.[88] Secondly, there is *substantive mistake*: if the Court of First Instance finds that it does not have jurisdiction to hear and determine an action in respect of which the Court of Justice has jurisdiction, it is to refer the action to the Court of Justice; likewise, where the Court of Justice finds that an action falls within the jurisdiction of the Court of First Instance, it is to refer it to the Court of

pursuant to an act of the Council founded on Title V of Part Three of the E.C. Treaty, relating to transport; (c) decisions addressed to undertakings or to associations of undertakings relating to the competition rules of the E.C. Treaty applicable to undertakings, including the rules relating to the control of concentrations of undertakings, or to Articles 65 and 66 of the ECSC Treaty; (d) decisions concerning aid granted by States and adopted pursuant to Article 88 (*ex Article 93*) (2) and (3) of the E.C. Treaty, to a Council regulation based on Article 89 (*ex Article 94*) of the E.C. Treaty or to an act of the Commission based on the first or second paragraphs of Article 95 of the ECSC Treaty; (e) acts adopted pursuant to a Council regulation concerning measures to protect trade within the meaning of Article 133 (*ex Article 113*) of the E.C. Treaty or to an act of the Commission relating to measures to protect trade in the sense contemplated by Article 74 of the ECSC Treaty, in cases of dumping, subsidies or in the exercise of the Community's rights under international trade rules in order to react against barriers to trade; (f) decisions adopted pursuant to an act of an institution creating a fund, a financial instrument or an action programme authorising the grant of Community financial support. As far as a proposed change in the jurisdiction of the Court of First Instance pursuant to an arbitration clause is concerned, see para.17–008, below. The Commission and the European Parliament are yet to give their opinion on this proposed transfer of jurisdiction. The Council has only just started to consider it.

[85] E.C. Treaty, Art. 236 (*ex Art. 179*); EAEC Treaty, Art. 152.

[86] See Chap. 15, below.

[87] ECSC Statute, Art. 47; EAEC Treaty, Art. 48.

[88] E.C. Statute, Art. 47, para. 1.

First Instance, whereupon that court may not decline jurisdiction.[89] As will be appreciated, the allocation of jurisdiction as between the Court of Justice and the Court of First Instance is based on objective grounds in so far as the court wrongly seised of a case falling within the jurisdiction of the other court is under an obligation to refer it to that other court. In case of doubt, the Court of Justice has the last word, since after it has referred a case to the Court of First Instance in that way, that court cannot decline jurisdiction. This system does not detract from the right of the Court of First Instance to decline jurisdiction where a case falls outside the sphere of action of the Community judiciary, regarded as a whole.

Thirdly, there is the case where the two courts are validly seised of cases in which *the object is identical.*[90] This will occur where a natural or legal person brings an action against a Community institution for annulment of an act or for failure to take a decision, and another Community institution or a Member State brings a similar action before the Court of Justice. Two examples may be given by way of illustration: a public undertaking brings an action before the Court of First Instance for the annulment of a Commission decision finding that it has abused a dominant position in the common market contrary to Article 82 (*ex Article 86*) of the E.C. Treaty, whilst the Member State responsible for the undertaking brings an action for the annulment of the same decision before the Court of Justice; an official claims before the Court of First Instance that his salary slip drawn up by the European Parliament should be annulled on the ground that the Council regulation laying down the weighting applicable to officials' salaries in the various places of employment is contrary to the Staff Regulations, whilst the Commission brings an action before the Court of Justice for the annulment of the same regulation. The third paragraph of Article 47 of the E.C. Statute resolves the matter as follows:

> "Where the Court of Justice and the Court of First Instance are seised of cases in which the same relief is sought, the same issue of interpretation is raised or the validity of the same act is called in question, the Court of First Instance may, after hearing the parties, stay the proceedings before it until such time as the Court of Justice shall have delivered judgment. Where applications are brought for the same act to be declared void, the Court of First Instance may also decline jurisdiction in order that the Court of Justice may rule on such

[89] E.C. Statute, Art. 47, para. 2. For practical examples, see (Order of May 23, 1990), Case C–72/90 *Asia Motor France v. Commission* [1990] E.C.R. I–2181, ECJ; (Order of June 4, 1991), Case C–66/90 *PTT v. Commission* [1991] E.C.R. I–2723, ECJ; (Order of May 3, 1993), Case C–424/92 *Ladbroke Racing v. Commission* [1993] E.C.R. I–2213, ECJ; (Order of March 21, 1997), Case C–95/97 *Région wallonne v. Commission* [1997] E.C.R. I–1787, ECJ; (Order of October 1, 1997), Case C–180/97 *Regione Toscana v. Commission* [1997] E.C.R. I–5245 at I–5250—5251, paras. 9–12, ECJ.

[90] Joliet and Vogel, "Le Tribunal de première instance des Communautés européennes" (1989) R.M.C. 423 at 429. See also the proposed further transfer of jurisdiction to the Court of First Instance designed to reduce the number of such situations to an absolute minimum (the proposal is explained in n. 84, above).

applications. In the cases referred to in this subparagraph [the above two sentences], the Court of Justice may also decide to stay the proceedings before it; in that event, the proceedings before the Court of First Instance shall continue."

This solution calls for a number of observations. The Court of Justice is not empowered to compel the Court of First Instance to stay proceedings or to decline jurisdiction (*se dessaisir*) in the case of an action for annulment.[91] This is a reflection of the judicial independence of the two courts, expressed by the words "the Court of First Instance may". But if that court decides to make use of that possibility, the Court of Justice can prevent it from doing so by staying proceedings on its part, thus causing the procedure to have to go through the Court of First Instance. In the event that the Court of First Instance has already declined jurisdiction in respect of an application for annulment, the Court of Justice can refer the case back to it by staying the parallel proceedings. The Court of Justice might decide to do so in a case such as that mentioned in the first example given above. The application for annulment of the Commission decision brought by the public undertaking may raise issues of great factual complexity on which the Court of Justice would like to have a ruling from the Court of First Instance before pronouncing on the application for annulment brought against the same Commission decision by the Member State concerned. The Court of Justice has in this respect a discretion to choose the most appropriate solution.[92]

[91] The expression "decline jurisdiction" (*se dessaisir* in the French version) in the E.C. Statute, Art. 47, para. 3, does not have the same meaning as it has in Art. 47, para. 2 (where the French reads "*décliner sa compétence*"). Where the Court of Justice refers a case to the Court of First Instance pursuant to Art. 47, para. 2, the Court of First Instance may no longer decline jurisdiction on account of the nature of the action, but it may refrain from deciding the case (*se dessaisir*), for example on jurisdictional grounds, and refer the case back to the Court of Justice. For examples, see (Order of June 21, 1991), Case T–42/91 *PTT v. Commission* [1991] E.C.R. II–273, CFI; (Order of February 1, 1995), Case T–88/94 *Société Commerciale des Potasses et de l'Azote and Others v. Commission* [1995] E.C.R. II–221, CFI (this case was decided by the Court of Justice: Joined Cases C–68/94 and C–30/95 *France v. Commission* [1998] E.C.R. I–1375, ECJ); (Order of February 23, 1995), Case T–488/93 *Hanseatische Industrie-Beteiligungen GmbH v. Commission* [1995] E.C.R. II–469, CFI; (Order of February 23, 1995), Case T–490/93 *Bremer Vulkan Verband A.G. v. Commission* [1995] E.C.R. II–477, CFI (these cases, too, were decided by the Court of Justice: Joined Cases C–329/93, C–62/95 and C–63/95 *Germany and Others v. Commission* [1996] E.C.R. I–5151, ECJ).

[92] An example is afforded by the action for annulment brought by a number of competitors of Air France against the Commission's decision under the E.C. Treaty, Art. 88 (*ex Art. 93*) (2) authorising an increase in the company's capital by France as state aid compatible with the common market, whilst the United Kingdom brought an action in the Court of Justice for the annulment of the same decision (Case C–274/94). The Court of Justice suspended the hearing of that case to allow the Court of First Instance to give judgment first. The latter court then gave judgment in Joined Cases T–371/94 and T–394/94 *British Airways and Others v. Commission*, [1998] E.C.R. II–2412, CFI, annulling the decision. After that judgment became *res judicata*—in the absence of an appeal—Case C–274/94 became to no purpose (since the application sought to annul a decision which had already been declared void).

CHAPTER 2

CO-OPERATION BETWEEN NATIONAL COURTS AND THE COURT OF JUSTICE: THE REFERENCE FOR A PRELIMINARY RULING

The primary responsibility of national courts for the correct application of Community law is rounded off by the preliminary ruling procedure, which, in the words of the Court of Justice, is "essential for preservation of the Community character of the law established by the Treaty and has the object of ensuring that in all circumstances this law is the same in all States of the Community".[1] **2–001**

Article 234 (*ex Article 177*) of the E.C. Treaty and Article 150 of the EAEC Treaty, which are virtually identical,[2] empower the Court of Justice to "give preliminary rulings" on the interpretation of Community law[3] and on the validity of acts of the Community institutions.[4] The new title of the **2–002**

---

[1] Case 166/73 *Rheinmühlen v. Einfuhr- und Vorratsstelle Getreide* [1974] E.C.R. 33 at 38, para. 2, ECJ.

[2] E.C. Treaty, Art. 234 (*ex Art. 177*):

The Court of Justice shall have jurisdiction to give preliminary rulings concerning:

(a) the interpretation of this Treaty;

(b) the validity and interpretation of acts of the institutions of the Community and of the ECB;

(c) the interpretation of the statutes of bodies established by an act of the Council, where those statutes so provide.

Where such a question is raised before any court or tribunal of a Member State, that court or tribunal may, if it considers that a decision of the question is necessary to enable it to give judgment, request the Court of Justice to give a ruling thereon.

Where any such question is raised in a case pending before a court or tribunal of a Member State against whose decisions there is no judicial remedy under national law, that court or tribunal shall bring the matter before the Court of Justice.

EAEC Treaty, Art. 150:

The Court of Justice shall have jurisdiction to give preliminary rulings concerning:

(a) the interpretation of this Treaty;

(b) the validity and interpretation of acts of the institutions of the Community;

(c) the interpretation of the statutes of bodies established by an act of the Council, save where those statutes provide otherwise.

Where such a question is raised before any court or tribunal of a Member State, that court or tribunal may, if it considers that a decision of the question is necessary to enable it to give judgment, request the Court of Justice to give a ruling thereon.

Where any such question is raised in a case pending before a court or tribunal of a Member State, against whose decisions there is no judicial remedy under national law, that court or tribunal shall bring the matter before the Court of Justice.

[3] See Chap. 6, below.

[4] See Chap. 10, below.

E.C. Treaty on visas, asylum and other policies related to free movement of persons, introduced by the Treaty of Amsterdam,[5] confers on the Court of Justice jurisdiction to give preliminary rulings on the interpretation of the title in question or on the validity or interpretation of acts of the Community institutions based on that title. Only national courts or tribunals against whose decisions there is no judicial remedy under national law may make such references for preliminary rulings. They are under a duty to make such a reference if they consider that a decision on the question is necessary to enable them to give judgment[6] (E.C. Treaty, Article 68 (*ex Article 73p*) (1)).[7]

The ECSC Treaty contains no provision relating to the Court's jurisdiction to give preliminary rulings on interpretation, but does provide that "The Court shall have sole jurisdiction to give preliminary rulings on the validity of acts of the High Authority [Commission] and of the Council where such validity is in issue in proceedings brought before a national court or tribunal" (Article 41). Nevertheless, the Court has held that it has jurisdiction to answer questions referred for a preliminary ruling on the interpretation of ECSC law, on the ground that it would be:

> "contrary to the objectives and the coherence of the Treaties if the determination of the meaning and scope of rules deriving from the EEC and EAEC Treaties were ultimately a matter for the Court of Justice, as is provided in identical terms by Article 177 *[now Article 234]* of the E[E]C Treaty and Article 150 of the EAEC Treaty, thereby enabling those rules to be applied in a uniform manner, but such jurisdiction in respect of rules deriving from the ECSC Treaty were to be retained exclusively by the various national courts, whose interpretations might differ, and the Court of Justice were to have no power to ensure that such rules were given a uniform interpretation."[8]

2–003 As far as the Court of Justice is concerned, Article 41 of the ECSC Treaty, Article 234 (*ex Article 177*) of the E.C. Treaty and Article 150 of the EAEC Treaty, "different though their actual terms may be", "all express a twofold need: to ensure the utmost uniformity in the application of

[5] [1997] O.J. C340.

[6] See paras 2–028—2–057, below.

[7] The new version of Title VI of the E.U. Treaty, "Provisions on police and judicial cooperation in criminal matters", also gives the Court of Justice jurisdiction to give preliminary rulings on the validity and interpretation of framework decisions and decisions on the interpretation of conventions established under that title and on the validity and interpretation of the measures implementing them (Art. 35 (*ex Art. K.7*) (1)). Under Art. 35(2), that jurisdiction to give preliminary rulings has to be accepted by Member States wishing to do so by a declaration made at the time of signature of the Treaty or at any time thereafter. On signature of the Amsterdam Treaty, Austria, Belgium, Germany, Greece and Luxembourg lodged declarations in which they accepted the jurisdiction of the Court of Justice on the conditions set out in Art. 35(3)(b) (in the case of those countries any national court or tribunal may make a reference for a preliminary ruling) (see Chap. 20, below).

[8] Case C–221/88 *Busseni* [1990] E.C.R. I–495 at I–524, para. 16, ECJ (case notes by Arnull (1990) E.L.Rev. 321–326, and Bebr (1991) C.M.L.Rev. 415–427).

Community law and to establish for that purpose effective co-operation between the Court of Justice and national courts".[9] That co-operation requires "the national court and the Court of Justice, both keeping within their respective jurisdiction, and with the aim of ensuring that Community law is applied in a uniform manner, to make direct and complementary contributions to the working out of a decision".[10]

That aim of the preliminary ruling procedure holds good no matter whether the ruling is sought on the interpretation of Community law or on the validity of a Community act.[11] This was the principal reason which prompted the Court to declare with regard to the application of Article 234 (*ex Article 177*) of the E.C. Treaty—which, unlike Article 41 of the ECSC Treaty, does not embody any formal stipulation in this regard—that it has the sole power to declare an act of a Community institution invalid.[12] This is because the uniform application of Community law is particularly necessary when the validity of a Community act is at stake. Divergences of view between courts in the Member States as to the validity of Community acts would be liable to place in jeopardy the very unity of the Community legal order and detract from the fundamental requirement of legal certainty.[13] Naturally, this does not alter the fact that reviewing the validity of acts of Community institutions is essentially a control of the legality of such acts, which is primarily designed to protect the rights of individuals.[14] **2–004**

A request for a preliminary ruling takes the form of a question put to the Court, which is subject to a number of rules. First, the *initiative* of referring the question must emanate from "a court or tribunal [*juridiction* in French] of a Member State", either of its own motion or acting on a request made by one of the parties in proceedings pending before it, and national (procedural) law may not put impediments in the way of the right to seek a preliminary ruling (which every national court or tribunal has by virtue of Community law).[15] Consequently, the *relevance* of the question falls to be **2–005**

---

9 *Busseni* (cited in n. 8, above), at I–523, para. 13.

10 Case 16/65 *Schwarze v. Einfuhr- und Vorratsstelle Getreide* [1965] E.C.R. 877 at 886, ECJ.

11 Case 66/80 *International Chemical Corporation v. Amministrazione delle Finanze dello Stato* [1981] E.C.R. 1191 at 1215, para. 11, ECJ.

12 Case 314/85 *Foto-Frost v. Hauptzollamt Lübeck-Ost* [1987] E.C.R. 4199 at 4231, para. 17, ECJ. See Bebr, "The Reinforcement of the Constitutional Review of Community Acts under Art. 177 *[now Art. 234]* EEC Treaty (cases 314/85 and 133 to 136/85)" (1988) C.M.L.Rev. 667 at 672–684; Glaesner, "Die Vorlagepflicht unterinstanzlicher Gerichte im Vorabentscheidungsverfahren" (1990) EuR. 143–157; Goffin, "De l'incompétence des juridictions nationales pour constater l'invalidité des actes d'institutions communautaires" (1990) C.D.E. 216–226.

13 *Foto-Frost v. Hauptzollamt Lübeck-Ost* (cited in n. 12, above), at 4231, para. 15.

14 Case 294/83 *Les Verts v. European Parliament* [1986] E.C.R. 1339 at 1365, para. 23, ECJ.

15 Case 166/73 *Rheinmühlen v. Einfuhr- und Vorratsstelle Getreide* [1974] E.C.R. 33 at 38, para. 2, ECJ; Case C–312/93 *Peterbroeck* [1995] E.C.R. I–4599 at I–4621, para. 13, ECJ. Note that where a potential question of Community law arises before a court not being a court of last resort, it has to decide whether a decision on the question is necessary in order to give judgment and, if so, whether the court should order a reference to be made. Matters taken into account in the United Kingdom include the importance of the point of law for the uniform interpretation of Community law; the question of delay and costs; the parties' wishes; the existence of parallel proceedings in other Member States and whether there is a need to consider a Community text in different languages: see *Brealey and Hoskins* (cited in Chap. 1, note 12, above), at pp. 214–224.

determined by the national court, albeit only within certain limits which the Court of Justice has placed upon its competence to answer questions referred for a preliminary ruling. Lastly, a "court or tribunal of a Member State against whose decisions there is no judicial remedy under national law" is in principle *obliged* to refer questions for a preliminary ruling which are raised in a case pending before it. These matters will be considered below.

I. The Initiative for Requesting a Preliminary Ruling

A. What is a "court or tribunal of a Member State"?

2–006 Generally, the expression "court or tribunal of a Member State" does not raise any difficulties. Where a Member State regards a public body as a "court or tribunal", Community law accepts it as such. This is because in that case the body manifestly fulfils the criteria which the Court of Justice has formulated in order to confer on a body which is not considered a court or tribunal under national law that capacity under Community law with a view to the application of the articles of the treaties relating to the preliminary ruling procedure.

2–007 There must be: (1) a body, (2) which is established by law, (3) permanent and independent[16] and (4) charged with the settlement of disputes defined in general terms, (5) which is bound by rules governing *inter partes* proceedings similar to those used by the ordinary courts of law,[17] (6) in so far as it acts as the "proper judicial body" for the disputes in question, which means that parties must be required to apply to the court or tribunal for the settlement of their dispute and its determination must be binding,[18] and (7) is bound to apply rules of law.[19] In accordance with that test, the Netherlands *Commissie van Beroep Huisartsgeneeskunde* (Appeals Committee for General Medicine) was regarded as being a "court or tribunal" even though it was part of a professional body and not considered to be a court or tribunal under Netherlands law.[20] The crucial factor appeared to be

[16] Case C–54/96 *Dorsch Consult* [1997] E.C.R. I–4961 at I–4992—4993, para. 23, ECJ. See also the particular analysis made by the Court of Justice of the condition of independence in order to decide whether the Tiroler Landesvergabeamt could be regarded as a court or tribunal within the meaning of the E.C. Treaty, Article 234 (*ex Article 177*), in (Judgment of February 4, 1999) Case C–103/97 *Köllensperger*, paras 16–25 (the answer was positive), ECJ (not yet reported).

[17] In the case of *Dorsch Consult* (*ibid.*, at I–4992—4996, paras 22–38), the Court held that "the requirement that the procedure before the hearing body concerned must be *inter partes* is not an absolute requirement", after which it found that the adjudicating body, the Federal German *Vergabeüberwachungsauschuss*, a statutory administrative body supervising the award of procurement contracts, had to hear the parties before making any determination (see at I–4994, para. 31). The Court of Justice held on that ground that the board in question was a "court or tribunal" within the meaning of the E.C. Treaty, Art. 234 *(ex Art. 177)*.

[18] *ibid.*, at I–4993—4994, paras 27–29.

[19] Case 61/65 *Vaassen (née Göbbels) v. Beambtenfonds Mijnbedrijf* [1966] E.C.R. 261 at 273, ECJ with case notes by Haardt (1966–67) C.M.L.Rev. 441–444; Storm (1967) C.D.E. 311–320.

[20] Case 246/80 *Broekmeulen v. Huisarts Registratie Commissie* [1981] E.C.R. 2311 at 2327, para. 11, ECJ.

that the decisions delivered by the Appeals Committee, after an adversarial procedure, were "in fact recognized as final", since "in a matter involving the application of Community law" (registration of general practitioners) there was "in practice [no] right of appeal to the ordinary courts", with the result that the absence of any opportunity of seeking a preliminary ruling from the Appeals Committee would constitute a threat to "the proper functioning of Community law".[21]

The position was completely different when the Court, of its own motion,[22] refused to answer a question referred for a preliminary ruling by the *Directeur des Contributions Directes et des Accises* (Director of Taxation and Excise Duties) of the Grand Duchy of Luxembourg on the ground that he was not a "court or tribunal".[23] The Court emphasised that that expression, which had to be defined under Community law, referred by its nature to an authority acting as a third party in relation to the authority which adopted the decision forming the subject-matter of the proceedings. This was clearly not so in the case of the *Directeur des Contributions*, who was in charge of the revenue departments which had made the contested assessment to tax. Furthermore, if the matter were to come before the Luxembourg *Conseil d'Etat* on appeal, the *Directeur des Contributions* would be the defendant, which was regarded as confirming that he was a party to proceedings and not an authority separating the parties to the proceedings as a neutral outsider.[24] In that respect, the Director should be compared with the British "Chief Adjudication Officer", who takes the administrative decision with regard to the grant of social security benefits. That "officer" is not a judicial authority, but a party who, as such, defends his decision on appeal before a "third party", namely the "Chief Social Security Commissioner", who is entitled, as a "court or tribunal" to make a reference to the Court for a preliminary ruling (not that there has been any dispute or doubt about this).[25] **2–008**

Bodies which act in an administrative capacity, but not as a judicial authority, or only submit opinions to the public authorities with a view to their taking a decision, are not entitled to refer questions for a preliminary ruling. Examples are bodies of professional organisations deciding on admission to a profession[26] or a consultative committee whose duty is to **2–009**

---

[21] *ibid.*, at 2328, paras 16, 17.

[22] The Commission and the Luxembourg Government, which alone submitted observations to the Court pursuant to Art. 20 of the E.C. Statute, did not take issue with the competence of the body requesting the preliminary ruling.

[23] Case C–24/92 *Corbiau* [1993] E.C.R. I–1277 at I–1304, para. 17, ECJ.

[24] *ibid.*, at I–1304, para. 16.

[25] Case 150/85 *Drake v. Chief Adjudication Officer* [1986] E.C.R. 1995, ECJ. See, to the same effect, Joined Cases C–74/95 and C–129/95 *Criminal proceedings against X* [1996] E.C.R. I–6609 at I–6635 paras 17–20, ECJ, in which the Court held that the Italian *Procura della Repubblica* could not be regarded as being a court or tribunal within the meaning of the E.C. Treaty, Art. 234 *(ex Art. 177)*, on the ground that its role in the main proceedings in the case in question was not to rule on an issue in complete independence but, acting as prosecutor in the proceedings, to submit that issue, if appropriate, for consideration by the competent judicial body.

[26] Case 65/77 *Razanatsimba* [1977] E.C.R. 2229 at 2237, para. 5, ECJ; (Order of June 18, 1980), Case 138/80 *Borker* [1980] E.C.R. 1975 at 1977, para. 4, ECJ.

submit reasoned—but not binding—opinions to the Treasury Minister on the sanctions to be imposed by that minister on persons infringing national legislation relating to transfers of foreign exchange.[27] In both cases, there was the possibility of an appeal after the final administrative decision to a judicial body which could, if necessary, make a reference for a preliminary ruling. In addition, none of the bodies concerned could be regarded as a "third party", either because they took the first—*ex hypothesi* subsequently contested—decision themselves or because they were directly involved in taking that decision.

2–010 The question arises as to whether national authorities responsible for settling disputes relating to the application of competition law (domestic as well as European) are entitled to refer questions for a preliminary ruling. Do the authorities in question give a ruling in like manner to a court on proceedings brought by the prosecuting party (the public department responsible for ensuring that competition law is complied with) against a defendant undertaking or do they instead take an administrative decision after a procedure in which the other party is entitled to give its views which they must subsequently defend before a court or tribunal to which the undertaking concerned has appealed?

The answer to this question depends on a prior analysis of the legal position of the authorities concerned in each Member State and hence is liable to differ from one Member State to another. Nevertheless, it appears that the Court of Justice may allow a preliminary reference to be made from the authorities concerned at the earliest possible stage. The need to maximise the protection of the uniform application—and hence the effectiveness—of European competition law is in fact strongly felt. This perhaps explains why the Court gave a ruling, without any reservation, on the questions referred for a preliminary ruling by the Spanish *Tribunal de Defensa de la Competencia*, after Advocate General Jacobs had pointed out that whilst, administratively, the "Tribunal" formed part of the Ministry of Trade, it nevertheless fulfilled the *Vaassen*[28] criteria.[29] In addition, the

[27] (Order of March 5, 1986), Case 318/85 *Greis Unterweger* [1986] E.C.R. 955 at 957, para. 4, ECJ. But see Case 36/73 *Nederlandse Spoorwegen v. Minister Verkeer en Waterstaat* [1973] E.C.R. 1299, ECJ together with Joined Cases C–69–79/96 *Garofalo and Others* [1997] E.C.R. I–5603 at I–5628—5630 paras 17–27, ECJ, in which the Court held that where the Italian *Consiglio di Stato* issues an opinion in relation to an extraordinary petition made to the President of the Republic for annulment of an administrative act, it constitutes a court or tribunal within the meaning of E.C. Treaty, Art. 234, (*ex Art. 177*). But see (Judgment of November 12, 1998) Case C–134/97 *Victoria Films A/S*, paras 15–19, ECJ (not yet reported),—the Swedish Skatterattsnamnden (tax authority) was not regarded as a court or tribunal within the meaning of the E.C. Treaty, Article 234 (*ex Article 177*), although there were factors which might make it possible to consider that it performs a judicial function, in particular the independence which its statutory origin confers on it and the power to deliver binding decisions in application of rules of law; other factors, however, led to the conclusion that it performs an essentially administrative function, such as that it does not have as its task to review the legality of the decision of the tax authorities but rather to adopt a view, for the first time, on how a specific transaction is to be assessed to tax, after which judicial review by a court competent in tax matters is possible.

[28] See para. 2–007, above.

[29] Opinion of Advocate General F.G. Jacobs in, Case C–67/91 *Asociación Española de Banca Privada and Others* [1992] E.C.R. I–4785 at I–4809, ECJ.

applicant in the proceedings was the "*Dirección General de Defensa de la Competencia*" and a number of banks, with the result that the "Tribunal" did in fact come across as a third party. The same reasoning would perhaps have to be followed in the case of the Belgian *Conseil de la Concurrence/ Raad voor de Mededinging* (Competition Council), which is regarded as a court under national law and determines cases brought against undertakings by the Competition Department (of the Ministry for Economic Affairs).[30] In the event of an appeal against decisions of the Competition Council to the Court of Appeal in Brussels, the defendant is not the Council, but the Belgian State, represented by the Minister for Economic Affairs.[31]

An arbitrator which does not fulfil *all* the *Vaassen* criteria cannot be regarded as a "court or tribunal of a Member State" within the meaning of Article 234 (*ex Article 177*) of the E.C. Treaty despite the fact that: **2–011**

> "there are certain similarities between the activities of the arbitration tribunal in question and those of an ordinary court or tribunal in as much as the arbitration is provided for within the framework of the law, the arbitrator must decide according to law and his award has, as between the parties, the force of *res judicata*, and may be enforceable if leave to issue execution is obtained".[32]

Those characteristics were not sufficient to give the arbitrator the status of a "court or tribunal of a Member State" because the parties to the contract were "free to leave their disputes to be resolved by the ordinary courts or to opt for arbitration by inserting a clause to that effect in the contract".[33] Consequently, the arbitrator did not act as the "proper judicial body" designated by law, with the result that at least that *Vaassen* criterion was not fulfilled. The parties were indeed under "no obligation, whether in law or in fact, to refer their disputes to arbitration".[34] Moreover, the Member State in which the arbitrator operated was not involved in the decision to opt for arbitration and was not called upon to intervene of its own motion in the proceedings before the arbitrator.[35] If questions of Community law arise in an arbitration resorted to by agreement, the Court reckons on the "ordinary courts" examining the issues and, where necessary, requesting a preliminary ruling. The ordinary courts will have an opportunity to do so "in the context of their collaboration" with arbitration tribunals, "in

30 Law of 5 August 1991, Art. 16 provides that the Competition Council constitutes an "administrative court" for the protection of economic competition (*Belgisch Staatsblad/ Moniteur belge*, October 11, 1991).

31 Law of 5 August 1991, Art. 40.

32 Case 102/81 *Nordsee v. Reederei Mond* [1982] E.C.R. 1095, at 1110, para. 10, ECJ (see the extensive case note by Hepting, "Art. 177 *[now Art. 234]* EWGV und die private Schiedsgerichtsbarkeit" (1982) EuR. 315–333).

33 *Nordsee v. Reederei Mond*, (cited in n. 32, above), at 1110, para. 11.

34 *ibid.*, at 1110, para. 11.

35 This consideration was perhaps intended to distinguish the *Broekmeulen* situation (*ibid.*, at 1110, para. 12); *cf.* n. 20, above and the associated passage in the body of the text.

particular in order to assist them in certain procedural matters or to interpret the law applicable", or when they are called upon to conduct a "review of an arbitration award" in the case of "an appeal or objection, in proceedings for leave to issue execution or by any other method of recourse available under the relevant national legislation".[36]

In this context, it makes no difference that, in reviewing the arbitration award, the ordinary court has, pursuant to the arbitration agreement concluded between the parties, to rule *ex aequo et bono*:

> "It follows from the principles of the primacy of Community law and of its uniform application, in conjunction with Article 5 *[now Article 10]* of the Treaty, that a court of a Member State to which an appeal against an arbitration award is made pursuant to national law must, even where it gives judgment having regard to fairness, observe the rules of Community law . . ."[37]

By declining jurisdiction to answer questions referred for a preliminary ruling by arbitrators, the Court sought to prevent contracting parties from creating "courts and tribunals" *of their own* and subsequently inducing (obliging) them to seek preliminary rulings. Indeed, Article 234 (*ex Article 177*) of the E.C. Treaty is intended to bring about a dialogue between courts in the Member States and the Court of Justice. National courts which have the monopoly right to seek preliminary rulings submit to the Court for such rulings only questions which are genuinely necessary in order to deliver a judgment with the authority of *res judicata*. In the Court's view this mechanism would be endangered if parties to a contract could circumvent it by setting up an arbitration board whose organisation is in no way based on action on the part of the public authorities and which is not regarded as the obligatory legal authority for dealing with a particular class of disputes. Where this is in fact the case and there is therefore a "sufficiently close connection" between the arbitration and the general system of legal protection in the Member State concerned, the "arbitrator" is deemed to be "a court or tribunal of a Member State" within the meaning of Article 234 (*ex Article 177*) of the E.C. Treaty (as in the case of the "arbitration tribunal" in the *Vaassen* case).[38]

---

[36] *ibid.*, at 1111, para. 14. Where a point of Community law is raised before an arbitrator and leave to appeal is sought against the award, an English judge will normally grant leave to appeal where the point is "capable of serious argument": *Bulk Oil (Zug) AG v. Sun International Ltd* [1984] 1 W.L.R. 147 at 154–155F, *per* Ackner L.J.

[37] Case C–393/92 *Almelo* [1994] E.C.R. I–1477 at I–1515, para. 23, ECJ.

[38] Case 109/88 *Handels- og Kontorfunktionærernes Forbund i Danemark v. Dansk Arbejdsgiverforening, Danfoss* [1989] E.C.R. 3199 at 3224–3225, paras 7–9, ECJ. See also Bebr, "Arbitration Tribunals and Art. 177 *[now Art. 234]* of the EEC Treaty" (1985) C.M.L.Rev. 489–504. For a critical commentary, see Kornblum, "Private Schiedsgerichte und Art. 177 *[now Art. 234]* EWGV", in *Jahrbuch für die Praxis des Schiedsgerichtsbarkeit*, Heidelberg, Verlag Recht und Wirtschaft GmbH, 1988, at 102–110. See, however, Storm, "Quod licet iovi. The Precarious Relationship between the Court of Justice of the European Communities and Arbitration", in *Essays on International and Comparative Law in Honour of Judge Erades*, The Hague, T.M.C. Asser Institute, 1983, at 144–177, who approves of the Court's case law on practical grounds.

The court or tribunal must be "of a Member State". Although this is generally obvious, it should be noted that the following courts qualify as such: courts and tribunals established in the Member States[39]; in the "French overseas departments"[40]; in the "overseas countries and territories" listed in Annex II to the Treaty to which the special association arrangements set out in Part Four of the Treaty apply[41]; in the "European territories for whose external relations a Member State is responsible", to which the Treaty applies[42]; and lastly in "the Channel Islands and the Isle of Man"[43] in so far as courts and tribunals established there refer to the Court questions concerning the interpretation of "Protocol No. 3",[44] the interpretation and validity of the Community legislation to which that Protocol refers, and the interpretation and validity of measures adopted by the Community institutions on the basis of Protocol No. 3. **2–012**

International courts, such as the International Court of Justice or the European Court of Human Rights, are not entitled to refer questions to the Court of Justice for a preliminary ruling, even though this might have been useful in some cases.[45] The position is different in the case of the Benelux Court of Justice. That court has the task of ensuring that the legal rules common to the three Benelux States are applied uniformly. The procedure before it is a step in the proceedings before the national courts leading to definitive interpretations of common Benelux legal rules. For those reasons, the Benelux Court of Justice is entitled—and, as a court against whose decisions there is no judicial remedy under national law, may be under a duty[46]—to refer a question to the Court of Justice in Luxembourg for a **2–013**

[39] E.C. Treaty, Art. 299 (*ex Art. 227*) (1). In England and Wales, references may be made, *e.g.* by magistrates' courts, the Crown Court, the High Court, the Court of Appeal, the House of Lords and specialist courts such as the Patent Court. The Social Security Commissioner, income tax commissioners, employment (formerly industrial) tribunals, the Employment Appeal Tribunal and the VAT Tribunal have also made successful requests for preliminary rulings. As has the Immigration Adjudicator: (Judgment of March 2, 1999), Case C–416/96 *El-Yassini*, paras 16–22, ECJ (not yet reported).

[40] E.C. Treaty, Art. 299(2).

[41] E.C. Treaty, Art. 299(3). For applications, see Joined Cases C–100/89 and C–101/89 *Kaefer and Procacci* [1990] E.C.R. I–4647, ECJ and Case C–260/90 *Leplat* [1992] E.C.R. I–643, ECJ, in which the *Tribunal Administratif* and the *Tribunal de Paix*, respectively, of Papeete in French Polynesia, were held to be courts or tribunals "of a Member State". For the Netherlands Antilles and Aruba, see Mischo, "The Competence of the Judiciary of the Netherlands Antilles and Aruba to request Preliminary Rulings from the Court of Justice of the European Communities", in *Met het oog op Europa*, Curaçao, Stichting Tijdschrift voor Antilliaans Recht-Justicia, 1991, at 140–145.

[42] E.C. Treaty, Art. 299(4); in practice, only Gibraltar.

[43] E.C. Treaty, Art. 299(5)(c).

[44] Protocol No. 3 constitutes the "arrangements for those islands set out" in the Accession Treaty signed on January 22, 1972. See Case C–335/89 *Barr and Montrose Holdings* [1991] E.C.R. I–3479 at I–3500—3501, paras 6–10, ECJ; Arnull, "The Evolution of the Court's Jurisdiction under Art. 177 *[now Art. 234]* EEC" (1993) E.L.Rev. 129 at 132–133.

[45] *Cf.* Schermers and Waelbroeck, *Judicial Protection*, s.701.

[46] See para. 2–044, below.

preliminary ruling where it is faced with the task of interpreting Community rules in the performance of its function.[47]

2–014 Of course, courts and tribunals established in non-member countries do not come under Article 234 (*ex Article 177*) of the E.C. Treaty. In the event that it is nevertheless intended to confer on such courts and tribunals to a certain extent the right to refer questions for a preliminary ruling, that right must be enshrined in an international agreement concluded between the Community and the non-member countries concerned. An example is the EEA Agreement, which authorises courts and tribunals of EFTA States to refer questions to the Court of Justice on the interpretation of an EEA rule.[48]

B. Types of proceedings in which a preliminary ruling may be requested

2–015 The Court has no jurisdiction to entertain a request for a preliminary ruling when at the time when it is made the procedure before the court making it has already been terminated.[49] Article 234 (*ex Article 177*) of the E.C. Treaty in fact restricts the right to make a reference to a court or tribunal which considers that the preliminary ruling requested is necessary to enable *it* to give judgment.[50] A national court is empowered to bring a matter before the Court by way of reference for a preliminary ruling only if a dispute is pending before it in the context of which it is called upon to give a decision capable of taking into account the preliminary ruling.[51] The preliminary ruling must actually be intended to make a contribution to the decision which the referring court is to take.

Since this is a question of securing the very essence of the preliminary ruling procedure, the Court does not shrink from going back to seek further information about the course of the procedure before the referring court with a view to ascertaining whether the proceedings were still pending

---

[47] Case C–337/95 *Parfums Christian Dior* [1977] E.C.R. I–6013 at I–6042—6043, paras 19–23, ECJ. It would be hard to argue that proceedings brought against a Member State in the European Court of Human Rights constitute "a step in the proceedings" before a national court. Proceedings before the European Court of Human Rights do not fall within any national proceedings and hence the reasoning employed by the Court of Justice in the *Christian Dior* case in order to hold that the Benelux Court of Justice constitutes a court or tribunal within the meaning of the E.C. Treaty, Art. 234 (*ex Art. 177*), cannot be used so as to allow the European Court of Human Rights to make a reference for a preliminary ruling to the Court of Justice.

[48] EEA Agreement, Art. 107 ([1994] O.J. L1/26) and Protocol 34 annexed to the EEA Agreement on the possibility for courts and tribunals of EFTA States to request the Court of Justice of the European Communities to decide on the interpretation of EEA rules corresponding to E.C. rules ([1994] O.J. L1/204); Arnull (n. 44, above), at 134. See also Lenaerts and Van Nuffel, *Constitutional Law of the European Union*, para. 20–017.

[49] Case 338/85 *Pardini v. Ministero del commercio con l'estero* [1988] E.C.R. 2041 at 2075, para. 11, 2nd sentence, ECJ; Case C–159/90 *Society for the Protection of Unborn Children Ireland v. Grogan and Others* [1991] E.C.R. I–4685 at I–4737, para. 12, ECJ. Once an English court has given judgment and its order has been drawn up, it is *functus officio* and may no longer make a reference: *SA Magnavision v. General Optical Council (No. 2)* [1987] 2 C.M.L.R. 262, para. 14–16, *per* Wilkins L.J.; *Chiron Corp. v. Murex Diagnostics Ltd* [1995] All E.R. (E.C.) 88 at 92g–93e, *per* Balcombe L.J.

[50] *Pardini v. Ministero del commercio con l'estero* (cited in n. 49, above), at 2074, para. 10.

[51] *ibid.*, at 2075, para. 11, first sentence.

before that court at the time when the request for a ruling was made. In *Pardini* the Court held—contrary to its first impressions—that, in view of the explanations which it had obtained, it had to be assumed that "the interlocutory proceedings which gave rise to the reference to the Court must be regarded as still pending before the *Pretore* [Magistrate], who may take account of the preliminary ruling for the purposes of his own decision confirming, varying or discharging his original order".[52]

All sorts of proceedings may give rise to a preliminary ruling: matters of civil law, criminal law, commercial and economic law, social law, revenue law, constitutional[53] and administrative law, and so on. Neither the substantive law at issue nor the type of proceedings has any bearing. Questions may be referred by an examining magistrate[54] and in interlocutory proceedings.[55] Even *ex parte* proceedings, at which the other party is not represented, may result in a reference for a preliminary ruling if the body making the reference is exercising the functions of a court or tribunal.[56] Furthermore, it does not matter if the body making the reference performs other functions in addition to its functions as a court or tribunal. Accordingly, the Court held that "the *Pretori* [Italian magistrates] are judges who, in proceedings such as those in which the questions referred . . . were raised, combine the functions of a public prosecutor and an examining magistrate". Yet it declared that it had jurisdiction to reply to the questions referred since the request emanated from: **2–016**

> "a court or tribunal which has acted in the general framework of its task of judging, independently and in accordance with the law, cases coming within the jurisdiction conferred on it by law, even though certain functions of that court or tribunal in the proceedings which gave rise to the reference for a preliminary ruling are not, strictly speaking, of a judicial nature".[57]

However, if in given proceedings the national court simply acts as an administrative authority and performs a non-judicial function, the Court of

---

52 *ibid.*, at 2075, para. 14.

53 Case C–93/97 *Fédération Belge des Chambres Syndicales de Médecins* [1998] E.C.R. I–4837, ECJ, in which the *Cour d'Arbitrage*, the Belgian Constitutional Court, made a reference for a preliminary ruling. For the judgment of the *Cour d'Arbitrage* of February 19, 1997, see (1997) J.T. 430, with a case note by Delgrange and van Ypersele.

54 Case 65/79 *Chatain* [1980] E.C.R. 1345 at 1379, para. 1, ECJ.

55 Case 29/69 *Stauder v. Ulm* [1969] E.C.R. 419 at 424, ECJ; Case 107/76 *Hoffmann-La Roche v. Centrafarm* [1977] E.C.R. 957 at 972, para. 4, ECJ. For an example, see Case C–213/89R *R. v. Secretary of State for Transport, ex p. Factortame Ltd and Others* (*Factortame I*) [1990] E.C.R. I–2433, ECJ. For England and Wales, see RSC, Ord. 114, r. 2—a reference may be made at any stage of the proceedings.

56 For examples, see the Italian proceedings for a court order in Case 70/77 *Simmenthal v. Amministrazione delle Finanze dello Stato* [1978] E.C.R. 1453 at 1467–1468, paras 4–11, ECJ; Case C–18/93 *Corsica Ferries* [1994] E.C.R. I–1783 at I–1818, para. 12, ECJ, and the cases referred to therein, and the proceedings for the protective sequestration of assets in Case 23/75 *Rey Soda v. Cassa Conguaglio Zucchero* [1975] E.C.R. 1279 at 1300, ECJ.

57 Case 14/86 *Pretore di Salò v. Persons Unknown* [1987] E.C.R. 2545 at 2567, para. 7, ECJ.

Justice considers that it has no jurisdiction to rule on questions referred for a preliminary ruling in the proceedings in question.[58]

2–017 Questions of jurisdiction which are apt to arise before national courts in connection with the classification of legal situations based on Community law cannot be determined by the Court of Justice. This is because it is for the legal system of each Member State to determine which court has jurisdiction to hear disputes involving individual rights derived from Community law. In such circumstances, a national court may make a reference for a preliminary ruling to the Court of Justice with a view to obtaining an explanation of points of Community law which may help to solve the problem of jurisdiction.[59]

C. Time and content of a request for a preliminary ruling

2–018 From the wording of Article 234 (*ex Article 177*) of the E.C. Treaty it merely appears that only the national court is entitled to apply to the Court of Justice for a preliminary ruling.[60]

Parties to the main proceedings, including the public prosecutor, cannot compel the national court to make a reference.[61] The national court has the right to refer questions of its own motion,[62] a right which Community law confers on *every* "court or tribunal of a Member State" within the meaning of Article 234 of the E.C. Treaty. National (procedural) law cannot detract from this. Accordingly, the Court has held that "the existence of a rule of domestic law whereby a court is bound on points of law by the rulings of the court superior to it cannot of itself take away the power provided for by Article 177 (*now Article 234*) of referring cases to the Court",[63] especially "if it considers that the ruling on law made by the superior court could lead it to give a judgment contrary to Community law".[64]

2–019 It is for the national court to determine the content of the preliminary questions. Of course, the parties to the main proceedings are at liberty to

---

[58] Case C–111/94 *Job Centre* [1995] E.C.R. I–3361 at I–3386—3387, paras 8–11, ECJ. *Cf.* the Opinion of Advocate General M.B. Elmer. In contrast, a preliminary question raised by a national court in proceedings brought for judicial review of a decision made in such non-contentious proceedings will be admissible (*ibid.*, para. 11; Case C–55/96 *Job Centre* [1997] E.C.R. I–7119, ECJ. See also Case 32/74 *Haaga* [1974] E.C.R. 1201 at 1206, para. 2, ECJ).

[59] Case 179/84 *Bozzetti v. Invernizzi* [1985] E.C.R. 2301 at 2317–2318, para 17, ECJ; Case C–446/93 *SEIM* [1996] E.C.R. I–73 at I–110, paras 32, 33, ECJ.

[60] Joined Cases 31 and 33/62 *Wöhrmann v. Commission* [1962] E.C.R. 501 at 507, ECJ. See *Portsmouth City Council v. Richards and Quietlynn* [1989] 1 C.M.L.R. 673 at 708, where Kerr L.J. stated that ". . . references by consent should not creep into our practice. All references must be by the court. The court itself must be satisfied of the need for a reference . . .". Nevertheless, it is the practice in the English courts for the parties to draft the questions for approval by the national court, but the necessity for a reference is for the court to determine.

[61] Case 93/78 *Mattheus v. Doego* [1978] E.C.R. 2203 at 2210, paras 4–6, ECJ.

[62] Case 166/73 *Rheinmühlen v. Einfuhr- und Vorratsstelle Getreide* [1974] E.C.R. 33 at 38, para. 3, ECJ; Case 126/80 *Salonia v. Poidomani and Giglio* [1981] E.C.R. 1563, at 1577, para. 7, ECJ; Case 283/81 *CILFIT v. Ministry of Health* [1982] E.C.R. 3415 at 3428, para. 9, ECJ; Case C–261/95 *Palmisani* [1997] E.C.R. I–4025 at I–4044, para. 20, ECJ. For England and Wales, see RSC, Ord. 114, r. 2 (an order for reference may be made by the court of its own motion at any stage in a cause or matter).

[63] *Rheinmühlen v. Einfuhr- und Vorratsstelle Getreide*, (cited in n. 62, above) at 39.

[64] *ibid.*, para. 4.

make proposals, but it is the judge alone who determines whether he or she accepts them wholly or in part or completely deviates from them. The Court does not allow parties to the main proceedings to seek to extend the request for a preliminary ruling to cover questions which they suggested to the national court, but it did not wish to ask.[65] It is immaterial in this connection that the Commission or one or more Member States support parties in their attempt to alter the subject-matter of the preliminary ruling procedure. The Court will not go against the referring court's (express or implicit) refusal to refer a particular question because that court "alone is competent under the system established by Article 177 *[now Article 234]* to assess the relevance of questions concerning the interpretation of Community law in order to resolve the dispute before it".[66]

This does not mean that the Court will shrink from giving a more precise definition of the subject-matter of the reference for a preliminary ruling or **2–020** even from altering it where this appears necessary in order to obtain a helpful answer, namely an answer which the national court can use.[67] But the adjustment of the questions referred must always be consonant with the actual objective of the referring court, which precludes any change running contrary to that court's intention. In a case in which the national court had not formulated *any* question, but had simply referred the parties to the Court, the Court itself defined the question of interpretation of Community law which had in fact arisen on the basis of the order for reference and the case-file directed to the Court through the Registry.[68]

Furthermore, the Court has not drawn the demarcation line over strictly between interpretation of Community law and assessing the validity of acts of the institutions. Questions which ostensibly relate to the interpretation of Community law, but, having regard to the whole content of the order for reference, rather probe the validity of a Community measure, are also answered as such.[69]

The opposite situation may also arise. That is to say, the Court may consider whether the question of validity is based on a correct interpretation of the Community act at issue. It may then find—after interpreting the act in question—that it is no longer necessary to inquire into its validity

[65] Case 247/86 *Alsatel v. Novasam* [1988] E.C.R. 5987 at 6007, para. 8, ECJ; *Palmisani*, (cited in n. 62, above), at I–4047, para. 31. Lord Denning put the matter bluntly: "The European court would not listen to any party who went moaning to them": *Bulmer v. Bollinger* [1974] Ch 401 at 420H.

[66] *Alsatel v. Novasam* (cited in n. 65, above) at 6007, para. 8.

[67] Bergerès, "La reformulation des questions préjudicielles en interprétation par la Cour de justice des Communautés européennes" (1985) Rec. Dalloz, Chronique 155–162.

[68] Case 101/63 *Wagner v. Fohrmann and Krier* [1964] E.C.R. 195 at 199–200, ECJ; but see (Order of December 21, 1995), Case C–307/95 *Max Mara* [1995] E.C.R. I–5083 at I–5087—5088, paras 5–10, ECJ, in which the Court found that the order for reference did not contain specific questions addressed to the Court and that it did not allow the questions on which the national court wished the Court to give a preliminary ruling to be discerned. The national court's order also did not contain enough information to permit the Court to give a useful interpretation. Accordingly, the Court held that the national court's request was manifestly inadmissible.

[69] Case 16/65 *Schwarze v. Einfuhr- und Vorratsstelle für Getreide und Futtermittel* [1965] E.C.R. 877 at 886–887, ECJ.

inasmuch as the argument that superior Community law has been breached is founded upon a different interpretation of the relevant Community act. If it so finds, the Court will also not go into the consequences which would have ensued from a finding that the act was invalid.[70]

However, in the event that the questions referred for a preliminary ruling are concerned with the validity of an individual decision against which no action for annulment has been brought, the Court of Justice will refuse to alter the substance of the questions referred in so far as the validity of the contested decision can no longer be called in question.[71] In those circumstances, to alter the substance of the questions referred would be incompatible with the Court's function under Article 234 (*ex Article 177*) of the E.C. Treaty and with its duty to ensure that the governments of the Member States and parties concerned are given the opportunity to submit observations under Article 20 of the E.C. Statute, bearing in mind that only the order for reference is notified to interested parties.[72] In the light of the order for reference, they may therefore confine their observations to the validity of the contested decision by arguing solely that the questions raised no longer require an answer. To amend the scope of the order for reference would infringe the right conferred on them by Article 20 of the E.C. Statute.

Also the Court does not shrink from supplementing the provisions of Community law of which the national courts seek an interpretation by provisions—as revealed by the national court in the order for reference—which it regards as relevant in the context of the main proceedings.[73] This is because it is the Court's duty to interpret all provisions of Community law which national courts need in order to decide the actions pending before them.[74] By the same token, the Court may even replace the provisions indicated by the national court in its preliminary question by those provisions of Community law which are actually relevant.[75] This can be explained in terms of the Court's concern for efficient collaboration with the national courts, whilst leaving the initiative to seek a preliminary ruling with the national courts.

2–021 The decision at which stage a reference should be made for a preliminary ruling pursuant to Article 234 (*ex Article 177*) is dictated by considerations of procedural economy and efficiency to be weighed by the national court alone and not the Court of Justice.[76] The national court is "in the best position to appreciate at which stage of the proceedings it requires a

[70] Case C–334/95 *Krüger* [1997] E.C.R. I–4517 at I–4547, para. 21, and at I–4550, para. 35, ECJ.

[71] See para. 10–010, below.

[72] Case C–178/95 *Wiljo* [1997] E.C.R. I–585 at I–606, para. 30, ECJ, and the Opinion of Advocate General F.G. Jacobs to the same effect.

[73] Case 12/82 *Ministère Public v. Trinon* [1982] E.C.R. 4089 at 4100, para. 5, ECJ.

[74] Case C–280/91 *Viessmann* [1993] E.C.R. I–971 at I–988, para. 17, ECJ; Case C–42/96 *Immobiliare SIF* [1997] E.C.R. I–7089 at I–7114, para. 28, ECJ.

[75] Case 294/82 *Einberger v. Hauptzollamt Freiburg* [1984] E.C.R. 1177 at 1185–1186, para. 6, ECJ; Case C–187/91 *Belovo* [1992] E.C.R. I–4937 at I–4969, para. 13, ECJ.

[76] Case 14/86 *Pretore di Salò v. Persons Unknown* [1987] E.C.R. 2545 at 2568, para. 11, ECJ.

preliminary ruling from the Court of Justice".[77] Nevertheless, the national court does not have unlimited latitude in this respect. It is only "in the best position" to appreciate the stage at which a reference should be made. In principle, the Court of Justice goes along with its assessment, unless it is manifestly premature. This will be clear from the content of the order for reference. If the national court has not yet sufficiently ascertained the factual and legal context of the case and therefore does not say anything about it in the order for reference, it leaves the Court uncertain about the way in which the preliminary ruling sought is intended to help resolve the main action pending before the national court. In those circumstances, there is a great risk that the Court will not reach a "helpful" determination. The upshot would be that the preliminary ruling would be ignored as a purely hypothetical "opinion" and the collaboration between the national court and the Court of Justice would not achieve its aim.

In order to avoid this the Court has gradually stepped up its requirements with regard to the content of the order for reference. As will become clear later, in order to satisfy those requirements the national court should make a request for a preliminary ruling to the Court only if it has determined the facts and non-Community aspects of the case to such an extent that it can indicate precisely how the preliminary ruling sought is to be applied. This inevitably restricts the national court's latitude to choose the stage at which the request for a preliminary ruling is made.

What requirements are imposed as regards the content of the order for **2–022**
reference? In the 1979 judgment in *Union Laitière Normande*, the Court held in the first place that "the need to afford a helpful interpretation of Community law makes it essential to define the legal context in which the interpretation requested should be placed".[78] Although in that case the national court had not stated why it sought an interpretation of Community law, the reasons for the questions referred were sufficiently clear from the case-file submitted to the Court and it consequently appeared that a "helpful interpretation of Community law" was possible and that the Court could give a ruling.

Two years later, in the 1981 *Irish Creamery Milk Suppliers Association* case, the Court enlarged upon that basic requirement:

> "From that aspect it might be *convenient*, in certain circumstances, for the facts in the case to be established and for questions of purely national law to be settled at the time the reference is made to the Court of Justice so as to enable the latter to take cognizance of all the features of fact and of law which may be relevant to the interpretation of Community law which it is called upon to give."[79]

---

[77] *ibid.*, at 2568, para. 11. See also an earlier case: Case 43/71 *Politi v. Italy* [1971] E.C.R. 1039 at 1048, para. 5, ECJ.

[78] Case 244/78 *Union Laitière Normande v. French Dairy Farmers* [1979] E.C.R. 2663 at 2681, para. 5, ECJ.

[79] Joined Cases 36 and 71/80 *Irish Creamery Milk Suppliers Association v. Ireland* [1981] E.C.R. 735 at 748, para. 6, ECJ, emphasis added.

This sounded like encouragement to formulate the order for reference in concrete terms, yet without taking away the national court's discretion to determine at what stage in the main proceedings it needed a preliminary ruling from the Court of Justice.[80] Plainly this is a compromise: the national court was given good advice in quite strong terms, but, at the same time, failure to follow it did not make the request for a preliminary ruling inadmissible. Where the Court of Justice could fill the gaps in the order for reference by using information gleaned from the national court's case-file or adduced in the proceedings before the Court, it was still generally prepared to answer the questions referred on that basis. Nonetheless, the Court has intimated that it is not entirely happy about this on account of the risk that the quality of judicial debate will suffer if it is based on insufficiently informative orders for reference. Indeed:

> "the information furnished in the decisions making the references does not serve only to enable the Court to give helpful answers but also to enable the Governments of the Member States and other interested parties to submit observations in accordance with Article 20 of the Statute of the Court . . . It is the Court's duty to ensure that the opportunity to submit observations is safeguarded, in view of the fact that, by virtue of the above-mentioned provision, only the decisions making the references are notified to the interested parties."[81]

2–023 In the 1993 judgment in *Telemarsicabruzzo*, the Court converted the good advice to national courts into a genuine requirement which, if not complied with, will cause the preliminary reference to be inadmissible.[82] The Court held that the need to provide an interpretation of Community law which would be of use to the national court made it necessary that the national court define the factual and legislative context of the questions it was asking or, at the very least, explain the factual circumstances on which those questions were based.[83] In fact, to a limited extent the Court had previously refused to consider particular parts of preliminary references, where they were insufficiently precise, but this had never resulted in the whole of the request for a ruling being declared inadmissible.[84] The reason for this

---

[80] *ibid.*, at 748, paras 7–9.

[81] Joined Cases 141–143/81 *Holdijk* [1982] E.C.R. 1299 at 1311–1312, para. 6, ECJ; (Order of March 20, 1996), Case C–2/96 *Sunino and Data* [1996] E.C.R. I–1543 at I–1547—1548, para. 5, ECJ; (Order of June 25, 1996), Case C–101/96 *Italia Testa* [1996] E.C.R. I–3081 at I–3085—3086, para. 5, ECJ; (Order of July 19, 1996), Case C–191/96 *Modesti* [1996] E.C.R. I–3937 at I–3941—3942, para. 5, ECJ; (Order of July 19, 1996), Case C–196/96 *Lahlou* [1996] E.C.R. I–3945 at I–3949—3950, para. 5, ECJ *Cf.* Case C–178/95 *Wiljo* [1997] E.C.R. I–585, ECJ.

[82] See also the Note for Guidance on References by National Courts for Preliminary Rulings (1997) C.M.L.Rev. 1319–1322 (reproduced in *Brealey and Hoskins* (para. 1–004, note 12, above, Appendix H, at 579).

[83] Joined Cases C–320–322/90 *Telemarsicabruzzo and Others* [1993] E.C.R. I–393 at I–426, para. 5, ECJ; Case C–378/92 *La Pyramide* [1994] E.C.R. I–3999 at I–4009, para. 17, ECJ.

[84] Case 52/76 *Benedetti v. Munari* [1977] E.C.R. 163 at 182, paras 20–22, ECJ; Joined Cases 205–215/82 *Deutsche Milchkontor v. Germany* [1983] E.C.R. 2633 at 2670, para. 36, ECJ. *Cf.* Case 222/78 *ICAP v. Beneventi* [1979] E.C.R. 1163 at 1178, paras 19 and 20, ECJ; Case 14/86 *Pretore di Salò v. Persons Unknown* [1987] E.C.R. 2545 at 2569, para. 16, ECJ.

change was that the Court considered it unrealistic—in particular in the light of the complex factual and legal situations arising in competition law, which was the subject of the main proceedings—to expect it to fill the *lacunae* in the order for reference (which was virtually unreasoned) with sufficient certainty from the information in the file provided by the national court and the observations submitted to the Court by the parties to the main proceedings, the Italian Government and the Commission pursuant to Article 20 of the E.C. Statute of the Court. The risk that the Court's judgment would be of no assistance to the national court was too great and hence co-operation with the referring court could not serve its purpose. The Court declined to give potentially ineffective rulings which would merely serve as an "opinion" for a hypothetical case and not contribute towards the determination of the main proceedings. In subsequent cases, the Court has even gone so far as to decide that the preliminary reference was *manifestly* inadmissible for the same reasons (in orders given pursuant to Article 92(1) of the ECJ Rules of Procedure).[85] The Court has recognised, however, that the requirement for the national court to define the factual and legislative context of the questions referred is less pressing where they relate to specific technical points and enable the Court to give a useful reply even where the national court has not given an exhaustive description of the legal and factual situation.[86]

The *Telemarsicabruzzo* requirement as to the precision of the order for reference in terms of its content does not completely negate the national court's discretion in determining at what stage in the proceedings pending before it, it should make a reference to the Court of Justice. It is sufficient for the national court to set out in the order for reference the factual and **2–024**

[85] (Order of March 19, 1993), Case C–157/92 *Banchero* [1993] E.C.R. I–1085, ECJ; (Order of April 26, 1993), Case C–386/92 *Monin Automobiles* [1993] E.C.R. I–2049, ECJ; (Order of March 23, 1993), Case C–458/93 *Saddik* [1995] E.C.R. I–511 at I–519, para. 19, ECJ; (Order of April 7, 1995), Case C–167/94 *Grau Gomis and Others* [1995] E.C.R. I–1023 at I–1029, para. 12, ECJ; (Order of February 2, 1996), Case C–257/95 *Bresle* [1996] E.C.R. I–233 at I–240—241, paras 16–18, ECJ; (Order of March 13, 1996), Case C–326/95 *Banco de Fomento e Exterior* [1996] E.C.R. I–1385, ECJ; (Order of March 20, 1996), Case C–2/96 *Sunino and Data* [1996] E.C.R. I–1543 at I–1548, paras 6 and 7, ECJ; (Order of June 25, 1996), Case C–101/96 *Italia Testa* [1996] E.C.R. I–3081 at I–3085, para. 4, ECJ; (Order of July 19, 1996), Case C–191/96 *Modesti* [1996] E.C.R. I–3937 at I–3941, para. 4, ECJ; (Order of July 19, 1996), Case C–196/96 *Lahlou* [1996] E.C.R. I–3945 at I–3949, para. 4, ECJ; (Order of June 30, 1997), Case C–66/97 *Banco de Fomento e Exterior* [1997] E.C.R. I–3757 at I–3765, para. 19, ECJ; (Order of April 30, 1998), Joined Cases C–128/97 and C–137/97 *Italia Testa and Modesti* [1998] E.C.R. I–2181 at I–2187—2189, paras 12–18, ECJ. See also Arnull, case note in (1994) C.M.L.Rev. 377; *cf.* Bergerès, "La CJCE et la pertinence de la question préjudicielle" (1993) Rec. Dalloz, Chronique 245; Wooldridge, "Disguised Contributions in Kind; the European Court refuses a Preliminary Ruling on Hypothetical Questions" (1993) 2 L.I.E.I. 69.

[86] Case C–316/93 *Vaneetveld* [1994] E.C.R. I–763 at I–783—784, para. 13, ECJ; (Order of March 13, 1996), Case C–326/95 *Banco de Fomento e Exterior* [1996] E.C.R. I–1385 at I–1390—1391, para. 8, ECJ. For a case in which the Court considered that the *Telemarsicabruzzo* requirement was not fulfilled in relation to preliminary questions concerning the interpretation of the E.C. Treaty, Articles 81 and 82 (*ex Articles 85 and 86*), but agreed to answer those concerning the interpretation of Articles 28 and 30 (*ex Articles 30 and 36*), see Case C–61/97 *Foreningen af danske Videogramdistributorer*, [1998] E.C.R. I–5171, ECJ.

national legal premises underlying the questions referred so as to enable the Court of Justice to arrive at a helpful answer. In contrast, the national court is not in principle required to have chosen between the legal premises or hypotheses at the time when it seeks the preliminary ruling. It may still be influenced by "considerations of procedural organization and efficiency"[87] and await the Court's answer to a preliminary question before making a definitive ruling on the factual and national legal aspects of the case. The only condition is that the national court's order for reference should interpret the various premises or hypotheses and explain the reasons why it is seeking a preliminary ruling so as to make it clear in what way Community law is relevant in the case of *each* of those premises or hypotheses. It goes without saying that the national court must have fully apprised itself of the case in order to fulfil this condition. This is at the heart of the *Telemarsicabruzzo* requirement, which is designed to give rise to a genuine dialogue between courts.

2–025 In one situation the order for reference has to contain more than an exposition of the various factual and national legal premises or hypotheses underlying the case, together with the reasons for seeking the preliminary ruling. This is where it appears that Community law is not relevant in every eventuality to the decision in the main proceedings. In such a case, it is the national court's task first to narrow down the legal debate to only those premises or hypotheses in which Community law is relevant *in any event*. In order to do so, it will perhaps have to make a full or partial determination of the facts and national legal aspects of the case before it makes a reference to the Court, which certainly restricts its discretion to determine at what stage the reference is made. The intention behind this restriction is to avoid a fruitless judgment from the Court in the event that the national court should subsequently find that Community law has no part to play at all, having regard to the facts or the relevant national law. The 1992 judgment in *Meilicke* illustrates this.[88] A German court had referred a long series of involved questions concerning the interpretation of the Second Company Law Directive in order to be able to rule on the compatibility with the directive of a principle of German company law enshrined in case law. However, the parties to the main proceedings did not agree whether that principle was applicable to the facts of the case. The national court had elected not to rule on that issue and first to submit the question of compatibility to the Court. Its idea was that if it should become clear from the Court's interpretation of the Second Company Law Directive that the principle of German company law conflicted therewith, the question as to the applicability of that principle to the facts of the case would be of no account, given that the principle would have in any event to yield to Community law, which took precedence. The Court of Justice was unable to accept the sequence of the national court's decision-making on the

[87] Joined Cases 36 and 71/80 *Irish Creamery Milk Suppliers Association v. Ireland* [1981] E.C.R. 735 at 748, para. 8, ECJ.

[88] Case C–83/91 *Meilicke* [1992] E.C.R. I–4871, ECJ (case note by Arnull (1993) C.M.L.Rev. 613–622).

ground that if, conversely, it were to appear from the preliminary ruling that the principle of German company law was compatible with the Second Company Law Directive, the judgment of the Court of Justice would have no practical effect as a contribution to the resolution of the main proceedings, if at that stage the national court were to decide that under national law the principle laid down by case law was not applicable to the facts of the case. The only way of eliminating the risk of a hypothetical ruling from the Court was to oblige the German court to determine the facts and rule on the applicability of the principle of national law at issue before considering making a reference to the Court for a preliminary ruling.

It should be borne in mind that, in preliminary ruling proceedings, any assessment of the facts in the case is a matter for the national court. The Court of Justice is empowered to rule on the interpretation or validity of Community provisions only on the basis of the facts which the national court places before it.[89]

D. Annulment of a request for a preliminary ruling

The Court considers that a request for a preliminary ruling made pursuant to Article 234 (*ex Article 177*) continues "so long as the request of the national court has not been withdrawn by the court from which it emanates or has not been quashed on appeal from a superior court".[90] Consequently, the Court refuses to go into objections to its jurisdiction raised in observations submitted pursuant to Article 20 of the E.C. Statute of the Court claiming that the questions are no longer relevant, for example on the ground that the national legislative provisions whose compatibility with Community law the preliminary reference seeks to assess have in the meantime been declared unconstitutional[91] or that the request for a preliminary ruling was the outcome of a decision which was not taken in accordance with the applicable national (procedural) law.[92] 2–026

[89] Case C–30/93 *AC–ATEL Electronics v. Hauptzollamt München-Mitte* [1994] E.C.R. I–2305 at I–2324, paras 16–17, ECJ; Case C–325/95 *Phytheron International v. Bourdon* [1997] E.C.R. I–1729 at I–1744—1745, paras 11–14, ECJ; Case C–235/95 *Dumon and Froment* [1998] E.C.R. I–4531 at I-4565, para. 25, ECJ.

[90] Case 127/73 *BRT v. SABAM* [1974] E.C.R. 51 at 62, para. 9, ECJ; Case 106/77 *Amministrazione delle Finanze dello Stato v. Simmenthal* [1978] E.C.R. 629 at 642, para. 10, ECJ. For an example, see Case 65/77 *Razanatsimba* [1977] E.C.R. 2229 at 2237, paras 5–6, ECJ; (Order of June 24, 1997), Case C–184/95 *Mercedes Lores Guillín* (not reported in the E.C.R.).

[91] *Amministrazione delle Finanze dello Stato v. Simmenthal*, (cited in n. 90, above) at 642–643, paras 8–12.

[92] Case 65/81 *Reina v. Landeskreditbank Baden-Württemberg* [1982] E.C.R. 33 at 42–43, para. 7, ECJ. *Cf.* the Opinions of Advocate General M. Lagrange in Case 13/61 *De Geus en Uitdenbogerd v. Bosch and Van Rijn* [1962] E.C.R. 45 at 56, ECJ; and of Advocate General H. Mayras in Case 127/73 *BRT v. SABAM* [1974] E.C.R. 51 at 68, ECJ; Joined Cases C–332–333 and C–335/92 *Eurico Italia and Others* [1994] E.C.R. I–711 at I–733, para. 13, ECJ; Case C–472/93 *Spano and Others* [1995] E.C.R. I–4321 at I–4345, para. 16, ECJ. But see the Opinion of Advocate General C. Gulmann in Joined Cases C–320–322/90 *Telemarsicabruzzo and Others* [1993] E.C.R. I–393 at I–410—415, ECJ.

"[I]n view of the distribution of functions between itself and the national court, it is not for the Court to determine whether the decision whereby a matter is brought before it was taken in accordance with the rules of national law governing the organization of the courts and their procedure. The Court is therefore bound by a decision of a court or tribunal of a Member State referring a matter to it, in so far as that decision has not been rescinded on the basis of a means of redress provided for by national law".[93]

However, the Court may find that the main proceedings are to no purpose and that for it to reply to the questions referred would therefore be of no avail to the national court. In those circumstances, it will hold that the reference is to no purpose and that there is no need to reply to the questions referred.[94]

2–027 In order for a request for a preliminary ruling to be admissible, it is not necessary that the order for reference should have the force of *res judicata* under national law.[95] Community law does not restrict the remedies available under national law against the order for reference.[96]

Where an appeal brought against the order for reference under national law has suspensory effect and the Court is officially notified of this by the national courts concerned, it will defer its ruling until it has received notification that the appeal has been decided.[97] If the appeal results in the annulment of the order for reference, the Court will order the case to be

[93] *Reina v. Landeskreditbank Baden-Württemberg*, (cited in n. 92, above) at 42–43, para. 7; Case C–39/94 *SFEI and Others* [1996] E.C.R. I–3547 at I–3586, para. 24, ECJ. If, however, the Court of Justice finds that, after making a reference for a preliminary ruling, the national court considers that it cannot terminate the main proceedings even though the defendant has acceded to the plaintiff's claims, on the ground that Community law debars it from doing so, it considers itself entitled to inquire into the reasons given by the national court. If it appears that Community law does not preclude the national court from terminating the main proceedings under national law, the Court considers that it has no jurisdiction to answer the questions referred for a preliminary ruling as long as the national court has not found that in national law the acts of the parties have not terminated the main proceedings: Joined Cases C–422, C–423 and C–424/93 *Zabala Erasun and Others* [1995] E.C.R. I–1567, ECJ.

[94] Case C–316/96 *Djabali* [1998] E.C.R. I–1149 at I–1162—1163, paras 17–23, ECJ.

[95] Case 13/61 *De Geus en Uitdenbogerd v. Bosch and Van Rijn* [1962] E.C.R. 45 at 49–50, ECJ; Joined Cases 2–4/82 *Delhaize Frères v. Belgium* [1983] E.C.R. 2973 at 2986, paras 8, 9, ECJ.

[96] Case 146/73 *Rheinmühlen Düsseldorf v. Einfuhr- und Vorratsstelle Getreide* [1974] E.C.R. 139 third subparagraph of paragraph 3, at 147, para. 3, subpara. 3, ECJ. Such a restriction may, however, ensue from national law itself; see, *e.g.* Walsh, "The Appeal of an Art. 177 *[now Art. 234]* EEC Referral" (1993) M.L.R. 881 at 885, n. 9. See also Pfeiffer, "Keine Beschwerde gegen EuGH-Vorlagen?" (1994) N.J.W. 1998–2002.

[97] See, by way of example (Order of the President of December 8, 1993), Case C–269/92 *Bosman*, not reported in the E.C.R., ECJ.

removed from the register.[98] In this way, the Court avoids giving a ruling which is no longer of any assistance for the purposes of making a determination in the main proceedings.[99]

II. Determination of the Relevance of the Request for a Preliminary Ruling

A. Task of the national court

Ever since the 1978 judgment in the *Pigs Marketing Board* case, it has been settled case law that: **2–028**

> "*[a]s regards the division of jurisdiction between national courts and the Court of Justice* under Article 177 *[now Article 234]* of the Treaty the national court, which is alone in having a direct knowledge of the facts of the case and of the arguments put forward by the parties, and which will have to give judgment in the case, *is in the best position* to appreciate, with full knowledge of the matter before it, the relevance of the questions of law raised by the dispute before it and the necessity for a preliminary ruling so as to enable it to give judgment."[1]

Consequently, the national court's responsibility for assessing the relevance of the questions referred for a preliminary ruling has a dual basis.

In the first place, that assessment falls to it as part of its *jurisdiction* to hear and determine the main proceedings, which is left intact by Article 234

[98] See (Order of June 3, 1969), Case 31/68 *Chanel v. Cepeha* [1970] E.C.R. 403 at 403–404, ECJ, and (Order of June 16, 1970), Case 31/68 *Chanel v. Cepeha* [1970] E.C.R. 404 at 405–406, ECJ; (Order of the President of January 16, 1996), Case C–310/94 *Garage Ardon SA and Others v. Garage Trabisco SA*, not reported in the E.C.R., paras 2–3, ECJ. By a recent order, the President of the Court instructed a case to be struck out where an appeal against the order for reference had been blocked for seven years because one of the parties to the main proceedings had been declared insolvent. The President took the view that in the circumstances it was no longer necessary to reply to the questions set out in the order for reference (Order of the President of February 20, 1997), Case C–205/90 *Les Assurances du Crédit Namur SA v. "Bowy" PVBA and Others*, not reported in the E.C.R., ECJ).

[99] *Cf.* the Opinion of Advocate General K. Roemer in *Chanel v. Cepeha* (cited n. 98, above), at 408–409.

[1] Case 83/78 *Pigs Marketing Board v. Redmond* [1978] E.C.R. 2347 at 2367, para. 25, ECJ (emphasis added). See also, among other cases, Joined Cases C–399, C–409 and C–425/92, C–34, C–50 and C–78/93 *Helmig and Others* [1994] E.C.R. I–5727 at I–5750, para. 8, ECJ; Case C–134/94 *Esso Española* [1995] E.C.R. I–4223 at I–4246, para. 9, ECJ; Joined Cases C–320, C–328, C–329, C–337, C–338 and C–339/94 *RTI and Others* [1996] E.C.R. I–6471 at I–6503, para. 21, ECJ. The judgment in Case C–193/94 *Skanavi and Chryssanthakopoulos* [1996] E.C.R. I–929 at I–950, paras 17, 18, ECJ, affords a good example. The facts material to the main proceedings had occurred three days before the E.U. Treaty entered into force. The question submitted for a preliminary ruling related in part to the E.C. Treaty, Art. 8a (*now Art. 18*), a new provision introduced by the E.U. Treaty, which, according to the national court, might preclude application of the national rules at issue in the criminal proceedings pending before it. The Court of Justice found that the national court could apply the principle, recognised by its national law, that the more favourable rule of criminal law should take retroactive effect and, consequently, set aside national law to the extent to which it was contrary to the provisions of the Treaty. For those reasons, the Court did not contest the need for the preliminary ruling or the relevance of the questions referred. To like effect, see Joined Cases C–163, C–165 and C–250/94 *Sanz de Lera and Others* [1995] E.C.R. I–4821 at I–4835, para. 14, ECJ.

(*ex Article 177*). This aspect of the national court's task was stressed above all during the first 20 years of preliminary rulings from the Court, when it repeatedly stated that, under Article 234 of the E.C. Treaty, which enshrines the principle of the mutual independence of the national and the Community courts, the Court of Justice has no jurisdiction to pronounce on the considerations which prompted the request for an interpretation or for the assessment of the validity of an act.[2] When the questions referred by the national court relate to the interpretation of a provision of Community law or to the validity of an act of a Community institution, "the Court is, *in principle*, bound to give a ruling".[3]

Secondly, it is for the national court to determine the relevance of the request for a preliminary ruling on account of its special *ability* to make the relevant assessment. This signifies that the national court's competence to determine the relevance of the preliminary questions constitutes the starting point, but is not absolute or subject to no possible correction in any circumstances (the Court is only obliged "in principle" to reply). The Court accordingly points out that, in the event of questions' having been improperly formulated or going beyond the scope of the powers conferred on the Court of Justice by Article 234 (*ex Article 177*), it is free to extract from all the factors provided by the national court and in particular from the statement of grounds contained in the reference, the elements of Community law requiring an interpretation—or, as the case may be, an assessment of validity—*having regard to the subject-matter of the dispute.*[4]

2–029 In other words, the national court's jurisdiction to adjudge the relevance of the questions referred for a preliminary ruling and, in that light, to determine their content is not exclusive. The Court of Justice itself must take heed that the questions do not go beyond the scope of its powers and, where necessary, adapt the questions, "having regard to the subject-matter of the dispute", so that the preliminary ruling achieves its aim of making an effective contribution towards resolving the dispute before the national court.

2–030 Consequently, in its subsequent case law, the Court has emphasised that the national court's power to determine the relevance of questions referred for a preliminary ruling is constrained by its aim.

"[I]n the use which it makes of the facilities provided by Article 177 *[now Article 234]* [the national court] should have regard to the proper function

[2] Case 13/68 *Salgoil* [1968] E.C.R. 453 at 459–460, ECJ; Case 5/77 *Tedeschi v. Denkavit* [1977] E.C.R. 1555 at 1574, paras 17–19, ECJ.

[3] Case C–231/89 *Gmurzynska-Bscher* [1990] E.C.R. I–4003 at I–4017, para. 20, ECJ; see also para. 19 (emphasis added). If the request for a preliminary ruling has nothing to do with the interpretation of the Treaty or the validity or interpretation of an act of the institutions, it will be inadmissible. The Court of Justice may then declare the request inadmissible by an order given pursuant to the ECJ Rules of Procedure, Art. 92(1). See (Order of June 12, 1996), Case C–95/96 *Urssaf v. Clinique de la Pointe Rouge SA*, not reported in the E.C.R., paras 6–7, ECJ; (Order of June 12, 1996), Case C–96/96 *Urssaf v. Clinique Florens SA*, not reported in the E.C.R., paras 6–7, ECJ.

[4] Case 83/78 *Pigs Marketing Board v. Redmond* [1978] E.C.R. 2347 at 2366, para. 26, ECJ (emphasis added).

of the Court of Justice in this field",[5] which is not that of "delivering advisory opinions on general or hypothetical questions but of assisting in the administration of justice in the Member States".[6] The Court of Justice must always examine whether the questions raised are connected with its own task in order—just as in the case of any other court—not to exceed the limits of its jurisdiction. That limit would be exceeded if it would be impossible for the ruling requested to contribute towards the resolution of the dispute pending before the national court because of a manifest error in assessing the relevance of the questions of Community law referred to the Court.

In order to enable the Court to ascertain whether it has jurisdiction, "it is **2–031**
essential for national courts to explain, when the reasons do not emerge beyond any doubt from the documents, why they consider that a reply to their questions is necessary to enable them to give judgment".[7] Failure to fulfil that duty to state reasons does not automatically mean that the request for a preliminary ruling is inadmissible,[8] but it does cause the Court to adopt a more critical attitude when it makes its substantive review of the assessment of relevance which the national court is implicitly deemed to have carried out.[9]

The assessment of relevance which the Court of Justice expects the national court to carry out in order to ensure that it does not exceed the limits of its jurisdiction in answering questions referred for a preliminary ruling is very close to the description given by Lord Denning M.R.:

> "The judge must have got to the stage when he says to himself: 'This clause of the Treaty is capable of two or more meanings. If it means this, I give judgment for the plaintiff. If it means that, I give judgment for the defendant.' In short, the point must be such that, whichever way the point is decided, it is conclusive of the case. Nothing more remains but to give judgment."[10]

B. The limits set by Community law

1. Obviously irrelevant questions

The Court will not follow the national court's assessment of relevance **2–032**
where "it is quite obvious that the interpretation of Community law or the examination of the validity of a rule of Community law sought by that court bears no relation to the actual nature of the case or to the subject-matter of

---

5 Case 244/80 *Foglia v. Novello* (*Foglia v. Novello II*) [1981] E.C.R. 3045 at 3063, paras 20 *et seq.*, ECJ.

6 *ibid.*, at 3062–3063, para. 18. *Cf.* Case 149/82 *Robards v. Insurance Officer* [1983] E.C.R. 171 at 187, para. 19, ECJ.

7 Case 244/80 *Foglia v. Novello* (*Foglia v. Novello II*) [1981] E.C.R. 3045 at 3062, para. 17, ECJ.

8 Joined Cases 98, 162 and 258/85 *Bertini v. Regione Lazio* [1986] E.C.R. 1885 at 1896–1897, paras 6, 7, ECJ.

9 See paras 2–035, 2–036, below.

10 *Bulmer v. Bollinger* [1974] C.M.L.R. 91, [1974] Ch 401.

the main action".[11] The request for a preliminary ruling is then inadmissible and will be dismissed on that account.[12]

In the words of the Court, it must be "obvious" that the preliminary questions are irrelevant. The question arises, however, as to how far the Court will take its examination of the facts and national legal aspects of the main action in order to ascertain whether the preliminary ruling sought has some chance of making an actual contribution towards the decision in the case. Is it not the case that the Court must exercise a degree of restraint, given that determining the facts and the national law comes under the national court's jurisdiction? The answer to that question is yes in so far as the Court may not pronounce upon facts or aspects of national law which are in issue between the parties and on which the national court has not yet made any determination. In contrast, where the facts and national legal aspects of the case have been determined in the order for reference or are clear from the case-file submitted to the Court, there is nothing to prevent the Court from having regard to them in testing the national court's assessment of the relevance of the preliminary questions against the requirements which arise out of the aims of the Court's jurisdiction under Article 234 (*ex Article 177*) of the E.C. Treaty. Two examples will serve to clarify the Court's approach.

2–033 In the 1982 judgment in *Vlaeminck* the Court undertook an in-depth appraisal of the facts set forth in the order for reference of the *Arbeidshof* (Labour Court), Ghent, and reached the following conclusion:

> "In view of that factual situation the preliminary question appears to lack any purpose. It is not possible to glean from it the factors necessary for an interpretation of Community law which the national court might usefully apply in order to resolve, in accordance with that law, the dispute before it. It follows that in the light of the factual and legal circumstances of the main proceedings no question of Community law is raised in the present case, so that the Court is unable to

[11] Case 126/80 *Salonia v. Poidomani and Giglio* [1981] E.C.R. 1563 at 1576–1577, para. 6 ECJ. See in particular also Case C–368/89 *Crispoltoni* [1991] E.C.R. I–3695 at I–3718—3719, para. 11, ECJ; Case C–186/90 *Durighello* [1991] E.C.R. I–5773 at I–5795, para. 9, ECJ; Case C–343/90 *Lourenço Dias* [1992] E.C.R. I–4673 at I–4709, para. 18, ECJ; Case C–67/91 *Asociación Española de Banca Privada and Others* [1992] E.C.R. I–4785 at I–4829, para. 26, ECJ; Joined Cases C–332—333 and C–335/92 *Eurico Italia and Others* [1994] E.C.R. I–711 at I–734, para. 17, ECJ; Case C–18/93 *Corsica Ferries* [1994] E.C.R. I–1783 at I–1818, para. 14, ECJ; Case C–62/93 *Soupergaz* [1995] E.C.R. I–1883 at I–1912, para. 10, ECJ; Case C–143/94 *Furlanis* [1995] E.C.R. I–3633 at I–3648—3649, para. 12, ECJ; Case C–415/93 *Bosman* [1995] E.C.R. I–4921 at I–5059—5060, para. 61, ECJ; Case C–118/94 *Associazione Italiana per il WWF and Others* [1996] E.C.R. I–1223 at I–1247, para. 15, ECJ; Case C–129/94 *Ruiz Bernáldez* [1996] E.C.R. I–1829 at I–1852, para. 7, ECJ; Case C–85/95 *Reisdorf* [1996] E.C.R. I–6257 at I–6279, para. 16, ECJ; Joined Cases C–320, C–328, C–329, C–337, C–338 and C–339/94 *RTI and Others* [1996] E.C.R. I–6471 at I–6503, para. 23, ECJ; Case C–104/95 *Kontogeorgas* [1996] E.C.R. I–6643 at I–6662, paras 10, 11, ECJ; Case C–261/95 *Palmisani* [1997] E.C.R. I–4025 at I–4044, paras 10, 11, ECJ; Case C–373/95 *Maso and Others* [1997] E.C.R. I–4051 at I–4071, para. 26, ECJ.

[12] See, *inter alia* (Order of May 16, 1994), Case C–428/93 *Monin Automobiles* [1994] E.C.R. I–1707 at I–1714, paras 13, 14, ECJ.

give a ruling, in the context of proceedings under Article 177 *[now Article 234]*, on the question referred to it by the *Arbeidshof*, Ghent."[13]

This judgment is noteworthy in that the facts and aspects of national law relating to a pension scheme applicable to a married couple where the husband and wife had worked in France and Belgium were particularly complicated. Nevertheless, the Court felt that it was in a position to decide on the basis of the particulars set out in the order for reference and the case-file submitted by the national court that the decision in the main proceedings could be reached without Community law having any part to play.

Matters were even more clear-cut in the 1990 order in *Falciola*.[14] The Court declined jurisdiction to answer a number of questions referred by an Italian court. The questions arose in proceedings purportedly relating to the award of a roadworks contract. According to the order for reference, the contract was subject to two Council directives by reason of its value. However, the questions referred exclusively to the compatibility with Community law of several aspects of Italian Law No. 117/88 of 13 April 1988 on compensation for damage caused in the exercise of judicial functions and the civil liability of the judiciary.[15] The Court plainly had no difficulty in finding that the questions bore no relation to "the subject-matter of the [main] action" since the request for a preliminary ruling was not concerned with the interpretation of the two Council directives; instead, it was clear "from the actual wording of the order for reference" that the national court was only in doubt "as to the possible psychological reactions of certain Italian judges as a result of the enactment of the Italian Law of 13 April 1988". Accordingly, the Court held that "the preliminary questions submitted to the Court do not involve an interpretation of Community law objectively required in order to settle the dispute in the main action".[16] **2–034**

Where the order for reference taken as a whole does not state the reasons why the national court considers that a preliminary ruling is necessary in order to determine the case before it, the Court gives itself greater latitude in testing the relevance of the questions referred. Such a situation occurred in the 1992 judgment in *Lourenço Dias*.[17] A Portuguese court had referred eight questions concerning the interpretation of Article 25 (*ex Article 12*) and Article 90 (*ex Article 95*) of the E.C. Treaty. The questions sought to ascertain the compatibility with Community law of various aspects of a new Portuguese law on motorvehicle taxation. The public prosecutor, who was a party in the main proceedings, the Portuguese and British Governments and the Commission claimed that the Court had **2–035**

[13] Case 132/81 *Rijksdienst voor Werknemerspensioenen v. Vlaeminck* [1982] E.C.R. 2953 at 2963–2964, paras 13, 14, ECJ.

[14] (Order of January 26, 1990), Case C–286/88 *Falciola* [1990] E.C.R. I–191, ECJ.

[15] (1988) GURI, No 88, 3.

[16] (Order of January 26, 1990), Case C–286/88 *Falciola* [1990] E.C.R. I–191 at I–195, para. 9, ECJ.

[17] Case C–343/90 *Lourenço Dias* [1992] E.C.R. I–4673, ECJ.

no jurisdiction on the ground that the questions, or at least some of them, bore no relation to the actual nature of the case or to the subject-matter of the main action.[18] The case was concerned with a vehicle which, upon importation into Portugal, was converted for goods transport, thus enjoying tax exemption. When a check was carried out some months later, it transpired, however, that the conversion had been reversed in order that passengers could be carried as well as goods. Consequently, the tax authorities claimed the tax, which the owner of the vehicle, Lourenço Dias, contested before the national court. The Court of Justice observed that the national court had expressed doubts about the compatibility with Community law of certain provisions of Portuguese law, but had omitted to inform the Court how those provisions were to be applied to the facts of the main proceedings. The Court itself then proceeded to identify the provisions of Portuguese law to which each of the eight preliminary questions referred and related them to the characteristics of the vehicle involved and the other factual circumstances which emerged, not only from the order for reference and the case-file submitted by the national court, but also—a much more radical step—from the observations submitted pursuant to Article 20 of the E.C. Statute of the Court, including those presented by an "outsider", the British Government. Having conducted that exercise, the Court held that the provisions of Portuguese law to which six of the eight preliminary questions referred, expressly or impliedly, were manifestly inapplicable to the facts of the main proceedings and that there was therefore no need to answer them. Whatever the Court's answer to them, it would have had no bearing on the outcome of the main proceedings.[19]

2–036 At first sight, that judgment may suggest that the Court trespassed over the borderline between interpreting Community law and interpreting national law. Yet its approach was perfectly proper since it did not pronounce upon any factual or national legal aspect of the main proceedings which was in issue between the parties.[20] The Court regarded itself as being obliged simply to supply the *lacunae* which the national court had left in its order, namely its omission to give reasons why it considered it needed an answer to the preliminary questions so as to decide the main action, in order not to exceed its jurisdiction. If the Court had answered all eight questions, it is clear that it would have done so without a prior thorough judicial debate of questions which in actual fact were not relevant from the point of view of the positions argued for by the parties to the main proceedings. For this reason too it is undesirable that the Court should be compelled to give a ruling—as it were in a vacuum—on hypothetical questions whose answers would not contribute towards the resolution of a dispute. In addition, it has to be borne in mind in this connection that a preliminary ruling has general value as a precedent in the Community legal

[18] This is the *Salonia* test: Case 126/80 *Salonia v. Poidomani and Giglio* [1981] E.C.R. 1563 at 1576–1577, para. 6, ECJ.

[19] See also Case C–297/93 *Grau-Hupka* [1994] E.C.R. I–5535 at I–5551, para. 19, ECJ.

[20] See para. 6–026, below.

order,[21] which makes the Court—in common with all courts—careful only to decide on what is necessary in order to bring a case to a conclusion and thereby to allow the whole mosaic of case law to build itself up incrementally. A court is not a legislative body laying down abstract rules of general scope.

2. Spurious disputes

The idea that the preliminary ruling should contribute towards bringing a dispute to a conclusion also underlies the Court's refusal to answer questions raised by means of spurious main proceedings. This means that the Court will refuse to give a preliminary ruling "where it appears that the procedure of Article 177 *[now Article 234]* of the Treaty has been misused and been resorted to, in fact, in order to elicit a ruling from the Court by means of a spurious dispute".[22] **2–037**

It is not, however, an easy matter for the Court to decide that it "appears" that the main proceedings are spurious, without in so doing exceeding the limits of its jurisdiction. It is a slippery slope from finding that preliminary questions have been raised "within the framework of procedural devices arranged by the parties in order to induce the Court to give its views on certain problems of Community law which do not correspond to an objective requirement inherent in the resolution of a dispute"[23] to assessing facts and aspects of national law on which no definitive finding has yet been made by the national court, a task which falls outside the limits of the Court's jurisdiction. **2–038**

In order to avoid this difficulty the Court will decide that the preliminary reference is inadmissible only where it is manifestly apparent from the facts set out in the order for reference that the dispute is in fact fictitious.[24] In this way, the Court confines its review to a species of "marginal review" of facts plainly set out in the order for reference, even without having regard to further particulars contained in the case-file from the national court or in observations submitted pursuant to Article 20 of the E.C. Statute of the Court.[25]

The only case to date in which the Court has declined jurisdiction on account of the spurious nature of the main proceedings was one in which the parties were concerned to obtain a ruling that a tax system in one Member State was invalid by the expedient of proceedings before a court in another Member State between two private individuals who were in agreement as to the result to be obtained and had inserted a clause in their **2–039**

---

[21] See para. 6–035, below.

[22] Case C–231/89 *Gmurzynska-Bcher* [1990] E.C.R. I–4003 at I–4018, para. 23, ECJ.

[23] Case 244/80 *Foglia v. Novello* (*Foglia v. Novello II*) [1981] E.C.R. 3045 at 3062–3063, para. 18, ECJ.

[24] Case 267/86 *Van Eycke v. ASPA* [1988] E.C.R. 4769 at 4790, para. 12, ECJ; Case C–118/94 *Associazione Italiana per il WWF and Others* [1996] E.C.R. I–1223 at I–1247, para. 12, ECJ; Case C–129/94 *Ruiz Bernáldez* [1996] E.C.R. I–1829 at I–1852, para. 7, ECJ.

[25] *Cf. Van Eycke v. ASPA* (cited in n. 24, above), Report for the Hearing, at 4774, second column.

contract in order to induce a court in another Member State to give a ruling on the point.[26] The Court held that the artificial nature of this expedient was underlined by the fact that the remedies available under the law of the first Member State to contest the tax in question had not been used.[27]

This judgment has been severely criticised by commentators on the ground that the Court exceeded its powers by going too deeply into the facts of the main proceedings, specifically with the intention of making the national court respect the limits of the Court's jurisdiction in so far as it is to give only preliminary rulings which actually contribute towards resolving the main dispute. It has been argued that this puts at risk the whole relationship of trust between the Court of Justice and the national courts on which the co-operation mechanism set in place by Article 234 (*ex Article 177*) of the E.C. Treaty is founded.[28] It is therefore not surprising that subsequently the Court has done everything to reduce the scope of this case law to a hard core of exceptional cases[29]: where it is clear from the factual data set out in the order for reference that the main proceedings are manifestly spurious, the Court will decline jurisdiction on the ground that answering the national court's preliminary questions will not assist it in giving judgment (which is unnecessary if there is no "dispute"). Clearly, such a situation will arise only exceptionally.[30]

---

[26] Case 104/79 *Foglia v. Novello* (*Foglia v. Novello I*) [1980] E.C.R. 745 at 759–760, para. 10, ECJ.

[27] *ibid.*, at 759, 760, para. 10.

[28] Barav, "Preliminary Censorship? The Judgment of the European Court in Foglia v. Novello" (1980) E.L.Rev. 443–468; Barav, "Imbroglio préjudiciel" (1982) R.T.D.E. 431–483; Bebr, "The Existence of a Genuine Dispute: an Indispensable Precondition for the Jurisdiction of the Court under Art. 177 (*now Art. 234*) EEC Treaty" (1980) C.M.L.Rev. 525–537; Lipstein, "Foglia v. Novello—Some Unexplored Aspects", in *Du droit international au droit de l'intégration—Liber amicorum Pierre Pescatore*, Baden-Baden, Nomos, 1987, at 373–385; Tizzano, "Litiges fictifs et compétence préjudicielle de la Cour de justice européenne" (1981) R.G.D.I.P. 514 at 524–525.

[29] Case 46/80 *Vinal v. Orbat* [1981] E.C.R. 77 at 91, paras 5–7, ECJ; and the Opinion of Advocate General G. Reischl in that case, at 98, which refers to the exceptional nature of *Foglia v. Novello*.

[30] Consequently, the case law on this point is in fact reverting to the Court's former stance: *cf.* Case 20/64 *Albatros v. Sopéco* [1965] E.C.R. 29 at 33–34; Case 261/81 *Rau v. De Smedt* [1982] E.C.R. 3961 at 3971, paras 8, 9, ECJ; Case 267/86 *Van Eycke v. ASPA* [1988] E.C.R. 4769 at 4790, para. 12, ECJ. But the principle that spurious proceedings are inadmissible remains: Joined Cases C–297/88 and C–197/89 *Dzodzi* [1990] E.C.R. I–3763 at I–3794, para. 40, ECJ; *Cf.* Case C–88/91 *Federconsorzi* [1992] E.C.R. I–4035 at I–4063—4064, paras 6–10, ECJ (Community law applicable through a contractual provision); Case C–412/93 *Leclerc-Siplec v. TF1 and Others* [1995] E.C.R. I–179 at I–215, para. 14, ECJ (the fact that the parties to the main proceedings are in agreement as to the result to be obtained makes the dispute no less real); Case C–408/95 *Eurotunnel and Others* [1997] E.C.R. I–6315 at I–6351, para. 22, ECJ (the reality of dispute may be inferred from the fact that all the arguments raised by the plaintiff in the main proceedings have been contested by the defendant in those proceedings).

III. The Duty to Request a Preliminary Ruling

The third paragraph of Article 234 (*ex Article 177*) of the E.C. Treaty provides that where a question concerning the interpretation of Community law or the validity of acts of Community institutions is raised in a national court and it considers that a decision on the question is necessary to enable it to give judgment, it is bound to bring the matter before the Court of Justice where "there is no judicial remedy under national law" against the national court's decisions. **2–040**

A. What national courts and tribunals are involved?

In the first place, the highest courts in the hierarchy are under a duty to make a preliminary reference, irrespective as to whether they have general competence (House of Lords) or specialised jurisdiction (for example, the Tariefcommissie voor Belastingzaken, a revenue court in the Netherlands[31]).[32] **2–041**

The idea behind this is that in the national legal systems decisions of the highest courts bind lower courts (in one way or another) with the result that the most efficient way of securing uniformity of Community law in all the Member States is to oblige courts of last resort to refer questions to the Court of Justice for a preliminary ruling.[33] If that obligation were to be extended to all courts and tribunals, the Court of Justice would be overloaded and there would be no real additional gain in terms of the uniformity of Community law since the lower courts have to follow decisions of courts of last resort which are the outcome of collaboration with the Court of Justice. Naturally, this does not detract from the *right* of *any* court to decide to refer a question to the Court of Justice of its own motion.

Secondly, courts other than those of last resort may in certain circumstances take decisions against which there is no remedy. Are those courts then under a duty to make a reference for a preliminary ruling under the third paragraph of Article 234 (*ex Article 177*) of the E.C. Treaty? The Court of Justice appears to have answered this question in the affirmative in an *obiter dictum* in the leading case of *Costa v. ENEL*, decided in 1964. It stated, with regard to a request for a preliminary ruling from an Italian *Giudice Conciliatore* (magistrate), that "By the terms of [Article 177 *[now Article 234]*] national courts against whose decisions, *as in the present case*, there is no judicial remedy, must refer the matter to the Court of Justice so **2–042**

---

31 Case 26/62 *Van Gend & Loos v. Nederlandse Administratie der Belastingen* [1963] E.C.R. 1, ECJ; Joined Cases 28–30/62 *Da Costa en Schaake v. Nederlandse Belastingadministratie* [1963] E.C.R. 31 at 38, ECJ.

32 Joliet, *Le contentieux*, at 180.

33 Case 107/76 *Hoffmann-La Roche v. Centrafarm* [1977] E.C.R. 957 at 973, para. 5, subpara. 1, ECJ: "[T]he particular object of the third paragraph [of Art. 177 (*now Art. 234*)] is to prevent a body of case-law not in accord with the rules of Community law from coming into existence in any Member State". See also, Joined Cases 35 and 36/82 *Morson and Jhanjan v. State of the Netherlands* [1982] E.C.R. 3723 at 3734, para. 8, ECJ.

that a preliminary ruling may be given . . .".[34] Accordingly, where a lower court has the power to prevent an appeal from it, it must make a reference if it is minded to exercise its power not to allow an appeal (for example in England and Wales where a court such as the Divisional Court declines to certify a question of law as fit for consideration by the House of Lords).

2–043 A judge hearing an application for *interim relief* where no judicial remedy is available against his order, is in a special position. In response to a preliminary question relating specifically to that situation the Court of Justice ruled that:

> "a national court or tribunal is not required to refer to the Court a question of interpretation or of validity mentioned in [Article 177 *[now Article 234]*] when the question is raised in interlocutory proceedings for [interim relief], even where no judicial remedy is available against the decision to be taken in the context of those proceedings provided that each of the parties is entitled to institute proceedings or to require proceedings to be instituted on the substance of the case and that during such proceedings the question provisionally decided in the summary proceedings may be re-examined and may be the subject of a reference to the Court under Article 177 *[now Article 234]*."[35]

Subsequently, the Court refined this by stating that the requirements of the third paragraph of Article 234 are observed even if only the unsuccessful party may bring proceedings as to the substance and the action is tried "before courts or tribunals belonging to a jurisdictional system different from that under which the interlocutory proceedings are conducted, provided that it is still possible to refer to the Court under Article 177 *[now Article 234]* any questions of Community law which are raised".[36]

2–044 Lastly, the Benelux Court of Justice,[37] which gives definitive rulings on questions of interpretation of uniform Benelux law, may be obliged to make a reference to the Court of Justice under Article 234 (*ex Article 177*) of the E.C. Treaty.[38] The Court of Justice has held, however, that if, before making a reference to the Benelux Court, a national court has submitted a question of Community law to the Court of Justice, the Benelux Court is released from its obligation to submit the question if it would be couched in "substantially the same terms".[39]

---

[34] Case 6/64 *Costa v. ENEL* [1964] E.C.R. 585, third paragraph, at 592, para. 3, ECJ (emphasis added).

[35] Case 107/76 *Hoffmann-La Roche v. Centrafarm* [1977] E.C.R. 957 at 973, para. 6, ECJ.

[36] Joined Cases 365 and 36/82 *Morson and Jhanjan v. State of the Netherlands* [1982] E.C.R. 3723 at 3734, paras 8, 9, ECJ.

[37] See para. 2–013, above.

[38] Case C–337/95 *Parfums Christian Dior* [1997] E.C.R. I–6013 at I–6044, para. 26, ECJ.

[39] See para. 2–049, below.

B. Decisions against which there is no judicial remedy under national law

2–045 The question as to against what decisions a "judicial remedy" exists is a matter of national law, as is clear from the actual wording of the third paragraph of Article 234 (*ex Article 177*). All the same, Community law does play a role, more specifically in ascertaining what type of possible "judicial remedy" precludes the obligation to make a reference for a preliminary ruling. The starting point for any inquiry should be the aim of the third paragraph of Article 234, which is to avoid the most authoritative case law in any given Member State developing contrary to Community law, thus putting all courts in that state at risk of going off in the same—wrong—direction.

Consequently, the obligation to make a preliminary reference arises whenever the national court finds that there is no judicial remedy available against its decisions which can normally be deployed against judicial decisions, no matter how the remedy is described. Whether the remedy is termed "ordinary" or "exceptional" has no bearing in this regard. The only test is whether the legal issues which the lower court has decided may, as a matter of course, be subjected to a fresh judicial assessment. This is clearly the case with an appeal on a point of law or in cassation proceedings, which must accordingly be deemed to be a "judicial remedy" within the meaning of the third paragraph of Article 234. Questions of Community law are in fact legal issues which are definitively settled in the highest courts.

2–046 In contrast, the existence of wholly exceptional judicial remedies—even where they may be available against decisions of the highest courts—may not be invoked in order to avoid the obligation to seek a preliminary ruling. Examples are applications for the revision of a judgment or *tierce-opposition* proceedings. The *Verfassungsbeschwerde* (constitutional appeal) which may be brought before the Federal Constitutional Court against a judgment of a court of last resort (for example the *Bundesgerichtshof* or the *Bundesfinanzhof*) is an example from Germany. The existence of such an exceptional remedy—which, moreover, does not enable all the legal issues decided by the court of last resort to be reviewed, but relates only to the compatibility of the contested judgment with the German Basic Law—does not detract from the obligation of the ordinary German courts of last resort to request a preliminary ruling from the Court of Justice.[40]

C. Limits set to the duty to request a preliminary ruling

2–047 First and foremost, courts coming within the scope of the third paragraph of Article 234 (*ex Article 177*) have a discretion to assess the *relevance* of a request for a preliminary ruling.[41] The Court of Justice enlarged upon this in the leading case of *CILFIT*, decided in 1982.[42] The mere fact that a party

[40] *Cf.* Lagrange, "L'action préjudicielle dans le droit interne des Etats membres et en droit communautaire" (1974) R.T.D.E. 268 at 284.

[41] See paras 2–028—2–031, above.

[42] Case 283/81 *CILFIT v. Ministry of Health* [1982] E.C.R. 3415, ECJ.

contends that the dispute gives rise to a question concerning the interpretation of Community law or the validity of an act of a Community institution does not mean that the court concerned is compelled to request a preliminary ruling.[43] The Court takes the view that:

> "it follows from the relationship between the second and third paragraphs of Article 177 *[now Article 234]* that the courts or tribunals referred to in the third paragraph have the same discretion as any other national court or tribunal to ascertain whether a decision on a question of Community law is necessary to enable them to give judgment. Accordingly, those courts or tribunals are not obliged to refer to the Court of Justice a question concerning the interpretation of Community law [or the validity of an act of a Community institution] raised before them if that question is not relevant, that is to say, if the answer to that question, regardless of what it may be, can in no way affect the outcome of the case".[44]

In such a case the Court of Justice would moreover dismiss the request for a preliminary ruling in any event on account of the irrelevance of the question referred (see the *Salonia* and *Lourenço Dias* cases).[45]

2–048 Next, it falls to consider the actual exceptions to the obligation to request a preliminary ruling where the question is manifestly relevant for the purposes of reaching a decision in the main proceedings. There are three instances in which the Court of Justice has tempered the obligation to seek a preliminary ruling in the interests of more efficiently achieving the aim of the third paragraph of Article 234 (*ex Article 177*), namely "to prevent the occurrence within the Community of divergences in judicial decisions on questions of Community law".[46]

2–049 *First*: in the 1963 judgment in *Da Costa en Schaake*, the Court ruled that:

> "the authority of an interpretation under Article 177 *[now Article 234]* already given by the Court may deprive the obligation [to seek a preliminary ruling] of its purpose and thus empty it of its substance. Such is the case especially when the question raised is materially

---

[43] *Cf. ibid.*, at 3428, para. 9. For the approach taken in the courts of England and Wales, see *Brealey and Hoskins* (cited in para. 1–004, n. 12, above), pp. 218–224. In *R v. International Stock Exchange, ex p. Else Ltd* [1993] Q.B. 534 at 545C–G, Sir Thomas Bingham said, "If the national court has any real doubt, it should ordinarily refer". Advocate General F.G. Jacobs expressed the view in his Opinion of July 10, 1997 in Case C–338/95 *Wiener v. Hauptzollamt Emmerich*, [1997] E.C.R. I–6495 at 6497, points 12–20, that national courts should show self-restraint in making references where there is no question of general importance or the ruling is not likely to promote the uniform application of Community law. In *Customs & Excise Commissioners v. APS Samex* [1983] 1 All E.R. 1042 at 1056f–g, Bingham J. called on judges to have regard to the expense and time needed for a preliminary ruling.

[44] *CILFIT* (cited in n. 42, above) at 3429, para. 10. For a case in which leave to make a reference for a preliminary ruling was refused on grounds of lack of relevance, see *R. v. Licensing Authority, ex p. Smith-Kline* [1990] 1 A.C. 64.

[45] See para. 2–032, above.

[46] *CILFIT* (cited in n. 42, above) at 3428, para. 7.

> identical with a question which has already been the subject of a preliminary ruling in a similar case."[47]

The national court which is obliged in principle under the third paragraph of Article 234 (*ex Article 177*) to make a reference to the Court of Justice is released from its obligation provided that it follows the existing preliminary ruling. It is only the obligation to make a reference which ceases to apply, not the possibility of seeking a ruling. More specifically, where the national court would like the Court of Justice to amend, qualify or limit its earlier preliminary ruling—for instance, in the light of the particular facts of the main action—the only solution is for the national court to make use of that possibility.[48]

Secondly: **2–050**

> "The same effect, as regards the limits set to the obligation laid down by the third paragraph of Article 177 *[now Article 234]*, may be produced where previous decisions of the Court have already dealt with the point of law in question, irrespective of the nature of the proceedings which led to those decisions, even though the questions at issue are not strictly identical."[49]

This is an extension of the first exception: it is no longer a requirement for the earlier judgment of the Court to have ruled on a virtually identical preliminary question. In contrast, it is sufficient that the earlier decision should provide an answer to the question of Community law which has arisen in the main proceedings, regardless of the procedural context in which it came about. This also provides an explanation as to why the questions at issue need not be completely identical, which would appear to be out of the question where the earlier judgment was not given in answer to a request for a preliminary ruling. The only critical point is whether the decision is capable of being regarded as "settled case law" or one of a number of "previous decisions" as the English translation has it, or, in other words, whether it can be definitely regarded as constituting the Court of Justice's answer to the question of Community law which has arisen. Thus, a judgment given pursuant to Articles 226 to 228 (*ex Articles 169 to 171*) of the E.C. Treaty in which the Court declared that a Member State had failed to fulfil its obligations under Community law will generally contain an interpretation of provisions and principles of that law. In so far as that is so, national courts subject to the third paragraph of Article 234 (*ex Article 177*) can extract from the judgment what they need in order to

[47] Joined Cases 28–30/62 *Da Costa en Schaake v. Nederlandse Belastingadministratie* [1963] E.C.R. 31 at 38 ECJ; confirmed by Case 283/81 *CILFIT v. Ministry of Health* [1982] E.C.R. 3415 paragraph 13, at 3429, para. 13, ECJ; and Case C–337/95 *Parfums Christian Dior* [1997] E.C.R. I–6013 at I–6045, paras 29, 30, ECJ (where it was held that the question had to be in "substantially the same terms").

[48] *CILFIT* (cited in n. 42 above) at 3430, para. 15.

[49] *ibid.*, at 3429, para. 14.

answer the questions concerning the interpretation of Community law which are determinative of the main proceedings pending before them. In common with any court, they are even obliged to do this,[50] unless they opt to exercise their right to bring the matter before the Court of Justice anew, perhaps with a view to an adjustment of the case law.[51]

2–051 *Thirdly*:

> "[T]he correct application of Community law may be so obvious as to leave no scope for any reasonable doubt as to the manner in which the question raised is to be resolved. Before it comes to the conclusion that such is the case, the national court or tribunal must be convinced that the matter is equally obvious to the courts of the other Member States and to the Court of Justice."

If that condition is satisfied, the national court may "refrain from submitting the question to the Court of Justice and take upon itself the responsibility for resolving it".[52] This exception is known as the *acte clair* doctrine.

The strict conditions to which implementation of the *acte clair* doctrine is subject are designed to prevent national courts from abusing the doctrine in order to evade their obligation to seek a preliminary ruling where they are disinclined to adhere to the Court's case law. Both the French *Conseil d'Etat* and the German *Bundesfinanzhof* at one time abused the *acte clair* doctrine in this way.[53] According to those courts, the wording of the third paragraph of Article 249 (*ex Article 189*) of the E.C. Treaty was so clear that it was unnecessary to seek a preliminary ruling from the Court of Justice on the effect within a Member State's national legal system of a directive which had failed to be implemented within the prescribed period. By reference to the plain words of Article 249 (*ex Article 189*), however, they decided, completely contrary to the settled case law of the Court of Justice,[54] that in the circumstances in question a directive could never have direct effect on account of its legal nature.

The *CILFIT* formulation of the *acte clair* doctrine is the expression of a particularly subtle compromise.[55] On the one hand, the Court sought to

---

[50] Joined Cases 314–316/81 and 83/82 *Waterkeyn* [1982] E.C.R. 4337 at 4360–4361, paras 13–16, ECJ.

[51] Case 283/81 *CILFIT v. Ministry of Health* [1982] E.C.R. 3415 at 3420, para. 15, ECJ.

[52] *ibid.*, para. 16.

[53] France: Conseil d'Etat, December 22, 1978, *Cohn-Bendit* (1979) R.T.D.E. 168–189. Germany: Bundesfinanzhof, July 16, 1981, (1981) EuR. 442–444. See Bebr, "The Rambling Ghost of 'Cohn-Bendit': *Acte clair* and the Court of Justice" (1983) C.M.L.Rev. 439–472. An explanation of the position taken by the *Conseil d'Etat* is to be found in Genevois, "Der Conseil d'Etat und das Gemeinschaftsrecht: Antagonismus oder Komplementarität?" (1985) EuR. 355–367. For English examples, see *R v. London Boroughs Transport Committee, ex p. Freight Transport Association Ltd* [1992] 1 C.M.L.R. 5 and *Kirklees Borough Council v. Wickes Building Supplies Ltd* [1992] 3 W.L.R. 170, discussed in Brealey and Hoskins, *Remedies in EC Law* (see para. 1–004, n. 12, above), pp. 227–228.

[54] For the direct effect of directives, see Lenaerts and Van Nuffel, *Constitutional Law of the European Union*, paras 14–101—14–106.

[55] *Cf.* the opposite view taken in the Opinion of Advocate General Capotorti in Case 283/81 *CILFIT v. Ministry of Health* [1982] E.C.R. 3415 at 3442, ECJ.

reinforce spontaneous collaboration on the part of the highest national courts by allowing them to take the responsibility upon themselves to decide questions of Community law where it is not reasonably conceivable that anyone would come to a different answer. A very limited category of extremely obvious questions of Community law is involved here. It would have been insensitive of the Court to have placed no trust in the judgment of the highest national courts with regard even to that sort of question. For other types of questions, the national courts have to place their trust in the Court of Justice once they realise that more than one answer is conceivable.[56] On the other hand, the Court seeks to constrain the judgment of the highest national courts as to the obvious nature of the—apparently only conceivable—answer to a question of Community law as much as possible in order to preclude *bona fide* inadvertence. To this end, the Court has listed three factors which the highest national courts have to take into account before they are entitled to consider that they may release themselves from their obligation to seek a preliminary ruling. Those factors have to do with the "characteristic features of Community law and the particular difficulties to which its interpretation gives rise".[57] These factors are as follows:

(1) the interpretation of a provision of Community law involves a comparison of the various language versions, all of which are authentic;

(2) given that Community law uses terminology peculiar to it, legal concepts do not necessarily have the same meaning as they do in the different national legal systems;

(3) every provision of Community law must be placed in its context and interpreted "in the light of the provisions of Community law as a whole, regard being had to the objectives thereof and to its state of evolution at the date on which the provision in question is to be applied".[58]

It is self-evident that if these three factors were scrupulously taken into account, the number of cases in which "the correct application of Community law is so obvious as to leave no scope for any reasonable doubt"[59] would be reduced to an absolute minimum.[60]

---

56 See to this effect Mancini and Keeling, "From *CILFIT* to *ERT*: the Constitutional Challenge facing the European Court" (1991) Y.E.L. 1 at 4–5; Rasmussen, "The European Court's Acte Clair Strategy in *CILFIT* (Or: 'Acte Clair, of course! But what does it mean?')" (1984) E.L.Rev. 242.

57 Case 283/81 *CILFIT v. Ministry of Health* [1982] E.C.R. 3415 at 3430, para. 17, ECJ.

58 *ibid.*, para. 18–20.

59 *ibid.*, at 3431, para. 21.

60 *CILFIT* may, however, also be abused: see Arnull, "The Use and Abuse of Art. 177 *[now Art. 234]* EEC" (1989) M.L.R. 622–639, in which the author cites a number of English cases which wrongly used the *CILFIT* judgment in order not to seek a preliminary ruling. For a general discussion of *CILFIT*, see Masclet, "Vers la fin d'une controverse? La Cour de justice tempère l'obligation de renvoi préjudiciel en interprétation faite aux juridictions suprêmes (art. 177 *[now Art. 234]*, alinéa 3, CEE)" (1983) R.M.C. 363–373.

D. Enforcement of the obligation to request a preliminary ruling

2–052 There is no remedy available from the Court of Justice to parties to the main proceedings against a refusal of a court of last resort to make a preliminary reference. The Commission or a Member State may, however, seek a declaration from the Court of Justice pursuant to Article 226 or 227 (*ex Article 169 or 170*) of the E.C. Treaty that, through its national court's refusal to seek a ruling, the Member State in question has infringed the third paragraph of Article 234 (*ex Article 177*). Courts and tribunals are in fact "institutions of the Member State concerned".[61]

The Commission acknowledges a duty to oversee the way in which national courts subject to the obligation to seek preliminary rulings make use of the *acte clair* doctrine enshrined in the judgment in *CILFIT*.[62]

2–053 The institution of proceedings for infringement of Community law on account of the failure of a national court to comply with its obligation under the third paragraph of Article 234 (*ex Article 177*) is not, however, an efficient way of enforcing that obligation. In the first place, the parties to the main proceedings are not directly assisted thereby. Secondly, whilst in such proceedings it is no defence for a Member State to plead the independence under its Constitution of the state institution responsible for the infringement of Community law,[63] in a "Community based on the rule of law"[64] the essential principle of the constitutional independence of the judiciary from the executive and the legislature nevertheless implies that a national government which is unsuccessful in an action brought against it under Article 226 (*ex Article 169*) can count on comprehension where it is not in a position to compel the offending court to change its position. Unlike other "independent" institutions of the State (for example, legislative bodies, states forming part of a federation, etc.), in respect of which it is felt that the Member State should, where necessary, adjust its internal structure in such a way that it is always in a position to ensure that those institutions effectively comply with Community law, even if this is at the expense of their independence, a certain reluctance is—properly—felt in advocating that idea as far as the highest national courts are concerned. Commentators are also at one in taking the view that it would be inappropriate to enforce the obligation laid down in the third paragraph of Article 234 (*ex Article 177*) by means of proceedings under Articles 226 and 227 (*ex Articles 169 and 170*) of the E.C. Treaty.[65]

The conclusion is that, as a matter of fact, the obligation to seek a preliminary ruling cannot be enforced. Instead, compliance with that obligation is based on the relationship of trust linking the highest national courts and the Court of Justice in a context of efficient collaboration.

---

[61] Joined Cases 314–316/81 and 83/82 *Waterkeyn* [1982] E.C.R. 4337 at 4360, para. 14, ECJ.

[62] Answer given by President G. Thorn on behalf of the Commission on July 25, 1983 to a written question from A. Tyrrell MEP [1983] O.J. C268/25.

[63] Rideau and Picod, *Code de procédures communautaires*, at 192.

[64] Case 294/83 *Les Verts v. European Parliament* [1986] E.C.R. 1339 at 1365, para. 23, ECJ.

[65] Joliet, *Le contentieux*, at 186.

Following the 1991 judgment in *Francovich*,[66] however, Community law may possibly require Member States to recognise the possibility of a claim in damages against the public authorities where an infringement by a court of last resort of its obligation to make a reference for a preliminary ruling demonstrably thwarts a right conferred on individuals by Community law. Especially in cases where the *acte clair* doctrine is abused and the court of last resort shirks its obligation to seek a preliminary ruling in order to ignore the settled case law of the Court of Justice on the interpretation of a particular provision on the purported ground that it is obvious, it may well be imagined that the interested individual may identify an individual right which is denied to him (loss or damage) as a result (causal link) of the national court's refusal to comply with the third paragraph of Article 234 (*ex Article 177*) of the E.C. Treaty (breach of Community law).[67] Moreover, such a development would accord well with the right recognised by a number of Member States in connection with State liability in damages for loss or damage caused to individuals as a result of a breach of Community law on the part of the judiciary.[68] **2–054**

E. Obligation to request a preliminary ruling *praeter legem*

Where a court or tribunal not subject to the third paragraph of Article 234 (*ex Article 177*) perceives that an act of a Community institution is invalid, it may not make such a finding itself, but *must* seek a preliminary ruling thereon from the Court of Justice.[69] At first sight, this obligation detracts from the national court's freedom under the second paragraph of Article 234 to decide whether or not to make a reference to the Court of Justice. But the Court has held that: **2–055**

> "In enabling national courts, against whose decisions there is a judicial remedy under national law, to refer to the Court for a preliminary ruling questions on interpretation or validity, Article 177 *[now Article 234]* did not settle the question whether those courts themselves may declare that acts of Community institutions are invalid."[70]

---

66 Joined Cases C–6 and C–9/90 *Francovich and Others* [1991] E.C.R. I–5357, ECJ.

67 By analogy with *Francovich* at I–5415, paras 39–40. The Member State concerned may incur liability under Community law all the more readily inasmuch as the highest national court has no discretion in applying Art. 234 (*ex Art. 177*) para. 3; see para. 3–023, below. See also Ter Kuile, "To Refer or not to Refer: About the Last Paragraph of Art. 177 *[now Art. 234]* of the E.C. Treaty", in Curtin and Heukels (eds), *Institutional Dynamics of European Integration. Essays in Honour of H.G. Schermers*, Dordrecht, Martinus Nijhoff, 1994, II, 381 at 388–389.

68 Belgium: Cass., 19 December 1991 (1992) J.T. 142. Netherlands: In principle there is no recognition of state liability on account of judicial conduct amounting to fault: Hoge Raad, 17 March 1978 (1979) NJ 204, but in a Judgment of October 11, 1991 ((1992) N.J. 62), the Hoge Raad recognised that there may be state liability for the wrong interpretation of a provision of the Code of Criminal Procedure by the public prosecutor's office.

69 Case 314/85 *Foto-Frost v. Hauptzollamt Lübeck-Ost* [1987] E.C.R. 4199, ECJ (with case notes by Arnull, "National Courts and the Validity of Community Acts" (1988) E.L.Rev. 125–131, and Bebr (see para. 2–004, note 12, above), at 678, who identifies the autonomous nature of Community law as an additional reason for the exclusive jurisdiction of the Court of Justice to declare a Community measure invalid).

70 *Foto-Frost* (cited in n. 69, above) at 4230, para. 13.

Consequently, the relevant provision of the Treaty has a *lacuna* which the Court has filled by answering that question in the negative. In the Court's view, this is necessary for three reasons:

(1) divergences between courts in the Member States as to the validity of Community acts would be liable to place in jeopardy the unity of Community law;

(2) since the Court has exclusive jurisdiction to declare void an act of a Community institution (E.C. Treaty, Article 230 (*ex Article 173*)), the coherence of the system of judicial protection established by the Treaty requires that where the validity of a Community act is challenged before a national court the power to declare the act invalid must also be reserved to the Court of Justice, since both proceedings are "designed to permit the Court of Justice to review the legality of measures adopted by the institutions"[71];

(3) the Court of Justice is in the best position to decide on the validity of Community acts, since Community institutions whose acts are challenged "are entitled [under Article 20 of the Protocol on the Statute of the Court of Justice of the E[E]C] to participate in the proceedings in order to defend the validity of the acts in question".[72]

2–056 What national courts not subject to the third paragraph of Article 234 (*ex Article 177*) may of course do is:

> "consider the validity of a Community act and, if they consider that the grounds put forward before them by the parties in support of invalidity are unfounded, they may reject them, concluding that the measure is completely valid. By taking that action they are not calling into question the existence of the Community measure."[73]

It is only where the validity of a Community act is contested before a court subject to the third paragraph of Article 234 that that court must seek a preliminary ruling from the Court of Justice, even if it itself does not share the view that the act is invalid.

2–057 According to some commentators,[74] the authority of the Court's case-law causes a second obligation to request a preliminary ruling *praeter legem* to arise. Where national courts against whose decisions a judicial remedy exists under national law are minded to diverge from the interpretation

[71] *ibid.*, at 4231, paras 16, 17.

[72] *ibid.*, para. 18. In addition, under the E.C. Statute, Art. 21, para. 2, the Court may require the Member States and institutions not being party to the case to supply all information which the Court considers necessary for the proceedings.

[73] *ibid.*, at 4230, para. 14.

[74] Joliet, "L'article 177 *[now Art. 234]* du traité CEE et le renvoi préjudiciel" (1991) Riv.dir.eur. 591 at 606–607; Schockweiler,"L'exécution des arrêts de la Cour", in *Du droit international au droit de l'intégration—Liber amicorum Pierre Pescatore*, Baden-Baden, Nomos, 1987, 613 at 630.

which the Court of Justice has given to a provision or a principle of Community law, they must first attempt to obtain a change in the Court's case law by making a request for a preliminary ruling.

It is only by so doing that such courts, as institutions of a Member State, can act in accordance with Article 10 (*ex Article 5*) of the E.C. Treaty (obligation to co-operate in good faith). It would indeed be illogical if national courts of last resort were bound by the "settled case law" of the Court of Justice, subject to the possibility of their raising the content of the case law afresh with the Court,[75] yet inferior courts were completely at liberty to diverge from that case law without having to refer to the Court of Justice.[76]

The different treatment of inferior and superior courts in Article 234 (*ex Article 177*) only comes into its own, therefore, where there is not as yet any case law of the Court of Justice on a question of interpretation of Community law. In such a case, the inferior court will be at liberty to answer the question itself, whilst the superior court will be under an obligation to make a reference to the Court of Justice.

[75] See para. 2–050, above.

[76] See to this effect the Opinion of Advocate General J.-P. Warner in Case 112/76 *Manzoni v. Fonds National de Retraite des Ouvriers Mineurs* [1977] E.C.R. 1647 at 1662, second column. Moreover, the effect of the European Communities Act 1972, s.3(1) is that, if no reference to the Court of Justice is made, the United Kingdom courts must follow "the principles laid down by any relevant decision of the European Court".

CHAPTER 3

THE PRINCIPLE OF THE FULL EFFECTIVENESS OF COMMUNITY LAW AND ITS IMPACT ON NATIONAL LAW RELATING TO PROCEDURE AND SANCTIONS

As has already been mentioned, Community law falls to be applied principally by national courts. Since the Community does not have procedural law or law governing sanctions of its own,[1] it is for the "domestic legal systems of each Member State to designate the courts having jurisdiction and to determine the procedural conditions governing actions at law intended to ensure the protection of the rights which citizens have from the direct effect of Community law".[2] **3–001**

This raises two difficulties. First, national rules on procedure and sanctions may impede the effective application of Community law, and thereby affect its primacy and direct effect.[3] Secondly, uniform application of Community law may be jeopardised as a result of diverging national laws.[4] **3–002**

---

[1] What is meant is all those rules of law which come into play in order to apply Community law in the Member States' legal systems. They may have to do with the conduct of judicial proceedings, such as rules on admissibility, procedural time-limits and rules of evidence, or with the execution of judgments. However, concepts of civil law or other substantive law (*e.g.* the concept of unjust enrichment) may sometimes be relevant.

[2] Case 33/76 *Rewe v. Landwirtschaftskammer Saarland* [1976] E.C.R. 1989, at 1997–1998, para. 5, subpara. 3, ECJ; Case 45/76 *Comet v. Produktschap voor Siergewassen* [1976] E.C.R. 2043 at 2053, para. 13, ECJ. The Court has further pointed out that "[w]here necessary, Arts 100 to 102 and 235 *[now Articles 94 to 97 and 308]* of the Treaty enable appropriate measures to be taken to remedy differences between the provisions laid down by law, regulation or administrative action in Member States if they are likely to distort or harm the functioning of the common market", but that "[i]n the absence of such harmonization the right conferred by Community law must be exercised before the national courts in accordance with the conditions laid down by national rules". See *Rewe v. Landwirtschaftskammer Saarland* at 1998, para. 5, subparas 4, 6; and *Comet v. Produktschap voor Siergewassen*, at 2053, paras 14, 15.

[3] The national law may apply very short limitation periods or deal with the burden of proof or admissible evidence in such a way that the party relying on Community law is unable or has extreme difficulty in proving its claims.

[4] Bridge, "Procedural Aspects of the Enforcement of European Community Law through the Legal Systems of the Member States" (1984) E.L.Rev. 28–42. For examples of judgments in which the Court has expressed regret at the lack of Community provisions harmonising procedures and time-limits, see Case 130/79 *Express Dairy Foods v. Intervention Board for Agricultural Produce* [1980] E.C.R. 1887 at 1900, para. 12, ECJ; and Case 54/81 *Fromme v. BALM* [1982] E.C.R. 1449 at 1462–1463, para. 4, ECJ.

3–003 In order to deal with these difficulties, Article 10 (*ex Article 5*) of the E.C. Treaty places national courts under a duty to ensure the "full effectiveness of Community law".[5] The Court of Justice has defined this duty by means of a number of Community constraints with which national procedural law and law relating to sanctions must comply.[6] Those constraints are a practical expression of the principles of the primacy and direct effect of Community law[7] and aim at enabling individuals to claim before national courts the *full* enforcement and protection of the rights which they derive from Community law.[8]

---

[5] Case C–213/89 *R. v. Secretary of State for Transport, ex p. Factortame Ltd and Others* (*Factortame II*) [1990] E.C.R. I–2433 at I–2474, para. 21, ECJ. For a useful discussion of this topic, see Brealey and Hoskins, *Remedies in EC Law* (see para. 1–004, note 12, above), at 99–117. In *R. v. Secretary of State for the Home Department, ex p. Gallagher* [1996] 2 C.M.L.R. 951, Lord Bingham C.J. referred to the "cardinal principle of Community law" that national laws should provide "effective and adequate redress for violations" of that law.

[6] The relevant case law is remarkable in that the Court of Justice does not have jurisdiction to rule directly on questions of national procedural law (indeed, it systematically refuses to answer preliminary questions relating to the interpretation or validity of national law), yet will nevertheless seize upon the basis in Community law of national courts' obligation to achieve a particular result in order to provide very concrete guidance as to how that obligation must be complied with.

[7] Grévisse and Bonichot, "Les incidences du droit communautaire sur l'organisation et l'exercice de la fonction juridictionnelle dans les Etats membres", in *L'Europe et le Droit—Mélanges en hommage à J. Boulouis*, Paris, Ed. Dalloz, 1991, 297 at 309, observe in this connection that "La Cour ne fixe pas les règles de procédure nationale, elle énonce les exigences du droit communautaire qu'elles doivent satisfaire" [The Court does not fix national procedural rules, it sets forth the Community-law requirements which they must fulfil]. See also in this connection Kakouris, "Do the Member States possess Judicial Procedural 'Autonomy'?" (1997) C.M.L.Rev. 1389–1412, who argues that Member States do not possess "procedural autonomy", but that national procedural law is an "ancillary body of law" whose function is to "ensure the effective application of substantive Community law". He points out that where national courts apply Community law, they belong, functionally, to the Community legal order and therefore cannot be said to possess procedural autonomy. *Cf.* the approach taken by Prechal, "Community Law in National Courts: the Lessons from Van Schijndel" (1998) C.M.L.Rev. 681 at 686–687, who emphasises that Community law is part of the national legal order and that the primacy of Community law only appiies within the realm of the substantive law.

[8] See also Barav, "La plénitude de compétence du juge national en sa qualité de juge communautaire", in *L'Europe et le Droit* (cited in n. 7, above), at 1–20; Curtin, "The Decentralized Enforcement of Community Law Rights. Judicial Snakes and Ladders", in *Constitutional Adjudication in European Community and National Law. Essays for the Hon. Mr Justice O'Higgins,* Dublin, Butterworths (Ireland), 1992 at 33–49; Jacobs, "Remedies in National Courts for the Enforcement of Community Rights", in *Liber amicorum Diez de Velasco,* Madrid, Editorial Tecnos, 1993, at 969–983; Michel, "La protection des droits conférés par l'ordre juridique européen", in Tercier, Volken and Michel (eds), *Aspects du droit européen,* Fribourg, Editions universitaires Fribourg Suisse, 1993, at 43–70; Oliver, "Le droit communautaire et les voies de recours nationales" (1992) C.D.E. 348–374; Röben, *Die Einwirkung der Rechtsprechung des Europäischen Gerichtshofs auf das Mitgliedstaatliche Verfahren in öffentlich-rechtlichen Streitigkeiten,* Berlin, Springer Verlag, 1998; Rodríguez Iglesias, "Zu den Grenzen der verfahrensrechtlichen Autonomie der Mitgliedstaaten bei der Anwendung des Gemeinschaftsrechts" (1997) Eu.Gr.Z. 289–295; Szyszczak, "Making Europe more Relevant to its Citizens: Effective Judicial Process" (1996) E.L.Rev. 351–364; Van Gerven, "Bridging the Gap between Community and National Laws: Towards a Principle of Homogeneity in the Field of Legal Remedies?" (1995) C.M.L.Rev. 679–702; see also Ward, "Government Liability in the United Kingdom for Breach of Individual Rights in European Community Law" (1990) 1 Anglo-Am.L.R. 2–11.

The concept of the full effectiveness of Community law is being developed on a case-by-case basis by the Court of Justice, which means that the constraints described below must be regarded as being open to enlargement. 3–004

I. Basic Rules

The Court of Justice laid down the two most important constraints at the same time as it held that, in principle, national procedural rules and rules on sanctions are to apply, namely: 3–005

(1) that those rules may not be less favourable than those governing similar domestic actions (principle of equivalence),[9] and

(2) that they may not render virtually impossible or excessively difficult the exercise of rights conferred by Community law (principle of effectiveness).[10]

Above all, there is the requirement of procedural equal treatment of claims based on Community law and national law, for example as regards the effects of the expiry of a time-limit for bringing proceedings or an error in drawing up the document originating proceedings. In addition, it must be possible for every type of action provided for by national law to be available for the purpose of ensuring observance of Community provisions having direct effect, although it is not intended to create new remedies in the national courts to ensure the observance of Community law.[11] 3–006

[9] Case 33/76 *Rewe v. Landwirtschaftskammer Saarland* [1976] E.C.R. 1989, at 1998 para. 5, subpara. 3, ECJ; Case 45/76 *Comet v. Produktschap voor Siergewassen* [1976] E.C.R. 2043 at 2053, para. 13, ECJ; Case 811/79 *Amministrazione delle Finanze dello Stato v. Ariete* [1980] E.C.R. 2545, at 2554–2555, para. 12, ECJ; Case 826/79 *Amministrazione delle Finanze dello Stato v. MIRECO* [1980] E.C.R. 2559 at 2574–2575, para. 13, ECJ; Case C–338/91 *Steenhorst-Neerings* [1993] E.C.R. I–5475 at I–5502, para. 15, ECJ; Case C–410/92 *Johnson* [1994] E.C.R. I–5483 at I–5509, para. 21, ECJ; Case C–180/95 *Draehmpaehl* [1997] E.C.R. I–2195 at I–2222, para. 29, ECJ.

[10] *Rewe v. Landwirtschaftskammer Saarland* at 1998, para. 5, subpara. 6; *Comet v. Produktschap voor Siergewassen* at 2053, para. 16; *Amministrazione delle Finanze dello Stato v. Ariete*, para. 12; and *Amministrazione delle Finanze dello Stato v. MIRECO*, para. 13 (all cited in n. 9, above). For a recent formulation of both the principle of equivalence (see n. 9, above) and the principle of effectiveness, see the judgments in Case C–231/96 *Edis v. Ministero delle Finanze* [1998] E.C.R. I–4951 at I–4986—I–4990, paras 19, 34, ECJ; Case C–290/96 *Spac*, [1998] E.C.R. I–4997 at I–5019, para. 18, ECJ; and Joined Cases C–279/96, C–280/96 and C–281/96, *Ansaldo Energia and Others*, [1998] E.C.R. I–5025 at I–5049, para. 27, ECJ.

[11] Case 158/80 *Rewe v. Hauptzollamt Kiel* [1981] E.C.R. 1805 at 1838, para. 44, ECJ. As far as the application of the principle of equivalence to procedural time-limits is concerned, the Court of Justice held in *Edis* and *Spac* (cited in n. 10 above) that Community law does not prohibit a Member State from resisting actions for repayment of charges levied in breach of Community law by relying on a three-year time-limit under national procedural law, by way of derogation from the ordinary rules governing actions between private individuals for the recovery of sums paid but not due, for which the period allowed is more favourable, provided that the time-limit applies in the same way to actions based on Community law for repayment of such charges as to those based on national law. Consequently, compliance with the principle of equivalence hinges on the correct identification of similar actions, *i.e.*

3–007 In addition, national procedural rules and rules relating to sanctions, albeit complying with the principle of equivalence, "may not be so framed as to render virtually impossible the exercise of rights conferred by Community law".[12]

This may be illustrated by the example of the recovery of a charge levied in accordance with national law but not due under Community law.[13] Community law accepts that, under national law, a charge which was unduly levied and could be passed on by the individuals concerned to others does not qualify for reimbursement,[14] but:

> "[a] Member State cannot make the repayment of national charges levied contrary to the requirements of Community law conditional

---

those based on Comunity law and those based on national law. It would seem advisable in this context to employ the most precise criterion of equivalence, which was in those cases recovering unduly paid charges (*i.e.* charges not due under Community law or national law). For another example of the principle of equivalence in operation, see *Ansaldo Energia and Others* (cited in n. 10, above), paragraphs 24–36 (Community law does not preclude, in the event of the repayment of charges levied in breach thereof, payment of interest calculated by methods less favourable than those applicable under the ordinary rules governing actions for the recovery of sums paid but not due between private individuals, provided that those methods apply in the same way to actions for the repayment of charges brought under Community law as to those brought under national law).

[12] Case 199/82 *Amministrazione delle Finanze dello Stato v. San Giorgio* [1983] E.C.R. 3595 at 3612, para. 12, ECJ (this phrase has tended to be rendered in English as "framed in such a way as *in practice* to make it impossible: Joined Cases C–46/93 and C–48/93 *Brasserie du Pêcheur and Factortame* (*Factortame IV*) [1996] E.C.R. I–1029 at I–1156, para. 74, ECJ); in his Opinion in Case 2/94 *Denkavit International* [1996] E.C.R. I–2829 at I–2851, point 75, ECJ, Advocate General F.G. Jacobs suggests "unduly difficult". See also Case 309/85 *Barra v. Belgium and Another* [1988] E.C.R. 355 at 376–377, paras 18, 19, ECJ, in which the Court held that a Belgian law which restricted the right to repayment of an enrolment fee undue under Community law in such a way as to exclude Community students who were not Belgian nationals rendered the exercise of rights conferred by the E.C. Treaty, Art. 12 (*ex Art. 6*), (at that time, the EEC Treaty, Art. 7) impossible; Case 240/87 *Deville v. Administration des Impôts* [1988] E.C.R. 3513 at 3527, paras 12, 13, ECJ, in which the Court held that legislation restricting the ability to recover tax unduly paid pursuant to a judgment of the Court of Justice was in breach of the principle of the full effectiveness of Community law; Case C–246/96 *Magorrian and Cunningham* [1997] E.C.R. I–7153 at I–7186—7188, paras 36–47, ECJ. The same basic rules, refined by the Court from case to case, also apply to the recovery of unduly paid Community subsidies: Case C–296/96 *Oelmühle Hamburg and Another v. Bundewsanstalt für Landwirtschaft und ErnähRung*, [1998] E.C.R. I–4767, ECJ (specification of the Community-law requirements for applying the principle of loss of unjust enrichment on which a recipient of unduly paid Community subsidies may rely in a proper case in order to avoid recovery on the part of the national authorities).

[13] A clear summary of all the aspects of this example may be found in Joined Cases C–192–218/95 *Comateb and Others* [1997] E.C.R. I–165 at I–188—192, paras 19–34, ECJ. For the English law of restitution in this context, see Brealey and Hoskins, *Remedies in EC Law* (see para. 1–004, n. 12, above) pp. 169–176.

[14] Case 68/79 *Just v. Danish Ministry for Fiscal Affairs* [1980] E.C.R. 501 at 523, para. 26, ECJ; Case 61/79 *Amministrazione delle Finanze dello Stato v. Denkavit Italiana* [1980] E.C.R. 1205 at 1226, para. 26, ECJ; Case 130/79 *Express Dairy Foods v. Intervention Board for Agricultural Produce* [1980] E.C.R. 1887 at 1900, para. 12, ECJ. For a critical commentary on this rule, see, *inter alia*, Hubeau, "La répétition de l'indu en droit communutaire" (1981) R.T.D.E. 442–470. The same principle is applied in respect of a claim for repayment of an invalid "Community charge": Case 66/80 *International Chemical Corporation v. Amministrazione delle Finanze dello Stato* [1981] E.C.R. 1191 at 1218–1219, paras 22–26, ECJ (in that case, the plaintiff sought recovery of a charge levied pursuant to a Community regulation which had been declared void).

upon the production of proof that those charges have not been passed on to other persons if the repayment is subject to rules of evidence which render the exercise of that right virtually impossible, even where the repayment of other taxes, charges or duties levied in breach of national law is subject to the same restrictive conditions."[15]

Furthermore, a Member State may not make the recovery of a sum which was paid to a public authority under a mistake of law and was not due under Community law depend upon the payment having been made under protest, since such a condition is liable to prejudice effective protection of the rights conferred by Community law on the individuals involved.[16]

In contrast, "the laying down of reasonable periods of limitation of actions" does satisfy the test imposed by the principle of effectiveness.[17]

The national court's obligation to give full effect to Community law **3–008** means that it must "if necessary, [refuse] of its own motion to apply any conflicting provisions of national legislation, even if adopted subsequently, and it is not necessary for the court to request or await the prior setting aside of such provisions by legislative or other constitutional means".[18] By that ruling, the Court of Justice debarred Member States from placing any restriction on their courts in declaring inapplicable provisions or principles of national law which conflict with Community law. If there is nevertheless such a restriction, national courts must simply set it aside on the basis of Community law, which is binding upon the Member State of which they are institutions.[19]

---

15 Case 199/82 *Amministrazione delle Finanze dello Stato v. San Giorgio* [1983] E.C.R. 3595, operative part, at 3615–3616, ECJ, for an application, see Joined Cases 331, 376 and 378/85 *Bianco and Girard v. Directeur Général des Douanes et Droits Indirects* [1988] E.C.R. 1099 at 1118, paras 12, 13, ECJ. The same rule applies to the production of proof that a provision of Community law having direct effect has been breached: Case C–242/95 *GT-Link* [1997] E.C.R. I–4449 at I–4463, para. 26, ECJ.

16 Case C–212/94 *FMC and Others* [1996] E.C.R. I–389 at I–427, para. 72, ECJ.

17 Case 33/76 *Rewe v. Landwirtschaftskammer Saarland* [1976] E.C.R. 1989 at 1998, para. 5, subparas 7, 8, ECJ; Case 45/76 *Comet v. Produktschap voor Siergewassen* [1976] E.C.R. 2043 at 2053, paras 17–18, ECJ; Case 61/79 *Denkavit Italiana* [1980] E.C.R. 1205 at 1225, para. 23, ECJ; Case C–261/95 *Palmisani* [1997] E.C.R. I–4025 at I–4046, para. 28, ECJ; Case C–90/94 *Haahr Petroleum* [1997] E.C.R. I–4085 at I–4158, para. 48, ECJ. Consequently, the three-year procedural time-limit at issue in the aforementioned judgments in *Edis*, *Spac* and *Ansaldo Energia* (cited in n. 10, above) was not in breach of the principle of effectiveness, see *Edis*, para. 35, *Spac*, para. 19, and *Ansaldo Energia*, paras 17–18. But compare (Judgment of December 1, 1998) Case C–326/96 *Levez*, ECJ (not yet reported). See also para. 3–013, below.

18 Case 106/77 *Amministrazione delle Finanze dello Stato v. Simmenthal* [1978] E.C.R. 629, operative part, at 645–646, ECJ.

19 *Cf.* Carreau, "Droit communautaire et droits nationaux: concurrence ou primauté? La contribution de l'arrêt 'Simmenthal'" (1978) R.T.D.E. 381–418. Community law does not, however, preclude the adoption by a Member State, following judgments of the Court of Justice declaring duties or charges contrary to Community law, of provisions which render the conditions for repayment applicable to those duties and charges less favourable than those which would otherwise have been applied, provided that the duties and charges in question are not specifically targeted by that amendment and the new provisions do not make it impossible or excessively difficult to exercise the right to repayment: see (Judgment of February 9, 1999) Case C–343/96 *Dilexport*, para. 43, ECJ (not yet reported).

II. The Need for Judicial Supervision

3–009 The full effectiveness of Community law can be attained only if individuals can assert the rights which they derive from Community law before a national court. Consequently, the Member States must provide them actual access to a court and to judicial proceedings. Those obligations are not only connected with the full effectiveness of Community law but also reflect a general principle of law which underlies the constitutional traditions common to the Member States and is laid down in Articles 6 and 13 of the ECHR.[20]

3–010 In addition, it is a corollary of the prohibition of discrimination enshrined in Article 12 (*ex Article 6*) of the E.C. Treaty that nationals of a Member State carrying out an economic activity on the market of another Member State must be able to bring actions in the courts of that Member State on the same footing as nationals of that state in order to resolve any disputes arising from their economic activities.[21] Consequently, a Member State is precluded from requiring provision of security for costs by a legal person established in another Member State or by a national of another Member State, even if the person concerned is also a national of a non-member country, in which he or she is resident,[22] where the legal person or national in question has brought an action against one of its nationals or a company established in its territory, security for costs cannot be required to be provided by legal persons from the state in question and the action is connected with the exercise of fundamental[23] freedoms guaranteed by Community law.[24]

3–011 In addition, national law must provide for effective judicial review.[25] To that end, the court before which the case is brought should generally be empowered to require the competent authority to state the reasons for any national decision which is contested on the basis of Community law.

Individuals must also be able to defend their rights in the best possible circumstances and be in a position to decide with a full knowledge of the facts whether they will benefit from going to court. The competent authority is therefore under a duty to inform them of the grounds for its

[20] Case 222/84 *Johnston v. Chief Constable of the Royal Ulster Constabulary* [1986] E.C.R. 1651 at 1682, paras 17, 18 ECJ; Case C–97/91 *Oleificio Borrelli v. Commission* [1992] E.C.R. I–6313 at I–6334, paras 13, 14, ECJ. Indirect confirmation of this is provided by Case C–54/96 *Dorsch Consult* [1997] E.C.R. I–4961 at I–4996, para. 40, ECJ.

[21] Case C–43/95 *Data Delecta and Forsberg* [1996] E.C.R. I–4661, ECJ.

[22] Case C–122/96 *Saldanha and MTS* [1997] E.C.R. I–5325 at I–5346, para. 30, ECJ.

[23] Case C–323/95 *Hayes v. Kronenberger* [1997] E.C.R. I–1711 at I–1722—1723, para. 13, ECJ.

[24] *ibid.*, at I–1726, para. 25. See Ackermann's case note to these three judgments (1998) C.M.L.Rev. 783–799. In *Fitzgerald v. Williams* [1996] 2 Q.B. 657, the Court of Appeal followed the emergent case law of the Court of Justice on the ground that to require security for costs under RSC, Ord. 23, from Irish nationals resident in Ireland would be discriminatory and not justified in view of the Brussels Convention on Jurisdiction and the Enforcement of Judgments in Civil and Commercial Matters.

[25] Case 222/86 *Unectef v. Heylens* [1987] E.C.R. 4097 at 4117, paras 14–16, ECJ; Case C–340/89 *Vlassopoulou* [1991] E.C.R. I–2357 at I–2385, para. 22, ECJ; Case C–104/91 *Aguirre Borrell and Others* [1992] E.C.R. I–3003 at I–3029, paras 23, 24, ECJ.

decision, either in the decision itself or in a subsequent communication made at their request.

The possibility of bringing legal proceedings and the duty to state reasons are designed, among other things, effectively to protect the fundamental rights conferred on individuals by Community law. These Community law requirements apply only to final decisions of national authorities, not to opinions or to measures taken at the preparatory or investigative stage.

Also the rules of national law relating to an individual's *locus standi* and interest in bringing proceedings may not detract from the full effectiveness of Community law. In a first attempt to define the Community law requirements in this regard, the Court of Justice has held that persons who do not come within the scope *ratione personae* of a provision of Community law may nevertheless have an interest in the provision being taken into account *vis-à-vis* the person protected.[26] In this way, they may have sufficient *locus standi* under Community law, which must be recognised in national law. **3–012**

As has already been stated, the laying down of reasonable time-limits which, if unobserved, bar proceedings, in principle complies with the two basic rules.[27] In the light of the "particular nature of directives", the Court has held, however, that: **3–013**

> "Community law precludes the competent authorities of a Member State from relying, in proceedings brought against them by an individual before the national courts in order to protect rights directly conferred upon him by . . . [a directive], on national procedural rules relating to time-limits for bringing proceedings so long as that Member State has not properly transposed that directive into its domestic legal system."[28]

However, this rule does not preclude a provision of national law from limiting the retroactive effect of a claim to a social security benefit, not even where the claim is based on a directive with direct effect which has not yet been properly implemented in national law. Accordingly, the period for which benefits are payable may be limited to one year before the date of claim, even though the right to benefits arose before that date as a result of expiry of the period prescribed for implementing the directive in national

---

26 Joined Cases C–87–89/90 *Verholen and Others* [1991] E.C.R. I–3757 at I–3790, paras 23, 24 ECJ.

27 See para. 3–007, above.

28 Case C–208/90 *Emmott* [1991] E.C.R. I–4269 at I–4298—4299, paras. 17, 24, ECJ (case note by Szyszczak (1992) C.M.L.Rev. 604–612; for a very critical commentary, see Hoskins, "Tilting the Balance: Supremacy and National Procedural Rules" (1996) E.L.Rev. 365–377). For a good exposition of the criticism levelled against *Emmott* and of the way in which the Court of Justice has subsequently distinguished that case, see Brealey and Hoskins, *Remedies in EC Law* (see para. 1–004, n. 12, above), pp. 115–117. As far as the "particular nature of directives" is concerned, see Case C–91/92 *Faccini Dori v. Recreb srl* [1994] E.C.R. I–3325, ECJ.

law.[29] On the same lines, it is now clear that Community law does not prevent:

(1) a Member State which has not correctly implemented a directive from relying, in the case of claims for recovery of charges levied contrary to the directive, on a five-year limitation period running from the date on which the charges became payable[30]; or

(2) a Member State from relying, in the case of claims for recovery of charges levied in breach of a directive, on a national procedural time-limit reckoned from the date of payment of the charges in question, even though the directive had not been correctly implemented in national law on that date.[31]

3–014 The principle of the full effectiveness of Community law does not require the national court to raise applicable Community law in all circumstances of its own motion. The national court has the *power* to do so if it considers that Community law must be applied,[32] but it is only where the parties have failed to invoke rules of Community law having direct effect that it may be *obliged* to raise those rules of its own motion. Depending on the case, the Court of Justice has identified different bases for this principle. Where there is an obligation for the national court to raise mandatory rules of law of its own motion by virtue of domestic law, there will be the same obligation to raise

[29] Case C–338/91 *Steenhorst-Neerings* [1993] E.C.R. I–5475 at I–5504, para. 24, ECJ, with a case note by Adiba Sohrab (1994) C.M.L.Rev. 875–887; ECJ, Case C–410/92 *Johnson* [1994] E.C.R. I–5483 at I–5513, para. 36, ECJ, with a case note clearly summarising this question by Docksey (1995) C.M.L.Rev. 1447–1459.

[30] Case C–188/95 *Fantask and Others* [1997] E.C.R. I–6783, ECJ.

[31] *Edis*, para. 40–49, *Spac*, paras 24–32, and *Ansaldo Energia*, paras 13–23 (all cited in n. 10 above). In each of those judgments, the Court stated that it did not appear from the documents before it or the arguments put forward by the parties to the main proceedings that the conduct of the Italian authorities, in conjunction with the existence of the contested time-limit, had the effect (as it had in *Emmott* (n. 28, above)) of depriving the plaintiff companies of any opportunity of enforcing their rights before the national courts. This may be taken to be the justification for the refinement which has undoubtedly been made to the case law on this question. Community law does not preclude the application of a period of limitation or prescription laid down by national law which restricts the period prior to the bringing of a claim in the national court in which reimbursement of undue payments may be obtained, where that rule is not discriminatory and does not prejudice the actual right conferred on individuals by a preliminary ruling on invalidity: Case C–212/94 *FMC and Others* [1996] E.C.R. I–389 at I–424—425, paras 63, 64, ECJ; Case C–90/94 *Haahr Petroleum and Others* [1997] E.C.R. I–4085 at I–4157—4159, paras 45–53, ECJ; Joined Cases C–114 and C–115/95 *Texaco and Olieselskabet Danmark* [1997] E.C.R. I–4263 at I–4286—4287, paras 44–49, ECJ. In contrast, a provision which renders a claim based on Community law impossible in practice is contrary to Community law. Thus, the Court held in Case C–246/96 *Magorrian and Cunningham* [1997] E.C.R. I–7153, ECJ, that Community law precludes the application, in procedures for recognition of the entitlement to join an occupational pension scheme, of a national rule under which such entitlement, in the event of a successful claim, is limited to a period which starts to run from a point in time two years prior to commencement of the proceedings. Such a rule strikes at the very essence of the right to join an occupational pension scheme which the claimants derived from the E.C. Treaty, Art. 141 (*ex Art. 119*).

[32] Joined Cases C–87–89/90 *Verholen and Others* [1991] E.C.R. I–3757 at I–3788, para. 13, ECJ.

Community rules by virtue of the aforementioned principle of procedural equal treatment. Where domestic law confers on national courts a discretion to apply mandatory rules of law of their own motion, the same obligation to raise Community rules remains pursuant to the principle of co-operation laid down in Article 10 (*ex Article 5*) of the E.C. Treaty, which requires national courts to use all the possibilities afforded by national law in order to ensure the legal protection which persons derive from the direct effect of provisions of Community law,[33] or alternatively pursuant to the duty on the courts, as authorities of the Member States, under the third paragraph of Article 249 (*ex Article 189*) of the E.C. Treaty to take all the measures necessary to achieve the result prescribed by a directive.[34] It follows that, in the absence of any Community provision governing the matter, there will be a requirement for the national courts to raise provisions of Community law of their own motion only if there exists a requirement or a discretion to raise mandatory rules by virtue of domestic law.[35] Where national courts are precluded from so doing under national procedural law, there is in principle no requirement for them to do so, provided, however, that this does not cause national procedural law to conflict with Community law. National procedural law must comply with the basic rules[36] to which reference has already been made,[37] in particular the requirement that it must not render the exercise of rights conferred by Community law virtually impossible or excessively difficult. In addition, it must not prevent the procedure laid down in Article 234 (*ex Article 177*) of the E.C. Treaty from being followed.[38] A rule of national procedural law which does not satisfy those conditions must be set aside,[39] with the result that the national court in question may nevertheless be subject to the requirement to raise rules of Community law of its own motion. In this regard, the Court of Justice tests the national procedural rules against Community law having regard to their role in the procedure, its

---

33 Joined Cases C–430 and C–431/93 *Van Schijndel and Van Veen* [1995] E.C.R. I–4705 at I–4736, paras 13–14, ECJ (case note by Heukels (1996) C.M.L.Rev. 337–353). That judgment has been given a somewhat critical reception: see, *inter alia*, Hoskins (cited in n. 28, above). For an application of the judgment in the French legal system, see Szyszczak and Delicostopoulos, "Intrusions into National Procedural Autonomy: The French Paradigm" (1997) E.L.Rev. 141–149.

34 Case C–72/95 *Kraaijeveld and Others* [1996] E.C.R. I–5403 at I–5451—5453, paras 54–61, ECJ.

35 *Van Schijndel and Van Veen* at I–4736, para. 15. The Court did not explain exactly why a requirement for national courts to raise of their own motion rules of Community law having direct effect exists only where it is possible to raise mandatory national rules of their own motion. In his opinion in that case, Advocate General F.G. Jacobs argued that if the view were taken that national procedural rules must always yield to Community law that would unduly subvert established principles underlying the legal systems of the Member States. It could be regarded as infringing the principles of proportionality and subsidiarity. It would also give rise to widespread anomalies, since the effect would be to afford greater protection to rights which are not, by virtue of being Community rights, inherently of greater importance than rights recognised by national law (Opinion of Advocate General F.G. Jacobs, point 27; see also the case note by Heukels, (cited in n. 33, above) at 349).

36 See paras 3–005—3–008, above.

37 *Van Schijndel and Van Veen*, at I–4737, para. 17.

38 *Van Schijndel and Van Veen*, at I–4737, para. 18, and Case 166/74 *Rheinmühlen v. Einfur- und Vorratsstelle für Getreide* [1974] E.C.R. 33 at 38, paras 2, 3, ECJ, cited therein.

39 See para. 3–008, above.

progress and its special features, viewed as a whole, before the various national instances. Frequently, the Court also has regard to the basic principles of the domestic legal system, such as protection of the rights of the defence, the principle of legal certainty and the proper conduct of the procedure.[40] Accordingly, the Court has held that civil courts are not required to abandon the passive role assigned to them by raising a rule of Community law of their own motion.[41] In contrast, a rule of the Belgian Income Tax Code which prevented the national court from inquiring of its own motion into the compatibility of a tax assessment with a provision of Community law in proceedings relating to that assessment, unless the taxpayer had raised the relevant provision within a specified time-limit was held by the Court to be contrary to Community law.[42]

III. Legal Protection in Proceedings for Interim Measures

3–015 The protracted nature of judicial proceedings may pose a threat to the actual enforcement of the rights conferred upon an individual by Community law. This explains the interest for the full effectiveness of Community law of a system of provisional legal protection which enables a real claim to those rights to be safeguarded by freezing a provision which is allegedly in conflict with (superior) Community law or by granting interim relief provisionally to settle or regulate disputed legal positions or relationships pending a judicial ruling in the main proceedings. Two situations need to be distinguished. First, there is the situation where the national court grants interim relief in order to freeze the effect of a national provision which is allegedly in breach of Community law. Secondly, the national court may grant interim relief in order to freeze the implementation of a Community measure which is allegedly in breach of the superior law (and therefore unlawful) or provisionally to settle or regulate disputed legal positions or relationships with reference to a national administrative measure based on a Community act whose validity is under consideration in proceedings for a preliminary ruling.

[40] *Van Schijndel and Van Veen*, at I–4738, para. 19. The criterion whereby the Court of Justice also considers the role of the provision under national law seems to go further than the criterion in Case 33/76 *Rewe v. Landwirtschaftskammer Saarland* case (cited in n. 9, above), whereby the Court of Justice considers only the effect of the relevant rule in a particular case; see Hoskins (cited in n. 28, above), at 373.

[41] *Van Schijndel and Van Veen*, at I–4738, para. 22: Community law does not require national courts to raise of their own motion an issue concerning the breach of provisions of Community law, where examination of that issue would oblige them to abandon the passive role assigned to them by going beyond the dispute defined by the parties themselves and relying on facts and circumstances other than those on which the party, with an interest in application of those provisions, bases his or her claim.

[42] Case C–312/93 *Peterbroeck* [1995] E.C.R. I–4599, ECJ (with a case note by Heukels (cited in n. 33, above)). Characteristics and circumstances to which the Court of Justice has regard in finding that such a procedural rule is incompatible with Community law include the fact that the national court is the first judicial authority to have cognizance of the case and to be able to request a preliminary ruling, the fact that another judicial authority in a further hearing is precluded from raising the question of compatibility with Community law of its own motion, and the fact that the impossibility for national courts to raise points of Community law of their own motion, does not appear to be reasonably justifiable by principles such as the requirement of legal certainty or proper conduct of the procedure.

3–016 As far as the first situation is concerned, the Court of Justice has held as follows: "Community law must be interpreted as meaning that a national court which, in a case before it concerning Community law, considers that the sole obstacle which precludes it from granting interim relief is a rule of national law must set aside that rule".[43] It is only in this way that the "full effectiveness of Community law" can be secured by "the judgment to be given on the existence of the rights claimed under Community law".[44]

This means that, where necessary, the national court can derive directly from Community law the power to suspend a provision of national law in interlocutory proceedings.[45] The nature of the measure whose suspension is sought is immaterial. Furthermore, Community law embodies no special requirements for the suspension of provisions of national law, although here too the principle applies that there must be equal treatment of suspension on grounds of domestic law and suspension on Community law grounds, together with the principle that the applicable domestic law must not subject the suspension to conditions such as to make it impossible in practice to obtain.

3–017 As far as the second situation is concerned, the Court of Justice has held as follows:

> "In cases where national authorities are responsible for the administrative application of Community regulations, the legal protection guaranteed by Community law includes the right of individuals to challenge, as a preliminary issue, the legality of such regulations before national courts and to induce those courts to refer questions to the Court of

---

43 Case C–213/89 *Factortame and Others* (*Factortame II*) [1990] E.C.R. I–2433, operative part, at I–2475. After the House of Lords had held that it could not give an interim injunction in judicial review proceedings seeking to set aside an Act of Parliament because courts had no such power under the Supreme Court Act 1981 and an Act of Parliament was presumed valid until declared otherwise (*R. v. Secretary of State for Transport, ex p. Factortame (no 2)* [1990] A.C. 603), the preliminary ruling in *Factortame II* was considered to give it the power to grant such an injunction (or at least to remove the common law rule that an interim injunction may not be granted against the Crown): see Brealey and Hoskins, *Remedies in EC Law* (cited in para. 1–004, n. 12, above), pp. 106–107 and 154–155. For the injunctions available under English law to secure the full effectiveness of Community law, see *ibid.*, pp. 149–164.

44 *Factortame II* (cited in n. 43, above), at I–2474, para. 21.

45 Barav, "Omnipotent Courts", in Curtin and Heukels (eds), *Institutional Dynamics of European Integration. Essays in Honour of H.G. Schermers*, Dordrecht, Martinus Nijhoff, 1994, II, 265 at 277, and "The Effectiveness of Judicial Protection and the Role of the National Courts", in *Judicial Protection of Rights in the Community Legal Order*, Brussels, Brulyant, 1997, at 259–296; Simon and Barav, "Le droit communautaire et la suspension provisoire des mesures nationales: Les enjeux de l'affaire Factortame" (1990) R.M.C. 591–597: "[L]'arrêt Factortame a le mérite d'établir, fût-ce d'une manière quelque peu indirecte, la compétence du juge national d'écarter, à titre provisoire, l'application d'une mesure nationale prétendue contraire au droit communautaire dans l'attente d'une décision définitive" [The *Factortame* judgment has the merit of establishing—albeit indirectly—jurisdiction on the part of a national court to set aside, provisionally, the application of a national measure alleged to be contrary to Community law pending a definitive decision]. See also case notes by Toth (1990) C.M.L.Rev. 573 at 586, and Joliet, "Coopération entre la Cour de justice des Communautés européennes et les juridictions nationales" (1993) 2 J.T.D.E. 4–5.

> Justice for a preliminary ruling. That right would be compromised if, pending delivery of a judgment of the Court, which alone has jurisdiction to declare that a Community regulation is invalid . . ., individuals were not in a position, where certain conditions are satisfied, to obtain a decision granting suspension of enforcement which would make it possible for the effects of the disputed regulation to be rendered for the time being inoperative as regards them."[46]

For this reason, Article 249 (*ex Article 189*) of the E.C. Treaty does not preclude national courts from "granting interim relief to settle or regulate the disputed legal positions or relationships with reference to a national administrative measure based on a Community regulation which is the subject of a reference for a preliminary ruling on its validity".[47]

The question arises as to what is meant by "where certain conditions are satisfied". The Court of Justice has held that "the rules of procedure of the courts are determined by national law and . . . those conditions differ according to the national law governing them, which may jeopardize the uniform application of Community law".[48] In order to reduce this danger, the Court of Justice has held that suspension of enforcement of national administrative measures based on a Community regulation or the grant of other interim measures "must in all the Member States be subject to conditions which are uniform".[49] The Court identifies those "uniform conditions" with "the conditions which must be satisfied for the Court of Justice [itself] to allow an application to it for interim measures".[50] The parallel between the conditions for the grant of interim relief applicable before the national court and the Court of Justice (and the Court of First Instance) is due to the fact that an assessment of validity via a request for a preliminary ruling and an action for annulment constitute two aspects of a single system of judicial review of legality. The coherence of the system demands uniformity in the procedural rules for provisional suspension or limitation of enforcement of contested Community measures until such time as the Court of Justice or the Court of First Instance has carried out its review of legality, whether by a preliminary ruling (Court of Justice) or by a judgment on an application for annulment (Court of Justice or Court of First Instance). As a result, the national court must base itself, as far as

---

[46] Joined Cases C–143/88 and C–92/89 *Zuckerfabrik Süderdithmarschen and Zuckerfabrik Soest* [1991] E.C.R. I–415 at I–540—541, paras 16, 17, ECJ. See Mongin, "Le juge national et les mesures provisoires ordonnées en vertu du droit communautaire", in Christianos (ed.), *Evolution récente du droit judiciaire communautaire*, Maastricht, European Institute of Public Administration, 1994, 125–131.

[47] Case C–465/93 *Atlanta Fruchthandelsgesellschaft and Others* [1995] E.C.R. I–3761 at I–3790, para. 30, ECJ. See Mehdi, "Le droit communautaire et les pouvoirs du juge national de l'urgence" (1996) R.T.D.E. 77–100.

[48] *Zuckerfabrik Süderdithmarschen and Zuckerfabrik Soest*, (cited in n. 46, above), at I–542, para. 25.

[49] *Atlanta Fruchthandelsgesellschaft and Others* (cited in n. 47, above) at I–3790—3791, paras 29, 33.

[50] *Zuckerfabrik Süderdithmarschen and Zuckerfabrik Soest* (cited in n. 46, above), at I–542—543, paras 26, 27.

the substantive conditions for suspension or limitation of enforcement of national administrative measures based on a Community regulation are concerned, on the case law of the Court of Justice concerning interim measures, and no longer on national law.[51] National law governs only "the making and examination of the application".[52]

Interim measures may be granted by a national court only if:

(1) that court entertains serious doubts as to the validity of the Community act and, if the validity of the contested act is not already in issue before the Court of Justice, itself refers that question to the Court[53];
(2) there is urgency, in that interim relief is necessary to avoid serious and irreparable damage to the party seeking the relief;
(3) the national court takes due account of the Community interest;
(4) in its assessment of all those conditions, it respects any decisions of the Court of Justice or the Court of First Instance ruling on the lawfulness of the act or on an application for interim measures seeking similar interim relief at Community level.[54]

As far as the first requirement is concerned, the Court of Justice has held that:

> "the national court cannot restrict itself to referring the question of the validity of the regulation to the Court for a preliminary ruling, but must set out, when making the interim order, the reasons for which it considers that the Court should find the regulation to be invalid. The national court must take into account here the extent of the discretion which, having regard to the Court's case-law, the Community institutions must be allowed in the sectors concerned."[55]

The Court has clarified the second requirement as follows:

> "With regard to the question of urgency, . . . damage invoked by the applicant must be liable to materialize before the Court of Justice has

[51] See E.C. Treaty, Arts. 242 and 243 (*ex Arts. 185 and 186*). For examples, see (Order of the President of October 25, 1985), Case 293/85R *Commission v. Belgium* [1985] E.C.R. 3521, with a case note by Watson (1987) C.M.L.Rev. 93; and (Order of July 12, 1990), Case C–195/90R *Commission v. Germany* [1990] E.C.R. I–3351, ECJ. *Cf.* Pastor and Van Ginderachter, "La procédure en référé" (1989) R.T.D.E. 561–621. See also Joliet, Bertrand and Nihoul, "Protection juridictionnelle provisoire et droit communautaire" (1992) Riv.dir.eur. 253–284.

[52] Joined Cases C–143/88 and C–92/89 *Zuckerfabrik Süderdithmarschen and Zuckerfabrik Soest* [1991] E.C.R. I–415 at I–542, para. 26, ECJ (with a case note by Schermers (1992) C.M.L.Rev. 133–139, who emphasises that that judgment places the interest of the protection of the individual above the interest of the primacy of Community law).

[53] *ibid.*, at I–544, para. 33. See also Case C–334/95 *Krüger* [1997] E.C.R. I–4517 at I–4553—4554, para. 47, ECJ.

[54] Case C–465/93 *Atlanta Fruchthandelsgesellschaft and Others* [1995] E.C.R. I–3761 at I–3795, para. 51, ECJ.

[55] *ibid.*, at I–3791—3792, paras 36, 37.

> been able to rule on the validity of the contested Community measure. With regard to the nature of that damage, purely financial damage cannot, as the Court has held on numerous occasions, be regarded in principle as irreparable. However, it is for the national court hearing the application for interim relief to examine the circumstances particular to the case before it. It must in this connection consider whether immediate enforcement of the measure which is the subject of the application for interim relief would be likely to result in irreversible damage to the applicant which could not be made good if the Community act were to be declared invalid."[56]

As far as the third requirement is concerned, the Court of Justice has observed that the national court "must first examine whether the Community measure in question would be deprived of all effectiveness if not immediately implemented"[57] and, "if suspension of enforcement is liable to involve a financial risk for the Community, the national court must also be in a position to require the applicant to provide adequate guarantees, such as the deposit of money or other security".[58] In assessing the Community interest, the national court is free to decide, in accordance with its own rules of procedure, which is the most appropriate way of obtaining all relevant information on the Community act in question.[59]

The fourth requirement signifies that if the Court of Justice has dismissed an action for annulment of the act in question or has held, in the context of a reference for a preliminary ruling on validity, that the reference disclosed nothing to affect the validity of that act, the national court can no longer order interim measures or must revoke any existing measures, unless the grounds of illegality put forward before it differ from the pleas in law or grounds of illegality rejected by the Court in its judgment. The same applies if the Court of First Instance, in a judgment which has become final and binding, has dismissed on the merits an action for annulment of the act or an objection of illegality.[60]

3–018 National procedural rules allowing an appeal to be brought against a decision granting interim measures in the form of suspension of enforcement of a national administrative measure are compatible with Community law, provided that they do not affect the national court's obligation in such a case to make a reference for a preliminary ruling on the validity of the Community act on which the suspended national administrative implementing measure is based and that they do not restrict the right conferred by Article 234 (*ex Article 177*) on every court or tribunal to make a reference to the Court of Justice.[61]

---

[56] Joined Cases C–143/88 and C–92/89 *Zuckerfabrik Süderdithmarschen and Zuckerfabrik Soest* [1991] E.C.R. I–415 at I–543, para. 29, ECJ.
[57] *ibid.*, at I–543, para. 31.
[58] *ibid.*, at I–544, para. 32.
[59] Case C–334/95 *Krüger* [1997] E.C.R. I–4517 at I–4553, para. 46, ECJ.
[60] Case C–465/93 *Atlanta Fruchthandelsgesellschaft and Others* [1995] E.C.R. I–3761 at I–3794, para. 46, ECJ.
[61] Case C–334/95 *Krüger* [1997] E.C.R. I–4517 at I–4554—4555, paras 49–54, ECJ.

National courts' power to grant interim relief under Community law in the two situations described above[62] is also based on the consideration that the supervision of the legality of Community acts which the Court of Justice carries out in the preliminary ruling procedure needs to retain its full effectiveness.[63] In both situations, the national court has the power or even a duty to make a reference to the Court of Justice for a preliminary ruling. In the first situation, it may, by referring a question on the interpretation of the applicable provision of Community law, indirectly determine whether the national provision at issue is, as alleged, contrary to Community law. In the second, it is under a duty, if the question concerning the validity of the disputed Community act has not yet been submitted to the Court, to raise that question with the Court itself.[64] Consequently, the interim relief granted by national courts in those two situations is the precise counterpart of the interim relief which the Court of Justice or the Court of First Instance grants under Articles 242–243 (*ex Articles 185–186*) of the E.C. Treaty in order to ensure the effectiveness of the judicial supervision which it carries out in direct actions.[65] The Court of Justice has held, in full accord with its concern to guarantee the coherence of the system of legal protection outlined in the Treaty, that the national courts are not empowered to grant interim relief in situations in which, by virtue of a Community regulation, the existence and scope of traders' rights must be established by a Commission measure which that institution has not yet adopted. This is because the Treaty makes no provision for a reference for a preliminary ruling by which the national court asks the Court of Justice to rule that an institution has failed to act.[66] The Court of Justice and the Court of First Instance may only make such a ruling in a direct action brought pursuant to Article 232 (*ex Article 175*) of the E.C. Treaty. **3–019**

IV. Imposition of Sanctions for an Infringement of Community Law

The division of powers as between the Community and the Member States as regards the imposition of sanctions is a controversial question.[67] The Community does not have the power to impose criminal sanctions.[68] It can, **3–020**

[62] See paras 3–016, 3–017, above.

[63] Joined Cases C–143/88 and C–92/89 *Zuckerfabrik Süderdithmarschen and Zuckerfabrik Soest* [1991] E.C.R. I–415 at I–541, para. 19, ECJ.

[64] See para. 2–055, above.

[65] For further particulars, see Lenaerts, "The Legal Protection of Private Parties under the EC Treaty: a Coherent and Complete System of Judicial Review", in *Scritti in onore di Giuseppe Federico Mancini*, Milan, Giuffrè editore, 1998, II, at 591–623.

[66] Case C–68/95 *T. Port v. Commission* [1996] E.C.R. I–6065 at I–6103—6104, paras 52, 53, ECJ.

[67] For an extensive survey of the case law, see Tesauro, "La sanction des infractions au droit communautaire", (1992) Riv.dir.eur. 477–509.

[68] Case 203/80 *Casati* [1981] E.C.R. 2595 at 2618, para. 27, ECJ; Case 186/87 *Cowan v. Trésor public* [1989] E.C.R. 195 at 221–222, para. 19, ECJ. But see Haguenau, "Sanctions pénales destinées à assurer le respect du droit communautaire" (1993) R.M.C. 351 at 359, who

however, impose other types of sanctions.[69] If it does not do so,[70] Member States are empowered to enforce compliance with Community law by imposing criminal sanctions or using sanctions available under other branches of the law.[71]

3–021 The Member States' power to impose penalties or other sanctions for infringement of Community law must, pursuant to Article 10 (*ex Article 5*) of the E.C. Treaty, be exercised in order to guarantee the full effectiveness of that law.[72] This power constitutes the corollary of the Member States' obligation to impose Community law in their territory.[73]

3–022 That obligation to act entails that the sanction imposed by a Member State in the event of infringement of a Community provision from which individuals derive rights be such as to guarantee real and effective legal protection and have a real deterrent effect.[74] To that end, not only the imposition, but also the enforcement, of the sanction is important. For example, it would appear not to be in accordance with Community law for an obligation to pay compensation imposed upon a Member State for infringement of a Community provision to be thwarted by a general executive immunity with regard to public goods.

In connection with their obligation to act and their power to impose sanctions, however, the Member States may not impose any measures of administrative or criminal law which go further than what is strictly necessary. They must comply with Community law and the general

argues that the Community has the power to impose criminal sanctions under the E.C. Treaty, Arts. 10 and 308 (*ex Arts. 5 and 235*); and Zuleeg, "Der Beitrag des Strafrechts zur europäischen Integration" (1992) J.Z. 761–769, who rightly points out that the criminal law of the Member States may be the subject of harmonisation of national legislation pursuant to the E.C. Treaty.

69 Case C–240/90 *Germany v. Commission* [1992] E.C.R. I–5383, ECJ.

70 If Community sanctions are imposed, the principle *nec bis in idem* would prevent the imposition of additional national sanctions for the same breach of Community law. Naturally, the position would be different where the same set of measures constituted an infringement of both Community and national law. In such case, penalties and other sanctions could be imposed for the infringement of national law alongside the sanctions provided for by the Community provision itself in respect of the infringement of Community law. See also Biancarelli, "Les principes généraux du droit communautaire applicables en matière pénale" (1987) R.S.C.D.P.C. 131–166.

71 Joined Cases C–58, C–75, C–112, C–119, C–123, C–135, C–140, C–141, C–154 and C–157/95 *Gallotti and Others* [1996] E.C.R. I–4345 at I–4369, paras 14, 15, ECJ.

72 Case 68/88 *Commission v. Greece* [1989] E.C.R. 2965 at 2984, para. 23, ECJ; Case C–326/88 *Hansen* [1990] E.C.R. I–2911 at I–2935, para. 17, ECJ; Case C–7/90 *Vandevenne* [1991] E.C.R. I–4371 at I–4387, para. 11, ECJ; Case C–382/92 *Commission v. United Kingdom* [1994] E.C.R. I–2435 at I–2475, para. 55, ECJ; Case C–383/92 *Commission v. United Kingdom* [1994] E.C.R. I–2479 at I–2494, para. 40, ECJ.

73 Temple Lang, "Art. 5 *[now Art. 10]* of the EEC Treaty: the Emergence of Constitutional Principles in the Case Law of the Court of Justice" (1987) Fordham I.L.J. 503 at 519–522.

74 Case 14/83 *Von Colson and Kamann v. Land Nordrhein-Westfalen* [1984] E.C.R. 1891 at 1908, para. 23, ECJ; Case 79/83 *Harz v. Deutsche Tradax* [1984] E.C.R. 1921 at 1941, paras 22, 23, ECJ (where a Member State chooses to penalise a breach of the prohibition of discrimination by the award of compensation, the compensation must be adequate in relation to the damage sustained). See also Case C–177/88 *Dekker* [1990] E.C.R. I–3941 at I–3975—3976, paras 23–26, ECJ; Case C–271/91 *Marshall* [1993] E.C.R. I–4367 at I–4407—4408, paras 24–26, ECJ.

principles of law embodied therein.[75] Furthermore, control procedures must not be conceived in such a manner as to restrict the freedoms required by the Treaty and must not be accompanied by a penalty which is so disproportionate to the seriousness of the infringement that it becomes an obstacle to those freedoms.[76]

Community law obliges Member States to provide for the specific **3–023**
"sanction" of a right to reparation where, by their action or failure to act, national authorities infringe Community law (unlawful act or omission) and this results (causal link) in damage to rights which individuals derive from Community law (loss or damage).[77] The Court of Justice takes the view that "the principle whereby a State must be liable for loss and damage caused to individuals as a result of breaches of Community law for which the State can be held responsible is inherent in the system of the Treaty".[78] "A further basis for the obligation of Member States to make good such loss and damage is to be found in [Article 5 *[now Article 10]*] of the Treaty".[79]

The basic conditions "under which that liability gives rise to a right to reparation depend on the nature of the breach of Community law giving rise to the loss and damage".[80] This means that these conditions invariably have to be assessed in the light of the particular situation.[81] In determining those conditions, the Court of Justice has regard to its case law on the non-contractual liability of the Community. Firstly, this is because the second paragraph of Article 288 (*ex Article 215*) of the E.C. Treaty refers to the general principles common to the laws of the Member States, from which, in the absence of written rules, the Court also draws inspiration in other areas of Community law and, secondly, because the conditions under which the State may incur liability for damage caused to individuals by a breach of Community law cannot differ from those governing the liability of the Community in like circumstances.[82] It appears from the case law on the

[75] Joined Cases 201 and 202/85 *Klensch v. Secrétaire d'Etat* [1986] E.C.R. 3477 at 3507, para. 8, ECJ; Case 5/88 *Wachauf v. Bundesamt für Ernährung und Forstwirtschaft* [1989] E.C.R. 2609 at 2639–2640, para. 19, ECJ; Case C–210/91 *Commission v. Greece* [1992] E.C.R. I–6735 at I–6753, para. 19, ECJ. It may be noted that the penalties imposed by a Member State for non-compliance with formalities lawfully required in order to establish a right conferred by Community law may not be such as to constitute an obstacle to the exercise of that right. Such penalties are disproportionate and contrary to Community law: Case C–193/94 *Skanavi and Chryssanthakopoulos* [1996] E.C.R. I–929 at I–955—956, paras 36–39 ECJ.

[76] Case 203/80 *Casati* [1981] E.C.R. 2595 at 2618, para. 27, ECJ; Joined Cases 286/82 and 26/83 *Luisi and Carbone v. Ministero del Tesoro* [1984] E.C.R. 377 at 406, para. 34, ECJ.

[77] Joined Cases C–6 and C–9/90 *Francovich and Others* [1991] E.C.R. I–5357, ECJ.

[78] *ibid.*, at I–5414, para. 35.

[79] *ibid.*, para. 36.

[80] *ibid.*, at I–5415, para. 38.

[81] Joined Cases C–178, C–179, C–188, C–189 and C–190/94 *Dillenkofer and Others* [1996] E.C.R. I–4845 at I–4879, para. 24, ECJ.

[82] Joined Cases C–46 and C–48/93 *Brasserie du Pêcheur and Factortame* (*Factortame IV*) [1996] E.C.R. I–1029 at I–1146—1147, paras 39–42, ECJ (case note by Oliver (1997) C.M.L.Rev. 635–680). Some commentators would have preferred it if the conditions for liability on the part of the Community had been equated with those for liability on the part of the Member States and not the other way around, while arguing for "clarification" of the interpretation of the E.C. Treaty, Art. 288 (*ex Art. 215*), in the light of the judgment in *Francovich* (see Caranta, "Judicial Protection against Member States: a New *Jus Commune* takes Shape" (1995) C.M.L.Rev. 703–726.

non-contractual liability of the Community that the Court takes account of the complexity of the situations to be regulated, difficulties in the application or interpretation of the texts and, more particularly, the margin of discretion available to the author of the act in question.[83]

Consequently, the margin of discretion available to the Member State in an area governed by Community law largely determines how the Court of Justice will determine and flesh out the basic conditions governing liability on the part of the state.

Where a Member State acts in an area in which it has a broad discretion, there will be a right to reparation under Community law where three conditions are met:

(1) the rule of law infringed must be intended to confer rights on individuals;

(2) the breach must be sufficiently serious; and

(3) there must be a direct causal link between the breach of the obligation resting on the state and the damage sustained by the injured parties.[84]

The decisive test for finding that a breach of Community law is sufficiently serious is whether the Member State concerned manifestly and gravely disregarded the limits on its discretion.[85] The factors to be taken into consideration in this regard include (a) the clarity and precision of the rule breached; (b) the measure of discretion left by that rule to the national or Community authorities; (c) whether the infringement and the damage caused was intentional or involuntary; (d) whether any error of law was excusable or inexcusable; (e) the fact that the position taken by a Community institution may have contributed towards the omission; and (f) the adoption or retention of national measures or practices contrary to Community law.[86]

---

[83] *Factortame IV*, at I–1147, para. 43.

[84] *ibid.*, at I–1149, para. 51. For the question as to whether a directive without direct effect confers "rights" on individuals, breach of which may give rise to an obligation to make reparation, see Case C–91/92 *Faccini Dori* [1994] E.C.R. I–3325 at I–3357, para. 27, ECJ; Case C–192/94 *El Corte Inglés* [1996] E.C.R. I–1281 at I–1304, para. 22, ECJ.

[85] *Factortame IV*, at I–1150, para. 55.

[86] *ibid.*, at I–1150, para. 56. In this judgment, the Court of Justice held that a breach of Community law will be sufficiently serious if it has persisted despite a judgment finding the infringement in question to be established, or a preliminary ruling or settled case law of the Court on the matter from which it is clear that the conduct in question constituted an infringement (*ibid.*, para. 57). In Case C–392/93 *British Telecommunications* [1996] E.C.R. I–1631 at I–1669, para. 43, ECJ, the Court held that the improper transposition of a particular directive into national law did not constitute a sufficiently serious breach of Community law on the ground that the directive at issue was imprecisely worded and was reasonably capable of bearing the interpretation given to it by the United Kingdom in good faith and on the basis of arguments which were not entirely devoid of substance and not manifestly contrary to the wording of the directive or its objectives. In Joined Cases C–283, C–291 and C–292/94 *Denkavit and Others* [1996] E.C.R. I–5063 at I–5102, paras 51–54, ECJ,

In contrast, where, at the time when it committed the infringement, the Member State in question was not called upon to make any legislative choices and had only considerably reduced, or even no, discretion, the same conditions apply, but the mere infringement of Community law may be enough to establish the existence of a sufficiently serious breach.[87]

In the absence of Community rules, the procedural organisation of the legal proceedings is left to national law, but the provisions of national law must not be less favourable for actions for damages for breach of Community law than they are for other actions for damages, or be so framed as to make it "virtually impossible or excessively difficult to obtain reparation".[88] In addition, traditional concepts applying in some Member States must where appropriate yield to state liability under Community law.[89] Accordingly, the principle that the state cannot be held liable for an unlawful act or omission on the part of the legislature, which applies in some Member States' legal systems, cannot restrict the principle of state liability for breaches of Community law. The reason for this is that state liability holds good for any case in which a Member State breaches Community law, whatever be the organ of the state whose act or omission

---

the Court of Justice held that its case law did not provide Germany with any interpretation as to how a provision of a particular directive had to be interpreted. Consequently, the erroneous interpretation which Germany had given to it, which had been adopted by almost all the other Member States following discussions within the Council, could not be regarded as a sufficiently serious breach of Community law. In Joined Cases C–178, C–179, C–188, C–189 and C–190/94 *Dillenkofer and Others* [1996] E.C.R. I–4845, ECJ, the Court held that failure to take any measure to transpose a directive into national law within the prescribed period in order to achieve the result sought thereby constituted a sufficiently serious breach of Community law. Compare, however, Case C–319/96 *Brinkmann Tabakfabriken* [1998] E.C.R. I–5255 at I–5281—5283, paras 27–33, ECJ, where no liability for the Member State arose in spite of the fact that the national authorities had not transposed a directive into national law because no causal link was found to exist between that breach of Community law and the damage allegedly suffered, as these authorities had applied the directive in their administrative practice (they did it wrongly but not in such a way as to amount to a sufficiently serious breach of the directive, as their interpretation, supported by the Commission and another Member State, was not "manifestly contrary to the wording" of the directive or to the aim pursued by it).

[87] Case C–5/94 *The Queen v. MAFF, ex p. Hedley Lomas* [1996] E.C.R. I–2553 at I–2613, para. 28, ECJ. In that case, the mere infringement of Art. 29 (*ex Art. 34*) of the E.C. Treaty by the United Kingdom in refusing to grant an export licence constituted a sufficiently serious breach of Community law on the ground that at the time of the infringement the United Kingdom was not called upon to make any legislative choices and had considerably reduced discretion, if any (para. 28); Case C–127/95 *Norbrook Laboratories Ltd and Ministry of Agriculture, Fisheries and Food* [1998] E.C.R. I–1531 at I–1599—1600, para. 109, ECJ.

[88] Joined Cases C–6 and C–9/90 *Francovich and Others* [1991] E.C.R. I–5357 at I–5416, para. 43, ECJ; Case C–66/95 *Sutton* [1997] E.C.R. I–2163 at I–2191, para. 33, ECJ.

[89] See Emiliou, "State Liability under Community Law: Shedding More Light on the *Francovich* Principle" (1996) E.L.Rev. 399–411; Tesauro, "Responsabilité des Etats membres pour violation du droit communautaire" (1996) R.M.U.E. 15–34; Vandersanden and Dony, *La responsabilité des Etats membres en cas de violation du droit communautaire*, Brussels, Bruylant, 1997; Van Gerven, "Bridging the unbridgeable: Community and National Tort Laws after Francovich and Brasserie" (1996) I.C.L.Q. 507–544; Dantonel-Cor, "La violation de la norme communautaire et la responsabilité extracontractuelle de l'Etat" (1998) R.T.D.E. 75–91. For actions in damages against the state in English law, see Brealey and Hoskins, *Remedies in EC Law* (para. 1–004 n. 12, above) pp. 128–148; for damages actions against private parties, see pp. 118–127.

was responsible for the breach.[90] In addition, it is conceivable that Community law requires individuals who have infringed a Community provision with direct effect to make reparation for the loss or damage caused thereby.[91]

The amount of the damages must be commensurate with the loss or damage sustained so as to ensure the effective protection of the rights of the injured parties.[92] In the case of late implementation of a directive, retroactive and proper application in full of the measures implementing the directive will suffice, unless the beneficiaries establish the existence of complementary loss sustained on account of the fact that they were unable to benefit at the appropriate time from the financial advantages guaranteed by the directive, with the result that such loss must also be made good.[93] Limiting compensation to an upper limit or a prohibition on the national court's granting interest on that basic amount are contrary to Community law in so far as they make it impossible to make reparation in full for the damage sustained.[94] The setting of reasonable limitation periods for

---

[90] Joined Cases C–46 and C–48/93 *Brasserie du Pêcheur and Factortame* (*Factortame IV*) [1996] E.C.R. I–1029 at I–1145, paras 32–36, ECJ, and the Opinion of Advocate General G. Tesauro, at I–1088—1090, points 35–38, ECJ. It appears from the same judgment that the Court of Justice considers that the condition imposed by German law where a law is in breach of higher-ranking national provisions, which makes reparation dependent upon the legislature's act or omission being referable to an individual situation, must be set aside in the case of a breach of Community law. The reason for this is that that condition would in practice make it impossible or extremely difficult to obtain effective reparation for loss or damage resulting from a breach of Community law, since the tasks falling to the national legislature relate, in principle, to the public at large and not to identifiable persons or classes of persons (at I–1154, paras 71, 72). The Court likewise held in *Factortame IV* that any condition that may be imposed by English law on state liability requiring proof of misfeasance in public office must be set aside because such an abuse of power is inconceivable in the case of the legislature and therefore the condition makes it impossible to obtain effective reparation for loss or damage resulting from a breach of Community law (at I–1154, para. 73).

[91] Opinion of Advocate W. General Van Gerven in Case C–128/92 *Banks* [1994] E.C.R. I–1209, at I–1243–1260. Banks claimed damages in the national court because British Coal had allegedly infringed the competition rules by asking for excessively high compensation for licences for extracting coal and by paying an excessively low price for coal supplied by Banks. The Court of Justice held that the legal framework for the proceedings was the ECSC Treaty, none of the provisions of which that had been invoked had direct effect. Moreover, the Commission had exclusive competence in that context to find that there had been infringements of those rules, with the result that individuals could not bring an action for damages before the courts until such time as the Commission had made a finding that there had been an infringement. Consequently, the Court of Justice did not have to consider whether an infringement by an individual of a directly applicable provision of Community law gave rise to an obligation under Community law to make reparation for the resulting loss or damage.

[92] Joined Cases C–46 and C–48/93 *Brasserie du Pêcheur and Factortame* (*Factortame IV*) [1996] E.C.R. I–1029 at I–1156, para. 41, ECJ.

[93] Joined Cases C–94 and C–95/95 *Bonifaci and Others and Berto and Others* [1997] E.C.R. I–3969 at I–4023, para. 54, ECJ; Case C–373/95 *Maso and Others* [1997] E.C.R. I–4051 at I–4075, para. 41, ECJ.

[94] Case C–271/91 *Marshall* [1993] E.C.R. I–4367 at I–4407—4409, paras 22–32, ECJ. To limit compensation to an upper limit may, where the loss or damage exceeds that upper limit, conflict with the requirement for an effective, deterrent sanction. This is also true of the prohibition on adding interest to the basic amount. If account cannot be taken of the

bringing an action for damages is compatible with the above requirements, provided that it does not make it virtually impossible or excessively difficult to obtain reparation.[95]

Also where the Community imposes a "sanction", which has then to be carried out in a manner laid down by national law, the applicable provisions of that law must not affect the scope and effectiveness of Community law. The recovery of state aid granted contrary to Community law provides a good example of this. The decision declaring the aid incompatible with the common market will generally require the authority which granted the aid to recover it in accordance with the rules of national law. But the application of those rules must not make it impossible in practice to recover the sums irregularly granted or be discriminatory in relation to comparable cases which are governed solely by national legislation.[96] **3–024**

In the field of criminal or disciplinary proceedings, the Court of Justice subscribes to the Commission's view that "the Member States are required by virtue of Article 5 *[now Article 10]* of the E[E]C Treaty to penalize any persons who infringe Community law in the same way as they penalize those who infringe national law".[97] The Hellenic Republic was charged with having infringed Community law "by omitting to initiate all the criminal or disciplinary proceedings provided for by national law against the perpetrators of the fraud and all those who collaborated in the commission and concealment of it".[98] This certainly places a restriction on the public prosecutor's freedom in principle to decide whether or not to bring criminal proceedings for breaches of Community law. Yet that freedom does not disappear altogether. The Court of Justice simply held that "the national authorities must proceed, with respect to infringements of Community law, with the same diligence as that which they bring to bear in implementing corresponding national laws",[99] or, in other words, that the public prosecutor must be able to show the same strictness in respect of breaches of Community law pursued under the criminal law as he or she does in respect of similar breaches of national law. This is consistent with the general **3–025**

---

effluxion of time, reparation will not be made for the whole of the damage. Consequently, the grant of interest under the applicable national law is essential in order to satisfy the requirement of the full effectiveness of Community law. See Fitzpatrick and Szyszczak, "Remedies and Effective Judicial Protection in Community Law" (1994) M.L.R. 434–441. In *Marshall*, the Employment Appeal Tribunal held that the employment (formerly industrial) tribunal had wrongly awarded interest on damages (for sex discrimination contrary to the Sex Discrimination Act 1975) under the Supreme Court Act 1981, s.35A, as it was not a court of record. On appeal the House of Lords restored the award. The question of jurisdiction to award such interest is now catered for by the Sex Discrimination and Equal Pay (Remedies) Regulations 1993 (S.I. 1993 No. 2798).

95 Case C–261/95 *Palmisani* [1997] E.C.R. I–4025 at I–4046, para. 28, ECJ.

96 Joined Cases 205–215/82 *Deutsche Milchkontor v. Germany* [1983] E.C.R. 2633 at 2665–2667, paras 17–24, ECJ; Case 94/87 *Commission v. Germany* [1989] E.C.R. 175 at 192, para. 12, ECJ; Case T–459/93 *Siemens v. Germany* [1995] E.C.R. II–1675 at II–1707—1708, para. 82, CFI. For an example in which various principles of national law were set aside, see Case C–24/95 *Land Rheinland-Pfalz v. Alcan Deutschland GmbH* [1997] E.C.R. I–1591, ECJ.

97 Case 68/88 *Commission v. Greece* [1989] E.C.R. 2965 at 2984, para. 22, 1st sentence, ECJ.

98 *ibid.* para. 22, 2nd sentence.

99 *ibid.*, at 2985, para. 25.

obligation for Member States to ensure that "infringements of Community law are penalized under conditions, both procedural and substantive, which are analogous to those applicable to infringements of national law of a similar nature and importance and which, in any event, make the penalty effective, proportionate and dissuasive".[1]

[1] *ibid.*, at 2985, para. 24. See, to the same effect, Case C–326/88 *Hansen* [1990] E.C.R. I–2911 at I–2935, para. 17.

Part II
ENFORCEMENT OF COMMUNITY LAW

CHAPTER 4

INTRODUCTION

The original version of Article L of the E.U. Treaty limited the exercise of powers by the Court of Justice[1] to the Treaty establishing the European Community, the Treaty establishing the European Coal and Steel Community, the Treaty establishing the European Atomic Energy Community, the former third subparagraph of Article K.3(2)(c) of the E.U. Treaty and Articles 46 to 53 (*ex Articles L to S*) of that Treaty.[2] Accordingly, the jurisdiction of the Court of Justice covered Community law, certain agreements concluded by the Member States outwith Community law[3] and the final provisions of the E.U. Treaty. The Treaty of Amsterdam introduced a new Article L (*now Article 46*) into the E.U. Treaty considerably extending the jurisdiction of the Court of Justice in the field of police and judicial co-operation in criminal matters[4] and expressly empowers the Court of Justice to review acts of the institutions in the light of fundamental rights protected in the Union (E.U. Treaty, Article 6 (*ex Article F*) (2)) in so far as the Court has jurisdiction under the Community Treaties or the E.U. Treaty.[5] **4–001**

Article 46 (*ex Article L*) of the E.U. Treaty does not prevent the Court of Justice itself from delimiting the scope of its jurisdiction. For instance, a measure which was purportedly adopted in connection with a pillar other than the Community pillar of the Union (for example sanctions imposed under the common foreign and security policy) may in fact be ascribable to a Community competence (for example the common commercial policy referred to in Article 133 (*ex Article 113*) of the E.C. Treaty), which would mean that the Court of Justice would be competent to review the measure for compatibility with the Community treaties. In the event of a dispute, it is the task of the Court of Justice or the Court of First Instance to define the pillars of the Union in relation to each other. That task cannot be **4–002**

[1] This covers the two courts comprising the "institution" known as the Court of Justice: the Court of Justice and the Court of First Instance: see para. 1–003, above. For an application of the original Art. L of the E.U. Treaty, see (Order of April 7, 1995), Case C–167/94 *Juan Carlos Grau Gomis and Others* [1995] E.C.R. I–1023 at I–1027, para. 6, ECJ.

[2] For a discussion of the structure of the Union, see Lenaerts and Van Nuffel, *Constitutional Law of the European Union*, paras 3–013—3–017.

[3] See Chap. 19, below.

[4] As far as the Court's jurisdiction in this connection is concerned, see Chap. 20, below.

[5] See para. 20–004, below. For further details, see Lenaerts, "Le respect des droits fondamentaux en tant que principe constitutionnel de l'Union européenne", in *Mélanges Michel Waelbroeck*, Brussels, Bruylant, 1999.

undertaken by any other institution, since it is a matter of interpreting and applying the Community treaties and hence within the jurisdiction of the Court of Justice and the Court of First Instance within the Community legal order, which, by virtue of the judicially enforceable Article 47 (*ex Article M*) of the E.U. Treaty, is not affected by any other provision of that Treaty.[6]

4–003 The Community is a Community based on the rule of law in which each legislative, executive or implementing act of an institution or a Member State must be compatible with the "constitutional charter" on which the Community is based.[7] The treaties set out to establish a complete system of legal remedies, whereby any act or failure to act on the part of an institution or a Member State can be subjected to review by the Community court,[8] which has to ensure that in the interpretation and application of the treaties the law is observed.[9]

4–004 The judiciary has a two-fold task in connection with the Community system of legal remedies. First, it is responsible for enforcing *all* the rules of Community law. As a result, it affords protection against any act or failure to act on the part of national authorities and persons which offends against such rules. In this respect, Community law acts as a sword for safeguarding the rights deriving from that law.[10] In addition, the judiciary secures the enforcement of written and unwritten *superior* rules of Community law[11] and affords protection against any act or failure to act of institutions and other bodies of the Community in breach of those rules. In this respect, Community law acts as a shield.[12]

---

[6] For an application, see Case C–170/96 *Commission v. Council* [1998] E.C.R. I–2763 at I–2787, paras 12–18, ECJ.

[7] Case 294/83 *Les Verts v. European Parliament* [1986] E.C.R. 1339 at 1365, para. 23, ECJ, Opinion 1/91 *Draft agreement between the Community, on the one hand, and the countries of the European Free Trade Association, on the other, relating to the creation of the European Economic Area* [1991] E.C.R. I–6079 at I–6102, para. 21, ECJ. As far as Community law is concerned, there is an exception under the E.C. Treaty Art. 68 (*ex Art. 73p*) (2). That Article provides that the Court of Justice shall not have jurisdiction to rule on any measure or decision taken pursuant to Art. 62 (*ex Art. 73j*) (1) relating to the maintenance of law and order or the safeguarding of internal security.

[8] For a concise review of the Community's system of legal remedies, see Lenz, "Rechtsschutz im Binnenmarkt: Stand und Probleme" (1994) N.J.W. 2063–2067.

[9] E.C. Treaty, Art. 220 (*ex Art. 164*); ECSC Treaty, Art. 31; EAEC Treaty, Art. 136.

[10] See Chaps. 5 and 6, below.

[11] For a survey of the hierarchy of norms in Community law, see Lenaerts and Van Nuffel, *Constitutional Law of the European Union*, paras 14–037—14–039.

[12] See Pt. III, below.

CHAPTER 5

ACTION FOR INFRINGEMENT OF COMMUNITY LAW BY A MEMBER STATE

I. SUBJECT-MATTER

A. GENERAL

The action for failure to fulfil obligations (or infringement proceedings)[1] is for the purpose of obtaining a declaration that the conduct of a Member State infringes Community law and of terminating that conduct.[2] The action is objective in nature and the only question raised is whether or not the defendant Member State has breached Community law.[3] In determining whether the alleged infringement took place, the Court of Justice takes no account of subjective factors invoked to justify the Member State's conduct or omission or of the fact that there is no evidence that the infringement of Community law was intentional.[4] No reasonableness test may be applied. **5–001**

[1] E.C. Treaty, Art. 226 (*ex Art. 169*); EAEC Treaty, Art. 141. A somewhat similar procedure under the third pillar may be found in the E.U. Treaty, Art. 35 (*ex Art. K.7*) (7) (see para. 20–002, below).

[2] Joined Cases 15 and 16/76 *France v. Commission* [1979] E.C.R. 321 at 339, para. 27, ECJ.

[3] See, *inter alia*, Case 7/68 *Commission v. Italy* [1968] E.C.R. 423 at 428, ECJ; Case 415/85 *Commission v. Ireland* [1988] E.C.R. 3097 at 3118, paras 8–9, ECJ; Case 416/85 *Commission v. United Kingdom* [1988] E.C.R. 3127 at 3151, paras 8, 9, ECJ. See also Case 301/81 *Commission v. Belgium* [1983] E.C.R. 467 at 477, para. 8, ECJ. The admissibility of an action under the E.C. Treaty, Art. 226 (*ex Art. 169*) depends only on an objective finding of a failure to fulfil obligations and not on proof of any inertia or opposition on the part of the Member State.

[4] See, for instance, the case law rejecting the following as pleas in justification: difficulties in the domestic decision-making process (Case 96/81 *Commission v. Netherlands* [1982] E.C.R. 1791 at 1804–1805, para. 12, ECJ; Case 97/81 *Commission v. Netherlands* [1982] E.C.R. 1819 at 1833, para. 12, ECJ; Case 301/81 *Commission v. Belgium* [1983] E.C.R. 467 at 477, para. 6, ECJ; Joined Cases 227–230/85 *Commission v. Belgium* [1988] E.C.R. 1 at 11, para. 9, ECJ; Case C–33/90 *Commission v. Italy* [1991] E.C.R. I–5987 at I–6008, para. 24, ECJ); the fact that other Member States are also guilty of the infringement (52/75 *Commission v. Italy* [1976] E.C.R. 277 at 284–285, para. 11, ECJ; Case 78/76 *Steinike & Weinlig v. Germany* [1977] E.C.R. 595 at 613–614, para. 24, ECJ; Case 232/78 *Commission v. France* [1979] E.C.R. 2729 at 2739, para. 9, ECJ; Case 325/82 *Commission v. Germany* [1984] E.C.R. 777 at 793, para. 11, ECJ; Case C–38/89 *Blanguernon* [1990] E.C.R. I–83 at I–92—93, para. 7, ECJ)). See also Dashwood and White, "Enforcement Actions Under Articles 169 and 170 *[now Articles 226 and 227]* EEC" (1989) E.L.Rev. 388 at 400–401; Joliet, *Le contentieux*, p. 20; Nafilyan, "La position des Etats membres et le recours en manquement des articles 169 *[now Article 226]* CEE et 141 CEEA" (1977) R.T.D.E. 214 at 215; *Commentaire Mégret*, pp. 74–76. See, however, Mertens de Wilmars and Verougstraete, "Proceedings against Member States for Failure to Fulfil their Obligations" (1970) C.M.L.Rev. 385, who at the time of the "breakthrough" of the action for failure to fulfil obligations in the Court's case law still advocated, with certain reservations, merging the objective nature of the action with full powers on the part of the Court to take account also of subjective factors. This does not seem to have been followed.

The objective nature of the action for failure to fulfil obligations does not mean, however, that the Court of Justice does not subject the relevant conduct of the Member State concerned to thorough examination, from the point of view of both the law and the facts. In contradistinction to the action for annulment,[5] the Court of Justice does not confine its examination to a number of "grounds" on which the application must be based. Any infringement of Community law may be "found" pursuant to Articles 226–228 (*ex Articles 169–171*) of the E.C. Treaty.[6]

5–002 The "finding" serves principally to enforce the actual application of Community law by the Member State in breach. In the first place, since *Francovich*,[7] a Member State may incur liability under Community law for a breach of a Community provision. The judgment finding the infringement may ground liability.[8] In addition, Article 228 (*ex Article 171*) of the E.C. Treaty provides for options for enforcing such a judgment.

5–003 The action may also be used as a means of determining the exact nature of the obligations of a Member State in the event of differences of interpretation of Community law.[9] After the Court of Justice has given judgment, the Member State concerned may no longer contest the extent of its Community obligations. If the Member State continues to be in breach of its obligations, this will constitute a sufficiently serious breach of Community law, which may cause it to incur liability *vis-à-vis* injured individuals.[10]

5–004 The procedure is set forth in Articles 226, 227 and 228 (*ex Articles 169, 170 and 171*) of the E.C. Treaty (Articles 141, 142 and 143 of the EAEC Treaty are identical).[11] The action for failure to fulfil obligations is the only procedure—apart from some special procedures[12]—which allows the Court of Justice to measure the conduct of a Member State *directly* against Community law.[13]

---

[5] See Chap. 7, below.

[6] For a wide-ranging discussion of the E.C. Treaty, Art. 226 (*ex Art. 169*) see Ebke, "Les techniques contentieuses d'application du droit des Communautés européennes" (1986) R.T.D.E. 209–230.

[7] Joined Cases C–6 and C–9/90 *Francovich and Others* [1991] E.C.R. I–5357 (see para. 3–023, above and para. 5–064, below).

[8] See the settled case law since Case 39/72 *Commission v. Italy* [1973] E.C.R. 101 at 112 para. 11, ECJ, in which it was held that "a judgment by the Court under [Articles 169 and 171 *[now Articles 226 and 228]*] may be of substantive interest as establishing the basis of a responsibility that a Member State can incur as a result of its default, as regards other Member States, the Community or private parties". See also para. 5–064, below.

[9] Case 7/71 *Commission v. France* [1971] E.C.R. 1003 at 1021, para. 49, ECJ.

[10] See para. 3–023, above.

[11] E.C. Treaty, Art. 237 (*ex Art. 180*) (d), provides that, after monetary union has come into force, actions may be brought against a national central bank for failure to fulfil obligations. Proceedings are to be brought by the future European Central Bank, which is to have the same powers as the Commission has under Art. 226 (*ex Art. 169*). Art. 104 (*ex Art. 104c*) (10) rules out the possibility of bringing an action against a Member State for failing to fulfil its obligations under Art. 104(1)–(9) by failing to avoid an excessive government deficit.

[12] See paras 5–014—5–021, below.

[13] Case 28/83 *Forcheri v. Commission* [1984] E.C.R. 1425 at 1440–1441, para. 12, ECJ; Case T–13/93 *Cordier v. Commission* [1993] E.C.R. II–1215 at II–1232, para. 52, CFI. Since *Van*

The procedure laid down in Article 88 of the ECSC Treaty pursues the same aims but is completely differently constructed. The Commission itself is empowered to find that a Member State has failed to fulfil its obligations under ECSC law in a reasoned decision and to impose certain financial sanctions with the assent of the Council acting by a two-thirds majority. A Member State may bring an action to an unlimited extent against either of those measures before the Court of Justice.[14] In addition, a person may bring an action for annulment against a refusal on the part of the Commission to find a failure to fulfil obligations.[15]

The following section will deal solely with the procedure under Articles 226, 227 and 228 (*ex Articles 169, 170 and 171*) of the E.C. Treaty.

B. Failure of a Member State to fulfil an obligation under the Treaty

1. What rules are covered by the expression "an obligation under this Treaty"?

The expression "an obligation under this Treaty" covers all rules of Community law which are binding on the Member States. These are all the Treaty provisions, binding acts of Community institutions, international agreements concluded by the Community[16] and the general principles of law recognised by the Court of Justice. A finding that those rules have been infringed may be made as a result of an action brought pursuant to Articles 226 and 227 (*ex Articles 169 and 170*) of the E.C. Treaty.[17] **5–005**

A finding that a Member State has infringed general principles of law, including fundamental rights, may be made only in so far as the national conduct falls within the scope of Community law. This will be so in particular where the Member State justifies its conduct on one of the grounds provided for in the Treaty.[18] **5–006**

It is an open question whether a Member State may be brought before the Court of Justice for infringing a convention concluded pursuant to Article 293 (*ex Article 220*) of the E.C. Treaty. Some commentators have argued that this is possible on the ground that Article 293 puts the Member States under a duty to enter into negotiations with each other in order to achieve clearly **5–007**

Gend & Loos (Case 26/62 *Van Gend & Loos v. Nederlandse Administratie der Belastingen* [1963] E.C.R. 1 at 10–13, ECJ), however, the Court of Justice has held that it can use the procedure for a preliminary ruling on interpretation in order to appraise a Member State's conduct *indirectly* against Community law (see paras 5–023 and 6–028, below).

14 ECJ, Case 20/59 *Italy v. High Authority* [1960] E.C.R. 325 at 339, ECJ.

15 Case 30/59 *De Gezamenlijke Steenkolenmijnen in Limburg v. High Authority* [1961] E.C.R. 1, at 15–17, ECJ.

16 E.C. Treaty, Art. 300 (*ex Art. 228*) (7); Case 104/81 *Hauptzollamt Mainz v. Kupferberg* [1982] E.C.R. 3641 at 3662, para. 11, ECJ, Case C–61/94 *Commission v. Germany* [1996] E.C.R. I–3989 at I–4012, para. 15, ECJ.

17 For a discussion of the sources of Community law, see Lenaerts and Van Nuffel, *Constitutional Law of the European Union*, paras 14–040 *et seq.*, and Brealey and Hoskins, *Remedies in EC Law*, London, Sweet and Maxwell, 1998 (2nd ed.), pp. 3–26.

18 Case C–260/89 *ERT* [1991] E.C.R. I–2925 at I–2964, para. 42, ECJ; Case C–159/90 *Society for the Protection of Unborn Children Ireland v. Grogan and Others* [1991] E.C.R. I–4685 at I–4741, para. 31, ECJ.

defined Community objectives.[19] Others contend that a distinction should be made between the obligation to conclude the convention under Article 293 and the obligations ensuing out of such a convention for Member States. They maintain that the latter obligations are not part of Community law.[20] The Court of Justice has not yet had to rule on the question. However, it has held that the fourth indent of Article 293 of the E.C. Treaty is not intended to lay down a "legal rule directly applicable as such" but

> "to facilitate the working of the common market through the adoption of rules of jurisdiction for disputes relating thereto and through the elimination, as far as is possible, of difficulties concerning the recognition and enforcement of judgments in the territory of the Contracting States".[21]

The provisions of the Brussels Convention, concluded by the Member States pursuant to the fourth indent of Article 293 and within the framework defined by it, together with the national provisions to which the Convention refers, are "linked to the E[E]C Treaty".[22] Admittedly, this has allowed the Court of Justice to assess the compatibility of those provisions with Article 12 (*ex Article 6*) of the E.C. Treaty (prohibition of discrimination on grounds of nationality), but has not provided any answer to the question whether infringements on the part of Member States of the Brussels Convention can be the subject of proceedings brought under Articles 226 and 227 (*ex Articles 169 and 170*) of the E.C. Treaty. It may be considered, however, that the answer must be in the negative, given that the Court of Justice mentioned the Brussels Convention and the national provisions to which it refers on an equal footing when it stated that they are linked to the E.C. Treaty and therefore "within the scope of application of this Treaty" within the meaning of Article 12 of the E.C. Treaty. As a result, the Brussels Convention comes over as a joint measure of the Member States, which, in common with unilateral national measures, must be compatible with Community law, but does not form part of it.

In any event, it is agreed that compliance with conventions concluded by the Member States outside Article 293 cannot be enforced by proceedings under Articles 226 and 227 of the E.C. Treaty, even if they do contribute to the attainment of the objectives of the E.C. Treaty.[23]

[19] See Dashwood and White (cited in n. 4, above), at 390; *cf.* Pescatore, "Remarques sur la nature juridique des 'décisions des représentants des Etats membres réunis au sein du Conseil'" (1966) S.E.W. 579 at 583–584.

[20] See Schwartz, "Voies d'uniformisation du droit dans la CEE: règlements de la Communauté ou conventions entre les Etats membres" (1978) J.D.I. 751 at 781.

[21] ECJ, Case C–398/92 *Mund & Fester* [1994] E.C.R. I–467 at I–478, para. 11, ECJ.

[22] *ibid.*, para. 12.

[23] See Dashwood and White (cited in n. 4, above), at 390, who refer to the Convention on the European Patent for the Common Market, which provides for a special procedure for failure of Member States to fulfil their obligations in Art. 101(2), (3) ([1976] O.J. L17/1).

2. What is meant by "failure to fulfil"?

Since the action for failure to fulfil obligations is objective in nature, *any* shortcoming by a Member State in respect of its obligations under Community law will ground a claim for a declaration that it is in breach. The frequency or extent of the shortcoming is irrelevant. A minimum, isolated and negligible infringement of Community law is sufficient for the action to be declared well founded. It lies with the Commission or the applicant Member State[24] to assess whether it is appropriate to bring an action. Once the action is pending, the Court of Justice has to consider whether or not the alleged infringement was committed.[25] **5–008**

Whether conduct of a Member State can be categorised as a "failure to fulfil" an obligation under the Treaty also depends on the nature of the contested conduct and on the content of the rule of Community law allegedly infringed. Accordingly, it will be easier to make a finding that there has been a failure to fulfil an obligation where it ensues from the existence of a provision of national law which infringes Community law[26] than where it ensues out of a so-called "administrative practice" of a Member State, which assumes that a particular pattern of behaviour can be discerned on the part of the authorities of the defendant Member State.[27] **5–009**

The failure to fulfil obligations can arise both out of an act and out of a failure to act on the part of the Member State.[28] The classic example of the latter is failure by a Member State to implement a directive in national law.[29] An example of conduct contrary to Community law is the imposition of administrative formalities restricting the import of goods and therefore infringing Article 28 (*ex Article 30*) of the E.C. Treaty.[30] **5–010**

---

[24] See paras 5–022, 5–027, below.

[25] Case C–209/89 *Commission v. Italy* [1991] E.C.R. I–1575 at I–1594, para. 9, ECJ.

[26] However, the scope of national laws, regulations or administrative provisions must be assessed in the light of the interpretation given to them by national courts: Case 300/95 *Commission v. United Kingdom* [1997] E.C.R. I–2649 at I–2672, para. 37, ECJ.

[27] See, *e.g.*, Case 21/84 *Commission v. France* [1985] E.C.R. 1355, ECJ; Case 35/84 *Commission v. Italy* [1986] E.C.R. 545, ECJ.

[28] Case 31/69 *Commission v. Italy* [1970] E.C.R. 25 at 32, para. 9, ECJ (when the application of Community regulations requires a modification of certain public services or of the rules governing them, the failure of the authorities concerned to take the necessary measures constitutes a failure within the meaning of Art. 226 (*ex Art. 169*)). The French authorities' failure to adopt all necessary measures to prevent the free movement of fruit and vegetables from being obstructed by actions by private individuals constituted a failure to fulfil obligations under Art. 28 (*ex Art. 30*), in conjunction with Art. 10 (*ex Art. 5*) of the E.C. Treaty, and under the common organisations of the markets in agricultural products (Case C–265/95 *Commission v. France* [1997] E.C.R. I–6959, ECJ).

[29] A few examples: Case 386/85 *Commission v. Italy* [1987] E.C.R. 1061, ECJ, Case 116/86 *Commission v. Italy* [1988] E.C.R. 1323, ECJ; Case C–290/89 *Commission v. Belgium* [1991] E.C.R. I–2851 at I–2865, paras 8–10, ECJ. The obligation to transpose directives into national law requires a "positive act of transposition" if the directive in question expressly requires the Member States to ensure that their measures transposing the directive include a reference to it and that such reference is made when they are officially published: Case C–137/96 *Commission v. Germany* [1997] E.C.R. I–6749 at I–6757, para. 8, ECJ; Case C–360/95 *Commission v. Spain* [1997] E.C.R. I–7337 at I–7349, para. 13, ECJ.

[30] A few examples: Case 154/85 *Commission v. Italy* [1987] E.C.R. 2717 at 2738, para. 12, ECJ; Case C–80/92 *Commission v. Belgium* [1994] E.C.R. I–1019 at I–1033, para. 18, ECJ.

5–011 The existence of a legal provision conflicting with the Treaty may also be categorised as a "failure", even if it is not or no longer being applied by the national authorities. The fact that such a provision exists is liable to create uncertainty in those subject to the law about the possibility of relying on Community law. That uncertainty impedes the operation of Community law and is regarded as a "failure to fulfil" an obligation.[31] Only where such a provision can have no effect at all which conflicts with Community law, will its mere existence be insufficient to constitute an infringement of Community law.[32]

5–012 Even acts of a Member State which are not binding under the domestic legal system, may result in a failure to fulfil obligations under Community law in so far as their potential effects are comparable with those resulting from binding measures. A large-scale campaign launched by the Irish Government to promote the sale of Irish goods on the home market was accordingly held to be a measure of equivalent effect contrary to Article 28 (*ex Article 30*) of the E.C. Treaty.[33]

5–013 Lastly, acts of a Member State which affect the jurisdiction of the Court of Justice will invariably contravene Community law. For instance, a Member State is prohibited from transposing a regulation, which has direct effect, into national law, thereby concealing its Community origin, which would be liable to jeopardise the making of preliminary references on the interpretation or validity of the regulation.[34]

C. Relationship with special legal procedures to obtain a declaration that a Member State has failed to fulfil its obligations under Community law

1. Relationship between Articles 226 and 227 (*ex Articles 169 and 170*) and Article 88 (*ex Article 93*) (2) of the E.C. Treaty

5–014 Under Article 88 (*ex Article 93*) of the E.C. Treaty, the Commission is empowered to rule on the compatibility of state aid with the common

[31] Case 167/73 *Commission v. France* [1974] E.C.R. 359, ECJ (see Barav, "Failure of Member States to Fulfil Their Obligations Under Community Law" (1975) C.M.L.Rev. 369 at 374–376); Case 159/78 *Commission v. Italy* [1979] E.C.R. 3247 at 3264, para. 22, ECJ; Case 168/85 *Commission v. Italy* [1986] E.C.R. 2945 at 2961, para. 14, ECJ; Case 104/86 *Commission v. Italy* [1988] E.C.R. 1799 at 1817, para. 12, ECJ; Case 74/86 *Commission v. Germany* [1988] E.C.R. 2139 at 2148, para. 10, ECJ; Case 38/87 *Commission v. Greece* [1988] E.C.R. 4415 at 4430, para. 9, ECJ.

[32] Case 28/69 *Commission v. Italy* [1970] E.C.R. 187 at 195, paras 14–17, ECJ. The excise duty which Italy imposed on cocoa shells and husks differed depending on whether they were imported or produced by the Italian processing industry. Nevertheless, they were exempt from the duty if they were used for certain specified purposes. The high level of duty made it impossible in practice to use the products for purposes other than those to which the exemption applied. The existence of differential taxation was therefore insufficient to constitute an infringement of the E.C. Treaty, Art. 90 (*ex Art. 95*).

[33] Case 249/81 *Commission v. Ireland* [1982] E.C.R. 4005 at 4023, para. 27, ECJ.

[34] Case 39/72 *Commission v. Italy* [1973] E.C.R. 101 at 113, paras 16–17, ECJ; Case 34/73 *Variola v. Amministrazione Italiana delle Finanze* [1973] E.C.R. 981 at 991, para. 11, ECJ; Case 50/76 *Amsterdam Bulb v. Produktschap voor Siergewassen* [1977] E.C.R. 137 at 146–147, paras 4–7, ECJ.

market.[35] Both existing aid and the introduction or alteration of aid are subject to supervision by the Commission.[36] Any plans to grant or alter aid must be notified to the Commission pursuant to Article 88(3) of the E.C. Treaty.[37]

The Commission may take action against aid which it considers, on the basis of Article 87 (*ex Article 92*) of the E.C. Treaty, to be incompatible with the common market in accordance with the procedure laid down in Article 88 (*ex Article 93*) (2). It makes a finding that the aid is incompatible and orders the Member State concerned to abolish or alter the aid within a specified period. If the Member State fails to comply with the decision within the prescribed period, the Commission or any other interested Member State may, by way of derogation from Articles 226 and 227 (*ex Articles 169 and 170*), refer the matter directly to the Court of Justice.[38] **5–015**

Article 88(2) of the E.C. Treaty secures all interested parties the right to submit observations.[39] In addition, on application by a Member State, the Council may, acting unanimously and by way of derogation from Article 87, decide that the aid must be considered to be compatible if such a decision is justified by exceptional circumstances.[40]

The question arises as to whether, despite the existence of the special procedure provided for in Article 88 (*ex Article 93*) (2), the general procedure set out in Article 226 (*ex Article 169*) may still be used by the Commission to find infringements of Article 87 (*ex Article 92*). **5–016**

In the first place, the procedure provided for in Article 88(2) affords all interested parties guarantees commensurate with the specific problems raised by state aid for competition in the common market; those guarantees are much more extensive than those afforded by the pre-litigation procedure under Article 226, in which only the Commission and the Member State concerned take part. Accordingly, if the Commission wishes to make a finding that a state aid is incompatible with the common market, it is obliged to follow the procedure set out in Article 88(2).[41]

However, the existence of the procedure laid down in Article 88(2) does not preclude an aid measure being found incompatible with rules of

[35] For a survey of the case law of the Court of Justice, see Winter, "Supervision of State Aid: Article 93 *[now Article 88]* in the Court of Justice" (1993) C.M.L.Rev. 311–329.

[36] For the distinction between "existing" and "new" aid and an explanation of the respective powers of the Commission and the national courts in supervising aid for compatibility with the common market, see Case C–44/93 *Namur—Les Assurances du Crédit* [1994] E.C.R. I–3829 at I–3869—3871, paras 10–17, ECJ.

[37] For a survey of the applicable procedural requirements as they emerge from the case law of the Court of Justice, see Slot, "Procedural Aspects of State Aids: the Guardian of Competition versus the Subsidy Villains?" (1990) C.M.L.Rev. 741–760.

[38] E.C. Treaty, Art. 88 (*ex Art. 93*) (2), subpara. 2.

[39] Case C–294/90 *British Aerospace and Rover v. Commission* [1992] E.C.R. I–493 at I–522, para. 13, ECJ.

[40] E.C. Treaty, Art. 88 (*ex Art. 93*) (2), subpara. 3.

[41] Case 290/83 *Commission v. France* [1985] E.C.R. 439 at 449–450, para. 17, ECJ.

Community law other than Article 87 by means of the Article 226 procedure.[42]

Lastly, in the event of an infringement of a decision made pursuant to the first subparagraph of Article 88(2), the Commission may elect either to bring the matter directly before the Court of Justice under the second subparagraph of Article 88(2) or to initiate the Article 226 procedure.[43]

5–017 The Commission also often has a choice between the Article 88 (*ex Article 93*) (2) procedure and that provided for in Article 226 (*ex Article 169*) where a Member State fails to inform the Commission in time, contrary to Article 88(3), of a plan to grant new aid or altered aid.[44] The fact that the duty to notify the Commission has been infringed, however, does not make the aid incompatible with the common market. Accordingly, the Commission must initiate an examination of the compatibility of the non-notified aid with the common market. In that event, it may require the aid to be suspended pending the outcome of its examination and order the Member State to provide information under a procedure pursuant to Article 88(2).[45] If the Member State refuses to suspend the aid, the Commission may bring the matter directly before the Court of Justice pursuant to the second subparagraph of Article 88(2)[46] or bring an action against the Member State under Article 226.[47]

A finding by the Commission, after carrying out an examination, that the non-notified aid measure is compatible with the common market does not retroactively remedy the infringement of the Treaty caused by the failure to notify. Since Article 88(3) of the E.C. Treaty has direct effect, national courts are obliged to regard as unlawful any acts performed to implement the non-notified aid before the Commission made its finding that the aid

[42] Case 72/79 *Commission v. Italy* [1980] E.C.R. 1411 at 1425–1426, para. 12, ECJ; Case 73/79 *Commission v. Italy* [1980] 1533 at 1547, para. 9, ECJ (for these two judgments, see Gilmour, "The Enforcement of Community Law by the Commission in the Context of State Aids: the Relationship Between Articles 93 and 169 *[now Articles 88 and 226]* and the Choice of Remedies" (1981) C.M.L.Rev. 63–77); Case 290/83 *Commission v. France* [1985] E.C.R. 439 at 449–450, para. 17, ECJ; Case C–35/88 *Commission v. Greece* [1990] E.C.R. I–3125 at I–3154, para. 11, ECJ.

[43] Case 70/72 *Commission v. Germany* [1973] E.C.R. 813 at 828–829, paras 8–13, ECJ (action based on Art. 88 (*ex Art. 93*) (2), subpara. 2); Case 130/83 *Commission v. Italy* [1984] E.C.R. 2849, ECJ (action based on Art. 226 (*ex Art. 169*)). *Cf.* Case C–294/90 *British Aerospace and Rover v. Commission* [1992] E.C.R. I–493 at I–522, para. 12, ECJ (the Commission may also take the approach that the infringement of its decision constitutes new aid within the meaning of Art. 88(3); if so, it must start up the special procedure under Art. 88(2), subpara. 1, afresh and if necessary take a fresh decision after having put interested parties on notice to submit observations, *ibid.*, para. 13). See the case note by Blumann, "Régime des aides d'Etat: jurisprudence récente de la Cour de justice (1989–1992)" (1992) R.M.C. 721 at 732–733.

[44] Case 173/73 *Italy v. Commission* [1974] E.C.R. 709 at 717, para. 9, ECJ. See also Biancarelli, "Le contrôle de la Cour de justice des Communautés européennes en matière d'aides publiques" (1993) A.J.D.A. 412 at 428.

[45] Case C–301/87 *France v. Commission* [1990] E.C.R. I–307 at I–356—357, paras 18–23, ECJ; Case C–142/87 *Belgium v. Commission* [1990] E.C.R. I–959 at I–1009—1010, paras 15–19, ECJ.

[46] Case C–301/87 *France v. Commission* (cited in n. 45, above) at I–357, para. 23.

[47] *ibid.*, para. 23.

was compatible with the common market, and impose the appropriate sanctions.[48]

Since: 5–018

> "the Council is entitled to lay down, within the context of the regulations establishing the common organization of the markets in agricultural products, provisions prohibiting wholly or partially certain forms of national aids for the production or marketing of the products in question and . . . an infringement of such a prohibition may be dealt with within the specific framework of such an organization,"

the procedure laid down by Article 226 (*ex Article 169*) is to be used in order to determine the infringement.[49] Under Article 36 (*ex Article 42*) of the E.C. Treaty, all the provisions of Articles 78 to 89 (*ex Articles 85 to 94*) are applicable to production of and trade in agricultural products only to the extent determined by the Council within the framework of measures adopted for the organisation of agricultural markets. This explains why recourse by a Member State to Articles 87 to 89 (*ex Articles 92 to 94*) on aid cannot receive priority over the provisions of a regulation on the organisation of a sector of the agricultural market.[50] Consequently, the fact that there is a special procedure in Article 88 (*ex Article 93*) of the E.C. Treaty for appraising the compatibility of state aid with the common market, cannot preclude recourse to the Article 226 procedure in the event that the Commission considers that an aid measure of a Member State infringes the provisions of a regulation organising a sector of the agricultural market, even though the aid measure is also open to criticism under Article 87 (*ex Article 92*) of the E.C. Treaty.

2. Relationship between Articles 226 and 227 (*ex Articles 169 and 170*) and Article 86 (*ex Article 90*) (3) of the E.C. Treaty

Article 86 (*ex Article 90*) (3) of the E.C. Treaty charges the Commission with supervising Member States' compliance with their obligations with regard to public undertakings and undertakings to which they have granted special or exclusive rights, and expressly confers on it the power to use two legal instruments to this end, namely directives and decisions. 5–019

The Commission is empowered to use *directives* to specify in general terms the obligations arising under Article 86(1) of the E.C. Treaty. It exercises that power where, without taking into consideration the particular situation existing in the various Member States, it defines in concrete terms the obligations imposed on them under that provision of the Treaty. In view

[48] Case 120/73 *Lorenz v. Germany* [1973] E.C.R. 1471, ECJ; Case C–354/90 *Fédération Nationale du Commerce Extérieur des Produits Alimentaires and Syndicat National des Négociants et Transformateurs de Saumon* [1991] E.C.R. I–5505, ECJ.

[49] Case 72/79 *Commission v. Italy* [1980] E.C.R. 1411 at 1425–1426, para. 12, ECJ. See also Case C–61/90 *Commission v. Greece* [1992] E.C.R. I–2407, ECJ.

[50] Case 177/78 *Pigs and Bacon Commission v. McCarren* [1979] E.C.R. 2161 at 2187, para. 11, and at 2191, para. 21, ECJ. See also Biancarelli (cited in n. 44, above) at 428.

of its very nature, such a power cannot be used to make a finding that a Member State has failed to fulfil a particular obligation under the E.C. Treaty.[51]

The powers exercised by the Commission under Article 86(3) by *decision* are different from those which it exercises by directive. Decisions are adopted in respect of a specific situation in one or more Member States and necessarily involve an appreciation of the situation in the light of Community law. They specify the consequences arising for the Member State concerned, regard being had to the requirements which the performance of the particular tasks assigned to an undertaking imposes on it where it is entrusted with the operation of services of general economic interest (Article 86(1) and (2)).[52] If the power to adopt decisions conferred on the Commission by Article 86(3) is not to be deprived of all practical effect, the Commission must be empowered to determine that a given state measure is incompatible with the rules of the Treaty and to indicate what measures the state to which the decision is addressed must take in order to comply with its obligations under Community law.[53] Even though there is no express provision to this effect in Article 86(3)—unlike in Article 226 (*ex Article 169*) and Article 88 (*ex Article 93*) (2)—the general principle of respect for the rights of the defence requires that the Member State concerned must receive an exact and complete statement of the objections which the Commission intends to raise against it. It must also be placed in a position in which it may effectively make known its views on the observations submitted by interested third parties.[54]

5–020 The Commission's power to appraise, in a decision adopted pursuant to Article 86 (*ex Article 90*) (3), the conformity with the Treaty of measures adopted or applied by Member States with regard to undertakings referred to in Article 86(1) does not run counter to the powers conferred on the Court of Justice by Article 226 (*ex Article 169*) of the E.C. Treaty. If the Member State does not comply with the decision, this may form the basis for infringement proceedings under Article 226.[55]

Whether the Commission may bring an action for failure to fulfil obligations before it has adopted a decision pursuant to Article 86(3), depends in all likelihood on the requirements of the rights of the defence. The procedure which affords the strongest guarantees for the Member State concerned should probably take precedence in the stage of the initial examination of the compatibility of a national measure with Article 86(1)

---

[51] Case C–202/88 *France v. Commission* [1991] E.C.R. I–1223 at I–1264, para. 17, ECJ. For the use of directives in specific cases, see EAEC Treaty, Arts. 38, 82. See also Lenaerts, "Nuclear Border Installations: A Case-Study" (1988) E.L.Rev. 159 at 171–179.

[52] Joined Cases C–48 and C–66/90 *Netherlands and Others v. Commission* [1992] E.C.R. I–565 at I–635, para. 27, ECJ.

[53] *ibid.*, para. 28.

[54] *ibid.*, at I–639, paras 45, 46.

[55] Case 226/87 *Commission v. Greece* [1988] E.C.R. 3611, ECJ: it appears from this judgment that if the Member State to which the Commission's decision is addressed contests its legality, it must bring an action for annulment within the time-limit laid down by Art. 230 (*ex Art. 173*); thereafter, the Member State may not plead the unlawfulness of the decision as a defence in proceedings for failure to fulfil obligations.

and (2) of the E.C. Treaty by analogy with the aforementioned case law on Article 88 (*ex Article 93*) (2)[56].[57] In any event, it is certain that Member States may invariably bring an action under Article 227 (*ex Article 170*) of the E.C. Treaty against a Member State for failure to fulfil its obligations under Article 86(1) and (2), even if the Commission has not yet exercised its powers under Article 86(3) to address a decision to the Member State concerned.

3. Relationship between Articles 226 and 227 (*ex Articles 169 and 170*) of the E.C. Treaty and special procedures relating to the improper use of derogating provisions

Apart from Article 88 (*ex Article 93*) (2), the E.C. Treaty provides for other cases in which, by way of derogation from the procedure laid down in Articles 226 and 227 (*ex Articles 169 and 170*), the Commission or a Member State may bring a Member State directly before the Court of Justice, namely where the derogating provisions provided for in the Treaty are misused (E.C. Treaty, Article 95 (*ex Article 100a*) (4) and Articles 296 to 298 (*ex Articles 223 to 225*)). The opportunity afforded to the Commission by Article 95(9)[58] of the E.C. Treaty in order to bring a matter directly before the Court of Justice without incurring the delay of a pre-litigation procedure is intended to serve the Community interest of protecting in full the establishment of the internal market. However, this does not preclude the Commission from opting to bring proceedings under Article 226 of the E.C. Treaty in the interests of the defendant Member State.[59] 5–021

The action that the Commission or any Member State may bring against a Member State, pursuant to the second paragraph of Article 298, if it considers that that state is making improper use of the powers provided for in Articles 296 and 297, does not involve a pre-litigation stage (which is precisely the difference compared with proceedings under Articles 226 and 227), but does afford the guarantee that the Court of Justice is to give its ruling *in camera*, this being essential in the case of a politically charged dispute.[60]

---

[56] See para. 5–016, above.

[57] Besides, the Court of Justice itself has strongly emphasised the parallel between Art. 86 (*ex Art. 90*) (3) and Art. 88 (*ex Art. 93*). See Joined Cases C–48 and C–66/90 *Netherlands and Others v. Commission* [1992] E.C.R. I–565 at I–636, paras 31–33, ECJ.

[58] This was formerly part of the E.C. Treaty, Art. 100(4).

[59] It is argued that proceedings should have to be brought under the E.C. Treaty, Art. 226 (*ex Art. 169*) against a failure of a Member State to notify the Commission of the application of a national measure conflicting with a harmonising measure adopted pursuant to Art. 95 (*ex Art. 100a*) (1). If proceedings under Art. 95(9) were to be allowed, this might also mean that a Member State would in some cases have the power not to notify the Commission of a national measure (although it is considered this is not the case) on the ground that such proceedings relate only to "improper use of the powers provided for in this Article." (see Flynn, "How will Article 100a (4) work? A Comparison with Article 93 *[now Article 88]*" (1987) C.M.L.Rev. 689 at 700–701).

[60] See (Order of the President of March 19, 1996), Case C–120/94 *Commission v. Greece* [1996] E.C.R. I–1513, ECJ. A case brought under the E.C. Treaty, Art. 226 or 227 (*ex Art. 169 or 170*) is heard in principle in public, although the Court of Justice may decide otherwise of its own motion or on application by the parties for serious reasons (E.C. Statute, Art. 28).

II. Identity of the parties

A. The applicant

5–022 Under Article 226 (*ex Article 169*) of the E.C. Treaty, only the Commission may bring an action against a Member State. That power is consistent with its task of ensuring that Community law is applied.[61] The Commission exercises its supervisory task of its own motion in the general interest of the Community[62] and does not have to show the existence of a specific interest in bringing proceedings.[63] It itself assesses whether it is appropriate to bring proceedings under Article 226 and has no obligation to do so in the event of an alleged infringement of the Treaty.[64] The decision to apply to the Court of Justice for a declaration that a Member State has failed to fulfil its obligations cannot be described as a measure of administration or management and hence may not be delegated; it must be taken by all the members of the college of Commissioners, who should bear collective responsibility for it.[65] The formal requirements for effective compliance with that principle of collegiate responsibility are less strict in this case than in the case of the adoption of decisions affecting the legal position of individuals.[66] The reason for this is that, whilst the decision to commence proceedings for failure to fulfil obligations before the Court constitutes an indispensable step for the purpose of enabling the Court to give judgment by way of a binding decision on the alleged failure to fulfil obligations, it does not *per se* alter the legal position of the Member State in question. Consequently, it is

---

[61] E.C. Treaty, Art. 211 (*ex Art. 155*), first indent. Case C–422/92 *Commission v. Germany* [1995] E.C.R. I–1097 at I–1130—1131, para. 16, ECJ.

[62] Case 167/73 *Commission v. France* [1974] E.C.R. 359 at 368–369, para. 15, ECJ. See also Goffin, "Le manquement d'un Etat membre selon la jurisprudence de la Cour de Justice des Communautés européennes", in *Mélanges Fernand Dehousse, La construction européenne*, Paris/Brussels, Nathan/Labor, 1979, II, 211 at 215; and Lenaerts and Van Nuffel, *Constitutional Law of the European Union*, paras 7–046 and 7–053.

[63] Case C–422/92 *Commission v. Germany* [1995] E.C.R. I–1097 at I–1130—1131, para. 16, ECJ; Case C–182/94 *Commission v. Italy* [1995] E.C.R. I–1465 at I–1471, para. 5, ECJ.

[64] Case C–87/89 *Sonito and Others v. Commission* [1990] E.C.R. I–1981 at I–2008—2009, paras 6–7, ECJ; Case C–200/88 *Commission v. Greece* [1990] E.C.R. I–4299 at I–4310, para. 9, ECJ; Case C–209/88 *Commission v. Italy* [1990] E.C.R. I–4313 at I–4326, para. 13, ECJ; Case C–243/89 *Commission v. Denmark* [1993] E.C.R. I–3353 at I–3393, para. 30, ECJ. See also the E.C. Treaty, Art. 226 (*ex Art. 169*), para. 2, which provides that the Commission *may* bring the matter before the Court of Justice if the Member State concerned fails to comply with the reasoned opinion within the period laid down. See Evans, "The Enforcement Procedure of Article 169 *[now Article 226]* EEC: Commission Discretion" (1979) E.L.Rev. 442–456. The controversy in academic writings as to whether or not the Commission has a discretion to bring an action and the allegedly different implications of Art. 226, paras. 1, 2 (see, *e.g. Smit and Herzog (now Campbell and Powers), The Law of the European Community*, New York, Matthew Bender & Co., 1976, 5–321) has been overtaken by case law. For a survey of the use of Art. 226, see Thomas, "Infractions et manquements des Etats membres au droit communautaire" (1991) R.M.C. 887–892.

[65] Case C–191/95 *Commission v. Germany* [1998] E.C.R. I–5449 at I–5496, paras 35–37, ECJ, in which the Court justified this position in terms, *inter alia*, of "the discretionary power of the institution", which "[i]n its role as guardian of the Treaty . . . is competent to decide whether it is appropriate to bring proceedings against a Member State for failure to fulfil its obligations".

[66] See Lenaerts and Van Nuffel, *Constitutional Law of the European Union*, para. 7–056.

sufficient that the decision to bring an action was the subject of collective deliberation by the college of Commissioners and that the information on which the decision was based was available to the members of the college. However, it is not necessary for the college itself formally to decide on the wording of the acts which give effect to the decision and put them in final form.[67]

The involvement of the Court is not always necessary or appropriate in order to ensure that the Member States effectively apply Community law. The Commission is therefore also free to determine the time when it brings any proceedings.[68] In contrast, the Commission is not empowered to determine conclusively whether given conduct of a Member State is compatible with the Treaty. The rights and duties of Member States may be determined, and their conduct appraised only by judgment of the Court of Justice.[69] Consequently, a decision by the Commission not to bring proceedings against a Member State does not mean that it is not in breach of Community law.[70]

Individuals may not bring actions for failure to fulfil obligations before **5–023**
the Court of Justice (or the Court of First Instance).[71] If the need arises, they must contest the conduct of the Member State in a national court. The latter may (or must) request a preliminary ruling from the Court of Justice[72] in order indirectly to have the conduct complained of reviewed in the light of the requirements of Community law.[73] Furthermore, persons considering that a Member State is infringing Community law may lay a complaint before the Commission. The Commission, however, is under no obligation to act on the complaint.

---

67 Case C–191/95 *Commission v. Germany* (cited in n. 65, above) at I–5499, paras 47–48.

68 Case 7/68 *Commission v. Italy* [1968] E.C.R. 423 at 428, ECJ; Case 7/71 *Commission v. France* [1971] E.C.R. 1003 at 1016, para. 5, ECJ; Case 324/82 *Commission v. Belgium* [1984] E.C.R. 1861 at 1878, para. 12, ECJ. See also Case C–422/92 *Commission v. Germany* [1995] E.C.R. I–1097 at I–1030—1031, paras 17, 18, ECJ. Although the Court was surprised at the Commission's having brought an action more than six years after the national legislation at issue had entered into force, it held that the Commission was not obliged to act within a specified period.

69 Joined Cases 142 and 143/80 *Amministrazione delle Finanze dello Stato v. Essevi and Salengo* [1981] E.C.R. 1413 at 1433, para. 16, E.C.J.

70 Where it subsequently appears that the Member State is indeed infringing Community law, the fact that the Commission did not bring an action for failure to fulfil obligations may, in certain circumstances, constitute a reason for limiting the temporal effects of a judgment of the Court on a reference for a preliminary ruling which brings the infringement to light (see para. 6–039, below). This may also be relevant in assessing whether the breach of Community law was sufficiently serious as to cause the Member State to incur liability *vis-à-vis* individuals which suffered loss or damage as a result of it, see para. 3–023, above.

71 Case 1/82 *D. v. Luxembourg* [1982] E.C.R. 3709 at 3716, para. 8, ECJ.

72 See Chap. 6, below.

73 Joined Cases C–106/90, C–317/90 and C–129/91 *Emerald Meats v. Commission* [1993] E.C.R. I–209 at I–303, para. 40, ECJ. For further discussion of this point, see Timmermans, "Judicial Protection against the Member States: Articles 169 *[now Article 226]* and 177 *[now Article 234]* revisited", in Curtin and Heukels (eds), *Institutional Dynamics of European Integration. Essays in Honour of H.G. Schermers*, Dordrecht, Martinus Nijhoff, 1994, II, at 391–407.

5–024 The Commission's decision rejecting a complaint cannot be challenged by an action for annulment,[74] since the Commission does not adopt any binding legal act in the course of the pre-litigation stage[75]: it does not determine the rights and duties of the Member State or afford any guarantee that a given line of conduct is compatible with the Treaty. Accordingly, an opinion of the Commission cannot release a Member State from its Treaty obligations and certainly does not give it a licence to restrict rights which individuals derive from the Treaty.[76] Consequently, the Commission's decision rejecting a complaint from individuals does not affect their legal position since the Commission is simply refusing to take measures which in no event would have legal effects for them.

5–025 If the Commission leaves the complaint unanswered, an action for failure to act will not lie, since the Commission has not infringed any duty to act.[77] The same is true where the Commission fails to bring proceedings in the Court in the event of a Member State's infringing a decision adopted pursuant to Article 88 (*ex Article 93*) (2) of the E.C. Treaty.[78] In addition, natural or legal persons may bring such an action against the Commission only if it failed to adopt an act addressed to them, other than a

[74] Case C–87/89 *Sonito and Others v. Commission* [1990] E.C.R. I–1981 at I–2008—2009, paras 5–9, ECJ; Case T–16/91 *Rendo and Others v. Commission* [1992] E.C.R. II–2417 at II–2435, para. 52, CFI; Case T–575/93 *Koelman v. Commission* [1996] E.C.R. II–1 at 31 para. 71, CFI; Case T–111/96 *ITT Promedia v. Commission* [1998] E.C.R. II–2937 at II–2973, para. 97, CFI. Since the Commission likewise has a broad discretion in carrying out the function conferred on it by the E.C. Treaty, Art. 86 (*ex Art. 90*) (3) of ensuring that Member States fulfil their obligations in respect of public undertakings and undertakings to which Member States grant special or exclusive rights, individuals who requested the Commission to intervene pursuant to Art. 86 may not bring an action for annulment against the decision by which the Commission refuses to take a decision against national legislation of general application (Case C–107/95 P *Bundesverband der Bilanzbuchhalter v. Commission* [1997] E.C.R. I–947 at I–964—965, paras 26–30, ECJ. *Cf.* however, the Opinion of Advocate General A.M. La Pergola, at I–953—956, points 14–21, who took a different view; (Order of January 23, 1995), Case T–84/94 *Bundesverband der Bilanzbuchhalter v. Commission* [1995] E.C.R. II–101 at II–110, para. 23, CFI). This case law does not immediately preclude an action for annulment of a refusal on the part of the Commission to act against Member States which infringe Art. 86(1) and (2) in granting rights or advantages to individual undertakings. See, by analogy, the possibilities for bringing an action where the Commission takes a decision, pursuant to Art. 88 (*ex Art. 93*) (3) of the Treaty, that a plan to grant or alter aid is not incompatible with the common market and that the procedure provided for in Art. 88(2) therefore does not have to be initiated; see para. 7–072, below and the case note by Moloney (1998) C.M.L.Rev. 731–745.

[75] Case 48/65 *Lütticke v. Commission* [1966] E.C.R. 19 at 27, ECJ where the Court held that "[n]o measure taken by the Commission during [the pre-litigation] stage has any binding force".

[76] Joined Cases 142 and 143/80 *Amministrazione delle Finanze v. Essevi and Salengo* [1981] E.C.R. 1431 at 1433, paras 16–18, ECJ.

[77] (Order of February 19, 1997), Case T–117/96 *Intertronic v. Commission* [1997] E.C.R. II–141 at II–152, para. 32, CFI.

[78] Case T–277/94 *AITEC v. Commission* [1996] E.C.R. II–351 at II–377—379, paras 65–72, CFI. See also para. 8–004, below.

recommendation or an opinion.[79] Since in a procedure pursuant to Article 226 (*ex Article 169*) of the E.C. Treaty the Commission addresses to the Member State concerned only a reasoned "opinion", natural or legal persons are precluded from bringing an action for failure to deliver such an opinion.[80]

A failure on the part of the Commission to bring an action for failure to fulfil obligations will not ground an action for damages either.[81] The reason for this is that the Commission's inaction does not infringe Article 226 (*ex Article 169*) of the E.C. Treaty and therefore cannot be regarded as constituting fault.[82] In such a case, the source of any damage lies in the Member State's infringement of the Treaty and not in any shortcoming of the Commission. **5–026**

Under Article 227 (*ex Article 170*) of the E.C. Treaty, a Member State may also bring a matter before the Court of Justice if it considers that another Member State has failed to fulfil an obligation under Community law.[83] The Member State must first submit a complaint to the Commission. The Commission delivers a reasoned opinion, after giving each of the states concerned the opportunity to submit its own case and its observations on the other party's case both orally and in writing. The opinion sets out the Commission's view as to whether or not the alleged infringement of Community obligations under the Treaty is made out. If the Commission has not delivered an opinion within three months of the date of receipt of the complaint, the matter may be brought before the Court of Justice. **5–027**

The Commission may also bring the matter before the Court itself pursuant to Article 226 (*ex Article 169*) of the E.C. Treaty. If it does so, it does not prevent the Member State from also bringing an action. In the event that the Commission's reasoned opinion falls short of the Member State's expectations, it may add to it in its application.

---

[79] Case 247/87 *Star Fruit v. Commission* [1989] E.C.R. 291 at 301, paras 10–14, ECJ; (Order of May 23, 1990), Case C–72/90 *Asia Motor France v. Commission* [1990] E.C.R. I–2181 at I–2185, para. 11, ECJ; (Order of December 14, 1993), Case T–29/93 *Calvo Alonso-Cortés v. Commission* [1993] E.C.R. II–1389 at II–1406, para. 55, CFI; (Order of May 27, 1994), Case T–5/94 *J. v. Commission* [1994] E.C.R. II–391 at II–399, para. 16, CFI; (Order of July 4, 1994), Case T–13/94 *Century Oils Hellas v. Commission* [1994] E.C.R. II–431 at II–438, para. 13, CFI.

[80] (Order of March 30, 1990), Case C–371/89 *Emrich v. Commission* [1990] E.C.R. I–1555, ECJ.

[81] (Order of May 23, 1990), Case C–72/90 *Asia Motor France v. Commission* [1990] E.C.R. I–2181 at I–2185, para. 13, ECJ.

[82] However, the Commission's conduct may possibly infringe other Treaty provisions and hence potentially make it liable in damages if all the necessary conditions are fulfilled (see Chap. 11 below). The Court of Justice has declared actions for damages for infringement of the E.C. Treaty, Art. 97, para. 2 (since repealed) and Arts. 88 (*ex Art. 93*) (2), 211 (*ex Art. 115*) and 226 (*ex Art. 169*), respectively, admissible but unfounded (Case 4/69 *Lütticke v. Commission* [1971] E.C.R. 325, ECJ; Case 40/75 *Produits Bertrand v. Commission* [1976] E.C.R. 1, ECJ).

[83] ECSC Treaty, Art. 89, provides for a similar remedy, yet without a pre-litigation stage requiring the involvement of the Commission.

To date, only a few actions have been brought under Article 227 of the E.C. Treaty, and only one of them resulted in a judgment.[84]

B. The defendant

5–028 An action under Articles 226–227 (*ex Articles 169–170*) may be brought in the Court of Justice only against a Member State.

5–029 By "Member State" is meant the entity under international law which acceded to the Treaties. Any act or failure to act by any agency of the state or constitutionally independent bodies or institutions which are to be regarded as public bodies, may potentially cause the Member State to become liable under Community law.[85] The domestic organisation of a Member State may not detract from the full effect of Community law.

5–030 Consequently, it may be that a Member State is found guilty of infringing Community law even though the infringement was committed by a sub-entity and the national government, which represents the "Member State" before the Court of Justice, was not at fault and has no defence under domestic law.[86] The rationale of the Court's case law is that the Member State is under a Community-law duty to construct its constitutional structure in such a way as to avoid that evil.

5–031 An act or omission of the legislative authority of a Member State can certainly give rise to an action for failure to fulfil obligations.[87]

5–032 Shortcomings in the way in which national courts apply Community law may also be imputed to the Member States.[88] In all likelihood, an ordinary judicial error is not sufficient. If a national court deliberately ignored or disregarded Community law, this could certainly bring the Community liability of the relevant Member State into play.[89]

---

[84] Case 141/78 *France v. United Kingdom* [1979] E.C.R. 2923, ECJ.

[85] Case 77/69 *Commission v. Belgium* [1970] E.C.R. 237 at 243, para. 15, ECJ; Case 169/82 *Commission v. Italy* [1984] E.C.R. 1603, ECJ; Case 1/86 *Commission v. Belgium* [1987] E.C.R. 2797, ECJ; Joined Cases 227–230/85 *Commission v. Belgium* [1988] E.C.R. 1, ECJ; Case 45/87 *Commission v. Ireland* [1988] E.C.R. 4929, ECJ; Case C–58/89 *Commission v. Germany* [1991] E.C.R. I–4983, ECJ; Case C–33/90 *Commission v. Italy* [1991] E.C.R. I–5987, ECJ. See also the definition of the expression "Member State" in (Order of March 21 1997), Case C–95/97 *Région Wallonne v. Commission* [1997] E.C.R. I–1787 at I–1795—1796; paras 16–17, ECJ.

[86] Case 239/85 *Commission v. Belgium* [1986] E.C.R. 3645 at 3660, paras 13, 14, ECJ. In Belgium there is a system of substitution whereby the federal authorities may, subject to certain conditions, invest themselves with powers of a sub-entity in order to give effect to a judgment of the Court of Justice finding Belgium guilty of an infringement of Community law by that entity (Belgian Constitution, Art. 169 and Art. 16(3) of the Special Law on Institutional Reform).

[87] Case 8/70 *Commission v. Italy* [1970] E.C.R. 961 at 966, paras 8–9, ECJ; Case 94/81 *Commission v. Italy* [1982] E.C.R. 739 at 744, para. 4, ECJ; Case 41/82 *Commission v. Italy* [1982] E.C.R. 4213 at 4221, para. 15, ECJ; Case 309/84 *Commission v. Italy* [1986] E.C.R. 599 at 607–608, para. 9, ECJ.

[88] De Bellescize, "L'article 169 du traité de Rome, et l'efficacité du contrôle communautaire sur les manquements des Etats membres" (1977) R.T.D.E. 173 at 178.

[89] Opinion of Advocate General J.-P. Warner in Case 30/77 *Regina v. Bouchereau* [1977] E.C.R. 1999 at 2021. See also paras 2–052, 2–053, above, for the possibility of bringing proceedings under the E.C. Treaty, Arts. 226, 227 (*ex Arts. 169–170*) against a Member State where one of its courts infringes the obligation to seek a preliminary ruling under Art. 234, (*ex Art. 177*) para. 3.

Lastly, acts of legal persons governed by private law which are controlled by the public authorities may result in an infringement of Community law on the part of the Member State concerned. An example is the Irish Goods Council which was set up to organise the "Buy Irish" campaign in Ireland. The acts of the Irish Goods Council had to be imputed to the Irish State, since its membership, funding and aims were determined by the Irish Government.[90] 5–033

III. Special Characteristics

A. The pre-litigation stage of the procedure

The aim of the pre-litigation stage of the procedure is to give the Member State an opportunity (1) of remedying the infringement before the matter is brought before the Court of Justice, and (2) of putting forward its defence to the Commission's complaints.[91] Moreover, during the pre-litigation stage the Commission and the Member State may come to an accommodation, thus rendering a court hearing unnecessary. Lastly, the proper conduct of the pre-litigation procedure constitutes an essential guarantee, not only in order to protect the rights of the Member States concerned, but also so as to ensure that any contentious procedure will have a clearly defined dispute as to its subject-matter.[92] The scope of the dispute is defined in the pre-litigation procedure. As a result, in the contentious proceedings the Court may only judge the merits of the pleas in law put forward by the Commission in the pre-litigation procedure.[93] 5–034

1. Letter before action

The Article 226 (*ex Article 169*) procedure formally commences on receipt of a letter before action from the Commission giving the Member State formal notice. As a rule, the letter will have been preceded by informal contacts between the Commission and the Member State by which the former starts its investigation into the possible infringements of Community law.[94] 5–035

The purpose of the letter before action or formal notice is to delimit the subject-matter of the dispute and to provide the Member State, which is asked to submit observations, with the information necessary in order for it to prepare its defence.[95] 5–036

---

[90] Case 249/81 *Commission v. Ireland* [1982] E.C.R. 4005 paragraph 15, at 4020, para. 15, ECJ. See also Dashwood and White (cited in n. 4, above), at 391.

[91] Case 74/82 *Commission v. Ireland* [1984] E.C.R. 317 at 338–339, para. 13, ECJ.

[92] (Order of July 11, 1995), Case C–266/94 *Commission v. Spain* [1995] E.C.R. I–1975 at I–1982, para. 17, ECJ.

[93] Case C–158/94 *Commission v. Italy* [1997] E.C.R. I–5789 at I–5810–5811, paras 59–60, ECJ; Case C–159/94 *Commission v. France* [1997] E.C.R. I–5815 at I–5846–5847, paras 106, 107, ECJ.

[94] For a more extensive survey of the Commission's activities in this "administrative stage", see Rideau and Picod, *Code de procédures communautaires*, pp. 186–190, and Brealey and Hoskins, *Remedies in EC Law* (cited in n. 17, above), pp. 250–254.

[95] Case 274/83 *Commission v. Italy* [1985] E.C.R. 1077 at 1090, para. 19, ECJ; Case 229/87 *Commission v. Greece* [1988] E.C.R. 6347 at 6360, para. 12, ECJ.

5–037 Consequently, the letter before action must precisely specify the obligation which the Commission maintains the Member State has failed to fulfil and the grounds on which the Commission takes this view. Any vagueness in the letter before action, depriving the Member State of the opportunity of submitting observations to good effect, may be remedied by the Commission sending a new letter before action setting out in time additional particulars or information.[96] However, at that point in the pre-litigation stage it is sufficient if the Member State receives an initial brief summary of the complaints.[97] The test is whether the Member State was placed in possession of all the relevant information needed for its defence.[98]

5–038 Because it gives the Member State concerned the opportunity to submit prior observations the letter before action constitutes an essential procedural requirement for the legality of the procedure for a declaration that a Member State has failed to fulfil its obligations.[99] Even if the Member State does not wish to make any observations, the Commission must comply with that requirement.[1]

In addition, the Member State must be put on notice of the whole of the alleged infringement of Community law. The complaints may not be subsequently extended in the reasoned opinion, since that would be in breach of the Commission's duty to give the Member State concerned a fair hearing.[2] The illegality cannot be regarded as cured even by the fact that the Member State put forward a defence in its observations on the reasoned opinion to the new complaints enlarging the scope of the dispute.[3]

5–039 The Member State must have a reasonable time in which to make its observations. The reasonableness of the period prescribed by the Commission has to be assessed in the light of the particular circumstances. Thus, the urgent nature of the case or the fact that the Member State was fully apprised of the Commission's position even before the letter before action may warrant setting a short period.[4] However, the urgency of the case may not be brought about by the Commission itself, for instance because it was tardy in bringing proceedings for failure to fulfil obligations. Moreover, a Member State cannot be regarded as having been fully apprised of the

[96] Case 211/81 *Commission v. Denmark* [1982] E.C.R. 4547 at 4558, paras 10, 11, ECJ.

[97] Case 274/83 *Commission v. Italy* [1985] E.C.R. 1077 at 1090, para. 21, ECJ; Case C–289/94 *Commission v. Italy* [1996] E.C.R. I–4405 at I–4423—4424, para. 16, ECJ; Case C–279/94 *Commission v. Italy* [1997] E.C.R. I–4743 at I–4766, para. 15, ECJ. If, in the letter before action, the Commission wrongly refers to the E.C. Treaty, Art. 226 (*ex Art. 169*) instead of EAEC Treaty, Art. 141, where the failure to fulfil an obligation relates to the latter Treaty, that irregularity cannot result in the application being inadmissible if, in the circumstances of the case, the rights of defence of the Member State concerned are not affected.

[98] Case 229/87 *Commission v. Greece* [1988] E.C.R. 6347 at 6360, para. 13, ECJ.

[99] Case C–306/91 *Commission v. Italy* [1993] E.C.R. I–2133 at I–2158, paras 22–24, ECJ; Case C–243/89 *Commission v. Denmark* [1993] E.C.R. I–3353 at I–3389, para. 13, ECJ.

[1] Case 31/69 *Commission v. Italy* [1970] E.C.R. 25 at 33, paras 13–14, ECJ; Case 124/81 *Commission v. United Kingdom* [1983] E.C.R. 203 at 233, para. 6, ECJ; Case 274/83 *Commission v. Italy* [1985] E.C.R. 1077 at 1090, para. 21, ECJ.

[2] Case 51/83 *Commission v. Italy* [1984] E.C.R. 2793 at 2804, para. 6, ECJ.

[3] *ibid.*, para. 7.

[4] Case C–473/93 *Commission v. Luxembourg* [1996] E.C.R. I–3207 at I–3254, para. 22, ECJ.

Commission's position before the letter before action where the Commission did not make any clear view known to it.[5]

2. Reasoned opinion

5–040 If the Member State fails to remedy the failure to fulfil obligations under Community law, the Commission may issue a reasoned opinion. That document describes the infringement of Community law in detail and enumerates the measures which the Member State should take within the prescribed period in order to bring it to an end. As in the case of the letter before action, delivery of a reasoned opinion is an essential procedural requirement for the purposes of the legality of the proceedings and the admissibility of any proceedings brought against the Member State in the Court of Justice.[6]

The issue of a reasoned opinion constitutes a preliminary procedure, which does not have any binding legal effect for the addressee. It is merely a pre-litigation stage of a procedure which may lead to an action before the Court. The purpose of that pre-litigation procedure provided for by Article 226 (*ex Article 169*) of the E.C. Treaty is to enable the Member State concerned to comply of its own accord with the requirements of the Treaty or, if appropriate, to justify its position. If that attempt at settlement is unsuccessful, the function of the reasoned opinion is to define the subject-matter of the dispute. However, the Commission is not empowered to determine conclusively, by reasoned opinions formulated pursuant to Article 226, the rights and duties of a Member State or to afford that state guarantees concerning the compatibility of a given line of conduct with the Treaty. According to the system embodied in Articles 226 to 228 (*ex Articles 169 to 171*) of the E.C. Treaty, the rights and duties of Member States may be determined and their conduct appraised only by a judgment of the Court. The reasoned opinion, therefore, has legal effect only in relation to the commencement of proceedings before the Court, so that where a Member State does not comply with that opinion within the period allowed, the Commission has the right, but not the duty, to commence proceedings before the Court.[7]

A decision to issue a reasoned opinion is subject to the principle of collegiate responsibility, since it is not a measure of administration or management and therefore may not be delegated. Here too, however, a less stringent approach to effective compliance with the principle of collegiate responsibility applies, having regard to the legal consequences attaching to reasoned opinions,[8] in that it is not necessary for the college itself formally

[5] Case 293/85 *Commission v. Belgium* [1988] E.C.R. 305 at 351–353, paras 10–20, ECJ.

[6] *Commentaire Mégret*, at 70. Case 325/82 *Commission v. Germany* [1984] E.C.R. 777 at 793, para. 8, ECJ; Case C–152/89 *Commission v. Luxembourg* [1991] E.C.R. I–3141 at I–3163, para. 9, ECJ.

[7] This summary is based on Case C–191/95 *Commission v. Germany*, [1998] E.C.R. I–5449 at I–5498, paras 44–46, ECJ, and the case law cited therein, ECJ.

[8] See para. 5–022, above.

to decide on the wording of the act which gives effect to the decision to issue a reasoned opinion and put it in final form. It is sufficient that the decision was the subject of collective deliberation by the college of Commissioners and that the information on which the decision was based was available to the members of the college.[9]

5–041 The opinion is sufficiently reasoned if it contains a coherent and detailed statement of the reasons which led the Commission to believe that the Member State in question has failed to fulfil an obligation under the Treaty.[10] As has already been mentioned,[11] the opinion may only relate to shortcomings of the Member State which were mentioned in the letter before action. But the complaints contained in the reasoned opinion may be set out in more detail and refined.[12] The Commission takes account in the reasoned opinion of the observations submitted by the Member State in response to the letter before action.[13] If, nevertheless, the reasoned opinion contains new complaints, the Court of Justice will have regard in the subsequent judicial proceedings only to those contained both in the letter before action and in the reasoned opinion, as the Member State was in a position to submit observations on those complaints in accordance with the first paragraph of Article 226 (*ex Article 169*) of the E.C. Treaty before the Commission delivered its reasoned opinion.[14]

5–042 The Commission also may—or possibly must[15]—set forth the measures which need to be taken in order to bring the infringement to an end. To this extent, the Member State's freedom to determine the manner in which it terminates the relevant infringement of Community law is restricted. The fact that the Court of Justice is confined to making a "finding" that there has been a failure to fulfil an obligation does not affect this power of the Commission. This is because the aim of Article 226 (*ex Article 169*) proceedings is to achieve the practical elimination of infringements.[16] Where the Commission indicates in its reasoned opinion the measures required to this end and the Member State does not act on it, the "finding"

---

[9] Case C–191/95 (cited in n. 7, above) at I–5496 and I–5499, paras 34–36 and 48.

[10] Case 7/61 *Commission v. Italy* [1961] E.C.R. 317 at 327, ECJ; *Commission v. Germany* (cited in n. 7, above), para. 8, ECJ; Case 74/82 *Commission v. Ireland* [1984] E.C.R. 317 at 340, para. 20, ECJ; Case C–279/94 *Commission v. Italy* [1997] E.C.R. I–4743 at I–4767, para. 19, ECJ.

[11] See para. 5–038, above.

[12] Case 274/83 *Commission v. Italy* [1985] E.C.R. 1077 at 1090, para. 21, ECJ.

[13] If the Commission takes no account in the reasoned opinion of the observations submitted by the Member State concerned in response to the letter before action, this may mean that the nature and scope of the dispute are not precisely defined at the time when the case is brought before the Court. If so, the Court will hold that the pre-litigation procedure was not properly conducted and declare the application manifestly inadmissible: (Order of July 11, 1995), Case C–266/94 *Commission v. Spain* [1995] E.C.R. I–1975 at I–1981—1983, paras 16–26, ECJ.

[14] Case 51/83 *Commission v. Italy* [1984] E.C.R. 2793 at 2804, paras 6–8, ECJ.

[15] Opinion of Advocate General M. Lagrange in Case 7/61 *Commission v. Italy* [1961] E.C.R. 317 at 334, who infers this duty from the E.C. Treaty, Art. 226 (*ex Art. 169*), para. 2, which reads "If the State concerned does not comply with the opinion . . .". On this view, the opinion should therefore set out the measures which the Commission considers that the Member State should take.

[16] Case 70/72 *Commission v. Germany* [1973] E.C.R. 813 at 828–829, paras 10–13, ECJ.

made by the Court of Justice refers both to the actual infringement of Community law and to the measures which could have been taken in order to bring the infringement to an end. As a result, the Member State then knows—from the reasoning of the Court's judgment finding the infringement—what measures indicated in the reasoned opinion are capable of bringing the failure to fulfil obligations to an end.

The Commission must prescribe in the reasoned opinion the time within **5–043** which the Member State must comply with it. The period must be reasonable having regard to the circumstances of the case.[17] The Court of Justice has no power to alter the period prescribed by the Commission.[18] An action for failure to fulfil obligations brought after the expiry of a period which was too short to enable the Member State to take the necessary measures or, as the case may be, to prepare its defence will be declared inadmissible.[19] However, the application may be declared admissible, if in the actual case the aims of the pre-litigation procedure were nevertheless achieved in spite of the unreasonably short period of time allowed to the Member State.[20]

B. The stage of the procedure held before the Court of Justice

1. Conditions of admissibility

(1) The requirement for the pre-litigation stage of the procedure to be properly conducted

The proper conduct of the pre-litigation stage of the procedure is, as noted **5–044** above, an essential guarantee required by the Treaty not only in order to protect the rights of the Member State concerned, but also so as to ensure that any contentious procedure will have a clearly defined dispute as its subject-matter. For those reasons, the Commission must take account in the reasoned opinion of the observations submitted by the Member State concerned in response to the letter before action, so that the Court may judge, when proceedings are brought, what specific obligations the Commission claims the Member State concerned has breached. If the Commission fails to satisfy this requirement, this may mean that the subject-matter of the dispute is not precisely defined. Such an irregularity in the conduct of the pre-litigation stage of the procedure may result in the application being declared manifestly inadmissible.[21]

---

[17] Case 74/82 *Commission v. Ireland* [1984] E.C.R. 317 at 338, paras 9–12, ECJ; Case 293/85 *Commission v. Belgium* [1988] E.C.R. 305 at 352, para, 14, ECJ; Case C–56/90 *Commission v. United Kingdom* [1993] E.C.R. I–4109 at I–4139, para. 18, ECJ. See also para. 5–039, above, in relation to the time prescribed for submitting observations on the letter before action.

[18] Case 28/81 *Commission v. Italy* [1981] E.C.R. 2577 at 2582, para. 6, ECJ; Case 29/81 *Commission v. Italy* [1981] E.C.R. 2585 at 2591, para. 6, ECJ.

[19] Case 293/85 *Commission v. Belgium* [1988] E.C.R. 305 at 353, para. 20, ECJ.

[20] For an example, see Case 74/82 *Commission v. Ireland* [1984] E.C.R. 317 at 338–339, para. 13, ECJ.

[21] (Order of July 11, 1995), Case C–266/94 *Commission v. Spain* [1995] E.C.R. I–1975, ECJ.

(2) The requirement for the reasoned opinion to accord with the application by which an action for failure to fulfil obligations is brought before the Court

5–045 Since the subject-matter of the proceedings is defined in the pre-litigation stage, the application by which the action for failure to fulfil obligations is brought before the Court of Justice must accord with the reasoned opinion.[22] This means that the alleged infringement of Community law must be defined in both the application and in the reasoned opinion in consistent, sufficiently precise terms, and that the application must be based on the same pleas and arguments as the reasoned opinion.[23] However, the statement of the subject-matter of the proceedings in the reasoned opinion does not invariably have to be exactly the same as the form of order sought in the application if the subject-matter of the proceedings has not been extended or altered but simply limited.[24] For example, the Commission cannot extend an action brought against a Member State, for failing to implement a directive in national law, to cover the infringement of failing in practice to comply with provisions of the directive where that complaint was not raised during the pre-litigation stage.[25] In contrast, a clarification by the Commission of the subject-matter of the proceedings in the application submitted to the Court of Justice is not ruled out.[26] A number of observations may be made in this connection.

5–046 Where an action for failure to fulfil obligations relates, not to a single act, but to a cluster of acts, each involving a separate infringement, the Member State must have been given an opportunity in the pre-litigation stage to set forth its defence to each breach of which it stands accused. If the letter before action referred only to certain isolated cases, the action cannot

---

[22] It goes without saying that the application must accord with the general requirements of the E.C. Statute, Art. 19 and the ECJ Rules of Procedure, Art. 38(1)(c) (see Case C–52/90 *Commission v. Denmark* [1992] E.C.R. I–2187 at I–2213—2214, para. 17, ECJ) (see paras 22–003—22–025, below).

[23] Case 193/80 *Commission v. Italy* [1981] E.C.R. 3019 at 3032, para. 12, ECJ; Case 211/81 *Commission v. Denmark* [1982] E.C.R. 4547 at 4558–4559, paras 14–15, ECJ; Case 186/85 *Commission v. Belgium* [1987] E.C.R. 2029 at 2051, para. 13, ECJ; Case 298/86 *Commission v. Belgium* [1988] E.C.R. 4343 at 4366, para. 10, ECJ; Case 76/86 *Commission v. Germany* [1989] E.C.R. 1021 at 1039, para. 8, ECJ; Case 290/87 *Commission v. Netherlands* [1989] E.C.R. 3083 at 3103, para. 8, ECJ; Case C–217/88 *Commission v. Germany* [1990] E.C.R. I–2879 at 2902, para. 10, ECJ; Case C–347/88 *Commission v. Greece* [1990] E.C.R. I–4747 at I–4784, para. 16, ECJ; Case C–61/90 *Commission v. Greece* [1992] E.C.R. I–2407 at I–2454, para. 29, ECJ; Case C–157/91 *Commission v. Netherlands* [1992] E.C.R. I–5899 at I–5914, para. 16, ECJ; Case 306/91 *Commission v. Italy* [1993] E.C.R. I–2133 at I–2158, para. 22, ECJ; Case C–243/89 *Commission v. Denmark* [1993] E.C.R. I–3353 at I–3389, para. 13, ECJ; Case C–296/92 *Commission v. Italy* [1994] E.C.R. I–1 at I–12, para. 11, ECJ.

[24] Case C–279/94 *Commission v. Italy* [1997] E.C.R. I–4743 at I–4768, para. 25, ECJ.

[25] Case C–237/90 *Commission v. Germany* [1992] E.C.R. I–5973 at I–6014—6015, paras 20–22, ECJ. Where the Commission has given a Member State formal notice of a failure to transpose a directive and the Member State adopts some implementing measures after the pre-litigation stage but not all those necessary in order to transpose the directive, the Commission may restrict the form of order sought in the application made to the Court to those provisions not yet implemented at that time: Case C–132/94 *Commission* v. *Ireland* [1995] E.C.R. I–4789 at I–4794—4795, paras 7–9, ECJ. But see Case C–274/93 *Commission v. Luxembourg* [1996] E.C.R. I–2019 at I–2040, paras 12, 13, ECJ.

[26] Case 205/84 *Commission v. Germany* [1986] E.C.R. 3755 at 3798–3799, paras 11–13, ECJ.

extend to the whole collection of acts categorised as infringements. In this event, the application will be admissible only to the extent to which the acts complained of in the application were also dealt with in the pre-litigation stage.[27]

If, in both the pre-litigation stage (the letter before action and the reasoned opinion) and in its application, the Commission complains of a specific shortcoming on the part of the Member State, the latter cannot claim that the application is irregular on the ground that the same shortcoming was due in the pre-litigation stage to a different national provision than the one to which it was attributable at the time when the action was brought. This is because the shortcoming with which the Member State is charged is not the existence of a specific provision incompatible with Community law, but the specific shortcoming arising as a result of such provision. As a result, a change in the national provision in the course of or after the pre-litigation procedure does not jeopardise the admissibility of the action for failure to fulfil obligations.[28] **5–047**

The requirement that the reasoned opinion and the application must accord with each other does not preclude infringements committed by the Member State after notification of the reasoned opinion from nevertheless being covered by the application, provided that the conduct at issue is of the same kind as that complained of in the opinion. Accordingly, the Court of Justice was entitled to take account of administrative practices which were applied after the reasoned opinion was given but were substantively the same as those referred to in the reasoned opinion.[29] Factual circumstances referred to in the reasoned opinion which continued after it was given may unquestionably be reviewed by the Court of Justice for the whole of their duration.[30] **5–048**

An infringement arising where a Member State takes measures in order to eliminate an infringement complained of by the Commission may be the subject of an action for failure to fulfil obligations only if a new pre-litigation stage is held. This is because the infringement resulting from the measures in question is not the same as the breach originally complained of. It is therefore impossible to bring a new action on the basis of the original pre-litigation procedure without infringing the requirement that the subject-matter of the reasoned opinion and the application must be the same.[31] **5–049**

If the Court declares an application inadmissible on the ground that the application does not square with the reasoned opinion, the Commission

[27] Case 309/84 *Commission v. Italy* [1986] E.C.R. 599 at 609, paras 15, 16, ECJ.

[28] Case 45/64 *Commission v. Italy* [1965] E.C.R. 857 at 864–865; ECJ; Case C–42/89 *Commission v. Belgium* [1990] E.C.R. I–2821 at I–2838, para. 11, ECJ; Case C–105/91 *Commission v. Greece* [1992] E.C.R. I–5871 at I–5895, para. 13, ECJ; Case C–11/95 *Commission v. Belgium* [1996] E.C.R. I–4115 at I–4177, para. 74, ECJ; Case C–375/95 *Commission v. Greece* [1997] E.C.R. I–5981 at I–6001, para. 38, ECJ.

[29] Case 42/82 *Commission v. France* [1983] E.C.R. 1013 at 1040, para. 20, ECJ; Case 113/86 *Commission v. Italy* [1988] E.C.R. 607 at 621, para. 11, ECJ.

[30] *Commission v. France* (cited in n. 29, above), para. 20.

[31] Case 7/69 *Commission v. Italy* [1970] E.C.R. 111 at 117, paras 4, 5, ECJ. For a further example, see Case 391/85 *Commission v. Belgium* [1988] E.C.R. 579.

may remedy the defects by submitting a new application based on the same complaints, pleas in law and arguments as the reasoned opinion. If it does this, it is not under a duty to start the pre-litigation stage afresh or to issue a supplementary reasoned opinion.[32]

(3) Existence of a failure to fulfil obligations

5–050 In principle, an action for failure to fulfil obligations is admissible only if the infringement complained of exists on the expiry of the period prescribed by the reasoned opinion. The action is to no purpose if the Member State has taken measures in time in order to eliminate the infringement at issue.[33]

5–051 If the Member State has not taken measures in time, the application will be admissible. Even if the Member State remedies the infringement after the prescribed period has expired but before the action is brought, the application will still be admissible. In the light of the potential liability on the part of the Member State, there remains an interest for the Community, other Member States and individuals in the Court making a finding that there has been an infringement. The finding may then serve as the basis for claims for damages.[34]

The Commission is always presumed to have an interest. Nevertheless, the Court of Justice will inquire into that interest in a case where the action was brought at a time when the infringement of Community law with which the Member State was charged had in fact come to an end (in the case cited the Court held that the Commission did have an interest in bringing the proceedings).[35] In another case, the Court of Justice declared the application inadmissible on the ground that all the legal effects of the national conduct at issue had been exhausted by the time when the reasoned opinion was given.[36]

5–052 The fact that the Member State acknowledges that it has failed to fulfil its obligations, and its resultant liability after the action has been brought,

---

[32] Case C–57/94 *Commission v. Italy* [1995] E.C.R. I–1249 at I–1268, para. 14, ECJ.

[33] *Cf.* the Opinion of Advocate General M. Lagrange in Case 7/61 *Commission v. Italy* [1961] E.C.R. 317 at 333, ECJ, who stated that the question whether the action is to no purpose goes to the substance and ought to be considered after the question of the admissibility of the application; Case 240/86 *Commission v. Greece* [1988] E.C.R. 1835 at 1856, para. 16, ECJ.

[34] Case 39/72 *Commission v. Italy* [1973] E.C.R. 101 at 112, para. 11, ECJ; Case 309/84 *Commission v. Italy* [1986] E.C.R. 599 at 609, para. 18, ECJ; Case 103/84 *Commission v. Italy* [1986] E.C.R. 1759 at 1771, para. 8, ECJ; Case 154/85 *Commission v. Italy* [1987] E.C.R. 2717 at 2737, para. 6, ECJ; Case 240/86 *Commission v. Greece* [1988] E.C.R. 1835 at 1855–1856, para. 14, ECJ; Case 283/86 *Commission v. Belgium* [1988] E.C.R. 3271 at 3278 at para. 6, ECJ; Case C–249/88 *Commission v. Belgium* [1991] E.C.R. I–1275 at I–1318, para. 41, ECJ; Case C–361/88 *Commission v. Germany* [1991] E.C.R. I–2567 at I–2605, para. 31, ECJ; Case C–59/89 *Commission v. Germany* [1991] E.C.R. I–2607 at I–2635, para. 35, ECJ; Case C–29/90 *Commission v. Greece* [1992] E.C.R. I–1971 at I–1986, para. 12; ECJ; Case C–280/89 *Commission v. Ireland* [1992] E.C.R. I–6185 at I–6205, para. 7, ECJ; Case C–317/92 *Commission v. Germany* [1994] E.C.R. I–2039 at I–2057, para. 3, ECJ; Case C–289/94 *Commission v. Italy* [1996] E.C.R. I–4405 at I–4424—4425, para. 20, ECJ. See also Goffin (cited in n. 62, above), at 215.

[35] Case 26/69 *Commission v. France* [1970] E.C.R. 565, at 575–576, para 9–13, ECJ.

[36] Case C–362/90 *Commission v. Italy* [1992] E.C.R. I–2353 at I–2373, paras 11–13, ECJ.

does not mean that the application is to no purpose. Otherwise, the Member State would be at liberty, at any time during the proceedings, to have them brought to an end without any judicial determination of the breach of obligations and of the basis of its liability and the exclusive jurisdiction of the Court of Justice to make a determination—after an action has been brought—as to whether or not Community law has been infringed would be impaired.[37]

(4) Time-limits

In exercising its powers in connection with an action for failure to fulfil obligations, the Commission does not have to comply with any time-limits. It is free to judge at what time it starts the pre-litigation stage and at what time after the expiry of the period prescribed by the reasoned opinion it brings an action before the Court of Justice.[38] Yet the Commission may not abuse its discretion. For instance, if the pre-litigation procedure is excessively long, the Member State may find it more difficult to refute the Commission's arguments and this may constitute an infringement of the rights of the defence. The Member State has to prove that the unusual length of the pre-litigation procedure had adverse effects on the way in which it conducted its defence.[39] Only if it succeeds in proving this, will the application be declared inadmissible. However, the burden of proof is difficult for the Member State to discharge, since there will generally be factors justifying the unusually long lapse of time between the "infringement" and the commencement of the procedure, or the unusual duration of the pre-litigation stage, and causing them not to be regarded as excessive.[40] **5–053**

2. Aspects of the treatment given to the substantive claim

(1) Burden of proof

The burden of proof has to be discharged by the Commission.[41] It has to adduce evidence to the Court of Justice that the infringement existed at the time when the period prescribed by the reasoned opinion expired.[42] The **5–054**

---

37 Case C–243/89 *Commission v. Denmark* [1993] E.C.R. I–3353 at I–3393, para. 30, ECJ.

38 Case 7/68 *Commission v. Italy* [1968] E.C.R. 423 at 428, ECJ; Case 7/71 *Commission v. France* [1971] E.C.R. 1003 at 1016, paras 2–8, ECJ; Case 324/82 *Commission v. Belgium* [1984] E.C.R. 1861 at 1878, para. 12, ECJ; Case C–56/90 *Commission v. United Kingdom* [1993] E.C.R. I–4109 at I–4138, para. 15, ECJ; Case C–317/92 *Commission v. Germany* [1994] E.C.R. I–2039 at I–2057, paras 4–5, ECJ.

39 Case C–96/89 *Commission v. Netherlands* [1991] E.C.R. I–2461 at I–2491—2492, paras 14–16, ECJ.

40 In Case 7/71 *Commission v. France* [1971] E.C.R. 1003, the Commission applied to the Court of Justice in 1971 to find an infringement which had existed since 1965. The infringement did not come to light until 1968 and the Commission formally started the procedure in April 1970 following informal contacts with the Member State. In Case 324/82 *Commission v. Belgium* [1984] E.C.R. 1861, the Commission waited until the directive concerned had been implemented in all the Member States before investigating the contested Belgian measures. In Case C–96/89 *Commission v. Netherlands* [1991] E.C.R. I–2461, the Commission waited for the Court of Justice to give judgment in another case and for the reaction of the Netherlands government.

41 Case 96/81 *Commission v. Netherlands* [1982] E.C.R. 1791 at 1803, para. 6, ECJ; Case C–

Commission may not rely on any presumptions (of law) in this connection.[43] It is settled case law that the scope of national laws, regulations or administrative provisions must be assessed in the light of the interpretation given to them by national courts. This means that if the Commission bases its application on the existence of a national provision which is in breach of Community law, it must prove that there are national judicial decisions which interpret the domestic provision at issue inconsistently with Community law.[44] Consequently, an application from the Commission for an expert's report to be commissioned by the Court will be refused, since if it were granted the Commission itself would not be providing evidence of the alleged failure to fulfil obligations.[45]

It is only when the Commission has produced sufficient evidence of the failure to fulfil obligations that the defendant Member State has to adduce its counter-arguments.[46]

5–055 Article 10 (*ex Article 5*) of the E.C. Treaty requires the Member States to facilitate the achievement of the Commission's tasks. As a result, they are under an obligation to provide the Commission with information about the way in which they apply Community law.[47] Many directives incorporate that duty to provide information in a specific provision. Such a provision will require Member States to provide clear, accurate information about the legal and administrative provisions adopted in order to implement the directive in question, which enables the Commission to ascertain whether the Member State has effectively and completely implemented it.[48]

249/88 *Commission v. Belgium* [1991] E.C.R. I–1275 at I–1310, para. 6, ECJ; Case C–210/91 *Commission v. Greece* [1992] E.C.R. I–6735 at I–6754 para. 22, ECJ; Case C–375/90 *Commission v. Greece* [1993] E.C.R. I–2055 at I–2091, para. 33. See also Louis, "Le rôle de la Commission dans la procédure en manquement selon la jurisprudence récente de la Cour de justice", in *Du droit international au droit de l'intégration. Liber amicorum Pierre Pescatore*, Baden-Baden , Nomos, 1987, 387 at 397–405.

[42] Case 121/84 *Commission v. Italy* [1986] E.C.R. 107 at 114, paras 10–12, ECJ; Case 188/84 *Commission v. France* [1986] E.C.R. 419 at 440, paras 38–39, ECJ; Case 298/86 *Commission v. Belgium* [1988] E.C.R. 4343 at 4367, para. 15, ECJ; Case C–157/91 *Commission v. Netherlands* [1992] E.C.R. I–5899 at I–5913, para. 12, ECJ.

[43] Case 290/87 *Commission v. Netherlands* [1989] E.C.R. 3083 at 3104, para. 11, ECJ; Case C–61/94 *Commission v. Germany* [1996] E.C.R. I–3989 at I–4023, para. 61, ECJ.

[44] Case C–382/92 *Commission v. United Kingdom* [1994] E.C.R. I–2435 at I–2471, para. 36, ECJ; Case C–300/95 *Commission v. United Kingdom* [1997] E.C.R. I–2649 at I–2672, para. 37, ECJ.

[45] Case 141/87 *Commission v. Italy* [1989] E.C.R. 943 at 979, para. 17, ECJ.

[46] Case 272/86 *Commission v. Greece* [1988] E.C.R. 4875 at 4901, para. 21, ECJ.

[47] Case 96/81 *Commission v. Netherlands* [1982] E.C.R. 1791 at 1803, paras 7–8, ECJ; Case 97/81 *Commission v. Netherlands* [1982] E.C.R. 1819 at 1832, paras 7–8, ECJ; Case 192/84 *Commission v. Greece* [1985] E.C.R. 3967 at 3979, para. 19, ECJ; Case 240/86 *Commission v. Greece* [1988] E.C.R. 1835 at 1857–1858, paras 23–28, ECJ; Case 272/86 *Commission v. Greece* [1988] E.C.R. 4875 at 4903, para. 30, ECJ; Case C–33/90 *Commission v. Italy* [1991] E.C.R. I–5987 at I–6006, para. 18, ECJ; Case C–65/91 *Commission v. Greece* [1992] E.C.R. I–5245 at I–5266, para. 14, ECJ.

[48] See, *e.g.* Case 274/83 *Commission v. Italy* [1985] E.C.R. 1077 at 1095, para. 42, ECJ.

(2) Substantive defence of the Member State

The chance of success of defence pleas which a Member State wishes to raise is determined first by the objective nature of actions for failure to fulfil obligations.[49] The Court of Justice pays no regard to the underlying reasons for the breach or to circumstances which in fact limited its adverse effects or explain the breach. It is virtually certain that a defence based on such pleas will fail. Accordingly, a Member State may not plead provisions, practices or circumstances existing in its internal legal system in order to justify a failure to comply with Community obligations.[50] Neither does the fact that a directive with direct effect produces the same result in practice, as if the directive had been implemented properly and in time, justify a failure to fulfil the obligation to implement it.[51] **5–056**

Secondly, the special nature of Community law prevents a Member State from relying on a number of common defences in international law. For instance, a Member State cannot justify its failure to perform its obligations by reference to the shortcomings of other Member States, since the Treaty did not merely create reciprocal obligations between the Member States, but also established a new legal order governing the procedures necessary for the purposes of having any infringement of Community law "declared and punished".[52] **5–057**

Lastly, a Member State is not entitled to raise the claim that a directive or a decision addressed to it is unlawful where it is accused of breaching such a measure and the time-limit for applying for its annulment has expired. The Court of Justice takes the view that to allow this defence would jeopardise the stability of the system of legal remedies established by the Treaty and the principle of legal certainty on which it is based.[53] **5–058**

In the exceptional case where the directive or decision infringed contained such serious and manifest defects that it could be deemed non-

---

[49] See para. 5–001, above.

[50] Case 52/75 *Commission v. Italy* [1976] E.C.R. 277 at 285, para. 14, ECJ.

[51] Case 102/79 *Commission v. Belgium* [1980] E.C.R. 1473 at 1487, para. 12, ECJ; Case 301/81 *Commission v. Belgium* [1983] E.C.R. 467 at 478–479, para. 13, ECJ; Case C–433/93 *Commission v. Germany* [1995] E.C.R. I–2303 at I–2318—2319, para. 24, ECJ; Case C–253/95 *Commission v. Germany* [1996] E.C.R. I–2423 at I–2430, para. 13, ECJ.

[52] Case 52/75 *Commission v. Italy* [1976] E.C.R. 277 at 284, para. 11, ECJ; Case C–11/95 *Commission v. Belgium* [1996] E.C.R. I–4115 at I–4165—4166, paras 36–37, ECJ.

[53] Case 156/77 *Commission v. Belgium* [1978] E.C.R. 1881 at 1896–1898, paras 15–25, ECJ; Case 52/83 *Commission v. France* [1983] E.C.R. 3707 at 3715–3716, para. 10, ECJ; Case 52/84 *Commission v. Belgium* [1986] E.C.R. 89 at 104, para. 13, ECJ; Case 226/87 *Commission v. Greece* [1988] E.C.R. 3611 at 3623–3624, para. 14, ECJ; Case C–74/91 *Commission v. Germany* [1992] E.C.R. I–5437 at I–5466, para. 10, ECJ; (concerning a directive); Case C–183/91 *Commission v. Greece* [1993] E.C.R. I–3131 at I–3149, para. 10, ECJ. There is some doubt whether the illegality of a regulation or similar act may be raised as a defence in an action for failure to fulfil obligations. The doubt arises because of the wording of the E.C. Treaty, Art. 241 (*ex Art. 184*), which allows an objection of illegality to be raised in "proceedings in which a regulation . . . is at issue". Thus the defence forms an express part of the system of legal remedies laid down in the Treaty and does not jeopardise the stability of that system, *cf.* Schermers and Waelbroeck, *Judicial Protection*, at 531, who argue that the defence may be raised; see also Goffin (cited in n. 62, above), at 217. The Court of Justice has not had to consider this question: see para. 9–002, below.

existent, the Court of Justice may be asked to declare it non-existent, thereby making the claim of an infringement to no purpose.[54]

5–059 The Member State's defence is not restricted to a limited number of pleas. Any plea, of law or fact, which refutes the alleged breach in an objective manner, is admissible.

5–060 Thus, a Member State may claim that it was "absolutely impossible" for it to have adopted measures capable of eliminating the infringement or, in proceedings based on Article 88 (*ex Article 93*) (2) of the E.C. Treaty, to implement the decision properly.[55] In such case it would have to prove the existence of such a situation of *force majeure*.[56] In compliance with the duty of cooperation imposed by Article 10 (*ex Article 5*) of the E.C. Treaty, the Member State should have informed the Commission of the difficulties arising in applying the Community provision, with a view to their seeking a solution together. If the Member State did not do so, its defence would fail because it would in any event be in breach of that obligation to co-operate.[57]

IV. Consequences

A. Result of the action

5–061 The Court of Justice either finds the infringement made out or dismisses the application.[58] The judgment finding the failure to fulfil obligations is purely declaratory. The infringement existed before the Court made its finding. It does not have the power to require specific measures to be taken in order to give effect to the judgment. At the most, it may indicate such measures as it considers necessary in order to eliminate the infringement found.[59] In addition, the Court may not set a period of time for compliance with its judgment, since Article 228 (*ex Article 171*) of the E.C. Treaty does not confer power on it to do so.[60] Equally, the Court may not declare acts

---

[54] Case 226/87 *Commission v. Greece*, (cited in n. 53 above) at 3624, paras 15–16. The beginnings of this case law can be found in Joined Cases 6 and 11/69 *Commission v. France* [1969] E.C.R. 523 at 539, paras 11–13, ECJ.

[55] See para. 5–015, above.

[56] Case 52/84 *Commission v. Belgium* [1986] E.C.R. 89 at 104, para. 14, ECJ; Case 213/85 *Commission v. Netherlands* [1988] E.C.R. 281 at 300–301, paras 22–25, ECJ.

[57] Case 52/84 *Commission v. Belgium*, (cited in n. 56, above), at 105, para. 16. See also Case C–349/93 *Commission v. Italy* [1995] E.C.R. I–343 at I–357, para. 13, ECJ; Case C–348/93 *Commission v. Italy* [1995] E.C.R. I–673 at I–694, para. 17, ECJ.

[58] If the Court does not have sufficient information to find that the act of the Member State constitutes a failure to fulfil obligations, it may ask the parties to resume examination of the question at issue and report to it, after which the Court will give final judgment (see Case 170/78 *Commission v. United Kingdom* [1980] E.C.R. 417 at 438, para. 24, ECJ).

[59] In the reasoned opinion, the Commission may prescribe the measures which it deems necessary in order to eliminate the infringement. In addition, in a procedure under the E.C. Treaty, Art. 88 (*ex Art. 93*) (2), the Commission may adopt a decision finding that a measure constitutes aid incompatible with the common market and requiring the unlawfully granted aid to be repaid. If the Member State concerned fails to comply with that decision, the Commission may bring an action in the Court for failure to fulfil the specific obligation to obtain repayment of the aid (Case 70/72 *Commission v. Germany* [1973] E.C.R. 813 at 829, para. 13, ECJ). See para. 5–016, above.

[60] Case C–473/93 *Commission v. Luxembourg* [1996] E.C.R. I–3207 at I–3262, para. 52, ECJ.

(or failures to act) on the part of a Member State unlawful, void or not applicable. Only the national courts have the power to do so under national law.[61] The Court of Justice may find only that the act (or failure to act) was or was not contrary to Community law.

B. Legal force of the judgment declaring that a Member State has failed to fulfil its obligations

Article 228 (*ex Article 171*) (1) of the E.C. Treaty puts the Member State which has been found by the Court of Justice to have failed to fulfil its Treaty obligations under a duty to take the necessary measures to comply with the Court's judgment. That duty, which also arises because the judgment has the force of *res judicata*, entails a prohibition having the full force of law against applying a national rule held to be incompatible with Community law and an obligation to take every measure to enable Community law to be fully applied.[62] The duty to give effect to the Court's judgment is borne by all institutions of the Member State concerned within the fields covered by their respective powers. The legislative and executive authorities have to bring the offending provisions of domestic law into conformity with the requirements of Community law. The courts of the Member State concerned have to disregard those provisions in determining cases.[63] **5–062**

The judgment finding the infringement of Community law does not as such confer any rights on individuals. Individuals may not rely directly on such a judgment before the national courts, but only on the "provision" of Community law having direct effect which the judgment finds has been infringed by the Member State.[64] **5–063**

In the event that an individual pleads a provision of Community law in his defence which does not have direct effect, but which has been found by the Court of Justice to have been infringed by the Member State concerned, the national court, as an institution of that Member State, must ensure in the exercise of its functions that it is complied with by applying national law in such a way that it is compatible with the obligations that—according to the judgment of the Court—ensue from Community law for that Member State.

The finding of a failure to fulfil obligations may potentially form the basis for liability on the part of the Member State concerned.[65] However, it appears from the case law that a Member State may incur liability only in **5–064**

---

[61] Opinion of Advocate General G. Reischl in Case 141/78 *France v. United Kingdom* [1979] E.C.R. 2923 at 2946.

[62] Case 48/71 *Commission v. Italy* [1972] E.C.R. 527 at 532, para. 7, ECJ; (Order of March 28, 1980), Joined Cases 24 and 97/80R *Commission v. France* [1980] E.C.R. 1319 at 1333. para. 16, ECJ; Case C–101/91 *Commission v. Italy* [1993] E.C.R. I–191 at I–206, para. 24, ECJ.

[63] Joined Cases 314–316/81 and 83/82 *Waterkeyn* [1982] E.C.R. 4337 at 4360–4361, para. 14, ECJ.

[64] *ibid.*, at 4361, paras 15–16.

[65] Case 39/72 *Commission v. Italy* [1973] E.C.R. 102 at 112, para. 11, ECJ; Case 309/84 *Commission v. Italy* [1986] E.C.R. 599 at 609. para. 18, ECJ; Case 240/86 *Commission v. Greece* [1988] E.C.R. 1835 at 1855–1856, para. 14, ECJ; Case C–287/87 *Commission v. Greece* [1990] E.C.R. I–125, ECJ; Case C–249/88 *Commission v. Belgium* [1991] E.C.R. I–1275 at I–1318, para. 41, ECJ.

the case of a sufficiently serious breach of Community law.[66] A judgment finding a failure to fulfil obligations is in itself not enough, certainly not for loss or damage which arose before judgment was given. The requirement for a "sufficiently serious breach" of Community law does not square completely with the strict or objective nature of an action for failure to fulfil obligations,[67] since the Court of Justice also takes other factors into account where the Member State had a discretion in applying Community law, such as whether or not the breach was intentional and whether any mistake of law was excusable. It is self-evident that if the failure to fulfil obligations continues after delivery of the judgment declaring the Member State concerned to be in breach of its obligations, that itself will constitute a sufficiently serious breach of Community law and cause the Member State to incur liability to make good any loss or damage which occurred in that period.[68]

In addition, it must be noted that the Community provision infringed must confer a "right" on individuals in order for the issue of state liability to arise.[69] It follows that a finding of an infringement in proceedings under Articles 226–227 (*ex Articles 169–170*) of the E.C. Treaty does not automatically result in the Member State concerned incurring liability under Community law. Yet it may well be that the Member State will incur liability in damages under national law for loss or damage caused by an infringement of a Community provision even though that provision does not directly confer any "right" on individuals.

5–065 The Treaty itself does not specify the period within which the judgment must be complied with, but the Court of Justice has held that the process must be initiated at once and completed as soon as possible.[70]

5–066 Because the judgment has the force of *res judicata*, the Commission may not make an application for interim measures pursuant to Article 243 (*ex Article 186*) of the E.C. Treaty in order to require the Member State to desist from an infringement of Community law which has already been found by judgment of the Court of Justice. This is because the Member State is required to take the necessary measures under Article 228 (*ex*

[66] Joined Cases C–46 and C–48/93 *Brasserie du Pêcheur and Factortame* (*Factortame IV*) [1996] E.C.R. I–1029 at I–1159, para. 93, ECJ.

[67] Moreover, there is no need for the Court of Justice to have made a finding that the Member State is in breach in order for the Member State to incur liability. The national courts may themselves find that the Member State has infringed Community law. If difficulties arise in this connection, they may always enlist the help of the Court of Justice by making a reference for a preliminary ruling. This power of the national courts is important. Since the Commission has a discretion whether to bring proceedings under the E.C. Treaty, Art. 226 (*ex Art. 169*), individuals may play a major, complementary role in enforcing Community law by invoking *Francovich* liability in national courts (*cf.* Case C–91/92 *Faccini Dori* [1994] E.C.R. I–3325 at I–3357–3358, paras 27–29, ECJ).

[68] See para. 3–023, above.

[69] Schockweiler, "La responsabilité de l'autorité nationale en cas de violation du droit communautaire" (1992) R.T.D.E. 27 at 48.

[70] Case 69/86 *Commission v. Italy* [1987] E.C.R. 773 at 780, para. 8, ECJ; Case 169/87 *Commission v. France* [1988] 4093 at 4118, para. 14, ECJ; Case C–345/92 *Commission v. Germany* [1993] E.C.R. I–1115 at I–1122, para. 6, ECJ; Case C–334/94 *Commission v. France* [1996] E.C.R. I–1307 at I–1343, para. 31, ECJ.

Article 171) (1) of the E.C. Treaty. No further decision of the Court, in interlocutory or other proceedings, is required. Where the Commission sought such interim measures, the Court held that they were not necessary within the meaning of Article 243 of the E.C. Treaty.[71]

C. Sanctions for failure to comply with the judgment

The Commission is responsible for ensuring that the judgment finding a breach of Community law is complied with. If the Member State fails to take the necessary measures, under Article 228 (*ex Article 171*) (2) of the E.C. Treaty the Commission must first give it written notice, giving it an opportunity to submit any observations. It then issues a reasoned opinion "specifying the points on which the Member State concerned has not complied with the judgment of the Court of Justice". If the Member State then fails to take the necessary measures within the time-limit laid down by the Commission, it may be brought before the Court of Justice again with a view to a finding that it has failed to comply with the original judgment (or to give effect to it in time or correctly). In bringing the case before the Court, the Commission may specify such lump sum or penalty payment to be paid by the Member State as it considers appropriate in the circumstances.[72] The Court may then impose a lump sum or penalty payment pursuant to the third subparagraph of Article 228(2) of the E.C. Treaty in the event that it finds that the original judgment has not been complied with. In such proceedings, the Court of Justice has jurisdiction to assess the suitability and effectiveness of any measures which the Member State has taken in compliance with the original judgment. As that judgment has the force of *res judicata*, the dispute as to the original failure to fulfil obligations may not be reopened in proceedings under Article 228(2) of the E.C. Treaty. The only matter in issue is the alleged failure to give effect to the original judgment. **5–067**

Failure to comply with a judgment constitutes an infringement of Article 228 of the E.C. Treaty and may therefore give rise in its turn to a finding of liability on the part of the Member State concerned. **5–068**

---

[71] (Order of March 28, 1980), Joined Cases 24 and 97/80R *Commission v. France* [1980] E.C.R. 1319 at 1333 para. 19, ECJ.

[72] In the "Communication from the Commission—Memorandum on applying Article 171 *[now Article 228]* of the EC Treaty" (96/C 242/07: [1996] O.J. C242/6), the Commission expresses a preference for penalty payments on the ground that this is the most appropriate instrument for securing compliance with the judgment as rapidly as possible. The amount of the payment should be calculated in the light of the seriousness of the infringement, its duration and the need to ensure that the penalty itself is a deterrent to future infringements.

CHAPTER 6

INTERPRETATION OF COMMUNITY LAW BY WAY OF PRELIMINARY RULING

The request for a preliminary ruling[1] on the interpretation of Community law raises three specific questions. The first relates to the *subject-matter* of the preliminary ruling on interpretation, in other words, to what provisions and principles may be interpreted by the Court of Justice. The second relates to the *content* of the preliminary ruling on interpretation and the related limits set to the jurisdiction of the Court of Justice. Thirdly, there is the question of the *consequences* of a preliminary ruling. **6–001**

These three questions will be considered in turn.

I. SUBJECT-MATTER OF AN INTERPRETATION BY WAY OF PRELIMINARY RULING

According to Article 234 (*ex Article 177*) of the E.C. Treaty, the jurisdiction of the Court of Justice to give preliminary rulings on interpretation extends to "this Treaty" and "acts of the institutions of the Community and of the ECB [European Central Bank]". The wording of Article 150 of the EAEC Treaty is similar, unlike Article 41 of the ECSC Treaty, which does provide for a preliminary rulings procedure, but only on the "validity of acts of the High Authority [Commission] and of the Council". As we have seen, the Court of Justice has given Article 41 of the ECSC Treaty the same scope as Article 234 of the E.C. Treaty and Article 150[2] of the EAEC Treaty.[3] As a result, henceforward the Court of Justice may give preliminary rulings pursuant to Article 41 of the ECSC Treaty also on the interpretation of that Treaty and on acts adopted by Community institutions pursuant thereto. **6–002**

The upshot is that, as far as the subject-matter of a reference for a preliminary ruling is concerned, the Court has parallel jurisdiction to give preliminary rulings on interpretation under each of the three Treaties. This covers the Treaties themselves, acts of the Community institutions, including international agreements concluded by the Community and acts of

[1] For the mechanism of cooperation between national courts and the Court of Justice and the general requirements which requests for preliminary rulings have to satisfy, see Chap. 2, above.

[2] See para. 2–003, above.

[3] Case C–221/88 *Busseni* [1990] E.C.R. I–495 at I–522—524, paras 8–17, ECJ.

bodies set up by such agreements, and provisions of Community law to which national law refers.

A. The Treaties

6–003 The Treaties establishing the European Communities (E.C., ECSC and EAEC Treaties) constitute the "basic constitutional charter".[4] They are the written constitution surmounting the hierarchy of Community norms and consequently are the first instruments whose interpretation may form the subject-matter of preliminary rulings by the Court of Justice.

6–004 What is meant is the Treaties establishing the Communities and all amendments thereto, the treaties and acts relating to the accession of new Member States, complementary "treaties", such as the former (1957) "Convention on Certain Institutions Common to the European Communities"[5] and the former (1965) "Treaty Establishing a Single Council and a Single Commission of the European Communities" (the "Merger Treaty"; see Article 30 thereof),[6] and all the annexes and protocols annexed to the Treaty, which have the same legal force as the treaties themselves.[7]

Not all of the Single European Act (1986) and the Treaty on European Union (1992) relate to the European Communities. Consequently, only those parts of them relating to Community law fall within the Court's jurisdiction to give preliminary rulings on interpretation under Article 234 (*ex Article 177*) of the E.C. Treaty (see the final provisions of the E.U. Treaty (Articles 46 to 53 (*ex Articles L to S*))).[8]

6–005 Treaty status also has to be given to such provisions, adopted by the Council by means of a special procedure, as it "shall recommend to the

---

[4] Case 294/93 *Les Verts v. European Parliament* [1986] E.C.R. 1339 at 1365, para. 23, ECJ.

[5] Convention on Certain Institutions Common to the European Communities, in *European Union/Selected instruments taken from the Treaties*, Book I, Volume I, Luxembourg, Office for Official Publications of the European Communities, 1995, pp. 683–696.

[6] *ibid.*, pp. 697–737. This Treaty and the Convention cited in the preceding note have been repealed by the Treaty of Amsterdam, Art. 9(1) ([1997] O.J. C340/76). Most of their provisions had been incorporated in the Community Treaties. As for the remainder, Art. 9(2) to (7) of the Amsterdam Treaty set out to retain their essential elements (*ibid.*).

[7] ECSC Treaty, Art. 84, paras 8–17, E.C. Treaty, Art. 311 (*ex Art. 239*); EAEC Treaty, Art. 207. The principal protocols are those on the Statute of the European Investment Bank, on the Statute of the Court of Justice, and on the privileges and immunities of the European Communities, together with the 16 protocols appended to the E.C. Treaty by the E.U. Treaty (a 17th protocol is appended to the E.U. Treaty itself and to the treaties establishing the European Communities). For the text of the protocols, see *European Union/Selected instruments taken from the Treaties*, Book I, Volume I (Luxembourg, Office for Official Publications of the European Communities, 1995). See also the further protocols annexed by the Treaty of Amsterdam to the E.C. Treaty ([1997] O.J. C340/103–110), to the E.U. Treaty and the E.C. Treaty (*ibid.*, pp. 93–102) and to the E.U. Treaty and the three Community Treaties (*ibid.*, pp. 111–114). For a practical example, see Case C–147/95 *Evrenopoulos* [1997] E.C.R. I–2057, ECJ, in which the Court of Justice gave a ruling on the interpretation of the Protocol of the E.C. Treaty, Art. 119 (*now Art. 141*). At the same time, a whole series of declarations of intergovernmental conferences relating to various provisions of the treaties accompany the treaties (especially the Single European Act, the E.U. Treaty and the Treaty of Amsterdam). Although those declarations do not have the status of legislation (and hence certainly not the status of the Treaties), their content may be taken into account in interpreting the provisions to which they relate (for the text of the declarations, see the references cited above).

[8] See para. 4–001, above.

Member States for adoption in accordance with their respective constitutional requirements".[9] The provisions decided upon by the Council do not enter into force until they have been adopted by all Member States (by act of parliament or after a referendum, depending on the "constitutional requirements" of each Member State). Once they have been so adopted, they obtain treaty status in the hierarchy of norms of Community law.[10]

6–006 The unwritten general principles of Community law, including fundamental rights, may also be the subject of a reference for a preliminary ruling on interpretation. Those principles form part of the "law" which the Court of Justice has to ensure is observed in the interpretation and application of the Treaties (ECSC Treaty, Article 31; E.C. Treaty, Article 220 (*ex Article 164*); EAEC Treaty, Article 136). Examples are the principles of equal treatment, proportionality and *nec bis in idem* and the rights of the defence prior to the adoption of an individual decision having adverse effect.[11] Naturally, a preliminary ruling on the interpretation of those principles may be sought only in connection with the application of substantive Community law, that is to say, in connection with main proceedings relating (at least to some extent) to Community law.[12]

B. Acts of Community institutions

6–007 All acts of Community institutions may be the subject of a request for a preliminary ruling on their interpretation, irrespective of whether the act is specifically mentioned in the treaties[13] or not,[14] whether it is binding or non-binding[15] or whether or not it has direct effect.[16]

---

[9] See, *inter alia*, E.C. Treaty, Art. 22 (*ex Art. 8e*) (adding to rights arising out of citizenship of the Union); Art. 190 (*ex Art. 138*) (4) (determining a uniform procedure for elections to the European Parliament; see the Act Concerning the Election of the Representatives of the Assembly by Direct Universal Suffrage, annexed to the Council Decision of September 20, 1976, [1976], O.J. L278/5, as amended by Council Decision of February 1, 1993, [1993] O.J. L33/15) and Art. 269 (*ex Art. 201*) (determining the system of the Community's own resources).

[10] See Isaac, *Droit communautaire général*, Paris, Masson, 1990, p. 281; *cf.* Joliet, *Le contentieux*, pp. 190–191.

[11] The "interpretation" of the principle concerned is concealed behind the appraisal of the "validity" of an inferior provision of Community law. See Joined Cases 41, 121 and 796/79 *Testa v. Bundesanstalt für Arbeit* [1980] E.C.R. 1979 at 1997–1998, para. 21, ECJ; Case 265/87 *Schräder v. Hauptzollamt Gronau* [1989] E.C.R. 2237 at 2269–2270, paras 20–24, ECJ; Case C–331/88 *Fedesa and Others* [1990] E.C.R. I–4023 at I–4062—4063, paras 12–14, ECJ.

[12] Case C–144/95 *Maurin* [1996] E.C.R. I–2909 at I–2919, paras 12–13, ECJ; Case C–299/95 *Kremzow v. Austria* [1997] E.C.R. I–2629 at I–2645—2646, paras 15–19, ECJ. For further particulars, see Lenaerts and Van Nuffel, *Constitutional Law of the European Union*, paras 14–046—14–066.

[13] In ECSC Treaty, Art. 14, E.C. Treaty, Art. 249 (*ex Art. 189*) or EAEC Treaty, Art. 161 or elsewhere, such as the Rules of Procedure of the institutions (E.C. Treaty, Arts. 199, 207(3) and 218(2) (*ex Arts 142, 151(3) and 162(2)*)), the Financial Regulation (E.C. Treaty, Art. 279 (*ex Art. 209*)), the measures provided for in the E.C. Treaty, Art. 202 (*ex Art. 145*), indent 3, ("Comitology" Decision of July 13, 1987, ([1987] O.J. L187/33) or Art. 225 (*ex Art. 168a*) (concerning the Court of First Instance), although it would seem virtually impossible in the last mentioned case for any question of interpretation to have any relevance to a decision in main proceedings.

[14] *e.g.* a Council resolution: Case 9/73 *Schlüter v. Hauptzollamt Lörrach* [1973] E.C.R. 1135 at

6–008 The sole criterion is whether the act may be ascribed to a Community institution. The Court of Justice has held that no such act was involved in the case of an agreement concluded between national central insurance bureaux relating to the Green Card Scheme pursuant to Council Directive 72/166 on insurance against civil liability in respect of the use of motor vehicles. The agreement could not be considered an act of a Community institution on the ground that "no Community institution or agency took part in its conclusion", even though the conclusion of the agreement was a precondition for the entry into force of the directive and the length of time for which the directive was applicable was determined by the agreement's duration. It made no difference that the Commission had consistently stated, in a recommendation and in successive decisions, that the agreement complied with the directive's requirements or that it was annexed to a Commission decision and published with it in the *Official Journal of the European Communities*. This did not mean that the agreement itself was the work of a Community institution.[17]

6–009 The test that a Community institution or body must have "taken part" in the conclusion of the act in order for it to be amenable to interpretation by the Court of Justice in Article 234 (*ex Article 177*) proceedings is, in all likelihood, open to flexible application. There are many ways in which a Community institution or body might conceivably "take part" in the conclusion of an act. Thus, the test is satisfied in the case of international agreements concluded by the Community and of (binding and non-binding)

1161, para. 40, ECJ.

[15] *e.g.* a recommendation (or opinion) within the meaning of the E.C. Treaty, Art. 249 (*ex Art. 189*): Case 113/75 *Frecassetti v. Amministrazione delle Finanze dello Stato* [1976] E.C.R. 983 at 993, paras 8–9, ECJ; Case C–322/88 *Grimaldi v. Fonds des Maladies Professionnelles* [1989] E.C.R. 4407 at 4418–4419, paras 7–9, ECJ. As a result of the principle of co-operation in good faith, national courts are bound to take recommendations into consideration in order to decide disputes referred to them, in particular where they cast light on the interpretation of national measures adopted in order to implement them or where they are designed to supplement binding Community provisions.

[16] *e.g.* Case 32/74 *Haaga* [1974] E.C.R. 1201 at 1205, para. 1, ECJ; Case 111/75 *Mazzalai v. Ferrovia del Renon* [1976] E.C.R. 657 at 665, para. 7/9, ECJ; Case 14/83 *Von Colson and Kamann v. Land Nordrhein-Westfalen* [1984] E.C.R. 1891 at 1909, para. 27, ECJ; Case C–261/95 *Palmisani* [1997] E.C.R. I–4025 at I–4045, para. 21, ECJ; Case C–373/95 *Maso and Others* [1997] E.C.R. I–4051 at I–4072, para. 28, ECJ. Irrespective of whether the Community measure has direct effect, its interpretation will be useful to the national court, which, as a public body, is required under the E.C. Treaty, Art. 10 (*ex Art. 5*) to apply its domestic legislation in conformity with the requirements of Community law (see also Case 31/87 *Beentjes v. Netherlands State* [1988] E.C.R. 4635 at 4662, para. 39, ECJ; Case C–106/89 *Marleasing* [1990] E.C.R. I–4135 at I–4159, paras 8–9, ECJ. See the case note by Stuyck and Wytinck (1991) C.M.L.Rev. 205–223).

[17] Case 152/83 *Demouche v. Fonds de Garantie Automobile* [1987] E.C.R. 3833 at 3852–3853, paras 15–21, ECJ. See also an earlier case, Case 116/83 *Bureau Belge des Assureurs Automobiles v. Fantozzi* [1984] E.C.R. 2481 at 2490, para. 11, ECJ. See also (Order of November 12, 1998) Case C-162/98 *Hartmann*, paras 8-14, ECJ (not yet reported)—the Court declined jurisdiction to give a preliminary ruling on the interpretation of an agreement concluded between Member States in spite of the fact that the agreement was the outcome of co-operation between two or more Member States authorised by a Community directive; that was not enough to justify the view that an agreement concluded for that purpose forms an integral part of Community law whose interpretation falls within the jurisdiction of the Court.

acts adopted by bodies set up by such agreements (since the Community participates in the operation of such bodies). But new forms of regulatory activity within the Community will make it necessary to take a creative approach to this test.

An example may be found in the title of the E.C. Treaty concerning social policy, as amended by the Treaty of Amsterdam. Under Article 139 (*ex Article 118b*) of the E.C. Treaty, management and labour may conclude agreements at Community level. The question is whether, in certain circumstances, such agreements may also be the subject of a reference for a preliminary ruling. Such agreements are intended to be an alternative to the Community legislation contemplated by Article 137 (*ex Article 118*) of the E.C. Treaty. In addition, before submitting proposals for legislation to the Council, the Commission has to consult management and labour and, if they express a wish to that effect, must give them the opportunity to conclude an agreement on the content of the proposal (E.C. Treaty, Article 138 (*ex Article 118a*)). Lastly, "[a]greements concluded at Community level shall be implemented . . ., in matters covered by Article 118 *[now Article 137]*, at the joint request of the signatory parties, by a Council decision on a proposal from the Commission" (adopted by the voting method specified in Article 137 (*ex Article 118*)) (E.C. Treaty, Article 139(2)). Although, strictly speaking, Community institutions or bodies do not play any part in drawing up the agreements to be concluded by management and labour at Community level, it may perhaps be accepted, in the light of the contribution they make, that they "take part" to a sufficient extent in the conferral of legal force on the agreements, as a result of the Council decisions implementing them, as to make them qualify for preliminary rulings by the Court of Justice.[18] The position will be different, of course, where the agreements are implemented, not by Council decision, but "in accordance with the procedures and practices specific to management and labour and the Member States" (the other alternative set out in Article 139 (*ex Article 118b*) (2) of the E.C. Treaty). The main reason for taking this view is that it is stated in Declaration No. 27 annexed to the Treaty of Amsterdam that "the content of [such] agreements" is to be developed "by collective bargaining according to the rules of each Member State" and that there is therefore "no obligation on the Member States to apply the agreements directly or to work out rules for their transposition, nor any obligation to amend national legislation in force to facilitate their implementation". Precisely the opposite situation obtains where the agreements are implemented by Council decision, which means that the aim of the procedure of preliminary rulings on interpretation may be achieved in full in that case.

The question also arises as to what is the precise meaning of the expression "institutions of the Community" in indent (b) of the first paragraph of Article 234 (*ex Article 177*) of the E.C. Treaty. The Court of Justice has interpreted it broadly by referring to a "Community institution **6–010**

[18] An action for annulment may lie against such a Council decision: see Case T–135/96 *UEAPME v. Council* [1998] E.C.R. II–2335, CFI.

or agency", which must have taken part in the conclusion of the relevant act.[19] It appears from this that the expression covers any Community body in addition to the "institutions of the Community" referred to in Article 7 (*ex Article 4*) of the E.C. Treaty.

6–011 It is self-evident that all measures adopted by the Council, the Commission or the European Parliament and the Council jointly may be the subject of a reference for a preliminary ruling on their interpretation. In the overwhelming majority of cases, Community decision-making results in such an act in one form or another (see E.C. Treaty, Article 249 (*ex Article 189*)).

6–012 Acts of the European Parliament and the Court of Auditors also come under the jurisdiction of the Court of Justice to give preliminary rulings on interpretation,[20] albeit it is rarer for the interpretation of such acts to be relevant to the determination of main proceedings before a national court.[21]

6–013 Preliminary rulings may also be sought on the interpretation of judgments of the Court of Justice. For instance, an interpretation of a previous judgment may be sought in the event that the national court has difficulty in understanding or applying it.[22] The judgment to be interpreted does not have to be a preliminary ruling; it may have been given in any sort of proceedings.[23]

Commentators have long been divided on this issue. Those arguing that judgments of the Court could be the subject of a reference for a preliminary ruling did so chiefly on the basis of the wording of Article 234 (*ex Article 177*) of the E.C. Treaty: the Court of Justice is an "institution" of the Community and so its "acts" (judgments/orders) may be interpreted by way of preliminary ruling.[24] Those taking the opposite view contended that the subject-matter of a reference for a preliminary ruling on the interpretation of an earlier judgment was in fact not the judgment as such but the provisions and principles of Community law applied or interpreted therein.[25]

---

[19] *Demouche v. Fonds de Garantie Automobile* (cited in n. 17, above) at 3853, para. 19.

[20] For acts of the European Parliament, see Dumon, "La Cour de justice: Questions préjudicielles", in *Les Novelles: Droit des Communautés européennes*, Brussels, Larcier, 1969, at 341–366; Vandersanden and Barav, *Contentieux communautaire*, p. 296. For acts of the Court of Auditors, see *Commentaire Mégret*, at 212.

[21] Rideau and Picod, *Code de procédures communautaires*, pp. 328–329.

[22] (Order of March 5, 1986), Case 69/85 *Wünsche v. Germany* [1986] E.C.R. 947 at 953, para. 15, ECJ; Case 14/86 *Pretore di Salò v. Persons Unknown* [1987] E.C.R. 2545 at 2568–2569, para. 12, ECJ. For an example, see Joined Cases C–363 and C–407–411/93 *Lancry and Others* [1994] E.C.R. I–3957, ECJ; Case C–280/94 *Posthuma-van Damme and Oztürk* [1996] E.C.R. I–179 at I–200, para. 13, ECJ; Case C–5/97 *Ballast Nedam Groep* [1997] E.C.R. I–7549 at I–7558, para. 1, ECJ.

[23] See, *e.g.* Joined Cases 314–316/81 and 83/82 *Waterkeyn* [1982] E.C.R. 4337, ECJ—interpretation of the scope and legal effects of a judgment given pursuant to the E.C. Treaty, Art. 226 (*ex Art. 169*).

[24] Chevallier and Maidani, *Guide pratique. Article 177* (now Art. 234), Luxembourg, Office for Official Publications of the European Communities, 1982; Vandersanden and Barav, *Contentieux communautaire*, p. 296.

[25] Joliet, *Le contentieux*, p. 193; Kovar, "Cour de justice. Recours préjudiciel en interprétation et en appréciation de validité—Examen de la question préjudicielle par la Cour de justice"

The distinction is perhaps not as clear-cut as it seems. The Court of Justice allows national courts and tribunals to refer questions to it on the interpretation of its previous judgments, but in answering them, it inevitably falls back on the provisions and principles of Community law underlying those judgments. This is also true where national courts apply to the Court of Justice for an interpretation of a judgment of the Court of First Instance. The possibility of making such a reference is of great practical importance for national courts where they query whether a judgment of the Court of First Instance against which no appeal has been brought before the Court of Justice correctly interprets the principles and provisions of Community law with which it deals.

Alongside acts of "institutions of the Community", since the E.U. Treaty entered into force, indent (b) of the first paragraph of Article 234 (*ex Article 177*) of the E.C. Treaty has expressly mentioned acts of the European Central Bank (which denoted, in the second stage of Economic and Monetary Union, the European Monetary Institute: see E.C. Treaty, Article 117 (*ex Article 109f*) (9)). Consequently, a preliminary ruling may also be sought from the Court of Justice on the interpretation of its acts. **6–014**

The fact that only the European Central Bank is also mentioned does not mean that acts of other Community bodies may not be the subject of a reference for a preliminary ruling. The correct position is that acts of bodies which have been established by Community institutions in the exercise of their powers and given specific executive tasks (and the associated power to take decisions) may form the subject of a request for a preliminary ruling. As has already been pointed out, the Court of Justice requires Community institutions or bodies to have taken part in the adoption of an act in order for it to be capable of being the subject of an Article 234 (*ex Article 177*) reference on its interpretation. That requirement is certainly fulfilled in the case of the agencies, offices, foundations and other "bodies" established by the Community institutions.[26] **6–015**

The Economic and Social Committee and the Committee of the Regions, which assist the Council and the Commission in an advisory capacity (E.C. Treaty, Article 7 (*ex Article 4*)), are not institutions or bodies whose acts are amenable to interpretation by the Court of Justice pursuant to Article 234 **6–016**

(1991) J.C.D.I. Vol. 161–26–2, No. 24, referring to Case 135/77 *Bosch v. Hauptzollamt Hildesheim* [1978] E.C.R. 855, ECJ and Joined Cases 87, 112 and 113/79 *Bagusat v. Hauptzollamt Berlin-Packhof* [1980] E.C.R. 1159, ECJ. See also the Opinion of Advocate General J.-P. Warner in Case 8/78 *Milac v. Hauptzollamt Freiburg* [1978] E.C.R. 1721 at 1740–1741, ECJ. Brealey and Hoskins, *Remedies in EC Law* (cited in para. 1–004, n. 12, above), p. 204, n. 62, also take the view that judgments of the Court of Justice are not open to review in the context of preliminary ruling proceedings; they refer to (Order of March 5, 1986), Case 69/85 *Wünsche Handelsgesellschaft v. Germany* [1986] E.C.R. 947 at 952–953, paras 10–16, ECJ.

26 See the list set out in Art. 1 of the Decision taken by common agreement between the Representatives of the Governments of the Member States, meeting at Head of State or Government level, on the location of the seats of certain bodies and departments of the European Communities and of Europol, [1993] O.J. C323/1. See also Lenaerts, "Regulating the Regulatory Process: 'Delegation of Powers' in the European Community" (1993) E.L.Rev. 23 at 45–46.

(*ex Article 177*) of the E.C. Treaty. The opinions which they deliver form part of the decision-making process carried out between the Commission, the Council and (generally) the European Parliament. They have no independent existence and could, at the most, be used to help interpret acts where they took part in the process of their adoption.[27]

6–017 The European Council is not an institution of the Community; in principle, its acts fall outwith the Court's jurisdiction to give preliminary rulings on interpretation. Nevertheless, some have argued that it should be equated with the Community institutions for the purposes of Article 234 (*ex Article 177*) on the ground that it has to provide the Union (and hence the Community) with the necessary impetus for its development and to define general political guidelines (E.U. Treaty, Article 4 (*ex Article D*)).[28] Exceptionally, the European Council itself plays a formal role in the Community's decision-making process[29] or serves as the forum for the adoption of a decision of the Heads of State or Government meeting in the European Council.[30] As such, those acts do not give rise to references for preliminary rulings from national courts, although they may well have to be interpreted by the Court of Justice in conjunction with the Community acts or Treaty provisions to which they relate in order to determine the precise implications of those acts or provisions.

C. International agreements concluded by the Community and acts of bodies established by such agreements

6–018 Not only acts adopted by Community institutions autonomously, but also "contractual" acts, are covered by indent (b) of the first paragraph of Article 234 (*ex Article 177*). Thus, the Court of Justice has held that it has jurisdiction to give preliminary rulings on the interpretation of international agreements concluded by the Community.[31]

The question arises as to whether in the case of a mixed agreement concluded by the Community and the Member States jointly with a third country the jurisdiction of the Court extends to rulings interpreting provisions of the agreement by which the Member States enter into commitments *vis-à-vis* that country by virtue of their own powers. So far, the Court of Justice has expressly left this question open.[32] It has been able

[27] *Commentaire Mégret*, pp. 212–213.

[28] Rideau and Picod, *Code de procédures communautaires*, p. 330.

[29] E.C. Treaty, Art. 99 (*ex Art. 103*)—adoption of a conclusion on the broad guidelines of the economic policies of the Member States and the Community, on the basis of which the Council is to adopt a recommendation.

[30] See with regard to the position of Denmark in the European Union ([1992] O.J. C348/1). See also Curtin and Van Ooik, "De bijzondere positie van Denemarken in de Europese Unie" (1993) S.E.W. 675–689.

[31] Case 181/73 *Haegeman v. Belgium* [1974] E.C.R. 449, at 459–460, paras 1–6, ECJ. For examples, see Case 87/75 *Bresciani v. Amministrazione Italiana delle Finanze* [1976] E.C.R. 129, ECJ; Case 65/77 *Razanatsimba* [1977] E.C.R. 2229; ECJ; Case C–18/90 *Kziber* [1991] E.C.R. I–199; ECJ; Case C–432/92 *Anastasiou and Others* [1994] E.C.R. I–3087, ECJ; Case C–113/97 *Babahenini* [1998] E.C.R. I–183, ECJ.

[32] Case 12/86 *Demirel v. Stadt Schwäbisch Gemünd* [1987] E.C.R. 3719 at 3751, para. 9, ECJ;

to do so because it could take the view that the provisions whose interpretation was sought fell partly within the Community's powers to guarantee commitments towards the non-member country concerned. The fact that the Member States had to carry out the commitments was irrelevant, because in doing so they were simply fulfilling an obligation in relation to the Community[33] and did not assume, *vis-à-vis* the non-member country, the Community's responsibility for the due performance of the agreement.

For the purposes of the Court's jurisdiction to give preliminary rulings on interpretation, international agreements by which the Community is bound by way of substitution for the Member States are treated in the same way as international agreements concluded by the Community. In this way, the Court of Justice has held that it has jurisdiction to give preliminary rulings on the interpretation of GATT (General Agreement on Tariffs and Trade) on the ground that, since the Common Customs Tariff entered into effect, the Community has been substituted for the Member States as regards fulfilment of the commitments laid down in GATT, the result being that "the provisions of GATT should, like the provisions of all other agreements binding the Community, receive uniform application throughout the Community".[34] **6–019**

It is striking that the Court of Justice assumed jurisdiction to give preliminary rulings simply by referring to the aim of that jurisdiction, namely "to ensure the uniform interpretation of Community law"[35] (thereby completely ignoring the lack of any actual connection between GATT and any act of a Community institution, whereas such a connection does, of course, exist in the case of international agreements concluded by the Community).

That same aim of the Court's jurisdiction to give preliminary rulings on interpretation has prompted it to hold that it may give preliminary rulings on the interpretation of binding and non-binding acts of bodies established by international agreements concluded by the Community. Thus, the Court has held that decisions of an association council form an integral part of Community law on account of their direct connection with the agreement itself.[36] Since the function of Article 234 (*ex Article 177*) of the E.C. Treaty is to ensure the uniform application throughout the Community of all provisions forming part of the Community legal system and to ensure that their effects do not vary according to the interpretation accorded to them in the various Member States, the Court of Justice must have jurisdiction to give preliminary rulings on the interpretation, not only of the agreement **6–020**

Case C–53/96 *Hermès International* [1998] E.C.R. I–3603 at I–3647—3649, paras 24–33, ECJ.

[33] E.C. Treaty, Art. 10 (*ex Art. 5*); Case 104/81 *Hauptzollamt Mainz v. Kupferberg* [1982] E.C.R. 3641, ECJ.

[34] Joined Cases 267–269/81 *Amministrazione delle Finanze dello Stato v. SPI and SAMI* [1983] E.C.R. 801 at 828, para. 14, and at 828–829, paras 15–19, ECJ.

[35] *ibid.*, para. 15.

[36] Case 30/88 *Greece v. Commission* [1989] E.C.R. 3711 at 3737–3738, para. 13, ECJ.

itself, but also of decisions of the body established by the agreement and entrusted with responsibility for its implementation.[37]

D. Provisions of Community law to which national law refers

6–021 In 1990 the Court of Justice considerably extended its jurisdiction to give preliminary rulings on interpretation (after Advocate General M. Darmon had delivered an Opinion proposing that it should not do so):

> "It does not appear either from the wording of Article 177 *[now Article 234]* or from the aim of the procedure introduced by that article that the authors of the Treaty intended to exclude from the jurisdiction of the Court requests for a preliminary ruling on a Community provision in the specific case where the national law of a Member State refers to the content of that provision in order to determine rules applicable to a situation which is purely internal to that State".[38]

The Court stated that it was "manifestly in the interest of the Community legal order that, in order to forestall future differences of interpretation, every Community provision should be given a uniform interpretation irrespective of the circumstances in which it is to be applied".[39]

6–022 The Court has jurisdiction only to interpret Community law; it cannot "take account of the general scheme of the provisions of domestic law which, while referring to Community law, define the extent of that reference". The Court drew the demarcation line between its own jurisdiction and that of the national court in the following terms:

> "Consideration of the limits which the national legislature may have placed on the application of Community law to purely internal situations, to which it is applicable only through the operation of the national legislation, is a matter for domestic law and hence falls within the exclusive jurisdiction of the courts of the Member States".[40]

---

[37] Case C–192/89 *Sevince* [1990] E.C.R. I–3461 at I–3501, paras. 9–11, ECJ. See also Case C–237/91 *Kus* [1992] E.C.R. I–6781, ECJ; Case C–188/91 *Deutsche Shell* [1993] E.C.R. I–363, ECJ (the latter case was concerned with the interpretation of a non-binding act, which was of interest to the national court because it wanted to apply its national law as consistently as possible with that act on account of the obligation of co-operation in good faith borne by the Member State of which that court was a body); Case C–277/94 *Taflan-Met and Others* [1996] E.C.R. I–4085, ECJ; Case C–171/95 *Tetik* [1997] E.C.R. I–329, ECJ; Case C–351/95 *Kadiman* [1997] E.C.R. I–2133, ECJ; Case C–386/95 *Eker* [1997] E.C.R. I–2697, ECJ; Case C–285/95 *Kol* [1997] E.C.R. I–3069, ECJ; Case C–36/96 *Günaydin* [1997] E.C.R. I–5143, ECJ; Case C–98/96 *Ertanir* [1997] E.C.R. I–5179, ECJ.

[38] Joined Cases C–297/88 and C–197/89 *Dzodzi* [1990] E.C.R. I–3763 at I–3793, para. 36, ECJ. See also Case C–28/95 *Leur-Bloem* [1997] E.C.R. I–4161 at I–4200, para. 27, ECJ; Case C–130/95 *Giloy* [1997] E.C.R. I–4291 at I–4302—4303, para. 23, ECJ.

[39] *Dzodzi, (*cited in n. 38, above), para. 37.

[40] *Dzodzi*, at I–3794—3795, para. 42. In *Leur-Bloem* and *Giloy*, the Court held, however, that in every case where it had held that it had jurisdiction to give preliminary rulings on questions concerning Community provisions in situations where the facts of the cases being considered by the national courts were outside the scope of Community law, the application

Indeed the Court has consistently held that it has no jurisdiction to rule on questions of national law which remain unanswered in the order for reference, even if this means that it has to consider different hypotheses in interpreting Community law.[41]

Moreover, it is on account of the same limitation of its jurisdiction to give preliminary rulings that the Court refuses to rule on the interpretation of provisions of international law (for example of an agreement) which are binding on Member States outside the confines of Community law.[42]

Dzodzi remains within the confines of the interpretation of Community law, although it breaks new ground because it accepts that Community law is being applied, not by virtue of its own authority, but by virtue of that of national law, and that this does not prevent the Court ruling on its interpretation.[43] The Court of Justice also accepts jurisdiction to give preliminary rulings on interpretation on the same terms where provisions of Community law are applicable for the resolution of a dispute by virtue of a contractual relationship between the parties.[44] **6–023**

II. Content of a Preliminary Ruling on Interpretation

The Treaty does not define precisely what is meant by "interpretation" of Community law in the context of the preliminary rulings procedure.[45] Initially, the Court of Justice strongly emphasised the distinction between **6–024**

---

of the provisions of Community law was manifestly not limited by provisions of domestic law or contractual provisions incorporating those Community provisions (*Leur-Bloem* at I–4200, para. 27; and *Giloy* at I–4302—4303, para. 23 (both cases cited in n. 38, above). The position was different in *Kleinwort Benson* (Case C–346/93 *Kleinwort Benson* [1995] E.C.R. I–615, ECJ). In that case, the Court of Appeal made a reference to the Court of Justice pursuant to the Protocol of June 3, 1971 on a provision of the Brussels Convention. The Court of Justice held that it had no jurisdiction to answer the question on the ground that the dispute in the main proceedings was concerned with the interpretation not of the relevant provision of the Brussels Convention as such, but of a provision of domestic law (the Civil Jurisdiction and Judgments Act 1982) modelled on the Convention and partially reproducing its terms. The Court of Justice further found that the Act provided for the national authorities to adopt modifications designed to produce divergence between provisions of the act and corresponding provisions of the Convention. The Court properly inferred from this that the provisions of the Convention could not be regarded as having been rendered applicable as such in cases outwith the scope of the Convention by the law of the contracting state concerned. The Court went on to observe that, in applying the provisions of national law modelled on the Brussels Convention, the national courts were not bound by its case law but were required only to have regard to it (see also the case note by Betlem (1996) C.M.L.Rev. 137–147, who even argues that the Court lacks jurisdiction to give preliminary rulings on questions such as those referred in the *Dzodzi* case; a less extreme position is taken by Poilvache, "Compétence préjudicielle et dispositions nationales inspirées du droit communautaire" (1998) J.T.D.E.121–125, who mentions some examples from Belgian law in which the legislature took over Community provisions expressly and unconditionally).

41 See Wils, *Prejudiciële vragen van Belgische rechters en hun gevolgen* (Preadvies, Vereniging voor de vergelijkende studie van het recht van België en Nederland), Zwolle, Tjeenk Willink, 1993, pp. 14–15.

42 Case 130/73 *Vandeweghe v. Berufsgenossenschaft Chemische Industrie* [1973] E.C.R. 1329 at 1333, para. 2, ECJ; Case 44/84 *Hurd v. Jones* [1986] E.C.R. 26 at 76–77, para. 20, ECJ.

43 For other applications, see Case C–231/89 *Gmurzynska-Bscher* [1990] E.C.R. I–4003, ECJ; Case C–384/89 *Tomatis and Fulchiron* [1991] E.C.R. I–127, ECJ.

44 Case C–88/91 *Federconsorzi* [1992] E.C.R. I–4035, ECJ.

45 See Case 13/61 *De Geus and Uitdenbogerd v. Bosch and Others* [1962] E.C.R. 45, at 50, ECJ,

interpretation and application, which was also to demarcate the respective functions of the Court of Justice and the national courts.[46] At the same time, however, it referred to:

> "the special field of judicial cooperation under Article 177 *[now Article 234]* which requires the national court and the Court of Justice, both keeping within their respective jurisdiction, and with the aim of ensuring that Community law is applied in a unified manner, to make direct and complementary contributions to the working out of a decision".[47]

Since then, the idea of "judicial cooperation" has got the upper hand over the distinction between interpretation and application, the aim being to ensure that the main proceedings are determined in a way which secures the uniform "application" of Community law.[48]

6–025 This is why the Court of Justice regularly refers to "the need to afford a helpful interpretation of Community law".[49] Such an interpretation can be confined very specifically to the facts and points of national law underlying the national proceedings as they emerge from the "documents before the Court".[50] The documents in the case from which the Court derives the relevant facts and points of national law include not only the order for reference and the file submitted by the national court, but also the observations of the parties to the main proceedings, the Member States, the Commission and the Council (where an act of the latter is at issue in the proceedings) submitted pursuant to Article 20 of the E.C. Statute of the Court of Justice.

6–026 It is essential in this connection that the "matters disclosed by the documents before the Court" are not disputed,[51] since the Court is not entitled to find the facts and points of national law in *inter partes* proceedings.[52] or to verify whether they are correct.[53] Where, however, the

---

where the Court of Justice held that "since the question what is meant in Article 177 *[now Article 234]* by 'the interpretation of Community law' may itself be a matter of interpretation, it is permissible for the national court to formulate its request in a simple and direct way".

[46] (Order of June 3, 1964), Case 6/64 *Costa v. ENEL* [1964] E.C.R. 614 at 614–615, ECJ; Case 20/64 *Albatros v. SOPECO* [1965] E.C.R. 29 at 34, ECJ; Case 13/68 *Salgoil* [1968] E.C.R. 453 at 459–460, ECJ.

[47] Case 16/65 *Schwarze v. Einfuhr- und Vorratsstelle für Getreide und Futtermittel* [1965] E.C.R. 877 at 886, ECJ.

[48] For a critical approach to the distinction between interpretation and application, see Donner, "Uitlegging en toepassing", in *Miscellanea W.J. Ganshof van der Meersch*, Brussels, Bruylant, 1972, II, at 103 *et seq.*

[49] Case 244/78 *Union Laitière Normande v. French Dairy Farmers Ltd* [1979] E.C.R. 2663 at 2681, ECJ.

[50] Case 311/85 *VVR v. Sociale Dienst van de Plaatselijke en Gewestelijke Overheidsdiensten* [1987] E.C.R. 3801 at 3826, para. 11, ECJ.

[51] It is for this reason that the Court refers to the fact that the observations submitted are "not disputed", see *ibid.* at 3826–3827, paras 13–17.

[52] Case 17/81 *Pabst & Richarz v. Hauptzollamt Oldenburg* [1982] E.C.R. 1331 at 1346, paras 10–12, ECJ.

[53] Case 104/77 *Oehlschläger v. Hauptzollamt Emmerich* [1978] E.C.R. 791 at 797, para. 4, ECJ.

facts and points of national law are agreed as between the "parties" (being all the parties participating in the legal debate before the Court under Article 20 of the E.C. Statute), there is nothing to prevent the Court from spelling out its understanding of the facts and points of national law as its starting point for its "useful" (*i.e.* specific) interpretation of the applicable provisions and principles of Community law.[54]

More specifically, in answering questions on interpretation which in fact are designed to bring to light a possible inconsistency of national law as compared with Community law.[55] it is important for the Court to be able to base itself on the undisputed facts and points of national law set out by the "defendant" government in its observations.[56]

The Court of Justice may also ask the government concerned to elucidate certain facts and points of national law and, if those explanations are not contested, take account of them in the judgment giving a preliminary ruling.[57] Generally, the request will be informal in the shape of a letter from the Registrar, but it may if necessary be made in the form of an order of the Court prescribing measures of inquiry within the meaning of Article 45(2) of the ECJ Rules of Procedure (request for information and production of documents).[58] Other measures of inquiry, such as taking oral testimony, commissioning an expert's report and inspections of a place or thing, are not formally precluded in proceedings for a preliminary ruling on the interpretation of Community law, but probably go too far in practice because they are intrinsically intended to determine or verify contested facts and points of national law and the Court of Justice has indeed no jurisdiction to do this.[59]

In order to arrive at a "useful interpretation", the Court of Justice often has to rework the questions to some extent before answering them.[60] It will do this where the questions referred are too vague, for instance where they do not refer specifically to any provision or principle of Community law,[61] **6–027**

---

[54] See, for a very explicit example, Case 311/85 *VVR v. Sociale Dienst van de Plaatselijke en Gewestelijke Overheidsdiensten* [1987] E.C.R. 3801 at 3827–3828, paras 16–18, ECJ.

[55] This is an accepted feature of the preliminary ruling procedure, see Case 26/62 *Van Gend & Loos v. Nederlandse Administratie der Belastingen* [1963] E.C.R. 1 at 10–11 and 13, ECJ.

[56] See, *e.g. Case 33/88 Allué and Others v. Università degli studi di Venezia* [1989] E.C.R. 1591 at 1610, para. 12.

[57] Case C–343/90 *Lourenço Dias* [1992] E.C.R. I–4673 at I–4717, para. 52, ECJ.

[58] See, *e.g.* Case 148/77 *Hansen v. Hauptzollamt Flensburg* [1978] E.C.R. 1787 at 1790, ECJ, from which it appears that the Court decided "to open the procedure without any preparatory inquiry", but "requested the Government of the Federal Republic of Germany, the Government of the French Republic and the Commission of the European Communities to provide written answers to a certain number of questions before the opening of the oral procedure". Germany had submitted observations to the Court pursuant to the E.C. Statute, Art. 20, but France had not, so that the questions were intended to involve that state in the proceedings, which is what happened, para. 5, see *ibid.*, at 1798–1799.

[59] See Pescatore, "Article 177 *[now Article 234]*", in *Traité instituant la CEE. Commentaire article par article*, Paris, Economica, 1992, 1073, No. 61, at 1115–1116.

[60] See para. 2–020, above.

[61] Case 10/71 *Ministère Public of Luxembourg v. Muller* [1971] E.C.R. 723, ECJ; Case 251/83 *Haug-Adrion v. Frankfurter Versicherungs-AG* [1984] E.C.R. 4277 at 4286–4287, paras 6–11, ECJ.

or are deficient in other respects.[62] In such cases, the Court will specify and flesh out the questions in the light of the particulars set out in the order for reference and in the national case-file. Sometimes, too, a great many questions are referred and the Court prunes them back somewhat[63] or the questions are put in a very complicated way (divided into propositions and sub-propositions) and the Court has first to identify the core issue raised.[64] This exercise often makes it unnecessary to answer some of the questions referred.[65]

6–028 The Court sometimes reworks the wording of the questions referred on account of the limits placed by the Treaty on its jurisdiction to give preliminary rulings. It has to do so because the Treaty "neither expressly nor by implication prescribes a particular form in which a national court must present its request for a preliminary ruling" and it therefore falls to the Court of Justice itself to decide "on that request only in so far as it has jurisdiction to do so, that is to say, only in so far as the decision relates to the interpretation" of Community law.[66]

This has occurred principally where questions were referred by which the national court sought a ruling on whether or not national provisions were consistent with Community law. Commonly, the national court puts the question of compatibility with Community law directly to the Court of Justice, as indeed is its right precisely because of the lack of any requirements as to the form in which questions are to be referred. Moreover, formulating questions directly in this way affords the advantage that there is no doubt as to the scope of the request for a preliminary ruling. Consequently, the referring court should not be concerned if the Court of Justice, referring to its settled case law,[67] prefaces its judgment with the words:

> "although in proceedings brought under Article 177 *[now Article 234]* of the Treaty, it is not for the Court to rule on the compatibility of national rules with provisions of Community law, the Court is compe-

---

[62] Joined Cases 141–143/81 *Holdijk* [1982] E.C.R. 1299, ECJ; Case C–237/94 *O'Flynn* [1996] E.C.R. I–2617 at I–2639—2640, paras 24, 25, ECJ.

[63] See, *e.g.* Joined Cases 115 and 116/81 *Adoui and Cornuaille v. Belgium* [1982] E.C.R. 1665, ECJ.

[64] See, *e.g.* Case 266/81 *Siot v. Ministero delle Finanze* [1983] E.C.R. 731 at 773–774, paras 10–13, ECJ; Joined Cases C–297/88 and C–197/89 *Dzodzi* [1990] E.C.R. I–3763 at I–3788, para. 11, ECJ: "The questions submitted for a preliminary ruling by the Tribunal de première instance essentially seek to establish whether, and in what circumstances, the Community provisions . . ."; at 3789, para. 14: "The questions submitted by the Cour d'appel, Brussels, ask the Court to interpret Arts. 8 and 9 of Directive 64/221 of February 25, 1964 . . .". Paras 11–15 of the judgment contain, under the heading "The object of the questions submitted to the Court", a meticulous analysis of the orders for reference (and the associated case-files) showing which provisions and principles of Community law raise difficulty for the referring courts.

[65] See, *e.g.* Case 352/85 *Bond van Adverteerders v. Netherlands State* [1988] E.C.R. 2085 at 2136, paras 40, 41, ECJ.

[66] Case 13/61 *De Geus and Uitdenbogerd v. Bosch and Others* [1962] E.C.R. 45 at 50, ECJ.

[67] For the first of those cases, see Case 6/64 *Costa v. ENEL* [1964] E.C.R. 585 at 592–593, ECJ.

tent to give a ruling on the interpretation of Community law in order to enable the national court to assess the compatibility of those rules with the Community provisions".[68]

That caveat which the Court enters as regards the limits placed on its jurisdiction, however, does not lead it to give a somewhat abstract interpretation of the Community law at issue. On the contrary, the Court will reformulate the national court's questions in a particularly concrete manner. As a result, although they are primarily based on the interpretation of provisions or principles of Community law, the answers given will be nevertheless at the same time determinative of the outcome of the question of compatibility.[69]

Where the Court of Justice interprets Community law in a case where **6–029**
certain relevant facts or points of national law have not yet been established in the main proceedings, it will indicate very precisely what findings the national court has to make in order to resolve the case in accordance with its interpretation.[70] However, the Court of Justice may not abuse this sort of reference back to the national court by evading its responsibility for making the necessary appraisals in interpreting Community law, especially the fundamental provisions and principles.[71] The Court is under a duty to give the national court an answer which, in principle, will lead directly to the resolution of the case (at least as far as Community law is concerned). Only where, in the concrete context of the main proceedings, some specific facts or points of national law require clarification when the preliminary ruling is applied in the final judgment, will that clarification have to be made by the national court after the Court of Justice has clearly identified which facts and points of national law require elucidation. Where, by contrast, the Court of Justice is itself apprised of the uncontested facts and points of

---

68 Case C–130/93 *Lamaire* [1994] E.C.R. I–3215 at I–3224, para. 10, ECJ.

69 See, as an example, *ibid.*, para. 11: "The national court's question asks essentially whether Articles 9 and 12 (*now Articles 23 and 25*) of the Treaty preclude national legislation from levying a compulsory contribution, such as the charge of BFR 2 per 100 kg of potatoes exported [to other Member States], provided for in Article 4(4) of the [Belgian] Royal Decree of 15 May 1986, as amended by the Royal Decree of 14 July 1987, on exports of agricultural products to other Member States". In answering that question, the Court of Justice came to the conclusion that "a compulsory contribution levied in respect of the exportation of potatoes, such as the charge levied for the National Board pursuant to Article 4(4) of the Belgian Royal Decree of 15 May 1986, as amended, must be regarded as a charge having equivalent effect to a customs duty on exports and as such prohibited by Articles 9 and 12 *[now Articles 23 and 25]* of the [EC] Treaty" (para. 20). It then gave the same answer, couched in somewhat more neutral terms, in the operative part. Sometimes, the Court does not formulate the operative part neutrally and refers expressly to the provisions of national law as being compatible or incompatible with Community law: Case C–130/92 *OTO v. Ministero delle Finanze* [1994] E.C.R. I–3281, ECJ.

70 For examples, see Joined Cases 286/82 and 26/83 *Luisi and Carbone v. Ministero del Tesoro* [1984] E.C.R. 377 at 407, para. 36, ECJ; Case 171/88 *Rinner-Kühn v. FWW Spezial Gebäudereinigung* [1989] E.C.R. 2743 at 2761, paras 14–15, ECJ; Joined Cases C–184 and C–221/91 *Oorburg and Van Messem* [1993] E.C.R. I–1633, ECJ; Case C–127/92 *Enderby* [1993] E.C.R. I–5535 at I–5575—5576, paras 26–29, ECJ.

71 See, for instance, the criticism in learned articles of Case C–145/88 *Torfaen Borough Council v. B & Q plc* [1989] E.C.R. 3851 at 3889, paras 15–17, ECJ: Gormley (1990) C.M.L.Rev. 141 at 148; Pisuisse (1990) S.E.W. 599 at 604.

national law which are necessary in order to reach a decision in the main proceedings, then it has to have regard to those facts and points of law as such in making the "useful interpretation" of Community law expected by the national court.[72]

6–030 Naturally, it falls in any event to the national court to dispose of the case. In that sense, the judgment giving a ruling on interpretation, no matter to what extent it determines the outcome of the main proceedings, is always "preliminary", that is to say, given before the national court gives final judgment in the main proceedings.[73] However, the Court of Justice does not shrink from giving guidance based on the case-file and the written and oral observations which have been submitted to it, with a view to enabling the national court to give judgment on the application of Community law in the specific case with which it is having to deal.[74] The Court went a step further in dealing with a request for a preliminary ruling in a factually complex case on state liability for an alleged breach of Community law. While recognising that it was in principle for the national courts to verify whether or not the conditions governing state liability for a breach of Community law are fulfilled, the Court held that in the case in question it had all the necessary information to assess the acts of the Member State concerned itself.[75]

III. Consequences of a Preliminary Ruling on Interpretation

A. As regards the national court deciding the case at issue in the main proceedings

6–031 A judgment given by the Court under Article 234 (*ex Article 177*) is binding on the national court hearing the case in which the decision is given.[76] This is to be understood as meaning that all courts and tribunals dealing with the case, also at a later stage of the proceedings, on appeal or upon an appeal on a point of law, are obliged to comply with the substance of the judgment giving the preliminary ruling.[77]

The binding effect attaches to the whole of the operative part and main body of the judgment, since the operative part has to be understood in the light of the reasoning on which it is based.[78]

---

[72] See also Lenaerts, "Form and Substance of the Preliminary Rulings Procedure", in Curtin and Heukels (eds), *Institutional Dynamics of European Integration. Essays in Honour of H.G. Schermers*, Dordrecht, Martinus Nijhoff, 1994, II, 355 at 364–370.

[73] *Cf.* Case 1/80 *Fonds National de Retraite des Ouvriers Mineurs v. Salmon* [1980] E.C.R. 1937 at 1945–1946, para. 6, ECJ.

[74] Case C–328/91 *Secretary of State for Social Security v. Thomas and Others* [1993] E.C.R. I–1247 at I–1273, para. 13, ECJ; Case C–278/93 *Freers and Speckmann* [1996] E.C.R. I–1165 at I–1191, para. 24, ECJ. See also the more cautious terms employed in Joined Cases C–46 and C–48/93 *Brasserie du Pêcheur and Factortame* (*Factortame IV*) [1996] E.C.R. I–1029 at I–1151, para. 58, ECJ.

[75] Case C–392/93 *British Telecommunications* [1996] E.C.R. I–1631 at I–1668, para. 41, ECJ; Joined Cases C–283, C–291 and C–292/94 *Denkavit and Others* [1996] E.C.R. I–5063 at I–5101, para. 49, ECJ.

[76] Case 29/68 *Milch-, Fett-, und Eierkontor v. Hauptzollamt Saarbrücken* [1969] E.C.R. 165 at 180, para. 2, ECJ.

[77] Pescatore (cited in n. 59, above), No. 65, at 1118. See also the general wording of Case 52/76 *Benedetti v. Munari* [1977] E.C.R. 163 at 183, para. 26, ECJ.

[78] Case 135/77 *Bosch v. Hauptzollamt Hildesheim* [1978] E.C.R. 855 at 859, para. 4, ECJ.

Nevertheless that binding effect does not preclude the courts to which the judgment is addressed, or another court involved in deciding the case, from making a further reference for a preliminary ruling to the Court of Justice if it considers such a step to be necessary in order to give judgment in the main proceedings.[79] Such a request will be justified "when the national court encounters difficulties in understanding or applying the judgment, when it refers a fresh question of law to the Court, or again when it submits new considerations which might lead the Court to give a different answer to a question submitted earlier".[80] **6–032**

The validity of the judgment delivered previously cannot be contested by means of a further reference for a preliminary ruling "as this would call in question the allocation of jurisdiction as between national courts and the Court of Justice under Article 177 *[now Article 234]* of the Treaty".[81]

Furthermore, the initiative for making a fresh request for a preliminary ruling lies with the national court dealing with the main proceedings alone. The parties to those proceedings are not entitled to ask the Court of Justice to interpret an earlier preliminary ruling.[82] More generally, moreover, the Court has held that:

> "Articles 38 to 41 of the Protocol on the Statute of the Court of Justice list exhaustively the exceptional review procedures available for challenging the authority of the Court's judgments; however, since there are no parties to proceedings in which the Court gives judgment by way of a preliminary ruling, the aforesaid articles do not apply to such a judgment".[83]

Naturally, the fact that the judgment given by way of preliminary ruling is binding does not mean that the national court has invariably to apply the provisions or principles of Community law elucidated thereby in reaching its decision in the main proceedings. It may be that that judgment specifically indicates why those provisions or principles are not applicable.[84] **6–033**

In the event that the national court fails to comply with its obligation to follow the judgment giving the preliminary ruling, that court, as an institution of its Member State, will be in breach of Community law. This means that proceedings may be brought against that Member State under Articles 226 to 228 (*ex Articles 169 to 171*) of the E.C. Treaty.[85] This may **6–034**

---

79 See Case 29/68 *Milch-, Fett-, und Eierkontor v. Hauptzollamt Saarbrücken* [1969] E.C.R. 165 at 180, para. 3, ECJ.

80 Case 14/86 *Pretore di Salò v. Persons Unknown* [1987] E.C.R. 2545 at 2568–2569, para. 12, ECJ.

81 (Order of March 5, 1986), Case 69/85 *Wünsche v. Germany* [1986] E.C.R. 947 at 953, para. 15, ECJ.

82 (Order of May 16, 1968), Case 13/67 *Becher v. Hauptzollamt München-Landesbergerstrasse* [1968] E.C.R. 196 at 197, ECJ; (Order of October 18, 1979), Case 40/70 *Sirena v. Eda* [1979] E.C.R. 3169 at 3170–3171, ECJ.

83 (Order of March 5, 1986), Case 69/85 *Wünsche v. Germany* [1986] E.C.R. 947 at 952, para. 14, ECJ.

84 Case 222/78 *ICAP v. Beneventi* [1979] E.C.R. 1163 at 1177, paras 7–12, ECJ.

85 Pescatore (cited in n. 59 above), No. 65, at 1118. See also para. 5–032, above.

also result in domestic remedies being taken with a view to reversing the infringement of Community law or at least its consequences.[86]

B. As regards national courts generally

6–035 The binding effect of a judgment by way of preliminary ruling extends further than merely what is necessary to determine the main proceedings. It also applies outside the specific dispute in respect of which it was given to all national courts and tribunals, subject, of course, to their right to make a further reference on interpretation to the Court of Justice.[87] In the United Kingdom, this has been given effect by section 3(1) of the European Communities Act 1972, under which questions of Community law shall, if not referred to the Court of Justice, be decided "in accordance with the principles laid down by and any relevant decision" of that Court. There are two arguments in favour of the generalisation of the binding effect of judgments by way of preliminary rulings.

6–036 First, there is the fact that the interpretation is declaratory; it does not lay down any new rule, but is incorporated into the body of provisions and principles of Community law on which it is based. Consequently, the binding effect of the interpretation coincides with the binding effect of the provisions and principles on which it is based and which all national courts must respect.[88] It is, moreover, precisely because the interpretation has, by its very nature, such effect *erga omnes* that there are no "parties to proceedings",[89] but in contrast a system in which, alongside the parties to the main proceedings, the Commission, the Council (where one of its acts is at issue), possibly the European Parliament (where the act at issue was adopted under the co-decision procedure) and all the Member States are entitled to submit observations pursuant to Article 20 of the E.C. Statute of the Court of Justice (and to take part in the oral procedure before the Court). The compass of the legal discussion which takes place before the Court accordingly corresponds with the scope of the judgment to be given.[90]

---

[86] For examples, see Rideau and Picod, *Code de procédures communautaires*, p. 359.

[87] For an example, see Case 68/74 *Alaimo v. Préfet du Rhône* [1975] E.C.R. 109, ECJ. See *Garland v. British Rail* [1983] 2 A.C. 751 at 771G (Lord Diplock).

[88] See to this effect Trabucchi, "L'effet *erga omnes* des décisions préjudicielles rendues par la CJCE" (1974) R.T.D.E. 56, at 76, para. 14, Jeantet, "Originalité de la procédure d'interprétation du traité de Rome" (1966) J.C.P. Doctrine No. 1987. See, in the United Kingdom, the European Communities Act 1972, s.3(1): "For the purposes of all legal proceedings any question as to the meaning or effect of any of the Treaties, or as to the validity, meaning or effect of any Community instrument, shall . . . if not referred to the European Court, be for determination . . . in accordance with the principles laid down by and any relevant decision of the European Court . . .", cited by Advocate General J.-P. Warner in his Opinion in Case 112/76 *Manzoni v. Fonds National de Retraite des Ouvriers Mineurs* [1977] E.C.R. 1647 at 1663.

[89] (Order of March 5, 1986), Case 69/85 *Wünsche v. Germany* [1986] E.C.R. 947 at 952, para. 14, ECJ.

[90] It would seem from Joined Cases 141–143/81 *Holdijk* [1982] E.C.R. 1299 at 1311–1312, para. 6, ECJ, that the Court of Justice takes the same view.

It would therefore be wrong to seize on the idea that a judgment given in preliminary ruling proceedings has effects only *inter partes* on the ground that it is designed primarily to help the national court reach its decision in the main proceedings in which the question referred for a preliminary ruling arose. The *inter partes* aspect attaches only to the judicial decision in the main proceedings, including the way in which that decision deals with the judgment given by way of preliminary ruling, but it does not extend to that judgment itself.[91]

Secondly, the purpose for which the preliminary rulings procedure exists, **6–037** which is to secure uniformity in the application of Community law throughout the Member States, would be defeated if it were to be considered that a ruling under Article 234 (*ex Article 177*) had "no binding effect at all except in the case in which it was given".[92] The Court of Justice assumes that, with the exception of any new feature necessitating a refinement or even a reversal of the existing case law, the preliminary ruling provides all national courts and tribunals with an answer to the question of Community law which gave rise to the interpretation given.[93] This is underscored by Article 104(3) of the ECJ Rules of Procedure:

> "Where a question referred to the Court for a preliminary ruling is manifestly identical to a question on which the Court has already ruled, the Court may, after informing the court or tribunal which referred the question to it, hearing any observations submitted by the persons referred to in Article 20 of the EC Statute . . . and hearing the Advocate General, give its decision by reasoned order in which reference is made to its previous judgment."

That provision combines with the practice of many years standing by which the Court informs the national court by letter from the Registrar that an earlier judgment has answered its question, and requests it to let it know whether in the circumstances it still wishes to pursue its request for a preliminary ruling (very often the national court will then withdraw its request).[94]

---

[91] See, for instance, Joliet, *Le contentieux*, pp. 212–213.

[92] Opinion of Advocate General J.-P. Warner in Case 112/76 *Manzoni v. Fonds National de Retraite des Ouvriers Mineurs* [1977] E.C.R. 1647 at 1662–1663, ECJ, where he went on to say as follows: "This, it seems to me, is where the doctrine of *stare decisis* must come into play. . . . It means that all Courts throughout the Community, with the exception of the Court itself, are bound by the *ratio decidendi* of a Judgment of this Court". He then referred to German legislation and the U.K. European Communities Act 1972 (see n. 88, above), which confirm this binding effect; *cf.* Toth, "The Authority of Judgments of the European Court of Justice: Binding Force and Legal Effects" (1984) Y.E.L. 1 at 24.

[93] Joined Cases 76, 86–89 and 149/87 *Seguela v. Administration des Impôts* [1988] E.C.R. 2397 at 2409, paras 11–14, ECJ. For an express reversal of the case law prompted by a new reference for a preliminary ruling, see Case C–10/89 *HAG GF* [1990] E.C.R. I–3711 at I–3757, para. 10, ECJ; Joined Cases C–267 and C–268/91 *Keck and Mithouard* [1993] E.C.R. I–6097, ECJ. *Cf.* Arnull, "Owning up to Fallibility: Precedent and the Court of Justice" (1993) C.M.L.Rev. 247.

[94] See Arnull (cited in n. 93, above), at 252.

C. Temporal effects

6–038 In principle, the interpretation simply expresses what was contained *ab initio* in the provisions and principles of Community law to which it relates. Consequently, its temporal effects are the same as the effects of those provisions and principles, in other words, it is effective as from their entry into force or *ex tunc*.[95] This is the starting point for the Court's case law:

> "The interpretation which, in the exercise of the jurisdiction conferred upon it by Article 177 *[now Article 234]*, the Court of Justice gives to a rule of Community law clarifies and defines where necessary the meaning and scope of that rule as it must be or ought to have been understood and applied from the time of its entry into force. It follows that the rule as thus interpreted may, and must, be applied by the courts even to legal relationships arising and established before the judgment ruling on the request for interpretation, provided that in other respects the conditions enabling an action relating to the application of that rule to be brought before the courts having jurisdiction, are satisfied".[96]

The proviso set out in the last sentence of that passage refers to the national procedural rules which continue to govern the conditions in which such a dispute may be brought before the courts (for example time limits and other procedural requirements). Admittedly the procedural rules must accord with Community law,[97] but their relevance—and hence the fact that they may prevent the dispute from being brought back before the courts—is not necessarily defeated by the effects *ex tunc* of the preliminary ruling on interpretation.

6–039 The only exception to the *ex tunc* rule arises out of "the general principle of legal certainty inherent in the Community legal order".[98] Pursuant to that principle, the Court may:

> "be moved to restrict for any person concerned the opportunity of relying upon the provision as . . . interpreted with a view to calling into question legal relationships established in good faith. As the Court has consistently held, such a restriction may be allowed only in the actual judgment ruling upon the interpretation sought".[99]

The national legislature or the domestic courts have no power to restrict the effects *ratione temporis* of a judgment given by way of preliminary ruling

---

[95] See Pescatore (cited in n. 59, above), No. 70, at 1120.

[96] Case 61/79 *Amministrazione delle Finanze dello Stato v. Denkavit Italiana* [1980] E.C.R. 1205 at 1223, para. 16, ECJ; Joined Cases 66, 127 and 128/79 *Amministrazione delle Finanze v. Salumi* [1980] E.C.R. 1237 at 1260, para. 9, ECJ; Case C–137/94 *Richardson* [1995] E.C.R. I–3407 at I–3433–3434, para. 31, ECJ.

[97] See paras. 3–005—3–008, above.

[98] Case 24/86 *Blaizot v. University of Liège* [1988] E.C.R. 379 at 406, para. 28, ECJ.

[99] *ibid.*

if the Court of Justice itself has not done so.[1] In practice, the Court of Justice weighs the principle of legal certainty—which is applied to obviate the serious effects which its judgment might have, as regards the past, on legal relationships entered into in good faith—against the principle of the uniform application of Community law.

Where the scales fall in favour of the principle of legal certainty, the Court declares that no reliance may be placed in the provision as interpreted in order to support claims concerning periods prior to the date of its judgment, except in the case of persons who have before that date initiated legal proceedings or raised an equivalent claim under national law.[2]

The preliminary ruling on interpretation will be limited in time only where "Member States and the circles concerned" were reasonably entitled to assume that the relevant provision of Community law did not apply to their situation and it was only the Court's judgment which showed that it in fact did so apply. The Commission's conduct in the period prior to the judgment will have a decisive bearing on the Court's decision in this regard,[3] alongside the Court's earlier case law[4] and any existing measures of other Community institutions.[5]

---

[1] Case 309/85 *Barra v. Belgium* [1988] E.C.R. 355 at 375, para. 13, ECJ. "[T]he Court has consistently held that such a restriction may be allowed only in the judgment ruling upon the interpretation sought. The fundamental need for a general and uniform application of Community law implies that it is for the Court of Justice alone to decide upon the temporal restrictions to be placed on the interpretation which it lays down." See also Alexander, "The Temporal Effects of Preliminary Rulings" (1988) Y.E.L. 11 at 25, para. 31, Bebr, "Preliminary Rulings of the Court of Justice: Their Authority and Temporal Effect" (1981) C.M.L.Rev. 475 at 503. Compare, however, para. 3–008 above, and in particular (Judgment of February 9, 1999) Case C-343/96 *Dilexport* (cited therein; n. 19).

[2] Case 43/75 *Defrenne v. Sabena* [1976] E.C.R. 455 at 480–481, paras 69–75, ECJ; Case 24/86 *Blaizot v. University of Liège* [1988] E.C.R. 379 at 407, para. 35, ECJ; Case C–262/88 *Barber* [1990] E.C.R. I–1889 at I–1956, paras 44–45, ECJ; Case C–163/90 *Legros and Others* [1992] E.C.R. I–4625 at I–4671, paras 34–35, ECJ; Joined Cases C–485 and C–486/93 *Simitzi* [1995] E.C.R. I–2655 at I–2680, para. 34, ECJ; Case C–126/94 *Cadi Surgelés and Others* [1996] E.C.R. I–5647 at I–5666—5667, paras 32–34, ECJ.

[3] See four of the six cases cited in the preceding note: *Defrenne v. Sabena*, at 480–481, paras 72–73, *Blaizot v. University of Liège*, at 407, paras 32–33, *Barber*, at I–1955, para. 40, *Legros and Others*, at I–4670, para. 32.

[4] Cited in favour of restricting the temporal effects of the preliminary ruling in Case 24/86 *Blaizot v. University of Liège* [1988] E.C.R. 379 at 406–407, para. 31, ECJ; and against in Case 61/79 *Amministrazione delle Finanze dello Stato v. Denkavit Italiana* [1980] E.C.R. 1205 at 1224–1225, paras 19–21, ECJ.

[5] Case C–262/88 *Barber* [1990] E.C.R. I–1889 at I–1995—1956, para. 42, ECJ. The Court of Justice will limit the effects of its judgment *ratione temporis* where, for *e.g.* there is a risk of serious economic repercussions owing in particular to the large number of legal relationships entered into in good faith on the basis of rules considered validly to be in force, or where it appears that both individuals and national authorities have been prompted to adopt practices which do not comply with Community law by reason of objective, significant uncertainty regarding the implications of Community provisions, to which the conduct of other Member States or the Commission may even have contributed (see, for instance, Case C–163/90 *Legros and Others* [1992] E.C.R. I–4625 at I–4670, para. 32, ECJ; Joined Cases C–197 and C–252/94 *Bautiaa and Société française maritime* [1996] E.C.R. I–505 at I–547—550, paras 44–56, ECJ).

6–040 Lastly, it should be noted that the precise scope of the temporal limitation of the effects of a preliminary ruling may be the subject of a further request for an interpretation by way of preliminary ruling.[6]

[6] See para. 6–013, above. See for instance, Case C–106/91 *Ten Oever* [1993] E.C.R. I–4879, ECJ; Case C–110/91, *Moroni* [1993] E.C.R. I–6591, ECJ (these two judgments interpret the restriction of the temporal effects of the judgment in *Barber* which the Court of Justice associated with its interpretation of the E.C. Treaty, Art. 141 (*ex Art. 119*). See also Joined Cases C–363 and C–407–411/93 *Lancry and Others* [1994] E.C.R. I–3957 at I–3995—3996, paras 42, 43, ECJ.

Part III
PROTECTION AGAINST ACTS OF THE INSTITUTIONS

CHAPTER 7

THE ACTION FOR ANNULMENT

I. SUBJECT-MATTER

A. GENERAL

The action for annulment (*i.e.* for a declaration that an act is void), which is provided for in Articles 33 and 38 of the ECSC Treaty, Article 230 (*ex Article 173*) of the E.C. Treaty and Article 146 of the EAEC Treaty, enables Community institutions, Member States and natural and legal persons to protect themselves against unlawful binding acts of Community institutions, provided that specific conditions as to admissibility are fulfilled.[1] By this procedure, the Court of Justice or the Court of First Instance reviews the contested act in the light of superior—written and unwritten—Community law. In the event that an infringement of that superior law is found, the action will result in the annulment of the contested act. **7–001**

B. THE TERM "ACT"

1. The requirement for there to be a contested act

An application for annulment is admissible only if it is directed against an existing act.[2] A non-existent act may not be declared void. **7–002**

Consequently, the applicant must identify precisely the act which it is seeking to have annulled. If it fails to do so, the application will be inadmissible on the ground that its subject-matter is unknown.[3] It may be **7–003**

---

[1] E.U. Treaty, Art. 35 (*ex Art. K.7*) (6) provides for a comparable, yet not identical, procedure in the context of the third pillar (see para. 20–002, below.)

[2] (Order of October 7, 1987), Case 248/86 *Brüggemann v. ESC* [1987] E.C.R. 3963, ECJ; Case T–64/89 *Automec v. Commission* [1990] E.C.R. II–367 at II–381, para. 41, CFI; Case T–16/91 *Rendo v. Commission* [1992] E.C.R. II–2417 at II–2432, para. 39, CFI. The Court of Justice (under the ECJ Rules of Procedure, Art. 92 (2)) and the Court of First Instance (under the CFI Rules of Procedure, Art. 113) may declare of its own motion that an act is non-existent.

[3] Case 30/68 *Lacroix v. Commission* [1970] E.C.R. 301 at 310–311, paras 20–27, ECJ; Case 247/87 *Star Fruit v. Commission* [1989] E.C.R. 291 at 301, para. 9, ECJ. See, however, Case 34/77 *Oslizlok v. Commission* [1978] E.C.R. 1099 at 1111, paras 5, 6, ECJ, where an application for annulment, which was not expressly directed against a specific Commission decision, was nevertheless regarded as being directed against that decision, in view of the arguments put forward in one of the applicant's pleas raised against other decisions related to the first decision, which were expressly mentioned as being the subject-matter of the application for annulment.

that an application for annulment which is formally directed against a particular act, is in fact directed against other acts which are linked with the contested act in such a way that they constitute a single whole.[4]

7–004 An application for annulment of an act which is no longer in force is not necessarily devoid of purpose. If the applicant has an interest in the annulment of an act which is no longer in force and it is within the time-limit prescribed by the fifth paragraph of Article 230 (*ex Article 173*) of the E.C. Treaty, the application will be admissible (at least from this point of view).[5] This also applies where the contested act has already been implemented at the time when the action is brought.[6]

7–005 In the interests of the due administration of justice and the requirements of procedural economy, an action for annulment of an act which is withdrawn in the course of the proceedings may be directed against a new, closely related act which replaces or simply revokes the contested act.[7] In such case, the new act is regarded as a new matter which has arisen in the course of the proceedings and the applicant may put forward new pleas in law.[8] Naturally, it is also possible to bring a new action for annulment. The new act is regarded as being of the same kind as the act which was withdrawn.[9]

7–006 The requirement that the contested measure must exist is applied in the special case of the doctrine of the non-existent act. Such a measure exhibits such particularly serious and manifest defects that it must be regarded as non-existent. If a measure is found to be non-existent, it loses the benefit of the normal presumption that an act is valid in so far as it has not been annulled or the institution which adopted it has not properly repealed or withdrawn it.[10] Moreover, the non-existent act cannot produce any legal

---

[4] Joined Cases 25 and 26/65 *Simet and Feram v. High Authority* [1967] E.C.R. 33 at 43–44, ECJ.

[5] For an example of a case where the applicant had an interest, see Case 207/86 *Apesco v. Commission* [1988] E.C.R. 2151 at 2176, paras 15, 16, ECJ (the interest which the Court of Justice considered sufficient was in preventing a repetition of the alleged illegality in similar future acts); for examples of cases in which the applicant was held not to have an interest, see Joined Cases 294/86 and 77/87 *Technointorg v. Commission and Council* [1988] E.C.R. 6077 at 6110, paras 11–14, ECJ (the application for annulment of a regulation imposing a provisional anti-dumping duty became devoid of purpose where, in the course of the proceedings, it was replaced by a definitive regulation, against which a new action for annulment had been brought); Joined Cases C–305/86 and C–160/87 *Neotype Techmashexport v. Commission and Council* [1990] E.C.R. I–2945 at I–2997, paras 14, 15, ECJ; Case T–239/94 *EISA v. Commission* [1997] E.C.R. II–1839 at II–1855, paras 34, 35, CFI (an action brought against a Commission decision authorising the grant of aid by a Member State pursuant to the ECSC Treaty, Art. 95, which was withdrawn in the course of the procedure, was held to be devoid of purpose because the contested decision had become "inapplicable").

[6] Case 53/85 *AKZO Chemie v. Commission* [1986] E.C.R. 1965 at 1990, para. 21, ECJ.

[7] Case 14/81 *Alpha Steel Ltd v. Commission* [1982] E.C.R. 749, ECJ (the withdrawal of an unlawful measure is permissible, provided that the withdrawal occurs within a reasonable time and that the Commission has had sufficient regard to how the applicant might have been led to rely on the lawfulness of the measure).

[8] ECJ Rules of Procedure, Art. 42(2); CFI Rules of Procedure, Art. 48(2).

[9] Schermers and Waelbroeck, *Judicial Protection*, p. 325.

[10] Joined Cases 7/56 and 3–7/57 *Algera and Others v. Common Assembly* [1957 and 1958] E.C.R. 39 at 60–61, ECJ; Case 15/85 *Consorzio Cooperative d'Abruzzo v. Commission* [1987] E.C.R. 1005 at 1036, para. 10, ECJ.

effects at all. Consequently, an application for annulment of a non-existent act will invariably be declared inadmissible.[11] Furthermore, an act may be declared non-existent after the period prescribed for bringing an action for annulment has run out. The case law, which shows every sign of reluctance,[12] affords only two instances in which a measure was actually declared non-existent (one of them being a case heard by the Court of First Instance, the judgment ultimately being set aside by the Court of Justice).[13]

2. The requirement for a binding act

It follows from Article 230 (*ex Article 173*) of the E.C. Treaty, which provides that opinions and recommendations may not be declared void, and Article 33 of the ECSC Treaty, which provides that only decisions or recommendations (within the meaning of Article 14 of the ECSC Treaty) may be annulled, that acts whose annulment is sought must be binding.[14] Binding acts are the outcome of "the exercise, upon the conclusion of an internal procedure laid down by law, of a power provided for by law which is intended to produce legal effects of such a nature as to affect adversely the interests of the applicant by modifying its legal position".[15] They must therefore have a legitimate legal basis, reflect the definitive position of a Community institution or body and be intended to have legal effects. **7–007**

(1) Content and not form determines whether the act is binding

The binding nature of an act is inferred only from its content.[16] The form in which an act is cast cannot alter its nature.[17] Consequently, an act which does not satisfy the relevant requirements as to form does not cease to be **7–008**

11 In view of the non-existence of the contested measure, the Court of Justice and the Court of First Instance may make an order for costs against the defendant in favour of the applicant (ECJ Rules of Procedure, Art. 69(3), subpara. 2; CFI Rules of Procedure, Art. 87(3), subpara. 2).

12 Joined Cases 7/56 and 3–7/57 *Algera and Others v. Common Assembly* [1957 and 1958] E.C.R. 39 at 60–61, ECJ; Joined Cases 15–33, 52–53, 57–109, 116–117, 123, 132, 135–137/73 *Schots-Kortner v. Council, Commission and European Parliament* [1974] E.C.R. 177 at 191, para. 33, ECJ; Case 15/85 *Consorzio Cooperative d'Abruzzo v. Commission* [1987] E.C.R. 1005 at 1036, para. 10, ECJ; Case 226/87 *Commission v. Greece* [1988] E.C.R. 3611 at 3624, para. 16, ECJ.

13 Joined Cases 1 and 14/57 *Société des Usines à Tubes de la Sarre v. High Authority* [1957 and 1958] E.C.R. 105 at 112–113, ECJ. It must be noted, however, that that judgment was not so much concerned with the non-existence of the measure in question, but to fathom its nature (Mathijsen, "Nullité et annulabilité des actes des institutions européennes", *Miscellanea W.J. Ganshof van der Meersch*, Brussels, Bruylant, 1972, II, at 272–276); Joined Cases T–79, T–84–86, T–89, T–91–92, T–94, T–96, T–98, T–102 and T–104/89 *BASF and Others v. Commission* [1992] E.C.R. II–315, CFI, set aside by Case C–137/92P *Commission v. BASF and Others* [1994] E.C.R. I–2555, ECJ (case note by Le Mire (1994) A.J.D.A. 724).

14 *Société des Usines à Tubes de la Sarre v. High Authority*, (cited in n. 13, above), at 114; Case 133/79 *Sucrimex v. Commission* [1980] E.C.R. 1299 at 1309–1310, paras 12–19, ECJ. For examples of acts which have been held open to review, see Brealey and Hoskins, *Remedies in EC Law*, London, Sweet and Maxwell, 1998 (2nd ed.), pp. 271 *et seq*.

15 Case 182/80 *Gauff v. Commission* [1982] E.C.R. 799 at 817, para. 18, ECJ.

16 For an application, see Case C–57/95 *France v. Commission* [1997] E.C.R. I–1627 at I–1647, para. 9, ECJ.

17 Case 101/76 *Koninklijke Scholten Honig v. Council and Commission* [1977] E.C.R. 797 at 806, para. 7, ECJ; (Order of April 28, 1994), Joined Cases T–452 and T–453/93 *Pevasa and Inpesca v. Commission* [1994] E.C.R. II–229 at II–242, para. 29, CFI.

binding as a result.[18] Thus, the Court of Justice held that it did not follow from non-compliance with the formal requirements prescribed by the High Authority "as a matter of obligation" for decisions within the meaning of Article 14 of the ECSC Treaty that a measure should not be considered a decision if it did not comply with those formal requirements, provided that it satisfied the substantive requirements which decisions had to fulfil under the Treaty.[19] In addition, the Court of First Instance has held that an action will lie against an act made simply orally—by means of a statement by the spokesman for the Commissioner responsible for competition matters, also reported by the press agency *Agence Europe*—on the ground that its contents were not contested by the parties and had subsequently been confirmed by the Commission itself, and that hence the Court of First Instance was in a position to investigate whether it had produced legal effects.[20]

7–009 In the legal sphere of the E.C. Treaty the class of measures against which an action for annulment will lie is not confined to the binding acts mentioned in Article 249 (*ex Article 189*) of that Treaty. The Court of Justice has held that to confine that class of measures in that way would conflict with the obligation under Article 220 (*ex Article 164*) of the E.C. Treaty to ensure observance of the law in the interpretation and application of the Treaty, and that an action for annulment, as a means of fulfilling that obligation, "must therefore be available in the case of all measures adopted by the institutions, whatever their nature or form, which are intended to have legal effects".[21]

In the judgment in the *AETR* case, the Court of Justice found that the Council's decision establishing a common negotiating position on the part of the Member States with a view to the conclusion of an international agreement, fell within the competence of the Community and therefore laid down a course of action binding on the institutions as well as on the Member States. Accordingly, the Court held that the decision constituted a binding act and hence one against which an action would lie, even though it

[18] Joined Cases 53 and 54/63 *Lemmerz-Werke v. High Authority* [1963] E.C.R. 239, ECJ. Once the Court has established that a measure contained in a letter satisfies the substantive requirements of a binding act, it cannot be declared inadmissible on that count: Joined Cases 15 and 29/59 *Société Métallurgique de Knutange v. High Authority* [1960] E.C.R. 1 at 7, ECJ; Joined Cases 8–11/66 *Cimenteries v. Commission* [1967] E.C.R. 75 at 90–91, ECJ; Case C–135/92 *Fiskano v. Commission* [1994] E.C.R. I–2885 at I–2905—2906, paras 21–26, ECJ (Commission letter to Sweden containing a binding act).

[19] Joined Cases 23–24 and 52/63 *Usines Henricot v. High Authority* [1963] E.C.R. 217 at 222, ECJ, where the Court of Justice held, however, that these "fundamental conditions" were not met, namely "a decision must appear as a measure taken by the High Authority, acting as a body, intended to produce legal effects and constituting the culmination of a procedure within the High Authority, whereby the High Authority gives its final ruling in a form from which its nature can be identified": at 224.

[20] Case T–3/93 *Air France v. Commission* [1994] E.C.R. II–121 at II–153—155, paras 55–60, CFI. In a staff case, the Court of Justice likewise accepted that a binding act could be communicated orally (Joined Cases 316/82 and 40/83 *Kohler v. Court of Auditors* [1984] E.C.R. 641 at 655–656, paras 8–13, ECJ).

[21] Case 22/70 *Commission v. Council* (the *AETR* case) [1971] E.C.R. 263 at 277, para. 42, ECJ. See also Case 60/81 *IBM v. Commission* [1981] E.C.R. 2639 at 2651, para. 8, ECJ; Case C–25/94 *Commission v. Council* [1996] E.C.R. I–1469 at I–1505—1506, para. 29, ECJ.

could not be brought within one of the classes of binding acts listed in Article 249 (*ex Article 189*) of the E.C. Treaty.[22]

In contrast, the Court of Justice did not find that a decision of the representatives of the Governments of the Member States meeting in the Council, made at the Commission's proposal, to grant special aid to Bangladesh was a binding act of the Council. The Court did not come to that view because of the name of the act in question,[23] but based its assessment on the precise content of the act and the context in which it was adopted.[24]

Unlike the wording of Article 230 (*ex Article 173*) of the E.C. Treaty and Article 146 of the EAEC Treaty, that of Article 33 of the ECSC Treaty affords, on the face of it, no scope for bringing an action for annulment against binding measures not listed in Article 14 of the ECSC Treaty. Nevertheless, the broad interpretation which the Court of Justice has given to the term "decision" does give scope for bringing any binding act adopted within the legal sphere of the ECSC Treaty within the ambit of Article 33 of that Treaty.[25]

Lastly, an institution may adopt a binding act only in so far as it has a **7–010** legitimate legal basis which empowers the institution to adopt a binding act.[26] No such power may be presumed to exist in the absence of a specific Community provision.[27] As a result of that requirement, the Court of Justice and the Court of First Instance often take the view that they have to consider whether the application for annulment is admissible together with the substance.[28]

[22] An action will even lie against an act by which the Commission concludes an international agreement on behalf of the Community: Case C–327/91 *France v. Commission* [1994] E.C.R. I–3641 at I–3672, paras 14–17, ECJ.

[23] Press release entitled "Aid for Bangladesh—Council conclusions" (reference 6004/91, Press 60–c).

[24] Joined Cases C–181 and C–248/91 *European Parliament v. Council and Commission* [1993] E.C.R. I–3685, ECJ.

[25] Case 8/55 *Fédération Charbonnière de Belgique v. High Authority* [1954 to 1956] E.C.R. 245 at 257, ECJ; Joined Cases 1 and 14/57 *Société des Usines à Tubes de la Sarre v. High Authority* [1957 and 1958] E.C.R. 105 at 114, ECJ: "[A]n act of the High Authority constitutes a decision when it lays down a rule capable of being applied, in other words, when by the said act the High Authority unequivocally determines the position which it decides to adopt if certain conditions are fulfilled".

[26] Case T–113/89 *Nefarma v. Commission* [1990] E.C.R. II–797 at II–816—817, paras 68 *et seq.*, CFI: See para. 7–097, below.

[27] (Order of September 30, 1987), Case 229/86 *Brother Industries v. Commission* [1987] E.C.R. 3757, ECJ; *Nefarma v. Commission* (cited in n. 26, above), at II–817, para. 69.

[28] The question whether the contested act has a legitimate legal basis coincides with the question whether the institution was empowered to adopt it: Joined Cases 358/85 and 51/86 *France v. European Parliament* [1988] E.C.R. 4821 at 4851, paras 13–15, ECJ; Case C–366/88 *France v. Commission* [1990] E.C.R. I–3571, ECJ; Case C–303/90 *France v. Commission* [1991] E.C.R. I–5315, ECJ; Case C–325/91 *France v. Commission* [1993] E.C.R. I–3283 at I–3308—3309, paras 8–11, ECJ.

(2) The act is intended to produce legal effects

7–011 Acts of a Community institution are binding in so far as they produce legal effects.[29] This means that they must be "capable of affecting the interests of the applicant by bringing about a distinct change in his legal position"[30] or adversely affect his legal position by restricting his rights.[31] If they are not, they are not binding and an action will not lie against them.[32]

7–012 Whether an act is capable of having adverse effect must be determined in the first place from its operative part.[33] But the explanations and recitals contained in the act in support of the operative part may also mean that the act has adverse effect and is amenable to review.[34]

---

[29] Joined Cases 8–11/66 *Cimenteries v. Commission* [1967] E.C.R. 75 at 91, ECJ; Case 22/70 *Commission v. Council* [1971] E.C.R. 263 at 276, para. 39, ECJ; Case C–312/90 *Spain v. Commission* [1992] E.C.R. I–4117 at I–4140—4143, paras 11–26, ECJ; and Case C–327/91 *France v. Commission* [1994] E.C.R. I–3641 at I–3672, paras 14, 15, ECJ (the application for annulment of an act by which the Commission purported to conclude an international agreement "between the Commission of the European Communities and the Government of the United States of America regarding the application of their competition laws" was declared admissible on the ground that, "as is apparent from its actual wording, the Agreement is intended to produce legal effects"); Case T–154/94 *CSF and CSME v. Commission* [1996] E.C.R. II–1377 at II–1392, paras 37 *et seq*., CFI (the binding nature of a letter from the Commission was considered in the light of a letter from the applicants which the Commission's letter answered).

[30] Case 60/81 *IBM v. Commission* [1981] E.C.R. 2639 at 2651, para. 9, ECJ; Case 53/85 *AKZO Chemie v. Commission* [1986] E.C.R. 1965 at 1989, para. 16, ECJ.

[31] For cases in which this was held not to be the case, see Case T–541/93 *Connaughton and Others v. Council* [1997] E.C.R. II–549, CFI; and Case T–554/93 *Saint and Murray v. Council and Commission* [1997] E.C.R. II–563, CFI.

[32] (Order of May 17, 1989), Case 151/88 *Italy v. Commission* [1989] E.C.R. 1255 at 1261, paras 22–23, ECJ; (Order of October 4, 1991), Case C–117/91 *Bosman v. Commission* [1991] E.C.R. I–4837 at I–4842, para. 14, ECJ; Case C–476/93P *Nutral v. Commission* [1995] E.C.R. I–4125 at I–4146—4147, paras 30–31, ECJ; Case C–58/94 *Netherlands v. Council* [1996] E.C.R. I–2169 at I–2196, para. 27, ECJ; Case C–180/96 *United Kingdom v. Commission* [1998] E.C.R. I–2265 at I–2280, para. 29, ECJ; Case T–113/89 *Nefarma v. Commission* [1990] E.C.R. II–797 at II–816—824, paras 66–99, CFI; Joined Cases T–10–12 and T–15/92 *Cimenteries CBR and Others v. Commission* [1992] E.C.R. II–2667 at II–2679, para. 28, CFI; Case T–277/94 *AITEC v. Commission* [1996] E.C.R. II–351 at II–372–374, paras 49–56, CFI; Case T–271/94 *Branco v. Commission* [1996] E.C.R. II–749 at II–761—762, para. 32, CFI; (Order of September 29, 1997), Case T–83/97 *Sateba v. Commission* [1997] E.C.R. II–1523 at II–1536—1539, paras 32–40, CFI: a Commission decision in the course of a procedure under the E.C. Treaty, Art. 226 (*ex Art. 169*), which it had initiated following a complaint from an individual, to shelve the complaint has no legal effects for the complainant. The complainant has no procedural rights on the basis of which it could require the Commission to keep it informed and hear its views. Moreover, the complainant has no right to a definitive decision from the Commission since the latter has a discretion whether or not to bring proceedings for failure to fulfil obligations.

[33] Case T–138/89 *Nederlandse Bankiersvereniging and Nederlandse Vereniging van Banken v. Commission* [1992] E.C.R. II–2181 at II–2191, para. 31, CFI.

[34] This is because the operative part of an act is indissociably linked to the statement of reasons for it, so that, when it has to be interpreted, account must be taken of the reasons which led to its adoption: Case C–355/95P *Textilwerke Deggendorf v. Commission* [1997] E.C.R. I–2549 at I–2574, para. 21, ECJ; Joined Cases T–213/95 and T–18/96 *SCK and FNK v. Commission* [1997] E.C.R. II–1739 at II–1780, para. 104, CFI, and the case law cited therein. Whether the operative part has adverse effect consequently extends to the recitals, which constitute the necessary support for the operative part. They may therefore also be the subject of an action for annulment: Case T–16/91 *Rendo and Others v. Commission* [1992] E.C.R. II–2417 at II–2432—2433, paras 40, 41, and at II–2436, para. 55, CFI.

(a) *Confirmatory acts*

7–013 An application for annulment of an act which merely confirms an irrevocable act which was previously adopted is inadmissible.[35] The confirmatory measure does not produce any new legal effects. If the Court of Justice or the Court of First Instance were to hold that an application for annulment of a confirmatory act was admissible despite the fact that the time-limit for bringing an action against the original act had run out, this would make it possible to circumvent that time-limit. An applicant who was out of time would then be able to reactivate the possibility of bringing proceedings by provoking the adoption of a confirmatory act, thereby jeopardizing legal certainty.[36]

So long as the time-limit for bringing an action against the original act has not expired, an action for annulment may be brought against the original act, the confirmatory act or both concurrently.[37] An action against a confirmatory measure will be inadmissible only in so far as it is a genuinely confirmatory act.[38] Thus, from the point of view of procedural law, a measure will be regarded as confirmatory of an earlier measure only if the latter is or was amenable to appeal.[39] Furthermore, a new fact which is of such a character as to alter the essential circumstances and conditions which governed the adoption of the original act causes the new act no longer to be confirmatory even though it has the same content as the original act. An action brought against such an ostensibly confirmatory act will be admissible.[40]

---

[35] Case 56/72 *Goeth v. Commission* [1973] E.C.R. 181 at 187, para. 15, ECJ; Case 1/76 *Wack v. Commission* [1976] E.C.R. 1017 at 1024, para. 7, ECJ; Case 26/76 *Metro v. Commission* [1977] E.C.R. 1875 at 1898, para. 4, ECJ; Joined Cases 166 and 220/86 *Irish Cement Ltd v. Commission* [1988] E.C.R. 6473 at 6499–6503, paras 1–16, ECJ; (Order of November 21, 1990), Case C–12/90 *Infortec v. Commission* [1990] E.C.R. I–4265 at I–4269, para. 10, ECJ; Case C–199/91 *Foyer Culturel du Sart-Tilman v. Commission* [1993] E.C.R. I–2667 at I–2694–2695, paras 20–24, ECJ; Case C–480/93P *Zunis Holding and Others v. Commission* [1996] E.C.R. I–1 at I–29, para. 14, ECJ; Case T–514/93 *Cobrecaf and Others v. Commission* [1995] E.C.R. II–621 at II–636, para. 44, CFI; Case T–275/94 *Groupement des Cartes Bancaires "CB" v. Commission* [1995] E.C.R. II–2169 at II–2182—2183, para. 27, CFI; (Order of March 16, 1998), Case T–235/95 *Goldstein v. Commission* [1998] E.C.R. II–523 at II–536—539, paras 36–48, CFI; (Order of June 10, 1998), Case T–116/95 *Cementir v. Commission* [1998] E.C.R. II–2261 at II–2268, paras 19–25, CFI; (Judgment of September 16, 1998), Case T–188/95 *Waterleiding Maatschappij Noord-West Brabant v. Commission*, paras 88–141, CFI (not yet reported) (a complaint made against state aid which the Commission had already declared to be compatible with the common market does not, where the decision has become definitive, cause time to start running afresh in order to bring an action for annulment of the decision by which the Commission rejects the complaint while confirming its earlier decision).

[36] Joined Cases 166 and 220/86 *Irish Cement Ltd v. Commission* [1988] E.C.R. 6473 at 6503, para. 16, ECJ; Case C–199/91 *Foyer Culturel du Sart-Tilman v. Commission* [1993] E.C.R. I–2667 at I–2694—2695, paras 23–24, ECJ; Joined Cases T–121/96 and T–151/96 *MAAS v. Commission* [1997] E.C.R. II–1355 at II–1370, para. 50, CFI.

[37] Joined Cases 193 and 194/87 *Maurissen and European Public Service Union v. Court of Auditors* [1989] E.C.R. 1045 at 1075, para. 26, ECJ.

[38] Case 9/81 *Williams v. Court of Auditors* [1982] E.C.R. 3301 at 3314, para. 15, ECJ.

[39] Joined Cases 193 and 194/87 *Maurissen and European Public Service Union v. Court of Auditors* [1989] E.C.R. 1045 at 1074, para. 23, ECJ.

[40] Joined Cases 42 and 49/59 *SNUPAT v. High Authority* [1961] E.C.R. 53 at 75–76, ECJ; Case T–331/94 *IPK v. Commission* [1997] E.C.R. II–1665 at II–1678, para. 26, CFI.

(b) *Resolutions*

7–014 Resolutions often express a political declaration of intent which embodies no binding commitments and therefore produces no legal effects. Accordingly, an action will not lie against a resolution,[41] unless it appears from its content that it affects the legal position of a Member State or a person.[42]

(c) *Internal instructions*

7–015 Internal instructions are usually simply guidelines for the adoption of acts of institutions. Generally, they do not produce legal effects. Consequently, an internal instruction of the Commission indicating the manner in which it intended to exercise its provisional power to compile a list of candidates for service contracts concluded within the framework of the Lomé Convention was not an act producing legal effects. It was not the line of conduct set out in the internal instruction which produced legal effects and reflected the Commission's definitive position, but the drawing up of the list itself.[43]

Even where internal instructions do have legal effects, they must create rights or obligations outside the institution concerned before third parties may bring an admissible application for their annulment.[44]

(d) *Preparatory acts and measures laying down a definitive position*

7–016 An action will lie against an act only if it definitively lays down the position of the institution which adopted it.[45]

7–017 Some acts of institutions are adopted by means of a procedure comprising different stages. Only the measure which concludes the procedure expresses the definitive position of the institution. Measures paving the way for the final measure do not determine a definitive position. Consequently,

---

[41] Joined Cases 90 and 91/63 *Commission v. Luxembourg and Belgium* [1964] E.C.R. 625 at 631, ECJ (in that judgment, given pursuant to the E.C. Treaty, Art. 169 (*now Art. 226*), the Court of Justice held that a resolution was not a binding measure); Case 9/73 *Schlüter v. Hauptzollamt Lörrach* [1973] E.C.R. 1135 at 1161, para. 40, ECJ (in that judgment, given in response to a request for a preliminary ruling, the Court of Justice held that the resolution in question was "primarily an expression of the policy favoured by the Council and Government Representatives of the Member States" and could not, "by reason of its content, create legal consequences of which parties might avail themselves in court").

[42] Case 108/83 *Luxembourg v. European Parliament* [1984] E.C.R. 1945 at 1957–1958, paras 19–23, ECJ; Joined Cases C–213/88 and C–39/89 *Luxembourg v. European Parliament* [1991] E.C.R. I–5643, ECJ.

[43] Case 114/86 *United Kingdom v. Commission* [1988] E.C.R. 5289, ECJ.

[44] For examples of cases in which the internal instruction produced only internal effects, see Case 20/58 *Phoenix-Rheinrohr v. High Authority* [1959] E.C.R. 25, ECJ; Case 190/84 *Les Verts v. European Parliament* [1988] E.C.R. 1017, ECJ. For a case in which the internal instruction had effects outside the institution and could therefore be challenged before the Court of Justice, see Case C–366/88 *France v. Commission* [1990] E.C.R. I–3571.

[45] Joined Cases 23–24 and 52/63 *Henricot v. High Authority* [1963] E.C.R. 217 at 223–224, ECJ; Case 60/81 *IBM v. Commission* [1981] E.C.R. 2639 at 2652, para. 10, ECJ. For an instance in which the contested act did not definitively lay down a position and therefore had no legal effects, see (Order of June 28, 1993), Case C–64/93 *Danotab and Others v. Commission* [1993] E.C.R. I–3595 at I–3601, paras 13, 14, ECJ.

preparatory acts may not be the subject of an action for annulment.[46] This is because an action brought against such a measure would make it necessary for the Court of Justice or the Court of First Instance to "arrive at a decision on questions on which the [institution] has not yet had an opportunity to state its position and would as a result anticipate the arguments on the substance of the case, confusing different procedural stages both administrative and judicial".[47]

Where an action for annulment is brought against the measure conclud- **7–018** ing the procedure, any irregularities in the preparatory acts may be raised in challenging the final act.[48]

(e) *Competition cases*

The processing of complaints and the investigation and prosecution of **7–019** infringements of Articles 81 and 82 (*ex Articles 85 and 86*) of the E.C. Treaty are governed by Regulation No. 17 and Regulation No. 99/63.[49] These regulations set out an administrative procedure involving the Commission adopting a number of acts, some of which may be challenged in court proceedings, others not.[50]

Acts which the Commission adopts during this administrative procedure **7–020** with regard to undertakings under investigation are generally only preparatory acts. Any irregularities in such acts may be raised in an action brought against the decision concluding the procedure.[51] Consequently, the initiation of an administrative procedure under Regulation No. 17[52] and the communication of a statement of objections within the meaning of Article 2 of Regulation No. 99/63[53] are not acts against which an application for annulment may be brought.[54] Likewise, notice given by the Commission

46 See, for instance, Case 346/87 *Bossi v. Commission* [1989] 303 at 332–333, para. 23, ECJ; Case T–64/89 *Automec v. Commission* [1990] E.C.R. II–367 at II–381, para. 42, CFI; Joined Cases T–17/90, T–28/91 and T–17/92 *Camara Alloisio and Others v. Commission* [1993] E.C.R. II–841 at II–857, para. 39, CFI.

47 Case 60/81 *IBM v. Commission* [1981] E.C.R. 2639 at 2654, para. 20, ECJ.

48 Joined Cases 12 and 29/64 *Ley v. Commission* [1965] E.C.R. 107 at 118, ECJ. See also n. 57, *infra*: Joined Cases T–10–12 and T–15/92 *Cimenteries CBR and Others v. Commission* [1992] E.C.R. II–2667, CFI.

49 [1963–1964] O.J. Spec. Ed. 47.

50 For an extensive discussion, see Kerse, *EEC Antitrust Procedure*, London, European Law Centre Ltd, 1994.

51 See para. 7–105, below.

52 In order to initiate the administrative procedure under Regulation No 17, Arts. 2, 3 or 6, there must be a "an authoritative act of the Commission, evidencing its intention of taking a decision under the said Articles" (Case 48/72 *Brasserie de Haecht v. Wilkin-Janssen* [1973] E.C.R. 77 at 88, para. 16, ECJ). This means that the undertaking addressed can be in no doubt that an administrative procedure is under way against it, and must be aware of its procedural position. Such notification does not constitute the definitive adoption of a position.

53 In its statement of objections, the Commission is obliged to apprise the undertaking charged with an infringement of the E.C. Treaty, Art. 81 or 82 (*ex Art. 85 or 86*) of the facts and arguments underlying its charges. That statement secures the right of the undertaking concerned to a fair hearing.

54 Case 60/81 *IBM v. Commission* [1981] E.C.R. 2639 at 2654, para. 21. ECJ. For another

pursuant to Article 19(3) of Regulation No. 17, indicating that it intends to adopt a favourable position with regard to an agreement which has been notified to it and inviting interested third parties to submit their comments, cannot form the subject-matter of an action for annulment.[55]

7–021 Nevertheless, an action will lie against some acts adopted in the course of the administrative procedure.

For instance, a decision by the Commission not to treat certain documents as confidential during the administrative procedure and to disclose them to third parties may form the subject-matter of an action.[56] Such a decision is independent of the final decision bringing the administrative procedure to an end. Moreover, the possibility of bringing an action for annulment of the final decision does not afford adequate protection. On the one hand, the administrative procedure does not always culminate in a final decision, which, at the same time, rules out any chance of bringing an action and would hence enable the right to confidential treatment of documents to be breached without any judicial sanction; on the other hand, an action against the final decision affords no guarantee of being able to prevent the disclosure of confidential documents from having irreparable consequences.[57]

A decision taken by the Commission pursuant to Article 11(5) of Regulation No. 17 in the context of a preliminary examination requesting an undertaking or an association of undertakings to provide information[58] or a decision ordering an investigation pursuant to Article 14(3) of that regulation, constitute acts against which an action will lie.[59]

---

example see (Order of June 24, 1998) *Dalmine v. Commission* [1998] E.C.R. II–2383 at II–2398—2399, paras 30–32, CFI, (the decision referred to in Article 16(1) of Regulation No. 17 imposing a periodic penalty payment expressed in terms of a number of units of account per day of delay, calculated from a date fixed by it, does not constitute a challengeable measure, since that decision does not determine the total amount of the periodic penalty payment and hence cannot be enforced; that amount can be definitively fixed only in another decision, which will be a challengeable act).

[55] Case T–74/92 *Ladbroke v. Commission* [1995] E.C.R. II–115 at II–142—143, para. 72, CFI.

[56] Case 53/85 *AKZO Chemie v. Commission* [1986] E.C.R. 1965, ECJ. But see (Order of May 2, 1997), Case T–136/96 *Automobiles Peugeot v. Commission* [1997] E.C.R. II–663, CFI: an action will not lie against a letter addressed by the Commission to an undertaking in which it expresses its intention to communicate purported business secrets of that undertaking and giving it one month to submit any comments to the hearing officer pursuant to Commission Decision 94/810, Art. 5, ECSC on the terms of reference of hearing officers in competition procedures before the Commission ([1994] O.J. L330/67). Such an act is only a preparatory act forming part of the first stage of the procedure set out in Decision 94/810, Art. 5.

[57] In contrast, a Commission decision refusing to comply with a request for disclosure of supplementary documents to undertakings affected by a statement of objections in order to guarantee their rights of defence does not constitute a challengeable act. The possible unlawfulness of that decision may be attacked in an application against the final decision (Joined Cases T–10–12 and T–15/92 *Cimenteries CBR and Others v. Commission* [1992] E.C.R. II–2667, CFI).

[58] Case 374/87 *Orkem v. Commission* [1989] E.C.R. 3282, ECJ.

[59] Regulation No. 17, Art. 11(5) and Art. 14(3) require the Commission's decision to mention the right to have the decision reviewed by the Court of Justice (now the Court of First Instance). It should be noted, however, that reports drawn up by Commission officials conducting the investigation noting oral explanations given by representatives of the undertaking or association of undertakings under investigation cannot constitute the

A communication pursuant to Article 15(6) of Regulation No. 17 by which the Commission withdraws exemption from a fine from an undertaking which has notified an agreement[60] is an act against which an action may be brought. The Commission takes such a decision where, after conducting a preliminary examination, it considers that the agreement notified is prohibited by Article 81 (*ex Article 85*) (1) of the E.C. Treaty and that a declaration under Article 81(3) that the first paragraph of that article is inapplicable is unjustified. The Court of Justice has held that if such a "preliminary measure" were excluded from all (direct) judicial review, there would be no other alternative for the undertakings concerned than to "take the risk of a serious threat of a fine or to terminate against their own interests an agreement which, if proceedings had been instituted, might have had a chance of escaping the prohibition".[61] That dilemma for the undertakings concerned generally leads to termination of the notified agreement, with the result that the Commission often does not have to take a final decision in order to impose its view of the merits. If no action could lie against a communication pursuant to Article 15(6) of Regulation No. 17, the Commission could effectually avoid any judicial review of its action.

Decisions by which the Commission imposes interim measures pending its final decision in order to avoid irreparable damage arising during investigations which cannot be remedied by the final decision must be "made in such a form that an action may be brought upon them . . . by any party who considers he has been injured".[62]

An action will lie against commitments entered into by undertakings in the context of a Commission investigation into infringements of competition law. Such commitments are to be equated to orders requiring an infringement to be brought to an end as provided for by Article 3 of Regulation No. 17. The undertakings acquiesce in fact to a decision which the Commission itself could have taken. Entry into such commitments is therefore not an act ascribable to the undertakings, but the corollary of an act of the Commission against which an action will lie.[63]

Acts adopted by the Commission during the administrative procedure, *vis-à-vis* persons who have lodged complaints about alleged breaches of the competition rules, are also not capable of forming the subject-matter of an action. **7–022**

Accordingly, an action will not lie against the notification to be served under Article 6 of Regulation 99/63 on persons submitting a complaint to

subject-matter of an action: (Order of June 9, 1997), Case T–9/97 *Elf Atochem v. Commission* [1997] E.C.R. II–909 at II–918—920, paras 18–27, CFI.

60 Regulation No 17, Art. 15 (5).

61 Joined Cases 8–11/66 *SA Cimenteries CBR Cementsbedrijven NV and Others v. Commission* [1967] E.C.R. 75 at 92–93, ECJ; Case T–19/91 *Vichy v. Commission* [1992] E.C.R. II–415 at II–420, para. 5, CFI; Joined Cases T–213/95 and T–18/96 *SCK and FNK v. Commission* [1997] E.C.R. II–1739 at II–1769, para. 68, CFI.

62 (Order of January 17, 1980), Case 792/79R *Camera Care v. Commission* [1980] E.C.R. 119 at 131, para. 19, ECJ. See also Joined Cases 228 and 229/82 *Ford v. Commission* [1984] E.C.R. 1129 at 1158, para. 10, ECJ.

63 Joined Cases C–89, C–104, C–114, C–116–117 and C–125–129/85 *Ahlström Osakeyhtiö v. Commission* [1993] E.C.R. I–1307 at I–1625, para. 181, ECJ.

the Commission pursuant to Article 3(2) of Regulation No. 17 which informs the complainants that the Commission is not going to take up the complaint and fixes a time-limit for them to submit any further comments, after which it takes its final decision.[64] The notification must make it quite clear that the complainant is entitled to submit comments on the proposed rejection of his or her complaint. If no such communication is made, the rejection of the complaint is final and, according to settled case law,[65] may be the subject of judicial proceedings.[66]

However, an action will lie against a decision of the Commission suspending an administrative procedure under Regulation No. 17 pending delivery of judgment in proceedings pursuant to Article 226 (*ex Article 169*) of the E.C. Treaty. This is because such a decision affects the procedural rights of persons who have submitted a complaint pursuant to Article 3(2) of Regulation No. 17, in particular the right to be informed beforehand of the Commission's intention not to uphold their complaint and to submit

---

[64] Case C–282/95P *Guérin Automobiles v. Commission* [1997] E.C.R. I–1503 at I–1542, para. 34, ECJ; Case T–64/89 *Automec v. Commission* [1990] E.C.R. II–367 at II–382—383, para. 46, CFI.

[65] Case 210/81 *Demo-Studio Schmidt v. Commission* [1983] E.C.R. 3045, ECJ; Case 298/83 *CICCE v. Commission* [1985] E.C.R. 1105, ECJ; Joined Cases 142 and 156/84 *BAT and Reynolds v. Commission* [1987] 4487, ECJ.

[66] See Case C–39/93P *SFEI and Others v. Commission* [1994] E.C.R. I–2681 at I–2709—2711, paras 24–33, ECJ, in which the Court of Justice set aside the order of the Court of First Instance in Case T–36/92 *SFEI and Others v. Commission* [1992] E.C.R. II–2479. The judgment given on appeal by the Court of Justice links up with the analysis carried out by the Court of First Instance in Case T–64/89 *Automec v. Commission* [1990] E.C.R. II–367 of the procedure to be applied where the Commission deals with a complaint alleging infringement of the Treaty competition rules. The Court of First Instance distinguished between three stages (*ibid.*, at II–382—383, paras 45–47). During the first of those stages, the Commission collects the information needed to decide what action to take on the complaint. That stage may include an informal exchange of views and information between the Commission and the complainant. In the view of the Court of First Instance, preliminary observations made by Commission officials in the context of those informal contacts cannot be regarded as measures open to challenge. In the second stage, the Commission *either* informs the complainant, in accordance with Regulation 99/63, Art. 6, that it does not intend to take up the complaint and sets a time-limit within which the complainant is to submit its observations, *or* serves on the undertaking allegedly in breach of the competition rules a statement of objections if it considers that the infringement raised in the complaint should be pursued. As already mentioned, neither of those acts may be challenged because they do not amount to a definitive position on the part of the Commission. If the Commission intends to reject the complaint, the Commission takes cognizance of the complainant's comments in the third stage. That stage may end with a final decision by which the Commission rejects the complaint. The complainant may bring an action to annul that decision. In its order in *SFEI and Others v. Commission*, the Court of First Instance took the view that the contested act formed part of the first stage of the investigation and was therefore not amenable to an action for annulment. On appeal, however, the Court of Justice held that the act constituted a final decision definitively rejecting the complaint, and annulled the order of the Court of First Instance. That judgment does not detract from the analysis of the Court of First Instance in *Automec*. It merely indicates—as also emerges from the judgment of the Court of First Instance in *Automec* (para. 48)—that the breakdown of the processing of a complaint into three stages for analytical purposes does not mean that an action will lie against the rejection of a complaint only if all three stages of the procedure have been completed (see, however, Spinks, note to *Automec v. Commission* (1991) C.M.L.Rev. 453 at 461; see also Case T–37/92 *BEUC and NCC v. Commission* [1994] E.C.R. II–285 at II–303—307, paras 27–36, CFI).

observations in that connection and the right to bring an action for annulment against the rejection of the complaint. In the case of proceedings under Article 226 of the Treaty, persons who have lodged a complaint do not have those rights. If some of the questions raised in the complaint pursuant to Regulation No. 17 are going to form the subject of infringement proceedings and the Commission therefore suspends judgment on the complaint as far as those questions are concerned, this deprives the complainant of its procedural rights. An action may consequently be brought against the decision suspending the administrative procedure.[67]

(f) *State aid cases*

Under Article 88 (*ex Article 93*) (2) of the E.C. Treaty, the Commission has to put "parties concerned" on notice to submit observations before it rules on the compatibility of state aid with the common market. **7–023**

That notice produces no legal effects where it relates to an existing aid[68] because the Member State may maintain the aid at that stage in the procedure.

If, in contrast, the notice relates to new aid,[69] the Member State concerned may not implement the proposed measure before the *inter partes* procedure provided for in Article 88(2) has resulted in a final decision (E.C. Treaty, Article 88(3)). In this case, the obligation to suspend implementation of the proposed aid measure produces legal effects which cannot be eradicated.[70] The delay in the implementation of the aid measure on account of the suspensory effect of the notice, is not remedied by a Commission decision finding the aid compatible with the common market or by a successful action for the annulment of the Commission's finding that the proposed aid is incompatible with the common market. In the latter case, any implementation of the new aid from the date of the notice

67 Case T–16/91 *Rendo and Others v. Commission* [1992] E.C.R. II–2417 at II–2435—2436, paras 51–55, CFI.

68 "[A]id which existed before the entry into force of the Treaty and aid which could be properly put into effect under the conditions laid down in Art. 93 (*now Art. 88*) (3), including those arising from the interpretation of that article given by the Court in its judgment in the *Lorenz* case, is to be regarded as existing aid within the meaning of Art. 93 (*now Art. 88*) (1)": Case C–44/93 *Namur - Les Assurances du Crédit* [1994] E.C.R. I–3829 at I–3870, para. 13, ECJ. It appears from *Lorenz* that if the Commission, after being informed by a Member State of a plan to grant or alter aid, fails to initiate the *inter partes* procedure, this state may, at the end of a period sufficient to enable a preliminary examination of the plan to be carried out, grant the proposed aid, provided that it has given prior notice to the Commission, and this aid will then be governed by the rules concerning existing aid (Case 120/73 *Lorenz v. Germany* [1973] E.C.R. 1471 at 1482, para. 6, ECJ. See also Case C–387/92 *Banco Exterior de España* [1994] E.C.R. I–877 at I–909, para. 19, ECJ).

69 "[M]easures to grant or alter aid, where the alterations may relate to existing aid or initial plans notified to the Commission, must be regarded as new aid subject to the obligation of notification laid down by Art. 93 (*now Art. 88*) (3)" (*Namur - Les Assurances du Crédit* (cited in n. 68, above), para. 13. For those two types of new aid, see also Joined Cases 91 and 127/83 *Heineken Brouwerijen BV v. Inspecteurs der Vennootschapsbelasting* [1984] E.C.R. 3435 at 3453, paras 17, 18, ECJ).

70 Case C–312/90 *Spain v. Commission* [1992] E.C.R. I–4117 at I–4141—4142, paras 14–20, ECJ; Case C–47/91 *Italy v. Commission* [1992] E.C.R. I–4145 at I–4160—4162, paras 22–26, ECJ.

until the time of the final decision is unlawful. For those reasons, notice under Article 88(2) of the E.C. Treaty cannot be regarded as merely a preparatory step.[71] Moreover, for the Member State concerned an action will lie against a decision by which the Commission classifies a measure as state aid within the meaning of Article 87 (*ex Article 92*) (1) of the E.C. Treaty and nevertheless declares it compatible with the common market.[72] The Court of Justice has given no specific reasons why this should be so, but it may be observed that classification of the measure at issue as state aid means that the Member State is obliged to notify it and implement it only after the Commission has taken its final decision. Furthermore, the decision by which the Commission holds the measure classified as state aid to be compatible with the common market does not cause the aid which has been disbursed during the administrative investigation no longer to be unlawful. Lastly, such a decision gives rise to an obligation to notify like measures to the Commission in the future.

(g) *Anti-dumping cases*

7–024 Regulation No. 384/96[73] confers extensive duties on the Commission in connection with the investigation of dumping and the provisional control thereof. It receives complaints, directly or indirectly, initiates investigations and decides whether or not protective measures are needed. Various acts adopted by the Commission pursuant to that regulation are preparatory and hence cannot be the subject of an application for annulment, the reason being that sufficient protection is afforded by bringing an action against the final decision.[74] In contrast, other acts adopted by the Commis-

[71] *Spain v. Commission* (cited in n. 70, above) at I–4142—4143, paras 21–24.

[72] Case C–241/94 *France v. Commission* [1996] E.C.R. I–4551, ECJ.

[73] Council Regulation No. 384/96 of December 22, 1995 on protection against dumped imports from countries not members of the European Community ([1996] O.J. L56/1).

[74] Accordingly, the Court of Justice held that an application for the annulment of a decision of the Commission rejecting an undertaking offered by the company concerned in return for the termination of the anti-dumping investigation (Regulation No. 384/96, Art. 8(3)) was inadmissible on the ground that the rejection constituted only an "intermediate measure" against which an action for annulment would not lie (Joined Cases C–133 and C–150/87 *Nashua Corporation and Others v. Commission and Council* [1990] E.C.R. I–719 at I–771, paras 8–11, ECJ; Case C–156/87 *Gestetner Holdings v. Council and Commission* [1990] E.C.R. I–781 at I–831, para. 8, ECJ). A Commission decision terminating an undertaking breached by an exporter (within the meaning of Regulation No. 384/96, Art. 8) is not an attackable act: (Order of July 10, 1996), Case T–208/95 *Miwon v. Commission* [1996] E.C.R. II–635 at II–646, para. 31, CFI. A decision to initiate an anti-dumping procedure is a purely preparatory act: (Order of March 14, 1996), Case T–134/95 *Dysan Magnetics and Review Magnetics v. Commission* [1996] E.C.R. II–181 at II–192, para. 23, CFI, and (Order of December 10, 1996), Case T–75/96 *Söktas v. Commission* [1996] E.C.R. II–1689 at II–1699—1703, paras 26–43, CFI. A proposal submitted by the Commission to the Council, following an objection raised in the Advisory Committee, to terminate the procedure without imposing protective measures (Regulation No. 384/96, Art. 9(2)) is a preparatory act, against which an action will not lie: Case T–212/95 *Oficemen v. Commission* [1997] E.C.R. II–1161 at II–1176—1178, paras 45–54, CFI.

sion in this context have legal effects and may be attacked by means of action for annulment.[75]

II. Identity of the Parties

A. In the E.C. Treaty

1. Defendants: against which institutions can an action for annulment be brought?

(1) Institutions

The first paragraph of Article 230 (*ex Article 173*) of the E.C. Treaty enables actions for annulment to be brought against acts adopted jointly by the European Parliament and the Council and acts of the Council, the Commission and the European Central Bank.[76] Acts of the European Parliament may also be reviewed if they are intended to produce legal effects *vis-à-vis* third parties.[77] This confirms the case law on the EEC Treaty with regard to the admissibility of applications for annulment of acts of the European Parliament.[78] **7–025**

[75] The following are to be regarded as acts producing legal effects: a decision to terminate the procedure without taking protective measures, a decision which is final unless the Council decides otherwise within one month, and a decision to impose a provisional anti-dumping duty (as far as the latter is concerned, see Joined Cases 294/86 and 77/87 *Technointorg v. Commission and Council* [1988] E.C.R. 6077 at 6109–6110, paras 10–14, ECJ: it was held that there was no need to proceed to judgment on the application for the annulment of the provisional anti-dumping duty, but the admissibility of the application was not denied). This does not prevent irregularities committed by the Commission in the course of the procedure leading to the imposition of provisional anti-dumping duties from being raised in order to claim that the Council regulation imposing definitive anti-dumping duties should be annulled, provided that the Council regulation takes the place of the Commission regulation. If, however, the defects were remedied in the course of the procedure resulting in the adoption of the definitive anti-dumping duties, the unlawfulness of the Commission regulation no longer affects the legality of the Council regulation: Joined Cases T–159/94 and T–160/94 *Ajinomoto and NutraSweet v. Council* [1997] E.C.R. II–2461 at II–2493, para. 87, CFI; a decision of the Commission denying a third party access to the non-confidential file also has legal effects: Case C–170/89 *BEUC v. Commission* [1991] E.C.R. I–5709 at I–5739, para. 11, ECJ.

[76] An example of an act which may be the subject of an action for annulment is the decision of the European Central Bank imposing a sanction on the basis of Council Regulation No. 2532/98 of November 23, 1998, concerning the powers of the European Central Bank to impose sanctions ([1998] O.J. L318/4).

[77] An application to annul an act of the European Council will be inadmissible since such acts do not fall within the jurisdiction of the Court of Justice or the Court of First Instance to conduct judicial review: (Order of July 14, 1994), Case T–179/94 *Bonnamy v. Council*, para. 10, CFI (not reported in the E.C.R.); (Order of July 14, 1994), Case T–584/94 *Roujansky v. Council* [1994] E.C.R. II–585 at II–591, para. 12, CFI.

[78] The EEC Treaty, Art. 173, para. 1 confined actions for annulment to acts of the Council or the Commission. That limitation stemmed from the original institutional structure of the Community in which only the Council and the Commission were empowered to adopt binding acts. The gradual expansion of the European Parliament's competence which enabled it to adopt binding acts prompted the Court of Justice to give a broad interpretation to the former Art. 173, para. 1, in order to avoid acts of the Parliament not being subject to judicial review with regard to their compatibility with the Treaty (Case

(2) Community bodies entrusted with the preparation or implementation of Community law

7–026 Community institutions may set up bodies (legal persons governed by private or public law) and delegate powers to them. Following on from the judgment in *Les Verts*, which made any binding act of any Community "institution" amenable to judicial review by the Court of Justice and the Court of First Instance, the question arises as to whether the Court of Justice and the Court of First Instance have jurisdiction under Article 230 (*ex Article 173*) of the E.C. Treaty to declare acts of such bodies void. As far as actions for damages are concerned, the Court of Justice has already held that "a Community body established by the Treaty and authorized to act in [the Community's] name and on its behalf" may be an "institution" of the Community for the purposes of the second paragraph of Article 288 (*ex Article 215*)[79] of the E.C. Treaty.[80] The same approach would not seem to be precluded in the case of actions for annulment.[81]

(3) What acts may be imputed to an institution?

7–027 An action for annulment will lie only against acts which may be imputed to a Community institution.[82] It is not enough that an institution was involved in bringing the act about in order for it to be imputed to that institution. The act must be the outcome of the institution's decision-making power.

294/83 *Les Verts v. European Parliament* [1986] E.C.R. 1339, ECJ, confirmed by Case 34/86 *Council v. European Parliament* [1986] E.C.R. 2155 at 2201, para. 5, ECJ).

[79] Case C–370/89 *SGEEM and Etroy v. European Investment Bank* [1992] E.C.R. I–6211 at I–6248, paras 15–16, ECJ.

[80] See para. 11–013, below.

[81] But only in so far as the Community act establishing the body in question does not provide for an effective procedure organising supervision of the legality of acts of that body. See also Lenaerts, "Regulating the Regulatory Process: 'Delegation of Powers' in the European Community" (1993) E.L.Rev. 23–49. For a survey of such bodies, see Lenaerts and Van Nuffel, *Constitutional Law of the European Union*, 7–095 and 11–056—11–060. It has become clear from Case C–25/94 *Commission v. Council* [1996] E.C.R. I–1469 at I–1504—1505, paras 21–28, ECJ, that Coreper is not an institution, but an auxiliary body of the Council, in that it carries out preparatory work and tasks assigned to it by the Council (E.C. Treaty, Art. 207 (*ex Art. 151*) (1)). Coreper's function of carrying out tasks assigned to it by the Council does not give it the power to take decisions which belongs, under the Treaty, to the Council. Acts adopted by Coreper in this context therefore cannot be regarded as binding acts of the Council. In an Order of November 26, 1993, the Court of First Instance held that Art. 180 (*now Art. 237*) (c) did not afford a legal basis for individuals to bring an action for annulment of decisions of the Board of Directors of the European Investment Bank. The Court took this view because the European Investment Bank, unlike the European Parliament, had not increased its original powers and because acts of the EIB did not have legal effects *vis-à-vis* third parties. Consequently, there was no need to give a broad interpretation to Art. 173 (*now Art. 230*) as the Court of Justice had done in the judgment in *Les Verts* in order to enable actions to be brought against acts of the European Parliament: (Order of November 26, 1993), Case T–460/93 *Tête and Others v. EIB* [1993] E.C.R. II–1257, CFI.

[82] Case C–201/89 *Le Pen* [1990] E.C.R. I–1183 at I–1200, para. 14, ECJ: acts of a political group of the European Parliament cannot be imputed to the Parliament *qua* institution; Case C–97/91 *Oleificio Borelli v. Commission* [1992] E.C.R. I–6313 at I–6333, paras 9–10, ECJ; Joined Cases C–181 and C–248/91 *European Parliament v. Council and Commission* [1993] E.C.R. I–3685, ECJ: acts adopted by representatives of the Member States' governments meeting in the Council cannot be imputed to the Council, a Community institution.

The classic example is a decision to award a tender in a public tendering procedure for works in the ACP States which, by virtue of the Lomé Convention,[83] are financed by the Community. The decision to award the tender is a sovereign decision of the ACP State concerned. The Commission's involvement, which is governed by legislation, in preparing the decision does not mean that that decision may be imputed to it.[84]

An act of a member or of a staff member of an institution is not necessarily to be imputed to the institution.[85] It will be so imputable only if the person who adopts the act makes it clear that he or she does so pursuant to his or her power to act in the name of the institution.[86] Furthermore, it must transpire from the content of the act that the person in question intended to express the position or the decision of the institution.[87] **7–028**

Treaty amendments and Acts relating to the accession of new Member States (adopted pursuant to Article 49 (*ex Article O*) of the E.U. Treaty, formerly Article 237 of the EEC Treaty) are not acts of Community institutions.[88] They are provisions of primary law which are not subject to the system of judicial review provided for in the Treaty. Even if modifications of acts of the institutions ensue out of those provisions, they still do not constitute acts of the institutions and are therefore not amenable to judicial review.[89] **7–029**

2. Applicants: who can bring an action for annulment?

(1) The Council, the Commission and the Member States

The Council, the Commission and the Member States derive from the second paragraph of Article 230 (*ex Article 173*) of the E.C. Treaty the right to bring actions for annulment. They are privileged applicants. They may, **7–030**

[83] [1991] O.J. L229/3.

[84] Case 126/83 *STS v. Commission* [1984] E.C.R. 2769, ECJ; Case 118/83 *CMC v. Commission* [1985] E.C.R. 2325, ECJ; Case C–257/90 *Italsolar v. Commission* [1993] E.C.R. I–9, ECJ. For an application of this principle in the agricultural sector, see Case T–93/95 *Laga v. Commission* [1998] E.C.R. II–195 at II–206—208, paras 33–42, CFI; Case T–94/95 *Landuyt v. Commission* [1998] E.C.R. II–213 at II–223—225, paras 33–42, CFI (in which the Court of First Instance held that the claim for annulment was essentially directed against the act of a national authority and not against an act of a Community institution). But see Case C–395/95P *Geotronics v. Commission* [1997] E.C.R. I–2271, ECJ.

[85] Joined Cases 42 and 49/59 *SNUPAT v. High Authority* [1961] E.C.R. 53 at 72, ECJ.

[86] Case 34/86 *Council v. European Parliament* [1986] E.C.R. 2155 at 2201–2202, paras 7–8, ECJ. A report commissioned by an institution from a private consultancy firm cannot be imputed to the institution. This is because such a report does not contain any act adopted by the institution itself ((Order of March 26, 1980), Case 51/79 *Buttner v. Commission* [1980] E.C.R. 1201, ECJ).

[87] Case T–113/89 *Nefarma v. Commission* [1990] E.C.R. II–797 at II–820, para. 81, CFI (a letter from the Member of the Commission responsible for competition to the Netherlands Government appeared to have been written in his own name and in the context of an exchange of views between politicians, and could therefore not be regarded as an act of the Commission).

[88] Case C–313/89 *Commission v. Spain* [1991] E.C.R. I–5231 at I–5250, para. 10, ECJ.

[89] Joined Cases 31 and 35/86 *LAISA and Others v. Council* [1988] E.C.R. 2285 at 2315–2319, paras 1–18 (with a case note by Vandersanden (1989) C.M.L.Rev. 551–561).

without proving that they have an interest in bringing proceedings,[90] bring an action for annulment against any binding act of a Community institution, whether general or individual, and may also rely on any plea in law permitted under Article 230 of the E.C. Treaty.[91] The right to bring an action for annulment is not dependent upon the position which they took up when the act at issue was adopted. Thus, the fact that an act was voted for in the Council by the representative of a Member State does not disentitle that Member State from bringing an application for its annulment.[92] Any Member State has a right to bring an action for annulment and that right is not dependent upon other Member States, the Council or the Commission participating in the proceedings before the Court of Justice.[93]

7–031 Local authorities (municipalities, federated states, etc.) are not equated to a Member State and are therefore not privileged applicants. If they have legal personality under national law, they may be regarded as legal persons within the meaning of the fourth paragraph of Article 230 (*ex Article 173*) of the E.C. Treaty and bring an action, provided that the admissibility requirements laid down in that provision of the Treaty are satisfied.[94]

(2) The European Parliament, the Court of Auditors and the European Central Bank

7–032 In the judgment in the *Chernobyl* case, the Court of Justice granted the European Parliament a right not conferred by the former Article 173 of the EEC Treaty to bring an action for annulment against acts of the Council or the Commission "provided that the action seeks only to safeguard its prerogatives and that it is founded only on submissions alleging their

[90] Case 45/86 *Commission v. Council* [1987] E.C.R. 1493 at 1518, para. 3, ECJ.

[91] Case 41/83 *Italy v. Commission* [1985] E.C.R. 873 at 888, para. 30, ECJ. One of the questions raised in that case was whether Italy could bring an action for annulment against a Commission decision finding that British Telecommunications, at that time a nationalised undertaking having a statutory monopoly in the United Kingdom over the running of telecommunications services, had infringed the EEC Treaty, Art. 86 (*now Art. 82*). Italy argued, amongst other things, that the Commission had disregarded Art. 90 (*now Art. 86*) (2) and that undertakings entrusted with the operation of services of general economic interest were subject to Community competition law only in so far as its application did not impede the performance of their particular tasks. The Court of Justice allowed Italy to raise that plea despite the fact that what was involved was a balancing of interests—described by the Commission as difficult—which affected only the United Kingdom.

[92] Case 166/78 *Italy v. Council* [1979] E.C.R. 2575 at 2596, paras 5–6, ECJ.

[93] Case 230/81 *Luxembourg v. European Parliament* [1983] E.C.R. 255 at 283–284, paras 22–26, ECJ (interpretation of the ECSC Treaty, Art. 38, para. 1, which also holds good for the E.C. Treaty, Art. 230 (*ex Art. 173*), para. 2 (formerly the EEC Treaty, Art. 173, para. 1)).

[94] Case 222/83 *Municipality of Differdange v. Commission* [1984] E.C.R. 2889 at 2896, para. 9, ECJ. See also the Opinion of Advocate General C.O. Lenz in Joined Cases 62 and 72/87 *Exécutif Régional Wallon v. Commission* [1988] E.C.R. 1573 at 1582, ECJ; Case C–298/89 *Gibraltar v. Council* [1993] E.C.R. I–3605 at I–3653, para. 14, ECJ; (Order of March 21, 1997), Case C–95/97 *Région Wallonne v. Commission* [1997] E.C.R. I–1787 at I–1791, para. 6, ECJ; (Order of October 1, 1997), Case C–180/97 *Regione Toscana v. Commission* [1997] E.C.R. I–5245 at I–5249—5250, paras 6–8, ECJ; Case T–214/95 *Vlaams Gewest v. Commission* [1998] E.C.R. II–717 at II–732, para. 28, CFI; (Order of June 16, 1998), Case T–238/97 *Comunidad Autónoma de Catanbria v. Council* [1998] E.C.R. II–2271, CFI.

infringement".[95] The primary intention of the Court in so ruling was to maintain the balance between the institutions laid down by the treaties.[96] The third paragraph of Article 230 (*ex Article 173*) of the E.C. Treaty has consolidated this judge-made rule, and confers a similarly limited right of action on the Court of Auditors and the European Central Bank.[97] The European Parliament, the Court of Auditors and the European Central Bank must clearly show which of their prerogatives should have been respected and in what way the prerogative in question has been infringed.[98]

(3) Individual applicants

Under the fourth paragraph of Article 230 (*ex Article 173*) of the E.C. Treaty, any natural or legal person has the right to institute proceedings against a decision addressed to that person or against a decision which, although in the form of a regulation or a decision addressed to another person, is of direct and individual concern to the former. **7–033**

(a) *Requirements as to admissibility relating to the person*

Any natural or legal person may bring an action for annulment.[99] **7–034**

The applicant's nationality is irrelevant as far as the admissibility of the application is concerned. **7–035**

The fourth paragraph of Article 230 (*ex Article 173*) of the E.C. Treaty, unlike Article 33 of the ECSC Treaty, does not require the applicant to belong to a particular sector of the economy. **7–036**

---

[95] Case C–70/88 *European Parliament v. Council* [1990] E.C.R. I–2041 at I–2073, para. 27, ECJ. In the judgment on the substance of the case, moreover, the Court of Justice declared the European Parliament's second and third pleas inadmissible in that they did not allege any infringement of its prerogatives: Case C–70/88 *European Parliament v. Council* [1991] E.C.R. I–4529 at I–4567, paras 19, 20, ECJ. That condition for admissibility has been confirmed in, for example, Case C–295/90 *European Parliament v. Council* [1992] E.C.R. I–4193 at I–4233, paras 8–10, ECJ; Case C–316/91 *European Parliament v. Council* [1994] E.C.R. I–625 at I–659, para. 19, ECJ; Case C–187/93 *European Parliament v. Council* [1994] E.C.R. I–2857 at I–2879—2880, paras 14–16, ECJ.

[96] *Cf.* Bradley, "The Variable Evolution of the Standing of the European Parliament in Proceedings before the Court of Justice" (1988) Y.E.L. 27–57; Darmon, "Le statut contentieux du Parlement européen", in *L'Europe et le Droit—Mélanges en hommage à J. Boulouis*, Paris, Ed. Dalloz, 1991, at 75–96.

[97] During the second stage of Economic and Monetary Union, the European Monetary Institute (E.C. Treaty, Art. 117 (*ex Art. 109f*) (9)).

[98] Case C–316/91 *European Parliament v. Council* [1994] E.C.R. I–625 at I–659, para. 16, ECJ; Case C–21/94 *European Parliament v. Council* [1995] E.C.R. I–1827 at I–1849, para. 8, ECJ; Case C–156/93 *European Parliament v. Commission* [1995] E.C.R. I–2019 at I–2045, para. 11, ECJ (infringement of the requirement to state the reasons on which acts are based cannot be relied upon by the European Parliament on the ground that it is not clear how that breaches its prerogatives); Case C–360/93 *European Parliament v. Council* [1996] E.C.R. I–1195 at I–1216, para. 18, ECJ; Case C–392/95 *European Parliament v. Council* [1997] E.C.R. I–3213 at I–3246—3247, paras 14, 15, ECJ; Case C–259/95 *European Parliament v. Council* [1997] E.C.R. I–5303, ECJ.

[99] In all probability this includes third countries; *cf.* (Order of February 23, 1983), Joined Cases 91 and 200/82 *Chris International Foods v. Commission* [1983] E.C.R. 417, in which the Court of Justice gave a third country leave to intervene in the proceedings on the ground that it was an interested "person" within the meaning of the E.C Statute of the Court of Justice, Art. 37, para. 2.

7–037 In principle, national law determines whether the applicant has legal personality.[1] Sometimes lack of legal personality precludes access to the Court of Justice or the Court of First Instance.[2] Often, however, entities without legal personality may nevertheless be admitted to bring an action for annulment. In order for them to bring an action, they must be entitled and in a position to act as a responsible body in legal matters.[3] As a result, the expression "legal persons" has been given an independent, Community meaning which is not necessarily the same one it has in national law. The fact that the applicant was recognised by the defendant as a negotiating partner before the proceedings arose[4] and the fact that an ad hoc association was allowed to take part in a tendering procedure organised by the Commission[5] have helped applicants to be recognised as legal persons within the meaning of the fourth paragraph of Article 230 (*ex Article 173*) of the E.C. Treaty.

(b) *Requirements as to admissibility based on the type of act*

7–038 **(i) The requirement that the contested act should be a decision.** The only Community acts which can, in principle, be challenged by natural or legal persons in an action for annulment are decisions addressed to them, decisions addressed to another person or decisions adopted in the form of a regulation.[6] In the last two cases, an action for annulment of the "decision" will lie only if it is of direct and individual concern to the applicant.

---

[1] Case 18/57 *Nold v. High Authority* [1959] E.C.R. 41 at 48–49, ECJ; Case 50/84 *Bensider v. Commission* [1984] E.C.R. 3991 at 3997, para. 7, ECJ; Case T–174/95 *Svenska Journalistförbundet v. Council* [1998] E.C.R. II–2289 at II–2306, para. 43, CFI. *Cf.* Case 294/83 *Les Verts v. European Parliament* [1986] E.C.R. 1339 at 1362–1363, paras 13–18, ECJ, in regard to merging associations and the assignment of a pending legal action to the new association.

[2] *Bensider v. Commission* (cited in n. 1, above), at 3997, para. 9.

[3] Case 175/73 *Union Syndicale, Massa and Kortner v. Council* [1974] E.C.R. 917 at 924–925, paras 7–17, ECJ; Case 18/74 *Syndicat Général du Personnel des Organismes européens v. Commission* [1974] E.C.R. 933 at 943–944, paras 3–11, ECJ.

[4] *Union Syndicale, Massa and Kortner v. Council* at 925, para. 12; *Syndicat Général du Personnel des Organismes européens v. Commission* at 944, para. 9, (both cases cited in n. 3, above); Case T–161/94 *Sinochem Heilongjiang v. Council* [1996] E.C.R. II–695 at II–710, para. 34, CFI; Case T–170/94 *Shanghai Bicycle v. Council* [1997] E.C.R. II–1383 at II–1397, para. 26, CFI.

[5] Case 135/81 *Groupement des Agences de Voyage v. Commission* [1982] E.C.R. 3799 at 3808, paras 10, 11, ECJ.

[6] Some applicants have argued that the term "decision" used in the E.C. Treaty, Art. 230, para. 4 (*then the EEC Treaty*, Art. 173, para. 2) had a wider meaning than it does in the E.C. Treaty, Art. 249 (*ex Art. 189*) and covers any binding act. That argument has been rejected by the Court of Justice (see Joined Cases 16 and 17/62 *Confédération nationale des producteurs de fruits et légumes and Others v. Council* [1962] E.C.R. 471 at 478–479, ECJ). The rationale for confining actions brought by individuals to decisions is probably that regulations are legislative in character. Moreover, regulations, being the outcome of hard-won compromises, ought to be given greater protection against possible actions for annulment.

The Court of Justice has held that: 7–039

> "[t]he essential characteristics of a decision arise from the limitation of the persons to whom it is addressed, whereas a regulation, being essentially of a legislative nature, is applicable not to a limited number of persons, defined or identifiable, but to categories of persons viewed abstractly and in their entirety".[7]

Consequently, a regulation differs on account of its general application. In order to determine the scope of a measure, the Court of Justice and the Court of First Instance assess "[t]he nature of the contested [measure] . . . and in particular the legal effects which it is intended to or does actually produce".[8]

This requires a substantive analysis of the contested measure.[9] If a measure lays down generally applicable principles, applies to objectively defined situations and produces legal effects for categories of persons determined in an abstract manner, the measure will be regarded as a regulation.[10] A measure does not lose its general character because: 7–040

---

[7] Joined Cases 16 and 17/62 *Confédération nationale des producteurs de fruits et légumes and Others v. Council* [1962] E.C.R. 471 at 478, ECJ; (Order of April 24, 1996), Case C–87/95P *Cassa Nazionale di Previdenza ed Assistenza a favore degli Avvocati et Procuratori v. Council* [1996] E.C.R. I–2003 at I–2015—2016, para. 33, ECJ. See also Greaves, "The Nature and Binding Effect of Decisions under Art. 189 (*now Art. 249*) EC" (1996) E.L.Rev. 3–16.

[8] Case 101/76 *Koninklijke Scholten Honig v. Council and Commission* [1977] E.C.R. 797 at 806, para. 10, ECJ.

[9] Joined Cases 789 and 790/79 *Calpak v. Commission* [1980] E.C.R. 1949 at 1961, para. 7, ECJ; "the choice of form cannot change the nature of the measure". For a Commission decision which was held to be a "measure of general application", see Case 231/82 *Spijker v. Commission* [1983] E.C.R. 2559 at 2566, para. 9, ECJ; and Joined Cases T–480/93 and T–483/93 *Antillean Rice Mills and Others v. Commission* [1995] E.C.R. II–2305 at II–2331, para. 65, CFI. See also (Judgment of February 11, 1999) Case T–86/96 *Arbeitsgemeinschaft Deutscher Luftfahrt-Unternehmen v. Commission*, CFI (not yet reported), in which the Court of First Instance dismissed as inadmissible an action for annulment brought against a Commission decision based on the E.C. Treaty, Article 88 (*ex Article 93*) (2), declaring incompatible with the common market fiscal aid given to German airlines in the form of a depreciation facility; according to the Court, "because it prohibits the extension of tax provisions having general application, the contested decision, although addressed to a Member State, appears, *vis-à-vis* the potential beneficiaries of those provisions, to be a measure of general application covering situations which are determined objectively and entailing legal effects for a class of persons envisaged in a general and abstract manner"(para. 45); that decision affected the applicant merely by virtue of its objective position as a potential beneficiary of the depreciation facility in question, in the same way as any other operator who was, or might in the future be, in the same situation (para. 46, where reference is made *inter alia* to the *Spijker* judgment, cited above, at para. 9).

[10] Joined Cases 36–38 and 40–41/58 *Simet v. High Authority* [1959] E.C.R. 157 at 166, ECJ; Case 147/83 *Binderer v. Commission* [1985] E.C.R. 257 at 270–271, paras 11–15, ECJ; Case C–244/88 *Usines coopératives de déshydratation du Vexin and Others v. Commission* [1989] E.C.R. 3811 at 3830, para. 13, ECJ; Case C–229/88 *Cargill and Others v. Commission* [1990] E.C.R. I–1303 at I–1320—1321, paras 13–19, ECJ; (Order of January 11, 1995), Case T–116/94 *Cassa Nazionale di Previdenza ed Assistenza a favore degli Avvocati e Procuratori* [1995] E.C.R. II–1 at II–11—13, paras 21–25, CFI; (Order of June 19, 1995), Case T–107/94 *Kik v. Council and Commission* [1995] E.C.R. II–1717 at II–1730—1731, para. 35, CFI; Case T–47/95 *Terres Rouges and Others v. Commission* [1997] E.C.R. II–481 at II–494, paras 40–41, CFI.

> "it may be possible to ascertain with a greater or lesser degree of accuracy the number or even the identity of the persons to which it applies at any given time as long as there is no doubt that the measure is applicable as a result of an objective situation of law or of fact which it specifies and which is in harmony with its ultimate objective".[11]

Even the fact that a legal provision may have different practical effects for the various persons to whom it applies is not inconsistent with its nature as a regulation when the circumstances in which it applies are objectively determined.[12]

7–041 Although, in principle, a single provision cannot at one and the same time have the character of a measure of general application and of an individual measure,[13] the admissibility of an action for annulment brought by a natural or legal person will not turn directly on the mere finding that the contested act is legislative in nature.[14]

7–042 In the first place, some provisions of acts which, *per se*, are to be regarded as regulations may be decisions against which a natural or legal person can

---

[11] Case 6/68 *Zuckerfabrik Watenstedt v. Commission* [1968] E.C.R. 409 at 415, ECJ. See also Case 64/69 *Compagnie Française Commerciale v. Commission* [1970] E.C.R. 221 at 226–227, para. 11, ECJ; Joined Cases 789 and 790/79 *Calpak v. Commission* [1980] E.C.R. 1949 at 1961, para. 9, ECJ; Case 242/81 *Roquette Frères v. Council* [1982] E.C.R. 3213 at 3230, para. 7, ECJ; Case 307/81 *Alusuisse v. Council and Commission* [1982] E.C.R. 3463 at 3472, para. 11, ECJ; Case 231/82 *Spijker v. Commission* [1983] E.C.R. 2559 at 2566, para. 10, ECJ; Case 26/86 *Deutz and Geldermann v. Council* [1987] E.C.R. 941 at 951, para. 8, ECJ; Joined Cases C–15 and C–108/91 *Buckl and Others v. Commission* [1992] E.C.R. I–6061 at I–6099, para. 25, ECJ; Case C–213/91 *Abertal and Others v. Commission* [1993] E.C.R. I–3177 at I–3200, para. 17, ECJ; Case C–264/91 *Abertal and Others v. Council* [1993] E.C.R. I–3265 at I–3278, para. 16, ECJ; (Order of October 28, 1993), Case T–476/93 *FRSEA and FNSEA v. Council* [1993] E.C.R. II–1187 at II–1194—1195, para. 19, CFI; Case T–489/93 *Unifruit Hellas v. Commission* [1994] E.C.R. II–1201, CFI; (Order of October 4, 1996), Case T–197/95 *Sveriges Betodlares and Henrikson v. Commission* [1996] E.C.R. II–1283 at II–1295, para. 28, CFI. *Cf.* Joined Cases 41–44/70 *International Fruit Company v. Commission* [1971] E.C.R. 411, ECJ, in which the contested "regulation" applied to a number of applications for import licences which was known at the time when the "regulation" was adopted and no new application could be added. The Court of Justice regarded the act as a conglomeration of individual decisions which, albeit adopted in the guise of a regulation, affected the legal position of each of the applicants for a licence. This indicates that the condition of admissibility to the effect that the contested act must be a decision is particularly closely linked with the condition of admissibility requiring a contested act not addressed to the applicant to be of direct and individual concern to him. *Cf.* paras 7–046—7–064, below. See also Case C–354/87 *Weddel v. Commission* [1990] E.C.R. I–3847 at I–3885—3886, paras 16–23, ECJ; Case T–70/94 *Comafrica and Dole Fresh Fruit Europe v. Commission* [1996] E.C.R. II–1741 at II–1761, paras 40–41, CFI, annulled however in (Judgment of January 21, 1999) Case C–73/97P *France v. Comafrica and Dole Fresh Fruit Europe*, (not yet reported), ECJ, putting a narrow construction on the judgment in *Weddel*.

[12] (Order of March 28, 1996), Case T–270/95P *Kik v. Council and Commission* [1996] E.C.R. I–1987 at I–1994, para. 13, ECJ.

[13] Case 18/57 *Nold v. High Authority* [1959] E.C.R. 41 at 50, ECJ; Case 45/81 *Moksel v. Commission* [1982] E.C.R. 1129 at 1144, para. 18, ECJ.

[14] *Cf.* Neuwahl, "Art. 173 (*now Art. 230*) paragraph 4 EC: Past, Present and Possible Future" (1996) E.L.Rev. 17 at 23; Waelbroeck and Verheyden, "Les conditions de recevabilité des recours en annulation des particuliers contre les actes normatifs communautaires" (1995) C.D.E. 399–441.

bring an action for annulment.[15] However, it will be possible to separate out provisions of a regulation only in so far as they do not constitute an indissoluble whole together with the remaining provisions of the regulation.[16] This will be so only where the intended aim of the regulation can be equally well attained after the provisions alleged to be decisions have been severed.[17]

Secondly, sometimes the dual nature of the contested act as a whole or of some of its provisions will nevertheless be recognised. Then, the act or some of its provisions will operate as a "decision" *vis-à-vis* some natural or legal persons, whilst remaining in essence a regulation.[18] The reason for this is that it appears from the case law that the fact that an act is of a legislative nature does not prevent it in certain circumstances from affecting some of the market participants concerned individually.[19] The requirement is that the market participants in question must be affected by the Community act by reason of attributes peculiar to them or by reason of factual circumstances differentiating them from all other persons as if it was a decision addressed to them.[20] In such a case, the analysis focuses on whether the requirement is met that the act, albeit not addressed to the applicant, nevertheless is of individual concern to it.[21] When that is the case the **7–043**

[15] Joined Cases 16 and 17/62 *Confédération nationale des producteurs de fruits et légumes and Others v. Council* [1962] E.C.R. 471 at 479, 1st para, ECJ.

[16] It will be hard to separate out transitional provisions from the legislative measure without this causing adverse effects as far as achievement of the intended objective is concerned. Generally, therefore, they will have the same nature as the contested measure: see, Case 64/80 *Giuffrida and Campogrande v. Council* [1981] E.C.R. 693 at 702–703, paras 4–7, ECJ.

[17] For some cases in which any severing of provisions appeared impossible, see Case 45/81 *Moksel v. Commission* [1982] E.C.R. 1129 at 1144–1145, paras 16–19; and Case 276/82 *Roomboterfabriek "De beste boter" v. Produktschap voor Zuivel* [1983] E.C.R. 3331 at 3342–3343, paras 12–17, ECJ. See also Schermers and Waelbroeck, *Judicial Protection*, pp. 278–280.

[18] Case 264/82 *Timex v. Council and Commission* [1985] E.C.R. 849 at 864–866, paras 8–17, ECJ; Joined Cases T–481 and T–484/93 *Exporteurs in Levende Varkens and Others v. Commission* [1995] E.C.R. II–2941 at II–2961, para. 50, CFI.

[19] Case C–152/88 *Sofrimport v. Commission* [1990] E.C.R. I–2477 at I–2507—2508, paras 8–13, ECJ; Case C–309/89 *Codorniu v. Council* [1994] E.C.R. I–1853 at I–1884—1887, paras 14–33, ECJ; (Order of November 24, 1995), Case C–10/95P *Asocarne v. Council* [1995] E.C.R. I–4149 at I–4163, para. 34, ECJ; (Order of April 24, 1996), Case C–87/95P *Cassa Nazionale di Previdenza ed Assistenza a favore degli Avvocati e Procuratori v. Council* [1996] E.C.R. I–2003 at I–2016, para. 36, ECJ; Joined Cases T–480 and T–483/93 *Antillean Rice Mills and Others v. Commission* [1995] E.C.R. II–2305 at II–2331, para. 66, CFI; (Order of October 4, 1996), Case T–197/95 *Sverige Betodlares and Henrikson v. Commission* [1996] E.C.R. II–1283 at II–1295—1296, para. 31, CFI; Case T–298/94 *Roquette Frères v. Council* [1996] E.C.R. II–1531 at II–1543, para. 37, CFI; (Order of December 10,1996), Case T–18/95 *Atlanta and Internationale Fruchtimport Gesellschaft Weichert v. Commission* [1996] E.C.R. II–1669 at II–1686, para. 47, CFI. See also Nihoul, "La recevabilité des recours en annulation introduits par un particulier à l'encontre d'un acte communautaire de portée générale" (1994) R.T.D.E. 173–174.

[20] See para. 7–052, below.

[21] Fulfilment of the requirement for the act to be of individual concern approximates closely to the test for determining that the contested act is essentially a decision. The two questions—whether the contested act is a decision and whether it is of individual concern to the applicant where it is not addressed to it—are directed towards the legal effects produced by the act and necessitate a similar inquiry into its content. For those reasons, the nature of the

applicant may bring an action for annulment against the contested "decision". For others, the regulation preserves its general legislative character and will not be amenable to an action for annulment. Anti-dumping cases afford striking illustrations. Undertakings which can prove that their identity is apparent from the contested regulation, or that the investigation which resulted in the imposition of anti-dumping duties related to them, may bring an action for annulment of the regulation or of the provisions of the regulation which imposed anti-dumping duties on them.[22] Another practical example was the admissibility of an application brought by a company for annulment of an intrinsically legislative regulation laying down general rules for the description and presentation of sparkling wines. The Court of Justice treated the regulation as far as the applicant was concerned as a decision of individual concern to it on the ground that the regulation prohibited use of a graphic trade mark which the applicant had officially registered before the regulation entered into force.[23] As a result,

contested act is not always expressly determined in the case law. The relationship between the two questions sometimes upsets the logical sequence of the admissibility requirements which may be inferred from the wording of the E.C. Treaty, Art. 230, para. 4, (*ex Art. 173*). Compare Case 123/77 *UNICME v. Council* [1978] E.C.R. 845 at 851, para. 7, ECJ; and Case 64/69 *Compagnie Française Commerciale v. Commission* [1970] E.C.R. 221 at 225–226, para. 3 *et seq.*, ECJ; Case C–264/91 *Abertal v. Council* [1993] E.C.R. I–3265 at I–3678, para. 16, ECJ. See also Case T–489/93 *Unifruit Hellas v. Commission* [1994] E.C.R. II–1201 at II–1213, para. 21, CFI, for a wide-ranging discussion, see Schermers and Waelbroeck, *Judicial Protection*, pp. 404–406; Harding, "The Review of EEC Regulations and Decisions" (1982) C.M.L.Rev. 311–323. See also Bleckmann, "Zur Klagebefugnis für die Individualklage vor dem Europäischen Gerichtshof", in *Festschrift für C.F. Menger—System des verwaltungsgerichtlichen Rechtsschutzes*, Cologne/Berlin/Bonn/Munich, Carl Heymanns Verlag KG, 1985, 871 at 883; Parkinson, "Admissibility of Direct Actions by Natural or Legal Persons in the European Court of Justice: Judicial Distinctions Between Decisions and Regulations" (1989) Texas I.L.J. 433 at 445–449.

[22] Case 113/77 *NTN Toyo Bearing Company v. Council* [1979] E.C.R. 1185 at 1204–1205, paras 10–11, ECJ; Case 118/77 *ISO v. Council* [1979] E.C.R. 1277 at 1292–1294, paras 17–27, ECJ; Case 119/77 *Nippon Seiko v. Council and Commission* [1979] E.C.R. 1303 at 1326–1327, paras 12–15, ECJ; Case 121/77 *Nachi Fujikoshi v. Council* [1979] E.C.R. 1363 at 1378–1379, paras 7–13, ECJ; Joined Cases 239 and 275/82 *Allied Corporation v. Commission* [1984] E.C.R. 1005 at 1028–1031, paras 7–16, ECJ; Case 53/83 *Allied Corporation v. Council* [1985] E.C.R. 1621 at 1655–1656, paras 2–5, ECJ; Case 240/84 *Toyo v. Council* [1987] E.C.R. 1809 at 1851–1852, paras 4–7, ECJ; Case 255/84 *Nachi Fujikoshi v. Council* [1987] E.C.R. 1861 at 1886–1887, paras 5–8, ECJ; Case 256/84 *Koyo Seiko v. Council* [1987] E.C.R. 1899 at 1914–1915, paras 4–7, ECJ; Case 258/84 *Nippon Seiko v. Council* [1987] E.C.R. 1923 at 1960–1961, paras 5–8, ECJ; (Order of July 8, 1987), Case 279/86 *Sermes v. Commission* [1987] E.C.R. 3109 at 3115, para. 21, ECJ; (Order of July 8, 1987), Case 301/86 *Frimodt Pedersen v. Commission* [1987] E.C.R. 3123 at 3129, para. 21, ECJ; Joined Cases C–133 and C–150/87 *Nashua Corporation and Others v. Commission and Council* [1990] E.C.R. I–719 at I–772—773, paras 12–21, ECJ; Case C–156/87 *Gestetner Holdings v. Council and Commission* [1990] E.C.R. I–781 at I–831—834, paras 7–24, ECJ; Joined Cases C–305/86 and C–160/87 *Neotype Techmashexport v. Commission and Council* [1990] E.C.R. I–2945 at I–2998, para. 19, ECJ; Case C–358/89 *Extramet Industrie v. Council* [1991] E.C.R. I–2501 at I–2531, paras 13–14, ECJ. See also Greaves, "Locus Standi under Article 173 *[now Article 230]* EEC when Seeking Annulment of a Regulation" (1986) E.L.Rev. 119, at 131; Nihoul (cited in n. 19, above) at 171–194. For a critical note, see Von Heydebrand und der Lasa, "Die Nichtigkeitsklage von Unternehmen aus Drittländern vor dem EuGH gegen 'Verordnungen' im Bereich des Antidumpingsrechts" (1985) N.J.W. 1257 at 1259.

[23] Case C–309/89 *Codorniu v. Council* [1994] E.C.R. I–1853 at I–1884—1887, paras 14–23, ECJ.

the contested regulation adversely affected "specific rights" of the applicant, which, as the Court held, the latter must be able to challenge by means of an action for annulment.[24]

In the light of this case law, an application brought by a natural or legal person for annulment of a directive is, in principle, inadmissible because, as a legislative act, a directive cannot be of individual concern to such persons.[25] Nevertheless, it is possible that an applicant may be directly and individually concerned by a directive if it can prove that it has a right which the Community institutions should have taken into account when they adopted the directive. This is because the mere existence of such a right means that its holder should be afforded legal protection.[26] **7–044**

The expression "decision addressed to another person" also covers decisions addressed to a Member State.[27] **7–045**

(ii) The requirement that, if the contested act is not addressed to the applicant, it should be of direct and individual concern to him. Under the fourth paragraph of Article 230 (*ex Article 173*) of the E.C. Treaty, an application brought by natural or legal persons against decisions adopted in the form of a regulation or addressed to another person will be admissible only in so far as they are of direct and individual concern to them. The justification for the restriction lies in the far-reaching consequences of the annulment of a Community act. Annulment applies *erga omnes* and is retroactive. To make the action for annulment generally available might mean permanent litigation about Community regulations and open the way to an *actio popularis*.[28] **7–046**

---

[24] See the interpretation of the Judgment in *Codorniu* to this effect in (Order of November 23, 1995), Case C–10/95P *Asocarne v. Council* [1995] E.C.R. I–4149 at I–4163, para. 43, ECJ (from which it also appears that the Court considers this to be an absolutely exceptional situation).

[25] (Order of December 7, 1988), Case 138/88 *Flourez v. Council* [1988] E.C.R. 6393 at 6997, paras 10–12, ECJ; (Order of December 7, 1988) Case 160/88 *Fédération européenne de la santé animale and Others v. Council* [1988] E.C.R. 6399 at 6403–6404, paras 12–14, ECJ; Case C–298/89 *Gibraltar v. Council* [1993] E.C.R. I–3605 at I–3653—3656, paras 14–24, ECJ; (Order of October 20, 1994), Case T–99/94 *Asocarne v. Council* [1994] E.C.R. II–871 at II–879—881, paras 17–19, CFI; (Order of November 23, 1995), Case C–10/95P *Asocarne v. Council* [1995] E.C.R. I–4149 at I–4159—4160, paras 29–34, ECJ. See also (Order of October 29, 1993), Case T–463/93 *GUNA v. Council* [1993] II–1206 at II–1210, para. 13, CFI, where the Court of First Instance raised the question of principle as to whether an application brought by an individual for the annulment of a directive would be admissible, but did not answer it, observing only that the provisions of the directive in question were not of direct and individual concern to the applicant. *Cf.* Schneider, "Effektiver Rechtsschutz Privater gegen EG-Richtlinien nach dem Maastricht-Urteil des Bundesverfassungsgerichts" (1994) Archiv des öffentlichen Rechts 294 at 302–308.

[26] Case T–135/96 *UEAPME v. Council* [1998] E.C.R. II–2335 at II–2371, para. 90, CFI.

[27] Case 25/62 *Plaumann & Co. v. Commission* [1963] E.C.R. 95 at 106–107, ECJ.

[28] Opinion of Advocate General A. Dutheillet de Lamothe in Joined Cases 9 and 11/71 *Cie d'Approvisionnement v. Commission* [1972] E.C.R. 391 at 411, ECJ; Opinion of Advocate General H. Mayras in Case 43/72 *Merkur v. Commission* [1973] E.C.R. 1055 at 1078, ECJ. See, to the same effect, Harding, "The Private Interest in Challenging Community Action" (1980) E.L.Rev. 354 at 358.

7–047 (a) *Direct concern.* The requirement that a decision not addressed to the applicant must be of direct concern to it expresses the rule that an applicant may bring an action for annulment only against acts of Community institutions which, as such, have legal effects on it.[29] By contrast, Community acts which are to be implemented by national authorities and in respect of which the latter have a discretion, do not obtain their precise scope until they have been implemented. Interested individuals are entitled to challenge the implementing measures before the national courts when they have been adopted. If it is argued that the implementing measures are unlawful on the ground that the Community act purported to be implemented is invalid, the national court may (or must) make a reference to the Court of Justice for a preliminary ruling.[30] In this way, the structure of legal protection reflects the structure of Community law-making.

7–048 In order for it to be found that an act is of direct concern to the applicant, the question whether the contested measure confers a discretion on the national authorities or on its addressee[31] with regard to its implementation must be answered in the negative.[32]

7–049 The contested act will not be of direct concern to the applicant only where, in implementing the act, the national authorities have a *genuine* discretion.[33] Where implementation is "purely automatic", no discretion on the part of the national authorities is involved and the Community act to be implemented is of direct concern to the applicant.[34]

---

[29] Case 294/83 *Les Verts v. European Parliament* [1986] E.C.R. 1339 at 1367, para. 31, ECJ: the contested measures are of direct concern to the applicant because they "constitute a complete set of rules which are sufficient in themselves and . . . require no implementing provisions". See also the Opinion of Advocate General K. Roemer in Case 25/62 *Plaumann & Co. v. Commission* [1963] E.C.R. 95 at 114–115, ECJ. For an example in which the measure was held not to be of direct concern to the applicants, see Case T–96/92 *CCE de la Société des Grandes Sources v. Commission* [1995] E.C.R. II–1213 at II–1236—1237, para. 45, CFI.

[30] See chap. 10, below.

[31] The fact that the Commission declares a concentration notified to it, pursuant to Regulation No. 4064/89, compatible with the common market on condition that the notifying parties implement "commitments" set forth in the notification does not prevent a third undertaking, which is affected by the implementation of those commitments, from being directly concerned by the Commission's decision. This is because there is no doubt that parties to the concentration have undertaken to implement those commitments, given that the Commission declared it compatible with the common market in return for compliance with those commitments and the Commission may always revoke its decision under Art. 8(5)(b) of the regulation if the undertakings concerned commit a breach of an obligation attached thereto (Joined Cases C–68/94 and C–30/95 *France and SCPA and EMC v. Commission* [1998] E.C.R. I–1375 at I–1470, para. 51, ECJ).

[32] For examples, see Joined Cases 41–44/70 *International Fruit Company v. Commission* [1971] E.C.R. 411 at 422–423 paras 23–28, ECJ; Joined Cases 87 and 130/77, 22/83, 9 and 10/84 *Salerno v. Commission* [1985] E.C.R. 2523 at 2535, paras 31–32, ECJ; Case 207/86 *Apesco v. Commission* [1988] E.C.R. 2151 at 2175, para. 12, ECJ.

[33] For examples, see Case 123/77 *UNICME v. Council* [1978] E.C.R. 845 at 852, para. 11, ECJ; Case 55/86 *Arposol v. Council* [1988] E.C.R. 13 at 26, paras 11–13, ECJ; (Order of October 21, 1993), Joined Cases T–492/93 and T–492/93R *Nutral v. Commission* [1993] E.C.R. II–1023 at II–1033—1034, paras 26–29, CFI.

[34] Case 113/77 *NTN Toyo Bearing Company v. Council* [1979] E.C.R. 1185 at 1205, para. 11, ECJ; Case 118/77 *ISO v. Council* [1979] E.C.R. 1277 at 1294, para. 26, ECJ; Case 119/77

A decision by which the Commission authorises Member States in some areas of Community law to diverge from the applicable general provisions may be of direct concern to individuals, depending on the circumstances. This will be so where, before they were given authorisation, the national authorities limited their discretion themselves. The Court of Justice has, therefore, held that where the Member State concerned makes it known beforehand that it will implement an authorising decision, that decision will be of direct concern to individuals.[35] The Member State's position does not have to be express, it may be inferred from all relevant factors.[36] If a Member State does not make its position known beforehand with regard to an authorising decision, it reserves its power of discretion and the decision is not of direct concern to individuals.[37] **7–050**

If an application from a Member State for authorisation is refused and this adversely affects an individual's interests, the requirement that the contested act must be of direct concern to the applicant is assessed just as if the authorisation had been granted.[38] Authorisation from the Commission of a protective measure already adopted by a Member State is of direct concern to individuals.[39]

In the context of aid programmes financed by the Community or the grant of Community loans to non-member countries, one and the same division of powers is generally instituted between the authorities of the beneficiary state and the Community institutions. The authorities of the beneficiary state have the power to select a contractual partner to carry out a particular project, to negotiate the contractual conditions and to conclude the agreement. The Commission is given the task only of examining whether the conditions for Community financing are met. Undertakings competing for the grant of a particular project are in a legal relationship only with the authorities of the beneficiary state. For its part, the Commission has legal relations only with the authorities of the beneficiary state. This pattern of legal relations means that the decision by which the Commission approves the financing of a contract concluded by the beneficiary state is not of direct concern to undertakings to which the contract is not granted.[40] This is because the Commission's decision to finance the **7–051**

Nippon Seiko v. Council and Commission [1979] E.C.R. 1303 at 1327, para. 14, ECJ; Case 120/77 *Koyo Seiko v. Council and Commission* [1979] E.C.R. 1337 at 1353, para. 25, ECJ; Case 121/77 *Nachi Fujikoshi v. Council* [1979] E.C.R. 1363 at 1379, para. 11, ECJ; Case T–155/94 *Climax Paper v. Council* [1996] E.C.R. II–873 at II–892, para. 53, CFI; Case T–170/94 *Shanghai Bicycle v. Council* [1997] E.C.R. II–1383 at II–1401, para. 41, CFI.

35 Case 62/70 *Bock v. Commission* [1971] E.C.R. 897 at 908, paras 6–8, ECJ; *contra*: Joined Cases 10 and 18/68 *Eridania v. Commission* [1969] E.C.R. 459, ECJ.

36 Case 11/82 *Piraiki-Patraiki v. Commission* [1985] E.C.R. 207 at 241–242, paras 7–10, ECJ.

37 *Cf.* Case 123/77 *UINICME v. Council* [1978] E.C.R. 845, ECJ (where derogating rules were provided for a Member State in a Council regulation).

38 Case 69/69 *Alcan v. Commission* [1970] E.C.R. 385 at 394, para. 15, ECJ: "The decision rejecting the request does not . . . concern the applicants in any other way than would the positive decision which they wish to obtain".

39 Joined Cases 106 and 107/63 *Töpfer and Others v. Commission* [1965] E.C.R. 405 at 411, ECJ.

40 Case 126/83 *STS v. Commission* [1984] E.C.R. 2769 at 2779, para. 18, ECJ; Case 118/83

project does not take the place of the decision of the beneficiary state granting the contract in question.[41] However, it is possible for the undertaking, to which the beneficiary state awarded a contract, to be directly concerned by the Commission decision refusing financing. This depends on the circumstances in which the Commission decision was adopted. If it appears that the Commission decision refusing Community financing deprived the applicant of any real possibility of performing the transaction entered into with the beneficiary state or of obtaining payment of the goods supplied on the agreed terms, the applicant's "legal situation" will be directly concerned. This will be the case where the contract with the beneficiary state was concluded on account of the commitments which the Commission would enter into in its capacity as "financing authority" once it found that the contract was in conformity with the Community rules.[42]

7–052 (b) *Individual concern.* An act not addressed to natural or legal persons will be of individual concern to them if it "affects them by reason of certain attributes which are peculiar to them or by reason of circumstances in which they are differentiated from all other persons and by virtue of these factors distinguishes them individually just as in the case of the person addressed [by the act]".[43] This means that the applicant must prove that the contested act, which, in terms of form, is not addressed to him, affects him substantively as if the act was a decision addressed to him. This is a

---

CMC v. Commission [1985] E.C.R. 2325 at 2345, para. 28, ECJ.

[41] But a Commission act which, by reason of its context, may be isolated from the procedure for the conclusion of a contract between the beneficiary state and an undertaking inasmuch as the Commission adopted it in the exercise of its own powers and specifically directed it to an individual undertaking, which loses any chance of actually being awarded the contract simply because that act is adopted, does give rise to binding legal effects as regards the undertaking in question and may therefore be regarded as an act adversely affecting it against which the undertaking concerned may bring an action for annulment: Case C–395/95P *Geotronics v. Commission* [1997] E.C.R. I–2271 at I–2295–2297, paras 12–15, ECJ.

[42] Case C–386/96P *Dreyfus v. Commission* [1998] E.C.R. I–2309 at I–2370—2374, paras 40–56, ECJ; Case C–391/96P *Compagnie Continentale v. Commission* [1998] E.C.R. I–2377 at I–2398—2402, paras 38–54, ECJ; Case C–403/96P *Glencore Grain v. Commission* [1998] E.C.R. I–2405 at I–2428—2432, paras 40–56, ECJ; Case C–404/96P *Glencore Grain v. Commission* [1998] E.C.R. I–2435 at I–2454—2458, paras 38–54, ECJ. The Court of Justice set aside the judgments given by the Court of First Instance in these cases in which the latter court held that the applicants were not directly concerned. In comparison with the approach taken by the Court of Justice, the Court of First Instance made a formal juridical analysis of the question whether the applicants' "legal situation" was affected, whereas the Court of Justice based its reasoning more on the "objective economic" finding that the third country could not execute the contracts concluded with the applicant for the supply of grain in the absence of Community aid.

[43] Case 25/62 *Plaumann & Co. v. Commission* [1963] E.C.R. 95 at 107, ECJ. A somewhat clearer English rendering is to be found in more recent case law, *e.g.* Case T–266/94 *Foreningen af Jernskibs- og Maskinbyggerier i Danmark, Skibsværftsforeningen and Others v. Commission* [1996] E.C.R. II–1339 at II–1418, para. 44, CFI: "persons other than those to whom a decision is addressed may claim to be individually concerned only if that decision affects them by reason of attributes peculiar to them or by reason of factual circumstances differentiating them from all other persons and, as a result, distinguishing them individually in like manner to the person addressed".

particularly strict requirement and it extensively curtails natural or legal persons' ability to bring actions for annulment.[44]

Where the contested measure is a "decision",[45] it is sufficient for the applicant to show that, at the time when that decision was adopted, he or she was part of a closed class of persons concerned by that act.[46] It makes no difference whether the class is large or small or whether its members are known by name. Various sets of circumstances may bring about a closed class. **7–053**

Accordingly, a closed class is involved where the contested decision affects only persons who satisfied certain conditions before it was adopted. This is a situation in which the decision has completely retroactive effect. Because the number of persons who satisfied the conditions laid down for the application of the decision in the past can no longer change, the act is applicable to a closed class. Accordingly, a Commission decision approving a national decision refusing to grant import licences concerns the closed class of importers who were refused an import licence before the Commission decision was taken. That group was known (or at least ascertainable) when the decision was adopted.[47] **7–054**

The contested decision may be intended to cover both events in the past and events to come about in the future. If provisions can be found in the contested decision which are applicable solely to events in the past, those provisions concern a closed class of persons.[48] **7–055**

If the applicant contests the partially retroactive effect of a regulation with a view to its being regarded, at least as far as the applicant is concerned, as a decision of direct and individual concern to it, the Court will examine the significance of the whole of the situation governed by the regulation. If it appears from that examination that, in order to achieve its aim, the regulation must be held to be applicable without distinction to facts which existed at the time when it was adopted and to similar facts which arose thereafter, the regulation does not cease to be of general **7–056**

---

[44] In recent years, commentators have been pressing for a broad interpretation to be placed on the admissibility requirements to be satisfied by applicants who are individuals: see, for instance, Moitinho de Almeida, "Le recours en annulation des particuliers (article 173, deuxième alinéa (*now Art. 230, fourth paragraph*), du traité CE): nouvelles réflexions sur l'expression 'la concernent . . . individuellement'", *Festschrift für Ulrich Everling*, Baden-Baden, Nomos, 1995, at 849–874. An attempt by Greenpeace to have this requirement less strictly interpreted in environmental cases was rejected by both the Court of First Instance and the Court of Justice (sitting as the full court): (Order of August 9, 1995), Case T–585/93 *Greenpeace v. Commission* [1995] E.C.R. II–2205, CFI, and Case C–321/95P *Greenpeace Council and Others v. Commission* [1998] E.C.R. I–1651, ECJ. For a critical case note, see Wegener, "Keine Klagebefugnis für Greenpeace and 18 andere. Anmerkung zu EuGH, Rs C–321/95P (Greenpeace)" (1998) Zeitschrift für Umweltrecht 131–135.

[45] That is to say, an act, irrespective of its name or form, which is *not* of general application, see para. 7–039, above.

[46] Case 97/85 *Deutsche Lebensmittelwerke v. Commission* [1987] E.C.R. 2265 at 2287, para. 11, ECJ. The Court of Justice uses the expression "closed circle". See also (Order of May 24, 1993), Case C–131/92 *Arnaud and Others v. Council* [1993] I–2573 at I–2579, para. 8, ECJ, where the applicant used the expression "closed class".

[47] Joined Cases 106 and 107/63 *Töpfer and Others v. Commission* [1965] E.C.R. 405 at 411–412, ECJ.

[48] Case 62/70 *Bock v. Commission* [1971] E.C.R. 897 at 907–908, paras 2–5, ECJ.

application and cannot therefore be regarded as being a decision *vis-à-vis* any person. The Court of Justice found, for instance, that a regulation suspending advance fixing of a Community subsidy in the agricultural sector related both to applications which were pending when the suspension entered into effect and to applications made during the period of suspension. The Court went on to hold that the regulation at issue was applicable to objectively determined situations and produced legal effects with respect to categories of persons envisaged in the abstract. Consequently, the regulation was of general application within the meaning of the second paragraph of Article 249 (*ex Article 189*) of the E.C. Treaty and therefore could not be of individual concern to the applicant within the meaning of the fourth paragraph of Article 230 (*ex Article 173*).[49]

The contested regulation may also ostensibly have effects in the future, but in actual fact concern only events situated in the past. In that case, the persons concerned form part of a closed class and are directly and individually concerned by a decision adopted in the form of a regulation.[50]

7–057 Where, in contrast, the contested act is of general application, the applicant must show that that intention was not achieved as far as it is concerned[51] in that its legal position is affected because of a factual situation which differentiates it from all other persons and distinguishes it individually in like manner to a person to whom it is addressed.[52]

7–058 To this end, it is not enough for the applicant to show that it belongs to a closed class. This is because such a class may be formed on the basis of a criterion which does not affect the legislative nature of the contested act as far as persons belonging to that class are concerned.[53] Thus, the fact that the persons to whom a regulation is applicable are identifiable does not affect the legislative nature of that act, provided that it is clear that the regulation is applicable as a result of an objective situation of law or of fact which it specifies and is in harmony with its ultimate objective.[54] The fact

---

[49] Case C–244/88 *Usines coopératives de déshydratation du Vexin and Others v. Commission* [1989] E.C.R. 3811 at 3830–3831, paras 11–14, ECJ; Case C–229/88 *Cargill and Others v. Commission* [1990] E.C.R. I–1303 at I–1320—1321, paras 13–18, ECJ.

[50] Case 100/74 *CAM v. Commission* [1975] E.C.R. 1393 at 1403, para. 16, ECJ.

[51] *Cf.* para. 7–043, above.

[52] Case T–489/93 *Unifruit Hellas v. Commission* [1994] E.C.R. II–1201 at II–1213, para. 21, CFI.

[53] Case T–482/93 *Weber v. Commission* [1996] E.C.R. II–609 at II–630, para. 65, CFI.

[54] Case 6/68 *Zuckerfabrik Watenstedt v. Council* [1968] E.C.R. 409, ECJ; Case 63/69 *Compagnie Française Commerciale v. Commission* [1970] E.C.R. 221 at 226–227, para. 11, ECJ; Case 123/77 *UNICME v. Council* [1978] E.C.R. 845 at 852, para. 16, ECJ; Case 242/81 *Roquette Frères v. Council* [1982] E.C.R. 3213 at 3230, para. 7, ECJ; Case 26/86 *Deutz and Geldermann v. Council* [1987] E.C.R. 941 at 951, para. 8, ECJ; Joined Cases 97, 193, 99 and 215/86 *Asteris v. Commission* [1988] E.C.R. 2181 at 2205, para. 13, ECJ; (Order of the President of July 13, 1988), Case 160/88R *Fédération européenne de la santé animale and Others v. Council* [1988] E.C.R. 4121 at 4130, para. 29, ECJ; Joined Cases C–15 and C–108/91 *Buckl and Others v. Commission* [1992] E.C.R. I–6061 at I–6099, para. 25, ECJ; (Order of May 24, 1993), Case C–131/92 *Arnaud v. Council* [1993] E.C.R. I–2573 at I–2580—2581, paras 13–17, ECJ; Case C–213/91 *Abertal and Others v. Commission* [1993] E.C.R. I–3177 at I–3200—3202, paras 17–24, ECJ; (Orders of June 21, 1993), Case C–256/93 *Pacific Fruit Company and Others v. Council and Commission*, not reported in the

that an act of general application is applicable only to one person is not enough to make it cease to be legislative in nature with regard to that person if the act is applicable as a result of an objective fact situation specified in the act.[55]

However, an applicant can show in various other ways that it is individually concerned by a legislative act. In the first place, it is sufficient to show that the act adversely affected specific rights of the applicant or its members.[56] **7–059**

Secondly, the applicant may argue that, in adopting the legislative act, the Community institution was under a duty to take account of its specific circumstances. Such specific protection distinguishes it sufficiently from other market participants to which the act applies. In addition, there is the fact that such a market participant must be able to assert that specific protection and therefore to bring an action.[57] **7–060**

Thirdly, an applicant will be individually concerned when the contested act mentions it by name (although it is not the addressee) and a situation specific to it is directly governed by the act.[58] **7–061**

An action for annulment may be brought by a natural or legal person against an institution's refusal to adopt an act only if an application brought against the act refused would have been admissible.[59] **7–062**

E.C.R.; Case C–257/93 *Van Parijs and Others v. Council and Commission* [1993] E.C.R. I–3335, ECJ; Case C–276/93 *Chiquita Banana and Others v. Council* [1993] E.C.R. I–3345, ECJ; Case C–282/93 *Comafrica and Others v. Council and Commission*, not reported in the E.C.R., and Case C–288/93 *CO.MA.CO v. Council*, not reported in the E.C.R.; Case C–298/89 *Gibraltar v. Council* [1993] E.C.R. I–3605 at I–3654, para. 17, ECJ. For the possibility that the contested act is also applicable to situations in the future, see Case 231/82 *Spijker v. Commission* [1983] E.C.R. 2559 at 2566–2567, paras 8–11, ECJ. For the possibility that the regulation is also applicable to individuals established in another Member State, see Case 1/64 *Glucoseries Réunies v. Commission* [1964] E.C.R. 413 at 417, ECJ.

55 Case 38/64 *Getreide-Import Gesellschaft v. Commission* [1965] E.C.R. 203 at 208, ECJ. In that case, the contested act was a decision addressed to all Member States valid for one day and laying down the basis for an import levy. The applicant was the only individual who had applied for an import certificate.

56 (Order of November 23, 1995), Case C–10/95P *Asocarne v. Council* [1995] E.C.R. I–4149 at I–4163, para. 43, ECJ.

57 Case 11/82 *Piraiki-Patraiki v. Commission* [1985] E.C.R. 207 at 243–246, paras 17–32, ECJ. For a discussion of the scope of that judgment, see Case C–209/94P *Buralux and Others v. Council* [1996] E.C.R. I–615 at I–647—648, paras 30–35, ECJ; Case C–152/88 *Sofrimport v. Commission* [1990] E.C.R. I–2477 at I–2507—2508, paras 8–13, ECJ; Joined Cases T–480 and T–483/93 *Antillean Rice Mills and Others v. Commission* [1995] E.C.R. II–2305 at II–2332—2335, paras 67–68, CFI (upheld on appeal); (Judgment of February 11, 1999) Case C–390/95P *Antillean Rice Mills and Others v. Commission* (not yet reported), paras 25–30, ECJ. See also case note by Waelbroeck and Fosselard (1996) C.M.L.Rev. 811–829.

58 Case 138/79 *Roquette Frères v. Council* [1980] E.C.R. 3333 at 3355–3356, paras 13–16, ECJ; Case 139/79 *Maizena v. Council* [1980] E.C.R. 3393 at 3418–3419, paras 13–16, ECJ; Joined Cases 239 and 275/82 *Allied Corporation v. Commission* [1984] E.C.R. 1005 at 1027, para. 4, and at 1030, para. 12, ECJ. *Cf.* para. 7–069, below, as regards independent importers being individually concerned where they seek the annulment of a regulation imposing anti-dumping duties.

59 Case 42/71 *Nordgetreide v. Commission* [1972] E.C.R. 105 at 110–111, para. 5, ECJ; Joined Cases 97, 193, 99 and 215/86 *Asteris v. Commission* [1988] E.C.R. 2181 at 2206, paras 17–18, ECJ; Case C–87/89 *Sonito and Others v. Commission* [1990] E.C.R. I–1981 at I–2009, para. 8, ECJ; Joined Cases C–15 and C–108/91 *Buckl and Others v. Commission* [1992] E.C.R. I–

7–063 In exceptional circumstances, the requirement that the contested act must be of individual concern to the applicant discriminates against persons who find themselves in a similar position. In such a case, the Court of Justice, applying the principle of equal treatment—part of superior Community law—will, if necessary, lower the hurdle of admissibility. The judgment in *Les Verts v. European Parliament*[60] provides an illustration. The decision of the Bureau of the European Parliament determining the allocation of financial assistance to political parties with a view to preparing for the European Elections applied both to political parties which were represented in the Parliament at the time when the decision was adopted, which were therefore identifiable, and to parties which were not so represented at that time and therefore were not identifiable, but which would be taking part in the elections. According to the wording of the judgment, there was no doubt that parties represented in the Parliament, which were identifiable, were individually concerned.[61] The question arose whether this was also true of parties not represented in the Parliament, who were therefore not identifiable. The Court of Justice held that the fact that the decision applied to all parties taking part in the elections placed the second class of parties in a similar position to the first, with the result that both classes had to be regarded as individually concerned by the decision in the same way.

7–064 The Court of Justice is not prepared to relax the criteria developed in its case law for individual concern where the rights which individuals derive from a superior rule of Community law are fully protected by the national courts which may, if need be, refer a question to the Court for a preliminary ruling under Article 234 (*ex Article 177*) of the E.C. Treaty.[62]

7–065 In anti-dumping, competition and state aid cases, the question often arises whether an individual applicant is individually concerned by the measure contested by way of an action for annulment. The question also arises on occasions as to the circumstances in which an association of undertakings is individually concerned.

7–066 *Anti-dumping cases.* Provisional and definitive anti-dumping duties or countervailing duties are imposed by regulation pursuant to Article 14(1) of Regulation No. 384/96.[63] What is involved is essentially a provision of general

6061 at I–6098, para. 22, ECJ; Case T–83/92 *Zunis Holding and Others v. Commission* [1993] E.C.R. II–1169 at II–1181—1182, para. 31, CFI.

[60] Case 294/83 *Les Verts v. European Parliament* [1986] E.C.R. 1339, ECJ.

[61] Commentators point to the specific character of the contested measure (Kovar (1987) C.D.E. 300–332; *cf.* Jacqué (1986) R.T.D.E. 500–511).

[62] Case C–321/95P *Greenpeace Council and Others v. Commission* [1998] E.C.R. I–1651 at I–1716, paras 33–34, ECJ (the fact that the subject-matter of proceedings before a national court and that of an action before the Court of First Instance are different does not change matters in so far as both proceedings are based on rights derived by individuals from a superior rule of Community law); see also (Order of March 12, 1998), Case T–207/97 *Berthu v. Council* [1998] E.C.R. II–509 at II–520, para. 29, CFI, and Lenaerts, "The Legal Protection of Private Parties under the EC Treaty: a Coherent and Complete System of Judicial Review", in *Scritti in onore di Giuseppe Federico Mancini*, Milan, Giuffrè editore, 1998, II, at 591–623.

[63] Council Regulation No. 384/96 of December 22, 1995 ([1996] O.J. L56/1).

application, which applies to all economic entities concerned. Nevertheless, some parts of such a "regulation" are of individual concern to some persons.[64]

Producers or exporters established outside the Community of products on which anti-dumping duties are imposed are individually concerned where information about their trading activities is used with a view to determining the duties. Generally speaking, this will be the case where manufacturing and exporting undertakings can establish that they were identified in measures adopted by the Commission or the Council or concerned by the preliminary investigation.[65] An action for annulment is often the only legal remedy available to them against the imposition of such duties.[66] This argument provides support for the Community Court in finding that such an action is admissible. **7–067**

Manufacturing and exporting undertakings, however, are not individually concerned by an anti-dumping duty which is imposed on other undertakings by the same regulation. They are, therefore, not entitled to challenge such a duty.[67]

Natural or legal persons or associations without legal personality, acting on behalf of the Community industry which lodge a complaint leading to a preliminary administrative procedure,[68] are entitled to bring an action for annulment against a refusal by the Commission to initiate the actual anti-dumping procedure on the grounds that there is insufficient evidence.[69] Their particular legal position founded upon the procedural guarantees conferred by Regulation No. 384/96[70] must be protected by the Community **7–068**

---

64 See paras 7–041—7–043, above. For a survey, see Ress and Ukrow, "Direct Actions before the EC Court of Justice. The Case of EEC Anti-dumping Law", in *Adjudication of International Trade Disputes in International and National Economic Law*, Pupil, volume 7, Freiburg, University Press, 1992, at 159–260.

65 Joined Cases 239 and 275/82 *Allied Corporation v. Commission* [1984] E.C.R. 1005 at 1030, para. 12, ECJ. See, however, Case T–161/94 *Sinochem Heilongjiang v. Council* [1996] E.C.R. II–695 at II–715, paras 45–48, CFI, where the Court of First Instance held that the preliminary investigation had concerned the applicant undertaking, even though the Commission had decided not to make use of the information which it had provided; Case T–155/94 *Climax Paper v. Council* [1996] E.C.R. II–873 at II–891—892, paras 46–51, CFI; Case T–170/94 *Shanghai Bicycle v. Council* [1997] E.C.R. II–1383 at II–1401, para. 39, CFI.

66 *Allied Corporation v. Commission* (cited in n. 65, above), para. 13.

67 Case 240/84 *Toyo v. Council* [1987] E.C.R. 1809 at 1851–1852, paras 4–7, ECJ; Case 258/84 *Nippon Seiko v. Council* [1987] E.C.R. 1923, para. 7, at 1960–1961, ECJ; Case C–156/87 *Gestetner Holdings v. Council and Commission* [1990] E.C.R. I–781, para. 12, at I–832, ECJ, Case C–174/87 *Ricoh v. Council* [1992] E.C.R. I–1335, paras 6–8, at I–1389, ECJ.

68 The "investigation" provided for by Regulation No. 384/96, Art. 6.

69 Case 191/82 *Fediol v. Commission* [1983] E.C.R. 2913 at 2932–2936, paras 15–33, ECJ. See also Bellis, "Judicial Review of EEC Anti-dumping and Anti-subsidy Determinations after *Fediol*: The Emergence of a New Admissibility Test" (1984) C.M.L.Rev. 539 at 549, who argues that there should be generalised access to the Court of Justice (now the Court of First Instance) for any natural or legal person who participated in the administrative investigation into the dumping in question.

70 The procedural guarantees conferred by the regulation are the right to lodge a complaint, the associated right that the complaint should be investigated with due care in accordance with the procedure laid down by the Commission and the right, upon written request, to inspect all information made available by any party to an investigation which is not confidential (Art. 6(7)).

Court. A decision refusing to initiate a procedure may not undermine those procedural safeguards.

An action brought against the regulation imposing a definitive anti-dumping duty is available only to a complainant whose involvement in the adoption of the regulation extends further than simply lodging the complaint which initiated the anti-dumping or anti-subsidy procedure. Only where the complainant's observations were determinative of the course of the investigation or where its specific position on the market was taken into account, will the complainant be individually concerned by the regulation imposing a definitive anti-dumping duty.[71] The fact that the complaint was lodged by a trade association of which the applicant is a member does not detract from the undertaking's right to bring an action.[72] If the aforementioned conditions are fulfilled by both the trade association and the undertaking, both of them can bring an action for annulment.

7–069 Importers associated with an exporter are individually concerned by a regulation imposing an anti-dumping duty where their resale prices, and not the export prices, of the products in question are considered in order to determine whether dumping is taking place[73] or the level of the anti-dumping duty.[74]

Generally speaking, importers not associated with an exporter are not individually concerned by a regulation imposing an anti-dumping duty.[75] The reason for this is that the imposition of the duty affects them in their objective capacity as importers of the product subjected to an anti-dumping duty. Consequently, the regulation remains a regulation, even if independent importers were involved in the procedure which led to its adoption[76] or if their identity emerges from the regulation.[77] The existence of dumping is not normally determined by reference to importers' resale prices, but by reference to the actual prices paid or payable on export.[78]

---

[71] Case 264/82 *Timex v. Council and Commission* [1985] E.C.R. 849 at 864–866, paras 8–17, ECJ.

[72] *ibid.*

[73] Case 118/77 *ISO v. Council* [1979] E.C.R. 1277, ECJ; Joined Cases 239 and 275/82 *Allied Corporation v. Commission* [1984] E.C.R. 1005 at 1031, para. 15, ECJ.

[74] Joined Cases C–305/86 and C–160/87 *Neotype Techmashexport v. Commission and Council* [1990] E.C.R. I–2945 at I–2999, paras 20–21, ECJ.

[75] Case 307/81 *Alusuisse v. Council and Commission* [1982] E.C.R. 3463, ECJ; (Order of July 8, 1987), Case 279/86 *Sermes v. Commission* [1987] E.C.R. 3109, ECJ; (Order of July 8, 1987), Case 301/86 *Frimodt Pedersen v. Commission* [1987] E.C.R. 3123, ECJ. A regulation which is confined to accepting price undertakings offered by an exporter in an anti-dumping investigation in relation to products imported by the applicant is of individual concern only to the exporter in question. The importer—even if he is the sole importer—is necessarily not party to the undertakings given: (Order of July 8, 1987), Case 295/86 *Garelly v. Commission* [1987] E.C.R. 3117 at 3122, para. 14, ECJ. For a critical discussion, see Van Ginderachter, "Recevabilité des recours en matière de dumping" (1987) C.D.E. 635–666. See also (Order of November 11, 1987), Case 205/87 *Nuova Ceam v. Commission* [1987] E.C.R. 4427 at 4431–4432, para. 14, ECJ.

[76] *Alusuisse v. Council and Commission* (cited in n. 75, above), at 3473, para. 13.

[77] (Order of July 8, 1987), Case 301/86 *Frimodt Pedersen v. Commission* [1987] E.C.R. 3123 at 3125, para. 3, ECJ.

[78] *ibid.*, at 3128, para. 17.

The restrictive scope of the case law relating to independent importers is mitigated by the fact that they can challenge the imposition of an anti-dumping duty in the national courts, which, in turn, may (or must) make a reference to the Court of Justice for a preliminary ruling on the validity of the regulation.[79]

The Court of Justice has recognised the particular economic situation of an independent importer as a specific circumstance causing the importer to be individually concerned by a regulation imposing an anti-dumping duty.[80] The Court pointed out that the applicant was the largest importer of the product and that its business activities depended to a very large extent on imports, given that there was only one Community producer of the product, which, moreover, was its direct competitor and had strengthened its position considerably *vis-à-vis* the applicant as a result of the restriction of imports. It made no difference that its resale price was not taken into account in adopting the regulation.[81]

An original equipment manufacturer (OEM), an undertaking selling **7–070** goods produced by other manufacturers under its own brand name,[82] will be individually concerned by a regulation imposing an anti-dumping duty where, in calculating the dumping margin, account was taken of the particular features of its business dealings with the manufacturers in respect of which anti-dumping duties are imposed by the regulation. An application by an OEM will be admissible only in so far as it seeks annulment of the specific anti-dumping duty imposed by the regulation on the producer from which the OEM obtains the goods which it sells.[83]

Competition cases. Article 3(2)(b) of Regulation No. 17 confers on inter- **7–071** ested individuals the right to lodge a complaint with the Commission on account of an alleged infringement of the Community competition rules by competitors, purchasers or suppliers. Article 19(2) entitles complainants to be heard by the Commission in the course of the investigation. Persons who have lodged a complaint with the Commission are entitled to bring an action for annulment against the full or partial rejection of their complaint or against a declaration that Article 81 (*ex Article 85*) (1) of the E.C. Treaty

---

79 See Chap. 10, below.

80 Case C–358/89 *Extramet Industry v. Council* [1991] E.C.R. I–2501, ECJ. For an extensive commentary, see Brouwer and Carlin, "Qualité pour agir dans les procédures anti-dumping après Extramet" (1981) D.P.C.I. 243–267. For a critical note, see Arnull, "Challenging EC Anti-dumping Regulations: The Problem of Admissibility" (1992) E.C.L.R. 73 at 79.

81 The question arises as to the extent to which this case law is confined to anti-dumping or as to whether it might open the door to claims from natural and legal persons who are especially concerned by a Community measure, yet do not form part of a closed class. It appears from Joined Cases C–15 and 108/91 *Buckl and Others v. Commission* [1992] E.C.R. I–6061, ECJ, that, for the present, the Court of Justice is limiting this "economic" approach.

82 It purchases the goods and sells them under its own brand name. Consequently, an OEM falls somewhere between a producer/exporter, on the one hand, and an importer, on the other.

83 Joined Cases C–133 and C–150/87 *Nashua Corporation and Others v. Commission and Council* [1990] E.C.R. I–719 at I–772—773, paras 16–21, ECJ; Case C–156/87 *Gestetner Holdings v. Council and Commission* [1990] E.C.R. I–781 at I–833—834, paras 19–24, ECJ.

is inapplicable[84] to the facts to which the complaint relates.[85] Also persons who submitted objections in writing to the Commission during the investigation in regard to a proposed declaration that Article 81 (*ex Article 85*) (1) of the E.C. Treaty is not applicable to the practices of a competitor or supplier, or persons who participated in the hearing organised by the Commission, are individually concerned by such declaration.[86] Those classes of person have been sufficiently involved in the procedure whereby the contested decision was adopted in order to constitute a closed class in the light of the act.[87]

In some circumstances, an undertaking will be individually concerned by a Commission decision addressed to two competing undertakings in which it comes to the conclusion that the concentration between the undertakings, under Council Regulation No. 4064/89 of December 21, 1989 on the control of concentrations between undertakings,[88] does not raise serious doubts as to its compatibility with the common market.[89] The Court of First Instance

---

[84] See E.C. Treaty, Art. 81 (*ex Art. 85*) (3).

[85] Case 26/76 *Metro v. Commission* [1977] E.C.R. 1875, ECJ. Mancini argues that the relaxation of the admissibility requirements for individuals effected by the judgment in *Metro* is justified by the overriding interest in enabling the application of competition law to be judicially reviewed (Mancini, "Access to Justice: Individual Undertakings and EEC Antitrust Law—Problems and Pitfalls" (1989) Fordham I.L.J. 189 at 203); Case 210/81 *Demo-Studio Schmidt v. Commission* [1983] E.C.R. 3045, ECJ; Case T–37/92 *BEUC and NCC v. Commission* [1994] E.C.R. II–285 at II–307, para. 36, CFI; Case T–114/92 *BEMIM v. Commission* [1995] E.C.R. II–147 at II–160, para. 27, ECJ.

[86] Case 75/84 *Metro v. Commission* [1986] E.C.R. 3021 at 3079–3080, paras 18–23, ECJ; Case T–19/92 *Leclerc v. Commission* [1996] E.C.R. II–1851 at II–1878—1881, paras 53–63, CFI, and Case T–88/92 *Leclerc v. Commission* [1996] E.C.R. II–1961 at II–1988—1989, paras 49–50, CFI. In these judgments, the Court of First Instance based its finding that the applicant—a co-operative society—was individually concerned also on the fact that it had taken part in the administrative procedure as a representative of its members, who, as potential competitors of the traders belonging to the selective distribution system to which the E.C. Treaty, Art. 85 (*now Art. 81*) (1) had been declared inapplicable, could have taken part in the administrative procedure, and been individually concerned thereby, as "interested third parties" under Regulation No. 17, Art. 19(3).

[87] Sometimes the case law goes even further: see Joined Cases T–528, T–542, T–543 and T–546/93 *Métropole Télévision and Others v. Commission* [1996] E.C.R. II–649, CFI, where the Court of First Instance held that it is sufficient for the applicant to be able to be regarded as an interested third party within the meaning of Regulation No. 17, Art. 19(3), which was entitled to be associated by the Commission with the administrative procedure for the adoption of the decision in order for it to be individually concerned thereby within the meaning of the E.C. Treaty, Art. 173 (*now Art. 230*), para. 4. The Court considered it irrelevant that the applicant had not availed itself of its procedural rights under Regulation No. 17, Art. 19(3). It considered that to make the capacity to bring proceedings of such interested third parties subject to their actually taking part in the administrative procedure would be tantamount to introducing an additional condition of admissibility in the form of a compulsory pre-litigation procedure not provided for in the E.C. Treaty, Art. 173 (*now Art. 230*). *Cf.*, however, Case T–87/92 *Kruidvat v. Commission* [1996] E.C.R. II–1931 at II–1954, paras 61–67, CFI.

[88] [1990] O.J. L257/1.

[89] Case T–2/93 *Air France v. Commission* [1994] E.C.R. II–323 at II–340—342, paras 40–48, CFI. *Cf.* Heidenhain, "Zur Klagebefugnis Dritter in der europäischen Fusionskontrolle" (1991) Eu.Z.W. 590–595. For a thorough analysis of admissibility problems in the case of actions against Commission decisions pursuant to Regulation No. 4064/89, see Langeheine, "Judicial Review in the Field of Merger Control" (1992) J.B.L. 121 at 121–131. For a recent application, see Joined Cases C–68/94 and C–30/95 *France and SCPA and EMC v.*

reached this view in the light of a number of factors. The applicant had been intensively involved in the investigation into the compatibility of the intended concentration with the common market by submitting observations and criticisms, clarifying, among other things, the effects of the concentration on its competitive position. Next, the Commission had judged the competitive structure of the market in question above all in the light of the applicant's competitive position. Lastly, some months before the concentration came about, the applicant undertaking had given up its interest in one of the undertakings concerned pursuant to an agreement concluded with the Commission. The Court of First Instance has also held in connection with Regulation No. 4064/89 that recognised employees' representatives of an undertaking involved in a concentration were individually concerned by a Commission decision adopted pursuant to that regulation on the ground that Regulation No. 4064/89 mentioned them expressly and specifically among the third persons showing a "sufficient interest" to submit observations to the Commission during the administrative investigation of the concentration's compatibility with the common market. The Court of First Instance regarded it as irrelevant whether the employees' representatives of the undertaking had actually taken part in the administrative procedure.[90]

State aid cases. As far as new aid[91] is concerned, the Commission is empowered to take decisions at two stages in the investigation into their compatibility with the common market. 7–072

First, there is the preliminary stage for reviewing aid pursuant to Article 88 (*ex Article 93*) (3) of the E.C. Treaty. Where, at the conclusion of its investigation, the Commission decides to initiate the procedure under Article 88(2) of the E.C. Treaty, that decision is of individual concern to the undertaking which was to benefit by the proposed aid.[92] Where, in contrast, the Commission considers at the end of the preliminary stage that the proposed aid is compatible with the common market and therefore decides not to initiate a procedure pursuant to Article 88(2), that decision is of individual concern to all the parties concerned which could have submitted observations in the course of that procedure.[93] Moreover, judicial

---

Commission [1998] E.C.R. I–1375 at I–1471—1472, paras 54–58, ECJ (the Court of Justice also took account in this case of the fact that the conditions attached to the declaration by which the concentration was stated to be compatible with the common market primarily touched the applicant's interests).

[90] Case T–96/92 *CCE de la Société générale des Grandes Sources and Others v. Commission* [1995] E.C.R. II–1213 at II–1232, para. 37, CFI; Case T–12/93 *CCE de Vittel and Others v. Commission* [1995] E.C.R. II–1247 at II–1270—1271, para. 48, CFI. In those cases, the Court of First Instance subsequently held that the applicants were directly affected by the contested decision only in so far as their procedural rights during the administrative procedure had been affected. Consequently, it considered only the plea alleging that those rights had been breached. For a critical note on that limited admissibility, see Arnull (1996) C.M.L.Rev. 319–335.

[91] For a definition, see para. 7–023, n. 69, above.

[92] This is because the Member State concerned may not implement the aid measure until a final decision has been reached.

[93] Case C–198/91 *Cook v. Commission* [1993] E.C.R. I–2487 at I–2526—2528, paras 13–26,

review is the only means whereby those parties concerned can enforce their procedural rights. "Parties concerned" within the meaning of Article 88(2) do not comprise only the undertaking or undertakings in receipt of aid (which in this event naturally have no interest in bringing an action for annulment), but also such persons, undertakings or associations whose interests might be affected by the grant of the aid, for instance, competing undertakings and trade associations.[94] Trade associations particularly closely involved in the adoption of Commission policy on aid in a given sector are individually concerned by a Commission decision refusing—implicitly—to initiate a formal investigation pursuant to Article 88(2) of the E.C. Treaty where such refusal is allegedly at odds with the policy traced out. This is because such a decision concerns the trade organisation *qua* negotiator of the policy.[95]

In addition, the Commission may also take a decision after the *inter partes* procedure provided for in Article 88(2) of the E.C. Treaty has been completed. Such a decision is addressed to the Member State concerned. If the Commission declares the aid incompatible with the common market, the undertaking for which the aid was intended will be individually concerned.[96] If, in contrast, the aid is declared compatible with the common

ECJ; Case C–225/91 *Matra v. Commission* [1993] E.C.R. I–3203 at I–3254—3255, paras 15–20, ECJ. This is also the case where the Commission considers that the measures at issue do not constitute State aid, with the result that competing undertakings which have submitted a complaint about the measures in question would be deprived of the procedural guarantees afforded by the E.C. Treaty, Art. 88(2). They are directly and individually concerned by such a Commission decision and entitled to rely on those procedural guarantees before the Community Court: Case C–367/95P *Commission v. Sytraval and Brink's France* [1998] E.C.R. I–1719 at I–1766, para. 47, ECJ; (Judgment of September 15, 1998), Case T–11/95 *BP Chemicals v. Commission*, paras 88–89 and 164–166, CFI (not yet reported).

94 Case 323/82 *Intermills v. Commission* [1984] E.C.R. 3809 at 3827, para. 16, ECJ. It is not enough for the competitive position of an undertaking to have been affected by the aid measure approved only potentially and incidentally in order for it to be regarded as a "party concerned" within the meaning of the E.C. Treaty, Art. 88(2). In so far as aid the potential beneficiaries of which are defined only in a general and abstract manner is approved, there can, in the Court's view, be no competing undertaking before individual aid is granted in application of the aid scheme: Case T–398/94 *Kahn Scheepvaart v. Commission* [1996] E.C.R. II–477 at II–494—495, paras 47–49, CFI. *Cf.* (Judgment of September 16, 1998), Case T–188/95 *Waterleiding Maatschappij Noord-West Brabant v. Commission*, paras 50–87, CFI (not yet reported).

95 Case C–313/90 *CIRFS and Others v. Commission* [1993] E.C.R. I–1125 at I–1184—1185, paras 28–31, ECJ.

96 Case 730/79 *Philip Morris v. Commission* [1980] E.C.R. 2671 at 2687, para. 5, ECJ; Case 323/82 *Intermills v. Commission* [1984] E.C.R. 3809 at 3824, para. 5, ECJ; Joined Cases 296 and 318/82 *Netherlands and Leeuwarder Papierwarenfabriek v. Commission* [1985] E.C.R. 809 at 821, para. 13, ECJ; Case T–358/94 *Air France v. Commission* [1996] E.C.R. II–2109 at II–2122, para. 31, CFI. Works councils and trade unions of undertakings in receipt of aid were, however, not held to be individually concerned by a Commission decision declaring the aid unlawful because the Commission was not given prior notification pursuant to Art. 88 (*ex Art. 93*) (3) and the aid was not compatible with the common market. Such works councils and trade unions are parties concerned within the meaning of Art. 88 (2), but that is not sufficient to render them individually concerned, not even if they submitted comments during the administrative procedure: (Order of February 18, 1998), Case T–189/97 *Comité d'entreprise de la Société française de production and Others v. Commission* [1998] E.C.R. II–335 at II–350—351, paras 42–44, CFI. But see (Judgment of February 11, 1999) Case T–

market, it will be of individual concern to competing undertakings which participated in the formal investigation pursuant to Article 88(2) and whose position on the market is put at risk by the aid measure.[97] In the case of trade organisations it is enough that their position as negotiator is affected[98] and that they were closely involved in the formal investigation[99] or that, in the context of a procedure under Article 88(2) of the E.C. Treaty, they protected the interests of some of their members in accordance with powers conferred on them by their statutes, without any objection from those members, provided that the contested decision is of direct and individual concern to those members within the meaning of Article 230 (*ex Article 173*) of the E.C. Treaty.[1]

Public contracts. Natural or legal persons who participate in a public tender procedure organised by the Community belong to a closed class. Each of them is individually concerned by a decision awarding the contract to one of their number.[2] The withdrawal of a definitive decision awarding the contract is of individual concern to the person to whom it was awarded.[3] **7–073**

Associations. The question whether trade associations are individually concerned is arising increasingly frequently. It appears from the case law that trade associations may be deemed to be sufficiently individually **7–074**

86/96 *Arbeitsgemeinschaft Deutscher Luftfahrt-Unternehmen v. Commission*, CFI (not yet reported), individual concern for the potential beneficiary of the aid was found to be lacking in this procedural setting, because the contested Commission decision appeared to be a measure of general application, see n. 9, above.

97 Case 169/84 *Cofaz v. Commission* [1986] E.C.R. 391 at 414–415, paras 22–25, ECJ (for a critical commentary, see Gyselen, "La transparence en matière d'aides d'Etat: Les droits des tiers" (1993) C.D.E. 417 at 433–434); Joined Cases T–477, T–478 and T–449/93 *AITEC and Others v. Commission* [1995] E.C.R. II–1871 at II–1988—1990, paras 3–42, and at II–2000—2002, paras 75–80, CFI; Case T–149/95 *Ducros v. Commission* [1997] E.C.R. II–2031 at II–2042—2045, paras 30–43, CFI. See also (Judgment of September 15, 1998) Case T–11/95 *BP Chemicals v. Commission*, paras 69–83, CFI (not yet reported).

98 In the case of a trade organisation, its position as a negotiator at both national and Community level is taken into account.

99 Joined Cases 67–68 and 70/85 *Van der Kooy v. Commission* [1988] E.C.R. 219 at 268–269, paras 20–25, ECJ; Case T–380/94 *AIUFFASS and AKT v. Commission* [1996] E.C.R. II–2169 at II–2187—2189, paras 44–52, CFI. In a recent judgment, however, the Court of First Instance accepted that undertakings which had not taken part in the formal investigation pursuant to the E.C. Treaty, Art. 88(2), could nevertheless be directly and individually concerned on the ground that the market in which the aid was granted was characterised by a limited number of producers (the applicants had a market share of 95 per cent) and by the significant increase in production capacity involved in the investments planned by the company in receipt of the aid in question. That special situation distinguished them from every other market participant as far as the aid in issue was concerned (Case T–435/93 *ASPEC and Others v. Commission* [1995] E.C.R. I–1281 at I–1309, para. 70, CFI).

1 Joined Cases T–447/, T–448 and T–449/93 *AITEC and Others v. Commission* [1995] E.C.R. II–1971 at II–1996, para. 60, CFI. The Court of First Instance took the view that a collective action brought by the association in question presented procedural advantages, since it avoided the institution of numerous separate actions against the same decision, whilst obviating any risk of the E.C. Treaty, Art. 230 (*ex Art. 173*) being circumvented by means of such a collective action.

2 Case 135/81 *Groupement des Agences de Voyages v. Commission* [1982] E.C.R. 3799, ECJ.

3 Case 232/81 *Agricola Commerciale Olio v. Commission* [1984] E.C.R. 3881, ECJ.

concerned in three types of situation.[4] First, a trade association may be individually concerned if it can show that a provision of Community law expressly grants it a series of procedural rights.[5] Secondly, this may be so where the association represents the interests of undertakings which would be entitled to bring proceedings in their own right.[6] Thirdly, a trade association will be sufficiently individually concerned where it is differentiated because its own interests as an association are affected by the contested measure, especially where its position as negotiator is affected.[7] In those three situations, the Court of Justice and the Court of First Instance also take account of the participation of the association in question in the decision-making procedure.

(c) *The requirement that there should be an interest in the annulment of the contested act*

7–075 Natural or legal persons may bring an action for annulment only in so far as they can establish that they have an interest. This means that they must benefit from the annulment of the contested act. That benefit consists in the elimination of the adverse repercussions on their legal position.[8]

---

[4] For a clear survey of the case law, see (Order of September 30, 1997), Case T–122/96 *Federolio v. Commission* [1997] E.C.R. II–1559 at II–1580 *et seq.*, paras 60 *et seq.*, CFI.

[5] Case 191/82 *Fediol v. Commission* [1983] E.C.R. 2913, ECJ (see also para. 7–068, above); Case T–12/93 *CCE de Vittel and Others v. Commission* [1995] E.C.R. II–1247, CFI (see para. 7–071, above).

[6] Joined Cases T–447, T–448 and T–449/93 *AITEC and Others v. Commission* [1995] E.C.R. II–1971, CFI.

[7] See, for instance, Joined Cases 67/85, 68/85 and 70/85 *Van der Kooy and Others v. Commission* [1988] E.C.R. 219, ECJ (see also para. 7–072, above).

[8] Opinion of Advocate General G.F. Mancini in Joined Cases 142 and 156/84 *BAT and Reynolds v. Commission* [1987] E.C.R. 4487 at 4549, ECJ. That requirement was not satisfied in the case of undertakings which had been granted negative clearance at their request in respect of the prohibition set out in the E.C. Treaty, Art. 85 (*now Art. 81*) (1), but nonetheless sought annulment of the decision granting negative clearance because they considered that the decision contained recitals which might be detrimental to their interests. Since the undertakings had ended up in the legal position which they had asked the Commission to grant them, they had no interest in the annulment of the decision: Case T–138/89 *Nederlandse Bankiersvereniging and Nederlandse Vereniging van Banken v. Commission* [1992] E.C.R. II–2181 at II–2192—2193, paras 32–34, CFI. An undertaking, which was declared bankrupt after it had brought an action for annulment of a Commission decision approving the grant of state aid to a competitor, had ceased to have an interest in bringing the proceedings on the ground that the competitive situation disappeared when the undertaking was declared bankrupt and it could not have been affected before the undertaking was placed in liquidation as the state aid had not yet been paid over at that date: Case T–443/93 *Casillo Grani v. Commission* [1995] E.C.R. II–1375, CFI. It has been held that a decision closing the file on the complaint of an applicant association representing members of a mutual provident association did not affect its legal position. In addition, the association in no way competed with the undertaking which allegedly benefited from the state aid which was the subject of the complaint: Case T–178/94 *ATM v. Commission* [1997] E.C.R. II–2529 at II–2549, paras 62, 63, CFI. An undertaking which brought an action for annulment of a regulation, which did not concern the product which it manufactured, was held not to be affected by the regulation and to have no legal interest in bringing proceedings for its annulment: Case T–117/95 *Corman v. Commission* [1997] E.C.R. II–95 at II–125, paras 82, 84. CFI; *ATM v. Commission* (cited above) at II–2549, para. 62 (the Court of First Instance found that a Commission decision terminating its

The interest must be personal to the applicant itself.[9] An applicant to which the contested act does not apply cannot claim a personal interest.[10] 7–076

A hypothetical interest is insufficient to ground an action for annulment.[11] However, an applicant may have an interest in the annulment of an act which is no longer in force.[12] The annulment of such a measure has the effect of preventing its author from adopting a similar act in the future.[13] The applicant may also have an interest in bringing an action against a measure which has been implemented in full,[14] the intention being for the defendant institution to do justice to the applicant immediately or for it to make the necessary amendments for the future to the legal system in the context of which the act was adopted.[15] Lastly, an applicant may have an interest in the annulment of a decision which has been repealed. The reason for this is that the repeal of a decision cannot invariably be equated with annulment by the Court since, by definition, it does not amount to recognition of the decision's illegality. Moreover, repeal generally takes effect *ex nunc*, whereas annulment within the meaning of Article 231 (*ex Article 174*) of the E.C. Treaty takes effect *ex tunc*. Accordingly, the judgment annulling a decision which has been withdrawn may put the originator of the act under an obligation to remove the effects of the illegal conduct found in the judgment by taking adequate steps to restore the 7–077

investigation into the compatibility of aid with Community law did not affect the applicant's legal sphere).

[9] Case 282/85 *DEFI v. Commission* [1986] E.C.R. 2469 at 2481, para. 18, ECJ; Case 204/85 *Stroghili v. Court of Auditors* [1987] E.C.R. 389 at 402, para. 9, ECJ. A federated state will often have autonomous policy-making powers which are not subject to the control of the federal state. Consequently, such a federated state has an interest of its own, distinct from the interest of the federal or central authorities, in challenging a Community act which restricts its policy-making powers: see Case T–214/95 *Vlaams Gewest v. Commission* [1998] E.C.R. II–717 at II–733, para. 30, CFI.

[10] Case 88/76 *Exportation des Sucres v. Commission* [1977] E.C.R. 709 at 726, paras 18–19, ECJ.

[11] Case 204/85 *Stroghili v. Court of Auditors* [1987] E.C.R. 389 at 402, para. 11, ECJ.

[12] Case 53/85 *AKZO v. Commission* [1986] E.C.R. 1965 at 1990, para. 21, ECJ; Case 207/86 *Apesco v. Commission* [1988] E.C.R. 2151 (see para. 7–004, above).

[13] If, however, the Court of First Instance finds that annulment of the act could not give rise to measures to comply with the judgment declaring the act void within the meaning of the E.C. Treaty, Art. 233 (*ex Art. 176*), the applicant will have no interest in obtaining its annulment: see (Order of June 13, 1997), Case T–13/96 *TEAM and Kolprojekt v. Commission* [1997] E.C.R. II–983 at II–994, para. 28, CFI.

[14] Case T–46/92 *The Scottish Football Association v. Commission* [1994] E.C.R. II–1039 at II–1050—1051, paras 13, 14, CFI. In litigation concerning access to documents of Community institutions, the Court of First Instance has held that it was irrelevant that the documents to which access had been refused were already in the public domain. The reason was that the Court found that the Commission and Council framework decisions on public access did not require members of the public to put forward reasons for seeking access to requested documents, since their aim was to give effect to the principle of the largest possible access for citizens to information with a view to strengthening the democratic character of the institutions and the public's trust in the administration. Consequently, a person who is refused access to a document has a sufficient interest in the annulment of the decision refusing such access (Case T–174/95 *Svenska Journalistförbundet v. Council* [1998] E.C.R. II–2289 at II–2312; paras 66–69, CFI (not yet reported).

[15] Case 92/78 *Simmenthal v. Commission* [1979] E.C.R. 777 at 799, para. 32, ECJ; Joined Cases T–480 and T–483/93 *Antillean Rice Mills v. Commission* [1995] E.C.R. II–2305 at II–2329—2330, para. 60, CFI.

applicant to its original position or to avoid the adoption of an identical measure.[16]

7–078 In order to obtain judgment on the substance, it is not enough that the applicant had an interest at the time when it brought its action.[17] If that interest disappears in the course of the proceedings (for example, if the defendant institution revokes the contested act in all its aspects), it is for the applicant to discontinue the proceedings. If it fails to do so, it may be ordered to pay the costs.[18]

7–079 Moreover, by and large the Court of Justice and the Court of First Instance are flexible about the requirement to establish an interest. Even if the contested act does not impose a fine on the applicant, it nevertheless has an interest in having the legality of the act reviewed.[19] In the event that, owing to the fact that bringing an action for annulment does not have suspensory effect, the applicant tailors its conduct to comply with the contested measure, that will not destroy its interest.[20] Neither does it have any effect on the applicant's interest that, in the event of annulment of the contested act, it will be impossible for the defendant institution to take all the measures necessary to comply with the judgment of the Court of Justice or the Court of First Instance.[21] The declaration of nullity can always constitute the basis for a damages claim.[22]

7–080 The applicant may adduce only pleas in law against the contested act which raise breaches of the law adversely affecting it—no matter how

[16] Joined Cases T–481 and T–484/93 *Exporteurs in Levende Varkens and Others v. Commission* [1995] E.C.R. II–2941 at II–2960—2961, paras 46–48, CFI. However, the withdrawal of the contested decision may take effect *ex tunc* and also have the same consequences as a declaration of nullity. In such case, the Court of Justice or the Court of First Instance, as the case may be, may decide in an order that the action for annulment is devoid of purpose and that there is no need to proceed to judgment: (Order of March 4, 1997), Case C–46/96 *Germany v. Commission* [1997] E.C.R. I–1189 ECJ; (Order of September 18, 1996), Case T–22/96 *Langdon v. Commission* [1996] E.C.R. II–1009 CFI; (Order of March 14, 1997), Case T–25/96 *Arbeitsgemeinschaft Deutscher Luftfahrt-Unternehmen and Hapag Lloyd v. Commission* [1997] E.C.R. II–363, CFI.

[17] Note, however, that the Court of First Instance has stressed that the applicant's interest in bringing proceedings must be determined "at the time when the application was lodged" and not assessed on the basis of a "future, hypothetical event" (Case T–16/96 *Cityflier Express v. Commission* [1998] E.C.R. II–757 at II–771, para. 30, CFI). In that state aid case, the Court of First Instance found that the matters which the Commission had relied on in order to argue that the competitor of the undertaking in receipt of the aid had no interest in bringing proceedings were purely speculative and hence could not affect the applicant's *locus standi*.

[18] Case 243/78 *Simmenthal v. Commission* [1980] E.C.R. 593 at 607, para. 9, ECJ (where the Court of Justice dismissed the application); Case 179/80 *Roquette Frères v. Commission* [1982] E.C.R. 3623 at 3634–3635, paras 8–12, ECJ (where the Court of Justice declared that there was no need to proceed to judgment). It should be noted that it is only the action for annulment which becomes to no purpose if the applicant's interest disappears in the course of the proceedings. This does not mean, however, that an action for damages cannot subsequently be brought against the defendant institution which was late in giving satisfaction to the applicant.

[19] Case 77/77 *BP v. Commission* [1978] E.C.R. 1513 at 1525, para. 13, ECJ.

[20] Joined Cases 172 and 226/83 *Hoogovens Groep v. Commission* [1985] E.C.R. 2831 at 2847, paras 18–19, ECJ.

[21] Case 76/79 *Könecke v. Commission* [1980] E.C.R. 665 at 678, paras 8–9, ECJ.

[22] Joined Cases C–68/94 and C–30/95 *France and SCPA and EMC v. Commission* [1998] E.C.R. I–1375 at I–1475, para. 74, ECJ.

indirectly. Pleas *solely* raised in the interests of the law or of the institutions are inadmissible.[23]

B. In the ECSC Treaty

1. Defendants: against which institutions will an action for annulment lie?

(1) The Commission

Article 33 of the ECSC Treaty provides that actions for annulment may be brought against decisions or recommendations of the Commission (within the meaning of Article 14 of the ECSC Treaty). **7–081**

(2) The Council and the European Parliament

Article 38 of the ECSC Treaty provides that the Court of Justice may declare void acts of the "Assembly" or of the Council. **7–082**

2. Applicants: who can bring an action for annulment?

(1) Actions against acts of the Commission

(a) *The Council, the Member States and the European Parliament*

Under Article 33 of the ECSC Treaty, an action for annulment may be brought against decisions or recommendations of the Commission by the Council, the Member States and the European Parliament. As in the case of the E.C. Treaty, the Council and the Member States are privileged applicants. They do not have to establish an interest. The European Parliament may bring an action for annulment only "for the purpose of protecting its prerogatives". **7–083**

---

[23] Case 85/82 *Schloh v. Council* [1983] E.C.R. 2105 at 2123, paras 13–14, ECJ. This will arise only in extremely rare cases. Thus, even where an individual raises, as applicant, a breach of the division of powers as between the institutions or as between the Community and the Member States, or breach of any procedural requirement in the course of the adoption of the contested act, he or she will never do so *exclusively* in the interests of the law or of the institutions, since all the superior rules of law in that connection are intended, *inter alia*, generally to protect individuals affected by acts of the institutions. See Case 138/79 *Roquette Frères v. Council* [1980] E.C.R. 3333 at 3352, para. 2, ECJ; Case 139/79 *Maizena v. Council* [1980] E.C.R. 3393 at 3415, para. 2, ECJ. A likely example of an inadmissible plea is where the applicant argues that the contested measure is discriminatory, while admitting that the discrimination operates only in his or her favour. Something somewhat similar arose moreover in *Schloh*: the applicant relied on the fact that the vacancy for the post for which his candidature had been rejected (which he was contesting) had not been brought to the notice of staff of Community institutions other than his own. Although that constituted a breach of the Staff Regulations, this had operated in the event only to the applicant's advantage, since there had been less competition for the post as a result.

(b) *Undertakings and associations*

7–084 The ECSC Treaty confers a right to bring an action for annulment on only a restricted class of persons.[24] Only undertakings and associations referred to in Article 48 of the ECSC Treaty may seek the annulment of Commission decisions and recommendations concerning them which are individual in character, or against general decisions and recommendations of the Commission which they consider involve a misuse of powers affecting them.

7–085 **(i) Requirements as to admissibility relating to the person.** For the purposes of the ECSC Treaty,[25] an undertaking is constituted by a single organisation of personal, tangible and intangible elements, attached to an autonomous legal entity and pursuing a given long-term economic aim,[26] which is engaged in the production of coal or steel or, for the purposes of the application of the competition rules,[27] in wholesale trade in those products.[28] In addition, the undertakings in question must carry on their activities in an area coming within the territorial scope of the Treaty as defined by Article 79. An undertaking is engaged in the "production" of coal or steel when its activities constitute processing causing the product to fall under a heading of the nomenclature of products (annexed to the Treaty) different from that under which it appeared previously. Crushing, screening and washing of anthracite does not cause it to fall under a different heading, and hence cannot be regarded as a form of "production".[29]

7–086 The associations referred to in Article 48 are associations of undertakings within the meaning of the above definition. If only one of the members of the association is engaged in the production of coal or steel, the association is not an association within the meaning of Article 48 of the ECSC Treaty and has no right to bring proceedings.[30]

7–087 **(ii) Requirements as to admissibility relating to the type of act.** Undertakings and associations may challenge both general and individual decisions and recommendations; however, actions for annulment of general decisions and recommendations may be brought only where the undertaking or association considers them to involve a misuse of powers affecting it. The view that, as a result, undertakings and associations may in fact challenge a general decision only where an individual decision has been

[24] (Order of September 29, 1997), Case T–4/97 *D'Orazio and Hublau v. Commission* [1997] E.C.R. II–1505 at II–1510, para. 15, CFI; (Order of September 29, 1997), Case T–70/97 *Région Wallonne v. Commission* [1997] E.C.R. II–1513 at II–1520—1521, paras 21–25, CFI.

[25] See ECSC Treaty, Art. 80.

[26] Joined Cases 17 and 20/61 *Klöckner-Werke and Others v. High Authority* [1962] E.C.R. 325 at 341, ECJ.

[27] ECSC Treaty, Arts. 65, 66.

[28] ECSC Treaty, Art. 80, reads: "regularly engaged in distribution other than sale to domestic consumers or small craft industries".

[29] Joined Cases 9 and 12/60 *Vloeberghs v. High Authority* [1961] E.C.R. 197 at 211–212, ECJ.

[30] Joined Cases 8 and 10/54 *Association des Utilisateurs de Charbon du Grand-Duché de Luxembourg v. High Authority* [1954 to 1956] E.C.R. 227 at 239–240, ECJ.

camouflaged beneath the external appearance of a general decision[31] has been rejected by the Court of Justice.[32] An action for annulment will lie against any general decision which, in the applicant's view, involves a misuse of powers. The fact that the only plea which may be raised is that of misuse of powers applies both to the issue of admissibility and to the substance.[33]

(iii) Requirements as to admissibility relating to the interest of the applicant undertaking or association. Undertakings and associations may seek a declaration of nullity relating to individual decisions which are addressed to them or which are addressed to another but nevertheless "concern them". This condition will be satisfied where the applicant undertaking or association gives sufficient reasons for its interest in seeking annulment of the contested act. The classic example is where the competitive position of the undertaking or association is affected by an individual decision addressed to another undertaking or association or to a Member State.[34] 7–088

Undertakings and associations are regarded as having an interest in bringing proceedings against general decisions if they adduce grounds alleging misuse of powers in their regard.[35] Proof of misuse of powers does not have to be adduced at the stage of determining the admissibility of the application.[36]

---

[31] The fact that general decisions may be challenged only on the ground of misuse of powers gave rise to this view. The idea was that the misuse of powers consisted in the Commission's having used a general decision rather than an individual decision in order to affect the undertaking or association. It was argued that the authors of the Treaty wished to provide undertakings and associations with an appropriate means of attacking general decisions camouflaging individual decisions and such decisions alone (see Schermers and Waelbroeck, *Judicial Protection*, p. 399).

[32] Case 8/55 *Fédération Charbonnière de Belgique v. High Authority* [1954 to 1956] E.C.R. 245 at 257–258, ECJ.

[33] *Fédération Charbonnière de Belgique v. High Authority*, (cited in n. 32, above), at 302–303; Case 250/83 *Finsider v. Commission* [1985] E.C.R. 131 at 151, para. 4, ECJ. For the meaning of the expression "misuse of powers", see paras 7–121—7–124, below.

[34] Joined Cases 24 and 34/58 *Chambre Syndicale de la Sidérurgie v. High Authority* [1960] E.C.R. 281 at 292, ECJ; Case 30/59 *De Gezamenlijke Steenkolenmijnen in Limburg v. High Authority* [1961] E.C.R. 1 at 16, ECJ; Joined Cases 172 and 226/83 *Hoogovens Groep v. Commission* [1985] E.C.R. 2831 at 2847, para. 15, ECJ; Case 236/86 *Dillinger Hüttenwerke v. Commission* [1988] E.C.R. 3761 at 3783, para. 8, ECJ; Case C–180/88 *Wirtschaftsvereinigung Eisen- und Stahlindustrie v. Commission* [1990] E.C.R. I–4413 at I–4440—4441, paras 22, 23, ECJ; Case T–239/94 *EISA v. Commission* [1997] E.C.R. II–1839 at II–1853–1854, paras 28–29, CFI.

[35] Joined Cases 140, 146, 221 and 226/82 *Walzstahl-Vereinigung and Thyssen v. Commission* [1984] E.C.R. 951 at 982–983, para. 18, ECJ.

[36] Case 3/54 *ASSIDER v. High Authority* [1954 to 1956] E.C.R. 63 at 69, ECJ; Case 4/54 *ISA v. High Authority* [1954 to 1956] E.C.R. 91 at 97–98, ECJ; Case 8/55 *Fédération Charbonnière de Belgique v. High Authority* [1954 to 1956] E.C.R. 245 at 257, ECJ; Case 9/55 *Société des Charbonnages de Beeringen and Others v. High Authority* [1954 to 1956] E.C.R. 311 at 325, ECJ; Joined Cases 55–59 and 61–63/63 *Acciaierie Fonderie Ferriere di Modena and Others v. High Authority* [1964] E.C.R. 211 at 228, ECJ; Joined Cases 3 and 4/64 *Chambre Syndicale de la Sidérurgie Française and Others v. High Authority* [1965] E.C.R. 441 at 454–455, ECJ; Joined Cases 140, 146, 221 and 226/82 *Walzstahl-Vereinigung and Thyssen v. Commission* [1984] E.C.R. 951 at 982–983, para. 18, ECJ; Joined Cases 32, 52 and 57/87 *ISA v. Commission* [1988] E.C.R. 3305 at 3327, paras 7, 8, ECJ.

(2) Actions against acts of the Council or the European Parliament

(a) *The Commission and the Member States*

7–089 Under Article 38 of the ECSC Treaty, an act of the Council or the European Parliament may be the subject of an action for annulment brought by a Member State or the Commission (High Authority).

(b) *Undertakings and associations*

7–090 Under the ECSC Treaty, an action for annulment brought by an undertaking or an association will not lie against an act of the Council or the European Parliament.[37]

III. Special Characteristics

A. Grounds for Annulment

7–091 Under Article 230 (*ex Article 173*) of the E.C. Treaty, Article 146 of the EAEC Treaty or Article 33 of the ECSC Treaty,[38] an act of a Community institution may be annulled on grounds of lack of competence, infringement of an essential procedural requirement, infringement of the treaties or of any rule of law relating to their application, or misuse of powers. Consequently, the review exercised under those articles must be limited to the legality of the disputed measure and does not extend to its expediency.[39]

7–092 It appears from the case law that the first three grounds for annulment may be subsumed under the heading of breach of superior law, since the rules on competence and essential procedural requirements form part of the treaties or of general rules adopted pursuant thereto. This blurs the distinction between the different grounds for annulment. Yet the distinction is not without importance.[40] The Court of Justice and the Court of First Instance may raise of their own motion pleas alleging lack of competence[41] and infringement of an essential procedural requirement[42] in

---

[37] Case 66/76 *CFDT v. Council* [1977] E.C.R. 305 at 310, paras 9–10, ECJ.

[38] Undertakings or associations of undertakings which seek the annulment under the ECSC Treaty, Art. 33, of general decisions can rely only on misuse of powers (see para. 7–084, above). Actions brought under the ECSC Treaty, Art. 38, may be based only on pleas alleging lack of competence or infringement of an essential procedural requirement.

[39] Case C–84/94 *United Kingdom v. Council* [1996] E.C.R. I–5755 at I–5802, para. 23, ECJ.

[40] Opinion of Advocate General M. Lagrange in Case 66/63 *Netherlands v. High Authority* [1964] E.C.R. 533 at 553–554, ECJ.

[41] Case 14/59 *Société des Fonderies de Pont-à-Mousson v. High Authority* [1959] E.C.R. 215 at 229, ECJ; Case T–182/94 *Marx Esser and Del Amo Martinez v. European Parliament* [1996] E.C.R.–S.C. II–1197 at II–1209, para. 44 (English abstract at I–A–411), CFI.

[42] Case 1/54 *France v. High Authority* [1954 to 1956] E.C.R. 1 at 15, ECJ; Case 6/54 *Netherlands v. High Authority* [1954 to 1956] E.C.R. 103 at 112, ECJ; Case 18/57 *Nold v. High Authority* [1959] E.C.R. 41, at 51–52, ECJ; Case C–291/89 *Interhotel v. Commission* [1991] E.C.R. I–2257 at I–228, para. 14, ECJ; Case 304/89 *Oliveira v. Commission* [1991] E.C.R. I–2283 at I–2312, para. 18, ECJ; Case T–32/91 *Solvay v. Commission* [1995] E.C.R. II–1825 at II–1841, para. 43, CFI; Case T–106/95 *FFSA and Others v. Commission* [1997] E.C.R. II–229 at II–253, para. 62, CFI.

relation to the adoption of the act (*la légalité externe*) in the light of the facts adduced. If the rule breached constitutes a matter of public interest, the Court of Justice or the Court of First Instance, as the case may be, may even be under a duty to raise the relevant ground for annulment of its own motion.[43] Pleas alleging infringement of the treaties or of any rules of law relating to their application, or misuse of powers, which relate to the content of the contested act (*la légalité interne*),[44] may only be considered by the Court of Justice or the Court of First Instance if they are raised by the applicant.[45] It is not necessary to that end for the grounds to be specified, it being "sufficient for the grounds for instituting the proceedings to be expressed in terms of their substance rather than the legal classification provided, however, that it is sufficiently clear from the application which of the grounds referred to in the Treaty is being invoked".[46]

The legality of an act is reviewed in the light of the facts and the state of **7–093**
the law at the time when it was adopted.[47] The content of the act being reviewed is determined as at that time also. Addenda and improvements effected by the institution subsequently are not capable of regularising the act and will not be taken into account.[48]

1. Lack of competence

As a ground for annulment, lack of competence has several aspects, namely **7–094**
substantive, territorial and personal aspects.

(1) Substantive competence

The Community is empowered only to act in policy areas assigned to it by **7–095**
the treaties. A Community act which falls outside those areas may be annulled.[49] That "external" lack of competence results, in some commenta-

[43] Case C–166/95P *Commission v. Daffix* [1997] E.C.R. I–983 at I–999, para. 24, ECJ; Case C–367/95P *Commission v. Sytraval and Brink's France* [1998] E.C.R. I–1719 at I–1771, para. 67, ECJ.

[44] Vandersanden and Barav, *Contentieux communautaire*, p. 187.

[45] Case C–367/95P *Commission v. Sytraval and Brink's France* [1998] E.C.R. I–1719 at I–1771, para. 67, ECJ.

[46] Joined Cases 19 and 21/60, 2 and 3/61 *Société Fives Lille Cail and Others v. High Authority* [1961] E.C.R. 281 at 295, ECJ.

[47] Joined Cases 9 and 11/71 *Cie d'Approvisionnement v. Commission* [1972] E.C.R. 391 at 406, para. 39, ECJ; Case 40/72 *Schroeder v. Germany* [1973] E.C.R. 125 at 142, para. 14, ECJ; Joined Cases 15 and 16/76 *France v. Commission* [1979] E.C.R. 321 at 336, para. 7, ECJ; Joined Cases T–79 and T–80/95 *SNCF and British Railways v. Commission* [1996] E.C.R. II–1491 at II–1510, para. 48, CFI; Case T–77/95 *SFEI and Others v. Commission* [1997] E.C.R. II–1 at II–26, para. 74, CFI; Case T–115/94 *Opel Austria v. Council* [1997] E.C.R. II–39 at II–69, para. 87, CFI; Joined Cases T–371/94 and T–394/94 *British Airways and Others v. Commission* [1998] E.C.R. II–2405 at II–2443, para. 81, CFI.

[48] Case 195/80 *Michel v. European Parliament* [1981] E.C.R. 2861 at 2876–2877, para. 22, ECJ (it seems from para. 27 that addenda or improvements effected by the defendant institution before the period prescribed for bringing proceedings has expired may indeed regularise the act); Case C–343/87 *Culin v. Commission* [1990] E.C.R. I–225 at I–244, para. 15, ECJ.

[49] Case 294/83 *Les Verts v. European Parliament* [1986] E.C.R. 1339 at 1372, paras 51–55, ECJ.

tors' view, in the act's being non-existent, and consequently not within the compass of the grounds for annulment under discussion in this section.[50]

7–096 The next question to be considered is the division of powers in the context of Community decision-making. An example may be found in the case law on the seat of the European Parliament: the scope of the Parliament's powers of internal organisation had to be delimited as against the powers of the national governments under Article 77 of the ECSC Treaty, Article 216 (*now Article 289*) of the E.C. Treaty and Article 189 of the EAEC Treaty to determine the seats of the institutions.[51]

7–097 Where an application for annulment is based on an alleged "lack of competence" of a Community institution which has acted, the case will generally consist of a dispute about the legal basis of the contested act. If the provision of superior law which is stated as being the legal basis for the act is substantively insufficient to support its content, at the same time the mode of decision-making laid down in that provision (including the powers provided for therein for the various Community institutions), together with the permitted legislative instruments (regulations, directives, decisions or still other—albeit unspecified—instruments), will clearly have been used unlawfully. In that sense, the institution which adopted the contested measure will have exceeded its powers (even if it could have adopted the same measure on the basis of some other provision of superior law). So it would seem that in such cases the ground for nullity of lack of competence fuses almost entirely with the ground of infringement of the treaties or of any rules of law relating to their application. From the procedural viewpoint, however, it is more a question of the correct application of the rules invoked as the legal basis for adopting a given act than a question purely of competence (or lack of it).[52]

(2) Territorial competence

7–098 A Community act may apply to natural or legal persons established in areas outside the territorial scope of the Treaty.[53] It must however be applied in conformity with international law.[54] As far as competition law is concerned,

[50] Joliet, *Le contentieux*, p. 96; Vandersanden and Barav, *Contentieux communautaire*, p. 213. See also Bergerès, *Contentieux communautaire*, Paris, Presses Universitaires de France, 1989, p. 203.

[51] Case 230/81 *Luxembourg v. European Parliament* [1983] E.C.R. 255 at 285–292, ECJ; Case 108/83 *Luxembourg v. European Parliament* [1984] E.C.R. 1945 at 1959–1960, ECJ; Joined Cases 358/85 and 51/86 *France v. European Parliament* [1988] E.C.R. 4821 at 4852–4857, ECJ. For a different example, see Joined Cases 281, 283–285 and 287/85 *Germany, France, Netherlands, Denmark and United Kingdom v. Commission* [1987] E.C.R. 3203 at 3253–3254, paras 28–32, ECJ; Case C–57/95 *France v. Commission* [1997] E.C.R. I–1627 at I–1651, para. 24, ECJ.

[52] For an analysis of the concept of legal basis and its function in Community constitutional law, see Lenaerts and Van Nuffel, *Constitutional Law of the European Union*, paras 4–025 *et seq*.

[53] See E.C. Treaty, Art. 299 (*ex Art. 227*).

[54] Case C–286/90 *Poulsen and Diva Navigation and Others* [1992] E.C.R. I–6019 at I–6055—6057, paras 21–29, ECJ.

it is enough that agreements concluded outside the Community are implemented in the territory of the Community.[55]

(3) Delegation of powers

In the Community legal order, an institution may, subject to certain conditions, delegate implementing powers[56] to itself or to other institutions,[57] to Member States,[58] to international organisations[59] or to agencies governed by public or private law not mentioned in the Treaty.[60] **7–099**

The term "implementation" has to be given a broad interpretation.[61] It is sufficient for the institution charged with a legislative task to determine the "general objectives" of the policy in compliance with the applicable mode of decision-making.[62] The execution of those general objectives may be delegated to the institution itself (using a simplified manner of decision-making), to another institution or to the Member States, even if a measure of discretion is involved. The delegating institution, however, must always be able to supervise and, if necessary, correct the exercise of the discretion. **7–100**

On those terms, the Council has the right to delegate (important) implementing powers to the Commission under the third indent of Article 202 (*ex Article 145*) and the last indent of Article 211 (*ex Article 155*) of the E.C. Treaty.[63] The delegation is often subject to the requirement that specific committees must be involved.[64] In implementing acts of the Council, the Commission must remain within the limits of the implementing powers conferred upon it. If it does not respect those limits, its decisions may be annulled for want of competence.[65]

In specific cases, the Council may exercise certain implementing powers itself (delegation to itself pursuant to the third indent of Article 202 of the E.C. Treaty). When it decides to do so, it must state in detail the grounds for its decision.[66]

---

[55] Joined Cases 89, 104, 114, 116–117 and 125–129/85 *Åhlström v. Commission* [1988] E.C.R. 5193 at 5242–5243, paras 11–18, ECJ.

[56] For a definition of "delegation" in the Community legal order and an extended discussion of this phenomenon, see Lenaerts (cited in para. 7–026, n. 81, above), at 23–49.

[57] Case 25/70 *Einfuhr- und Vorratsstelle für Getreide v. Köster* [1970] E.C.R. 1161 at 1171, para. 9, ECJ.

[58] As a result of the E.C. Treaty, Art. 10 (*ex Art. 5*) para. 1, it is implicit in every Community act that the Member States are under a duty to implement it, although the extent of the obligation and the detailed rules relating to it may also be expressly defined in the act itself (see Case 5/77 *Tedeschi v. Denkavit* [1977] E.C.R. 1555, ECJ; Joined Cases 213–215/81 *Norddeutsches Vieh- und Fleischkontor v. Balm* [1982] E.C.R. 3583, ECJ).

[59] Opinion 1/76 *Draft Agreement establishing a European laying-up fund for inland waterway vessels* [1977] E.C.R. 741 at 755–756, para. 5, ECJ.

[60] Case 9/56 *Meroni & Co. v. High Authority* [1957 and 1958] E.C.R. 133 at 151, ECJ.

[61] Case 23/75 *Rey Soda v. Cassa Conguaglio Zucchero* [1975] E.C.R. 1279 at 1300, para. 10, ECJ.

[62] *ibid.*, at 1301, para. 14.

[63] Case C–240/90 *Germany v. Commission* [1992] E.C.R. I–5383 at I–5432—5435, paras 30–43, ECJ.

[64] Council Decision of July 13, 1987 laying down the procedures for the exercise of implementing powers conferred on the Commission: [1987] O.J. L197/33.

[65] *Cf.* Case 22/88 *Vreugdenhil and Others v. Minister van Landbouw en Visserij* [1989] E.C.R. 2049, ECJ.

[66] Case 16/88 *Commission v. Council* [1989] E.C.R. 3457 at 3485, para. 10, ECJ.

7–101 The Community is also empowered to assign "powers of decision" to an international body.[67] Such a delegation of powers, however, may not detract from the requirement for the objectives of the Community to be attained by common action on the part of the institutions, each one acting within the limits of the powers conferred on it. If they did otherwise, it would constitute a surrender of the independence of Community action in its external relations and a change in the internal constitution of the Community as regards both the prerogatives of the institutions and the position of the Member States *vis-à-vis* one another.[68] Consequently, the possibility of delegating "powers of decision" is confined to implementing powers.

7–102 Lastly, agencies governed by public or private law may exceptionally be set up to carry out support tasks.[69] Such agencies must help to attain the objectives underlying the substantive Community competence pursuant to which they are set up.[70] In addition, the delegation of powers to such agencies may not detract from the balance of powers as between the institutions, which constitutes a safeguard against institutions' exceeding their powers.[71] Consequently, no discretionary power may be delegated. Moreover, an institution may not delegate powers broader than those which it itself derives from the treaties.[72]

In exercising their powers, such agencies are subject to the same conditions as the delegating institution (in particular, as regards the duty to state reasons and judicial supervision of their acts). They carry out mainly preparatory or strictly executive work.[73]

7–103 The Commission may—provided that it does not detract from the principle of collective responsibility[74]—empower one or more of its members to take, on its behalf and under its responsibility, clearly defined management or administrative measures.[75] Measures adopted pursuant to such a delegation of authority are still ascribed to the Commission, which, as a collegiate body, has the last word.[76]

7–104 In so far as it is compatible with the intention behind the provision conferring a power on the Commission,[77] that institution may also delegate

[67] Opinion 1/76 *Draft Agreement establishing a European laying-up fund for inland waterway vessels* [1977] E.C.R. 741 at 755–756, para. 5, ECJ.

[68] *ibid.*, at 758, para. 12.

[69] Case 9/56 *Meroni & Co. v. High Authority* [1957 and 1958] E.C.R. 133, ECJ.

[70] *ibid.*, at 151.

[71] *ibid.*, at 152.

[72] *ibid.*, at 150.

[73] For a survey of these agencies, see Lenaerts and Van Nuffel, *Constitutional Law of the European Union*, paras 7–095 and 11–056—11–060.

[74] E.C. Treaty, Art. 219 (*ex Art. 163*): "The Commission shall act by a majority of the number of Members provided for in Article 213 *[ex Article 157]*. A meeting of the Commission shall be valid only if the number of Members laid down in its Rules of Procedure is present."

[75] Rules of Procedure of the Commission of February 17, 1993, Art. 11 ([1993] O.J. L230/15) as amended on March 8, 1995 ([1995] O.J. L97/82).

[76] Case 5/85 *AKZO Chemie v. Commission* [1986] E.C.R. 2585 at 2613–2616, paras 28–40, ECJ; Joined Cases 97–99/87 *Dow Chemical Ibérica and Others v. Commission* [1989] E.C.R. 3165 at 3195, paras 58–59, ECJ.

[77] Case 35/67 *A.J. Van Eick v. Commission* [1968] E.C.R. 329 at 344–345, ECJ. In that case, the

powers to its officials. In exceptional cases, a delegation of powers properly so called is involved where officials take decisions in the name of the Commission[78]; usually, however, what is involved is a delegation of signature, which, as a matter of the internal organisation of the institution, authorises an official to notify a decision taken by the Commission[79]; sometimes both aspects arise in the same case.[80] Where a delegation of powers properly so called is involved, the limits imposed on the Commission's ability to delegate powers to its members apply *a fortiori*.[81]

2. Infringement of essential procedural requirements

An essential procedural requirement is a procedural rule intended to ensure that measures are formulated with due care, compliance with which may influence the content of the measure[82]; essential procedural requirements enable the legality of an act to be reviewed or may express a fundamental institutional rule. The fact that such a rule has been breached in the preparation or adoption of a measure will constitute a ground for its annulment only if the Court of Justice or the Court of First Instance finds that in the absence of the irregularity in question the contested measure might have been substantively different,[83] that the irregularity makes judicial review impossible,[84] or that, on account of the irregularity which it contains, the act in question breaches a fundamental institutional rule.[85] If a procedural provision is infringed but this does not prevent the aims of the provision from being achieved, no "substantial procedural defect" will be **7–105**

point at issue was whether the appointing authority was entitled to delegate to an official its duty under the Staff Regulations, Annex IX, Art. 7, para. 3, to hear an official concerned by disciplinary proceedings before taking its decision in those proceedings. The Court of Justice held that the article in question constituted a peremptory legal requirement which did not authorise any delegation of powers.

78 Case 48/70 *Bernardi v. European Parliament* [1971] E.C.R. 175 at 185–186, paras 30–36, ECJ. This arises in all institutions as far as decisions in staff matters are concerned.

79 Case 48/69 *ICI v. Commission* [1972] E.C.R. 619 at 649–650, paras 11–15, ECJ; Case 8/72 *Cementhandelaren v. Commission* [1972] E.C.R. 977 at 988–989, paras 10–14, ECJ; Joined Cases 43 and 63/82 *VBVB and VBBB v. Commission* [1984] E.C.R. 19 at 56–57, para. 14, ECJ; Case C–220/89 *FUNOC v. Commission* [1990] E.C.R. I–3669 at I–3692, para. 14, ECJ; Case T–450/93 *Lisrestal v. Commission* [1994] E.C.R. II–1177 at II–1191—1192, para. 34, CFI.

80 Case C–200/89 *FUNOC v. Commission* [1990] E.C.R. I–3669 at I–3692, paras 13–14, ECJ.

81 See para. 7–103, above.

82 Case 6/54 *Netherlands v. High Authority* [1954 to 1956] E.C.R. 103 at 111–112, ECJ.

83 Joined Cases 209–215 and 218/78 *Van Landewyck v. Commission* [1980] E.C.R. 3125 at 3239, para. 47, ECJ; Case 150/84 *Bernardi v. European Parliament* [1986] E.C.R. 1375 at 1394–1395, para. 28, ECJ. See also the Opinion of Advocate General G. Reischl in Joined Cases 275/80 and 24/81 *Krupp v. Commission* [1981] E.C.R. 2489 at 2524.

84 This is why the duty to give a statement of reasons is strictly enforced (paras 7–112—7–115, below). See also Case C–137/92P *Commission v. BASF and Others* [1994] E.C.R. I–2555 at I–2652—2653, paras 75–76, ECJ, in which the Court of Justice held that authentication of a Commission decision is intended to guarantee legal certainty by ensuring that the text adopted by the college of Commissioners becomes fixed in the languages in which it is binding. Thus, in the event of a dispute, it can be verified that the texts notified or published correspond precisely to the text adopted by the college and so with the intention of the author. On those grounds, the Court held that authentication was an essential procedural requirement because failure to comply therewith makes judicial review impossible.

85 Case 138/79 *Roquette Frères v. Council* [1980] E.C.R. 3333 at 3360, para. 33, ECJ; Case 139/79 *Maizena v. Council* [1980] E.C.R. 3393 at 3424, para. 34, ECJ.

involved.[86] An express obligation to comply with certain procedural requirements when carrying out a particular act may not be extended to other acts by way of interpretation.[87] As has already been mentioned, the Court of Justice or the Court of First Instance may raise the issue of an infringement of an essential procedural requirement of its own motion and is even under a duty to do so where the rule breached raises a matter of public interest.[88]

(1) Requirement to consult

7–106 In the Community decision-making process, the body or institution adopting or implementing an act is sometimes under a duty (imposed by superior Community law) to seek the opinion of a body or institution before acting.[89] The requirement to consult constitutes an essential procedural requirement.[90] This is because consultation may affect the substance of the measure adopted.[91]

Furthermore, the Court of Justice has held that the consultation of the European Parliament required by the Treaty in certain cases constitutes a fundamental rule designed to guarantee the institutional balance intended by the Treaty, which reflects the fundamental democratic principle that the peoples should take part in the exercise of power through a representative assembly.[92]

7–107 It is not sufficient merely to ask the body having to be consulted for its opinion; that body must have made its views known before the act was

[86] Case 282/81 *Ragusa v. Commission* [1983] E.C.R. 1245 at 1259, para. 22, ECJ; Case 207/81 *Ditterich v. Commission* [1983] E.C.R. 1359 at 1373, para. 19, ECJ.

[87] Case 21/64 *Macchiorlati Dalmas v. Commission* [1965] E.C.R. 175 at 190–191, ECJ; Case 22/70 *Commission v. Council* [1971] E.C.R. 263 at 283, para. 98, ECJ.

[88] See para. 7–092, above. See also Case 1/54 *France v. High Authority* [1954 to 1956] E.C.R. 1 at 15, ECJ; Case 2/54 *Italy v. High Authority* [1954 to 1956] E.C.R. 37 at 52, ECJ; Case 18/57 *Nold v. High Authority* [1959] E.C.R. 41 at 51–52, ECJ; Joined Cases 73–74/63 *Handelsvereniging Rotterdam v. Minister van Landbouw* [1964] E.C.R. 1 at 13–14, ECJ; Case 185/85 *Usinor v. Commission* [1986] E.C.R. 2079 at 2098, para. 19, ECJ; Case C–166/95P *Commission v. Daffix* [1997] E.C.R. I–983 at I–999, para. 24, ECJ. See further para. 7–115, below.

[89] In the case of legislative action, the bodies or institutions concerned are the Consultative Committee and the Council under the ECSC Treaty and the European Parliament, the Economic and Social Committee and the Committee of the Regions under the E.C. Treaty; in the case of implementing action, they are the Advisory Committee on Restrictive Practices and Monopolies (Regulation No. 17, Art. 10 (1)) and the committees involved in the various procedures prescribed by the Council Decision of July 13, 1987 laying down the procedures for the exercise of implementing powers conferred on the Commission ([1987] O.J. L197/33).

[90] Case 1/54 *France v. High Authority* [1954 to 1956] E.C.R. 1 at 15, ECJ; Case 2/54 *Italy v. High Authority* [1954 to 1956] E.C.R. 37 at 52, ECJ.

[91] Case 165/87 *Commission v. Council* [1988] E.C.R. 5545 at 5562, para. 20, ECJ. See also Bradley, "Maintaining the Balance: the Role of the Court of Justice in Defining the Institutional Position of the European Parliament" (1987) C.M.L.Rev. 41 at 57.

[92] Case 138/79 *Roquette Frères v. Council* [1980] E.C.R. 3333 at 3360, para. 33, ECJ; Case 139/79 *Maizena v. Council* [1980] E.C.R. 3393 at 3424, para. 34, ECJ; Case 1253/79 *Battaglia v. Commission* [1982] E.C.R. 297 at 316, para. 17, ECJ; Case C–417/93 *European Parliament v. Council* [1995] E.C.R. I–1185 at I–1213, para. 9, ECJ; Case C–21/94 *European Parliament v. Council* [1995] E.C.R. I–1827 at I–1851—1852, para. 17, ECJ.

adopted,[93] unless a derogating provision provides otherwise[94] or the body requesting the advice exhausted all possibilities of obtaining a preliminary opinion.[95] In addition, the draft instrument submitted to the consultative body must basically correspond to the instrument ultimately adopted, unless the amendments made to the draft are specifically intended to comply with the wishes expressed by the consultative body in its opinion.[96]

It is sufficient, however, that the opinion be delivered before the act is adopted. The institution seeking the opinion is not obliged to allow a certain period of time to elapse between receipt of the opinion and adoption of the act in order to be able better to consider the opinion. Consequently, a regulation which is adopted only a matter of days after the European Parliament delivered its opinion will be validly adopted.[97]

(2) Requirement to hear the addressee

Before an act adversely affecting a person is adopted, the addressee of the act or interested third parties must be heard by the institution concerned.[98] That obligation is prescribed either by the Treaty[99] or by secondary Community law[1] or arises out of the general legal principle that "a person whose interests are perceptibly affected by a decision taken by a public authority must be given the opportunity to make his point of view known".[2] This obligation is an essential procedural requirement.[3] **7–108**

The person concerned must be informed in time[4] and effectively[5] of all the information in the file which might be useful for his or her defence[6] and

93 *Roquette Frères v. Council*, para. 34; *Maizena v. Council*, para. 35, (both cases cited in n. 92, above).

94 Case 128/86 *Spain v. Commission* [1987] E.C.R. 4171 at 4195–4196, paras 22–26, ECJ.

95 Case 138/79 *Roquette Frères v. Council* [1980] E.C.R. 3333 at 3360, para. 36, ECJ; Case 139/79 *Maizena v. Council* [1980] E.C.R. 3393 at 3424, para. 37, ECJ.

96 Case 41/69 *ACF Chemiefarma v. Commission* [1970] E.C.R. 661 at 688–689, paras 68–69, ECJ; Case 817/79 *Buyl v. Commission* [1982] E.C.R. 245 at 261–265, paras 14–24, ECJ; Case 828/79 *Adam v. Commission* [1982] E.C.R. 269 at 288–290, paras 18–25, ECJ; Case C–65/90 *European Parliament v. Council* [1992] E.C.R. I–4593, ECJ, whereby the Court of Justice annulled a Council regulation on the ground that the Council had not reconsulted the European Parliament, whereas the regulation ultimately adopted by the Council departed substantially from the text on which the Parliament had originally been consulted; Joined Cases C–13–16/92 *Driessen and Others* [1993] E.C.R. I–4751 at I–4789, para. 23, ECJ; Case C–388/92 *European Parliament v. Council* [1994] E.C.R. I–2067 at I–2085, para. 10, ECJ; Case C–280/93 *Germany v. Council* [1994] E.C.R. I–4973 at I–5054—5055, para. 38, ECJ.

97 Case 114/81 *Tunnel Refineries v. Council* [1982] E.C.R. 3189 at 3209–3210, para. 18, ECJ.

98 Case 17/74 *Transocean Marine Paint v. Commission* [1974] E.C.R. 1063 at 1080, para. 15, ECJ; Joined Cases 209–215 and 218/78 *Van Landewyck v. Commission* [1980] E.C.R. 3125 at 3232, para. 17, ECJ. For a discussion of the duty to hear parties in competition cases, see Kerse, "Procedures in EC Competition Cases: The Oral Hearing" (1994) E.C.L.R. 40–43; Joliet, *Le contentieux*, pp. 98–99.

99 See, *e.g.* E.C. Treaty, Art. 88 (*ex Art. 93*) (2).

1 See, *e.g.* Regulation No. 17, Art. 19; Regulation 384/96, Art. 6(7) (anti-dumping) and Regulation No. 4064/89, Art. 18(3) (control of concentrations).

2 Case 17/74 *Transocean Marine Paint v. Commission* [1974] E.C.R. 1063 at 1080, para. 15, ECJ. See to the same effect Case 85/76 *Hoffmann-La Roche v. Commission* [1979] E.C.R. 461 at 511, para. 9, ECJ.

3 Case 31/69 *Commission v. Italy* [1970] E.C.R. 25 at 33, para. 13, ECJ (proceedings brought pursuant to the E.C. Treaty, Art. 169 (*now Art. 226*)).

4 Case 55/69 *Cassella v. Commission* [1972] E.C.R. 887 at 911, paras 13–15, ECJ (12 days'

of the grounds of the proposed act so that he or she is in a position to challenge it with full knowledge of the facts.[7]

(3) Duty of confidentiality

7–109 Article 287 (*ex Article 214*) of the E.C. Treaty imposes an obligation not to disclose information of the kind covered by the obligation of professional secrecy, in particular information about undertakings, their business relations or their cost components.[8] The question often arises in the Commission's administrative procedure for investigating infringements of competition law[9] or for determining dumping practices.[10] It is the institution to which the purportedly confidential information is made available itself which has to judge whether or not the duty of confidentiality is applicable after giving the party concerned the opportunity to state its views. In addition, before implementing its decision, the institution must give that party the opportunity of bringing an action before the Court of First Instance with a view to having its assessments reviewed and to preventing disclosure.[11] Unlawful disclosure of confidential information will be regarded as an infringement of an essential procedural requirement only in so far as it resulted in the act to which it gave rise having a different

notice of the hearing did not jeopardise the defence).

[5] Joined Cases 56 and 58/64 *Consten and Grundig v. Commission* [1964] E.C.R. 299 at 338, ECJ; Case T–7/89 *Hercules Chemicals v. Commission* [1991] E.C.R. II–1711 at II–1738—1740, paras 51–54, CFI; Joined Cases T–10–12 and T–15/92 *Cimenteries CBR and Others v. Commission* [1992] E.C.R. II–2667 at II–2682, para. 38, CFI; Case T–65/89 *BPB Industries and British Gypsum v. Commission* [1993] E.C.R. II–389 at II–404—405, paras 29, 30, CFI.

[6] Case T–36/91 *ICI v. Commission* [1995] E.C.R. II–1847 at II–1880, paras 69–70, CFI; Case T–37/91 *ICI v. Commission* [1995] E.C.R. II–1901 at II–1922—1923, paras 49, 50, ECJ. The question whether in competition cases the Commission infringed the rights of the defence by granting no access to certain matters in the file compiled during the administrative investigation must be examined in the light of the specific circumstances of each particular case, since the infringement of the rights of the defence depends essentially on the objections raised by the Commission in order to prove the infringement which the undertaking concerned is alleged to have committed. The Commission will infringe the rights of the defence if it appears that certain documents to which the undertaking did not obtain access might have been useful for its defence in the light of the infringement alleged against it. For customs cases, see Case T–42/96 *Eyckeler & Malt v. Commission* [1998] E.C.R. II–401 at II–425, para. 80, CFI. See Lenaerts and Vanhamme, "Procedural Rights of Private Parties in the Community Administrative Process" (1997) C.M.L.Rev. 531–569.

[7] Case 121/76 *Milo v. Commission* [1977] E.C.R. 1971 at 1979, paras 19–20, ECJ; Case 75/77 *Mollet v. Commission* [1978] E.C.R. 897 at 907–908, paras 18–21, ECJ.

[8] There are specific applications of this duty of confidentiality in regulations and directives: see, *e.g.* Council Regulation No. 288/82, Art. 8(2), on common rules for imports ([1982] O.J. L35/1).

[9] See Regulation No. 17, Art. 20(2), in connection with the specific duty of confidentiality in competition cases; Case C–36/92P *SEP v. Commission* [1994] E.C.R. I–1911 at I–1942—1943, paras 36–38, ECJ. For an extensive discussion of the difficulty of reconciling the duty of confidentiality with the right to a fair hearing, see Joshua, "Balancing the Public Interests: Confidentiality, Trade Secret and Disclosure of Evidence in EC Competition Procedures" (1994) E.C.L.R. 68–80.

[10] See Regulation No. 384/96, Art. 19(5), in relation to the duty of confidentiality in the investigation procedure for determining dumping practices ([1996] O.J. L56/1).

[11] Case 53/85 *AKZO Chemie v. Commission* [1986] E.C.R. 1965 at 1992, para. 29, ECJ.

content. Consequently, it does not inevitably result in the act's being declared void.[12]

(4) Internal procedural rules

The institutions adopt internal procedural rules in their Rules of Procedure[13] and thereafter are obliged to comply with them.[14] Such rules may be categorised as essential procedural requirements. For instance, in one case the Court of Justice annulled a Council directive which was adopted in breach of Article 6 of that institution's Rules of Procedure.[15] The directive was adopted by the so-called written procedure, even though two Member States had expressed objections to its use. Article 6 provides that recourse to a written vote on an urgent matter may be had only if all members of the Council agree.[16] **7–110**

Natural or legal persons may plead infringement of internal procedural rules which confer rights on them and guarantee legal certainty.[17] This qualifies the view that internal procedural rules are intended to guarantee the sound functioning of internal decision-making while respecting the prerogatives of each of the members of the institution, and that they are therefore not intended to ensure protection for individuals.[18] **7–111**

(5) Requirement to provide a statement of reasons

The statement of reasons required by Article 253 (*ex Article 190*) of the E.C. Treaty must disclose in a clear and unequivocal fashion the reasoning followed by the Community authority which adopted the measure in **7–112**

---

[12] *Cf.* Joined Cases 209–215 and 218/78 *Van Landewyck v. Commission* [1980] E.C.R. 3125 at 3239, para. 47, ECJ. Naturally, this does not preclude the person who has been disadvantaged by disclosure from bringing an action for damages against the institution responsible: Case 145/83 *Adams v. Commission* [1985] E.C.R. 3539 at 3587–3590, paras 34–44, ECJ.

[13] See E.C. Treaty, Art. 199 (*ex Art. 142*) (European Parliament), Art. 207 (*ex Art. 151*) (3) (Council) and Art. 218 (*ex Art. 162*) (2) (Commission).

[14] Sometimes internal procedural rules are adopted in a different connection, *e.g.* in regard to staff matters, see Case 282/81 *Ragusa v. Commission* [1983] E.C.R. 1245 at 1258, para. 18, ECJ.

[15] [1979] O.J. L268/1.

[16] Case 68/86 *United Kingdom v. Council* [1988] E.C.R. 855 at 900–902, paras 40–49, ECJ. For a case in which the Rules of Procedure of the Economic and Social Committee were invoked, yet no infringement was found, see Case 307/85 *Gavanas v. ESC and Council* [1987] E.C.R. 2435, ECJ. For a case in which a Commission decision was annulled because a prior opinion was adopted in breach of the Rules of Procedure of the Standing Committee on Construction which assists the Commission in implementing a regulation in that a draft document was not sent to two addressees within the time-limit laid down and the vote was not postponed despite the request made to that effect by a Member State, see Case C–263/95 *Germany v. Commission* [1998] E.C.R. I–441 at I–478, para. 32, ECJ.

[17] Case C–137/92P *BASF and Others v. Commission* [1994] E.C.R. I–2555 at I–2652—2653, paras 72–78, ECJ, in which the Court of Justice annulled a Commission decision on the ground that it infringed of the Commission's Rules of Procedure, Art. 12. *Cf.* Case T–32/91 *Solvay v. Commission* [1995] E.C.R. II–1825 at II–1842—1845, paras 46–54, CFI. See also Case C–280/93 *Germany v. Council* [1994] E.C.R. I–4973 at I–5054, para. 36, ECJ, from which it appears that in adopting acts which directly affect individuals, the procedural requirements applicable to such acts must be strictly complied with.

[18] Case C–69/89 *Nakajima v. Council* [1991] E.C.R. I–2069 at I–2183, para. 48–51, ECJ.

question in such a way as to make the persons concerned aware of the reasons for the measure and thus enable them to defend their rights and the Court to exercise its supervisory jurisdiction.[19] The reasoning must be logically compatible with the content of the measure.[20] A minimal, merely formal statement of reasons is not enough, because it does not effectively enable interested parties[21] and the Court to verify the legality of the act.[22] However, the Community authority is not under a duty to go into all the arguments raised by interested parties during the administrative procedure which led to the adoption of the act.[23] It is sufficient if it sets out the facts and legal considerations having decisive importance in the context of the decision so as to enable its reasoning to be clearly understood.[24]

In any case, it is essential for the legal basis of the contested measure to be clearly indicated[25] or to be capable of being determined with certainty from other parts of the measure.[26]

In principle, the various relevant factual and legal aspects should be set out in the statement of reasons. There is a consistent line of cases, however, to the effect that this is not always necessary on the ground that, in considering whether the statement of reasons of an act satisfies the requirements of Article 253 of the E.C. Treaty, regard must be had not only to its wording but also to its context and to all the legal rules governing the matter in question.[27]

---

[19] Case C–350/88 *Delacre and Others v. Commission* [1990] E.C.R. I–395 at I–422, para. 15, ECJ (see also the case law cited in that judgment). *Cf.* Case 18/57 *Nold v. High Authority* [1959] E.C.R. 41 at 51–52, ECJ; Case 24/62 *Germany v. Commission* [1963] E.C.R. 63 at 68–69, ECJ; Case 294/81 *Control Data v. Commission* [1983] E.C.R. 911 at 928, para. 14, ECJ.

[20] Case 2/56 *Geitling v. High Authority* [1957] E.C.R. 3 at 16, ECJ.

[21] Interested parties comprise not only the addressee of an act, but also persons to whom the act is of direct and individual concern. The latters' interest in obtaining an explanation of the act should therefore be taken into account in determining the extent of the obligation to provide a statement of reasons: Case 41/83 *Italy v. Commission* [1985] E.C.R. 873 at 891, para. 46, ECJ; Case C–367/95P *Commission v. Sytraval and Brink's France* [1998] E.C.R. I–1719 at I–1770, para. 63, ECJ; Case T–16/91 RV *Rendo and Others v. Commission* [1996] E.C.R. II–1827 at II–1843, para. 43, CFI.

[22] Case C–269/90 *Technische Universität München* [1991] E.C.R. I–5469 at I–5501—5502, para. 26–27, ECJ.

[23] Case 55/69 *Cassella v. Commission* [1972] E.C.R. 887 at 912–913, para. 22, ECJ; Case 56/69 *Hoechst v. Commission* [1972] E.C.R. 927, ECJ; Joined Cases 209–215 and 218/78 *Van Landewyck v. Commission* [1980] E.C.R. 3125 at 3244, para. 66, ECJ; Joined Cases 43 and 63/82 *VBVB and VBBB v. Commission* [1984] E.C.R. 19 at 58, para. 19, ECJ; Case 42/84 *Remia v. Commission* [1985] E.C.R. 2545 at 2572–2573, para. 26, ECJ; Joined Cases 240–242, 261, 262, 268 and 269/82 *Stichting Sigarettenindustrie v. Commission* [1985] E.C.R. 3831 at 3882, para. 88, ECJ; Case C–41/93 *France v. Commission* [1994] E.C.R. I–1829 at I–1850, para. 36, ECJ; Case T–8/89 *DSM v. Commission* [1991] E.C.R. II–1833 at II–1920, para. 257, CFI; Case T–9/89 *Hüls v. Commission* [1992] E.C.R. II–499 at II–614—615, para. 332, CFI.

[24] Case T–44/90 *La Cinq v. Commission* [1992] E.C.R. II–1 at II–16—17, paras 40–44, CFI; Case T–7/92 *Asia Motor France and Others v. Commission* [1993] E.C.R. II–669 at II–683, para. 31, CFI. *Cf.* Case 24/62 *Germany v. Commission* [1963] E.C.R. 63 at 69, ECJ.

[25] Case 203/86 *Spain v. Council* [1988] E.C.R. 4563 at 4605, para. 37, ECJ. Failure to indicate the legal basis also infringes the principle of legal certainty (Case C–325/91 *France v. Commission* [1993] E.C.R. I–3283 at I–3312, para. 30, ECJ).

[26] Case 45/86 *Commission v. Council* [1987] E.C.R. 1493 at 1519–1520, para. 9, ECJ.

[27] Case C–350/88 *Delacre and Others v. Commission* [1990] E.C.R. I–395 at I–422, para. 16, ECJ, and the case law cited in that judgment; see also Case 25/68 *Schertzer v. European*

The nature of the contested measure is one aspect of its context which goes to determine the extent of the obligation to provide a statement of reasons.[28] In the case of an act of general application, such as a regulation, it is enough for the circumstances which led to its adoption, together with its general objectives, to be mentioned.[29] If the need for the act is obvious from its content, additional reasoning is unnecessary.[30]

The degree of precision of the statement of reasons of an individual measure depends on the practical realities and the time and technical facilities available for drawing it up.[31] Furthermore, an individual measure which fits into a well-established line of decisions may be reasoned in a summary manner, for instance, by reference to the practice in question. If, in contrast, the measure deviates from previous practice, for example, by going appreciably further than previous decisions, the Community authority which adopted the measure must expressly explain why this is so.[32]

Lastly, the degree to which the addressee was involved in the process by which an act was drawn up has a bearing on the extent of the duty to provide a statement of reasons.[33] In addition, persons concerned by a decision may be expected to make a certain effort to interpret the reasons if the meaning of the text is not immediately clear. The duty to give a statement of reasons is not infringed if it is possible to resolve ambiguities in the statement of reasons by means of such interpretation.[34]

Parliament [1977] E.C.R. 1729 at 1743, para. 39, ECJ; Case 35/80 *Denkavit v. Produktschap voor Zuivel* [1981] E.C.R. 45 at 64, para. 33, ECJ.

[28] Case T–26/90 *Finsider v. Commission* [1992] E.C.R. II–1789 at II–1812, para. 70, CFI.

[29] Case 5/67 *Beus v. Hauptzollamt München* [1968] E.C.R. 83 at 95; ECJ; Case 244/81 *Klöckner-Werke v. Commission* [1983] E.C.R. 1451 at 1484, para. 33, ECJ.

[30] Case 57/72 *Westzucker v. Einfuhr-und Vorratsstelle Zucker* [1973] E.C.R. 321 at 342, para. 19, ECJ.

[31] Settled case law ever since Case 16/65 *Schwarze v. Einfuhr- und Vorratsstelle Getreide* [1965] E.C.R. 877 at 888, ECJ. For examples of the influence of "practical realities" on the obligation to provide a statement of reasons, see Case 89/79 *Bonu v. Council* [1980] E.C.R. 553 at 563, para. 6, ECJ; Case 64/82 *Tradax v. Commission* [1984] E.C.R. 1359 at 1379, para. 21, ECJ.

[32] Case 73/74 *Papiers peints v. Commission* [1975] E.C.R. 1491 at 1514, para. 31, ECJ.

[33] Case 13/72 *Netherlands v. Commission* [1973] E.C.R. 27 at 39, paras 11–13, ECJ; Case 819/79 *Germany v. Commission* [1981] E.C.R. 21 at 36, paras 15–21, ECJ; Case 1251/79 *Italy v. Commission* [1981] E.C.R. 205 at 221–222, paras 20–21, ECJ; Case 347/85 *United Kingdom v. Commission* [1988] E.C.R. 1749 at 1797, para. 60, ECJ; Case 14/88 *Italy v. Commission* [1989] E.C.R. 3677 at 3703, para. 11, ECJ. In staff cases, previous memoranda and staff notices influence the duty to provide a statement of reasons in the same way: Case 61/76 *Geist v. Commission* [1977] E.C.R. 1419 at 1431–1432, paras 21–26, ECJ; Case 86/77 *Ditterich v. Commission* [1978] E.C.R. 1855 at 1866–1867, paras 34–42, ECJ; Joined Cases 36, 37 and 218/81 *Seton v. Commission* [1983] E.C.R. 1789 at 1813, paras 47–49, ECJ; Case T–80/92 *Turner v. Commission* [1993] E.C.R. II–1465 at II–1484, paras 62, 63, CFI. The fact that an official was involved in the reorganisation of his department may justify a decision adversely affecting him or her having a summary statement of reasons: Case 125/80 *Arning v. Commission* [1981] E.C.R. 2539 at 2553, para. 14, ECJ.

[34] Case T–16/91 RV *Rendo and Others v. Commission* [1996] E.C.R. II–1827 at II–1844, para. 46, CFI.

7–113 A shortcoming in the material accuracy of the statement of reasons, such as a factual inaccuracy or a wrong legal categorisation, is considered an infringement of the Treaty or of a rule relating to its application.[35]

7–114 A sufficient statement of reasons should be notified at the same time as the person concerned has notice of the act.[36] The absence of such a statement of reasons cannot be regularised after proceedings have been brought.[37]

7–115 The Court of Justice or the Court of First Instance must[38] raise of its own motion the question as to whether the requirement for a statement of reasons has been fulfilled.[39]

(6) Notification of the act

7–116 Irregularities in the publication or notification of an act are not classed as infringements of an essential procedural requirement because they do not affect the act itself. Such irregularities may at most prevent time from beginning to run for the purposes of bringing proceedings.[40]

---

[35] Case 8/65 *Acciaierie e Ferriere Pugliesi v. High Authority* [1966] E.C.R. 1 at 7–8, ECJ; Case T–17/93 *Matra Hachette v. Commission* [1994] E.C.R. II–595 at II–617, para. 57, CFI. *Cf.* Case 119/86 *Spain v. Council and Commission* [1987] E.C.R. 4121 at 4168, para. 51, ECJ. As can be seen from Case C–360/92 *Publishers Association v. Commission* [1995] E.C.R. I–23 at I–71—74, paras 39–48, ECJ; Joined Cases C–329/93, C–62/95 and C–63/95 *Germany and Others v. Commission* [1996] E.C.R. I–5151 at I–5211—5220, paras 23–58, ECJ; and Case C–367/95 P, *Commission v. Sytraval and Brink's France* [1998] E.C.R. I–1719 at I–1771—1774, paras 65–78, ECJ, it is not always easy to draw a clear distinction in this connection.

[36] Case 195/80 *Michel v. European Parliament* [1981] E.C.R. 2861 at 2876–2877, para. 22, ECJ.

[37] Case C–343/87 *Culin v. Commission* [1990] E.C.R. I–225 at 244, para. 15, ECJ; Case T–52/90 *Volger v. European Parliament* [1992] E.C.R. II–121 at II–137—139, paras 40–42, CFI, upheld by Case C–115/92P *European Parliament v. Volger* [1993] E.C.R. I–6549 at I–6588, para. 23, ECJ; Joined Cases T–371/94 and T–394/94 *British Airways and Others v. Commission*, [1998] E.C.R. II–2405 at II–2454, paras 114–118, CFI. At most, in staff cases the Court allows a concise statement of reasons to be completed in the course of the proceedings: Case 111/83 *Picciolo v. European Parliament* [1984] E.C.R. 2323 at 2339, para. 22, ECJ; Joined Cases 64, 71–73 and 78/86 *Sergio v. Commission* [1988] E.C.R. 1399 at 1439, para. 52, ECJ; Case T–37/89 *Hanning v. European Parliament* [1990] E.C.R. II–463 at II–478—479, para. 42, CFI; Joined Cases T–160 and T–161/89 *Kalavros v. Court of Justice* [1990] E.C.R. II–871 at II–894, para. 72, CFI; Case T–1/90 *Pérez-Mínguez Casariego v. Commission* [1991] E.C.R. II–143 at II–173, para. 87, CFI; Case T–156/89 *Valverde Mordt v. Court of Justice* [1991] E.C.R. II–407 at II–456—457, paras 130–133, CFI; Case T–25/92 *Vela Palacios v. ESC* [1993] E.C.R. II–201 at II–211—212, para. 26, CFI.

[38] Case C–166/95P *Commission v. Daffix* [1997] E.C.R. I–983 at I–999, para. 24, ECJ; Case C–367/95 P, *Commission v. Sytraval and Brink's France* [1998] E.C.R. I–1719 at I–1771, para. 67, ECJ.

[39] See para. 7–092, above, and Case 18/57 *Nold v. High Authority* [1959] E.C.R. 41 at 51–52, ECJ; Case 185/85 *Usinor v. Commission* [1986] E.C.R. 2079 at 2098, para. 19, ECJ; Case T–37/89 *Hanning v. European Parliament* [1990] E.C.R. II–463 at II–477—478, para. 38, CFI; Case T–115/89 *González Holguera v. European Parliament* [1990] E.C.R. II–831 at II–836–837, para. 37, CFI; Case T–61/89 *Dansk Pelsdyravlerforening v. Commission* [1992] E.C.R. II–1931 at II–1982—1983, para. 129, CFI; Case T–534/93 *Grynberg v. Commission* [1994] E.C.R.–S.C. II–595 at II–616, para. 59, CFI (English abstract at [1994] E.C.R.–S.C. I–A–179); Case T–12/94 *Daffix v. Commission* [1995] E.C.R.–S.C. II–233 at II–244, para. 31, CFI (English abstract at I–A–71); Case T–106/95 *FFSA and Others v. Commission* [1997] E.C.R. II–229 at II–253, para. 62, CFI; Case T–4/96 *S. v. Court of Justice* [1997] E.C.R. II–1125 at II–1144—1145, para. 53, CFI.

[40] Case 48/69 *ICI v. Commission* [1972] E.C.R. 619 at 652, para. 40, ECJ; Case 185/73 *Hauptzollamt Bielefeld v. König* [1974] E.C.R. 607 at 617, para. 6, ECJ.

3. Infringement of the Treaty or of any rule of law relating to its application

This ground for annulment encompasses any infringement of any provision of superior Community law.[41] 7–117

By "Treaty" is meant the Treaties establishing the Communities (as amended), the Protocols annexed thereto[42] and the Accession Treaties and Acts. The pleas raised by the applicant do not necessarily have to be confined to infringements of the Treaty on the basis of which the action is brought. An action for annulment based on the E.C. Treaty may embody admissible pleas referring to infringements of provisions of the ECSC Treaty or the EAEC Treaty.[43] 7–118

"Any rule of law relating to [the] application [of the Treaty]" covers all other binding provisions of the Community legal order. These include in the first place provisions of international law, in particular provisions originating in treaties concluded by Member States before the E.C. Treaty was concluded (by which the Community is bound—GATT),[44] agreements concluded by the Community itself[45] and customary international law.[46] Secondly, there is the group made up of the general principles of Community law.[47] Lastly, there are all valid, binding acts of Community institutions or bodies. 7–119

The "infringement" of Community law for which annulment is imposed under this head may consist equally of a misapplication of the law (including an erroneous legal categorisation of the facts in question or a misinterpretation of the applicable rule) or of an error in determining the factual basis on which the application of Community law is founded.[48] 7–120

---

[41] See, by way of example, Case 92/78 *Simmenthal v. Commission* [1979] E.C.R. 777 at 811, para. 106, ECJ. See also Boulouis and Darmon, *Contentieux communautaire*, Paris, Dalloz, 1997, at 214–217, nos 436–444.

[42] Treaty, Art. 84; E.C. Treaty, Art. 311 (*ex Art. 239*); EAEC Treaty, Art. 207.

[43] Case C–62/88 *Greece v. Council* [1990] E.C.R. I–1527 at I–1548, para. 8, ECJ.

[44] Joined Cases 21–24/72 *International Fruit Company v. Produktschap voor Groenten en Fruit* [1972] E.C.R. 1219 at 1228, paras 6–7, ECJ.

[45] E.C. Treaty, Art. 300 (*ex Art. 228*) (7); Case 181/73 *Haegeman v. Belgium* [1974] E.C.R. 449 at 460, para. 5, ECJ. For an example arising in connection with an action for annulment, see Case 30/88 *Greece v. Commission* [1989] E.C.R. 3711, ECJ.

[46] Joined Cases 89, 104, 114, 116–117 and 125–129/85 *Åhlström Osakeyhtiö v. Commission* [1988] E.C.R. 5193, ECJ.

[47] Case 4/73 *Nold v. Commission* [1974] E.C.R. 491 at 507–508, para. 13, ECJ; Case 114/76 *Bela-Mühle v. Grows-Farm* [1977] E.C.R. 1211 at 1220–1221, paras 5–7, ECJ; Case 224/82 *Meiko-Konservenfabrik v. Germany* [1983] E.C.R. 2539 at 2548, para. 11, ECJ; Case C–325/91 *France v. Commission* [1993] E.C.R. I–3283 at I–3312, para. 30, ECJ.

[48] Case 18/62 *Barge v. High Authority* [1963] E.C.R. 259 at 279–281, ECJ. For an analytical breakdown of those two aspects, see Case T–1/89 *Rhône-Poulenc v. Commission* [1991] E.C.R. II–867 at II–1048—1075, paras 31–128, CFI; Case T–4/89 *BASF v. Commission* [1991] E.C.R. II–1523 at II–1549—1610, paras 54–258, CFI; Case T–9/89 *Hüls v. Commission* [1992] E.C.R. II–499 at II–539—613, paras 90–328, ECJ. It also transpires from these judgments that the Court of First Instance thoroughly reviews the findings of fact which the Commission regards as constituting an infringement of the E.C. Treaty, Art. 81(1) or Art. 82 (*ex Art. 85 (1) or Art. 86*). See also Joined Cases T–68, T–77 and T–78/89 *SIV and Others v. Commission* [1992] E.C.R. II–1403 at II–1467—1551, paras 172–369, CFI. The Court effects its review by inquiring into the correctness of the factual claims set out in the

It is only in areas in which the institutions have a broad discretion that the Court of Justice and the Court of First Instance show great reluctance in reviewing the assessment of economic facts and circumstances which played a determinative role in the adoption of the contested act.[49] In such a case, there will have to be a manifestly wrong assessment or a misuse of power if the act is to be annulled (apart, of course, from any misapplication of Community law in some other respect).[50]

4. Misuse of powers

7–121 An institution is said to misuse its powers when it uses them for a purpose other than that for which they were conferred (*détournement de pouvoir*).[51] An act may be annulled on that ground. The Court of Justice has evolved from a subjective approach to an objective approach, principally in the context of the ECSC Treaty, of the concept of misuse of powers.[52] It is not always necessary to know the actual grounds which motivated the institution (subjective approach). When the outcome of the contested act diverges from the objectives for which the power was conferred, this can afford a sufficient basis for annulling the contested act for misuse of powers (objective approach).[53] Thus, the Court of Justice has equated with "disregard for the lawful aim" pursuing "objectively", through a serious

---

Commission decision by testing it against the admissible evidence from the parties to the proceedings.

[49] See ECSC Treaty, Art. 33; ECJ, Case 6/54 *Netherlands v. High Authority* [1954 to 1956] E.C.R. 103 at 114–115, ECJ. In agricultural cases: Case 138/79 *Roquette Frères v. Council* [1980] E.C.R. 3333 at 3358–3359, para. 25, ECJ. In competition cases: Case 42/84 *Remia v. Commission* [1985] E.C.R. 2545 at 2575, para. 34, ECJ; Joined Cases 142 and 156/84 *BAT and Reynolds v. Commission* [1987] E.C.R. 4487 at 4583, para. 62, ECJ; Case T–44/90 *La Cinq v. Commission* [1992] E.C.R. II–1 at II–28, para. 85, CFI; Case T–7/92 *Asia Motor France and Others v. Commission* [1993] E.C.R. II–669 at II–683, para. 33, CFI; Joined Cases T–39 and T–40/92 *CB and Europay v. Commission* [1994] E.C.R. II–49 at II–90, para. 109, CFI; Case T–17/93 *Matra Hachette SA v. Commission* [1994] E.C.R. II–595 at II–631—632, para. 104, CFI. In anti-dumping cases: Case 240/84 *Toyo v. Council* [1987] E.C.R. 1809 at 1854, para. 19, ECJ; Case 187/85 *Fediol v. Commission* [1988] E.C.R. 4155 at 4186–4187, para. 6, ECJ; Case C–156/87 *Gestetner Holdings v. Council and Commission* [1990] E.C.R. I–781 at I–843, para. 63, ECJ; Case C–174/87 *Ricoh v. Council* [1992] E.C.R. I–1335 at I–1404, para. 68, ECJ. In transport cases: Case C–354/89 *Schiocchet v. Commission* [1991] E.C.R. I–1775 at I–1795, para. 14, ECJ. In state aid cases: Case C–225/91 *Matra v. Commission* [1993] E.C.R. I–3203 at I–3256, paras 24–25, ECJ.

[50] Case 29/77 *Roquette Frères v. France* [1977] E.C.R. 1835 at 1843, paras 19–20, ECJ.

[51] Case 8/55 *Fédération Charbonnière de Belgique v. High Authority* [1954 to 1956] E.C.R. 292 at 303, ECJ; Case 15/57 *Compagnie des Hauts Fourneaux de Chasse v. High Authority* [1957 and 1958] E.C.R. 211 at 230, ECJ; Case 92/78 *Simmenthal v. Commission* [1979] E.C.R. 777 at 811, para. 106, ECJ; Case 817/79 *Buyl v. Commission* [1982] E.C.R. 245 at 266, para. 28, ECJ; Case T–38/89 *Hochbaum v. Commission* [1990] E.C.R. II–43 at II–51, para. 22, CFI; Case T–108/89 *Scheuer v. Commission* [1990] E.C.R. II–411 at II–425, para. 49, CFI; Case T–46/89 *Pitrone v. Commission* [1990] E.C.R. II–577 at II–594, para. 70, CFI. For an extensive discussion, see Schockweiler, "La notion de détournement de pouvoir en droit communautaire" (1990) A.J.D.A. 435.

[52] See Schockweiler (cited in n. 51, above), at 439–441.

[53] Joined Cases 351 and 360/85 *Fabrique de Fer de Charleroi v. Commission* [1987] E.C.R. 3639 at 3674–3675, paras 19, 20, ECJ; Joined Cases 32, 52 and 57/87 *ISA v. Commission* [1988] E.C.R. 3305 at 3330, para. 19, ECJ; Joined Cases 33, 44, 110, 226 and 285/86 *Peine-Salzgitter and Others v. Commission* [1988] E.C.R. 4309 at 4340, paras 27–28, ECJ.

lack of care or attention in the exercise of a power, purposes other than those for which the power was conferred.[54] An unlawful choice of a decision-making procedure in order to evade other procedures which would normally be applicable also constitutes a misuse of powers.[55]

An act which pursues both unauthorised and authorised aims may be annulled only if this detracts from the main aim for which the power was conferred[56] or if the unauthorised aim constitutes the main reason for exercising the power.[57] **7–122**

The Court subjects claims alleging misuse of powers to strict requirements as to proof. Only if the applicant proves, on the basis of objective, relevant and consistent facts, that the act was adopted for unauthorised purposes, will the Court of Justice or the Court of First Instance entertain a claim of misuse of powers.[58] A misuse of powers cannot be presumed.[59] **7–123**

In spite of the prominent role which this ground of nullity plays in the ECSC Treaty,[60] it is only seldom that the Court of Justice and the Court of First Instance declare an act void for misuse of powers.[61] **7–124**

---

54 Case 8/55 *Fédération Charbonnière de Belgique v. High Authority* [1954 to 1956] E.C.R. 292 at 303, ECJ; Case 13/57 *Wirtschaftsvereinigung Eisen- und Stahlindustrie and Others v. High Authority* [1957 and 1958] E.C.R. 265 at 282, ECJ.

55 Case 2/57 *Compagnie des Hauts Fourneaux de Chasse v. High Authority* [1957 and 1958] E.C.R. 199 at 207, ECJ; Joined Cases 140, 146, 221 and 226/82 *Walzstahl-Vereinigung and Thyssen v. Commission* [1984] E.C.R. 951 at 985, paras 27 *et seq.*, ECJ; Joined Cases 32, 52 and 57/87 *ISA v. Commission* [1988] E.C.R. 3305 at 3330, para. 19, ECJ; Joined Cases 33, 44, 110, 226 and 285/86 *Peine-Salzgitter and Others v. Commission* [1988] E.C.R. 4309 at 4339–4340, paras 27–28, ECJ.

56 Case 1/54 *France v. High Authority* [1954 to 1956] E.C.R. 1 at 16, ECJ; Case 8/55 *Fédération Charbonnière de Belgique v. High Authority* [1954 to 1956] E.C.R. 292 at 301, ECJ.

57 Case 2/57 *Compagnie des Hauts Fourneaux de Chasse v. High Authority* [1957 and 1958] E.C.R. 199 at 232, ECJ.

58 Joined Cases 18 and 35/65 *Gutmann v. Commission* [1966] E.C.R. 103 at 117, ECJ; Case 69/83 *Lux v. Court of Auditors* [1984] E.C.R. 2447 at 2465, para. 30, ECJ; Case 52/86 *Banner v. European Parliament* [1987] E.C.R. 979 at 992, para. 6, ECJ; Joined Cases 361 and 362/87 *Caturla-Poch and de la Fuente Pascual v. European Parliament* [1989] E.C.R. 2471 at 2489, para. 21, ECJ; Case C–323/88 *Sermes* [1990] E.C.R. I–3027 at I–3054, para. 33, ECJ; Case C–331/88 *Fedesa and Others* [1990] E.C.R. I–4023 at I–4065, para. 24, ECJ; Case T–46/89 *Pitrone v. Commission* [1990] E.C.R. II–577 at II–595, para. 71, CFI; Case T–23/91 *Maurissen v. Court of Auditors* [1992] E.C.R. II–2377 at II–2391, para. 28, CFI; Case T–80/92 *Turner v. Commission* [1993] E.C.R. II–1465 at II–1485—1486, para. 70, CFI; Case T–109/92 *Lacruz Bassols v. Court of Justice* [1994] E.C.R.–S.C. II–105 at II–123, para. 52 (English abstract at [1994] E.C.R.–S.C. I–A–31), CFI; Case T–46/93 *Michaël-Chiou v. Commission* [1994] E.C.R.–S.C. II–929 at II–939, para. 35 (English abstract at [1994] E.C.R.–S.C. I–A–297), CFI; Case T–143/89 *Ferriere Nord v. Commission* [1995] E.C.R. II–917 at II–943, para. 68, CFI; Joined Cases T–551/93, T–231, T–232, T–233 and T–234/94 *Industrias Pesqueras Campos and Others v. Commission* [1996] E.C.R. II–247 at II–308, para. 168, CFI.

59 Case 23/76 *Pellegrini v. Commission* [1976] E.C.R. 1807 at 1821, para. 30, and the Opinion of Advocate General H. Mayras, at 1829–1830, ECJ; Case T–146/89 *Williams v. Court of Auditors* [1991] E.C.R. II–1293 at II–1320, para. 89, CFI.

60 See para. 7–084, above.

61 Joined Cases 18 and 35/65 *Gutmann v. Commission* [1966] E.C.R. 103 at 117, ECJ; Case 105/75 *Giuffrida v. Council* [1976] E.C.R. 1395 at 1404, para. 18, ECJ; Case 92/78 *Simmenthal v. Commission* [1979] E.C.R. 777 at 811, para. 106, ECJ; Joined Cases 59 and 129/80 *Turner v. Commission* [1981] E.C.R. 1883 at 1920, para. 71, ECJ; Joined Cases 33, 44, 110, 226 and 285/86 *Peine-Salzitter and Others v. Commission* [1988] E.C.R. 4309 at 4340, para. 28, ECJ; Case T–106/92 *Frederiksen v. Parliament* [1995] E.C.R.–S.C. II–99 at II–112—123, paras 46–60 (English abstract at [1995] E.C.R.–S.C. I–A–29), CFI.

B. Limitation Periods

7–125 Under Article 230 (*ex Article 173*) of the E.C. Treaty, annulment proceedings "shall be instituted within two months of the publication of the measure, or its notification to the plaintiff, or, in the absence thereof, of the day on which it came to the knowledge of the latter, as the case may be". Article 33 of the ECSC Treaty provides that proceedings are to be "instituted within one month of the notification or publication, as the case may be, of the decision or recommendation".[62]

1. Publication

7–126 Under Article 254 (*ex Article 191*) (2) of the E.C. Treaty, regulations and directives addressed to all the Member States must be published in the *Official Journal of the European Communities*.[63] Time for bringing proceedings against such acts starts to run from the 15th day after their publication in the *Official Journal*.[64] There is a rebuttable presumption that the date of publication is the date borne by the issue of the *Official Journal* containing the contested act.[65] Since publication is necessary in order for such acts to enter into effect,[66] time for bringing proceedings cannot start to run until they have been published in full in the *Official Journal*.[67] It makes no difference if the applicant became aware of the content of the regulation in some other way. The same is true of acts which do not have to be published in order to enter into force where there is a consistent practice of publishing them. In those circumstances, and in the absence of notification of the act to the applicant, the latter is entitled to see the act published in the *Official Journal* and the starting point of the period for instituting proceedings is the date of publication, regardless of whether the applicant had earlier notice by some other means of the existence and content of the act in question.[68]

---

[62] For the method for calculating time-limits in general, which is also applicable to limitation periods, see paras 22–177–22–183, below. This section deals only with factors determining the onset of the period for bringing an action for annulment.

[63] The same applies to regulations, directives and decisions adopted in accordance with the E.C. Treaty, Art. 251 (*ex Art. 189b*) (co-decision as between the Council and the European Parliament) by virtue of Art. 254 (*ex Art. 191*) (1).

[64] ECJ Rules of Procedure, Art. 81(1); CFI Rules of Procedure, Art. 102(1). This rule applies not only to regulations and directives addressed to all the Member States, but to *all* acts of Community institutions in relation to which time for bringing proceedings against them starts to run after their publication in the *Official Journal of the European Communities*. See (Judgment of September 15, 1998) Case T–140/95 *Ryanair v. Commission*, para. 28, CFI (not yet reported).

[65] Case 98/78 *Racke v. Hauptzollamt Mainz* [1979] E.C.R. 69 at 85, paras 15–17, ECJ; Case T–115/94 *Opel Austria v. Council* [1997] E.C.R. II–39 at II–83, para. 127, CFI.

[66] Case 185/73 *Hauptzollamt Bielefeld v. König* [1974] E.C.R. 607 at 617, para. 6, ECJ.

[67] *Cf.* Opinion of Advocate General K. Roemer in Joined Cases 10 and 18/68 *Eridania v. Commission* [1969] E.C.R. 459 at 488–489, ECJ.

[68] Case C–122/95 *Germany v. Council* [1998] E.C.R. I–973 at I–1009—1010, paras 34–39, ECJ, in which the Court of Justice held that there was a consistent practice for Council decisions embodying the conclusion of international agreements binding on the European Community to be published in the *Official Journal* (compare Case C–309/95 *Commission v.*

2. Notification to the applicant

Under Article 254 (*ex Article 191*) (3) of the E.C. Treaty,[69] all other directives and decisions take effect upon notification to the addressee. The period of time for commencing proceedings against such a measure runs from the day following the receipt by the person concerned of due notification,[70] where any delay in notification is not attributable to that person.[71] 7–127

Due notification requires that the act be communicated to the person to whom it is addressed[72] and should put that person in a position to take cognizance of its content and of the grounds on which it is based.[73] Registered mail with an acknowledgment slip is accepted as an appropriate means of notification since it enables the Court to determine with certainty when time started to run.[74] In such case, only unforeseen circumstances, *force majeure* or excusable error which prevented the applicant from actually taking cognizance of the act notified may justify exceeding the time-limit for instituting proceedings.[75] The burden of proof is a difficult 7–128

Council [1998] E.C.R. I–655, ECJ, for acts which are not published). See also (Judgment of September 15, 1998) Case T–11/95 *BP Chemicals v. Commission* (not yet reported), paras 46–51, CFI; (Judgment of January 28, 1999) Case T-14/96 *Bretagne Angleterre Irlande (BAI) v. Commission* (not yet reported), paras 32–37, CFI; and para. 7–129 below.

[69] See the ECSC Treaty, Art. 15, para. 2, as far as individual decisions and recommendations are concerned.

[70] However, a purely formal error in the notification (*e.g.* a mistake in the name of the addressee) does not prevent the time-limits laid down in the Treaty from applying, provided that the act in question actually reached the addressee and the latter realised that he or she actually was the addressee: (Order of July 4, 1984), Case 82/84 *Metalgoi v. Commission* [1984] E.C.R. 2585 at 2586, ECJ; (Order of February 13, 1998), Case T–275/97 *Guérin Automobiles v. Commission* [1998] E.C.R. II–253 at II–258—259, para. 14, CFI; (Order of February 13, 1998), Case T–276/97 *Guérin Automobiles v. Commission* [1998] E.C.R. II–261 at II–268, para. 18, CFI.

[71] Case 5/76 *Jänsch v. Commission* [1976] E.C.R. 1027 at 1034, para. 9, ECJ. ECJ Rules of Procedure, Art. 81(1); CFI Rules of Procedure, Art. 102(1). This rule is applicable to *all* acts of Community institutions which enter into force upon notification.

[72] In the case of companies, the rule is that measures addressed to the parent company may not be validly notified to subsidiaries (Case 48/69 *ICI v. Commission* [1972] E.C.R. 619 at 651–652, paras 34–38, ECJ. In that case, however, the parent company had had full knowledge of the contested act and exercised the right to bring proceedings within the prescribed period. Consequently, the finding that notification might not have been properly effected had no bearing on the case: paras 39–44).

[73] Case 6/72 *Europemballage and Continental Can v. Commission* [1973] E.C.R. 215 at 241, para. 10, ECJ; Case T–196/95 *H. v. Commission* [1997] E.C.R.–S.C. II–403 at II–410, para. 31, (English abstract at I–A–133), CFI. Consequently, to send only a brief summary of the contents of the act is not sufficient and will not start time running for the purposes of bringing proceedings: Case C–143/95P *Commission v. Socurte and Others* [1997] E.C.R. I–1 at 22, para. 32, ECJ.

[74] Joined Cases 32 and 33/58 *SNUPAT v. High Authority* [1959] E.C.R. 127 at 136, ECJ; Case 224/83 *Ferriera Vittoria v. Commission* [1984] E.C.R. 2349 at 2355, para. 9, ECJ.

[75] Joined Cases 220 and 221/78 *ALA and ALFER v. Commission* [1979] E.C.R. 1693 at 1698, para. 9, ECJ; (Order of April 27, 1988), Case 352/87 *Farzoo v. Commission* [1988] E.C.R. 2281 at 2284, para. 7, ECJ; (Order of February 5, 1992), Case C–59/91 *France v. Commission* [1992] E.C.R. I–525 at I–529, para. 8, ECJ.

one for the applicant to discharge. In order for legal certainty not to suffer too much, these exceptions are strictly interpreted.[76]

7–129 If the act is addressed to a company, notification to the registered office suffices. Companies have no right to require the Commission to give notice at a place other than the registered office or to a particular person.[77]

The person to whom the act is addressed cannot prevent time from starting to run by refusing to take cognizance of a properly notified act.[78]

Publication in the *Official Journal* of an act which takes effect upon notification to the addressee, has no effect on when time starts running.[79]

7–130 The party alleging that the time-limit for bringing proceedings has run out has to prove the date on which the act was notified.[80]

3. Date on which the applicant had notice of the act

7–131 The period for commencing proceedings, in the case of interested third parties seeking annulment of an act addressed to another person, begins on the day on which that person acquired knowledge of the existence and the precise contents of the measure, and of the reasons on which it is based, in such a way as to enable him profitably to exercise his right of action.[81]

If the act is published in the *Official Journal*[82] or in an official publication of a Member State[83] or if it is brought to the notice of interested third parties, this will constitute sufficient notice, with the result that time will start running. However, whether an action for annulment brought by an interested third party against an act directed to another person is admissible does not depend on the fact of publication or notification. An application lodged before publication or notification will be admissible.[84] A third party who acquires precise knowledge of the content of an act before

[76] Case 284/82 *Busseni v. Commission* [1984] E.C.R. 557 at 566–567, paras 11–12, ECJ; Case 224/83 *Ferriera Vittoria v. Commission* [1984] E.C.R. 2349 at 2356, para. 13, ECJ; Case 209/83 *Valsabbia v. Commission* [1984] E.C.R. 3089 at 3097–3098, paras 21–22, ECJ; Case T–12/90 *Bayer v. Commission* [1991] E.C.R. II–219, CFI; Joined Cases T–33 and T–74/89 *Blackman v. European Parliament* [1993] E.C.R. II–249 at II–263—264, paras 32–36, CFI; Case T–514/93 *Cobrecaf and Others v. Commission* [1995] E.C.R. II–621 at II–635, para. 40, CFI.

[77] Case 42/85 *Cockerill-Sambre v. Commission* [1985] E.C.R. 3749 at 3756, paras 10–11, ECJ.

[78] Case 6/72 *Europemballage and Continental Can v. Commission* [1973] E.C.R. 215 at 240, para. 10, ECJ.

[79] Case 31/76 *Macevicius v. European Parliament* [1977] E.C.R. 883 at 890, para. 13, ECJ. See also *BP Chemicals v. Commission* (cited in n. 68 above), para. 52; *Bretagne Angleterre Irlande (BAI) v. Commission* (cited in n. 68, above), para. 36.

[80] Joined Cases T–70 and T–71/92 *Florimex and VGB v. Commission* [1997] E.C.R. II–693 at II–723, para. 74, CFI.

[81] Case 236/86 *Dillinger Hüttenwerke v. Commission* [1988] E.C.R. 3761 at 3784, para. 15, ECJ; Case 378/87 *Top Hit Holzvertrieb v. Commission* [1989] E.C.R. 1359 at 1383, para. 15, ECJ.

[82] Case 76/79 *Könecke v. Commission* [1980] E.C.R. 665 at 677, para. 7, ECJ; Case T–380/94 *AIUFFASS and AKT v. Commission* [1996] E.C.R. II–2169 at II–2186, para. 42, CFI.

[83] Joined Cases 31 and 33/62 *Wöhrmann and Others v. Commission* [1962] E.C.R. 501 at 508, ECJ.

[84] Joined Cases 172 and 226/83 *Hoogovens Groep v. Commission* [1985] E.C.R. 2831 at 2845–2846, para. 8, ECJ.

the person to whom it is addressed was notified of it, within the meaning of Article 254 (*ex Article 191*) (3) of the Treaty, must bring proceedings within two months of the moment at which it acquired that precise knowledge.[85] It has been held that where the applicant had knowledge of the contested act from a letter of which the date of receipt could not be definitely established, the period for commencing proceedings began on the date on which the applicant itself referred to the act in a letter.[86]

If the content of the act is not notified, yet interested parties are put on notice of its existence, they are under an obligation to request the complete text of the act within a reasonable period.[87]

IV. Consequences

A. Result of an Application for Annulment

If the action is well founded, the Court of Justice or the Court of First Instance will declare the contested act void.[88] If the application is not well founded, it will be dismissed. **7–132**

The annulment of an act causes it to disappear from the Community legal order from the date on which it came into force (*ex tunc*), so that the parties to the proceedings are restored to the situation which they were in before it entered into force.[89] **7–133**

---

[85] Case C–309/95 *Commission v. Council* [1998] E.C.R. I–655 at I–677—678, paras 18–22, ECJ. It could be inferred from the wording of this judgment that interested third parties invariably have to comply with this time-limit, irrespective as to whether or not the contested act has entered into force. But the objection to this interpretation is that if the act does not enter into force within two months of the time at which the third party acquired knowledge of it, the action would have to be brought against an act which does not yet produce any legal effects. In *Commission v. Council*, the addressee was notified during the two-month period and the problem did not arise.

[86] (Order of April 28, 1994), Joined Cases T–452 and T–453/93 *Pevasa and Inpesca v. Commission* [1994] II–229 at II–243—244, paras 33–36, CFI.

[87] Case 59/84 *Tezi v. Commission* [1986] E.C.R. 887 at 919, paras 9–11, ECJ (period of 14 months held to be reasonable); Case C–180/88 *Wirtschaftsvereinigung Eisen- und Stahlindustrie v. Commission* [1990] E.C.R. I–4413 at I–4440, para. 22, ECJ (two years held to be unreasonable); (Order of March 5, 1993), Case C–102/92 *Ferriere Acciaierie Sarde v. Commission* [1993] E.C.R. I–801 at I–807, paras 18, 19, ECJ (two months held to be unreasonable); (Order of February 10, 1994), Case T–468/93 *Frinil v. Commission* [1994] E.C.R. II–33 at II–44—45, paras 33, 34, CFI (one year and 10 months held to be unreasonable); Case T–465/93 *Consorzio gruppo di azione locale "Murgia Messapica" v. Commission* [1994] E.C.R. II–361, CFI (7.5 months held to be reasonable); Joined Cases T–432, T–433 and T–434/93 *Socurte and Others v. Commission* [1995] E.C.R. II–503 at II–520—521, para. 49, CFI; Case T–109/94 *Windpark Groothusen v. Commission* [1995] E.C.R. II–3007 at II–3017—3018, paras 24–28, CFI (seven months held to be unreasonable); (Order of September 30, 1997), Case T–151/95 *INEF v. Commission* [1997] E.C.R. II–1541 at II–1557, para. 48, CFI (18 months held to be unreasonable).

[88] E.C. Treaty, Art. 231 (*ex Art. 174*), para. 1; EAEC Treaty, Art. 147, para. 1. By implication, the ECSC Treaty, Arts. 33, 34.

[89] Case 22/70 *Commission v. Council* [1971] E.C.R. 263 at 278–279, paras 59–60, ECJ; Joined Cases 97, 193, 99 and 215/86 *Asteris v. Commission* [1988] E.C.R. 2181 at 2209, para. 30, ECJ.

7–134 The retroactive force of a declaration of nullity may be attenuated, pursuant to the second paragraph of Article 231 (*ex Article 174*) of the E.C. Treaty, in the light of the aim behind the action or on grounds of legal certainty.[90] Thus, the Court of Justice and the Court of First Instance may preserve the effects of the annulled act[91] or even declare that it is to remain in force until the competent institution has taken the necessary measures to give effect to the judgment annulling the act.[92]

7–135 The Court of Justice and the Court of First Instance may also declare part of the contested act void, either by annulling some of its provisions or by confining the declaration of nullity to some substantive or personal aspect.[93] The applicant may have sought partial annulment[94] or the Court of Justice or the Court of First Instance may itself take the view that only some provisions of the contested act must be annulled.[95] An act cannot be annulled in part if the contested part of the act cannot be severed from its other provisions.[96] Partial annulment is also impossible where it would result in the content of the remaining part ceasing to have its original effect.[97]

90 The power of the Court of Justice to state which effects of the annulled regulation are to be considered as definitive has also been exercised with regard to other types of act: see Case 92/78 *Simmenthal v. Commission* [1979] E.C.R. 777 at 811, para. 107, ECJ—annulment of a decision; Case 34/86 *Council v. European Parliament* [1986] E.C.R. 2155 at 2212, para. 48, ECJ—annulment of the act by which the President of the European Parliament declares the budget finally adopted; Case C–295/90 *European Parliament v. Council* [1992] E.C.R. I–4193 at I–4236—4237, paras 22–27, ECJ—annulment of a directive; Case C–106/96 *United Kingdom v. Commission* [1998] E.C.R. I–2729 at I–2759, paras 39–42, ECJ—annulment of a decision pursuant to which contracts had been concluded under a Community action programme.

91 Case 45/86 *Commission v. Council* [1987] E.C.R. 1493 at 1522, para. 23, ECJ; Case 51/87 *Commission v. Council* [1988] E.C.R. 5459 at 5481, para. 22, ECJ; Case C–360/93 *European Parliament v. Council* [1996] E.C.R. I–1195 at I–1219, paras 32–36, ECJ; Case C–271/94 *European Parliament v. Council* [1996] E.C.R. I–1689 at I–1718—1719, para. 40, ECJ; Case C–22/96 *European Parliament v. Council* [1998] E.C.R. I–3231 at I–3254, para. 42, ECJ.

92 Case 81/72 *Commission v. Council* [1973] E.C.R. 575 at 586, para. 15, ECJ; Case 264/82 *Timex v. Council and Commission* [1985] E.C.R. 849 at 870–871, para. 32, ECJ; Case 275/87 *Commission v. Council* [1989] E.C.R. 259 at 261, ECJ; Case C–295/90 *European Parliament v. Council* [1992] E.C.R. I–4193 at I–4236—4237, paras 22–27, ECJ; Case C–65/90 *European Parliament v. Council* [1992] E.C.R. I–4593 at I–4623, paras 22–24, ECJ.

93 See, by way of example, Joined Cases 33, 44, 110, 226 and 285/86 *Peine-Salzgitter and Others v. Commission* [1988] E.C.R. 4309 at 4341, point 1 of the operative part, ECJ; Case T–26/90 *Finsider v. Commission* [1992] E.C.R. II–1789 at II–1806—1808, paras 52–57, CFI.

94 If the applicant seeks only partial annulment of an act and the Court of Justice or the Court of First Instance considers that only annulment of the complete act is possible, it may not rule *ultra petita* (Case 37/71 *Jamet v. Commission* [1972] E.C.R. 483 at 490, para. 12, ECJ), but would have to declare the application inadmissible (see Joliet, *Le contentieux*, p. 108).

95 Case 27/76 *United Brands v. Commission* [1978] E.C.R. 207 at 303, para. 268, ECJ.

96 Case 17/74 *Transocean Marine Paint v. Commission* [1974] E.C.R. 1063 at 1081, para. 21, ECJ; Joined Cases C–68/94 and C–30/95 *France and Others v. Commission* [1998] E.C.R. I–1375 at I–1527—1528, paras 251–259, ECJ.

97 See Case 34/86 *Council v. European Parliament* [1986] E.C.R. 2155 at 2210—2211, paras 40–42, ECJ. But see Joined Cases T–68, T–77 and T–78/89 *SIV and Others v. Commission* [1992] E.C.R. II–1403 at II–1535—1542, paras 318–339, CFI.

B. Authority of the Judgment

1. Declaration of nullity

The declaration of nullity applies *erga omnes*. Consequently, an action for annulment of a measure which has already been declared void is to no purpose. This is because the annulled act can no longer compromise the applicant's rights or interests.[98] In exceptional cases, the Court of Justice or the Court of First Instance may be prompted to curtail the general effect of the declaration of nullity on grounds of legal certainty.[99] **7–136**

The institution whose act has been declared void is required by the first paragraph of Article 233 (*ex Article 176*) of the E.C. Treaty to take the necessary measures to comply with the judgment. The Court of Justice and the Court of First Instance have no power to indicate what measures should be taken.[1] The extent of the obligation to comply with the judgment is determined both by the operative part and by the grounds underlying the operative part.[2] Accordingly, the institution concerned must not only replace the annulled act by a new one not tainted by the same illegality, it must also eliminate provisions exhibiting the same shortcoming from all other measures.[3] **7–137**

[98] Case 3/54 *ASSIDER v. High Authority* [1954 to 1956] E.C.R. 63 at 70, ECJ. See also para. 1–029, n. 92, above.

[99] Case 92/78 *Simmenthal v. Commission* [1979] E.C.R. 777 at 811, para. 107, ECJ.

[1] Case 53/85 *AKZO Chemie v. Commission* [1986] E.C.R. 1965 at 1990, para. 23, ECJ; Case C–199/91 *Foyer Culturel du Sart-Tilman v. Commission* [1993] E.C.R. I–2667 at I–2693, para. 7, ECJ; Case T–37/89 *Hanning v. European Parliament* [1990] E.C.R. II–463 at II–488—489, para. 79, CFI; Case T–26/90 *Finsider v. Commission* [1992] E.C.R. II–1789 at II–1810, para. 65, CFI; Case T–84/91 *Meskens v. European Parliament* [1992] E.C.R. II–2335 at II–2357—2359, paras 71–80, CFI, upheld on appeal by Case C–412/92P *European Parliament v. Meskens* [1994] E.C.R. I–3757 at I–3775, para. 24, ECJ; Case T–508/93 *Mancini v. Commission* [1994] E.C.R.–S.C.–761 at II–774, para. 51 (English abstract at I–A–239), CFI; Case T–75/95 *Günzler Aluminium v. Commission* [1996] E.C.R. II–497 at II–506, para. 18, CFI. See also the ECSC Treaty, Art. 34, and Case 30/59 *De Gezamenlijke Steenkolenmijnen in Limburg v. High Authority* [1961] E.C.R. 1 at 17, ECJ.

[2] Joined Cases 97, 193, 99 and 215/86 *Asteris v. Commission* [1988] E.C.R. 2181 at 2208, para. 27, ECJ; Case T–224/95 *Tremblay and Others v. Commission* [1997] E.C.R. II–2215 at II–2241, para. 72, CFI. For further applications see (Judgment of November 12, 1998) Case C–415/96 *Spain v. Commission*, paras 23–35, ECJ (not yet reported): following the annulment for insufficient reasoning of a first Commission decision declaring aid incompatible with the common market, the Commission could legally adopt a second decision with the same tenor stating proper reasons without having to re-open the procedure provided for in the E.C. Treaty, Art. 88 (*ex Art. 93*) (2), since the annulment of a Community measure does not necessarily affect the preparatory acts; in this case it had not been held in the Court's judgment that, at the time of adoption of the first Commission decision, the investigation measures completed by the Commission within the framework of the aforementioned procedure had not allowed an exhaustive analysis to be made of the compatibility of the aid with the E.C. Treaty, Art. 87 (*ex Art. 92*) (3); it followed that the procedure for replacing that decision could be resumed at that point by means of a fresh analysis of the investigation measures, the reliability of which had not been challenged; implementation of the Court's judgment did not therefore require the Commission to repeat the whole procedure provided for in Art. 88; (Judgment of April 20, 1999) Joined Cases T–305/94, T–306/94, T–307/94, T–313/94, T–314/94, T–315/94, T–316/94, T–318/94, T–325/94, T–328/94, T–329/94 and T–335/94, *Limburgse Vinyl Maatschappij NV and Others v. Commission*, paras 183–193, CFI (not yet reported).

[3] *Asteris v. Commission* (cited in n. 2, above) paras 29–31; Case T–120/89 *Stahlwerke Peine-Salzgitter v. Commission* [1991] E.C.R. II–279 at II–380, para. 47, CFI.

7–138 In addition, the institution concerned may be required to consider whether, in the light of the reasoning of the judgment annulling the contested act, it needs to take measures in relation not only to the successful parties but also to the addressees of the partly annulled act who did not bring an action for annulment.[4]

7–139 The institution has a reasonable time in which to comply with the judgment.[5] What constitutes a reasonable time depends on the nature of the measures having to be taken in order to carry out the judgment declaring the contested act void and on the attendant circumstances.[6] In the event that there are special difficulties in giving effect to the judgment annulling the contested act, the institution may comply with its obligation to give effect to the judgment by adopting any measure which fairly compensates for the disadvantage suffered by the applicant as a result of the unlawful conduct found.[7]

2. Dismissal of an application for annulment

7–140 After a judgment has been given dismissing an application for annulment, the applicant may probably not raise the same pleas in another action brought against the same act.[8] An action for annulment which is brought after a judgment dismissing an action brought between the same parties and has the same purpose and is based on the same submissions as the application which led to the first judgment will be inadmissible on the ground that the first judgment has the authority of *res judicata*.[9] But the principle of *res judicata* extends only to matters of fact and law actually or necessarily settled in the judicial decision in question.[10]

---

[4] Case T–227/95 *AssiDomän Kraft Products and Others v. Commission* [1997] E.C.R. II–1185 at II–1213, para. 72, CFI. In this case a number of Swedish wood-pulp producers, who had not brought an action for annulment of a Commission decision finding an infringement of the E.C. Treaty, Art. 81 (*ex Art. 85*) (1), on account of concerted practices, and imposing fines, brought an action for annulment of a Commission decision rejecting a claim for repayment of the fines. The undertakings concerned had lodged a request for repayment with the Commission after the Court of Justice had annulled the original decision finding an infringement of Art. 81 (*ex Art. 85*) (1) as far as the undertakings which had brought an action against it were concerned. The Court of First Instance held that it would be inconsistent with the principle of legality for the Commission not to have a duty to examine its initial position in relation to undertakings which had not brought an action for annulment of the original decision after the Court had held that the alleged concerted practice was not proved. The Commission has appealed against this judgment to the Court of Justice (Case C–310/97P).

[5] ECSC Treaty, Art. 34; Case 266/82 *Turner v. Commission* [1984] E.C.R. 1 at 10–11, para. 5, ECJ; *Stahlwerke Peine-Salzgitter v. Commission* (cited in n. 3, above) at II–386, para. 66; Case T–81/96 *Apostolidis and Others v. Commission* [1997] E.C.R. II–607 at II–616, para. 37, CFI.

[6] Case T–73/95 *Oliveira v. Commission* [1997] E.C.R. II–381 at II–397–398, para. 41, CFI.

[7] Case T–91/95 *De Nil and Impens v. Council* [1996] E.C.R.–S.C. II–959 at II–970, para. 34 (English abstract at I–A–327), CFI.

[8] Case 62/82 *Italy v. Commission* [1983] E.C.R. 687 at 705, paras 17, 18, ECJ.

[9] (Order of April 1, 1987), Joined Cases 159 and 267/84, 12 and 264/85 *Ainsworth v. Commission* [1987] E.C.R. 1579 at 1581, para. 2, ECJ.

[10] (Order of November 28, 1996), Case C–277/95P *Lenz v. Commission* [1996] E.C.R. I–6109 at I–6125, para. 50, ECJ.

CHAPTER 8

THE ACTION FOR FAILURE TO ACT

I. SUBJECT-MATTER

A. GENERAL

The action for failure to act is provided for in Article 35 of the ECSC Treaty, Article 232 (*ex Article 175*) of the E.C. Treaty and Article 148 of the EAEC Treaty. Its object is a declaration on the part of the Court of Justice or the Court of First Instance that the defendant institution acted unlawfully by failing to take a decision.[1] Accordingly, the action for failure to act forms part of the whole system of judicial review, which covers both action and inaction on the part of Community institutions. **8–001**

B. SUBJECT-MATTER OF AN ACTION FOR FAILURE TO ACT

The subject-matter of the action is confined to an inquiry into whether the omission to take a given decision was lawful. **8–002**

In the first place, the institution against which the proceedings are brought must have failed to take a decision.[2] An action for failure to act will be admissible only if the institution concerned has first been called upon to act. If, within two months of being so called upon, the institution concerned has not defined its position, the action may be brought within a further period of two months.[3] **8–003**

The subject-matter of the action will cease to exist if the act to which it relates is adopted after the action was brought but before judgment, since then a declaration by the Court of Justice or the Court of First Instance that the initial failure to act was unlawful can no longer bring about the consequences prescribed by Article 233 (*ex Article 176*) of the E.C. Treaty.[4]

---

[1] Case 377/87 *European Parliament v. Council* [1988] E.C.R. 4017 at 4048, para. 9, ECJ; Case 383/87 *Commission v. Council* [1988] E.C.R. 4051 at 4064, para.9, ECJ.

[2] Opinion of Advocate General J. Mischo in Case 377/87 *European Parliament v. Council* [1988] E.C.R. 4017 at 4027, ECJ. See also Case 8/71 *Komponistenverband v. Commission* [1971] E.C.R. 705 at 710–711, ECJ.

[3] Under the ECSC Treaty, the applicant can challenge the implied decision of refusal which is to be inferred from the Commission's failure to take the decision or make the recommendation requested. In such case, the action for failure to act takes the form of an action for annulment.

[4] Case 377/87 *European Parliament v. Council* [1988] E.C.R. 4017 at 4048, para. 10, ECJ; Case 383/87 *Commission v. Council* [1988] E.C.R. 4051 at 4064, para. 10, ECJ; Joined Cases C–15 and C–108/91 *Buckl and Others v. Commission* [1992] E.C.R. I–6061 at I–6096—6098,

8–004 Furthermore, a failure to take a decision is unlawful only if the defendant institution was under a duty to act.[5] The duty to act must derive from superior Community law. The reference in Article 232 (*ex Article 175*) of the E.C. Treaty to "this Treaty" does not mean that only a duty to act enshrined in an article of the Treaty may be enforced by means of an action for failure to act. In fact, an action will lie on the basis of any rule of Community law which is as such binding on the defendant institution and contains a duty to act.[6]

8–005 The applicant must state what act the defendant institution has failed to adopt, failing which its application will be inadmissible.[7] It must also describe the act sufficiently precisely in order that the Court of Justice or the Court of First Instance may give a judgment which will enable the defendant institution to take the necessary measures to comply with it in accordance with Article 233 (*ex Article 176*) of the E.C. Treaty.[8]

8–006 The duty to take a decision must, in the case of the E.C. Treaty, give rise to an act which is capable of having legal effects.[9] The nature of the legal effects required, however, is not always the same.

If the action for failure to act is brought by a natural or legal person, the defendant institution must have failed to "address to that person any act other than a recommendation or an opinion" (E.C. Treaty, Article 232 (*ex*

---

paras 13–18, ECJ; Case C–25/91 *Pesqueras Echebastar v. Commission* [1993] E.C.R. I–1719 at I–1758, paras 11, 12, ECJ; (Order of June 10, 1993), Case C–41/92 *The Liberal Democrats v. European Parliament* [1993] E.C.R. I–3153 at I–3176, para. 4, ECJ; Case T–28/90 *Asia Motor France and Others v. Commission* [1992] E.C.R. II–2285 at II–2299—2301, paras 34–38, CFI; (Order of November 29, 1993), Case T–56/92 *Koelman v. Commission* [1993] E.C.R. II–1267 at II–1277—1278, para. 28, CFI; Case T–32/93 *Ladbroke Racing Limited v. Commission* [1994] E.C.R. II–1015 at II–1026, para. 22, CFI; (Order of November 26, 1996), Case T–164/95 *Kuchlenz-Winter v. European Parliament* [1996] E.C.R. II–1593 at II–1604, para. 36, CFI; (Order of November 26, 1996), Case T–226/95 *Kuchlenz-Winter v. Commission* [1996] E.C.R. II–1619 at II–1628, para. 30, CFI; Case T–212/95 *Oficemen v. Commission* [1997] E.C.R. II–1161 at II–1181, paras 65–68, CFI; (Order of November 26, 1997), Case T–39/97 *T. Port v. Commission* [1997] E.C.R. II–2125 at II–2134, para. 22, CFI.

[5] Case 64/82 *Tradax v. Commission* [1984] E.C.R. 1359 at 1379, paras 22–23, ECJ; Case T–277/94 *AITEC v. Commission* [1996] E.C.R. II–351 at II–377—379, paras 65–72, CFI (as for the question whether an action should be brought in the Court of Justice, either under Art. 226 (*ex Art. 169*) or under Art. 88 (*ex Art. 93*) (2) (concerning State aid), this depends on how the Commission uses its discretion; it does not entail any obligation which may be invoked by the applicant for the purposes of establishing a failure to act on the part of the defendant. Such a claim will be inadmissible); (Order of November 26, 1996), Case T–167/95 *Kuchlenz-Winter v. Council* [1996] E.C.R. II–1607 at II–1616, para. 24, CFI. Under the ECSC Treaty, Art. 35, para. 2, where the Commission has the *power* to act or not to act, its refraining from acting will be unlawful if it constitutes a misuse of powers.

[6] Joined Cases 10 and 18/68 *Eridania v. Commission* [1969] E.C.R. 459 at 483, para. 16, ECJ, where the Court of Justice used the expression "provision of Community law". See also (Judgment of September 15, 1998), Case T–95/96 *Gestevisión Telecinco v. Commission*, CFI (not yet reported), in which it was held that the Commission's failure to deal with a complaint lodged by a competitor of a recipient of non-notified State aid constituted a failure to act.

[7] (Order of May 7, 1980), Joined Cases 114–117/79 *Fournier v. Commission* [1980] E.C.R. 1529 at 1531, ECJ.

[8] Case 13/83 *European Parliament v. Council* [1985] E.C.R. 1513 at 1592–1593, paras 35–37, ECJ.

[9] Opinion of Advocate General J. Mischo in Case 377/87 *European Parliament v. Council* [1988] E.C.R. 4017 at 4029, point 30, ECJ.

Article 175), third paragraph). It follows that where an action for failure to act is brought by a natural or legal person, it will be admissible only if it relates to the defendant institution's failure to adopt a binding act.[10]

If, in contrast, the action for failure to act is brought by a Member State or a Community institution, the act which was not performed does not necessarily have to be binding in order to have legal effects and so an action may be brought in this case too. For instance, an action may be brought against the Commission if it fails to submit a proposal for a legislative measure to the Council relating to a matter on which the Community is under an obligation to legislate.[11] The rationale is that the Commission proposal is necessary in order to enable the Council and the European Parliament to play their respective roles in the legislative process.[12]

Under the ECSC Treaty, an action for failure to act is available only against a tacit refusal to take a decision or make a recommendation.

C. Relationship between the action for annulment and the action for failure to act

In the case of the E.C. Treaty, there is no necessary link between the action for annulment and the action for failure to act.[13] **8–007**

The *dictum* of the Court of Justice in *Chevalley v. Commission*[14] that "[t]he concept of a measure capable of giving rise to an action is identical in Articles 173 and 175 *(now Articles 230 and 232)*" is true only in the case of actions brought by natural or legal persons. But, even in the case of natural or legal persons, this does not mean that the only way in which the defendant institution can rectify its failure to act is to adopt a binding act. The definition of a position which brings the failure to act to an end will sometimes be a non-binding act against which an action for annulment would not lie. Since the failure to act has been terminated, an action for

[10] Consequently, individuals cannot challenge an institution's failure to adopt a non-binding act, not even where the failure to act takes the form of an express refusal, see Case 15/70 *Chevalley v. Commission* [1970] E.C.R. 975, ECJ.

[11] (Order of July 11, 1996), Case C–445/93 *European Parliament v. Commission*, ECJ, not reported in the E.C.R. (failure of the Commission to submit the necessary proposals pursuant to the E.C. Treaty, Arts. 7a and 155 (*now Arts. 14 and 211*), for the liberalisation of the movement of persons; on an application from the European Parliament, an order was given declaring that there was no need to proceed to judgment following the submission of the relevant proposal by the Commission). If the Council is not under a duty to legislate, the Commission cannot be obliged to submit a proposal for a legislative measure to the Council (Lauwaars, *Lawfulness and Legal Force of Community Decisions*, Leyden, Sijthoff, 1973, p. 109). For a case in which the Council was under a duty to legislate, see Case 13/83 *European Parliament v. Council* [1985] E.C.R. 1513 at 1597–1601, paras 54–71, ECJ.

[12] The same reasoning applies to decision-making in connection with the Community budget: Case 377/87 *European Parliament v. Council* [1988] E.C.R. 4017, ECJ (action brought against the Council for failure to act on the ground that it had failed to place before the European Parliament, in accordance with the E.C. Treaty, Art. 203 (*now Art. 272*) (4), a draft general budget of the Community for the following financial year by no later than October 5).

[13] Case 302/87 *European Parliament v. Council* [1988] E.C.R. 5615 at 5641, para. 16, ECJ.

[14] Case 15/70 *Chevalley v. Commission* [1970] E.C.R. 975 at 979, para. 6, ECJ.

failure to act will no longer lie, unless at a later stage a further failure to act on the part of the defendant institution can be established in the light of new circumstances.[15]

In addition, Member States or Community institutions may compel an institution to adopt a measure by means of an action for failure to act, even though no action for annulment would be available against the act in question. Accordingly, the European Parliament is entitled to a declaration from the Court of Justice that the Council's failure to lay before it a draft budget is unlawful. Yet once the draft budget has been adopted, no action for annulment will lie against it since it is a preparatory act.[16]

8–008 Once the institution adopts a binding act, an action will lie against it. The act in question may be a refusal to adopt the act sought[17] or the adoption of an act different from the one requested.[18] If, however, the failure to act is terminated by a definition of a position not constituting a binding act,[19] no action may be brought.[20]

8–009 Under the ECSC Treaty, however, it remains possible to bring an action for failure to act as long as the Commission has not taken a decision or made a recommendation.[21] An express refusal to take the decision or make the recommendation requested is regarded as a negative decision or recommendation, and therefore has to be challenged by an action for annulment.[22] The same is true where the Commission adopts an act different from the act requested.[23] An act which explains the Commission's position in relation to the act requested, but cannot be classed as a decision or a recommendation, does not cure the failure to act. In such a case, the application for a declaration that the Commission has failed to act remains admissible. Under the ECSC rules, the action for failure to act supplements

---

[15] See para. 8–020, below.

[16] Case 302/87 *European Parliament v. Council* [1988] E.C.R. 5615 at 5641, para. 16, ECJ.

[17] Case 42/71 *Nordgetreide v. Commission* [1972] E.C.R. 105 at 110, para. 4, ECJ (an action for annulment brought by an individual will then be admissible if the measure sought, constituting the subject-matter of the refusal, satisfies the conditions laid down in the E.C. Treaty, Art. 230 (*ex Art. 173*) para. 4; Case 44/81 *Germany v. Commission* [1982] E.C.R. 1855 at 1874, para. 6, ECJ.

[18] Case 8/71 *Komponistenverband v. Commission* [1971] E.C.R. 705 at 710, para. 2, ECJ.

[19] See para. 8–020, below.

[20] Case 48/65 *Lütticke v. Commission* [1966] E.C.R. 19 at 27, ECJ; Case 42/71 *Nordgetreide v. Commission* [1972] E.C.R. 105, ECJ.

[21] Once the period of two months after the failure to act has been raised has expired, the applicant has a definitive right to institute proceedings. The fact that the Commission subsequently sets out its reasons for the tacit refusal in a letter does not mean that the refusal is no longer tacit but express and the action remains admissible (Joined Cases 7 and 9/54 *Groupement des Industries Sidérurgiques Luxembourgeoises v. High Authority* [1954 to 1956] E.C.R. 175 at 193–194, ECJ). But see Joined Cases 5–11 and 13–15/62 *San Michele and Others v. High Authority* [1962] E.C.R. 449 at 459–460, ECJ, in which the Court of Justice declared an action for failure to act inadmissible on the ground that the applicant had no longer any interest when the High Authority had taken a decision after the two months following the applicant's having raised the matter had expired but before proceedings were brought.

[22] Case 30/59 *De Gezamenlijke Steenkolenmijnen in Limburg v. High Authority* [1961] E.C.R. 1 at 15–16, ECJ.

[23] Joined Cases 5–11 and 13–15/62 *San Michele and Others v. High Authority* [1962] E.C.R. 449 at 459, ECJ.

the action for annulment, thereby securing a seamless system of judicial review.[24]

As has already been mentioned, under the E.C. Treaty not all definitions of a position on the part of the defendant institution constitute binding acts against which an action for annulment will lie, with the result that a seamless system does not invariably obtain.[25]

The Court of Justice and the Court of First Instance will not tolerate any improper use of the action for failure to act. In the event that an institution has adopted a binding act, only an action for annulment will be available to challenge it. If the applicant has allowed the period for bringing an action to expire, it cannot provoke a failure to act by addressing a request to the institution concerned to revoke the measure adversely affecting it.[26] If the institution does not comply with such a request, moreover, it is not in breach of any obligation to act. **8–010**

II. The Identity of the Parties

A. Defendants

Under Article 232 (*ex Article 175*) of the E.C. Treaty, an action for failure to act may be brought against the Council, the Commission, the European Parliament or the European Central Bank. Under Article 35 of the ECSC Treaty, such proceedings may be instituted only against the Commission (High Authority). **8–011**

B. Applicants

1. Institutions and Member States

Article 232 (*ex Article 175*) of the E.C. Treaty authorises "the Member States and the other institutions of the Community" to bring an action for failure to act. It confers that right of action on *all* the Community institutions.[27] The European Central Bank has the right to bring an action for failure to act "in the areas falling within [its] competence". Only the Court of Justice and the Court of First Instance have no such right of action. This is because they are responsible for legal protection and do not themselves seek it.[28] **8–012**

24 Schermers and Waelbroeck, *Judicial Protection*, pp. 350–453; Toth, "The Law as it stands on the Appeal for Failure to Act" (1975) 2 L.I.E.I. 65 at 82–83.

25 See paras 8–005, 8–006, above.

26 Joined Cases 10 and 18/68 *Eridania v. Commission* [1969] E.C.R. 459 at 483, para. 17, ECJ.

27 Case 13/83 *European Parliament v. Council* [1985] E.C.R. 1513 at 1588, paras 17–18, ECJ. Now that the Court of Auditors is an "institution" (E.C. Treaty, Art. 7 (*ex Art. 4*)), it may also bring an action for failure to act.

28 Opinion of Advocate General C.O. Lenz in Case 13/83 *European Parliament v. Council* [1985] E.C.R. 1513 at 1519, ECJ.

2. Individual applicants

8–013 Under the third paragraph of Article 232 (*ex Article 175*) of the E.C. Treaty, a natural or legal person may complain to the Court of First Instance that "an institution of the Community has failed to address to that person any act other than a recommendation or an opinion". An action brought by a natural or legal person can therefore relate only to a failure to adopt an act which has a direct influence on that person's legal position.[29]

8–014 The words "address to" preclude an applicant who is a natural or legal person from bringing an action for failure to adopt an act of general application.[30] On the other hand, in spite of the more stringent wording of the third paragraph of Article 232 (*ex Article 175*) by comparison with the fourth paragraph of Article 230 (*ex Article 173*) of the E.C. Treaty,[31] it is enough for a natural or legal person to be directly and individually concerned by the act which the institution failed to adopt and which, formally, ought to have been addressed to another person (for example a Member State). This is because the Court of Justice has held that Articles 230 and 232 (*ex Articles 173 and 175*) of the E.C. Treaty merely prescribe one and the same method of recourse.[32] Consequently, the subject-matter of the right of action of a natural or legal person is not confined to the defendant institution's failure expressly to address a particular act to the applicant.[33] The idea behind this is to underscore the parallel between the

---

[29] Case 6/70 *Borromeo v. Commission* [1970] E.C.R. 815, ECJ; Case 15/70 *Chevalley v. Commission* [1970] E.C.R. 975; ECJ; (Order of October 17, 1984), Joined Cases 83 and 84/84 *N.M. v. Commission and Council* [1984] E.C.R. 3571 at 3575, para. 10, ECJ; (Order of March 30, 1990), Case C–371/89 *Emrich v. Commission* [1990] E.C.R. I–1555 at I–1558, para. 6, ECJ; (Order of May 27, 1994), Case T–5/94 *J. v. Commission* [1994] E.C.R. II–391 at II–399, para. 16, CFI; (Order of July 4, 1994), Case T–13/94 *Century Oils Hellas v. Commission* [1994] E.C.R. II–431 at II–438, para. 13, CFI.

[30] Case 15/71 *Mackprang v. Commission* [1971] E.C.R. 797 at 804, para. 4, ECJ; Case 134/73 *Holtz v. Council* [1974] E.C.R. 1 at 10–11, para. 5, ECJ; Case 90/78 *Granaria v. Council and Commission* [1979] E.C.R. 1081 at 1092–1093, paras 12–15, ECJ; (Order of July 11, 1979), Case 60/79 *Producteurs de Vins de Table v. Commission* [1979] E.C.R. 2429 at 2433, ECJ; (Order of November 26, 1996), Case T–167/95 *Kuchlenz-Winter v. Council* [1996] E.C.R. II–1607 at II–1615—1616, para. 21, CFI. *Cf.* McDonagh, "Pour un élargissement des conditions de recevabilité des recours en contrôle de la légalité par des personnes privées en droit communautaire: le cas de l'article 175 *(now Article 232)* du traité CE" (1994) C.D.E. 607–637.

[31] See also E.C. Treaty, Art. 232 (*ex Art. 175*), para. 3, of which the French and German versions are consistent in this regard: "de lui addresser un acte autre qu'une recommendation ou un avis"; "einen anderen Akt als eine Empfehlung oder eine Stellungnahme an sie zu richten".

[32] Case 15/70 *Chevally v. Commission* [1970] E.C.R. 975 at 979, para. 6, ECJ; Case C–68/95 *T. Port v. Commission* [1996] E.C.R. I–6065 at I–6105, para. 59, ECJ.

[33] See Case 134/73 *Holtz v. Council* [1974] E.C.R. 1 at 10–11, para. 5, ECJ. "It appears that the action commenced by the applicant has the object of procuring a provision of a general regulatory character having the same legal scope as Regulation No 1336/72 and not an act concerning it directly and individually". An indirect interest which a natural or legal person might have in the adoption of the act requested is completely insufficient for him to be regarded as a potential addressee of the act, Case 246/81 *Lord Bethell v. Commission* [1982] E.C.R. 2277 at 2291, para. 16, ECJ. *Cf.* (Order of January 23, 1991), Case T–3/90 *Prodifarma v. Commission* [1991] E.C.R. II–1 at II–13—16, paras 34, 35, CFI; Case T–32/93 *Ladbroke Racing Ltd v. Commission* [1994] E.C.R. II–1015 at II–1032—1034, paras 40–43, CFI.

action for annulment and the action for failure to act as far as the measure at issue is concerned[34] on the ground that the possibility for individuals to assert their rights should not depend upon whether the institution concerned has acted or failed to act.[35]

3. Applicants in relation to Article 35 of the ECSC Treaty

"As the case may be", Member States, the Council and undertakings and associations[36] are entitled to bring an action for failure to act. The action is directed against the tacit refusal embodied in the failure to act. **8–015**

III. Special Characteristics

A. Pre-litigation procedure

1. The duty to raise the matter

An action for failure to act is admissible only if, before proceedings are brought, the defendant institution is requested to adopt the measure in question. The idea behind raising the matter with the institution in this way is to prompt it to adopt the measure within two months or at least to define its position in regard to the alleged failure to act.[37] The matter must be raised within a reasonable time after the applicant initially finds that there has been a failure to act. An eighteen-month period is unreasonable.[38] **8–016**

2. What has to be raised

The communication calling upon the defendant institution to act must make it clear that it is made pursuant to Article 232 (*ex Article 175*) of the E.C. Treaty or Article 35 of the ECSC Treaty, as the case may be.[39] In addition, it must indicate precisely what measure(s) of Community law the applicant expects the defendant to adopt.[40] Since only the person who calls upon the institution to act is entitled to bring an action, it is important that he or she should make his or her identity clear. **8–017**

---

[34] Case 247/87 *Star Fruit v. Commission* [1989] E.C.R. 291 at 301, para. 13, ECJ.

[35] Case C–68/95 *T. Port v. Commission* [1996] E.C.R. I–6065 at I–6105, para. 59, ECJ; (Judgment of September 15, 1998), Case T–95/96 *Gestevisión Telecinco v. Commission*, CFI (not yet reported) (finding of a failure to act on the part of the Commission following a complaint lodged by a competitor of the recipient of state aid, whereas the decision sought by the applicant would have had to be addressed to the Member State granting the aid).

[36] See paras 7–083, 7–084, above.

[37] Case 17/57 *De Gezamenlijke Steenkolenmijnen in Limburg v. High Authority* [1959] E.C.R. 1 at 8, ECJ.

[38] Case 59/70 *Netherlands v. Commission* [1971] E.C.R. 639 at 652–654, paras 12–24, ECJ.

[39] Case 13/83 *European Parliament v. Council* [1985] E.C.R. 1513 at 1589, para. 24, ECJ; Case 84/82 *Germany v. Commission* [1984] E.C.R. 1451 at 1491, para. 23, ECJ.

[40] Case 25/85 *Nuovo Campsider v. Commission* [1986] E.C.R. 1531 at 1539, para. 8, ECJ; Case T–28/90 *Asia Motor France and Others v. Commission* [1992] E.C.R. II–2285 at II–2297, para. 28, CFI.

3. Reaction of the institution put on notice

8–018 In order to have brought the failure to act in question to an end, the defendant institution must have "defined its position" within two months of its having been called upon to act (E.C. Treaty, Article 232 (*ex Article 175*), second paragraph). Once the defendant institution has defined its position, an action for failure to act will be inadmissible.

8–019 The reaction of the institution which has been called upon to act will be deemed to be a definition of a position within the meaning of the second paragraph of Article 232 (*ex Article 175*) of the E.C. Treaty only in so far as it explains the institution's stance with regard to the measure requested. It is the content and not the form of the definition of a position which determines whether this condition has been met. Accordingly, the institution called upon to act may reject a request to adopt a particular measure by letter,[41] telex[42] or impliedly by adopting a measure other than the one requested.

8–020 Although a definition of a position brings the failure to act to an end, thereby making it impossible to bring an action for failure to act any more,[43] it is not always in the nature of a binding act against which an action for annulment will lie.[44]

This will, of course, be the case where the invitation to act is made by a Community institution or a Member State with a view to the adoption of a preparatory act needed for the purpose of the Community's decision-making procedure.[45] The only way in which the Court of Justice can secure legal protection for the applicant in such a situation is to be relatively exacting in adjudging whether the content of the definition of a position is such as to bring the failure to act to an end. The reason is that, since an action for annulment is ruled out in any event as a potential means of

---

[41] Case 125/78 *Gema v. Commission* [1979] E.C.R. 3173 at 3188–3190, paras 14–23, ECJ.

[42] Case 42/71 *Nordgetreide v. Commission* [1972] E.C.R. 105 at 110, para. 4, ECJ.

[43] If the position defined by the institution concerned does not come up to the expectations of the person who requested the institution to act, that person may no longer challenge the position defined by means of an action for failure to act. This is because the E.C. Treaty, Art. 232 (*ex Art. 175*), refers to failure to take a decision or to define a position, and not to the adoption of a measure different from that desired or considered necessary by the person concerned: Case 8/71 *Komponistenverband v. Commission* [1971] E.C.R. 705 at 710, para. 2, ECJ; Joined Cases 166 and 220/86 *Irish Cement Ltd v. Commission* [1988] E.C.R. 6473 at 6503, para. 17, ECJ; (Order of November 12, 1996), Case T–47/96 *SDDDA v. Commission* [1996] E.C.R. II–1559 at II–1574, para. 40, CFI; (Order of November 26, 1996), Case T–164/95 *Kuchlenz-Winter v. European Parliament* [1996] E.C.R. II–1593 at II–1604—1605, para. 37, CFI; (Order of November 26, 1996), Case T–226/95 *Kuchlenz-Winter v. Commission* [1996] E.C.R. II–1619 at II–1629, para. 31, CFI; Case T–107/96 *Pantochim v. Commission* [1998] E.C.R. II–311 at 325, para. 30, CFI. Note also that, in a technical sense, proceedings under Art. 232 (*ex Art. 175*) may not be truly devoid of purpose once the institution has acted, since the applicant may wish to bring an action for damages under Art. 288 (*ex Art. 215*). But the applicant does not have to obtain judgment under Art. 232 before bringing an action for damages as the failure to act may be established in the Art. 288 proceedings, see Brealey and Hoskins, *Remedies in EC Law*, (cited in para. 1–004, n. 12, above) pp. 345–346.

[44] *Cf.* Barav, "Considérations sur la spécificité du recours en carence en droit communautaire" (1975) R.T.D.E. 53 at 61.

[45] See paras 7–016—7–018, 8–006, above.

recourse, the only avenue remaining is an action for failure to act if the defendant institution is not fulfilling its obligations and so blocking the Community's decision-making process.[46]

Even where the invitation to act comes from a natural or legal person, who, in principle, therefore has in mind the adoption of a binding act against which an action for annulment will lie, it is possible for the failure to act to be brought to an end by a non-binding definition of a position. The procedure for the investigation of complaints made pursuant to Article 3(2) of Regulation No. 17 affords an illustration. A complaint is lodged in the hope that the Commission will find that there has been an infringement of Article 81 or 82 (*ex Article 85 or 86*) of the E.C. Treaty. But the complainant is not entitled to a definitive decision from the Commission on the existence of the alleged infringement.[47] Yet it does have the right to a decision on the outcome which the Commission is to give to its complaint, so that, in the event that the complaint is rejected, it can be ensured of being able to bring an action against the decision rejecting the complaint and hence of securing judicial review by the Court of First Instance (and, possibly, the Court of Justice).[48] As we know, before the complaint is rejected, the Commission should send a letter to the complainant pursuant to Article 6 of Regulation No. 99/63 informing it of the reasons why it considers that on the basis of the information in its possession there are insufficient grounds for upholding the complaint and fixing a time-limit within which the complainant may make its views known in writing. Such a letter constitutes a definition of a position within the meaning of the second paragraph of Article 232 (*ex Article 175*) of the E.C. Treaty,[49] even though it is not a binding act against which an action for annulment will lie.[50] If the complainant wishes to avail itself of the procedure provided for in Article 232 (*ex Article 175*) of the E.C. Treaty in order to induce the Commission to take a decision on the outcome of its complaint, it will call on the Commission to take that decision (which, moreover, the complainant hopes will be favourable to it), not to send off a letter pursuant to Article 6 of

[46] Case 13/83 *European Parliament v. Council* [1985] E.C.R. 1513 at 1590, para. 25, ECJ. Moreover, it was in an interinstitutional context that the Court of Justice held—in all likelihood for these reasons—that an express refusal to act does not put an end to a failure to act: Case 302/87 *European Parliament v. Council* [1988] E.C.R. 5615 at 5641, para. 17, ECJ.

[47] Case 125/78 *Gema v. Commission* [1979] E.C.R. 3173 at 3189–3190, paras 17–18, ECJ.

[48] Case T–7/92 *Asia Motor France and Others v. Commission* [1993] E.C.R. II–669, CFI; *Cf.* (Order of November 29, 1993), Case T–56/92 *Koelman v. Commission* [1993] E.C.R. II–1267 at II–1277, paras 26–28, CFI (action for failure to act held to be to no purpose because the Commission had definitively rejected the complaint) and Case T–575/93 *Koelman v. Commission* [1996] E.C.R. II–1, CFI in which the applicant sought the annulment of the definitive rejection of its complaint.

[49] Case 125/78 *Gema v. Commission* [1979] E.C.R. 3173 at 3190, para. 21, ECJ; Case C–282/95P *Guérin Automobiles v. Commission* [1997] E.C.R. I–1503 at I–1541, para. 30, ECJ; (*cf.* the Opinion of Advocate General G. Tesauro in that case); Case T–186/94 *Guérin Automobiles v. Commission* [1995] E.C.R. II–1753 at II–1767, para. 26, CFI.

[50] Case T–64/89 *Automec v. Commission* [1990] E.C.R. II–367 at II–382—383, para. 46, CFI; Case T–186/94 *Guérin Automobiles v. Commission* (cited in n. 49, above) at II–1772, para. 41; Case T–38/96 *Guérin Automobiles v. Commission* [1997] E.C.R. II–1223 at II–1233, para. 31, CFI.

Regulation No. 99/63.[51] Only if the Commission is planning to reject its complaint, will it receive, under the normal procedure in such a case, a letter pursuant to Article 6 of Regulation No. 99/63, *i.e.* a definition of a position which is not a binding act.[52] This provisionally exhausts the complainant's possibilities of recourse, but not necessarily for long. This is because the initiative reverts to it. If it submits written observations within the prescribed period, the Commission must take a final decision on the outcome of the complaint in the light of those observations in a reasonable time.[53] If necessary, the complainant can call on the Commission pursuant to Article 232 (*ex Article 175*) of the E.C. Treaty to take the decision.[54] If the Commission rejects the complaint, the complainant may bring an action for annulment; if the Commission does nothing at all, an action for failure to act will lie.[55]

8–021 Under the ECSC Treaty, only a positive decision or a decision refusing the request on the part of the institution called upon to act can bring the failure to act to an end.[56] A mere expression of the institution's position which cannot be regarded as a decision does not terminate the failure to act.[57] However, the decision does not have to deal expressly with all the points raised in the invitation to act. An indirect answer suffices.[58]

8–022 The letter before action marks the starting point of the two-month period which the institution has in order to bring the failure to act to an end. If, during that period, the institution persists in its failure to act, Member States, institutions or natural or legal persons who have called upon it to act may bring an action before the Court of Justice or the Court of First

---

[51] Case T–28/90 *Asia Motor France and Others v. Commission* [1992] E.C.R. II–2285 at II–2297, para. 28, CFI.

[52] The fact that a complainant which requests that a decision be taken has to be satisfied in the first instance with an act which does not have the force of a decision, namely a definition of a position which does not bring the failure to act to an end, has to do with the Commission's obligation to take the intermediate step—designed to protect the complainant's interests—of notifying the draft decision, following which the complainant is entitled to submit observations. Sometimes, however, the decision is taken directly, whereupon an action will lie against it, see Case C–39/93P *SFEI and Others v. Commission* [1994] E.C.R. I–2681 at I–2709—2711, paras 24–33, ECJ.

[53] Case C–282/95P *Guérin Automobiles v. Commission* [1997] E.C.R. I–1503 at I–1543, para. 37, ECJ.

[54] *Cf.* Opinion of Judge D.A.O. Edward, appointed to act as Advocate General, in Case T–24/90 *Automec v. Commission* [1992] E.C.R. II–2223 at II–2230, point 23, CFI.

[55] An action for failure to act will not be held to have lost its purpose merely because the restriction of competition referred to in the complaint has been terminated following the intervention of the Commission, since that did not dispense the Commission from defining its position on the applicant's complaint in conformity with the procedural guarantees provided for in Regulation No. 17, Art. 3, and in Regulation No. 99/63, Art. 6. If, therefore, the Commission has failed to define its position on the complaint, the action does not lose its purpose in those circumstances: Case T–74/92 *Ladbroke v. Commission* [1995] E.C.R. II–115 at II–140—141, paras 66–67, CFI.

[56] Joined Cases 42 and 49/59 *SNUPAT v. High Authority* [1961] E.C.R. 101 at 73–74, para. 51, ECJ.

[57] Joined Cases 21–26/61 *Meroni & Co. v. High Authority* [1962] E.C.R. 73, ECJ.

[58] Joined Cases 5–11 and 13–15/62 *San Michele and Others v. High Authority* [1962] E.C.R. 449 at 459, ECJ.

Instance "within a further period of two months" (E.C. Treaty).[59] If the act in question is adopted after the action for failure to act has been brought but before judgment is given, the application becomes to no purpose.[60] In such a case, the defendant institution exposes itself to having an order for costs made against it.[61]

The letter before action also determines the subject-matter of the action. The action can relate only to a failure to act which has been previously so raised with the defendant institution.[62] **8–023**

B. Pleas in law

Under Article 232 (*ex Article 175*) of the E.C. Treaty, the only plea open to the applicant is that the failure to act constitutes "an infringement of this Treaty". As has already been mentioned, the expression "infringement of the Treaty" covers any Community provision under which an obligation to act arises for the defendant institution.[63] Some commentators maintain that an action will lie also against the defendant institution's failure to exercise a discretionary power where that failure amounts to a misuse of powers.[64] **8–024**

IV. Consequences

If the Court of First Instance or the Court of Justice finds that an institution has infringed the Treaty by failing to act, the institution is required under Article 233 (*ex Article 176*) of the E.C. Treaty to take the necessary measures to comply with the judgment. The scope of the judgment is limited. It merely reinforces the duty on the institution to act, but it does not take the place of the act which the institution failed to adopt. At most, the Court of Justice or the Court of First Instance may indicate what act is necessary in order to comply with its judgment.[65] **8–025**

---

59 *Cf.* ECSC Treaty, Art. 35, para. 3: "If at the end of two months the High Authority has not taken any decision or made any recommendation, proceedings may be instituted before the Court within one month against the implied decision of refusal which is to be inferred from the silence of the High Authority on the matter."

60 See para. 8–003, above.

61 Case 377/87 *European Parliament v. Council* [1988] E.C.R. 4017 at 4048, paras 8–10, ECJ; Case T–212/95 *Oficemen v. Commission* [1997] E.C.R. II–1161 at II–1182—1183, paras 72–75, CFI. See, however, (Order of November 26, 1997), Case T–39/97 *T. Port v. Commission* [1997] E.C.R. II–2125 at II–2135 para, 29, CFI.

62 Joined Cases 24 and 34/58 *Chambre Syndicale de la Sidérurgie de l'Est de la France and Others v. High Authority* [1960] E.C.R. 281 at 299, ECJ; Joined Cases 41 and 50/59 *Hamborner Bergbau v. High Authority* [1960] E.C.R. 493, ECJ; Case 75/69 *Hake v. Commission* [1970] E.C.R. 535 at 543, paras 8, 9, ECJ.

63 See para. 8–004, above.

64 Waelbroeck and Waelbroeck, *Répertoire du droit communautaire*, keyword: Carence (recours en), Paris, Ed. Dalloz, 1994/1, s.28. The argument is that the defendant institution's obligation is to bring to an end the "misuse of powers" (brought about by its failure to exercise the power). In practice, this comes very close to reading into the E.C. Treaty, Art. 232 (*ex Art. 175*) the case expressly contemplated by the ECSC Treaty, Art. 35, para. 2.

65 The Court does this in the body of the judgment, which helps to determine the scope of the operative part, *cf.* Joined Cases 97, 193, 99 and 215/86 *Asteris v. Commission* [1988] E.C.R. 2181 at 2208, paras 26–27, ECJ.

Chapter 9

THE OBJECTION OF ILLEGALITY

I. Subject-Matter

A. General

The objection of illegality as provided for in Article 241 (*ex Article 184*) of the E.C. Treaty (the third paragraph of Article 36 of the ECSC Treaty and Article 156 of the EAEC Treaty) does not constitute an independent right of action.[1] It is an incidental plea in law[2] intended to avoid the application of unlawful Community acts of general application to the detriment of persons who are not—or no longer[3]—entitled to challenge them.[4] **9–001**

Article 241 (*ex Article 184*) of the E.C. Treaty (just as the third paragraph of Article 36 of the ECSC Treaty): **9–002**

> "gives expression to a general principle conferring upon any party to proceedings the right to challenge, for the purpose of obtaining the annulment of a decision of direct and individual concern to that party, the validity of previous acts of the institutions which form the legal basis of the decision which is being attacked, if that party was not entitled under Article 173 (*now Article 230*) of the Treaty to bring a direct action challenging those acts by which it was thus affected without having been in a position to ask that they be declared void".[5]

---

1 Case 33/80 *Albini v. Council and Commission* [1981] E.C.R. 2141 at 2157, para. 17, ECJ; Joined Cases 87 and 130/77, 22/83, 9 and 10/84 *Salerno v. Commission and Council* [1985] E.C.R. 2523 at 2536 para. 36, ECJ.

2 See Van Rijn, *Exceptie van onwettigheid en prejudiciële procedure inzake geldigheid van gemeenschapshandelingen*, Deventer, Kluwer, 1978, pp. 140–143, Smit and Herzog (now Campbell and Powers), *The Law of the European Community*, New York, Matthew Bender & Co., 1976, paras 5–540—541; Brealey and Hoskins, *Remedies in EC Law*, (cited in para. 1–004, n. 12, above), pp. 331–332.

3 For the question of who is entitled to raise an objection of illegality, see paras 9–007—9–012, below.

4 Joined Cases 31 and 33/62 *Wöhrmann and Others v. Commission* [1962] E.C.R. 501 at 507, ECJ. See also Barav, "The Exception of Illegality in Community Law: A Critical Analysis" (1974) C.M.L.Rev. 366 at 368.

5 Case 92/78 *Simmenthal v. Commission* [1979] E.C.R. 777 at 800, para. 39, ECJ. See also Case 9/56 *Meroni & Co. v. High Authority* [1957 and 1958] E.C.R. 133 at 140, ECJ; Case 10/56 *Meroni & Co. v. High Authority* [1957 and 1958] E.C.R. 156 at 162–163, ECJ; Case 15/57 *Compagnie des Hauts Fournaux de Chasse v. High Authority* [1957 and 1958] E.C.R. 211 at 224–225, ECJ; Case 262/80 *Andersen v. European Parliament* [1984] E.C.R. 195 at 203, para. 6, ECJ; Joined Cases T–6 and T–52/92 *Reinarz v. Commission* [1993] E.C.R. II–1047 at II–1072, para. 56, CFI; Case T–64/92 *Chavane de Dalmassy and Others v. Commission* [1994] E.C.R.–S.C. II–723 at II–736 para. 41 (English abstract at I–A-227), CFI.

It follows that the field of application of Article 241 (*ex Article 184*)—according to which an objection of illegality may be raised only against a regulation—extends to "acts of the institutions which, although they are not in the form of a regulation, nevertheless produce similar effects and on those grounds may not be challenged under Article 173 (*now Article 230*) by natural or legal persons other than Community institutions or Member States".[6] In so deciding, the Court of Justice intimated that the essential function of the objection of illegality is to enable natural and legal persons to have set aside an act against which they cannot bring an action for annulment under the fourth paragraph of Article 230 of the E.C. Treaty, in a case where they seek the annulment by the Court of First Instance of an implementing measure adopted by the Community on the basis of that act. As yet, the case law affords no answer to the question whether this is the only function of the objection of illegality.[7]

B. Acts against which an objection of illegality may be raised

9–003 Under Article 241 (*ex Article 184*) of the E.C. Treaty, an objection of illegality may be raised in respect of "a regulation of the Council, of the Commission, or of the ECB [European Central Bank]" or "a regulation adopted jointly by the European Parliament and the Council". But, as has already been mentioned, for the purposes of the application of Article 241, any measure having similar effects to a regulation will be treated as if it were a regulation provided that natural or legal persons cannot bring an action for annulment against it pursuant to the fourth paragraph of Article 231 (*ex Article 173*) of the E.C. Treaty.[8]

9–004 The third paragraph of Article 36 of the ECSC Treaty enables an applicant to raise an objection of illegality in support of an application for annulment brought against a "decision or a recommendation" which it has allegedly not observed. Because the objection of illegality is deemed to be the application of a "general principle" also in the context of the ECSC Treaty, it may in fact be raised against any act constituting the legal basis of an individual act, even outside the context of the imposition of fines and periodic penalty payments with which the first and second paragraphs of Article 36 of the ECSC Treaty deal.[9]

9–005 Although a literal interpretation of the third paragraph of Article 36 of the ECSC Treaty might perhaps have allowed applicants to raise an objection of illegality in respect of individual decisions which they could have contested in an action, the case law is resolutely opposed to such a possibility.[10] Also in the context of the E.C. Treaty, a party to proceedings is

---

[6] Case 92/78 *Simmenthal v. Commission*, (cited in n. 5, above), para. 40.

[7] See para. 9–009, below.

[8] See para. 9–002, above.

[9] Case 9/56 *Meroni & Co. v. High Authority* [1957 and 1958] E.C.R. 133 at 140, ECJ.

[10] Case 3/59 *Germany v. High Authority* [1960] E.C.R. 53 at 61, ECJ; Case 270/82 *Estel v. Commission* [1984] E.C.R. 1195 at 1214, para. 11, ECJ; Case 81/83 *Busseni v. Commission* [1984] E.C.R1. 2951 at 2961, para. 12, ECJ; Case 64/84 *Queenborough Rolling Mill Company v. Commission* [1985] E.C.R. 1829 at 1853, para. 16, ECJ; Case 67/84 *Sideradria v. Commission* [1985] E.C.R. 3983 at 3992–3993, para. 15, ECJ; Case T–26/90 *Finsider v. Commission* [1992] E.C.R. II–1789 at II–1809, para. 61, CFI.

not entitled to rely on Article 241 (*ex Article 184*) in order to challenge the legality of a decision addressed to it when it could have applied for its annulment under Article 230 (*ex Article 173*).[11] Legal certainty would be jeopardised if a party could still challenge such a decision by means of an objection of illegality after the time-limit for bringing proceedings against it had expired.[12] The only case in which such an objection might be upheld is the exceptional one in which the contested decision contained such particularly serious and manifest defects that it must be deemed non-existent.[13]

Article 241 of the E.C. Treaty requires the regulation in respect of which the objection of illegality is raised to be "at issue". In the light of the essential function of the objection,[14] the case law has interpreted that requirement as meaning that the general measure against which the objection is raised must constitute the legal basis of the individual measure which is being directly challenged.[15] The upshot is that, in principle, an objection of illegality may be raised only against the provisions of a general act which the individual act implements.[16] Nevertheless, other provisions of the general act may be affected by the objection if they are applicable to "the issue with which the application is concerned".[17]

With the same concern to guarantee the essential function of the objection of illegality, it is considered in the case law that such an objection may be raised against any act which cannot be contested for one reason or another, but whose content was nevertheless determinative in the adoption of individual acts which may be directly challenged.[18] Thus, the Court of Justice has assessed, via an objection of illegality, the lawfulness of a letter in which the High Authority gave directions for interpretation to a body which had to apply only articles of the Treaty and secondary Community legislation, after finding that the letter did not constitute an act against **9–006**

---

[11] Case 156/77 *Commission v. Belgium* [1978] E.C.R. 1881 at 1896, para. 20, ECJ. See also para. 9–009, below.

[12] *ibid.*, at 1896, para. 21.

[13] Case 226/87 *Commission v. Greece* [1988] E.C.R. 3611 at 3624, para. 16, ECJ.

[14] See para. 9–002, above.

[15] Case 21/64 *Macchiorlati Dalmas v. High Authority* [1965] E.C.R. 175 at 187–188, ECJ (where the Court of Justice referred to a "direct legal connection between the contested measure and the . . . general decisions").

[16] Joined Cases 275/80 and 24/81 *Krupp v. Commission* [1981] E.C.R. 2489 at 2517–2518, para. 32, ECJ.

[17] Case 32/65 *Italy v. Council and Commission* [1966] E.C.R. 389 at 409, ECJ. *Cf.* Case 18/62 *Barge v. High Authority* [1963] E.C.R. 259 at 279–280, ECJ; Joined Cases 140, 146, 221 and 226/82 *Walzstahl-Vereinigung and Thyssen v. Commission* [1984] E.C.R. 951 at 983, para. 20, ECJ. See also Van Rijn, (cited in n. 2, above), p. 194.

[18] Waelbroeck therefore suggests that an objection of illegality should be allowed to be raised against any general act, such as decisions approving the budget or directives addressed to all the Member States (see *Commentaire Mégret*, at 389, together with the academic writings cited in support in n. 9); see also the considerations put forward by Van Rijn (cited in n. 2, above), pp. 167–186, who considers the availability of the objection of illegality against various sorts of acts in detail; in contrast, Lauwaars argues, on the basis of the clear wording of E.C. Treaty, Art. 241 (*ex Art. 184)*, that objections of illegality should be able to be raised only against "regulations" (naturally in the substantive sense of the term) (Lauwaars (cited in para. 8–006, n. 11, above), p. 276).

which an action would lie.[19] In practice, however, the inquiry into the legality of such directions for interpretation will generally coincide with the Court's interpretation of the provisions of Community law to which they relate. If the directions for interpretation are consistent with the Court's interpretation, they will be "lawful", otherwise not. The legality of the individual act therefore does not actually depend so much on the "legality" of the directions for interpretation, as on whether the interpretation of the provisions of Community law which they apply is or is not correct.

II. Identity of the Parties

9–007 Under Article 241 (*ex Article 184*) of the E.C. Treaty, "any party" may raise an objection of illegality.

9–008 Those words cover, first, natural or legal persons who are unable to challenge before the Court of First Instance the act against which the objection is raised.[20]

Even if the act is only formally a regulation which is of direct and individual concern to a given natural or legal person within the meaning of the fourth paragraph of Article 230 (*ex Article 173*) of the E.C. Treaty, it must nevertheless still be possible to raise an objection of illegality against that "regulation". The natural or legal person must in fact be able to proceed on the basis of the impression created by the Community institution which adopted the act (even if that does not prevent that person—if he or she so elects—to transcend that impression by bringing an action for annulment pursuant to the fourth paragraph of Article 230).[21]

9–009 There is a school of thought in the literature to the effect that the fact that Member States and Community institutions may bring an action for annulment against *any* binding Community act precludes them from making use of the objection of illegality on the ground that, if they could, they would effectually be able to start time running again in breach of the principle of legal certainty.[22] But this view is not shared by all commentators. Some argue that Member States and Community institutions may also have recourse to Article 241 (*ex Article 184*) of the E.C. Treaty with a view to a finding that regulations and similar acts which are "at issue" are unlawful, even though they have not taken advantage of their right to bring an action for annulment against the acts in question within the period prescribed for bringing proceedings. This argument relies principally on the wording of Article 241 ("any party"), whilst referring at the same time to the ancillary function of the objection of illegality of avoiding the application of regulations and similar acts whose deficiencies and possible

[19] Joined Cases 32 and 33/58 *SNUPAT v. High Authority* [1959] E.C.R. 127 at 141, ECJ.
[20] See para. 9–002, above.
[21] *Cf. Commentaire Mégret*, at 389.
[22] Bebr, "Judicial Remedy of Private Parties against Normative Acts of the European Communities: The Role of Exception of Illegality" (1966) C.M.L.Rev. 7 at 11–13; Usher, "The Interrelationship of Articles 173, 177 and 184 *[now Articles 230, 234 and 241]* EEC" (1979) E.L.Rev. 36 at 37; Joliet, *Le contentieux*, pp, 134 *et seq.*

illegality become apparent to Member States or Community institutions after the time-limit for bringing proceedings has passed when they are implemented or raised in judicial proceedings.[23] The unlawful nature of an act may not in fact appear so much on its face as from the manner in which it is interpreted and applied.

A number of Advocates General of the Court of Justice have expressed the view in opinions that the wording of Article 241 does not preclude Member States and Community institutions from raising an objection of illegality.[24] On this view, the possibility of Member States' or Community institutions' raising such an objection is not even subject to any limitation, because Article 241 does not so provide. Thus, a Member State does not have to show that there was a good reason why it did not act in time in bringing an action for annulment against the regulation or similar act at issue or that it was taken by surprise—after the time-limit for bringing an action for annulment had passed—by the interpretation given to the act, which raised doubts as to its legality.[25]

The Court of Justice has yet to rule expressly on this question. It has, however, implicitly accepted the position argued for by certain of its Advocates General when a Member State raised an objection of illegality against provisions of a Council regulation and a Commission regulation in an action for the annulment of another Council regulation. Although it did not consider whether Member States were entitled to invoke Article 241, it did reject the objection on the ground that it was directed against provisions of regulations which were not applicable to the issue with which the application was concerned.[26]

This reasoning does not lose its force because the Court of Justice has not accepted that a Member State may raise an objection of illegality to contest decisions addressed to it, when it did not bring an action for annulment against them within the prescribed time-limit.[27] This is because the relevant case law is based on the consideration that "the objection provided for in Article 184 *[now Article 241]* of the Treaty is limited under

[23] See to that effect Lauwaars (cited in para. 8–006, n. 11, above), pp. 277–279, who systematically refutes Bebr's arguments (cited in n. 22, above). See also Barav (cited in n. 4, above), at 371; Van Rijn (cited in n. 2, above), p. 160; Dubois, "L'exception d'illégalité devant la Cour de Justice des Communautés européennes" (1978) C.D.E. 407 at 411–413.

[24] Opinion of Advocate General K. Roemer in Case 32/65 *Italy v. Council and Commission* [1966] E.C.R. 389 at 414, ECJ; Opinion of Advocate General Sir Gordon Slynn in Case 181/85 *France v. Commission* [1987] E.C.R. 689 at 702–703, ECJ; Opinion of Advocate General G.F. Mancini in Case 204/86 *Greece v. Council* [1988] E.C.R. 5323 at 5343–5345, ECJ.

[25] Opinion of Advocate General Sir Gordon Slynn in Case 181/85 *France v. Commission* [1987] E.C.R. 689 at 703, ECJ.

[26] Case 32/65 *Italy v. Council and Commission* [1966] E.C.R. 389 at 409–410, ECJ. However, in a somehat ambiguous *obiter dictum* in Case C–135/93 *Spain v. Commission* [1995] E.C.R. I–1651 at I–1679, para. 17, ECJ, the Court of Justice held that, in an action for annulment, Member States could not "raise a plea of illegality" against an earlier act of the same kind, "annulment of which [they] could have sought directly". The decision at issue in that case, which could not be classified as a regulation or a decision at first sight, was concerned with extending the validity of a Community framework for state aid to the motor vehicle industry adopted under the EEC Treaty, Art. 93 (*now Art. 88*) (1).

[27] Case 156/77 *Commission v. Belgium* [1978] E.C.R. 1881 at 1896, para. 21, ECJ.

that provision to proceedings 'in which a regulation of the Council or of the Commission is [at] issue' " and therefore can in no case be raised by an addressee of an individual decision against that decision.[28] As such, that consideration equally applies to natural or legal persons raising objections of illegality against decisions addressed to them. Consequently, it is impossible to infer from this any conclusion whatsoever with regard to Member States' or Community institutions' capacity to raise an objection of illegality in respect of regulations and similar acts.[29]

As far as the possibility of raising an objection of illegality against a directive is concerned, the position is still not quite clear. The argument raised against this possibility is that Article 241 (*ex Article 184*) refers only to "regulations", that is to say, acts of general application which enter into effect as a result of publication and not of notification since they are not addressed to specific persons. On the other hand, just like some decisions, directives are addressed to the Member States and, precisely like decisions, must be contested within the time-limit for bringing proceedings prescribed by the fifth paragraph of Article 230 (*ex Article 173*) of the E.C. Treaty.[30] However, a somewhat different complexion has been put on this by the new Article 254 (*ex Article 191*) (2) of the E.C. Treaty (introduced by the E.U. Treaty). Directives which are addressed to all the Member States are henceforth to be published in the *Official Journal of the European Communities* in the same way as regulations and are to enter into force, no longer upon notification to the Member States, but—again as in the case of regulations—on the 20th day following that of their publication (unless they specify otherwise). What is involved therefore is directives of a general legislative character whose content and possible illegality might only become apparent—precisely as in the case of regulations and similar acts—after the time for bringing proceedings has run out, for example, when the Commission informs the Member States of the precise content of their obligations in terms of implementation.

It is to be expected that the question as to whether Member States may raise an objection of illegality in respect of regulations and similar acts, and also of directives addressed to all Member States within the meaning of Article 254 (*ex Article 191*) (2) of the E.C. Treaty, will arise in its most acute form where a Member State raises such an objection as a defence against an action for failure to fulfil obligations brought by the Commission or another Member State.[31]

9–010 Both applicants and defendants are entitled to raise an objection of illegality with a view to having a case decided in their favour.[32]

[28] *ibid.*, at 1897, para. 22.

[29] See also Van Rijn, case note to Case 156/77 *Commission v. Belgium* (1980) C.D.E. 190 at 193.

[30] See, to that effect, Case C–74/91 *Commission v. Germany* [1992] E.C.R. I–5437 at I–5466, para. 10, ECJ.

[31] See para. 5–058, above.

[32] Waelbroeck and Waelbroeck (cited in para. 8–024, n. 64, above), key words: Exception d'illégalité, 1994/2.

In principle, an objection of illegality must be raised by one of the parties. Nevertheless, exceptionally, the Court of Justice or the Court of First Instance may consider whether a general act constituting the basis for the measure contested in the proceedings is unlawful of its own motion.[33] The Court may do so in particular where the general act may possibly be unlawful for lack of competence or infringement of an essential procedural requirement.[34] **9–011**

III. Special Characteristics

A. Requirements for admissibility

An objection of illegality will be admissible only in so far as the direct action in connection with which it is raised is admissible.[35] The applicant's interest in successfully raising an objection of illegality against the general act on which the contested individual measure is based coincides with its interest in its succeeding with its application for the annulment of that measure. If the general act is declared inapplicable, the individual measure loses its legal basis and the action for annulment of that measure will succeed. If the objection is raised by the defendant, its interest in obtaining a declaration that a Community act which it has allegedly infringed is inapplicable is likewise self-evident. **9–012**

As already noted, an objection of illegality may be raised only in respect of a general act which is applicable to the issue with which the application is concerned.[36] **9–013**

An objection of illegality may be raised against general acts outside the time-limit for bringing an action for annulment against them. This follows from the essential nature of the objection[37]; it is also confirmed by Article 241 (*ex Article 184*) of the E.C. Treaty. **9–014**

B. Actions in which an objection of illegality may be raised

An objection of illegality may be raised after any direct action has been brought before the Court of Justice or the Court of First Instance. As we have already seen, objections of illegality are raised most often after an action for annulment has been brought. **9–015**

Such an objection may also be raised, however, in proceedings for failure to act, either by the defendant institution, where it asserts that the general act which—the applicant claims—gives rise to an obligation for it to act is

[33] Case 14/59 *Société des Fonderies de Pont-à-Mousson v. High Authority* [1959] E.C.R. 215 at 230, ECJ.
[34] See para. 7–092, above.
[35] Opinion of Advocate General F. Capotorti in Case 48/76 *Reinarz v. Commission* [1977] E.C.R. 291 at 301, ECJ.
[36] See para. 9–005, above.
[37] Case 185/85 *Usinor v. Commission* [1986] E.C.R. 2079 at 2096, para. 11, ECJ.

unlawful, or by the applicant, where it argues that a general act which the defendant institution invokes in order to deny the existence of any obligation to act is unlawful.[38]

In addition, according to a major school of thought among academic writers and consistently with indirect indications in the case law, it should be possible for a Member State to defend itself against an action for failure to fulfil obligations by raising an objection of illegality against a regulation or similar act and, possibly, against a directive addressed to all Member States within the meaning of Article 254 (*ex Article 191*) (2) of the E.C. Treaty which it is alleged to have infringed.[39]

In principle, it is also possible to raise an objection of illegality in an action for damages.[40] In practice, however, recourse to such an objection in this connection will be of little utility. The illegality of the general act against which the objection is raised admittedly results in the act being declared inapplicable, but it does not as such result in a determination that the Community has incurred liability, irrespective of whether the general act allegedly caused damage as a result of its direct effect or because it served as the legal basis for individual implementing measures.[41]

Lastly, an objection of illegality assumes importance in staff cases.[42]

9–016 An objection of illegality *cannot* be raised before the Court of Justice in proceedings for a preliminary ruling. That procedure simply reflects a relationship of co-operation between the national courts and the Court of Justice. The national court determines the question(s) to be brought before the Court of Justice and the parties to the main proceedings are not entitled to alter their scope.[43] Yet, "according to a general principle of law which finds its expression in Article 184 *[now Article 241]* of the E[E]C Treaty", interested parties in the main proceedings must be able to plead the illegality of the Community act on which the national decision adopted in their regard was based.[44] If they do so, the national court may (or must) apply to the Court of Justice for a preliminary ruling on the validity of the Community act at issue.[45]

---

[38] Joined Cases 32 and 33/58 *SNUPAT v. High Authority* [1959] E.C.R. 127 at 139, ECJ (in that ECSC case, the action for failure to act was in fact an action to annul a tacit refusal). It is not as easy to raise an objection of illegality in proceedings for failure to act brought pursuant to the E.C. Treaty, Art. 232 (*ex Art. 175*). Where the institution concerned has failed to act, the applicant can only presume on what general measure the failure to act is based. Once the institution indicates the general act on which its failure to act is based, it has defined its position and the action for failure to act becomes inadmissible, see Van Rijn (cited in n. 2, above), p. 151.

[39] See para. 9–009, above.

[40] Lauwaars (cited in para. 8–006, n. 11, above), p. 279.

[41] *Cf.* Dubois (cited in n. 23, above), at 433.

[42] Case 102/63 *Boursin v. High Authority* [1964] E.C.R. 691, ECJ; Joined Cases 75 and 117/82 *Razzouk and Beydoun v. Commission* [1984] E.C.R. 1509 at 1529–1530, paras 15–18, ECJ.

[43] Case 44/65 *Hessische Knappschaft v. Singer* [1965] E.C.R. 965 at 970, ECJ.

[44] Case 216/82 *Universität Hamburg v. Hauptzollamt Hamburg-Kehrwieder* [1983] E.C.R. 2771 at 2787–2788, para. 10, ECJ.

[45] See Chap. 10, below.

C. Pleas in law

By virtue of Article 241 (*ex Article 184*) of the E.C. Treaty, any party may plead "the grounds specified in the second paragraph of Article 173 *[now Article 230]*" in order to claim that an allegedly unlawful regulation is inapplicable. The pleas of lack of competence, infringement of an essential procedural requirement, infringement of the Treaty or of any rule of law relating to its application or misuse of powers[46] are therefore potentially available in support of an objection of illegality.[47] **9–017**

IV. Consequences

If an objection of illegality is successfully raised, the general act to which it relates is declared inapplicable for the purposes of the proceedings in which the objection was raised. It is inapplicable only in relation to the parties involved in those proceedings.[48] The general act subsists as far as third parties are concerned.[49] **9–018**

Nevertheless the institution which adopted the act declared inapplicable is under a duty to withdraw or adjust the act in order to eliminate the illegality found.[50] **9–019**

---

46 See paras 7–091 *et seq.*, above.

47 This also applies where an objection is raised pursuant to the ECSC Treaty, Art. 36, para. 3, alleging that a general decision or recommendation is "illegal". See also Case 9/56 *Meroni and Co. v. High Authority* [1957 and 1958] E.C.R. 133 at 139–140, ECJ; Case 10/56 *Meroni and Co. v. High Authority* [1957 and 1958] E.C.R. 157 at 162, ECJ. See also Van Rijn (cited in n. 2, above), pp. 195–199.

48 Joined Cases 15–33, 52–53, 57–109, 116–117, 123, 132, 135–137/73 *Schots-Kortner v. Commission and European Parliament* [1974] E.C.R. 177 at 191, para. 36, ECJ. See also Van Rijn (see n. 2, above), pp. 199–205.

49 Nevertheless, the declaration that the act is inapplicable may have indirect effects on third parties. For example, if the implementation of the general act was determined by an individual act which was addressed to a number of persons, the annulment of the implementing measure on account of the non-applicability of the general act might also alter the legal position of persons to whom the implementing measure was addressed but who did not bring proceedings against it (Lauwaars (cited in para. 8–004, n. 11, above), pp. 283–284). In such an event, the Court of Justice or the Court of First Instance may of course restrict the effects of the declaration of nullity if such a step is necessary to protect the interests of third parties (see paras 7–134, 7–135, above). For an example, see, Case C–242/90P *Commission v. Albani and Others* [1993] E.C.R. I–3839 at I–3869—3870, paras 13–16, ECJ.

50 Opinion of Advocate General M. Lagrange in Case 14/59 *Société des Fonderies de Pont-à-Mousson v. High Authority* [1959] E.C.R. 215 at 242, ECJ who refers to "the need—moral if not legal—to adopt a new decision", and in Joined Cases 14, 16–17, 20, 24, 26–27/60 and 1/61 *Meroni & Co. v. High Authority* [1961] E.C.R. 161 at 174, ECJ; Opinion of Advocate General K. Roemer in Joined Cases 9 and 12/60 *Vloeberghs v. High Authority* [1961] E.C.R. 197 at 227, ECJ. *Cf.* Joined Cases 75 and 117/82 *Razzouk and Beydoun v. Commission* [1984] E.C.R. 1509 at 1530–1531, para. 19, ECJ.

CHAPTER 10

DETERMINATION OF THE VALIDITY OF COMMUNITY ACTS BY REFERENCES FOR PRELIMINARY RULINGS

The three Treaties confer jurisdiction on the Court of Justice to give preliminary rulings[1] on the "validity" of Community acts ("acts of the institutions of the Communities and of the ECB [European Central Bank]": E.C. Treaty, Article 234 (*ex Article 177*), first paragraph, indent (b); EAEC Treaty, Article 150, which has the same wording but makes no reference to the ECB; ECSC Treaty, Article 41: "acts of the High Authority and the Council"). What this involves is a review of the validity of a given Community act as a step in proceedings before a national court in which the validity of that act is in issue, but the national court does not resolve that question itself, referring it instead to the Court of Justice for its assessment. Article 41 of the ECSC Treaty puts the national court under an obligation to do so. Article 234 (*ex Article 177*) of the E.C. Treaty and Article 150 of the EAEC Treaty contain no such obligation or at least not for courts and tribunals against whose decisions there is a "judicial remedy under national law"[2] but, as already mentioned, the Court of Justice has decided that even the former have no jurisdiction themselves to declare that Community acts are invalid. Consequently, they too are under an obligation to submit the question of validity to the Court of Justice[3] whenever they regard a Community act as invalid.[4] **10–001**

The subject-matter covered by the review of validity will now be considered, followed by its content and consequences.

I. SUBJECT-MATTER OF PRELIMINARY RULING PROCEEDINGS RELATING TO THE VALIDITY OF A COMMUNITY ACT

The Treaties themselves and all other rules of constitutional rank fall outside the ambit of preliminary rulings on the validity of Community acts. Those rules constitute in fact the yardstick against which the validity of such acts is reviewed. **10–002**

---

[1] See paras 2–001 *et seq.*, above.
[2] See paras 2–045, 2–046, above.
[3] See para. 2–055, above.
[4] Case 314/85 *Foto-Frost v. Hauptzollamt Lübeck-Ost* [1987] E.C.R. 4199 at 4230–4232, paras 12–20, ECJ.

10–003 In addition, the Court of Justice has held that "a preliminary ruling of the Court does not rank among the acts of the Community institutions whose validity is open to review in proceedings under Article 177 *[now Article 234]*".[5] Undoubtedly, that ruling must be extended to cover any judgment of the Court of Justice, which, as a result, remains outside the scope of review by way of preliminary rulings on validity.

10–004 A trickier question is whether the validity of international agreements concluded by the Community may be reviewed in preliminary ruling proceedings. Textbook writers have voiced great reservations,[6] chiefly on the ground that, in the event that it failed to give effect to such agreements, the Community might stand to incur liability at international level. Moreover, it was for that reason that the Treaty introduced a procedure whereby the Court of Justice gives a prior opinion on the compatibility of proposed international agreements with the provisions of the treaties (which means in practice with Community constitutional law as a whole).[7] However, it is no simple matter to exclude international agreements concluded by the Community from the scope of the review of validity under the preliminary ruling procedure.

In the first place, this is because the Court of Justice has regarded such agreements as acts of the institutions coming under its jurisdiction to give preliminary rulings.[8] Since indent (b) of the first paragraph of Article 234 (*ex Article 177*) of the E.C. Treaty draws no distinction between preliminary rulings on the validity of acts of the institutions as opposed to preliminary rulings on their interpretation, if the Court of Justice holds that it has jurisdiction to interpret international agreements by preliminary ruling, it creates the impression that it also has jurisdiction to review their validity.

What is more, a *dictum* of the Court of Justice has further reinforced this impression:

> "The question whether the conclusion of a given agreement is within the power of the Community and whether, in a given case, such power has been exercised in conformity with the provisions of the Treaty is, in principle, a question which may be submitted to the Court of Justice . . . in accordance with the preliminary procedure".[9]

This passage has been understood to mean that the Court of Justice should review the validity of the act whereby the Community purported to conclude the agreement, but not the validity of the agreement itself.[10] But that reading of the Court's case law does not resolve the question of the

[5] (Order of March 5, 1986), Case 69/85 *Wünsche v. Germany* [1986] E.C.R. 947 at 953, para. 16, ECJ.

[6] See Joliet, *Le contentieux*, p. 198; *Commentaire Mégret*, at 214–215.

[7] See Chap. 12, below.

[8] See para. 6–018, above.

[9] Opinion 1/75 [1975] E.C.R. 1355 at 1361, ECJ.

[10] Joliet, *Le contentieux*, pp. 59–60 and 198; Bebr, *Development of Judicial Control of the European Communities*, The Hague, Martinus Nijhoff, 1981, p. 469; Van Rijn (cited in para. 9–001, n. 2, above), p. 236.

possible liability of the Community at international level, since if the act by which the Community purported to conclude an international agreement is declared invalid, it will lose all binding force in the Community legal order, just as if the agreement itself was to be declared invalid.[11]

Yet this did not stop the Court of Justice in its 1994 judgment in *France v. Commission* from declaring void "the act whereby the Commission of the European Communities sought to conclude the Agreement with the United States of America regarding the application of the competition laws of the European Communities and the United States, which was signed and entered into force on 23 September 1991"[12] (essentially on the ground that the Commission had disregarded the Council's powers under Article 228 *[now Article 300]* of the EEC Treaty). Although "[i]n the event of non-performance of the Agreement by the Commission . . . the Community could incur liability at international level",[13] the Court of Justice held that the action for annulment of the act whereby the Commission sought to conclude the agreement was admissible, on the ground that, "as is apparent from its actual wording, the Agreement [on which that act was based was] intended to produce legal effects" within the meaning of the *AETR Case*.[14] In addition, it held that "[e]xercise of the powers delegated to the Community institutions in international matters cannot escape judicial review, under Article 173 *[now Article 230]* of the Treaty, of the legality of the acts adopted".[15]

Given that the Court of Justice considers the action for annulment and the preliminary ruling on validity to be two mechanisms in the same system of judicial review at Community level,[16] it would seem probable that the Court would not assess the legality of an act by which the Community sought to conclude an international agreement any differently if this question were to be raised by a national court in a reference for a preliminary ruling on the validity of that act.

In principle, when it comes to reviewing the validity of "acts of the institutions" in preliminary ruling proceedings, the expression is to be given a broad interpretation in order to ensure that the system of legal protection is as "full" as possible.[17] Consequently, the validity of acts of the Council, the Commission, the European Parliament and the Court of Auditors, all **10–005**

---

[11] *Commentaire Mégret*, at 214.

[12] Case C–327/91 *France v. Commission* [1994] E.C.R. I–3641, ECJ. For a critical commentary, see Kaddous, "L'arrêt *France* c. *Commission* de 1994 (Accord concurrence) et le contrôle de la 'légalité' des accords externes en vertu de l'art. 173 *[now Article 230]* CE: la difficile réconciliation de l'orthodoxie communautaire avec l'orthodoxie internationale" (1996) C.D.E. 613–633.

[13] *ibid.*, at I–3674, para. 25.

[14] Case 22/70 *Commission v. Council* [1971] E.C.R. 263 at 274, paras 14–15, ECJ.

[15] Case C–327/91 *France v. Commission* [1994] E.C.R. I–3641 at I–3672, para. 16, ECJ.

[16] Case 112/83 *Produits de Maïs v. Administration des Douanes et Droits Indirects* [1985] E.C.R. 719 at 747–748, para. 17, ECJ; Case 294/83 *Les Verts v. European Parliament* [1986] E.C.R. 1339 at 1365, para. 23, ECJ; Case 314/85 *Foto-Frost v. Hauptzollamt Lübeck-Ost* [1987] E.C.R. 4199 at 4231, para. 16, ECJ.

[17] *Cf.* Case 25/62 *Plaumann & Co. v. Commission* [1963] E.C.R. 95 at 107, ECJ: provisions of the Treaty regarding the right of interested persons to bring an action must not be interpreted restrictively.

institutions of the Community within the meaning of Article 7 (*ex Article 4*) of the E.C. Treaty, may unquestionably all be reviewed under the preliminary ruling procedure.[18] It goes without saying that this also applies to acts adopted jointly by the European Parliament and the Council under the co-decision procedure provided for in Article 251 (*ex Article 189b*) of the E.C. Treaty. In addition, indent (b) of the first paragraph of Article 234 (*ex Article 177*) also makes acts of the European Central Bank (E.C. Treaty, Article 8 (*ex Article 4a*) subject to review of their validity under the preliminary ruling procedure.[19]

10–006 Acts of bodies or agencies set up by Community institutions to which powers of executive decision have been delegated by those institutions also come within the jurisdiction of the Court of Justice to give preliminary rulings on validity.[20] This is because the Court of Justice has made the compatibility with the Treaty of such a delegation of powers dependent upon its complying with the Treaty provisions to which the exercise of the powers by the delegating institution would have been subject, including the Treaty provisions on judicial supervision, had that institution exercised the powers itself.[21]

10–007 The question whether acts of a body established by an international agreement concluded by the Community may be subjected to a review of their validity under the preliminary ruling procedure is more difficult to answer. Also in the case of such bodies, the Court of Justice emphasises the need for a system of judicial supervision which provides effective legal protection for all individuals,[22] but so far has left it undecided whether the Court of Justice itself ought to provide the judicial protection in so far as the international agreement in question provides for no (or an insufficient) system of judicial supervision of the bodies which it establishes. Here too, the possibility of the Community incurring liability at international level counsels caution, but even so the requirement for a full system of judicial review is an argument in favour of allowing validity to be tested by references for preliminary rulings, especially since Community institutions contributed, within the framework of the bodies concerned, towards the adoption of the acts in question.[23]

10–008 The validity of *all* acts of Community institutions and bodies may be reviewed in the context of a reference for a preliminary ruling irrespective

---

[18] As far as the European Parliament is concerned, see Pescatore, "Reconnaissance et contrôle judiciaire des actes du Parlement européen" (1978) R.T.D.E. 581 at 590; for the Court of Auditors, see *Commentaire Mégret*, at 212.

[19] During the second stage of economic and monetary union, the European Monetary Institute: E.C. Treaty, Art. 117 (*ex Art. 109f*) (9).

[20] See Lauwaars, "Auxiliary Organs and Agencies in the EEC" (1979) C.M.L.Rev. 365 at 379–380.

[21] Case 9/56 *Meroni & Co. v. High Authority* [1957 and 1958] E.C.R. 133 at 149–150, ECJ. See also Lenaerts (cited in para. 7–026, n. 81, above), at 44–46.

[22] Opinion 1/76 *Draft Agreement establishing a European laying-up fund for inland waterway vessels* [1977] E.C.R. 741 at 761, para. 21, ECJ.

[23] *Cf.* Case C–192/89 *Sevince* [1990] E.C.R. I–3461 at I–3499, para. 3, ECJ.

as to what they are called[24] and whether or not they have direct effect.[25] The acts may be non-binding.[26] Reviewing the validity of non-binding acts in preliminary rulings can be of considerable interest: in the Court's words, such acts:

> "cannot . . . be regarded as having no legal effect. The national courts are bound to take recommendations[27] into consideration in order to decide disputes submitted to them, in particular where they cast light on the interpretation of national measures adopted in order to implement them or where they are designed to supplement binding Community provisions".[28]

Sometimes it will be sufficient for the Court to interpret a non-binding act (for example a communication), thereby appraising its compatibility with the Community provisions which it is intended to elucidate.[29]

Since the review of validity effected by means of a reference for a preliminary ruling is a species of review incidental to the main proceedings, some commentators have argued—by analogy with the objection of illegality (E.C. Treaty, Article 241 (*ex Article 184*)—that only acts of general application may be so reviewed.[30] The Court of Justice has also given the impression of acceding to that view by referring to the "complete system" of judicial review of acts of the institutions: **10–009**

> "Where the Community institutions are responsible for the administrative implementation of . . . measures [of general application], natural or legal persons may bring a direct action before the Court against administrative measures which are addressed to them or which are of direct and individual concern to them and, in support of such an action, plead the illegality of the general measure on which they are based. Where implementation is a matter for the national authorities, such persons may plead the invalidity of general measures before the national courts and cause the latter to request the Court of Justice for a preliminary ruling".[31]

---

24 For the indirect review in a preliminary ruling of the validity of a Council resolution, see Case 59/75 *Pubblico Ministero v. Manghera* [1976] E.C.R. 91 at 102, paras 19–22, ECJ.

25 For a cogent argument to this effect, see Bebr, "Examen en validité au titre de l'article 177 *[now Article 234]* du Traité CEE et cohésion juridique de la Communauté" (1975) C.D.E. 379 at 398–399.

26 Case C–322/88 *Grimaldi v. Fonds de Maladies Professionnelles* [1989] E.C.R. 4407 at 4419, para. 8, ECJ, where the Court of Justice compared the wording of Art. 173 and 177 (*now Arts. 230 and 234*), reaching the conclusion that "all acts of the institutions of the Community without exception" are covered by Art. 177 (*now Art. 234*).

27 Recommendations are not binding as a result of the E.C. Treaty, Art. 249 (*ex Art. 189*).

28 *Grimaldi v. Fonds des Maladies Professionnelles* (cited in n.26, above), at 4421, para. 18.

29 Case C–94/91 *Wagner* [1992] E.C.R. I–2765 at I–2792—2793, paras 16–17, ECJ.

30 See, for instance, Lagrange, "L'action préjudicielle dans le droit interne des Etats membres et en droit communautaire" (1974) R.T.D.E. 268 at 281; Mertens de Wilmars, "La procédure suivant l'article 177 *[now Article 234]* CEE" (1965) S.E.W. 437 at 445.

31 Case 294/83 *Les Verts v. European Parliament* [1986] E.C.R. 1339 at 1365, para. 23, ECJ.

It is clear, however, that while that passage correctly reproduces the *rationale* of judicial review of validity by means of the preliminary ruling procedure, it does not necessarily mean that such review may in no circumstances be carried out in respect of an individual act.[32]

10–010 What is actually behind the question whether it is possible to review by preliminary ruling the validity of an individual act of a Community institution often seems to arise under a different aspect, namely whether it is still possible for a party to the main proceedings to request the national court to apply to the Court of Justice for a preliminary ruling on the validity of an act where that party could have brought an action for annulment against the act in question within the prescribed time-limit (E.C. Treaty, Article 230 (*ex Article 173*), fifth paragraph), but neglected to do so.[33] The Court of Justice has answered this question in the negative[34]: a natural or legal person who undoubtedly has the right under Article 230 of the E.C. Treaty to seek the annulment of a Community act[35] and has been informed

---

[32] See Joined Cases 133–136/85 *Rau v. BALM* [1987] E.C.R. 2289 at 2344, point 1 of the operative part, ECJ: "The possibility of bringing a direct action under the [fourth] para. of Article 173 *[now Article 230]* of the [EC] Treaty against a decision adopted by a Community institution does not preclude the possibility of bringing an action in a national court against a measure adopted by a national authority for the implementation of that decision on the ground that the latter decision is unlawful". That case was concerned with a Commission decision addressed to the Federal Republic of Germany within the meaning of the E.C. Treaty, Art. 189, para. 4 *(now Art. 249)*, consequently an individual act, which a German authority had implemented with respect to the plaintiffs in the main proceedings, whereupon the plaintiffs brought an action for annulment of the Commission decision in the Court of Justice and an action for annulment of the German implementing decision in the national courts. It was in this context that the Court of Justice held that it had jurisdiction to conduct judicial review of an individual act of a Community institution in a preliminary ruling procedure on the basis of the *rationale* of that jurisdiction set out above. See, to the same effect, (Judgment of November 17, 1998), Case C–70/97P *Kruidvat v. Commission*, paras 47–49 (not yet reported), ECJ (relating to a Commission decision declaring Art. 81 (*ex Art. 85*) (1) inapplicable to a selective distribution system pursuant to Art. 81(3)).

[33] This goes back as far as Tomuschat, *Die gerichtliche Vorabentscheidung nach den Verträgen über die Europäischen Gemeinschaften*, Berlin/Heidelberg/New York, Springer-Verlag, 1964, pp. 89–92.

[34] Case C–188/92 *TWD Textilwerke Deggendorf* [1994] E.C.R. I–833, ECJ: in this case, the Court of Justice held that a beneficiary of an aid measure in respect of which the Commission had taken a decision was entitled to bring an action for annulment, Case C–178/95 *Wiljo* [1997] E.C.R. I–585 at I–603—604, paras 19–24, ECJ; in this case the Court held that the validity of a Commission decision set out in a letter addressed to the undertaking concerned could no longer be challenged since the undertaking had failed to bring an action for annulment. In two other cases, the Court of Justice held that a party could plead the illegality of a Community act in national proceedings on the ground that it was not obvious that an action for annulment pursuant to the E.C. Treaty, Art. 173, para. 4 *(now Art. 230)* would have been admissible: in Case C–241/95 *Accrington Beef* [1996] E.C.R. I–6699, at I–6727, para. 15, ECJ, where the applicants in the main proceeedings alleged that a regulation was invalid, the Court found that, in view of the fact that the contested act was in the nature of a regulation, it was improbable that an action brought by the applicants for its annulment would have been declared admissible. A similar ruling, but relating to a directive, is contained in Case C–408/95 *Eurotunnel and Others* [1997] E.C.R. I–6315, at I–6352—6353, paras 29–30, ECJ.

[35] What springs to mind in the first place is the obvious case where a Community act is addressed to a natural or legal person or where in a specific area of Community law a natural or legal person is manifestly directly and individually concerned within the meaning of the E.C. Treaty, Art. 230 *(now Art. 173)*, para. 4, such as a recipient of state aid which the

of that right but does not make use of it, may not plead the illegality of that act in subsequent proceedings before the national courts. To have decided otherwise would have detracted excessively from the legal certainty which the limitation period prescribed by the fifth paragraph of Article 230 is intended to secure. The national courts must regard the act in question as valid *vis-à-vis* the party in question and therefore apply it in any event. As a result, there is no point in making a reference to the Court of Justice for a preliminary ruling or at least not with a view to protecting a party to the main proceedings who is no longer entitled to plead that the act is unlawful. Another party to the main proceedings, who was not entitled to challenge the act in question pursuant to Article 230 may persuade the national court to make a reference for a preliminary ruling on the validity of the act. There is nothing to prevent the national court from inquiring into this question or from raising it with the Court of Justice of its own motion. If the Court then finds that the act is invalid, it will be for it to determine what consequences that finding should have for the party to the main proceedings for whom the act has become unappealable because of its failure to bring an action for annulment.[36]

However, in proceedings for a preliminary ruling the Court of Justice has no power to rule that a Community institution has failed to act.[37] Consequently, an action brought on the basis of Article 232 (*ex Article 175*) of the E.C. Treaty[38] is the only procedure for challenging an unlawful failure to act on the part of an institution. **10–011**

II. Substance of the Review of Validity of a Community Act in Preliminary Ruling Proceedings

The review of the validity of a Community act by preliminary ruling, in common with the action for annulment, is a form of judicial review of the legality of acts of Community institutions[39]: since Article 230 (*ex Article 173*) gives the Court of Justice exclusive jurisdiction to declare void an act of a Community institution, the coherence of the system requires that where the validity of a Community act is challenged before a national court, the power to declare the act invalid must also be reserved to the Court of Justice.[40] The Court, moreover, is "in the best position" to decide on the validity of Community acts, since "[u]nder Article 20 of the Protocol on the Statute of the Court of Justice of the [EC], Community institutions whose **10–012**

Commission has found to be incompatible with the common market in a decision addressed to the Member State in question: Case 730/79 *Philip Morris v. Commission* [1980] E.C.R. 2671, ECJ. See also *TWD Textilwerke Deggendorf*, (cited in n. 34, above), at I–852 and I–855, paras 14, 24. See in this regard Pache, "Keine Vorlage ohne Anfechtung?" (1994) Eu.Z.W. 615–620.

[36] *Cf. Commentaire Mégret*, at 210.

[37] Case C–68/95 *T. Port v. Commission* [1996] E.C.R. I–6065 at I–6104, para. 53, ECJ.

[38] See paras 8–001 *et seq.*, above.

[39] Case 314/85 *Foto-Frost v. Hauptzollamt Lübeck-Ost* [1987] E.C.R. 4199 at 4231, para. 16, ECJ.

[40] *ibid.*, at 4231, para. 17.

acts are challenged are entitled to participate in the proceedings in order to defend the validity of the acts in question".[41]

10–013 The most important differences between the action for annulment and the review of validity in preliminary ruling proceedings are that the latter is not subject to any time-limit and cannot be "limited by the grounds on which the validity of [Community] measures may be contested"[42] and that the initiative for seeking a preliminary ruling on validity comes from the national court and not from interested natural or legal persons. In the main proceedings, the parties may try to move the national court to make a reference to the Court of Justice, but they cannot compel the Court to rule on the validity of a measure if the national court has not put a question to that effect.[43]

10–014 The parties to the main proceedings or Community institutions and Member States submitting observations pursuant to Article 20 of the E.C. Statute cannot oblige the Court of Justice to appraise the validity of an act in the light of "submissions" or "grounds" of illegality not raised in the order for reference.[44] This does not mean, however, that the Court has no latitude at all in the matter.

10–015 In the first place, the national court may request the Court of Justice merely to interpret a Community act, but the Court, having regard to the whole of the content of the order for reference, may consider the reference to be concerned with the validity of the act with a view to promoting the efficiency of judicial cooperation.[45] It is important in such a case that the order for reference may be construed as a request for a ruling on validity even though it is couched as a request for a ruling on interpretation. The reason for this is that only in such case may the parties to the main proceedings, the Commission, the Council (if one of its acts is in issue), possibly the European Parliament (if the act in issue was adopted under the co-decision procedure), and the Member States correctly assess what the Court's ruling may cover and formulate their views thereon.[46]

---

[41] *ibid.*, para. 18, the wording of this passage of the judgment is more consonant with the procedure in the case of a direct action, see Chap. 22, below, than with the formally non-contentious procedure of a reference for a preliminary ruling. The Court of Justice added that, furthermore, under the E.C. Statute, Art. 21, para. 2, the Court may require the Member States and "institutions which are not participating in the proceedings" to supply all information which it considers necessary for the purposes of the case before it. It has done so already on one occasion in order to enable the European Parliament, which was not entitled to submit observations to the Court under Art. 20, to defend its prerogatives in proceedings for a preliminary ruling on validity: Case 20/85 *Roviello v. Landesversicherungsanstalt Schwaben* [1988] E.C.R. 2805 at 2816, ECJ.

[42] Joined Cases 21–24/72 *International Fruit Company v. Produktschap voor Groenten en Fruit* [1972] E.C.R. 1219 at 1226, para. 5, ECJ; Case C–162/96 *Racke v. Hauptzollamt Mainz* [1998] E.C.R. I–3655 at I–3700, para. 26, ECJ (where the Court reviewed the validity of a Community act in the light of customary international law).

[43] Case 44/65 *Hessische Knappschaft v. Singer* [1965] E.C.R. 965 at 970, ECJ.

[44] Joined Cases 50–58/82 *Affaires Maritimes, Bayonne v. Dorca Marina* [1982] E.C.R. 3949 at 3959, para. 13, ECJ.

[45] Case 16/65 *Schwarze v. Einfuhr- und Vorratsstelle für Getreide und Futtermittel* [1965] E.C.R. 877 at 886, ECJ.

[46] *Cf.* Case 62/76 *Strehl v. Pensioenfonds Mijnwerkers* [1977] E.C.R. 211 at 217, ECJ, where the Court of Justice held of its own motion that a provision of a regulation, of which only the interpretation had been sought, was invalid having regard to a decided case.

Next, the Court of Justice may supplement the "submissions" or "grounds" of illegality of the Community act at issue as set forth in the order for reference in the light of matters which come to light in the course of legal argument before the Court itself. **10–016**

One situation occurs where the national court raises the question of the validity of an act in general terms only. In such a case, the Court of Justice will answer that question in the light of an assessment of the submissions which are set out by the plaintiff in the main proceedings in its observations to the Court concerning the validity of the act[47] or which emerge from the statement of reasons of the order for reference.[48]

Secondly, the Court of Justice has held that it is empowered to find of its own motion infringements of essential procedural requirements by which an act is vitiated, thereby, if necessary, supplementing the submissions set out in the order for reference alleging that the act is invalid.[49] The case law to this effect is related to the rule applicable to actions for annulment that the Court of Justice or the Court of First Instance *may* find infringements of essential procedural requirements of its own motion.[50] Lack of competence on the part of the institution which adopted the contested act should also perhaps be regarded as a peremptory plea, with the result that, as in the case of an infringement of an essential procedural requirement, it may be raised by the Court of its own motion in conducting judicial review of a contested act in preliminary ruling proceedings.[51]

In arriving at its preliminary ruling on the validity of a given act, the Court of Justice may go no deeper into the facts of the main proceedings than it may in the case of a preliminary ruling on interpretation.[52] There is a slight difference, however, in that the Court may make all the findings of fact necessary to assess the legality of the contested act.[53] In this respect, the Court's powers are no different if it reviews the legality of an act under Article 230 (*ex Article 173*) or Article 234 (*ex Article 177*) of the E.C. Treaty.[54] In this connection, it would be perfectly possible for measures of **10–017**

47 Joined Cases 103 and 145/77 *Royal Scholten Honig v. Intervention Board for Agricultural Produce* [1978] E.C.R. 2037 at 2071, paras 16 and 17, ECJ.

48 Case 41/72 *Getreide-Import v. Einfuhr- und Vorratsstelle Getreide* [1973] E.C.R. 1 at 5, para. 2, ECJ.

49 Joined Cases 73–74/63 *Internationale Crediet- en Handelsvereniging Rotterdam v. Minister van Landbouw en Visserij* [1964] E.C.R. 1, at 14, ECJ.

50 See Case C–291/89 *Interhotel v. Commission* [1991] E.C.R. I–2257, at I–2280, para. 14, ECJ; Case C–304/89 *Oliveira v. Commission* [1991] E.C.R. I–2283 at I–2312, para. 18, ECJ.

51 See, to this effect, the Opinion of Advocate General J. Gand in Case 5/67 *Beus v. Hauptzollamt München-Landsbergerstrasse* [1968] E.C.R. 83 at 108–109, ECJ, who added that, in his view, the Court would not raise the question of misuse of powers of its own motion and that "there is doubt about the situation where there is a question of a breach of the Treaty or a rule of law". *Cf.* para. 7–092, above.

52 Joliet, *Le contentieux*, p. 210. See also para. 6–026, above.

53 For an example, see Case C–323/88 *Sermes* [1990] E.C.R. I–3027 at I–3051—3054, paras 21–31, ECJ.

54 The parallel between the two procedures as adverted to by the Court in Case 314/85 *Foto-Frost v. Hauptzollamt Lübeck-Ost* [1987] E.C.R. 4199, ECJ, emerges clearly here; for an example, see Case C–16/90 *Nölle* [1991] E.C.R. I–5163 at I–5204—5206, paras 17, 23 and 24, ECJ.

inquiry to be ordered pursuant to Article 45 of the ECJ Rules of Procedure.[55]

III. Consequences of the Review of the Validity of a Community Act in Preliminary Ruling Proceedings

10–018 Where the Court of Justice comes to the conclusion that the contested measure should not be declared invalid, the answer which it gives to the national court is not that the act is valid but as follows: "Examination of the question raised has revealed no factor of such a kind as to affect the validity of [the act]".[56] That answer does not preclude the court to which it is addressed from referring other questions to the Court of Justice which might call in question the validity of the same act.[57]

10–019 Where, in contrast, the Court of Justice declares the act in question invalid, its answer is binding on the national court to which it is made. It may no longer apply the act. The same applies to "any other national court" where there is "sufficient reason [for it] to regard that act as void for the purposes of a judgment which it has to give".[58] The effect *erga omnes* of the preliminary ruling on validity is justified as being the inevitable corollary of:

> "particularly imperative requirements concerning legal certainty in addition to those concerning the uniform application of Community law. It follows from the very nature of such a declaration that a national court may not apply the act declared to be void without once more creating serious uncertainty as to the Community law applicable".[59]

10–020 The declaration that an act is invalid is definitive, as in the case of a declaration of nullity (hence the Court's exclusive jurisdiction to declare an act void results in its also having exclusive jurisdiction to declare an act invalid).[60]

Nevertheless, the Court of Justice endeavours to reconcile the absolute effect of the declaration that a given act is invalid with the requirements of the preliminary ruling procedure as laid down by Article 234 (*ex Article 177*). Consequently, it acknowledges that the declaration of invalidity:

---

[55] See as long ago as Case 5/67 *Beus v. Hauptzollamt München-Landsbergerstrasse* [1968] E.C.R. 83 at 86, ECJ.

[56] For an example, see Case C–323/88 *Sermes* [1990] E.C.R. I–3027 at I–3058, operative part, ECJ.

[57] Case 8/78 *Milac v. Hauptzollamt Freiburg* [1978] E.C.R. 1721 at 1729–1730, paras 4–9, ECJ.

[58] Case 66/80 *International Chemical Corporation v. Amministrazione delle Finanze dello Stato* [1981] E.C.R. 1191 at 1223, operative part, point 1, ECJ.

[59] *ibid.*, at 1215, para. 12. For the effects in practice, see Bebr, "Direct and Indirect Judicial Control of Community Acts in Practice: the Relation Between Articles 173 and 177 *[now Articles 230 and 234]* of the EEC Treaty" (1984) Mich.L.Rev. 1229 at 1239–1248; Harding, "The Impact of Article 177 *[now Article 234]* of the EEC Treaty on the Review of Community Action" (1981) Y.E.L. 93 at 101–106.

[60] Case 314/85 *Foto-Frost v. Hauptzollamt Lübeck-Ost* [1987] E.C.R. 4199 at 4231, para. 16, ECJ.

> "does not mean . . . that national courts are deprived of the power given to them by Article 177 (*now Article 234*) of the Treaty and it rests with those courts to decide whether there is a need to raise once again a question which has already been settled by the Court where the Court has previously declared an act of a Community institution [invalid]".[61]

The Court does not mean that the declaration of invalidity may be reversed, but that *any* national court (including the one which obtained the ruling that the act in question was invalid) may possibly have an interest in referring further questions for a preliminary ruling "if questions arise as to the grounds, the scope and possibly the consequences of the invalidity established earlier".[62]

It is for the national court to decide disputes concerning the con- **10–021**
sequences of the declaration that a Community act is invalid in accordance with its national law in so far as Community law does not provide otherwise. In principle, therefore, national law governs the formal and substantive requirements for the refund of amounts collected on behalf of the Community—on the basis of a regulation subsequently declared invalid—unless a rule of Community law specifically deals with such refunds.[63]

On a more general level, all national authorities in the Member States have to draw the necessary conclusions from a declaration that a Community measure is invalid. Action by the national authorities may no longer be based on that measure and any action previously taken on the basis of that measure must be withdrawn (and, where necessary, its consequences rectified).[64] However, the consequences which may be drawn in the national legal systems from such a ruling of invalidity depend directly on Community law as it stands in the light of that ruling.[65]

Sometimes the Court of Justice spells out the consequences of the **10–022**
declaration that an act is invalid in the national legal system, either in the judgment ruling that it is invalid or in a subsequent judgment following a request for an interpretation of the consequences of the declaration of invalidity.

The first scenario presented itself when an agricultural regulation which denied the benefit of exemption from a levy to a particular group of traders, thereby discriminating against them, was declared invalid. As far as the "scope of the preliminary ruling" was concerned, the Court of Justice inferred from that declaration that the Community legislature had to act upon the judgment by adopting such measures as might be appropriate in

---

[61] Case 66/80 *International Chemical Corporation v. Amministrazione delle Finanze dello Stato* [1981] E.C.R. 1191 at 1215, para. 14, ECJ.

[62] *ibid.*

[63] Case 199/86 *Raiffeisen v. BALM* [1988] E.C.R. 1169 at 1186–1188, paras 12–19, ECJ.

[64] Case 23/75 *Rey Soda v. Cassa Conguaglio Zucchero* [1975] E.C.R. 1279 at 1306, paras 50–51, ECJ.

[65] Case C–127/94 *Ecroyd* [1996] E.C.R. I–2731 at I–2786—2787, para. 58, ECJ.

order to establish equal treatment for the traders concerned as regards the rules governing exemption from the levy.[66] In so doing, the Court implicitly applied Article 176 *(now Article 233)* of the E.C. Treaty (governing the consequences of a declaration of nullity) by analogy to a declaration by way of preliminary ruling that an act of a Community institution was invalid. Next, the Court noted that, in the particular circumstances of the case, in which the discrimination did not arise from what the offending provision provided but from what it did not provide, a straightforward declaration that it was invalid would have had the result that, pending the adoption of new provisions, all exemptions would be precluded.[67] In order to avoid such a situation, the Court expressly held that the second paragraph of Article 174 (*now Article 231*) of the E.C. Treaty[68] had to be applied "by analogy" for the same reasons of legal certainty which underlay that provision. Specifically, this meant that, pending such new provisions, "the competent authorities must continue to apply the exemption provided for in the provision declared invalid but they must also grant it to the operators affected by the discrimination found to exist".[69]

Next, there is the case where the national court comes back to the Court of Justice with a new request for a preliminary ruling for guidance on how it should react to the declaration of invalidity in deciding the case before it in the main proceedings. Such a request gives the Court of Justice an opportunity to give a precise indication of the consequences of its declaration of invalidity.[70]

10–023 So it is clear that the Court of Justice in fact attaches similar consequences to the declaration of invalidity and the declaration of nullity, especially as far as the application of the second paragraph of Article 231 (*ex Article 174*) and Article 233 (*ex Article 176*) of the E.C. Treaty is concerned. The act which has been declared invalid may no longer be applied by a national court or a national authority, the institution which adopted the offending act must take appropriate steps to cure the illegality and, if necessary, adopt a new measure, and the Court of Justice is prepared in certain circumstances to maintain certain aspects of the act which has been declared void in force until another measure has been adopted.

[66] Case 300/86 *Van Landschoot v. MERA* [1988] E.C.R. 3443 at 3463, para. 22, ECJ.

[67] *ibid.*, at 3464, para. 23.

[68] "In the case of a regulation, however, the Court of Justice shall, if it considers this necessary, state which of the effects of the regulation which it has declared void shall be considered as definitive."

[69] *Van Landschoot v. Mera* (cited in n. 66, above) at 3464, para. 24. *Cf.* Case 264/82 *Timex v. Council and Commission* [1985] E.C.R. 849 at 870–871, para. 32, ECJ.

[70] Case 359/87 *Pinna v. Caisse d'Allocations Familiales de la Savoie* [1989] E.C.R. 585 at 612–616, ECJ, where the Court explained the consequences of its declaration that Regulation No. 1408/71, Art. 73(2) was invalid for "those authorities [which were obliged] to draw the inferences in their legal system from a declaration of invalidity made in the context of Article 177 *[now Article 234]* of the Treaty" "so long as the Council has failed, following the judgment of the Court, to lay down new rules", *ibid.*, at 614–615, para. 13; the earlier judgment containing the declaration of invalidity is reported at Case 41/84 *Pinna v. Caisse d'Allocations Familiales de la Savoie* [1986] E.C.R. 1, ECJ.

As far as temporal effects are concerned, the declaration of invalidity and the declaration of nullity run on parallel lines. The Court of Justice has held that "a judgment of the Court in proceedings for a preliminary ruling declaring a Community act invalid in principle has retroactive effect, like a judgment annulling an act".[71] **10–024**

However, a problem may arise as a result of the fact that there is no temporal restriction on a national court's requesting the Court of Justice to declare a Community act invalid, in contrast to an action for annulment, which has to be brought within the limitation period laid down. Consequently, the idea that the legal uncertainty resulting from the effect *ex tunc* of a declaration of nullity (*i.e.* from the date on which the measure declared void took effect) is mitigated by the relatively short period within which an action for annulment must be brought has no relevance to a declaration of invalidity. This may explain why the Court of Justice has inferred from Article 234 (*ex Article 177*) the power to modulate the temporal effects of preliminary rulings declaring Community acts invalid, depending on the case.[72] In order to justify that power, the Court had recourse to the argument that the declaration of nullity and the declaration of invalidity were "two mechanisms provided for by the Treaty for reviewing the legality of acts of the Community institutions" and that the "necessary consistency" between the two mechanisms warranted interpreting the second paragraph of Article 174 *(now Article 231)* of the E.C. Treaty as enabling the Court to impose "temporal limits on the invalidity of a Community regulation, whether under Article 173 *(now Article 230)* or Article 177 *(now Article 234)* . . . in the interest of the uniform application of Community law throughout the Community" (in the event of the declaration's having full effect *ex tunc*, it would perhaps be impossible under the procedural law of some Member States to undo all the effects which the act declared invalid had already had, which would be at the expense of the uniform non-application of the act as far as the past was concerned).[73]

As far as limiting the temporal effects of its judgments is concerned, the Court of Justice will decide "in each particular case" whether: **10–025**

---

[71] Case C–228/92 *Roquette Frères* [1994] E.C.R. I–1445 at I–1471, para. 17, ECJ, from which it follows that the national authorities must ensure the repayment of sums unduly charged on the basis of Community regulations which are subsequently declared invalid by the Court, *ibid.*, at I–1471, para. 18; See also Case 130/79 *Express Dairy Foods v. Intervention Board for Agricultural Produce* [1980] E.C.R. 1887 at 1900–1901, para. 14, ECJ. *Cf.* Pescatore, "Article 177 *[now Article 234]*", in *Traité instituant la CEE. Commentaire article par article*, Paris, Economica, 1200–1121, no. 70. See also Hyland, "Temporal Limitation of the Effects of Judgments of the Court of Justice—A review of recent case-law" (1995) Ir.J.E.L. 208–233, para. 14, Isaac, "La modulation par la Cour de justice des Communautés européennes des effets dans le temps de ses arrêts d'invalidité" (1987) C.D.E. 444–470; Weiss, "Die Einschränkung der zeitlichen Wirkungen von Vorabentscheidungen nach Art. 177 EGV" (1995) EuR. 377–397.

[72] Case 112/83 *Produits de Maïs v. Administration des Douanes et Droits Indirects* [1985] E.C.R. 719, ECJ. For a case in which the Court of Justice refused to restrict the effect *ex tunc* of a declaration of invalidity, see Joined Cases C–363 and C–407–411/93 *Lancry and Others* [1994] E.C.R. I–3957 at I–3995–3997, paras 40–45, ECJ.

[73] *Produits de Maïs v. Administration des Douanes et Droits Indirects* (cited in n. 72, above), at 747, para. 17.

> "an exception to that temporal limitation . . . may be made in favour of the party who brought the action before the national court or of any other trader which took similar steps before the declaration of invalidity or whether, conversely, a declaration of invalidity applicable only to the future constitutes an adequate remedy".[74]

In the latter case, the Court has in fact considered that the parties which took the initiative of challenging in the national courts the act ultimately declared invalid are sufficiently rewarded for their efforts by seeing the act eliminated from the legal system for the future.[75] That approach has come in for criticism on the ground that it effectively deprives the party who successfully pleaded the invalidity of the Community act of the benefit of his or her success, since that party only shares in the general benefit which anyone may have in an invalid Community act which is detrimental to his or her interests being no longer applied.[76] This is patently insufficient to act as a stimulus to setting judicial review in train.

10–026 The Court of Justice recognised this when it was faced with this question on a subsequent occasion and had to consider whether:

> "an importer who, like the plaintiff in the main proceedings, has brought an administrative complaint followed by judicial proceedings, challenging a notice to pay MCAs [monetary compensatory amounts] on the ground that the Community regulation on the basis of which the notice was adopted was invalid, is entitled to rely for the purposes of those proceedings on the invalidity of a regulation declared by the Court of Justice in the same proceedings".[77]

If the Court were to have held that "a declaration of invalidity applicable only to the future is an adequate remedy even for that party", this would have meant that "the national court would dismiss the action brought against the notice in question, even though the regulation on the basis of which that notice was adopted had been declared invalid by the Court in the same proceedings".[78] The Court found that that outcome would be unacceptable: "An economic agent such as the plaintiff in the main proceedings would thereby be deprived of its right to effective judicial protection in the event of a breach of Community law by the institutions, and the practical effect of Article 177 *[now Article 234]* of the Treaty would

---

[74] *ibid.*, at 748, para. 18.

[75] Case 4/79 *Providence Agricole de la Champagne v. ONIC* [1980] E.C.R. 2823 at 2852–2854, paras 42–46, ECJ; Case 109/79 *Maïseries de Beauce v. ONIC* [1980] E.C.R. 2883 at 2912–2914, paras 42–46, ECJ; Case 145/79 *Roquette Frères v. French Customs Administration* [1980] E.C.R. 2917 at 2946–2947, paras 50–53, ECJ.

[76] See, among others, Labayle, "La Cour de justice des Communautés et les effets d'une déclaration d'invalidité" (1982) R.T.D.E. 484–510; Waelbroeck, "Le principe de la non-rétroactivité en droit communautaire à la lumière des arrêts 'isoglucose'" (1983) R.T.D.E. 363.

[77] Case C–-228/92 *Roquette Frères* [1994] E.C.R. I–1445 at I–1472, para. 24, ECJ.

[78] *ibid.*, at I–1472—1473, paras 25–26.

thereby be jeopardized".[79] Consequently, it came to the conclusion that "a trader who before the date of the present judgment has brought an action in a national court challenging a notice to pay MCAs adopted on the basis of a Community regulation declared invalid by the present judgment is entitled to rely on that invalidity in the national proceedings".[80] This meant not only the plaintiff in the main proceedings which had resulted in the reference to the Court of Justice, but also anyone who had brought judicial proceedings or "submitted an administrative complaint" before the date of the declaration of invalidity.[81]

Since the Court of Justice reached that decision sitting as the full Court and it is based on the fundamental "right to effective judicial protection" and on guaranteeing the "practical effect [*effet utile*] of Article 177 *[now Article 234]* of the Treaty", it seems unlikely that in future the Court will revert to the option, which still exists in theory, of holding that a declaration of invalidity is applicable to parties to the main proceedings and others whose position may be equated with theirs "only for the future".

[79] *ibid.*, at I–1473, para. 27.
[80] *ibid.*, at I–1473, para. 30.
[81] *ibid.* See also the earlier case, Case 41/84 *Pinna v. Caisse d'Allocations Familiales de la Savoie* [1986] E.C.R. 1 at 26–27, paras 29–30, ECJ.

Chapter 11

THE ACTION FOR DAMAGES

I. Subject-matter

A. General

An action for damages seeks to have the Community held non-contractually liable to make good any damage caused by its institutions or by its servants in the performance of their duties. The conditions for incurring liability are determined by the Court of Justice and the Court of First Instance "in accordance with the general principles common to the laws of the Member States" (E.C. Treaty, Article 288 (*ex Article 215*), second paragraph). The Court of Justice has drawn on those general principles—in so far as they could be identified—only as a source of inspiration with a view to developing an independent Community law on liability.[1] Liability on the part of the Community "presupposes the existence of a set of circumstances comprising actual damage, a causal link between the damage claimed and conduct alleged against the institution, and the illegality of such conduct".[2] **11–001**

Article 235 (*ex Article 178*) of the E.C. Treaty confers on the Court of Justice exclusive jurisdiction to find the Community non-contractually liable.[3] This jurisdiction is now vested in the Court of First Instance by virtue of Article 3(1)(b)(c) and (d) of the CFI Decision as regards actions brought by natural or legal persons. The exclusive jurisdiction of the Court of First Instance—and of the Court of Justice on appeal—to find the Community non-contractually liable guarantees the Community's independence in so far as its acts are not reviewed in the light of national law by national courts; in addition, it has the advantage of ensuring that there are uniform rules on liability for unlawful acts of the Community. **11–002**

---

1 For an extensive discussion, see Fines, "Etude de la responsabilité extracontractuelle de la Communauté économique européenne", in *Bibliothèque de droit international*, Vol. 101, Paris, Librairie générale de droit et de jurisprudence, 1990, and *Brealey and Hoskins* (cited in para. 1–004, n. 12, above), pp. 350–372.

2 Case 4/69 *Lütticke v. Commission* [1971] E.C.R. 325, at 337, para. 10, ECJ. For non-contractual liability under the rules of the ECSC Treaty, see Arts. 34 and 40. See also Case T–120/89 *Stahlwerke Peine-Salzgitter v. Commission* [1991] E.C.R. II–279, CFI, which should be compared with Case C–220/91P *Commission v. Stahlwerke Peine-Salzgitter* [1993] E.C.R. I–2393, ECJ.

3 The Court has the same exclusive jurisdiction under the ECSC Treaty, Arts. 34, 40 and the EAEC Treaty, Art. 151.

B. Independent nature of the action for damages

11–003 The question arises as to the extent to which the independent nature of the action for damages is influenced by the existence of other procedures which are available to an applicant in order to have the legality of an act causing damage reviewed by the Community Court. More specifically, the question is whether the action for damages is an independent form of action or whether the applicant may bring such proceedings only after it has been determined in some other proceedings that the act in question is unlawful.[4]

11–004 Originally, the case law seemed to take the second of these two approaches in that actions for damages seemed to be regarded as admissible only if an action for the annulment of the contested act had been brought.[5] Shortly after, however, matters took a different turn when the Court of Justice described the action for damages as "an independent form of action with a particular purpose to fulfil within the system of actions and subject to conditions for its use, conceived with a view to its specific purpose".[6] Consequently, an action for damages will be admissible even if no prior action for annulment[7] or for failure to act[8] has been brought and if no preliminary ruling declaring the offending act invalid has been obtained. The purpose of an action for damages is solely to obtain financial compensation and, on that ground, differs from that of other forms of

[4] Mead, "The Relationship between an Action for Damages and an Action for Annulment: the Return of Plaumann", in Heukels and McDonnell (eds), *The Action for Damages in Community Law*, The Hague, London, Boston, Kluwer Law International, 1997, pp. 243–258.

[5] Case 25/62 *Plaumann & Co. v. Commission* [1963] E.C.R. 95 at 108, ECJ: "An administrative measure which has not been annulled cannot of itself constitute a wrongful act on the part of the administration inflicting damage on those whom it affects". On this view, a finding of an unlawful failure to act or a declaration by way of preliminary ruling that a measure was invalid was to be equated with a declaration that the measure was void.

[6] Case 4/69 *Lütticke v. Commission* [1971] E.C.R. 325 at 336, ECJ. See also (Order of June 21, 1993), Case C–257/93 *Van Parijs and Others v. Council and Commission* [1993] E.C.R. I–3335 at I–3342, para. 14, ECJ. In his Opinion in Joined Cases 9 and 11/71 *Cie d'Approvisionnement v. Commission* [1972] E.C.R. 391 at 411, ECJ, Advocate General A. Dutheillet de Lamothe argued cogently that the action for damages should be independent of any action for annulment. He pointed out that a declaration of nullity applies *erga omnes* and is retroactive. In his view, those far-reaching consequences explained why the authors of the Treaty had restricted individuals' access to the Court of Justice (now the Court of First Instance) on the basis of the E.C. Treaty, Art. 173 *[now Art. 230]* and why Art. 174 *[now Art. 231]*, para. 2 of that Treaty had conferred on the Court of Justice the power to restrict the retroactive effect of a declaration of nullity. In contrast, the action for damages was an action for a declaration of subjective rights (*i.e.* rights appertaining to the applicant personally) and did not have the same far-reaching results. Consequently, the same stringent conditions as to admissibility ought not to apply. The argument that the authors of the Treaty had sought—irrespective of the type of dispute—to prevent the Court of Justice from ruling on the legality of a general act on an application from individuals was therefore misconceived. A similar argument with regard to the independent nature of the action for damages in the context of the ECSC Treaty is to be found in Joined Cases 9 and 12/60 *Vloeberghs v. High Authority* [1961] E.C.R. 197 at 212–213. For staff cases, however, see para. 16–018, below.

[7] Case 5/71 *Zuckerfabrik Schöppenstedt v. Council* [1971] E.C.R. 975 at 983, para. 3, ECJ.

[8] Case 4/69 *Lütticke v. Commission* [1971] E.C.R. 325, ECJ.

action.[9] What is more, the requirements in order for liability to be incurred are substantively very different from the criteria for reviewing the legality of an action or an alleged failure to act on the part of the Community.[10] The fact that an action for annulment of an act of a Community institution which at the same time is the subject of an action for damages is inadmissible does not necessarily make the claim for damages inadmissible.[11]

However, an action for damages will be inadmissible where it is used improperly as an action for annulment or for failure to act. An applicant who seeks to use an action for damages in order to obtain the specific outcome sought by one of those forms of action will be denied access to the Community Court. To use an action for damages for that purpose would amount to an abuse of process. Accordingly, an action for damages may not be brought in order to avoid the consequences of time having run out for bringing an action for annulment against an act against which the applicant could have brought such an action. The covert, unlawful purpose of the action for damages will be inferred from the fact that the reparation sought coincides with the benefit which the applicant would have obtained as a result of the annulment of the contested Community act[12] or from the close connection between the damage which arose and the applicant's own failure to have recourse to another form of action.[13] No matter how comprehensible this case law may be, textbook writers correctly point out that it detracts from the autonomous nature of the action for damages.[14] **11–005**

---

[9] See, for instance, the Opinion of Advocate General F. Capotorti in Case 68/77 *IFG v. Commission* [1978] E.C.R. 353 at 375, ECJ.

[10] Consequently, a finding that an act is unlawful or that the Community has failed to act does not as such give rise to a right to compensation. But an action for damages which is brought together with an action for annulment and seeks compensation for damage allegedly caused solely by the unlawfulness of an act of an institution will be inadmissible if it appears from examination of the application for annulment that the act has no legal effects: (Order of June 13, 1991), Case C–50/90 *Sunzest v. Commission* [1991] E.C.R. I–2917 at I–2924, para. 19, ECJ; (Order of October 4, 1991), Case C–117/91 *Bosman v. Commission* [1991] E.C.R. I–4837 at I–4843, para. 20, ECJ; (Order of October 10, 1996), Case T–75/96 *Söktas v. Commission* [1996] E.C.R. II–1689 at II–1704, para. 49, CFI.

[11] Case 175/84 *Krohn v. Commission* [1986] E.C.R. 735 at 770, para. 32, Case T–185/94 *Geotronics v. Commission* [1995] E.C.R. II–2795 at II–2809, para. 38, CFI; Case T–485/93 *Dreyfus v. Commission* [1996] E.C.R. II–1101 at II–1126, para. 67, CFI; Case T–491/93 *Richco v. Commission* [1996] E.C.R. II–1131 at II–1155, para. 64, CFI.

[12] Case 59/65 *Schreckenberg v. Commission* [1966] E.C.R. 543 at 550, ECJ; *Krohn v. Commission* (cited in n. 11 above) at 770, para. 33; Joined Cases C–199 and C–200/94P *Pevasa and Inpesca v. Commission* [1995] E.C.R. I–3709 at I–3721, para. 28, ECJ; Case T–514/93 *Cobrecaf and Others v. Commission* [1995] E.C.R. II–621, at II–641, paras 59, 60, CFI; *Dreyfus v. Commission*, (cited in n. 11 above) at II–1126—1127, para. 68; *Richco v. Commission*, (cited in n. 11 above), at II–1155, para. 65, (Order of February 3, 1998), Case T–68/96 *Polyvios v. Commission* [1998] E.C.R. II–153 at II–165—169, para 32–45, CFI; Case T–93/95 *Laga v. Commission* [1997] E.C.R. II–195 at II–210—211, paras 48–49, CFI; Case T–94/95 *Landuyt v. Commission* [1997] E.C.R. II–213 at II–227—228, paras 48–49, CFI.

[13] Case 4/67 *Muller (née Collignon) v. Commission* [1967] E.C.R. 365 at 373, ECJ.

[14] Waelbroeck and Waelbroeck, *Répertoire de droit communautaire*, key words: Responsabilité (de la Communauté), Paris, Ed. Dalloz, 1994/3, s.14. Note also, Case 153/73 *Holtz & Willemsen v. Council and Commission* [1974] E.C.R. 675 at 692, paras 3–5, ECJ; Joined Cases 197–200, 243, 245 and 247/80 *Ludwigshafener Walzmühle v. Council and Commission*

II. Identity of the Parties

A. Applicants

11–006 Any natural or legal person who claims to have been injured by acts or conduct of a Community institution or its officials or agents may bring an action for damages in the Court of First Instance.[15]

11–007 There is no requirement as to the applicant's nationality in the case of such an action.[16]

11–008 The injury for which the applicant seeks reparation must affect its own personal assets. Legal persons in particular must show that the damage sustained affected their own separate assets and not (exclusively) the personal assets of their members.[17] They may also not claim compensation for the collective damage suffered by their members.[18]

11–009 Nevertheless, a person who suffers injury may assign his or her right which was infringed, together with his or her claim to damages, to another person who will consequently be entitled to bring an action by subrogation.[19] Once the injured party has assigned his or her claim, that party ceases to have the right to bring an action.[20] If the assignment is of a fraudulent nature—if the assignor and/or the assignee is not in good faith—it may not be relied upon as against the defendant.[21]

11–010 Article 235 (*ex Article 178*) and the second paragraph of Article 288 (*ex Article 215*) of the E.C. Treaty do not preclude Member States from bringing an action for damages before the Court of Justice. To date, no Member State has done so and hence there is no case law concerning the conditions that such an action has to satisfy.

B. Defendants

11–011 The Community may incur liability under the second paragraph of Article 288 (*ex Article 215*) of the E.C. Treaty as a result of damage caused by its institutions[22] or by its servants in the performance of their duties.[23]

[1981] E.C.R. 3211 at 3243, paras 4–5, ECJ; Case C–87/89 *Sonito and Others v. Commission* [1990] E.C.R. I–1981 at I–2010, para. 14, ECJ.

15 Case 118/83 *CMC v. Commission* [1985] E.C.R. 2325 at 2346, para. 31, ECJ. For the ECSC Treaty, see Joined Cases 9 and 12/60 *Vloeberghs v. High Authority* [1961] E.C.R. 197 at 214, ECJ, in which it was also indicated that the applicant does not have to be an undertaking within the meaning of the ECSC Treaty, Art. 80 (or an association within the meaning of Article 48 of that Treaty), unlike in the case of an action for annulment.

16 *Cf.* Case 119/77 *Nippon Seiko v. Council and Commission* [1979] E.C.R. 1303, ECJ, Joined Cases 239 and 275/82 *Allied Corporation v. Commission* [1984] E.C.R. 1005, ECJ.

17 Case 114/83 *Société d'Initiatives et de Coopération Agricoles v. Commission* [1984] E.C.R. 2589 at 2597, paras 3–5, ECJ; Case 289/83 *GAARM v. Commission* [1984] E.C.R. 4295 at 4304, paras 4, 5, ECJ; Joined Cases T–481 and T–484/93 *Exporteurs in Levende Varkens and Others v. Commission* [1995] E.C.R. II–2941 at II–2968, para. 76, CFI.

18 Case 72/74 *Union Syndicale v. Council* [1975] E.C.R. 401 at 411, para. 21, ECJ.

19 Case 238/78 *Ireks-Arkady v. Council and Commission* [1979] E.C.R. 2955 at 2971, para. 5, ECJ; Joined Cases 256–257, 265, 267/80, 5 and 51/81 and 282/82 *Birra Wührer v. Council and Commission* [1984] E.C.R. 3693 at 3727, para. 12, ECJ.

20 *Birra Wührer v. Council and Commission* (cited in n. 19, above) at 3726, para. 12, ECJ.

21 Case 250/78 *DEKA v. EEC* [1983] E.C.R. 421, ECJ.

22 See para. 11–013, below.

23 See paras 11–014—11–017, below.

Community liability may also arise in conjunction with liability on the part of the Member States.[24] However, the Community cannot incur non-contractual liability for an act of primary Community law (such as amendments to the treaties), since such an act cannot be imputed to a Community institution.[25]

Substantively, it is the Community which has to be regarded as being the defendant and not the institutions, since they have no legal personality.[26] Yet it is the Community institution to which the harmful act is attributable which has to be summoned before the Court of First Instance or the Court of Justice as representing the Community.[27] The Commission has no general right to represent the Community.[28] It is advisable for the applicant to specify the institution against which its action is brought in its application, even though the Court of Justice takes a flexible, non-formalistic approach in this regard.[29] If the damage was caused by more than one institution, they must all be brought into the proceedings. **11–012**

1. Damage caused by institutions

The "institutions" which may cause the Community to incur liability under the second paragraph of Article 288 (*ex Article 215*) of the E.C. Treaty are not only those listed in Article 7 (*ex Article 4*) (1) of that Treaty, but also all bodies and agencies active in the sphere of Community law, such as the European Investment Bank.[30] This broad interpretation is designed to prevent the Community from escaping possible liability where it acts through bodies and agencies which are not institutions within the meaning of Article 7(1) of the E.C. Treaty,[31] by putting a strict interpretation on the **11–013**

---

24 See paras 11–018—11–029, below.

25 Case T–113/96 *Dubois et fils v. Council and Commission* [1998] E.C.R. II–125 at II–142, para. 47, CFI.

26 Case 302/87 *European Parliament v. Council* [1988] E.C.R. 5615 at 5640, para. 9, ECJ.

27 Joined Cases 63–69/72 *Werhahn v. Council* [1973] E.C.R. 1229 at 1247, para. 7, ECJ; Opinion of Advocate General C.O. Lenz in Case 62/83 *Eximo v. Commission* [1984] E.C.R. 2295 at 2317–2318, ECJ.

28 E.C. Treaty, Art. 282 (*ex Art. 211*) is concerned only with the Community's power to act and its representation in the various Member States.

29 Case 106/81 *Kind v. EEC* [1982] E.C.R. 2885, ECJ. Compare Case T–246/93 *Bühring v. Council and Commission* [1998] E.C.R. II–171, at II–182, para. 26, CFI, in which the defendant institutions argued that the application was inadmissible on the ground that it designated the Council and the Commission as defendants and not the Community. The Court of First Instance held that this could not render the application inadmissible where it did not affect the rights of the defence.

30 Case C–370/89 *SGEEM and Etroy v. European Investment Bank (EIB)* [1992] E.C.R. I–6211 at I–6248, para. 16, ECJ.

31 Some bodies have legal personality. The Court of Justice or the Court of First Instance may hold that these bodies have incurred non-contractual liability pursuant to a specific provision in the decisions establishing them. See European Centre for the Development of Vocational Training: Regulation No. 337/75 of the Council of February 10, 1975 establishing a European Centre for the Development of Vocational Training ([1975] O.J. L39/1), Art. 17(2) subparas 1, 2; European Foundation for the Improvement of Living and Working Conditions: Regulation No. 1365/75 of the Council of May 26, 1975 on the creation of a European Foundation for the Improvement of Living and Working Conditions, ([1975] O.J. L139/1), Art. 21(2), subparas 1, 2; European Agency for Cooperation: Council Regulation (EEC) No 3245/81 of October 26,

jurisdiction of the Court of Justice and the Court of First Instance under Article 235 (*ex Article 178*) and the second paragraph of Article 288 (*ex Article 215*) when the national courts have no jurisdiction over such cases in any event. Lastly, the third paragraph of Article 288 of the E.C. Treaty states that the second paragraph of that Article is to apply under the same conditions to damage caused by the European Central Bank.[32]

2. Damage caused by servants of institutions in the performance of their duties

11–014 The Court of Justice has regarded only a limited class of acts of servants of the institutions as acts carried out "in the performance of their duties" which are potentially capable of causing the Community to incur liability. The Community may be held liable only for damage caused by acts which are the "necessary extension" of the tasks entrusted to the institution to which the staff member belongs.[33]

11–015 Where a servant drives his or her own car pursuant to a travel order, this does not satisfy that test, except in the case of *force majeure* or in exceptional circumstances of such overriding importance that the Community would otherwise have been unable to carry out the tasks entrusted to it. A servant who causes a road accident with his or her own car pursuant

1981 setting up a European Agency for Cooperation ([1981] O.J. L328/1), Art. 18(2), subparas 1, 2; European Environment Agency and the European Environment Information and Observation Network: Council Regulation No. 1210/90 of May 7, 1990 on the establishment of the European Environment Agency and the European Environment Information and Observation Network ([1990] O.J. L120/1), Art. 18(2), subparas 1, 2; European Training Foundation: Council Regulation No. 1360/90 of May 7, 1990 establishing a European Training Foundation ([1990] O.J. L131/1), Art. 15(2), subparas 1, 2; European Monitoring Centre for Drugs and Drug Addiction: Council Regulation No. 302/93 of February 8, 1993 on the establishment of a European Monitoring Centre for Drugs and Drug Addiction ([1993] O.J. L36/1) Art. 16(2); European Agency for the Evaluation of Medicinal Products: Council Regulation No. 2309/93 of July 22, 1993 laying down Community procedures for the authorisation and supervision of medicinal products for human and veterinary use and establishing a European Agency for the Evaluation of Medicinal Products ([1993] O.J. L214/1) Art. 60(2); Office for Harmonization in the Internal Market (Trade Marks and Designs): Council Regulation No. 40/94 of December 20, 1993 on the Community trade mark ([1994] O.J. L11/1) Art. 114(3), (4); European Agency for Safety and Health at Work: Council Regulation No. 2062/94 of July 18, 1994 establishing a European Agency for Safety and Health at Work ([1994] O.J. L216/1), Art. 21(2), subparas 1, 2; Community Plant Variety Office: Council Regulation No. 2100/94 of July 27, 1994 on Community plant variety rights ([1994] O.J. L227/1) Art. 33(3), (4); Translation Centre for Bodies of the European Union: Council Regulation No. 2965/94 of November 28, 1994 setting up a Translation Centre for Bodies of the European Union ([1994] O.J. L314/1) Art. 18(2), subparas 1, 2; European Monitoring Centre on Racism and Xenophobia: Council Regulation No. 1035/97 of June 2, 1997 ([1997] O.J. L151/1), Art. 15(2). Other "bodies" include the Economic and Social Committee (E.C. Treaty, Art. 7 ((*ex Art. 4*) (2)) and the Committee of the Regions (E.C. Treaty, Art. 7(2)).

[32] During the second stage of economic and monetary union, the expression "European Central Bank" is to be read as referring to the European Monetary Institute (E.C. Treaty, Art. 117 (*ex Art. 109f*)(9)).

[33] Case 9/69 *Sayag v. Leduc* [1969] E.C.R. 329 at 335–336, para. 7, ECJ. The staff members concerned are the servants of any "institution" within the meaning of the E.C. Treaty, Art. 288 (*ex Art. 215*), para. 2, including the European Central Bank (E.C. Treaty, Art. 288, para. 3).

to a travel order issued by his or her institution, therefore, does not cause his or her institution to incur liability for the ensuing damage in the absence of *force majeure* or exceptional circumstances.[34]

Servants are liable for acts not performed in pursuance of their duties. They are not immune from legal proceedings in respect of such acts under Article 12(a) of the Protocol on the Privileges and Immunities of the European Communities, since such immunity is limited to "acts performed by them in their official capacity, including their words spoken or written". **11–016**

There is no parallel between the possible liability of the Community and the staff member's immunity from legal proceedings.[35] If the staff member's immunity is waived, this does not prevent the wrongful act from causing the Community to incur liability. Consequently, an act which cannot be regarded as having been performed by the staff member in an "official capacity" within the meaning of Article 12(a) of the Protocol may nevertheless be deemed an act carried out "in the performance of his duties" and imputed to the Community.[36] The idea behind this case law is to avoid the Community getting out of a claim all too easily by simply waiving the immunity of the staff member concerned, which would ultimately result in the injured party's risking coming up against an insolvent debtor—the staff member as opposed to the Community. As a result, concurrent claims against the Community (before the Court of First Instance) and against the staff member himself or herself (before the national courts) are not ruled out either. **11–017**

3. Liability concurrent with that of Member States

The Member States make an extensive contribution to the implementation of Community law. If they act unlawfully in this connection, this may affect the assets of individuals.[37] **11–018**

Sometimes the financial loss is exclusively ascribable to the Member State's infringing Community law in performing its executive task. But it may also arise because of the illegality of a Community act which was still **11–019**

[34] *ibid.*, at 336, paras 8–13. Note that this judgment refers to the EAEC Treaty, Arts. 151, 188, para. 2, the provisions corresponding to the E.C. Treaty, Art. 235 (*ex Art. 178*), Art. 288 (*ex Art. 215*), para. 2.

[35] Case 5/68 *Sayag v. Leduc* [1968] E.C.R. 395 at 402, ECJ.

[36] Schermers and Swaak suggest that a single concept of an "official act" should be used both for the scope of the immunity from legal proceedings and for determining the ambit of liability on the part of the Community. They argue that this concept should be given a broad interpretation so that the Community may be held liable for any official act, yet that immunity should invariably be waived where this does not conflict with the interests of the Community. The injured party would virtually always be able to make a claim against both the Community and the staff member concerned and so the fear of the Court of Justice that the Community might escape liability by acting quickly to waive the staff member's immunity would be groundless: "Official Acts of Community Servants and Article 215 *[now Article 288]* (4) EC", in Heukels and McDonnell (eds) (cited in n. 4, above), pp. 167–178.

[37] For an extensive discussion, see Wils, "Concurrent Liability of the Community and a Member State" (1992) E.L.Rev. 191–206; Schockweiler, "Die Haftung der EG-Mitgliedstaaten genüber dem einzelnen bei Verletzung des Gemeinschaftsrechts" (1993) EuR. 107 *et seq.*. See also Goffin, "La recevabilité du recours en indemnité devant la Cour de justice des Communautés européennes" (1981) J.T. 1–5.

regarded as valid at the time when it was implemented by the Member State. Lastly, the pecuniary loss may be the result of unlawful joint action on the part of the Community and a Member State.

11–020 In principle, the financial loss must be made good by the authority which caused it through its unlawful action. Accordingly, the Community must make good the financial loss caused by its institutions or by servants of its institutions in the performance of their duties, whilst the Member State will be liable for the financial loss caused by national authorities.[38]

11–021 Having stated this principle, however, the question remains as to the grounds on which an unlawful act may be attributed to a Community institution or a national authority. This is the central question. The answer determines the extent to which the Community may be held liable for financial loss arising as a result of illegality vitiating the application of a Community provision by a national authority.

11–022 The decisive criterion appears to be the respective decision-making powers of the Community and the Member States.

In *Mulder*[39] the Court of Justice held that, on the basis of Community law in force, the Member States did not have the power to carry out the act which individuals had claimed, namely allocation of a milk quota. The refusal to perform the act sought could not therefore, be attributed to them. The ensuing financial loss was in fact the result of the illegality of the underlying Community act which had not provided for the grant of milk quota, even though the mere instrumental application of the act was entrusted to the Member States. The conclusion reached was that the loss of earnings had to be made good by the Community.

In *Etoile Commerciale*,[40] in contrast, the Court of Justice considered that the sole cause of the damage was a decision taken by a national authority pursuant to a general obligation imposed upon it by a Community regulation which did not, however, instruct it to take the specific decision that gave rise to the damage. Consequently, the national authority had in fact a genuine discretion in carrying out the general obligation imposed by the Community regulation and hence could have taken a different decision. The financial loss incurred therefore had to be made good by the Member

---

[38] Case 175/84 *Krohn v. Commission* [1986] E.C.R. 753 at 767, para. 18, ECJ; Joined Cases 89 and 91/86 *Etoile Commerciale and CNTA v. Commission* [1987] E.C.R. 3005 at 3026–3027, paras 16–21, ECJ. See also Meij, "Article 215 *[now Article 288]* (2) EC and Local Remedies", in Heukels and McDonnell (eds) (cited in n. 4 above), pp. 273–284. The same principle applies in the event of financial loss arising where a non-member country (*e.g.* an ACP country) and the Community act jointly. The non-member country is liable for the financial loss attributable to its acts and the Community for the loss attributable to its acts: Case 118/83 *CMC v. Commission* [1985] E.C.R. 2325 at 2346, para. 31, ECJ; Case 33/82 *Murri Frères v. Commission* [1985] E.C.R. 2759 at 2789–2790, paras 4–8, ECJ; Case 267/82 *Développement SA and Clemessy v. Commission* [1986] E.C.R. 1907 at 1917–1918, paras 16–17, ECJ; Case C–370/89 *SGEEM and Etroy v. EIB* [1993] E.C.R. I–2583 at I–2611–2612, paras 29–31, ECJ.

[39] Joined Cases C–104/89 and C–37/90 *Mulder and Others v. Council and Commission* [1992] E.C.R. I–3061 at I–3131, para. 9, ECJ.

[40] Joined Cases 89 and 91/86 *Etoile Commerciale and CNTA v. Commission* [1987] E.C.R. 3005 at 3026–3027, ECJ.

State.[41] Moreover, the underlying Community regulation as a whole was not unlawful.

A Member State which follows an opinion given by the Commission at its request remains liable for any damage which may nevertheless ensue from any infringement of Community law. This is because opinions are not binding and hence do not restrict the Member State's discretion. Such co-operation cannot make the Community liable.[42]

The position will be different only where, acting on the basis of a power conferred on it by Community law, the Commission imposes a requirement or a prohibition on a Member State, which has no choice other than to comply. Although, on the face of it, the financial loss results from the national "decision", it is really the outcome of the Commission's binding direction. The illegality on which the action for damages is based regards that direction alone and must therefore be attributed to the Commission, making an action for damages admissible.[43]

Consequently, an infringement of Community law committed by a Member State which has a genuine discretion in implementing that law must be distinguished from a merely instrumental application by a Member State of an unlawful Community act where the Member State has no real discretion. **11–023**

(1) Pecuniary loss resulting from an infringement of Community law by a Member State

The principle that a Member State will be liable for loss and damage caused to individuals as a result of breaches of Community law for which the state can be held responsible is inherent in the system of the Treaty. A further basis for the obligation of Member States to make good such loss and damage is to be found in Article 10 (*ex Article 5*) of the E.C. Treaty, under which the Member States are required to take all appropriate measures, whether general or particular, to ensure fulfilment of their obligations under Community law. Among these is the obligation to nullify the unlawful consequences of a breach of Community law.[44] **11–024**

For those reasons, the Court of Justice has held that "it is a principle of Community law that the Member States are obliged to make good loss and damage caused to individuals by breaches of Community law for which they can be held responsible".[45] The action for damages must be brought in the national courts.[46] The conditions on which a Member State's liability under

[41] Case T–93/95 *Laga v. Commission* [1998] E.C.R. II–195 at II–210, para. 47; Case T–94/95 *Landuyt v. Commission* [1998] E.C.R. II–213 at II–227, para. 47, CFI.

[42] Case 133/79 *Sucrimex v. Commission* [1980] E.C.R. 1299 at 1310–1311, para. 22, ECJ; Case 217/81 *Interagra v. Commission* [1982] E.C.R. 2233 at 2247–2248, paras 8–9, ECJ.

[43] Case 175/84 *Krohn v. Commission* [1986] E.C.R. 753 at 767–768, paras 19–23, ECJ.

[44] Joined Cases C–6 and C–9/90 *Francovich and Others* [1991] E.C.R. I–5357 at I–5414, paras 35–36, ECJ. See, in relation to the ECSC Treaty, Art. 86, Case 6/60 *Humblet v. Belgium* [1960] E.C.R. 559, ECJ.

[45] *Francovich and Others* (cited in n. 44, above) at I–5415, para. 37.

[46] (Order of May 23, 1990), Case C–72/90 *Asia Motor France v. Commission* [1990] E.C.R. I–2181 at I–2185, paras 14–15, ECJ.

Community law will give rise to a right to damages are to be determined by national law, unless they have already been prescribed by Community law.[47] The applicable national law must result in effective legal redress and the rules on liability for loss or damage ensuing from breaches of Community law must be at least equivalent to the rules governing liability for loss or damage resulting from breaches of domestic law.[48]

(2) Pecuniary loss resulting from the unlawfulness of the Community measure implemented

11–025 Where a Member State carries out an allegedly unlawful Community act,[49] an action for damages brought pursuant to Article 235 (*ex Article 178*) and the second paragraph of Article 288 (*ex Article 215*) will be inadmissible where the alleged damage can be made good by bringing a claim before the national courts. The Court of Justice has described the circumstances in which this is most likely to occur as follows:

> "Where an individual considers that he has been injured by the application of a Community legislative measure that he considers illegal, he may, when the implementation of the measure is left to the national authorities, contest the validity of the measure, when it is implemented, before a national court in an action against the national authorities. That court may, or even must, as provided for in Article 177 (*now Article 234*), refer the question of the validity of the Community measure in dispute to the Court of Justice".[50]

This means that, in order to decide on the admissibility of an action for damages brought before it, the Court of First Instance has to consider whether bringing a claim before the national courts would be capable of securing full compensation for the alleged damage. This will depend first on the type of pecuniary loss which purportedly constitutes the damage, together with the possibility that the declaration of the invalidity of the Community act in question by preliminary ruling will constitute a direct basis for the national courts to remedy the pecuniary loss suffered. This has to be considered in the light of the particular circumstances. Only if on

---

[47] For the procedural conditions, see Joined Cases C–6 and C–9/90 *Francovich and Others* [1991] E.C.R. I–5357 at I–5415—5416, para. 42; the basic conditions "depend on the nature of the breach of Community law giving rise to the loss and damage", *ibid.*, at I–5415, para. 38, and the Court of Justice has specified them accordingly. They are designed to secure the full effect of the principle of state liability and hence the applicable national law must always satisfy them, *cf.* Case 101/78 *Granaria v. Hoofdproduktschap voor Akkerbouwprodukten* [1979] E.C.R. 623 at 638, paras 12–14, ECJ.

[48] See para. 3–023, above.

[49] If the act has already been annulled or declared invalid at the time when it is implemented by the Member State, the latter will be guilty of a breach of Community law and the question of compensation for any pecuniary loss will be dealt with in accordance with the previous section (see para. 11–024, above).

[50] Case 281/82 *Unifrex v. Commission and Council* [1984] E.C.R. 1969 at 1982, para. 11, ECJ. See also Case 175/84 *Krohn v. Commission* [1986] E.C.R. 753 at 769, para. 27, ECJ; Case 81/86 *De Boer Buizen v. Council and Commission* [1987] E.C.R. 3677 at 3692, para. 9, ECJ.

account of the type of the alleged damage or of the limited extent of the consequences of any declaration of invalidity by way of preliminary ruling, compensation cannot be obtained from the national courts, will an action for damages lie against the Community institution from which the act implemented by the Member State originated.

First, it may be that the pecuniary loss simply stems from a payment which the individual concerned made to a national authority pursuant to what he or she considers to be an unlawful Community act. In order to recover the undue amount paid over, together with the applicable interest at the legal rate, the individual concerned must apply to the national courts.[51] Community law obliges the Member States to provide for legal proceedings enabling undue amounts paid to be recovered.[52] The national courts have no jurisdiction themselves to declare that the Community act on the basis of which payment was made is invalid, but if they consider that there are grounds for doubting whether the act is lawful, they must make a reference to the Court of Justice for a preliminary ruling on its validity.[53] If the Court of Justice declares the Community act at issue invalid, it provides the national court in principle with a sufficient basis for ordering restitution of the undue amount. Hence, it is not possible to bring an action for damages under Article 235 (*ex Article 178*) and the second paragraph of Article 288 (*ex Article 215*) of the E.C. Treaty in respect of this kind of pecuniary loss.[54] An action for damages under those provisions will lie only in the exceptional case where the Court of Justice limits the effects as regards the part of a preliminary ruling declaring an act invalid. In such case, the national court cannot order restitution of the undue payment. Since in such a case compensation for the alleged damage cannot be secured by bringing proceedings in the national courts, an action for damages may unquestionably be brought in the Court of First Instance against the institution in which the act in question originated.[55] **11–026**

Secondly, the pecuniary loss may possibly be caused by a national authority's refusal to effect a payment or to perform some other act, whilst the individual concerned takes the view that the refusal is based on an unlawful Community act. In so far as individuals seek only reparation for the pecuniary loss resulting from the refusal, namely payment of what they **11–027**

[51] Case 26/74 *Roquette v. Commission* [1976] E.C.R. 677 at 686, paras 11, 12, ECJ. See also Case 96/71 *Haegeman v. Commission* [1972] E.C.R. 1005 at 1016, paras 15–16, ECJ, and Regulation 1430/79 ([1979] O.J. L175/1) Arts. 2, 4, as amended by Regulation No. 1854/89 ([1989] O.J. L/168/1), in connection with the recovery of overpaid import and export levies.

[52] *Cf.* Tatham, "Restitution of Charges and Duties levied by the Public Administration in Breach of Community Law: a Comparative Analysis" (1994) E.L.Rev. 146–168.

[53] Case 314/85 *Foto-Frost v. Hauptzollamt Lübeck-Ost* [1987] E.C.R. 4199, ECJ. See also para. 2–055, above.

[54] Naturally, this does not mean that the Community does not have to bear the financial burden of repayment. Repayment occurs as a result of a preliminary ruling by the Court of Justice declaring the Community act in question invalid, which is binding on all Community institutions. For the question of settlement as between the Community and the Member States, see Oliver, "Joint Liability of the Community and the Member States", in Heukels and McDonnell (eds) (cited in n. 4, above), pp. 285–310.

[55] Case 20/88 *Roquette Frères v. Commission* [1989] E.C.R. 1553 at 1587, paras 18–20, ECJ.

maintain they are owed, or adoption of the act to which they consider they are entitled (*i.e.* compensation in kind), the only question arising in principle is whether the declaration by preliminary ruling of the Court of Justice that the Community act on which the refusal is based is invalid affords *in itself* the legal basis needed by the national court in order to order the payment requested or, as the case may be, the adoption of the act requested. If the answer to that question is in the affirmative, an action for damages brought in the Court of First Instance against the institution from which the act originated will be inadmissible.[56] If, in contrast, the answer to that question is in the negative, such an action for damages will be admissible.[57]

It should not come as a surprise in the light of the above that the admissibility of an action for damages should turn on a close analysis of the individual case. A degree of unpredictability of the outcome is therefore inevitable. For example, the importance of the time factor should not be underestimated. Even if a declaration of invalidity in preliminary ruling proceedings results in the national court's annulling the refusal to adopt the act requested (for example the grant of import licences), the loss of a number of years can no longer be made good. Consequently, an action for damages brought against the Community institution from which the act declared invalid originated will be admissible.[58]

11–028 Thirdly, the pecuniary loss may take the form of actual "injury", possibly alongside the financial loss resulting from an undue payment or from the fact that a payment or an act was unlawfully withheld. Examples include an undertaking becoming the subject of insolvency proceedings, a weakening of the undertaking's competitive position or the price of having at short

---

[56] *e.g.*, see Case 99/74 *Grands Moulins v. Commission* [1975] E.C.R. 1531, ECJ; Case 12/79 *Hans-Otto Wagner v. Commission* [1979] E.C.R. 3657 at 3671–3672, paras 11–14, ECJ; Case C–119/88 *AERPO and Others v. Commission* [1990] E.C.R. I–2189 at I–2210, paras 12–14, ECJ. Here, too, the mechanism for settlement of the financial burden operates, see Oliver (cited in n. 54, above).

[57] The examples in the case law are generally concerned with cases in which the Community act was unlawful because it exhibited a *lacuna* which could be filled only by the necessary political decisions; on the basis of the mere finding that the act is invalid, the national court cannot order compensation to be paid for the "alleged damage" and hence the injured party will be entitled to bring proceedings in the Court of First Instance: see, for instance, Joined Cases 9 and 11/71 *Cie d'Approvisionnement v. Commission* [1972] E.C.R. 391, ECJ; Case 43/72 *Merkur v. Commission* [1973] E.C.R. 1055; ECJ, Case 153/73 *Holtz & Willemsen v. Council and Commission* [1974] E.C.R. 675; ECJ, Case 281/82 *Unifrex v. Council and Commission* [1984] E.C.R. 1969 at 1982, para. 12, ECJ; Case 81/86 *De Boer Buizen v. Council and Commission* [1987] E.C.R. 3677 at 3692, para. 10, ECJ. More exceptionally, the Court itself limits the effects of the declaration of invalidity by way of preliminary ruling, with the result that that ruling no longer constitutes a legal basis justifying the national court ordering reparation of the financial loss: see Case 238/78 *Ireks-Arkady v. Council and Commission* [1979] E.C.R. 2955 at 2971, para. 6, ECJ; Joined Cases 241–242, 245–250/78 *DGV v. Council and Commission* [1979] E.C.R. 3017 at 3037, para. 6, ECJ; Joined Cases 261 and 262/78 *Interquell Stärke-Chemie v. Council and Commission* [1979] E.C.R. 3045 at 3062, para. 6, ECJ.

[58] Case 62/83 *Eximo v. Commission* [1984] E.C.R. 2295 at 2310–2311, paras 15–17, ECJ; Case 175/84 *Krohn v. Commission* [1986] E.C.R. 753 at 769, paras 27–28, ECJ.

notice to obtain credit. Compensation for such injury may be obtained only by bringing an action for damages in the Court of First Instance.[59]

The Court of First Instance and the Court of Justice have exclusive jurisdiction to find the Community liable to make good actual injury following actions brought pursuant to Article 235 (*ex Article 178*) and the second paragraph of Article 288 (*ex Article 215*) of the E.C. Treaty.[60] If the Court of Justice has found that the illegality of the Community provision at issue does not cause the Community to incur liability because the relevant requirements are not satisfied, that finding makes it impossible to bring a claim before the national courts for a declaration that the Member State which implemented that provision is liable on account of the same illegality.[61] The judgment of the Court of Justice does not preclude "an action on grounds other than the unlawfulness of the Community measure in issue in that judgment brought against the competent national authorities for damage caused to individuals by the national authorities, even where they were acting within the framework of Community law".[62] In other words, a claim may be brought against Member States only where the damage stemmed from a wrongful act or omission on their part and not where the act or omission consisted in the due implementation of a Community measure which was later declared invalid.

(3) Pecuniary loss resulting from unlawful joint action on the part of the Community and a Member State

The Community and a Member State act jointly where they both contribute to the adoption of a measure through the exercise of their own discretion. An example is where Member States adopt protective measures with the agreement of the Community.[63] If such action is unlawful, here again a distinction has to be drawn between the three types of pecuniary loss mentioned above.[64] As far as the first two types of pecuniary loss are concerned, that is to say recovery of an undue payment or a claim for a payment or for an act which was wrongfully refused, proceedings must in principle be brought before the national courts.[65] In contrast, where actual "injury" is involved, although an action brought against the Community will be admissible before national remedies have been exhausted, the extent of the Community's liability will not be determined until the national courts **11–029**

[59] *e.g.*, see Case 26/74 *Roquette v. Commission* [1976] E.C.R. 677 at 687–688, paras 15–25, ECJ; Joined Cases 116 and 124/77 *Amylum v. Council and Commission* [1979] E.C.R. 3479 at 3559, para. 9, ECJ; Case T–167/94 *Nölle v. Council and Commission* [1995] E.C.R. II–2589 at II–2607—2608, paras 41–42, CFI. *Cf.* Harding, "The Choice of Court Problem in Cases of Non-Contractual Liability under EEC Law" (1979) C.M.L.Rev. 389 at 392–397.

[60] Case 101/78 *Granaria v. Hoofdproduktschap voor Akkerbouwprodukten* [1979] E.C.R. 623 at 637–638, para. 10, ECJ.

[61] Joined Cases 106–120/87 *Asteris v. Greece* [1988] E.C.R. 5515 at 5538–5539, paras 17–18, ECJ.

[62] *ibid.*, at 5539, para. 19.

[63] Joined Cases 5, 7 and 13–24/66 *Kampffmeyer and Others v. Commission* [1967] E.C.R. 245, ECJ.

[64] See paras 11–026—11–028, above.

[65] *Kampffmeyer and Others v. Commission* (cited in n. 63 above), at 263–264.

have determined the proportion of the liability to be borne by the Member State under national law. The Court of Justice has held in that connection that "it is necessary to avoid the applicants' being insufficiently or excessively compensated for the same damage by the different assessment of two different courts applying different rules of law".[66]

III. Special Characteristics

A. Requirements for liability

11–030 The classic requirements for liability—a wrongful Community act, loss or damage, and a causal connection between that act and the loss or damage—must be fulfilled[67] if the Community is to be held liable.[68]

1. The unlawful act

(1) What test for unlawfulness?

11–031 The case law is not always clear as to whether the unlawfulness of a Community act is based simply on the breach of a rule of superior law (objective or strict liability) or whether "fault" is also required on the part of the institution or person responsible for the act (subjective liability).[69]

11–032 In the case of the ECSC Treaty, "fault" or "a wrongful act or omission on the part of the Community in the performance of its functions" (*faute de service*: maladministration) is required in order for the Community to incur liability (see Articles 34 and 40). Such a requirement to show fault means that actual "blame" must attach to the act.[70] The criterion for determining blame is derived on an individual basis from the whole of the particular facts.[71] The complexity of the situations with which the institution has to deal, the difficulties in applying the Treaty provisions and the discretion which the institution has under those provisions are taken into account.[72] In addition, the fault must be of a particular nature. Thus, only "unjustifiably bad administration"[73] or "a lack of adequate supervision"[74] may be

---

[66] *ibid.*, at 226.

[67] See para. 11–001, above.

[68] Case 153/73 *Holz & Willemsen v. Council and Commission* [1974] E.C.R. 675 at 693, para. 7, ECJ.

[69] Hermann-Rodeville, "Un exemple de contentieux économique: le recours en indemnité devant la Cour de justice des Communautés européennes" (1986) R.T.D.E. 5 at 13–27.

[70] Heukels, "De niet-contractuele aansprakelijkheid van de Gemeenschap ex art. 215 *[now Article 288]*, lid 2, EEG: Dynamiek en continuïteit (1983–1991) (II)" (1992) S.E.W. 317–347.

[71] Case C–220/91P *Commission v. Stahlwerke Peine-Salzgitter* [1993] E.C.R. I–2393 at I–2447, para. 37, ECJ. See also Lysén, "Three Questions on the Non-Contractual Liability of the EEC" (1985) 2 L.I.E.I. 108.

[72] Joined Cases C–363 and C–364/88 *Finsider and Others v. Commission* [1992] E.C.R. I–359 at I–417, para. 24, ECJ (these criteria for determining the type of fault which must have been committed in order for the Community to incur liability apply in connection with both Art. 34 and Art. 40).

[73] Joined Cases 14, 16–17, 20, 24, 26–27/60 and 1/61 *Meroni & Co. v. High Authority* [1961] E.C.R. 161 at 169.

[74] Joined Cases 19 and 21/60, 2 and 3/61 *Société Fives Lille Cail and Others v. High Authority* [1961] E.C.R. 281 at 297, ECJ. See, to the same effect, Joined Cases 29, 31, 36, 39–47, 50 and 51/63 *SA des Laminoirs, Hauts Fournaux, Forges, Fonderies et Usines de la Providence and Others v. High Authority* [1965] E.C.R. 911 at 937, ECJ.

regarded as constituting fault capable of causing the Community to incur liability. Consequently, the fact that a Community act is unlawful does not necessarily mean that it has to be regarded as constituting "fault" giving rise to Community liability.

The second paragraph of Article 288 (*ex Article 215*) of the E.C. Treaty puts the Court of Justice and the Court of First Instance under a duty to determine any liability incurred by the Community "in accordance with the general principles common to the laws of the Member States". In theory, that provision provides an opportunity for formulating a system of objective or strict liability, in which a generally applicable criterion of unlawfulness is determined in advance, without having regard to the particular circumstances surrounding the Community act at issue.[75] In that case, a breach of a superior rule of law would be sufficient in itself to cause the act to be regarded as unlawful and hence to cause the Community to incur liability, regardless as to whether the act was actually blameworthy and hence vitiated by fault. This theoretical possibility has not achieved any success in the case law. **11–033**

The concept of fault has in fact not disappeared from the system of liability founded upon the second paragraph of Article 288 (*ex Article 215*) of the E.C. Treaty.[76] The case law has swung between mentioning fault[77] **11–034**

[75] Lysén (cited in n. 71 above), at 109. See also Van Gerven, "Non-Contractual Liability of Member States, Community Institutions and Individuals for Breaches of Community Law with a View to a Common Law for Europe" (1994) Maastricht Journal of European and Comparative Law 6, at 28 and 37–38. This definition even affords room for objective, no-fault liability arising out of a lawful act which infringes the principle of "*egalité devant les charges publiques*" (a principle of French administrative law to the effect that public charges should be discharged equally). To date, the Court of Justice has not yet accepted that type of liability, but has also not ruled it out. *Cf.* Joined Cases 9 and 11/71 *Cie d'Approvisionnement v. Commission* [1972] E.C.R. 391 at 407–408, para. 46, ECJ; Case 59/83 *Biovilac v. EEC* [1984] E.C.R. 4057 at 4080–4081, para. 28, ECJ; Case 267/82 *Développement SA and Clemessy v. Commission* [1986] E.C.R. 1907 at 1922, para. 33, ECJ; Case T–113/96 *Dubois et fils v. Council and Commission* [1998] E.C.R. II–125 at II–141, para. 42, CFI. Although the Court of First Instance has specified the circumstances in which the Community may be held liable for a lawful act, it has not stated whether this form of liability should in principle be recognised. The Court of First Instance has stated that such liability could be incurred only if the damage alleged affects a particular circle of economic operators in a disproportionate manner by comparison with others (unusual damage) and exceeds the limits of the economic risks inherent in operating in the sector concerned (special damage), without the legislative measure that gave rise to the alleged damage being justified by a general economic interest (CFI, Case T–184/95 *Dorsch Consult v. Council and Commission* [1998] E.C.R. II–667 at II–696, para. 80, CFI). See Bronkhorst, "The Valid Legislative Act as a Cause of Liability of the Communities", in Heukels and McDonnell (eds) (cited in n. 4, above), pp. 153–165.

[76] See Case T–120/89 *Stahlwerke Peine-Salzgitter v. Commission* [1991] E.C.R. II–279 at II–388—389, para. 74, CFI, which reiterates the conditions having to be fulfilled before there can be "fault of such a nature as to render the Community liable under the second para. of Article 215 *[now Article 288]* of the E[E]C Treaty". Academics are divided on this point. Some maintain that the Court has abandoned the requirement for fault, at least in the case of liability for legislative acts, and regards the illegality of the act at issue sufficient in certain circumstances to cause the Community to incur liability (Schockweiler, Wivines and Godart, "Le régime de la responsabilité extra-contractuelle du fait d'actes juridiques dans la Communauté européenne" (1990) R.T.D.E. 27–74). Others still adhere to the concept of fault, considering that it imposes requirements additional to the unlawful nature of the act

and not mentioning it,[78] but it is of course in the background whenever the mere unlawfulness of a Community act is insufficient to render the Community liable.[79]

11–035 That the term "fault" is used in connection with both the ECSC Treaty and the E.C. Treaty does not necessarily signify that it must be given the same meaning under the two Treaties. The Court of First Instance fleshed out the term "fault" within the meaning of the first paragraph of Article 34 of the ECSC Treaty by employing the criteria developed by the Court of Justice in its case law on the second paragraph of Article 215 (*now Article 288*) of the E.C. Treaty in order to secure uniform application of Community law on non-contractual liability on the part of the Community for unlawful legislative acts.[80] On appeal, the Court of Justice did not take issue with the actual manner in which the Court of First Instance had fleshed out the concept of fault, but stressed that Community liability under the ECSC Treaty had to be determined in the light of the criteria evolved for the application of Articles 34 and 40 of that Treaty.[81] Consequently, the concept of "fault" may receive a different interpretation depending on which of the different Treaties is involved.

(2) Unlawfulness of administrative measures

11–036 Various shortcomings in the performance of administrative acts have been held to constitute fault.[82] They may cause the Community to incur liability. The shortcomings in question include lack of care in exercising implement-

---

at issue (see, *e.g.*, Couzinet, "La faute dans le régime de la responsabilité non contractuelle des Communautés européennes" (1986) R.T.D.E. 367–390). The debate may perhaps be reduced to what is to be understood by "fault" and, to that extent, is purely epistemological (see, *e.g.*, Cornelis, "De extra-contractuele aansprakelijkheid van de Gemeenschap (1976–1982)" (1984) S.E.W. 5 at 11, who argues that the distinction between "fault" and "illegality" is superfluous on the ground that both concepts are objective, the concept of "fault" being based on the objective criterion of "a normal, prudent person").

[77] See, *e.g.* Case 25/62 *Plaumann & Co. v. Commission* [1963] E.C.R. 95 at 108, ECJ; Joined Cases 5, 7 and 13–24/66 *Kampffmeyer and Others v. Commission* [1967] E.C.R. 245 at 262, ECJ; Case 30/66 *Becher v. Commission* [1967] E.C.R. 285 at 296, ECJ; Case 16/67 *Labeyrie v. Commission* [1968] E.C.R. 293 at 304, ECJ; Joined Cases 19–20, 25 and 30/69 *Richez-Parise v. Commission* [1970] E.C.R. 325 at 338, para. 31, ECJ; Case 257/78 *Devred v. Commission* [1979] E.C.R. 3767 at 3784, para. 22, ECJ; Case 137/79 *Kohl v. Commission* [1980] E.C.R. 2601 at 2614, para. 14, ECJ.

[78] Case 5/71 *Zuckerfabrik Schöppenstedt v. Council* [1971] E.C.R. 975, ECJ. See, however, para. 11–037, below, where it appears that the rules on liability for legislative acts do in fact contain the requirement for fault in question.

[79] See Mahieu, "Illégalité et responsabilité en droit communautaire", *Mélanges Roger O. Dalcq*, Brussels, Larcier, 1994, 388 at 400–401. *Cf.* Fuss, "La responsabilité des Communautés européennes pour le comportement illégal de leurs organes" (1981) R.T.D.E. 1 at 14–15.

[80] CFI, Case T–120/89 *Stahlwerke Peine-Salzgitter v. Commission* [1991] E.C.R. II–279 at II–388–390, paras 74–78, CFI.

[81] Case C–220/91P *Commission v. Peine-Salzgitter* [1993] E.C.R. I–2393 at I–2445, para. 30, ECJ.

[82] For a survey, see Schermers and Waelbroeck, *Judicial Protection*, pp. 571–583, and Heukels (cited in n. 70, above), at 322–323. See also Van der Woude, "Liability for Administrative Acts under Article 215 *[now Article 288]* (2) EC", in Heukels and McDonnell (eds) (cited in n. 4, above), pp. 109–128. What is involved is the usual form taken by unlawful conduct attributed to the institutions: Case C–55/90 *Cato v. Commission* [1992] E.C.R. I–2533 at I–

ing powers,[83] misuse of powers,[84] failure to adopt a required act,[85] defective system adopted by an authority which can be attributed to the Community,[86] lack of supervision,[87] failure to rectify information in time once it becomes clear that the information provided was incorrect,[88] failure to comply with internal rules,[89] and breach of the duty of confidentiality.[90]

(3) Unlawfulness of legislative measures

A special rule on liability applies in the case of legislative acts: according to the rule in *Schöppenstedt*, "[w]here legislative action involving measures of economic policy is concerned", the Community will be liable only for damage suffered by individuals as a consequence of that action where there has been "a sufficiently flagrant violation of a superior rule of law for the protection of the individual".[91] That rule reflects the reluctance of the Court of Justice and the Court of First Instance to assess the legality of acts which inevitably involve choices made on the basis of considerations of expediency. The particular nature of the function played by the courts means that they have to accept such choices as such. On those grounds, moreover, the Member States have sharply curtailed or even ruled out altogether state liability for action taken under "statute law".[92] On the other **11–037**

2570–2571, para. 18, ECJ.

83 Case 169/73 *Compagnie Continentale v. Council* [1975] E.C.R. 117 at 134, para. 21, ECJ; Case T–514/93 *Cobrecaf and Others v. Commission* [1995] E.C.R. II–621 at II–642—643, paras 63–70, CFI (by waiting 15 months before rectifying a manifest error in paying a promised Community subsidy, the Commission exhibited an obvious lack of care).

84 Joined Cases 5, 7 and 13–24/66 *Kampffmeyer and Others v. Commission* [1967] E.C.R. 245 at 262, ECJ.

85 Joined Cases 9 and 12/60 *Vloeberghs v. High Authority* [1961] E.C.R. 197 at 213, ECJ.

86 Case 23/59 *FERAM v. High Authority* [1959] E.C.R. 245 at 251–252, ECJ (system adopted held not defective); Case 33/59 *Compagnie des Hauts Fournaux de Chasse v. High Authority* [1962] E.C.R. 381 at 389, ECJ (system held not defective); Joined Cases 46 and 47/59 *Meroni & Co. v. High Authority* [1962] E.C.R. 411 at 422–423, ECJ.

87 Joined Cases 19 and 21/60, 2 and 3/61 *Société Fives Lille Cail and Others v. High Authority* [1961] E.C.R. 281 at 297, ECJ.

88 Joined Cases 19–20, 25 and 30/69 *Richez-Parise v. Commission* [1970] E.C.R. 325 at 339–340, paras 38–42, ECJ.

89 Joined Cases 10 and 47/72 *Di Pillo v. Commission* [1973] E.C.R. 763 at 772, para. 24, ECJ.

90 Case 145/83 *Adams v. Commission* [1985] E.C.R. 3539 at 3585–3590, paras 28–44, ECJ.

91 ECJ, Case 5/71 *Zuckerfabrik Schöppenstedt v Council* [1971] E.C.R. 975 at 984, para. 11, ECJ. A more recent formulation of the rule in English is "the Community does not incur liability on account of a measure involving *choices of economic policy* unless a *sufficiently serious* breach of a superior rule of law for the protection of the individual has occurred" (Joined Cases C–104/89 and C–37/90 *Mulder and Others v. Council and Commission* [1992] E.C.R. I–3061 at I–3131—3132, para. 12, ECJ, italics supplied).

92 Joined Cases 83 and 94/76, 4, 15 and 40/77 *HNL v. Council and Commission* [1978] E.C.R. 1209 at 1224–1225, paras 5, 6, ECJ: "This restrictive view is explained by the consideration that the legislative authority, even where the validity of its measures is subject to judicial review, cannot always be hindered in making its decisions by the prospect of applications for damages whenever it has occasion to adopt legislative measures in the public interest which may adversely affect the interests of individuals. It follows from these considerations that individuals may be required, in the sectors coming within the economic policy of the Community, to accept within reasonable limits certain harmful effects on their economic interests as a result of a legislative measure without being able to obtain compensation from public funds even if that measure has been declared null and void". See also Schockweiler, Wivines and Godart (cited in n. 76, above), at 54.

hand, the existence of rules governing such liability—no matter how restrictive they may be—expresses a genuine concern to afford individuals the widest possible legal protection in the absence of effective parliamentary control.[93]

11–038 Community liability on account of a failure to act in a sphere where legislative action is required must also be tested against the same criteria.[94]

(a) *The expression legislative measure involving choices of economic policy*

11–039 Legislative measures to which the rule in *Schöppenstedt* applies are of general application and involve choices of (economic) policy.[95] It is irrelevant for this purpose whether the act in question is, in an institutional sense, a "legislative" or an "executive/implementing" measure.[96]

It is only the content of the act which is determinative: if it discloses a general policy choice made by the Community institution in the exercise of its discretion, the act will come under the rule in *Schöppenstedt*; if, in contrast, it constitutes simply an individual application of a general provision and/or contains no genuine policy choice, it will be merely an administrative measure[97] subject to the usual rules on liability.[98]

11–040 The type of measure involved may provide an indication of its legislative nature. Accordingly, as a rule decisions are not legislative acts since they do not apply to objectively defined classes of persons.[99]

---

[93] See also the Opinion of Advocate General K. Roemer in Case 5/71 *Zuckerfabrik Schöppenstedt v. Council* [1971] E.C.R. 975 at 989, ECJ.

[94] Case 50/86 *Grands Moulins de Paris v. Council and Commission* [1987] E.C.R. 4833 at 4857, para. 9, ECJ.

[95] Case C–119/88 *AERPO and Others v. Commission* [1990] E.C.R. I–2189 at I–2211, para. 17, ECJ.

[96] The distinction between legislation and implementation of legislation is not reflected in the Community legal order in a distinction between "authorities" or "institutions" charged with rule-making at the legislative or implementation levels. The distinction between "legislation" and "implementation" depends on the legal basis pursuant to which the act of the relevant Community institution is adopted. Any act which is based directly on an article of the Treaty will be a legislative act. Any act based on secondary legislation will be an implementing or executive act. It is to be expected that legislative acts will tend more often to be rule-making in comparison with implementing measures. For further particulars, see Lenaerts (cited in para. 7–026, n. 81, above), at 27–36.

[97] See para. 11–036, above.

[98] A legislative act which is found in an action for annulment to be of individual concern to a natural or legal person continues to be regarded as a legislative act *vis-à-vis* that person in the context of a claim for damages: Joined Cases T–480 and T–483/93 *Antillean Rice Mills and Others v. Commission* [1995] E.C.R. II–2305 at II–2367—2369, paras 180–186, CFI, upheld on appeal in (Judgment of February 11, 1999) Case C–390/95P *Antillean Rice Mills and Others v. Commission*, paras 56–63, ECJ (not yet reported). Accordingly the *Schöppenstedt* test is applied.

[99] E.C. Treaty, Art. 249 (*ex Art. 189*), para. 4. If, however, a decision is addressed to all the Member States, it may perhaps be legislative in nature. *Cf.* Heukels (cited in n. 70, above), at 328, who observes that even decisions which have a legislative slant because they approve a national measure are not regarded as legislative measures: Case 59/84 *Tezi v. Commission* [1986] E.C.R. 887 at 930, paras 69–73, ECJ, Case 253/84 *GAEC de la Ségaude v. Council and Commission* [1987] E.C.R. 123, ECJ; Opinion of Advocate General M. Darmon in Case C–55/90 *Cato v. Commission* [1992] E.C.R. I–2533 at I–2555—2556, ECJ.

In contrast, regulations[1] and directives[2] are pre-eminently the legal instruments which embody a legislative act.

The Community cannot incur liability on account of the Treaties themselves or amendments thereto.[3] **11–041**

Although the rule in *Schöppenstedt* refers only to legislative acts involving choices of economic policy, it is possible that legislative acts involving other policy choices are also covered by this special rule on Community liability.[4] **11–042**

(b) *Superior rule of law for the protection of individuals*

Any judicial review of the legality of an act involves checking whether it conflicts with superior law. This necessitates ascertaining the rank of the measure at issue in the hierarchy of norms.[5] **11–043**

The superior rules of law are the provisions of the treaties, the general principles of law and the Community measures on which the contested act is based. **11–044**

The Treaty provisions which have already been used to test the legality of an act include Article 12 (*ex Article 6*), Article 28 (*ex Article 30*), Article 29 (*ex Article 34*), Article 33 (*ex Article 39*) (1) and Article 34 (*ex Article 40*) (3) of the E.C. Treaty.[6] **11–045**

---

[1] *e.g.* Case 43/72 *Merkur v. Commission* [1973] E.C.R. 1055, ECJ; Joined Cases 63–69/72 *Werhahn v. Council* [1973] E.C.R. 1229; ECJ; Case 97/76 *Merkur v. Commission* [1977] E.C.R. 1063, ECJ. The fact that a regulation is of direct and individual concern to a particular person within the meaning of the E.C. Treaty, Art. 230 (*ex Art. 173*), para. 4, does not mean that it loses its legislative nature for the purposes of an action for damages brought pursuant to the second paragraph of Art. 288 (*ex Art. 215*), para. 2 (see, *e.g.* Case C–152/88 *Sofrimport v. Commission* [1990] E.C.R. I–2477 at I–2510, ECJ).

[2] Case C–63/89 *Assurances du Crédit v. Council and Commission* [1991] E.C.R. I–1799 at I–1846, para. 12, ECJ.

[3] Case 169/73 *Compagnie Continentale v. Council* [1975] E.C.R. 117 at 134, para. 16, ECJ; Joined Cases 31 and 35/86 *LAISA and Others v. Council* [1988] E.C.R. 2285 at 2319–2320, paras 19–22, ECJ.

[4] See, *e.g.* Van Gerven, "De niet-contractuele aansprakelijkheid van de Gemeenschap wegens normatieve handelingen" (1976) S.E.W. 2, at 10; Lysén (cited in n. 71, above), at 109.

[5] The following hierarchy of norms obtains in the legal order of the European Community: at the top, the Treaties and the Acts of Accession, which constitute the basic constitutional charter (see Case 294/83 *Les Verts v. European Parliament* [1986] E.C.R. 1339 at 1365, para. 23, ECJ). In addition, there is a series of decisions of a quasi-constitutional nature, such as the Decision on Own Resources (based on the E.C. Treaty, Art. 269 (*ex Art. 201*)) or the decision and the act concerning the direct election of the European Parliament (based on Art. 190 (*ex Art. 138*) (3)). The general principles of law, including fundamental rights, constitute the unwritten constitutional norms, which are on an equal footing with the Treaties and the other written constitutional rules. Next come the rules of international law which permeate the legal order of the Community, *i.e.* agreements and customary international law. At the third level, there are acts of Community institutions directly based on Treaty provisions. Finally, there are acts of Community institutions implementing earlier acts. For further details, see Lenaerts and Van Nuffel, *Constitutional Law of the European Union*, paras 14–037 *et seq.*

[6] See, as regards the EEC Treaty, Art. 7, (*now Art. 12 of the E.C. Treaty*), Joined Cases 71 and 72/84 *Surcouf and Vidou v. EEC* [1985] E.C.R. 2925, ECJ; as regards Arts. 28 and 29 (*ex Arts. 30 and 34*), Case 265/85 *Van den Bergh and Jurgens v. Commission* [1987] E.C.R. 1155, ECJ; as regards Art. 33 (*ex Art. 39*) (1), Case 27/85 *Vandemoortele v. Commission* [1987] E.C.R. 1129, ECJ; and, as regards Art. 34 (*ex Art. 40*) (3), Case 281/82 *Unifrex v. Council and Commission* [1984] E.C.R. 1969, ECJ. Art. 32 (*ex Art. 38*) (4) and Art. 37 (*ex Art. 43*) (2), do not constitute superior rules of law for the protection of individuals: Case T–571/93 *Lefebvre and Others v. Commission* [1995] E.C.R. II–2379 at II–2398, para. 41, CFI.

The general rules of law which operate as superior rules of law include the principle of protection of legitimate expectation,[7] the principle of proportionality,[8] the principle of equal treatment (also known as the principle of equality or the prohibition of discrimination),[9] the principle of care,[10] the principle of proper administration[11] and the prohibition of misuse of powers.[12] Fundamental rights, such as the right to property,[13] the

---

[7] Case 74/74 *CNTA v. Commission* [1975] E.C.R. 533 at 548–550, ECJ (manifest infringement of the principle of protection of legitimate expectation); Case C–152/88 *Sofrimport v. Commission* [1990] E.C.R. I–2477 at I–2511 para. 26, ECJ (manifest infringement of that principle); Joined Cases C–104/89 and C–37/90 *Mulder and Others v. Council and Commission* [1992] E.C.R. I–3061 at I–3132, para. 15, ECJ (manifest infringement of that principle); CFI, Case T–472/93 *Campo Ebro and Others v. Council* [1995] E.C.R. II–421 at II–441, para. 52, CFI (no infringement of the principle of protection of legitimate expectation); Joined Cases T–481/93 and T–484/93 *Exporteurs in Levende Varkens and Others v. Commission* [1995] E.C.R. II–2941 at II–2989, paras 148–150, CFI (no infringement of the principle of protection of legitimate expectation); Case T–521/93 *Atlanta and Others v. European Communities* [1996] E.C.R. II–1707 at II–1728, paras 55–58, CFI (no infringement of the principle of protection of legitimate expectation); Case T–105/96 *Pharos v. Commission* [1998] E.C.R. II–285 at II–305—307, paras 63–72, CFI (no infringement of the principle of protection of legitimate expectation).

[8] Joined Cases 63–69/72 *Werhahn v. Council* [1973] E.C.R. 1229 at 1250–1251, paras 18–20, ECJ; Joined Cases 279–280, 285 and 286/84 *Rau v. Commission* [1987] E.C.R. 1069 at 1125–1126, paras 33–37, ECJ; Case 27/85 *Vandemoortele v. Commission* [1987] E.C.R. 1129 at 1150–1151, paras 30–34, ECJ; Case 265/85 *Van den Bergh and Jurgens v. Commission* [1987] E.C.R. 1155 at 1177–1178, paras 30–34, CFI; Case T–152/95 *Petrides v. Commission* [1997] E.C.R. II–2427 at II–2443—2445, paras 48–53, CFI (no infringement of the principle of proportionality).

[9] Joined Cases 83 and 94/76, 4, 15 and 40/77 *HNL v. Council and Commission* [1978] E.C.R. 1209 at 1224, para. 5, ECJ; Joined Cases 64 and 113/76, 167 and 239/78, 27–28 and 45/79 *Dumortier v. Council* [1979] E.C.R. 3091 at 3114, para. 11, ECJ; Case 238/78 *Ireks-Arkady v. Council and Commission* [1979] E.C.R. 2955 at 2973, para. 11, ECJ; Joined Cases 241–242, 245–250/78 *DGV v. Council and Commission* [1979] E.C.R. 3017 at 3038–3039, para. 11, ECJ; Joined Cases 261 and 262/78 *Interquell Stärke-Chemie v. Council and Commission* [1979] E.C.R. 3045 at 3064, para. 14, ECJ; Case 106/81 *Kind v. EEC* [1982] E.C.R. 2885 at 2921–2922, paras 22–25, ECJ (no infringement of the principle of equal treatment); Case C–63/89 *Assurances du Crédit v. Council and Commission* [1991] E.C.R. I–1799 at I–1846–1848, paras 14–23, ECJ (no infringement of the principle of equal treatment); Case T–120/89 *Stahlwerke Peine-Salzgitter v. Commission* [1991] E.C.R. II–279 at II–394, para. 92, CFI (manifest infringement of the principle of equal treatment); Case T–489/93 *Unifruit Hellas v. Commission* [1994] E.C.R. II–1201 at II–1230—1231, paras 76–80, CFI (no infringement of the principle of equal treatment); Case T–472/93 *Campo Ebro and Others v. Commission* [1995] E.C.R. II–421 at II–449, para. 52, CFI; Joined Cases T–481 and T–484/93 *Exporteurs in Levende Varkens and Others v. Commission* [1995] E.C.R. II–2941 at II–2976, para. 102, CFI (no infringement of the principle of equal treatment); Case T–152/95 *Petrides v. Commission* [1997] E.C.R. II–2427 at II–2445—2447, paras 54–60, CFI (no infringement of the principle of equal treatment).

[10] Case T–167/94 *Nölle v. Council and Commission* [1995] E.C.R. II–2589 at II–2619, para. 76, CFI (no infringement of the principle of care).

[11] Case T–105/96 *Pharos v. Commission* [1998] E.C.R. II–285 at II–307—308, paras 73–78, CFI (no infringement of the principle of proper administration).

[12] Case C–119/88 *AERPO and Others v. Commission* [1990] E.C.R. I–2189 at I–2211—2212, para. 19, CFI; Joined Cases T–481 and T–484/93 *Exporteurs in Levende Varkens and Others v. Commission* [1995] E.C.R. II–2941 at II–2976, paras 134, 135, CFI (no infringement of the prohibition of misuse of powers).

[13] Case 59/83 *Biovilac v. EEC* [1984] E.C.R. 4057 at 4079, paras 21–22, ECJ; Case 281/84 *Zuckerfabrik Bedburg v. Council and Commission* [1987] E.C.R. 49 at 91–93, paras 25–28, ECJ.

right to be heard (*audi alteram partem*)[14] and freedom to pursue an economic activity,[15] are also recognised as being superior rules of law.

A breach of a superior rule of law can only cause the Community to incur liability if that superior rule of law is intended to protect an interest peculiar to the person concerned.[16] This doctrine of the *Schutznorm*,[17] which originates in German law and may be found also in some other jurisdictions,[18] has the aim of limiting liability. Yet it is applied flexibly. The Court of Justice does not rule out the possibility of superior rules of law protecting both general and individual interests.[19] Accordingly, the prohibition of discrimination laid down in the third paragraph of Article 34 (*ex Article 40*) of the E.C. Treaty assists the common organisation of the agricultural markets and, at the same time, protects the interests of individual market participants.[20] In contrast, the requirement laid down by Article 253 (*ex Article 190*) of the E.C. Treaty for a statement of reasons is intended only to enable the Court of Justice or the Court of First Instance to review the legality of acts and does not serve any individual interest, with the result that an infringement of that requirement cannot make the Community liable.[21] The same is true of "the system of the division of powers between the various Community institutions", which is designed to "ensure that the balance between the institutions provided for in the [E.C.] Treaty is maintained, and not to protect individuals".[22] For those reasons, a declaration in a preliminary ruling that a provision which the Commission adopted *ultra vires*, and hence in disregard of that system of institutional balance, is invalid does not render the Community liable. 11–046

---

14 Joined Cases T–481 and T–484/93 *Exporteurs in Levende Varkens and Others v. Commission* [1995] E.C.R. II–2941 at II–2991, para. 154, CFI (no infringement of the right to be heard).

15 Case T–521/93 *Atlanta and Others v. European Communities* [1996] E.C.R. II–1707 at II–1730, paras 62–64, CFI (no infringement of the freedom to pursue an economic activity).

16 This requirement was expressed for the first time in, Joined Cases 9 and 12/60 *Vloeberghs v. High Authority* [1961] E.C.R. 197 at 217, ECJ, where the Court of Justice dismissed a claim for damages brought under the ECSC Treaty, Art. 40, on the ground that the article of the Treaty which the Commission had allegedly infringed had been adopted only in the interests of the Community.

17 Under German law, the public authorities are liable only if they cause damage and breach a "*Schutznorm*" protecting an individual right, not of individuals in general, but of a specific group to which the interested party belongs: see Arnull, "Liability for Legislative Acts under Article 215 *[now Article 288]* (2) EC", in Heukels and McDonnell (eds) (cited in para. 11–003, n. 4, above), 129, at 136.

18 See Schockweiler, Wivines and Godart (cited in n. 76, above), at 53, who mention Denmark, Greece, Italy, the Netherlands and Portugal in this connection.

19 Joined Cases 5, 7 and 13–24/66 *Kampffmeyer v. Commission* [1967] E.C.R. 245 at 262–263, ECJ.

20 Joined Cases 83 and 94/76, 4, 15 and 40/77 *HNL v. Council and Commission* [1978] E.C.R. 1209 at 1224, para. 5, ECJ; Case 238/78 *Ireks-Arkady v. Council and Commission* [1979] E.C.R. 2955 at 2973, para. 11, ECJ; Joined Cases 241–242, 245–250/78 *DGV v. Council and Commission* [1979] E.C.R. 3017 at 3038–3039, para. 11, ECJ; Joined Cases 261 and 262/78 *Interquell Stärke-Chemie v. Council and Commission* [1979] E.C.R. 3045 at 3064–3065, para. 14, ECJ.

21 Case 106/81 *Kind v. EEC* [1982] E.C.R. 2885 at 2918, para. 14, ECJ; Case C–119/88 *AERPO and Others v. Commission* [1990] E.C.R. I–2189 at I–2212, para. 20, ECJ.

22 Case C–282/90 *Vreugdenhil v. Commission* [1992] E.C.R. I–1937 at I–1967—1968, paras 19–24, ECJ.

(c) *The requirement for a sufficiently serious breach*

11–047 The requirement for there to have been a sufficiently serious breach reflects once again the judiciary's reluctance to find the Community liable for loss or damage caused by its legislative acts. There can have been a sufficiently serious breach of a superior rule of law only in the event that the Community institution in question manifestly and gravely disregarded the limits on the exercise of its powers.[23]

11–048 Accordingly, the "breach" of a superior rule of law is sometimes justified, *inter alia* on the ground that an important general interest takes precedence over the individual interest of the injured party[24] or that the breach was the result of an erroneous, but excusable, approach to an unresolved legal question.[25] The absence of such justification raises a presumption that the Community institution acted "arbitrarily" as a result of which the breach of the relevant superior rule of law is deemed to be sufficiently serious.[26]

11–049 The Court of Justice has also tackled the question as to whether the Community institution concerned manifestly and gravely disregarded its powers in the light of an appraisal of the loss or damage caused thereby.[27] The particular intensity of the damage and the fact that a limited or ascertainable number of persons were affected determine the matter.[28]

2. The loss or damage

11–050 The requirement for loss or damage is the second pillar on which Community liability is based. The requirement is satisfied when the existence and the extent of the damage have been proved.[29] In practice, these constituent aspects of the concept of damage—existence and extent on the one hand, and proof, on the other—are merged. For the purposes of the following survey, they will be considered separately.

---

[23] Joined Cases 83 and 94/76, 4, 15 and 40/77 *HNL v. Council and Commission* [1978] E.C.R. 1209 at 1224, para. 6, ECJ; Case 50/86 *Grands Moulins de Paris v. Council and Commission* [1987] E.C.R. 4833 at 4856–4857, para. 8, ECJ; Case 20/88 *Roquette Frères v. Commission* [1989] E.C.R. 1553 at 1588–1589, paras 23–26, ECJ. *Cf.* Mahieu (cited in n. 79, above), at 400–401.

[24] Case 97/76 *Merkur v. Commission* [1977] E.C.R. 1063 at 1077–1078, para. 5, ECJ; Case 281/84 *Zuckerfabrik Bedburg v. Council and Commission* [1987] E.C.R. 49 at 95, para. 38, ECJ; Case 50/86 *Grands Moulins de Paris v. Council and Commission* [1987] E.C.R. 4833 at 4859, para. 21, ECJ.

[25] Case T–120/89 *Stahlwerke Peine-Salzgitter v. Commission* [1991] E.C.R. II–279 at II–398—400, paras 108–118, CFI.

[26] Joined Cases 116 and 124/77 *Amylum v. Council and Commission* [1979] E.C.R. 3497 at 3561, para. 19, ECJ; Case 106/81 *Kind v. Commission* [1982] E.C.R. 2885 at 2921, para. 22, ECJ.

[27] Joined Cases 83 and 94/76, 4, 15 and 40/77 *HNL v. Council and Commission* [1978] E.C.R. 1209 at 1225, para. 7, ECJ.

[28] *ibid. Cf.* Case T–120/89 *Stahlwerke Peine-Salzgitter v. Commission* [1991] E.C.R. II–279 at II–403, para. 131, CFI (ruling under the ECSC Treaty). See also Case 50/86 *Grands Moulins de Paris v. Council and Commission* [1987] E.C.R. 4833 at 4859, para. 21, ECJ. The fact that the number of persons involved was ascertainable in *Mulder* (Joined Cases C–104/89 and C–37/90 *Mulder and Others v. Council and Commission* [1992] E.C.R. I–3061, ECJ) was not mentioned as a requirement for liability. See the case note by Heukels (1993) C.M.L.Rev. 368 at 381.

[29] Toth, "The Concepts of Damage and Causality as Elements of Non-contractual Liability", in Heukels and McDonnell (eds) (cited in para. 11–003, note 4, above) pp. 179–198.

(1) Existence and extent of the damage

The loss or damage caused by an unlawful Community act will found a claim for damages only if its existence is sufficiently certain,[30] in the form of a reduction in a person's assets (*damnum emergens*) or loss of earnings (*lucrum cessans*)[31] or else of future[32] or non-material[33] damage. 11–051

As has already been mentioned, there are no objections in principle to an award of damages for loss of profit.[34] The applicant must show that it was legitimately entitled in all the circumstances to make the profit and was only frustrated by the unlawful act of the Community institution.[35] 11–052

There has been a change as far as recovery of future loss or damage is concerned. Originally, the Court of Justice held, with regard to the ECSC Treaty, that a claim for compensation for damage which had not yet materialized was inadmissible.[36] It moderated its stance under the second paragraph of Article 288 (*ex Article 215*) of the E.C. Treaty when it held that a claim for compensation for damage which was to materialise only in the future, yet was foreseeable with sufficient certainty, was admissible.[37] It reached this view on the grounds that it might prove necessary to prevent even greater damage to bring the matter before the Court of Justice as soon as the cause of damage was certain and that most Member States recognised an action for declaration of liability based on future damage which was sufficiently certain. 11–053

Where non-material damage is found, equitable[38] or sometimes symbolic[39] damages may be awarded. 11–054

---

[30] See, *e.g.* Joined Cases 19–20, 25 and 30/69 *Richez-Parise v. Commission* [1970] E.C.R. 325 at 338, para. 31, ECJ.

[31] Opinion of Advocate General F. Capotorti in Case 238/78 *Ireks-Arkady v. Council and Commission* [1979] E.C.R. 2955 at 2998–2999, ECJ.

[32] Damage not yet sustained at the time when it is being appraised.

[33] Such damage is not an actual reduction in assets, but the "reflection" of unreasonable inconvenience caused to an individual on account of an unlawful act or failure to act of a Community institution.

[34] Joined Cases 5, 7 and 13–24/66 *Kampffmeyer and Others v. Commission* [1967] E.C.R. 245 at 266, ECJ: the alleged loss must not be essentially speculative in nature; consequently, the Court of Justice held in that case that the intended transaction must at least have been begun to be performed.

[35] Case 74/74 *CNTA v. Commission* [1975] E.C.R. 533 at 550, para. 45, ECJ.

[36] Joined Cases 9 and 25/64 *FERAM v. High Authority* [1965] E.C.R. 311 at 320–321, ECJ.

[37] Joined Cases 56–60/74 *Kampffmeyer and Others v. Commission* [1976] E.C.R. 711 at 741–742, paras 6–8, ECJ.

[38] Joined Cases 7/56 and 3–7/57 *Algera and Others v. Common Assembly* [1957 and 1958] E.C.R. 39 at 66–67, ECJ; Case 110/63 *Willame v. Commission* [1965] E.C.R. 649 at 667, ECJ; Joined Cases 10 and 47/72 *Di Pillo v. Commission* [1973] E.C.R. 763 at 772, paras 23–25, ECJ; Case 75/77 *Mollet v. Commission* [1978] E.C.R. 897 at 908–909, paras 27–29, ECJ; Case 207/81 *Ditterich v. Commission* [1983] E.C.R. 1359 at 1374–1375, paras 28–29, ECJ; Joined Cases 169/83 and 136/84 *Leussink-Brummelhuis v. Commission* [1986] E.C.R. 2801 at 2827, para. 18, ECJ; Case T–13/92 *Moat v. Commission* [1993] E.C.R. II–287 at II–301, para. 49, CFI; Case T–59/92 *Caronna v. Commission* [1993] E.C.R. II–1129 at II–1166, para. 107, CFI.

[39] See, *e.g.* Case T–18/93 *Marcato v. Commission* [1994] E.C.R.–S.C. II–681 at II–706, para. 80, CFI (English abstract at [1994] E.C.R.–S.C. I–A–215). The Court sometimes considers that the judgment itself, together with its reasoning, affords sufficient redress for the damage

11–055 The award of damages is intended to restore the injured party's financial situation to what it would have been in the absence of the unlawful act or as close as possible thereto.[40] The quantum of the damage is therefore determined by comparing the actual assets of the person concerned with his notional assets in the event that he had not been affected by the wrongful act.

11–056 The damage must be quantifiable,[41] since under Articles 34 and 40 of the ECSC Treaty and Article 235 (*ex Article 178*) and the second paragraph of Article 288 (*ex Article 215*) of the E.C. Treaty, the Court of Justice and the Court of First Instance are empowered only to make an award of money. The damages are expressed in national currency or in euro. An "exact assessment" of the damage sustained is needed, but an approximate determination based on sufficiently reliable facts, preferably collected by an expert, will suffice if it is not possible to make an exact assessment.[42]

11–057 The question of the determination of the quantum of the damages will be reserved in the event that the necessary information is not available at the time when the finding of liability is made.[43] In that event, the Court will indicate as far as possible a number of calculation criteria and invite the parties to reach agreement on the amount of the damages within a specified period and to submit the result to it. If the parties fail to reach

---

sustained (Joined Cases 59 and 129/80 *Turner v. Commission* [1981] E.C.R. 1883 at 1921, ECJ). See also Joined Cases 44, 77, 294 and 295/85 *Hochbaum and Rawes v. Commission* [1987] E.C.R. 3259 at 3279, para. 22, ECJ; Case T–37/89 *Hanning v. European Parliament* [1990] E.C.R. II–463 at II–490, para. 83, CFI; Case T–158/89 *Van Hecken v. ESC* [1991] E.C.R. II–1341 at II–1357, para. 37, CFI; Case T–52/90 *Volger v. European Parliament* [1992] E.C.R. II–121 at II–139, para. 46, CFI (annulment of the contested decision constituted sufficient redress for the non-material damage sustained). But see Case C–343/87 *Culin v. Commission* [1990] E.C.R. I–225 at I–246, para. 29, ECJ (annulment of the contested decision held not to constitute appropriate and sufficient redress for non-material damage suffered); Case T–165/89 *Plug v. Commission* [1992] E.C.R. II–367 at II–413, para. 118, CFI.

[40] Opinion of Advocate General F. Capotorti in Case 238/78 *Ireks-Arkady v. Council and Commission* [1979] E.C.R. 2955 at 2999, ECJ. Van Gerven (cited in n. 75, above), at 31, points out that the principle of "full compensation" applies; (Order of the President of December 19, 1990), Case C–385/90R *Compagnia Italiana Alcool v. Commission* [1990] E.C.R. I–4887 at I–4894, para. 26, ECJ. *Cf.* Case T–59/92 *Caronna v. Commission* [1993] E.C.R. II–1129, CFI.

[41] Toth (cited in n. 29, above), p. 185.

[42] Joined Cases 29, 31, 36, 39–47, 50 and 51/63 *SA des Laminoirs, Hauts Fourneaux, Forges, Fonderies et Usines de la Providence and Others v. High Authority* [1965] E.C.R. 911 at 939, ECJ.

[43] Joined Cases 95–98/74, 15 and 100/75 *Coopératives Agricoles de Céréales and Others v. Commission and Council* [1975] E.C.R. 1615 at 1635. para. 5, ECJ. The Court may find that liability exists in principle, indicating the wrongful act or omission, the type of damage and the causal connection between them, while deferring only the determination of the amount of damages (*SA des Laminoirs, Hauts Fourneaux, Forges, Fonderies et Usines de la Providence and Others v. High Authority*, (cited in n. 42 above) at 940–941. See also Case C–152/88 *Sofrimport v. Commission* [1990] E.C.R. I–2477 at I–2511, para. 30, ECJ; Joined Cases C–104/89 and C–37/90 *Mulder and Others v. Council and Commission* [1992] E.C.R. I–3061 at I–3137—3138, paras 37–38, ECJ; Case T–120/89 *Stahlwerke Peine-Salzgitter v. Commission* [1991] E.C.R. II–279 at II–405, para. 137, CFI). Initially, the Court may confine itself to the unlawful nature of the act at issue and defer finding the causal connection and the damage (Case 90/78 *Granaria v. Council and Commission* [1979] E.C.R. 1081 at 1090–1091, paras 4–6, ECJ).

agreement, the Court will itself determine the amount of the damages. The following paragraphs set out a number of general calculation criteria.

If the damage originated in the unlawful collection of a charge or the unlawful withholding of a payment, the amount of the charge or payment in question will form the basis for calculating the damages.[44] The fact that the amount of the damages coincides precisely with the charge or payment at issue does not detract from the autonomous nature of the action for damages. The payment of compensation is founded upon a legal basis—the second paragraph of Article 288 (*ex Article 215*) of the E.C. Treaty—different from that of the contested charge or payment. **11–058**

Loss or damage which the individual passes or could pass on to others is not eligible for an award of damages.[45] So, if financial aid is withdrawn, a producer may recover his loss by increasing the price of his products. In so far as that price increase offsets the loss, it must be taken into account when quantifying the damage.[46] However, it must be certain that the producer concerned did pass on the loss or could have done so.[47] **11–059**

Default interest, calculated at the normal legal rate as from the date of judgment, may be awarded.[48] Interest is not due until the date of judgment since the extent of the damage is also determined at that date, which means that any increase in the damage from the time at which it arose until the date of judgment is therefore taken into account.[49] In staff cases, interest is **11–060**

---

44 Case 238/78 *Ireks-Arkady v. Council and Commission* [1979] E.C.R. 2955 at 2973, para. 13, ECJ; Joined Cases 64 and 113/76, 167 and 239/78, 27–28 and 45/79 *Dumortier v. Council* [1982] E.C.R. 1733 at 1745–1746, paras 9–10, ECJ.

45 *Ireks-Arkady v. Council and Commission*, cited in n. 44 above) at 2974, para. 14, ECJ; Case 256/81 *Pauls Agriculture v. Council and Commission* [1983] E.C.R. 1707 at 1719–1720, paras 8–10, ECJ; Joined Cases 256–257, 265, 267/80 and 51/81 and 282/82 *Birra Wührer v. Council and Commission* [1984] E.C.R. 3693 at 3730–3731, paras 26–30, ECJ. See, however, Case 199/82 *Amministrazione delle Finanze dello Stato v. San Giorgio* [1983] E.C.R. 3595 at 3613, para. 15, ECJ: "In a market economy based on freedom of competition, the question whether, and to what extent, a fiscal charge imposed on an importer has actually been passed on in subsequent transactions involves a degree of uncertainty for which the person obliged to pay a charge contrary to Community law cannot be systematically held responsible."

46 Toth (cited in n. 29, above), pp. 189–190, sharply criticises this approach. His principal arguments are that pricing policy depends on factors other than the withdrawal of financial aid and that this approach places an unreasonable burden on the individual concerned inasmuch as he has to pass on the loss to others, with the end result that the Community passes on its duty to pay compensation to the community in general and consumers in particular.

47 Seemingly, there is an obligation on a prudent vendor to pass on the loss brought about by an unlawful act of a public authority in his or her selling prices if market conditions so permit.

48 Case 238/78 *Ireks-Arkady v. Council and Commission* [1979] E.C.R. 2955 at 2975, para. 20, ECJ.

49 Joined Cases 64 and 113/76, 167 and 239/78, 27–28 and 45/79 *Dumortier v. Council* [1982] E.C.R. 1733 at 1746, para. 11, ECJ; Opinion of Advocate General G.F. Mancini in Case 256/81 *Pauls Agriculture v. Council and Commission* [1983] E.C.R. 1707 at 1723–1729, ECJ; Joined Cases 256–257, 265, 267/80 and 51/81 and 282/82 *Birra Wührer v. Council and Commission* [1984] E.C.R. 3693 at 3732, para. 37, ECJ; Case C–152/88 *Sofrimport v. Commission* [1990] E.C.R. I–2477 at I–2512, para. 32, ECJ; Joined Cases C–104/89 and C–37/90 *Mulder and Others v. Council and Commission* [1992] E.C.R. I–3061 at I–3137, para. 35, ECJ. The award of interest, however, may be a means of assessing the total amount of

due from the date on which the staff member lodged his complaint with the administration concerned pursuant to Article 90(2) of the Staff Regulations or from the date on which a debt not paid by the administration became payable if that date occurred after the day on which the complaint was lodged.[50]

11–061 The exchange rate for an award of damages expressed in ECUs was that ruling on the date of judgment.[51]

11–062 The extent of the compensation awarded also depends on the manner in which the requirement for there to be a causal connection between the unlawful Community act and the loss or damage is fulfilled.[52]

11–063 Furthermore, as has already been mentioned, in the case of legislative acts the extent and the specific characteristics of the damage suffered play a particular role with a view to determining whether the relevant breach of a superior rule of law was sufficiently serious.[53]

(2) Proof of damage

11–064 The burden of proof has to be discharged by the applicant.[54] He or she has to convince the Court of the existence of the damage and of its extent. The defendant may adduce factual evidence which casts doubt on the existence and extent of the damage.[55] As a public authority, the defendant may sometimes be compelled to disclose information to which it alone has access.[56]

11–065 If the applicant does not succeed in proving that damage occurred and its extent, the application will be inadmissible[57] or, albeit declared admissible, will be dismissed.[58] The application must indicate the nature and extent of

---

the damage at the date of judgment. In that case, it is due from the day on which the damage materialised (Case 185/80 *Garganese v. Commission* [1981] E.C.R. 1785 at 1796, paras 19–21, ECJ).

[50] Joined Cases 75 and 117/82 *Razzouk and Beydoun v. Commission* [1984] E.C.R. 1509 at 1530–1531, para. 19, ECJ; Case 158/79 *Roumengous Carpentier v. Commission* [1985] E.C.R. 39 at 51–52, para. 11, ECJ; Joined Cases 532, 534, 567, 600, 618, 660/79 and 543/79 *Amesz v. Commission* [1985] E.C.R. 55 at 67, para. 14, ECJ; Case 737/79 *Battaglia v. Commission* [1985] E.C.R. 71 at 80, para. 10, ECJ.

[51] Joined Cases 64 and 113/76, 167 and 239/78, 27–28 and 45/79 *Dumortier v. Council* [1982] E.C.R. 1733 at 1746, para. 12, ECJ.

[52] See paras 11–067—11–071, below.

[53] See para. 11–049, above. For an application, see CFI, Joined Cases T–480/93 and T–483/93 *Antillean Rice Mills and Others v. Commission* [1995] E.C.R. II–2305 at II–2373, paras 200–208, CFI.

[54] ECJ, Case 26/74 *Roquette v. Commission* [1976] E.C.R. 677 at 688, paras 22–24, ECJ.

[55] See the cases on passing on the loss (para. 11–059, above). The defendant has to show that the loss was actually passed on. The applicant may counter the defendant's evidence by showing that the loss was not passed on or that a price increase was attributable to other factors.

[56] Opinion of Advocate General M. Lagrange in, Joined Cases 29, 31, 36, 39–47, 50 and 51/63 *SA des Laminoirs, Hauts Fourneaux, Forges, Fonderies et Usines de la Providence and Others v. High Authority* [1965] E.C.R. 911 at 943–944, ECJ.

[57] Case 68/63 *Luhleich v. Commission* [1965] E.C.R. 581 at 605, ECJ; Case T–64/89 *Automec v. Commission* [1990] E.C.R. II–367 at II–390—391, paras 72–75, CFI; Case T–461/93 *An Taisce and WWF UK v. Commission* [1994] E.C.R. II–733 at II–752, paras 42–43, CFI.

[58] Case 10/55 *Mirossevich v. High Authority* [1954 to 1956] E.C.R. 333 at 344–345, ECJ; Joined Cases 14, 16–17, 20, 24, 26–27/60 and 1/61 *Meroni & Co. v. High Authority* [1961] E.C.R. 161

the damage sufficiently precisely.[59] For example, it is not sufficient for the applicant to allege that he or she suffered "serious damage". He or she must at least adduce factual evidence on the basis of which the nature and the extent of the damage may be assessed. The Court of Justice recognises that to hold an action inadmissible on this ground requires an assessment of the facts, in particular of whether the appellant has sufficiently proved the amount of compensation claimed by it in the application and the reply. It lies beyond the jurisdiction of the Court of Justice on appeal to rule on whether the assessment made by the Court of First Instance was well founded.[60]

Uncertainty about the *extent* of the damage does not mean that the application will be declared inadmissible, provided that the case discloses a real possibility that damage has been suffered.[61] Mention has already been made of the fact that where the Court finds the Community liable in an interlocutory judgment, it can set the parties a time within which they are to agree on the amount of damages.[62] If they do not succeed and, in addition, the applicant does not adduce sufficiently precise evidence of the extent of the damage within the prescribed period, the application will be dismissed.[63] **11–066**

3. The causal connection

The Community will be liable only for damage which is a direct consequence of its unlawful acts.[64] The principle is reflected in the Treaties[65] and links up with the law of the Member States. It is for the applicant to prove the causal connection.[66] **11–067**

---

at 171, ECJ; Case 15/63 *Lassalle v. European Parliament* [1964] E.C.R. 31 at 39, ECJ; Case 26/74 *Roquette v. Commission* [1976] E.C.R. 677, ECJ; Case 49/79 *Pool v. Council* [1980] E.C.R. 569 at 582, para. 12, ECJ. For further particulars, see Toth (cited in n. 29, above), pp. 184–185.

59 Case 5/71 *Zuckerfabrik Schöppenstedt v. Council* [1971] E.C.R. 975 at 984, para. 9, ECJ; Case T–64/89 *Automec v. Commission* [1990] E.C.R. II–367 at II–390—391, para. 73, CFI; (Order of November 21, 1996), Case T–53/96 *Syndicat des Producteurs de Viande Bovine and Others v. Commission* [1996] E.C.R. II–1579 at II–1589, paras 22–23, CFI.

60 Case C–209/94P *Buralux and Others v. Council* [1996] E.C.R. I–615 at I–645, para. 21, ECJ.

61 Case 74/74 *CNTA v. Commission* [1975] E.C.R. 533, ECJ; Case 90/78 *Granaria v. Council and Commission* [1979] E.C.R. 1081 at 1090–1091, paras 4–6, ECJ.

62 See para. 11–057, above.

63 Case 74/74 *CNTA v. Commission* [1976] E.C.R. 797, ECJ.

64 Case 18/60 *Worms v. High Authority* [1962] E.C.R. 195 at 206, ECJ; Opinion of Advocate General A. Dutheillet de Lamothe in Case 4/69 *Lütticke v. Commission* [1971] E.C.R. 325 at 346, ECJ; Joined Cases 64 and 113/76, 167 and 239/78, 27–28 and 45/79 *Dumortier v. Council* [1979] E.C.R. 3091 at 3117, para. 21, ECJ; Case T–175/94 *International Procurement Services v. Commission* [1996] E.C.R. II–729 at II–745, para. 55, CFI; Case T–7/96 *Perillo v. Commission* [1997] E.C.R. II–1061 at II–1076, para. 41, CFI; Joined Cases T–213/95 and T–18/96 *SCK and FNK v. Commission* [1997] E.C.R. II–1739 at II–1776, paras 94–98, CFI.

65 ECSC Treaty, Art. 40 refers to "any injury *caused* in carrying out this Treaty by a wrongful act or omission on the part of the Community in the performance of its functions" and "any injury *caused* by a personal wrong" and the E.C. Treaty Art. 288 (*ex Art. 215*) para. 2, provides that the Community is liable to make good any damage "*caused* by its institutions or by its servants in the performance of their duties" (italics supplied).

66 Joined Cases 197–200, 243, 245 and 247/80 *Ludwigshafener Walzmühle v. Council and*

11–068 Whether or not the damage was a direct consequence of the Community act will depend on various circumstances.

11–069 Damage which is a consequence of damage caused in the first place by the Community act does not flow directly from that act and hence is too remote. Accordingly, loss suffered by members of the family of a member of the Commission's staff, on account of the personal injuries and psychological *sequelae* suffered by that person as a result of a road accident attributable to careless maintenance of the car on the part of the Commission, could not be indemnified.[67]

11–070 The person concerned may also break the chain of causation if he or she contributed to the damage arising. He or she is under a duty to take all such measures within his or her sphere as may help to obviate the damage or limit its extent. Only damage arising to the detriment of a person who showed normal prudence is recoverable from the Community.[68] If the person concerned did not show reasonable prudence, the Community will either not be liable[69] or liable only for part of the damage suffered.[70]

11–071 The Community will not be answerable for damage which is attributable exclusively to action by a Member State.[71] However, a shortcoming by the Community in exercising its supervisory duties, in particular if it fails to take action against a national measure which is contrary to Community law, may be regarded as the direct cause of damage ensuing from the application of that measure and hence render the Community liable.[72] Express Community approval of a national measure which is in breach of Community law may, *a fortiori*, be regarded as the direct cause of any damage flowing from that measure.[73]

Commission [1981] E.C.R. 3211 at 3254–3255, paras 51–56, ECJ; Case 310/81 *EISS v. Commission* [1984] E.C.R. 1341 at 1353–1354, paras 16, 17, ECJ.

[67] Joined Cases 169/83 and 136/84 *Leussink-Brummelhuis v. Commission* [1986] E.C.R. 2801 at 2828, para. 22, ECJ. See also the Opinion of Advocate General Sir Gordon Slynn, at 2819.

[68] Case 36/62 *Société des Aciéries du Temple v. High Authority* [1963] E.C.R. 289 at 296, ECJ.

[69] Joined Cases 14, 16–17, 20, 24, 26–27/60 and 1/61 *Meroni & Co. v. High Authority* [1961] E.C.R. 161 at 171, ECJ; Case 4/67 *Muller (née Collignon) v. Commission* [1967] E.C.R. 365 at 373 (application inadmissible); Case 169/73 *Compagnie Continentale v. Council* [1975] E.C.R. 117 at 135–137, paras 22–32, ECJ; Case 58/75 *Sergy v. Commission* [1976] E.C.R. 1139 at 1154, paras 46–47, ECJ; Case 26/81 *Oleifici Mediterranei v. EEC* [1982] E.C.R. 3057 at 3079, para. 24, ECJ; Joined Cases C–104/89 and C–37/90 *Mulder and Others v. Council and Commission* [1992] E.C.R. I–3061 at I–3136—3137, para. 33, and the Opinion of Advocate General W. Van Gerven, at I–3122—3123.

[70] Case 145/83 *Adams v. Commission* [1985] E.C.R. 3539 at 3592, paras 53–55, ECJ; Case C–308/87 *Grifoni v. Commission* [1990] E.C.R. I–1203 at I–1227, paras 16–17, ECJ.

[71] Case 132/77 *Exportation des Sucres v. Commission* [1978] E.C.R. 1061 at 1073, para. 27, ECJ.

[72] Joined Cases 9 and 12/60 *Vloeberghs v. High Authority* [1961] E.C.R. 197 at 215–216, ECJ. See also the Opinion of Advocate General K. Roemer, at 236.

[73] Joined Cases 5, 7 and 13–24/66 *Kampffmeyer and Others v. Commission* [1967] E.C.R. 245 at 260 *et seq.*, ECJ.

B. Limitation period

1. Commencement and duration

A claim against the Community for non-contractual liability becomes time-barred after a period of five years from the occurrence of the event giving rise thereto.[74] 11–072

The event that causes the claim to arise is the materialisation of the damage.[75] It is not until that time that all the conditions for liability to be incurred are fulfilled.[76] It is then that time starts running. 11–073

If the full extent of the damage does not materialise immediately but only over a period of time, the damages claim will be admissible only for compensation for the damage which arose during the period starting five years before the date on which the action was brought.[77]

The possibility of bringing a claim for compensation for future damage or damage which has not yet been assessed does not influence when time starts to run. Time under the limitation period always starts to run when the damage materialises and not from the time when it became possible to bring an action for damages. If that were not the case, the claim for damages could be time-barred before the damage had actually materialised.[78] 11–074

The limitation period for Community liability for unlawful legislative acts also does not begin until the resulting damage materialises.[79] Neither notification of the act nor its entry into force as such causes the limitation period to begin running. 11–075

Expiry of the limitation period cannot be pleaded against an applicant who was not aware in time of the event which gave rise to the damage and therefore did not have a reasonable time before the limitation period ran out in order to bring a claim.[80] The fact that the applicant was unaware must be excusable.[81] This means that a normally prudent person who had done everything possible to become apprised of the facts which resulted in 11–076

---

[74] E.C. Statute, Art. 43; EAEC Statute, Art. 44; ECSC Statute, Art. 40.

[75] Joined Cases 46 and 47/59 *Meroni & Co. v. High Authority* [1962] E.C.R. 411 at 420, ECJ.

[76] Case T–152/97 *Petrides v. Commission* [1997] E.C.R. II–2427 at II–2438—2439, paras 25–31, ECJ: the applicant has to show that there is a link between the allegedly unlawful act and time when the damage arose. If it fails to do so the claim will be inadmissible in any event in so far as it is based on an act which took place more than five years before the application was lodged.

[77] Case T–571/93 *Lefebvre and Others v. Commission* [1995] E.C.R. II–2379 at II–2394, para. 26, CFI.

[78] Cornelis (cited in para. 11–034, n. 76, above), at 9–10.

[79] Joined Cases 256–257, 265, 267/80 and 5/81 *Birra Wührer v. Council and Commission* [1982] E.C.R. 85 at 106–107, paras 9–12, ECJ; Case 51/81 *De Franceschi v. Council* [1982] E.C.R. 117 at 134, paras 9–11, ECJ; Joined Cases 256–257, 265, 267/80, 5 and 51/81 and 282/82 *Birra Wührer v. Council and Commission* [1984] E.C.R. 3693 at 3727, para. 15, ECJ. For an example of how to calculate the limitation period, see how it was done for each of the applicants in the 1984 *Birra Wührer* case, *ibid.*, at 3728–3729, paras 16–24; Case T–20/94 *Hartmann v. Council and Commission* [1997] E.C.R. II–595 at II–626, para. 107, CFI.

[80] Case 145/83 *Adams v. Commission* [1985] E.C.R. 3539 at 3591, para. 50, ECJ.

[81] Opinion of Advocate General G.F. Mancini in Case 145/85 *Adams v. Commission* [1985] E.C.R. 3539 at 3550, ECJ.

the damage would not have been in a position in the same circumstances to have been aware of the event which led to the damage.[82]

11–077 As in most Member States, expiry of the limitation period cannot be raised by the Court of its own motion.[83]

2. Interruption of the limitation period

11–078 Article 43 of the E.C. Statute of the Court of Justice provides that the period of limitation is to be interrupted if proceedings are instituted before the Court of Justice (or the Court of First Instance)[84] or if prior to such proceedings an application is made by the aggrieved party to the relevant Community institution. In the latter event, proceedings must be instituted within the two-month period provided for in Article 230 (*ex Article 173*); the provisions of the second paragraph of Article 232 (*ex Article 175*) apply where appropriate.

11–079 Reference to Articles 230 and 232 (*ex Articles 173 and 175*) is made solely in connection with the possibility of interrupting the five-year limitation period prescribed by the first sentence of Article 37 (*ex Article 43*). This reference is not intended to shorten the five-year limitation period, but simply to protect interested parties by preventing certain periods from being taken into account in calculating that limitation period. Its aim is merely "to postpone the expiration of the period of five years when proceedings instituted or a prior application made within this period start time to run in respect of the periods provided for in Article 173 or 175 *[now Article 230 or 232]*".[85]

If a prior application is addressed by the aggrieved party to the institution concerned, interruption will occur only if that application is followed by an application to the Court within the time-limits determined by reference to Articles 230 and 232 of the E.C. Treaty.[86] If the aggrieved party does not bring proceedings within those time-limits, the initial five-year limitation period continues to run in spite of the application made to the defendant institution. On the other hand, the limitation period is not reduced as a result.[87]

---

[82] Heukels and McDonnell, "Limitation of the Action for Damages against the Community: Considerations and New Developments, in Heukels and McDonnell (eds) (cited in para. 11–003, n. 4, above) pp. 225–229.

[83] Case 20/88 *Roquette Frères v. Commission* [1989] E.C.R. 1553 at 1586, para. 12 ECJ. See also Goffin, "La Cour de justice: Recours en indemnité", in *Les Novelles: Droit des Communautés européennes*, Brussels, Larcier, 1969, 333 at 337.

[84] The institution of proceedings before the national courts does not constitute an act interrupting the limitation period under the E.C. Statute, Art. 43: Case T–246/93 *Bühring v. Council and Commission* [1998] E.C.R. II–171 at II–192, para. 72, CFI.

[85] Joined Cases 5, 7 and 13–24/66 *Kampffmeyer and Others v. Commission* [1967] E.C.R. 245 at 260, ECJ.

[86] Case 11/72 *Giordano v. Commission* [1973] E.C.R. 417 at 424–425, para. 6, ECJ.

[87] *ibid.*, at 425, para. 7; Case T–167/94 *Nölle v. Council and Commission* [1995] E.C.R. II–2589 at II–2603—2604, para. 30, CFI.

IV. Consequences

A. Judgment holding the Community liable

If the Court of Justice or the Court of First Instance finds the Community liable, the Community will be obliged under the second paragraph of Article 288 (*ex Article 215*) of the E.C. Treaty to pay the necessary damages to the person concerned. **11–080**

By virtue of Articles 244 and 256 (*ex Articles 187 and 192*) of the E.C. Treaty, judgments of the Court of Justice and of the Court of First Instance are enforceable.[88] Enforcement is carried out in accordance with the law of the Member State on whose territory it takes place. However, the property and assets of the Communities shall not be the subject of any administrative or legal measure of constraint without the authorisation of the Court of Justice.[89] **11–081**

B. Judgment dismissing the action for damages

A judgment dismissing an application for damages does not take effect *erga omnes*.[90] Its force as *res judicata* extends only to the parties to the proceedings: they are no longer entitled to bring the same claim before the Court on the basis of the same facts. Other persons wishing to bring an action for damages on the basis of the same facts may indeed do so. **11–082**

---

88 Judgments of the Court of First Instance are enforceable even if an appeal has been brought before the Court of Justice. Appeals do not have suspensory effect (E.C. Statute, Art. 53, para. 1). Yet the Court of Justice may order application of the judgment of the Court of First Instance to be suspended for the duration of the appeal proceedings pursuant to the E.C. Treaty, Arts. 242 and 243 (*ex Arts. 185 and 186*) (see *ibid.*).

89 Protocol on the Privileges and Immunities of the European Communities, Art. 1.

90 Plouvier, *Les décisions de la Cour de Justice des Communautés européennes et leurs effets juridiques*, Brussels, Bruylant, 1975, p. 147.

CHAPTER 12

APPLICATION FOR AN OPINION ON THE COMPATIBILITY OF AN INTERNATIONAL AGREEMENT TO BE CONCLUDED BY THE COMMUNITY WITH THE PROVISIONS OF THE E.C. TREATY

I. SUBJECT-MATTER

A. GENERAL

The jurisdiction of the Court of Justice to give opinions under Article 300 (*ex Article 228*) (6) of the E.C. Treaty is intended to avoid potential complications arising out of legal disputes concerning the compatibility with provisions of the E.C. Treaty of international agreements concluded by the Community.[1] **12–001**

The Court has described such complications in the following terms:

> "[A] possible decision of the Court to the effect that such an agreement is, either by reason of its content or of the procedure adopted for its conclusion, incompatible with the provisions of the Treaty could not fail to provoke, not only in the Community context but also in that of international relations, serious difficulties and might give rise to adverse consequences for all interested parties, including third countries."[2]

Consequently, such opinions perform a preventive function.[3] The Court of Justice has described the procedure as:

> "a special procedure of collaboration between the Court of Justice on the one hand and the other Community institutions and the Member

[1] The Court of Justice also has the power to give opinions under the ECSC Treaty, Art. 95 (in connection with the so-called minor amendments procedure) and the EAEC Treaty, Art. 103 (see Ruling 1/78 *Draft Convention of the International Energy Agency on the Physical Protection of Nuclear Materials, Facilities and Transports* [1978] E.C.R. 2151. E.C.J.).

[2] Opinion 1/75 *Opinion of the Court given pursuant to Article 228 of the EEC Treaty* [1975] E.C.R. 1355 at 1360–1361, ECJ.

[3] For further details see Kovar, "La compétence consultative de la Cour de justice et la procédure de conclusion des accords internationaux par la Communauté économique européenne", in *Mélanges offerts à P. Reuter*, Paris, Pedone, 1981, at 357–377.

> States on the other whereby, at a stage prior to conclusion of an agreement which is capable of giving rise to a dispute concerning the legality of a Community act which concludes, implements or applies it, the Court is called upon to ensure, in accordance with Article 164 *[now Article 220]* of the Treaty, that in the interpretation and application of the Treaty the law is observed."[4]

The existence of this judicial procedure, however, does not mean that the Court of Justice will not conduct judicial review *ex post* of the act by which a Community institution intended to conclude an international agreement.[5] In other words, whilst the procedure for obtaining the opinion of the Court of Justice is intended to obviate the adoption of unlawful acts, if it does not succeed in this, the usual channels for judicial review of the acts in question remain open.[6]

12–002 To date, the Court has given a limited number of opinions, but recently the pace has quickened.[7]

B. The expression "agreement envisaged"

12–003 The term "agreement" in Article 300 (*ex Article 228*) (6) refers to any undertaking entered into by entities subject to international law which has binding force, whatever its formal designation.[8] Provided that it is a "'standard' [norm], that is to say a rule of conduct, covering a specific field, determined by precise provisions, which is binding upon the participants", the Court of Justice has jurisdiction to give an opinion on its compatibility with the provisions of the E.C. Treaty.[9]

12–004 Since the Court's power to give opinions is provided for in Article 300 (*ex Article 228*) of the E.C. Treaty, which lays down the Community decision-making procedure with regard to the conclusion of international agreements, the power extends only to agreements in which the Community

---

[4] Opinion 2/94 *Accession by the Communities to the Convention for the Protection of Human Rights and Fundamental Freedoms* [1996] E.C.R. I–1759 at I–1784, para. 6, ECJ.

[5] Case C–327/91 *France v. Commission* [1994] E.C.R. I–3641 at I–3672, paras 15–17, ECJ.

[6] For the action for annulment, see paras 7–009, 7–010, above. For the preliminary ruling on validity, see para. 10–004, above.

[7] See Opinion 1/75 [1975] E.C.R. 1355, ECJ; Opinion 1/76 *Draft Agreement establishing a European laying-up fund for inland waterway vessels* [1977] E.C.R. 741, ECJ; Opinion 1/78 *International Agreement on Natural Rubber* [1979] E.C.R. 2871, ECJ; Opinion 1/91 Draft agreement between the Community, on the one hand, and the countries of the European Free Trade Association, on the other, relating to the creation of the European Economic Area [1991] E.C.R. I–6079, ECJ; Opinion 2/91 *Convention No 170 of the International Labour Organization concerning safety in the use of chemicals at work* [1993] E.C.R. I–1061, ECJ; Opinion 1/94 *Agreement establishing the World Trade Organization* [1994] E.C.R. I–5267, ECJ; Opinion 2/92 *Competence of the Community or one of its institutions to participate in the Third Revised Decision of the OECD on national treatment* [1995] E.C.R. I–521, ECJ; Opinion 2/94 *Accession by the Communities to the Convention for the Protection of Human Rights and Fundamental Freedoms* [1996] E.C.R. I–1759, ECJ; Opinion 3/94 *GATT—WTO—Framework Agreement on Bananas* [1995] E.C.R. I–4577, ECJ.

[8] Opinion 1/75 *Opinion of the Court given pursuant to Article 228 of the EEC Treaty* [1975] E.C.R. 1355 at 1359–1360. ECJ.

[9] *ibid.*, at 1360.

proposes to participate.[10] This relates to the aim of the opinion procedure, which is "to forestall . . . legal disputes concerning the compatibility with the Treaty of international agreements binding upon the Community".[11] By the same token, the Court of Justice is entitled to give opinions on the compatibility with the Treaty of mixed agreements to which both the Community and some or all Member States are parties.[12]

II. Identity of the Applicants

The Council, the Commission or a Member State may request the Court of Justice to deliver an opinion.[13] Under Article 300(6), the European Parliament is not entitled to make such a request, notwithstanding its increased role in the decision-making procedure leading up to the conclusion by the Community of international agreements[14] and its right to bring an action for the annulment of acts of the Council and the Commission in so far as the action is intended to protect its prerogatives.[15] In the light of those two factors, it is possible to conceive of a situation in which the Council and the Parliament take different views on whether a given envisaged international agreement may be concluded after merely consulting the Parliament (Article 300 (*ex Article 228*) (3), first subparagraph) or after obtaining its assent (Article 300 (3), second subparagraph), with the end result being the Parliament's bringing an action for annulment of the 12–005

[10] One commentator considers that it can be inferred from the vague wording of Opinion 2/91 that all "agreements", including those concluded by Member States, may be submitted to the Court of Justice for its opinion (see case note by Neuwahl in (1993) C.M.L.Rev. 1185 at 1190–1191). The possibility has to be ruled out. Unlike the EAEC Treaty, Art. 103, the E.C. Treaty affords no textual basis therefor. What is more, such agreements are not binding on the Community and hence, if they are subsequently found to be incompatible with the Treaty, there will be no likelihood of the Community incurring liability under international law. In contrast, in the case of mixed agreements, the Court of Justice is entitled to test Member States' obligations against the requirements of the E.C. Treaty, Art. 10 (*ex Art. 5*) see Kovar (cited in n. 3, above), at 366.

[11] Opinion 1/75 *Opinion of the Court given pursuant to Article 228 of the EEC Treaty* [1975] E.C.R. 1355 at 1360, ECJ.

[12] See, for instance, Opinion 1/76 *Draft Agreement establishing a European laying-up fund for inland waterway vessels* [1977] E.C.R. 741, ECJ.

[13] To date, all requests for opinions have been made by the Commission with the exception of Opinion 2/92 *Competence of the Community or one of its institutions to participate in the Third Revised Decision of the OECD on national treatment* [1995] E.C.R. I–521, ECJ (Belgium); Opinion 2/94 *Accession by the Communities to the Convention for the Protection of Human Rights and Fundamental Freedoms* [1996] E.C.R. I–1759, ECJ (the Council); Opinion 3/94 *GATT—WTO—Framework Agreement on Bananas* [1995] E.C.R. I–4577, ECJ (Germany).

[14] Under the E.C. Treaty, Art. 300 (*ex Art. 228*) (3), subpara. 2, "agreements referred to in Article 301 *[ex Article 238]*, other agreements establishing a specific institutional framework by organising co-operation procedures, agreements having important budgetary implications for the Community and agreements entailing amendment of an act adopted under the procedure referred to in Article 251 *[ex Article 189b]* shall be concluded after the assent of the European Parliament has been obtained".

[15] E.C. Treaty, Art. 230 (*ex Art. 173*), para. 3, linking up with Case C–70/88 *European Parliament v. Council* [1990] E.C.R. I–2041, ECJ (see para. 7–032, above). See also Auvret-Finck, "Les avis 1/91 and 1/92 relatifs au projet d'accord sur la création de l'Espace économique européen" (1993) C.D.E. 38 at 58–59.

act by which the Council concluded the agreement. That would be an unsatisfactory outcome which would detract from the preventive role of the Court of Justice. Consequently, it would seem appropriate for the Court to interpret Article 300 (6) of the E.C. Treaty in parallel with the text of the third paragraph of Article 230 (*ex Article 173*) by allowing the Parliament to request an opinion in order to protect its prerogatives.[16] The Court of Justice has recognised for some considerable time that the opinion procedure is appropriate for settling questions relating to the division of powers between the Community and the Member States or between Community institutions before an international agreement is concluded on the ground that this helps to determine beforehand that the way in which the agreement came into being was lawful.[17]

It is perhaps on those grounds that the Court of Justice recently gave the Parliament leave at its request—without any written basis in the Court's Statute or Rules of Procedure—to submit observations within the meaning of Article 107 (1) of the ECJ Rules of Procedure following submission of a request for an opinion.[18]

12–006 It is optional whether a request for an opinion is made. The Community can validly conclude an international agreement without seeking the opinion of the Court.[19]

III. Special Characteristics

A. Extent of the jurisdiction to give opinions

12–007 The Court of Justice has interpreted its jurisdiction to review "whether an agreement envisaged is compatible with the provisions of the [E.C.] Treaty" in the sense that its judgement may depend not only on provisions of substantive law but also on those concerning the powers, procedure or organisation of the institutions of the Community. This approach is also expressed in Article 107(2) of the ECJ Rules of Procedure.[20]

---

[16] Barents, "The Court of Justice and the EEA Agreement: Between Constitutional Values and Political Realities", in Stuyck and Looijestijn-Clearie (eds), *The European Economic Area EC-EFTA: Institutional Aspects and Financial Services*, Deventer, Kluwer, 1994, 57 at 58.

[17] Opinion 1/78 *International Agreement on Natural Rubber* [1979] E.C.R. 2871 at 2906–2908, paras 29–31, ECJ.

[18] Opinion 1/92 *Draft agreement between the Community, on the one hand, and the countries of the European Free Trade Association, on the other, relating to the creation of the European Economic Area* [1992] E.C.R. I–2821 at I–2826, ECJ.

[19] *Cf.* Christianos, "La compétence consultative de la Cour de justice à la lumière du traité sur l'Union européenne" (1994) R.M.C.U.E. 37 at 39.

[20] Opinion 1/75 [1975] E.C.R. 1355, ECJ Opinion 1/76 *Draft Agreement establishing a European laying-up fund for inland waterway vessels* [1977] E.C.R. 741, ECJ; Opinion 1/78 *International Agreement on Natural Rubber* [1979] E.C.R. 2871 at 2907, para. 30, ECJ; Opinion 2/91 *Convention No 170 of the International Labour Organization concerning safety in the use of chemicals at work* [1993] E.C.R. I–1061 at I–1075, para. 3, ECJ; Opinion 2/94 *Accession by the Communities to the Convention for the Protection of Human Rights and Fundamental Freedoms* [1996] E.C.R. I–1759 at I–1784, para. 9, ECJ. The ECJ Rules of Procedure, Art. 107(2), provides as follows: "The Opinion may deal not only with the question whether the envisaged agreement is compatible with the provisions of the E.C. Treaty but also with the question whether the Community or any Community institution has the power to enter into that agreement."

The Court's review is limited, however, to the envisaged agreement's compatibility with the Treaty. The requirements imposed upon the Community by international law are not covered. Thus, the Court did not inquire into the provisions establishing the International Labour Organisation to see whether the Community was entitled to join that organisation.[21] In addition, the review as to compatibility covers only the legal aspects of the envisaged agreement. Judicial review does not extend to political expediency. As a result of the broad compass of the Court's review, conflicting powers often form the basis of requests for opinions. **12–008**

Alongside the question as against what provisions the Court of Justice reviews the compatibility of an envisaged agreement with the Treaty, the question arises as to whether in the case of a given request the Court must examine the whole agreement or simply part of it. In Opinion 1/91, the Court, at the Commission's request, considered only the provisions of the envisaged EEA Agreement which related to the system of judicial supervision provided for therein.[22] In Opinion 1/92, the Court confined its review to those provisions of the EEA Agreement which had been amended following Opinion 1/91 finding the Agreement incompatible with the Treaty, despite the request made by the European Parliament in its observations submitted to the Court that it should consider the influence of the EEA Agreement on the role and powers of the Parliament.[23] **12–009**

B. Time-limit

Article 300 (*ex Article 228*) (6) sets no time-limit. Nevertheless, the preventive nature of these judicial proceedings and the extent of the Court's jurisdiction to give opinions place restrictions on the time within which a request may be made to the Court.[24] **12–010**

First, a request for an opinion may be made to the Court only as from the time when the subject-matter of the envisaged agreement is known.[25] It is hard to conceive that the Court would be requested to give an opinion at a time when the subject-matter of the envisaged agreement is still uncertain. But as soon as the subject-matter is known, the Court's opinion may be sought, even before the negotiations have started.[26] From that time, the Court is in a position to adjudge whether the Community is competent to conclude the agreement in question. Indeed, in the event of any conflicts **12–011**

---

[21] Opinion 2/91, (cited in n. 20, above) at I–1075, para. 4.

[22] Opinion 1/91 *Draft agreement between the Community, on the one hand, and the countries of the European Free Trade Association, on the other, relating to the creation of the European Economic Area* [1991] E.C.R. I–6079 at I–6099, para. 1, ECJ.

[23] Opinion 1/92 *Draft agreement between the Community, on the one hand, and the countries of the European Free Trade Association, on the other, relating to the creation of the European Economic Area* [1992] E.C.R. I–2821 at I–2838, para. 1, ECJ.

[24] See Karagiannis, "L'expression 'accord envisagé' dans l'article 228 *[now Article 300]*, §6 du traité CE" (1998) C.D.E. 105–136.

[25] Opinion 1/78 *International Agreement on Natural Rubber* [1979] E.C.R. 2871 at 2908–2909, paras 32–34, ECJ.

[26] Opinion 2/94 *Accession by the Communities to the Convention for the Protection of Human Rights and Fundamental Freedoms* [1996] E.C.R. I–1759 at I–1785—1786, paras 11–12, ECJ.

of jurisdiction it is of essential importance for the Community, the Member States and third countries or international organisations concerned to be certain about the precise powers of the parties at the beginning of the negotiations.

12–012 But the Court will not be in a position to give its opinion on the compatibility of an envisaged agreement so long as it does not have sufficient information about the content and institutional machinery of the agreement. Consequently, a request for an opinion raising the question of the compatibility of an envisaged agreement with the Treaty will be admissible only in so far as the Court can have access to such information.[27]

12–013 Secondly, a request may be made to the Court only in so far as the Community is not yet bound by the agreement.[28] Failing this, the opinion would not play its preventive role.[29] It makes no difference in this connection at what stage in the process of concluding the international agreement the opinion is sought, provided that the Community is not yet bound by it. Accordingly, an opinion may be obtained from the Court before the Commission has made any recommendations to the Council pursuant to Article 300 (*ex Article 228*) (1) of the E.C. Treaty with a view to opening negotiations and before the Council has given it the necessary authorisation. The Court's opinion may also be sought after the negotiations have closed, but before the Council concludes the agreement pursuant to Article 300(2) of the E.C. Treaty.[30]

12–014 If, however, the envisaged agreement is concluded after the request for an opinion was submitted but before the Court has given its opinion, the request becomes devoid of purpose. The preventive intent of the procedure provided for in Article 300 (*ex Article 228*) (6) of the E.C. Treaty requires the "envisaged" agreement to be still only envisaged at the time when the Court gives its opinion. Moreover, if the Court were to give an adverse opinion on the compatibility with the Treaty of an agreement which had already been concluded, that opinion would not be capable of having the legal effect prescribed by the second sentence of Article 300 (6), namely that, if the Court has given an adverse opinion, the agreement may enter into force only after the Treaty has been amended in accordance with the procedure provided for in Article 48 (*ex Article N*) of the E.U. Treaty.[31] In those circumstances the Court will not respond to the request for an opinion.[32]

---

[27] *ibid.*

[28] Kovar (cited in n. 3, above), at 362; Christianos (cited in n. 19, above), at 40–41.

[29] An opinion dealing with the compatibility with the Treaty of an international agreement which has already entered into force may be given where the Community is not yet bound by it, but is considering acceding to it.

[30] Opinion 1/94 *Agreement establishing the World Trade Organization* [1994] E.C.R. I–5267 at I–5392, para. 12, ECJ.

[31] See para. 12–017, below.

[32] Opinion 3/94 *GATT—WTO—Framework Agreement on Bananas* [1995] E.C.R. I–4577, ECJ.

C. Procedure before the Court

Since a request for an opinion pursuant to Article 300 (*ex Article 228*) (6) of the E.C. Treaty does not introduce normal contentious proceedings, the decision is reached in the Court of Justice in accordance with a special procedure held behind closed doors. It is traced out in Articles 107 and 108 of the ECJ Rules of Procedure. The request for an opinion has to be lodged with the Registry. If it is lodged by the Council, it has to be served on the Commission and the European Parliament.[33] If the request is lodged by the Commission, it must be served on the Council, the European Parliament and the Member States. If a Member State requests an opinion, the request has to be served on the Council, the Commission, the European Parliament and the other Member States.[34] The President of the Court prescribes a period within which the institutions and the Member States which have been served with the request may submit written observations.[35] **12–015**

The Court, sitting in closed session, delivers its reasoned opinion after hearing all the advocates general.[36] No provision is made for a hearing, although the Court may hear the institutions and Member States in closed session.[37] The opinion is signed by the President, by the judges who took part in the deliberations and by the Registrar, following which it is served on the Council, the Commission, the European Parliament and the Member States.[38] **12–016**

IV. Consequences

An agreement on which the Court of Justice has given an adverse opinion may enter into effect only if the conditions set out in Article 48 *(ex Article N)* of the E.U. Treaty are complied with. This means first that the E.C. Treaty must be amended in accordance with the applicable procedure (E.C. Treaty, Article 300 (*ex Article 228*) (6)).[39] Naturally, it is also possible for the envisaged agreement to be amended in consultation with the third countries and international organisations concerned in order to meet the objections raised by the Court.[40] **12–017**

A favourable opinion leaves the way free for the Community to enter into the agreement, but naturally does not compel it to do so. However, the **12–018**

---

33 The Member States, as "members" of the Council, are always apprised of the fact that a request is to be lodged.

34 ECJ Rules of Procedure, Art. 107 (1).

35 ECJ Rules of Procedure, Art. 107 (1), subpara. 2.

36 ECJ Rules of Procedure, Art. 108(2).

37 Christianos (cited in n. 19, above), at 41.

38 ECJ Rules of Procedure, Art. 108(3).

39 For further details, see Kheitmi, "La fonction consultative de la Cour de justice des Communautés européennes" (1967) R.T.D.E. 553 at 576; Gray, "Advisory Opinions and the European Court of Justice" (1983) E.L.Rev. 24 at 36, who argues that there are only procedural differences between an opinion and a declaratory judgment.

40 See, *e.g.* the EEA Agreement: the proposed system of judicial supervision was amended following Opinion 1/91: *cf.* Opinions 1/91 and 1/92 (see note 7, above).

opinion does not prevent the legality of the act by which the Community concludes the agreement from being raised in some other judicial proceedings, especially where the opinion considered the compatibility of the agreement with the Treaty only from a clearly specified point of view.[41]

[41] See para. 12–009, above.

Part IV
SPECIAL FORMS OF PROCEDURE

CHAPTER 13

PROCEEDINGS FOR INTERIM MEASURES BEFORE THE COURT OF JUSTICE AND THE COURT OF FIRST INSTANCE

I. SUBJECT-MATTER

A. GENERAL

Actions brought before the Court of Justice or the Court of First Instance do not have suspensory effect.[1] As a result of the time which elapses between the bringing of proceedings and judgment, that principle may detract from the effectiveness of legal protection. Consequently, interim measures which the Court may impose as necessary in interlocutory proceedings are intended, *inter alia*, to secure full effect for the application in the event that the dispute is decided in the applicant's favour.[2] **13–001**

B. TYPES OF MEASURES

First, under Article 242 (*ex Article 185*) of the E.C. Treaty, the Court may order that application of the contested act be suspended. Only the operation of "enforceable" measures may be suspended.[3] On that ground an administrative authority's refusal to grant a request made to it may not be suspended, generally speaking, unless, as such, it alters the applicant's legal position.[4] The judge dealing with applications for interim relief must **13–002**

[1] E.C. Treaty, Art. 242 (*ex Art. 185*), first sentence; ECSC Treaty, Art. 39, para. 1; EAEC Treaty, Art. 157, first sentence.

[2] (Order of the President of May 3, 1996), Case C–399/95R *Germany v. Commission* [1996] E.C.R. I–2441 at I–2456, para. 46, ECJ.

[3] (Order of the President of June 7, 1991), Case T–19/91R *Vichy v. Commission* [1991] E.C.R. II–265 at II–271—272, para. 20, CFI; Van Ginderachter, "Le référé en droit communautaire" (1993) Rev.dr.ULB 113 at 118. For the Commission's powers to order interim measures in competition and state aid cases, see Bellamy and Child, *The Common Market Law of Competition* (4th ed.), Sweet and Maxwell, London, 1993 pp. 740–743; Kerse, *EC Antitrust Procedure* (3rd ed.), Sweet and Maxwell, London, 1994 pp. 191–200.

[4] Joliet, Bertrand and Nihoul, "Protection juridictionnelle provisoire et droit communautaire" (1992) *Riv.dir.eur.* 253 at 258, take the view that suspension of operation may be granted only if the decision rejecting the request is "enforceable", as in (Order of the President of March 23, 1988), Case 76/88R *La Terza v. Court of Justice* [1988] E.C.R. 1741, ECJ, in which the decision rejecting the applicant's request for an extension of her authorisation to work part time was suspended. The decision rejecting her request meant that she had to start working full time with immediate effect, which altered her legal position as an official. In principle, suspension of the operation of a negative administrative decision is impossible, however, since suspension would not be capable of effecting any change in the applicant's situation: (Order of the President of April 30, 1997), Case C–89/97 P(R) *Moccia Irme v. Commission* [1997] E.C.R. I–2327 at I–2339, para. 45, ECJ.

not encroach upon the domain of the "executive".[5] If he or she did so, suspension of the operation of the rejection of a request would be tantamount to performing the act requested, which would entail the judge acting in place of the administrative authority. At the same time, the purpose of the main action would disappear in that the applicant would obtain the act which it sought to obtain by means of its action for failure to act.[6]

13–003 In some cases, suspension of the operation of the contested act does not suffice in order to prevent irreparable damage from occurring. Consequently, under Article 243 (*ex Article 186*) of the E.C. Treaty, the Court may prescribe "any necessary interim measures".[7] The range of possible measures is not predetermined,[8] but the judge who imposes them may not exercise a power which is vested first and foremost in another institution as this would jeopardise the balance between the institutions.[9] The measure imposed is tailored to the case. Consequently, suspension of operation may be ordered of only part of the contested act or may be made subject to specific conditions.[10] Sometimes security may be required to be lodged.[11] The judge hearing applications for interim relief may also remind a party to

---

[5] See the Opinion of Advocate General J. Gand in (Order of October 5, 1969), Case 50/69R *Germany v. Commission* [1969] E.C.R. 449 at 454–455, ECJ.

[6] (Order of the President of October 15, 1976), Case 91/76 *De Lacroix v. Court of Justice* [1976] E.C.R. 1563 at 1564, para. 2, ECJ; in general, judges hearing applications for interim relief may not grant measures which cause the main action to become nugatory: (Order of the President of September 26, 1986), Case 231/86R *Breda-Geomineraria v. Commission* [1986] E.C.R. 2639 at 2645, para. 18, ECJ. For further particulars, see Boulouis and Darmon, *Contentieux communautaire*, Paris, Dalloz, 1997, 136, No. 257.

[7] See also ECSC Treaty, Art. 39, and EAEC Treaty, Arts. 157 and 158.

[8] See, by way of example, (Order of the President of July 16, 1992), Case T–29/92R *SPO and Others v. Commission* [1992] E.C.R. II–2161, CFI. See also *Commentaire Mégret*, at 406–407; Joliet, Bertrand and Nihoul, (cited in n. 4, above), at 261; Borchardt, "The Award of Interim Measures by the European Court of Justice" (1985) C.M.L.Rev. 203 at 226–229.

[9] (Order of the President of October 22, 1975), Case 109/75R *National Carbonising Company v. Commission* [1975] E.C.R. 1193 at 1202, para. 8, ECJ. For the Commission's power to impose interim measures during an investigation into infringements of the competition rules, see (Order of January 17, 1980), Case 792/79R *Camera Care v. Commission* [1980] E.C.R. 119, ECJ; Case T–44/90 *La Cinq v. Commission* [1992] E.C.R. II–1, CFI; (Order of the President of December 2, 1994), Case T–322/94R *Union Carbide Corporation v. Commission* [1994] E.C.R. II–1159 at II–1172—1173, paras 26–27, CFI. See also Ferry, "Interim Relief under the Rome Treaty—The European Commission's Powers" (1980) E.I.P.R. 330–335; Piroche, "Les mesures provisoires de la Commission des Communautés européennes dans le domaine de la concurrence" (1989) R.T.D.E. 439–469.

[10] For examples, see (Order of the President of October 15, 1974), Cases 71/74 R and RR *Fruit- en Groentenimporthandel and Others v. Commission* [1974] E.C.R. 1031 at 1034, ECJ; (Order of the President of March 31, 1982), Joined Cases 43 and 63/82R *VBVB and VBBB v. Commission* [1982] E.C.R. 1241 at 1249, para. 11, ECJ; (Order of the President of June 16, 1992), Joined Cases T–24 and T–28/92R *Langnese-Iglo and Schöller Lebensmittel v. Commission* [1992] E.C.R. II–1839, CFI.

[11] ECJ Rules of Procedure, Art. 86(2); CFI Rules of Procedure, Art. 107(2). For applications, see (Order of the President of May 7, 1982), Case 86/82R *Hasselblad v. Commission* [1982] E.C.R. 1555, ECJ; (Order of the President of October 26, 1994), Joined Cases T–231R, T–232R and T–234/94R *Transacciones Maritimas and Others v. Commission* [1994] E.C.R. II–885 at II–902, para. 46, CFI.

comply with existing provisions where this may provisionally ensure appropriate protection of the applicant's rights.[12]

C. The ancillary nature of proceedings for interim measures

The ancillary nature of proceedings for interim measures clearly emerges from Article 242 *(ex Article 185)* of the E.C. Treaty, which merely permits application of the "contested act" to be suspended, and from Article 243 *(ex Article 186)* of that Treaty, which provides only for interim measures in cases before the Court of Justice or the Court of First Instance.[13] **13–004**

Accordingly, the Rules of Procedure of the two courts provide that an application to suspend the operation of a measure shall be admissible only if the applicant is challenging it in main proceedings[14] and that an application for any other interim measure must be made by a party to a pending case and must relate to that case.[15] These requirements are not interpreted in a strictly formalistic manner. For instance, the applicant may seek suspension of the operation of an act which is not the immediate

[12] (Order of the President of December 12, 1995), Case T–203/95R *Connolly v. Commission* [1995] E.C.R. II–2919 at II–2930, para. 25, CFI.

[13] See also ECJ Rules of Procedure, Art. 83(1); CFI Rules of Procedure, Art. 104(1). See also Cruz Vilaça, "La procédure en référé comme instrument de protection juridictionnelle des particuliers en droit communautaire", in *Scritti in onore di Giuseppe Federico Mancini*, Milan, Giuffrè editore, 1998, II, 257 at 265–269.

[14] ECJ Rules of Procedure, Art. 83(1), subpara. 1; CFI Rules of Procedure, Art. 104(1), subpara. 1. See, (Order of the President of November 22, 1995), Case T–395/94R *Atlantic Container and Others v. Commission* [1995] E.C.R. II–2893 at II–2910—2911, para. 39, CFI, in which the President of the Court of First Instance rejected an application for an interim order forestalling the application of an (as yet untaken) Commission decision withdrawing immunity from fines in respect of a notified agreement pursuant to Regulation No 17, Art. 15(6). The action in the main proceedings was directed against a Commission decision finding an earlier version of the agreement to be contrary to the E.C. Treaty, Art. 85 (*now Art. 81*) (1). An amended version of the agreement had since been notified to the Commission. It was with regard to that new agreement that the Commission had communicated its intention to adopt a decision pursuant to Regulation No. 17, Art. 15(6).

[15] ECJ Rules of Procedure, Art. 83(1), subpara. 2; CFI Rules of Procedure, Art. 104(1), subpara. 2. For examples of applications for interim measures held not to be related to the relevant case before the Court, see (Order of the President of October 19, 1976), Case 88/76R *Exportation de Sucres* [1976] E.C.R. 1585 at 1587, ECJ; (Order of the President of November 3, 1980), Case 186/80R *Suss v. Commission* [1980] E.C.R. 3501 at 3506, paras 15–16, ECJ; (Order of the President of December 16, 1980), Case 258/80R *Rumi v. Commission* [1980] E.C.R. 3867 at 3879, paras 20–22, ECJ; (Order of the President of May 17, 1991), Case C–313/90R *CIRFS and Others v. Commission* [1991] E.C.R. I–2557 at I–2564, para. 23, ECJ; in which the applicants sought, by way of interim measure, an order requiring repayment of allegedly unlawful aid, whilst in the main proceedings they had applied for annulment of the Commission decision declaring that there was no obligation for prior notification of the aid in question under the E.C. Treaty, Art. 93 (*now Art. 88*) (3). The President of the Court pointed out that annulment of the contested decision would not result in the contested aid being unlawful. Consequently, the application for repayment of the aid exceeded the scope of the application in the main proceedings. See also (Order of the President of December 14, 1993), Case T–543/93R *Gestevisión Telecinco v. Commission* [1993] E.C.R. II–1411 at II–1420, para. 25, CFI; (Order of the President of December 2, 1994), Case T–322/94R *Union Carbide v. Commission* [1994] E.C.R. II–1159 at II–1173, para. 28, CFI; (Order of the President of February 27, 1996), Case T–235/95R *Goldstein v. Commission*, not reported in the E.C.R., para. 38, CFI. For a clear, more extensive exposition, see Barents, Procedures, at 83–95.

subject-matter of the main proceedings, but the consequence of the act challenged in those proceedings.[16]

13–005 In principle, an application for interim measures may be made after any direct action has been brought.[17] However, the interim relief sought may not make the claim in the main proceedings nugatory.

Accordingly, there would seem to be little chance of successfully applying for suspension of operation in connection with an action for failure to act, since the very object of that action is to procure the adoption of a measure.[18] The question whether, in connection with an action for damages, suspension of the operation of the act which allegedly caused the damage may be sought remains for the present an open question.[19] In any event, it is now clear that it is not possible:

> "to rule out in advance, in a general and abstract manner, that payment, by way of advance, even of an amount corresponding to that sought in the main application, may be necessary in order to ensure the practical effect of the judgment in the main action and may, in certain cases, appear justified with regard to the interests involved".[20]

The Court of Justice may order the adoption of interim measures under Article 243 (*ex Article 186*) of the E.C. Treaty in the context of an action for failure to fulfil obligations.[21] The interim relief most often sought is—full or partial, conditional or unconditional—suspension of the operation of a contested national measure.[22] The fact that the judgment finding the failure to fulfil obligations is declaratory in nature does not preclude the imposition of interim measures. The Court's interlocutory order does not derive its binding force from the Court's power to give judgment in the main proceedings. If a contested national measure threatens to cause irreparable damage to one of the parties, the judge hearing the application for interim relief must be able to order the necessary measures to secure the full

---

[16] (Order of the President of April 8, 1965), Case 18/65R *Gutmann v. Commission* [1966] E.C.R. 135 at 136–137, ECJ; but see (Order of the President of July 16, 1963), Joined Cases 35/62 and 16/63 R *Leroy v. High Authority* [1963] E.C.R. 213 at 215, ECJ. See also Pastor and Van Ginderachter, "La procédure en référé" (1989) R.T.D.E. 561 at 567.

[17] *Commentaire Mégret*, at 395 and 405; Mertens de Wilmars, "Het kort geding voor het Hof van Justitie van de Europese Gemeenschappen" (1986) S.E.W. 32 at 40.

[18] See paras 8–002—8–004, above.

[19] (Order of the President of May 23, 1990), Joined Cases C–51 and C–59/90R *Comos-Tank and Others v. Commission* [1990] E.C.R. I–2167 at I–2175, para. 33, ECJ.

[20] (Order of the President of January 29, 1997), Case C–393/96P(R) *Antonissen v. Council and Commission* [1997] E.C.R. I–441 at I–457, para. 37, ECJ. For the opposite view, see (Order of the President of November 29, 1996), Case T–179/96R *Antonissen v. Council and Commission* [1996] E.C.R. II–1641 at II–1653—1654, para. 30, CFI.

[21] (Order of May 21, 1977), Cases 31 and 53/77R *Commission v. United Kingdom* [1977] E.C.R. 921, ECJ; (Order of May 22, 1977), Case 61/77R *Commission v. Ireland* [1977] E.C.R. 937, ECJ; (Order of July 13, 1977), Case 61/77RII *Commission v. Ireland* [1977] E.C.R. 1411, ECJ. For a commentary, see Wainwright, "Art. 186 *[now Art. 243]* EEC: Interim Measures and Member States" (1977) E.L.Rev. 349–354.

[22] ECJ (Order of the President of October 25, 1985), Case 293/85R *Commission v. Belgium* [1985] E.C.R. 3521, ECJ.

effectiveness of the action in the main proceedings. This view is firmly established in the case law.[23]

If the application aims at the adoption of a measure which would be contrary to Community law, the application will be dismissed.[24] Consequently, an application for measures amounting to the judge's assuming the role of the defendant institution, not merely reviewing its activity, may not be granted unless the application contains evidence from which the judge hearing the interim application can find that there are exceptional circumstances justifying the adoption of the measures requested.[25] **13–006**

A party who has brought an appeal may apply for interim measures in the form of suspension of the operation of the judgment of the Court of First Instance or other interim relief. The application must be made to the Court of Justice under Article 53 of the E.C. Statute of the Court of Justice.[26]

The Court of Justice takes the view that it is not empowered to order interim measures in preliminary ruling procedures. However, in the judgments in *Factortame II*,[27] *Zuckerfabrik*[28] and *Atlanta Fruchthandelsgesellschaft*[29] it provided indications as to the interim relief which the national courts are under a duty to provide following the bringing of proceedings relating to the application of Community law.[30]

D. The provisional nature of interim measures

Interim measures are only provisional. There are two aspects to this[31]: the measures are valid only for a limited period and may not prejudice the judgment in the main proceedings. **13–007**

The period of time for which the measures are to apply may be expressly specified in the order.[32] If no time-limit is mentioned in the order, the order will expire when judgment is given in the main proceedings. At the request **13–008**

---

23 See all the orders cited in this chapter in connection with actions for failure to fulfil obligations.

24 (Order of the President of October 21, 1996), Case T–107/96R *Pantochim v. Commission* [1996] E.C.R. II–1361 at II–1375, paras 41–42, CFI.

25 (Order of the President of July 12, 1996), Case T–52/96R *Sogecable v. Commission* [1996] E.C.R. II–797 at II–812—813, paras 38–41, CFI, and the case law cited therein.

26 See (Order of the President of November 22, 1991), Case T–77/91R *Hochbaum v. Commission* [1991] E.C.R. II–1285 at II–1291, paras 19–22, CFI. Operation of the judgment of the Court of First Instance is automatically suspended during the period in which an appeal may be brought, and, in case of an appeal, until the dismissal of the appeal, when that court annuls a regulation. An application for interim measures may then be lodged with the Court of Justice for the suspension of the effects of the regulation which has been declared void or for the prescription of any other interim measure.

27 Case C–213/89 *R v. Secretary of State for Transport, ex p. Ltd* [1990] E.C.R. I–2433, ECJ ("*Factortame II*").

28 Joined Cases C–143/88 and C–92/89 *Zuckerfabrik Süderdithmarschen and Zuckerfabrik Soest* [1991] E.C.R. I–415, ECJ.

29 Case C–465/93 *Atlanta Fruchthandelsgesellschaft and Others* [1995] E.C.R. I–3761, ECJ.

30 See paras 3–015—3–019, above.

31 E.C. Statute, Art. 36, para. 3.

32 (Order of the President of April 8, 1965), Case 18/65R *Gutmann v. Commission* [1966] E.C.R. 135 at 138, ECJ; (Order of the President of July 5, 1983), Case 78/83R *Usinor v. Commission* [1983] E.C.R. 2183 at 2189, para. 9, ECJ; (Order of the President of July 16,

of one of the parties[33] or by order given by the Court of its own motion,[34] interim measures may at any time be varied, extended[35] or cancelled on account of a change in circumstances.[36]

13–009 The order giving interim relief may not prejudge the decision to be given in the main proceedings.[37] It may not decide disputed points of law or fact or neutralise in advance the consequences of the decision to be taken subsequently on the substance.[38] The judge hearing applications for interim relief may not order measures which are irrevocable and would confront the judges responsible for the substantive decision with an irreversible situation[39] or which would make the main application devoid of purpose.[40] Indeed, proceedings for interim relief do not lend themselves to an in-depth investigation of the facts and the parties' pleas. In addition, an excessively far-reaching pronouncement would completely reverse the relationship between interim measures and the main proceedings, which is not the intention behind interim relief.[41] Sometimes, however, interim measures unavoidably create an irreversible situation, which the judges hearing the main case have to accept.[42]

1984), Case 160/84R *Oryzomyli Kavallas v. Commission* [1984] E.C.R. 3217 at 3222, para. 9, ECJ; (Order of the President of March 17, 1986), Case 23/86R *United Kingdom v. European Parliament* [1986] E.C.R. 1085 at 1099, operative part, ECJ; (Order of the President of April 2, 1993), Case T–12/93R *CCE Vittel and CE Pierval v. Commission* [1993] E.C.R. II–449 at II–461, para. 33, CFI; (Order of the President of January 12, 1994), Case T–554/93R *Abbott Trust v. Council and Commission* [1994] E.C.R. II–1 at II–8, para. 19, CFI.

[33] ECJ Rules of Procedure, Art. 87; CFI Rules of Procedure, Art. 108.

[34] ECJ Rules of Procedure, Art. 84(2); CFI Rules of Procedure, Art. 105(2).

[35] (Order of the President of July 8, 1974), Case 20/74R II *Kali-Chemie v. Commission* [1974] E.C.R. 787.

[36] (Order of the President of June 12, 1992), Case C–272/91R *Commission v. Italy* [1992] E.C.R. I–3929 at I–3932–3933, paras 7–8, ECJ.

[37] (Order of the President of June 25, 1963), Case 65/63 *Prakash v. Commission* [1965] E.C.R. 576 at 579, ECJ; (Order of the President of July 7, 1981), Joined Cases 60 and 190/81R *IBM v. Commission* [1981] E.C.R. 1857 at 1862, para. 4, ECJ; (Order of the President of March 17, 1986), Case 23/86R *United Kingdom v. European Parliament* [1986] E.C.R. 1085 at 1095, para 32 *et seq.*, ECJ; (Order of the President of April 30, 1986), Case 62/86R *AKZO v. Commission* [1986] E.C.R. 1503 at 1508 para. 18, ECJ; (Order of the President of March 26, 1987), Case 46/87R *Hoechst v. Commission* [1987] E.C.R. 1549 at 1557–1558, paras 29–31, ECJ; (Order of the President of June 3, 1996), Case T–41/96R *Bayer v. Commission* [1996] E.C.R. II–381 at II–387–388, para. 13, CFI.

[38] (Order of the President of February 26, 1981), Case 20/81R *Arbed v. Commission* [1981] E.C.R. 721 at 730–731, para. 13, ECJ; (Order of the President of July 20, 1981), Case 206/81R *Alvarez v. European Parliament* [1981] E.C.R. 2187 at 2190, para. 6, ECJ.

[39] (Order of the President of May 28, 1975), Case 44/75R *Könecke v. Commission* [1975] E.C.R. 637 at 641, para. 4, ECJ.

[40] (Order of the President of October 15, 1976), Case 91/76R *De Lacroix v. Court of Justice* [1976] E.C.R. 1563 at 1564, para. 2, ECJ.

[41] Opinion of Advocate General F. Capotorti in (Order of March 28, 1988), Joined Cases 24 and 97/80R *Commission v. France* [1980] E.C.R. 1319 at 1338–1339, ECJ.

[42] (Order of January 17, 1980), Case 792/79R *Camera Care v. Commission* [1980] E.C.R. 119, ECJ; in which the Court of Justice recognised the Commission's power to adopt interim measures.

II. Identity of the Parties

A. The applicant

The ancillary nature of interim measures also determines the identity of the parties who may apply to the Court for such relief. An application for suspension of the operation of an act may be made only by the party who is challenging that measure in proceedings before the Court.[43] Other interim measures may be sought by any party to the main proceedings.[44] 13–010

Textbook writers are divided over the question whether a party intervening in the main proceedings is entitled to apply for interim measures regardless of the stance taken by the party in support of whose submissions it has intervened.[45] It is perhaps preferable not to grant interveners a right of their own to apply for interim measures, since if they were given such a right they might obtain the initiative in the litigation, something which Article 37 of the E.C. Statute of the Court of Justice sought specifically to avoid by allowing them only to intervene in support of the submissions of one of the parties. However, they may join in proceedings for interim measures provided that they show a sufficient interest. If they satisfy that requirement, it appears even to be unnecessary for them to have already intervened in the main proceedings.[46] In such case, the view of the judge hearing the application for interim relief as to whether leave should be granted to intervene in those proceedings would not be binding on the judges hearing the main application. A party which has been given leave to intervene in proceedings for interim measures may seek relief different from that applied for by the party which it is supporting.[47] 13–011

A party may request interim measures only in order to protect his or her own interests,[48] not in order to avoid disadvantages which the failure to grant the relief would cause third parties to suffer.[49] 13–012

[43] ECJ Rules of Procedure, Art. 83(1), subpara. 1; CFI Rules of Procedure, Art. 104(1), subpara. 1.

[44] ECJ Rules of Procedure, Art. 83(1), subpara. 2; CFI Rules of Procedure, Art. 104(1), subpara. 2.

[45] See E.C. Statute, Art. 37. *In favour of this proposition*: *Commentaire Mégret*, at 407; Pastor and Van Ginderachter (cited in n. 16, above) at 577, who tie in the intervener's status with the distinction between suspension—which may be sought only by the applicant—and other interim measures, for which any party may apply. They argue that suspension is in fact far too drastic a measure for the purposes of safeguarding the intervener's interests, whereas other interim measures might well be appropriate to this end. *Cf.* Lasok, *The European Court of Justice: Practice and Procedure*, London, Butterworths, 1994, p. 289; *against the proposition*: Mertens de Wilmars (cited in n. 17, above), at 38.

[46] See, by implication, (Order of the President of May 13, 1993), Case T–24/93R *CMBT v. Commission* [1993] E.C.R. II–543 at II–548, paras 14–16, CFI.

[47] Mertens de Wilmars (cited in n. 17 above), at 38.

[48] (Order of the President of May 4, 1964), Case 12/64R *Ley v. Commission* [1965] E.C.R. 132 at 134, ECJ.

[49] (Order of the President of February 25, 1975), Case 22/75 *Küster v. European Parliament* [1975] E.C.R. 277 at 278, paras 6–8, ECJ.

B. The defendant

13–013 The defendant in proceedings for interim measures is the opponent in the main proceedings of the party which lodged the application for interim relief. There has been one wholly exceptional case in which the Commission was obliged to comply with an interim measure addressed to it in the context of proceedings concerning the Community's budget which were brought by the United Kingdom against the European Parliament.[50]

III. Special Characteristics

A. Competent Judge

13–014 The President of the Court of Justice or the President of the Court of First Instance, depending on the court before which the main proceedings have been brought, is empowered to rule on applications for interim measures.[51] The President may refer the application to his or her respective court for decision.[52] Such a reference will generally be made on the ground of the difficulty or exceptional interest of the case.[53] If the application is so referred, the Court of Justice or the Court of First Instance, as the case may be, has to give it priority over all other cases.[54]

B. Procedure before the Court

13–015 An application for interim relief is adjudicated upon "by way of summary procedure".[55] The application is served on the opposite party; the President of the Court of Justice or the Court of First Instance, as the case may be, prescribes a short period within which that party may submit written or oral observations.[56] The President may grant the application even before the observations of the opposite party have been submitted.[57] In most cases, a hearing is held at which the parties put their case and the President puts

---

50 (Order of the President of March 17, 1986), Case 23/86R *United Kingdom v. European Parliament* [1986] E.C.R. 1085 at 1093, paras 23, 24, ECJ. *Cf.,* however, (Order of the President of June 25, 1987), Case 133/87R *Nashua Corporation v. Commission* [1987] E.C.R. 2883 at 2887, para. 8, ECJ; (Order of the President of December 14, 1993), Case T–543/93R *Gestevisión Telecinco v. Commission* [1993] E.C.R. II–1411 at II–1420, para. 25, CFI.

51 E.C. Statute, Art. 36, para. 1. If that provision is read together with Art. 50, paras 2, 3, it appears that, in principle, the President of the Court of Justice is empowered to rule on appeals brought against orders given by the (President of the) Court of First Instance in applications for interim relief.

52 ECJ Rules of Procedure, Art. 85, para. 1; CFI Rules of Procedure, Art. 106, para. 1 (in this case the President will in fact refer the application to the chamber to which the main case has been assigned).

53 See Pastor and Van Ginderachter (cited in n. 16 above), at 579, and the cases cited therein.

54 ECJ Rules of Procedure, Art. 85, para. 3; CFI Rules of Procedure, Art. 106, para. 3.

55 E.C. Statute, Art. 36. See also Pastor and Van Ginderachter (see n. 16, above), at 581–583.

56 ECJ Rules of Procedure, Art. 84(1); CFI Rules of Procedure, Art. 105(1).

57 ECJ Rules of Procedure, Art. 84(2), subpara. 2; CFI Rules of Procedure, Art. 105(2), subpara. 2. It is provided therein that the decision may be varied or cancelled even without any application being made by any party. For an example, see (Order of the President of June 28, 1990), Case C–195/90R *Commission v. Germany* [1990] E.C.R. I–2715, ECJ, followed by (Order of July 12, 1990), Case C–195/90R *Commission v. Germany* [1990] E.C.R. I–3351.

questions.[58] If necessary a preparatory inquiry may be ordered in so far as this is compatible with the objectives of the interim proceedings.[59]

C. Other requirements for admissibility

1. Admissibility of the application in the main proceedings

Again on account of the ancillary nature of proceedings for interim relief, whether an application for interim measures is admissible will be contingent upon the admissibility of the application in the main proceedings.[60] Proceedings for interim relief would acquire an impermissible degree of autonomy if interim measures could be ordered in connection with an inadmissible application in the main proceedings. This requirement faces the judge hearing the application for interim relief with a dilemma: because of the provisional nature of such relief he or she may not prejudge in any way the final judgment, yet in order to determine the admissibility of the application for interim measures, he or she must make a reasonably accurate determination of whether the main application will be declared admissible. **13–016**

Consequently, the judge hearing the application for interim relief takes a cautious approach to this question. It has been consistently held that the issue of the admissibility of the main application should not be examined in proceedings relating to an application for interim measures in order not to prejudice the substantive proceedings.[61] Yet where the opposite party contends that the main application is manifestly inadmissible, it will be necessary nevertheless for the judge hearing the application for interim relief to establish whether there are any grounds for concluding prima facie

---

58 If the judge hearing applications for interim relief considers that the case-file contains all the information which is required to make a pronouncement, he or she may lawfully dispense with oral explanations from the parties: (Order of the President of January 29, 1997), Case C–393/96P(R) *Antonissen v. Council and Commission* [1997] E.C.R. I–441 at I–454, para. 24, ECJ.

59 ECJ Rules of Procedure, Art. 84(2), subpara. 1; CFI Rules of Procedure, Art. 105(2), subpara. 1.

60 (Order of the President of May 23, 1990), Case C–68/90R *Blot and Front National v. European Parliament* [1990] E.C.R. I–2177 at I–2179, paras 4–5, ECJ; (Order of the President of June 27, 1991), Case C–117/91R *Bosman v. Commission* [1991] E.C.R. I–3353 at I–3356, para. 6, ECJ; (Order of the President of July 6, 1993), Case C–257/93R *Van Parijs and Others v. Council and Commission* [1993] E.C.R. I–3917 at I–3920, para. 4, ECJ; (Order of the President of July 9, 1993), Case C–64/93R *Donatab and Others v. Commission* [1993] E.C.R. I–3955 at I–3958, para. 4, ECJ; (Order of the President of July 16, 1993), Case C–107/93R *AEFMA v. Commission* [1993] E.C.R. I–4177 at I–4179, para. 4, ECJ.

61 (Order of the President of November 21, 1962), Case 25/62R *Plaumann & Co. v. Commission* [1963] E.C.R. 126 at 129, ECJ; (Order of the President of July 7, 1965), Case 28/65R *Fonzi v. Commission* [1966] E.C.R. 508 at 509, ECJ; (Order of the President of November 30, 1972), Case 75/72R *Perinciolo v. Council* [1972] E.C.R. 1201 at 1203, para. 7, ECJ; (Order of the President of November 3, 1980), Case 186/80R *Suss v. Commission* [1980] E.C.R. 3501 at 3505–3506, paras 13–14, ECJ; (Order of the President of March 17, 1986), Case 23/86R *United Kingdom v. European Parliament* [1986] E.C.R. 1085 at 1092, para. 21, ECJ; (Order of the President of April 22, 1986), Case 351/85R *Fabrique de Fer de Charleroi v. Commission* [1986] E.C.R. 1307 at 1311, para. 13, ECJ; (Order of the President of October 16, 1986), Case 221/86R *Group of the European Right and National Front Party v. European Parliament* [1986] E.C.R. 2969 at 2975, para. 19, ECJ; (Order of the President of April 8, 1987), Case 65/87R *Pfizer v. Commission* [1987] E.C.R. 1691 at 1696, para. 15, ECJ.

that the main application is admissible.[62] He or she will always take care that the judges hearing the main case retain their latitude. The assessment made by the judge hearing applications for interim relief does not preclude interim measures being granted following the bringing of an action which is subsequently declared inadmissible,[63] but it does avoid an application which is manifestly inadmissible giving rise to proceedings for interim relief which enable the application or effects of a Community act to be temporarily averted.[64]

The judge hearing applications for interim measures takes the view that the application in the main proceedings may be admissible where he or she finds that that application discloses prima facie grounds for concluding that there is a certain probability that it is admissible.[65] Such grounds will be lacking where, in the light of settled case law, the main application is manifestly inadmissible. For instance, an application for annulment of the Commission's refusal to initiate proceedings for failure to fulfil obligations is manifestly inadmissible.[66] Accordingly, an application for interim measures brought in connection with such an action will also be inadmissible.[67] Other examples of manifest inadmissibility of the main application are when the applicant has failed to comply with certain formal requirements[68]

---

[62] See, for example, (Order of the President of August 5, 1983), Case 118/83R *CMC v. Commission* [1983] E.C.R. 2583 at 2595, para. 37, ECJ; (Order of the President of May 8, 1987), Case 82/87R *Autexpo v. Commission* [1987] E.C.R. 2131 at 2137, paras 15–16, ECJ; (Order of the President of August 10, 1987), Case 209/87R *EISA v. Commission* [1987] E.C.R. 3453 at 3457, para. 10, ECJ; (Order of the President of August 10, 1987), Case 214/87R *Cockerill Sambre v. Commission* [1987] E.C.R. 3463 at 3467, para. 10, ECJ; (Order of the President of August 10, 1987), Case 223/87R *Assider v. Commission* [1987] E.C.R. 3473 at 3477, para. 10, ECJ; (Order of the President of July 13, 1988), Case 160/88R *Fédération Européenne de la Santé Animale and Others v. Council* [1988] E.C.R. 4121 at 4128, para. 22, ECJ; (Order of the President of June 27, 1991), Case C–117/91R *Bosman v. Commission* [1991] E.C.R. I–3353 at 3357, para. 7, ECJ; (Order of the President of October 12, 1992), Case C–295/92R *Landbouwschap v. Commission* [1992] E.C.R. I–5069, ECJ; (Order of the President of March 23, 1992), Joined Cases T–10–12/92R and T–14–15/92R *Cimenteries CBR SA and Others v. Commission* [1992] E.C.R. II–1571 at II–1585, para. 44, CFI; (Order of the President of December 15, 1992), Case T–96/92R *CCE de la Société des Grandes Sources and Others v. Commission* [1992] E.C.R. II–2579 at II–2592, para. 31, CFI; (Order of the President of March 2, 1998), Case T–310/97R *Government of the Netherlands Antilles v. Council* [1998] E.C.R. II–455 at II–467—469, paras 30–37, CFI.

[63] For an example, see (Order of the President of October 25, 1985), Case 293/85R *Commission v. Belgium* [1985] E.C.R. 3521, ECJ; followed by Case 293/85 *Commission v. Belgium* [1988] E.C.R. 305, ECJ.

[64] (Order of the President of January 27, 1988), Case 376/87R *Distrivet v. Council* [1988] E.C.R. 209 at 216, para. 22, ECJ. This also applies to the requirement for a prima facie case (paras 13–023, 13–024, below).

[65] (Order of the President of February 1, 1984), Case 1/84R *Ilford v. Commission* [1984] E.C.R. 423 at 428, paras 6–7, ECJ; (Order of the President of April 2, 1993), Case T–12/93R *CCE Vittel and CE Pierval v. Commission* [1993] E.C.R. II–449 at II–457—459, paras 20–26, CFI; (Order of the President of May 13 1993), Case T–24/93R *CMBT v. Commission* [1993] E.C.R. II–543 at II–551—552, paras 27–30, CFI.

[66] See para. 5–024, above.

[67] (Order of the President of May 5, 1994), Case C–97/94P-R *Schulz v. Commission* [1994] E.C.R. I–1701 at I–1705—1706, paras 12–15, ECJ.

[68] (Order of the President of February 26, 1981), Case 10/81 *Farrall v. Commission* [1981] E.C.R. 717, ECJ (application not lodged by a lawyer).

or to lodge the application within the prescribed time-limit[69] and where individuals have brought an action against an act which is unmistakeably of general application[70] or against an action which produces no legal effects.[71] An action brought by individuals against a decision addressed to a Member State which the judge hearing applications for interim relief finds, prima facie, not to be of individual concern to them will be held to be manifestly inadmissible.[72]

2. Time-limits

An application for interim measures will be admissible only as from the time when the application in the main proceedings has been brought.[73] As long as the main action is pending, an application for interim measures can in principle be made. Nevertheless, the judge hearing applications for interim relief will not hold an application admissible if it is lodged after the written and oral procedures in the main case have been concluded and only a matter of weeks before final judgment is given.[74] In addition, the applicant should take care that its decision as to the time when it submits an application for interim measures does not prejudice its chance of the measures being granted. If the applicant delays too long, there is a danger that the judge hearing the application for interim relief will draw inferences detracting from the urgency of the measures sought.[75] **13–017**

In staff cases, an application may be made for interim measures from the time when the applicant lodges his or her complaint with the appointing authority. At the same time, the main action must have been brought before the Court of First Instance.[76] The proceedings in the principal action **13–018**

---

[69] (Order of the President of May 23, 1984), Case 50/84R *Bensider v. Commission* [1984] E.C.R. 2247 at 2252, para. 24, ECJ.

[70] (Order of the President of July 13, 1988), Case 160/88R *Fédération Européenne de la Santé Animale and Others v. Council* [1988] E.C.R. 4121 at 4128–4130, paras 23–30, ECJ.

[71] (Order of the President of August 26, 1996), Case T–75/96R *Söktas v. Commission* [1996] E.C.R. II–859 at II–867—870, paras 16–30, CFI; (Order of the President of October 14, 1996), Case T–137/96R *Valio v. Commission* [1996] E.C.R. II–1327 at II–1338—1341, paras 27–37, CFI.

[72] (Order of the President of December 22, 1995), Case T–219/95R *Danielsson v. Commission* [1995] E.C.R. II–3051 at II–3071—3074, paras 66–76, CFI.

[73] ECJ Rules of Procedure, Art. 83(1), subpara. 1; CFI Rules of Procedure, Art. 104(1), subpara. 1.

[74] (Order of the President of April 11, 1960), Joined Cases 3–16, 18 and 25–26/58R *Barbara Erzbergbau v. High Authority* [1960] E.C.R. 220 at 223–224, ECJ.

[75] (Order of the President of April 22, 1994), Case C–87/94R *Commission v. Belgium* [1994] E.C.R. I–1395 at I–1406—1407, paras 38 and 42, ECJ. In this order, the President of the Court of Justice held that the Commission had not displayed the diligence to be expected of a party lodging an application for interim measures who relied on the urgency of the measures sought. On October 29, 1993, the Commission received a complaint from the bus manufacturer Van Hool alleging irregularities in the choice of suppliers of new buses by the Walloon regional transport company (*Société régionale wallonne de transport*). The Commission did not announce its intention to seek interim measures until its reasoned opinion of February 8, 1994. The President held that this was too late. For a commentary, see Mattera, "L'ordonnance du 22 avril 1994 sur les 'bus wallons'" (1994) R.M.U.E. 161–171.

[76] In principle, an application to the Court of First Instance will be admissible in staff cases only after the administrative phase has run its course: the official lodges a complaint with his

are then suspended until such time as an express or implied decision rejecting the complaint is taken.[77]

3. Requirement for a separate application

13–019 Under Article 83(3) of the ECJ Rules of Procedure and Article 104(3) of the CFI Rules of Procedure, an application for interim measures must be made by a separate document and in accordance with the formal requirements applying to procedural documents in general and applications in particular.[78] A request for interim relief contained in the application initiating the main proceedings will be inadmissible.[79] Applications for interim measures must state the subject-matter of the proceedings, the circumstances giving rise to urgency and the pleas of fact and law establishing a prima facie case for the interim measures applied for.[80]

13–020 The application may be "varied" in the course of the oral procedure if the variation falls within the framework of the measures requested in the application for interim relief and has less of an effect on the defendant.[81] If those requirements are not fulfilled and the varied application substantially differs in kind from the original application, the application to vary the initial request for interim measures will be inadmissible.[82]

D. Substantive requirements

13–021 All the following three requirements have to be met if the application for interim measures is to be granted:

(1) the application must establish a prima facie case, which means that the application in the main proceedings with which it is associated must, at first sight, have a reasonable chance of succeeding;

(2) the application must be urgent; and

(3) the applicant's interest in the imposition of interim measures must outweigh the other interests at stake in the proceedings.

The first two requirements arise under Article 83(2) of the ECJ Rules of Procedure and Article 104(2) of the CFI Rules of Procedure. The third has

---

or her appointing authority, which then has four months to take a decision. If no decision is taken within that four-month period, the complaint is deemed to have been impliedly refused (Staff Regulations, Art. 90(2)).

[77] Staff Regulations, Art. 91(4).

[78] ECJ Rules of Procedure, Arts. 37 and 38; CFI Rules of Procedure, Arts. 43 and 44 (paras 22–003—22–029, below).

[79] Case 108/63 *Merlini v. High Authority* [1965] E.C.R. 1 at 9, ECJ; Case 32/64 *Italy v. Commission* [1965] E.C.R. 365 at 372, ECJ; (Order of June 19 1995), Case T–107/94 *Kik v. Council and Commission* [1995] E.C.R. II–1717, CFI; Case T–140/94 *Gutiérrez de Quijano y Llorens v. European Parliament* [1996] E.C.R.-S.C. II–689 at II–700, para. 32, (English abstract at I–A–241), CFI; Case T–146/95 *Bernardi v. European Parliament* [1996] E.C.R. II–769 at II–782, para. 30, CFI; (Order of September 29, 1997), Case T–4/97 *D'Orazio and Hublau v. Commission* [1997] E.C.R. II–1505 at II–1510, para. 14, CFI.

[80] ECJ Rules of Procedure, Art. 83(2); CFI Rules of Procedure, Art. 104(2).

[81] (Order of June 29, 1993), Case C–280/93R *Germany v. Council* [1993] E.C.R. I–3667 at I–3674, para. 15, ECJ.

[82] *ibid.*, at I–3675, para. 16.

come out of the case law, sometimes in connection with the determination whether the application in the main proceedings is potentially well founded or with the urgency of the application for interim relief.

The order in which the judge hearing applications for interim relief considers these substantive requirements is of little consequence. Once one of the requirements is not satisfied, interim measures may not be imposed. In practice, the determination of the urgency of the measures sought is often decisive and the other requirements do not have to be considered. It may be noted in this connection that the judge hearing the application for interim relief is not required to reply explicitly to all the points of law and fact raised in the course of the interlocutory proceedings. It is sufficient that the reasons given validly justify the order given in the light of the circumstances of the case.[83] **13–022**

1. Prima facie case

The requirement for a prima facie case to be made out (also referred to as *fumus boni juris*) is designed—just as in the case of the determination that the main application is not manifestly inadmissible—to prevent improper use being made of applications for interim relief.[84] **13–023**

The main case must have a reasonable chance of succeeding. Since the judge hearing applications for interim relief may not prejudge the decision in the proceedings on the substance his or her assessment in this regard will be confined to whether the arguments put forward by the applicant in the main proceedings are, prima facie, basically sound or are certainly doomed to fail.[85] The case law, which is influenced greatly by the particular circumstances, exhibits in practice quite considerable subtle differences in its interpretation of this requirement. Sometimes the judge hearing applications for interim relief holds that there should be "a strong presumption that the application in the main action is well founded".[86] In other cases, it is found that there is substantial prima facie evidence that the applicant is in the right[87] or that the legality of the contested act is, to say the least, **13–024**

[83] Case C–248/97P(R) *Chaves Fonseca Ferrão v. Office for Harmonization in the Internal Market (Trade Marks and Designs)* [1997] E.C.R. I–4729 at I–4739, para. 20, ECJ.

[84] See para. 13–016, above.

[85] See, *e.g.* (Order of the President of April 5, 1993), Case T–21/93 *Peixoto v. Commission* [1993] E.C.R. II–463 at II–472, para. 27, CFI, where it was found that the arguments advanced provided a "firm basis" for the applicant's claims in the main proceedings. *Cf.* (Order of the President of May 26, 1998), Case T–60/98R *Ecord Consortium for Russian Cooperation v. Commission*, [1998] E.C.R. II–2205, CFI, where the President clearly held that the plea alleging infringement of the principle of protection of legitimate expectation appeared unfounded.

[86] (Order of the President of October 20, 1959), Joined Cases 43, 44 and 45/59 *Von Lachmüller and Others v. Commission* [1960] E.C.R. 489 at 492, ECJ. See, to the same effect, (Order of the President of June 25, 1963), Case 65/63 *Prakash v. Commission* [1965] E.C.R. 576 at 578, ECJ, in which the President dismissed the application for interim measures on the ground that he did not have sufficient information to assess whether the main application was prima facie well founded.

[87] (Order of March 4, 1982), Case 42/82R *Commission v. France* [1982] E.C.R. 841 at 856, paras 13–14, ECJ.

doubtful.[88] In other cases still, the judge hearing applications for interim relief takes the opposite approach and finds that there are no grounds for holding that the substantive application is manifestly without foundation.[89] That formula expresses the view of the judge hearing the application that the arguments put forward by the person seeking the interim measures cannot be rejected at that stage of the proceedings in the absence of an in-depth consideration of the case.[90] Thus *fumus boni juris* is slowly but surely turning into *fumus non mali juris*. Moreover, it would seem that the judge hearing interim applications is no longer required to be of the opinion that the main action will succeed in order to grant the measures requested, merely having to be persuaded that the main application is reasonable.[91]

If the application in the main proceedings raises questions of legal principle which the Court of Justice has not yet had occasion to determine and the pleas adduced relate to those questions, the application will be regarded as not being manifestly unfounded and the judge hearing the application for interim relief will hold that the requirement for a prima facie case has been made out.[92]

2. Urgent nature of the application for interim measures

13–025 An application for interim relief is urgent where the absence of the judgment in the main proceedings threatens to cause the person seeking the relief serious and irreparable damage. The urgent nature of the interim application is therefore determined by the nature of the damage which is liable to arise as a result of the duration of the main proceedings. It was

---

[88] (Order of the President of August 21, 1981), Case 232/81R *Agricola Commerciale Olio v. Commission* [1981] E.C.R. 2193 at 2199, para. 5, ECJ.

[89] (Order of the President of January 16, 1975), Case 3/75R *Johnson & Firth Brown v. Commission* [1975] E.C.R. 1 at 6, ECJ.

[90] (Order of the President of June 13, 1989), Case 56/89R *Publishers Association v. Commission* [1989] E.C.R. 1693 at 1700, para. 33, ECJ; (Order of the President of October 10, 1989), Case 246/89R *Commission v. United Kingdom* [1989] E.C.R. 3125 at 3134, para. 33, ECJ; (Order of the President of June 28, 1990), Case C–195/90R *Commission v. Germany* [1990] E.C.R. I–2715 at I–2719, para. 19, ECJ; (Order of the President of January 31, 1992), Case C–272/91R *Commission v. Italy* [1992] E.C.R. I–457 at I–464, para. 24, ECJ; (Order of the President of June 20, 1993), Case C–280/93R *Germany v. Council* [1993] E.C.R. I–3667 at I–3676, para. 21, ECJ; (Order of the President of July 19, 1995), Case C–149/95P(R) *Commission v. Atlantic Container Line and Others* [1995] E.C.R. I–2165 at I–2179, para. 26, ECJ.

[91] (Order of the President of July 7, 1998), Case T–65/98R *Van den Bergh Foods Ltd v. Commission* [1998] E.C.R. II–2641 at II–2660, para. 61 ("In view of all of the foregoing, the pleas in law put forward by the applicants cannot be held prima facie to lack any foundation").

[92] (Order of the President of January 31, 1991), Case C–345/90P-R *European Parliament v. Hanning* [1991] E.C.R. I–231 at I–238, paras 29–30, ECJ. *Cf.* (Order of the President of April 15, 1991), Case T–13/91R *Harrison v. Commission* [1991] E.C.R. II–179 at II–185, para. 26, CFI. The President found first that the pleas adduced in support of the application in the main proceedings did not bear out the applicant's claims, before going on to hold that "the applicant has failed to make out a *prima facie* case suggesting that his main application is well founded". In ECJ (Order of the President of January 31, 1992), Case C–272/91R *Commission v. Italy* [1992] E.C.R. I–457 at I–462—464, paras 19–24, ECJ, the President of the Court of Justice set forth the Commission's and Italy's arguments alongside each other before holding that the Commission's application did not appear to be without substance.

therefore not by chance that the serious and irreparable nature of the damage has emerged in the case law as the yardstick for determining the urgency of an application for interim measures. That two-fold criterion is intended to restrict the grant of interim measures to cases in which the judgment in the main proceedings would not afford any legal redress in the absence of the interim relief sought.[93] The case law does not provide any conclusive definitions of the two terms. Moreover, the seriousness and the irreparable nature of the alleged damage are not always considered separately.[94] Although the damage must be both serious and irreparable,[95] the case law seems to attach the most importance to the question of irreparability.

The damage is irreparable where it will not be eliminated by a judgment in the main proceedings in favour of the applicant.[96] In addition, the damage must be serious, which gives a relative aspect to the urgency of an application for interim relief. Thus, a small undertaking has less of an ability to bear financial or economic burdens than a multinational or a 13–026

[93] (Order of the President of November 28, 1966), Case 29/66R *Gutmann v. Commission* [1967] E.C.R. 241 at 242, ECJ.

[94] See the Opinion of Advocate General F. Capotorti in (Order of March 28, 1980), Joined Cases 24 and 97/80R *Commission v. France* [1980] E.C.R. 1319 at 1341–1342, ECJ, who equated irreparable with serious. In (Order of the President of June, 26 1959), Case 31/59 *Acciaieria e Tubificio di Brescia v. High Authority* [1960] E.C.R. 98 at 99, ECJ, the requirement for urgency was defined in terms of the applicant's having to show that the implementation of the contested measure would cause "irreparable or at least serious damage".

[95] (Order of the President of January 13, 1978), Case 4/78R *Salerno v. Commission* [1978] E.C.R. 1 at 3, para. 11, ECJ.

[96] Joliet, Bertrand and Nihoul (cited in n. 4, above), at 269, reject the view that damage is irreparable only if compensation may not be given therefor (for this view, see *Commentaire Mégret*, at 399). They argue that the fiction that any damage may be made good applies only to damage which has already arisen. In contrast, the judge hearing applications for interim relief has to forestall the damage. He or she must therefore regard as irreparable damage for which the applicant would have to claim compensation in separate proceedings after a judgment in his or her favour in the main proceedings on the ground of the illegal aspects found in that judgment. See, *inter alia* (Order of the President of October 25, 1990), Case C–257/90R *Italsolar v. Commission* [1990] E.C.R. I–3841 at I–3845, para. 15, ECJ: financial loss is in principle regarded as serious and irreparable damage only in the event that it would not be fully compensated if the applicant in the main proceedings were to be successful. This may be so, for instance, where the alleged damage threatens the existence of the undertaking concerned or where the damage, even when it occurs, cannot be quantified: (Order of the President of May 23, 1990), Joined Cases C–51 and C–59/90R *Comos-Tank and Others v. Commission* [1990] E.C.R. I–2167 at I–2173—2174, para. 24, ECJ; (Order of the President of March 21, 1997), Case T–41/97R *Antillean Rice Mills v. Council* [1997] E.C.R. II–447 at II–463, para. 47, CFI. That approach does not conflict with the case law holding that pure financial loss is not regarded as irreparable or even as difficult to repair: see (Order of the President of November 23, 1990), Case T–45/90R *Speybrouck v. European Parliament* [1990] E.C.R. II–705 at II–711, para. 23, CFI; (Order of the President of August 1, 1991), Case T–51/91R *Hoyer v. Commission* [1991] E.C.R. II–679 at II–685, para. 19, CFI; (Order of the President of March 23, 1993), Case T–115/92R *Hogan v. European Parliament* [1993] E.C.R. II–339 at II–334, para. 17, CFI; (Order of the President of September 29, 1993), Case T–497/93 *Hogan v. Court of Justice* [1993] E.C.R. II–1005 at II–1011, para. 17, CFI. This is because such loss, *e.g.* recovery of an unlawfully imposed levy or grant of a subsidy, may be awarded in full pursuant to the judgment in the main proceedings: see, *e.g.* (Order of the President of June 19, 1983), Case 120/83R *Raznoimport v. Commission* [1983] E.C.R. 2573 at 2580, para. 15, ECJ.

Member State.[97] In addition, the requirement for the damage to be serious prevents interim measures being imposed in order to avert irreparable, but negligible, damage.[98] Lastly, in assessing the seriousness of the damage and the related urgency of the measures requested, the judge may take account of the stance adopted by the applicant. Accordingly, the European Parliament was held not to be entitled to maintain that to give immediate effect to a judgment of the Court of First Instance annulling the appointment of an official would cause it serious damage, since it had left the post vacant for some six months.[99]

13–027 Interim measures serve only to avoid damage from arising. This requirement is considered separately.[1] If the judge hearing the application for interim relief finds that the contested act has been completely implemented and produced all its effects, damage can no longer be averted by imposing interim measures. If that is so, the application for interim measures is to no purpose. It may happen that a measure which had already produced damage before the application for interim measures was brought is continuing to cause damage, in which case interim measures may be imposed to prevent any increase in the damage.

Furthermore, the threat of damage must be a real one. Indefinite potential damage does not suffice.[2] The judge hearing the application for interim measures may have regard, in assessing the imminence of damage, to whether or not effective relief is available from the national courts.[3] The fact that both material and non-material damage is imminent may result in the grant of interim measures.[4]

---

[97] (Order of the President of February 26, 1981), Case 20/81R *Arbed v. Commission* [1981] E.C.R. 721 at 731, para. 14, ECJ; (Order of the President of September 24, 1986), Case 214/86R *Greece v. Commission* [1986] E.C.R. 2631 at 2637, para. 20, ECJ; (Order of the President of December 17, 1986), Case 294/86R *Technointorg v. Commission* [1986] E.C.R. 3979 at 3987, para. 28, ECJ; (Order of the President of August, 10, 1987), Case 223/87R *Assider v. Commission* [1987] E.C.R. 3473 at 3480, para. 22, ECJ; (Order of the President of May 6, 1988), Case 111/88R *Greece v. Commission* [1988] E.C.R. 2591 at 2596, para. 18, ECJ; (Order of the President of June 10, 1988), Case 152/88R *Sofrimport v. Commission* [1988] E.C.R. 2931 at 2941, paras 31–32, ECJ.

[98] This concern is very much to the fore in the case of the third substantive requirement that the applicant's interest must outweigh the interest of the opposite party/third parties (see paras 13–029—13–031, below).

[99] (Order of the President of April 3, 1992), Case C–35/92P-R *European Parliament v. Frederiksen* [1992] E.C.R. I–2399 at I–2405, para. 20, ECJ.

[1] (Order of the President of August 28, 1978), Case 166/78R *Italy v. Council* [1978] E.C.R. 1745 at 1748, para. 14, ECJ.

[2] (Order of the President of June 15, 1987), Case 142/87R *Belgium v. Commission* [1987] E.C.R. 2589 at 2597, para. 25, indefinite potential damage cannot be regarded as serious and irreparable damage, ECJ; (Order of the President of July 16, 1993), Case C–296/93R *France v. Commission* [1993] E.C.R. I–4181 at I–4188—4189, para. 26, ECJ (Order of the President of 7 June 1991), Case T–19/91R *Vichy v. Commission* [1991] E.C.R. II–265 at II–271, para. 19, CFI; (Order of the President of May 13, 1993), Case T–24/93R *CMBT v. Commission* [1993] E.C.R. II–543 at II–553, para. 34, CFI.

[3] (Order of the President of June 15, 1987), Case 142/87R *Belgium v. Commission* [1987] E.C.R. 2589 at 2597, para. 26, ECJ.

[4] This may be inferred from (Order of the President of June 26, 1959) Case 31/59 *Acciaieria e Tubificio di Brescia v. High Authority* [1960] E.C.R. 98 at 100, ECJ, and (Order of the President of November 30, 1993), Case T–549/93R *D. v. Commission* [1993] E.C.R. II–1347 at II–1359, para. 44, CFI.

The applicant for interim relief must show that damage affecting him or her personally is imminent.[5] A Member State may rely on damage allegedly suffered by a domestic industrial sector[6] on the ground that it is the guardian of national economic and social interests.[7] Furthermore, by virtue of its participation in the exercise of legislative and budgetary powers and contribution to the Community budget, a Member State may rely on the damage which would arise from expenditure being incurred contrary to the rules governing the powers of the Community and its institutions.[8] All the same, it does not appear sufficient for a Member State to refer to damage specifically suffered by an individual undertaking.[9] In connection with an action for failure to fulfil obligations, the Commission is entitled to adduce evidence of damage to its own interests as guardian of Community law[10] or to the interests of nationals of other Member States[11] or even of the Member State concerned.[12] **13–028**

3. Balance of interests

Even where the judge hearing the application for interim relief has found that the application in the main proceedings is prima facie not unreasonable and that the interim measures sought are urgent, he or she is not obliged to give an order imposing those measures. He or she will withhold consent if the applicant's interest does not outweigh the possible effects of the measures on the interests of the opposite party[13] or third parties[14] or the **13–029**

---

[5] (Order of the President of May 6, 1988), Case 111/88R *Greece v. Commission* [1988] E.C.R. 2591 at 2595, para. 15; ECJ (Order of the President of May 6, 1988), Case 112/88R *Crete Citron Producers Association v. Commission* [1988] E.C.R. 2597 at 2602, para. 20, ECJ.

[6] (Order of the President of August 28, 1978), Case 166/78R *Italy v. Council* [1978] E.C.R. 1745, ECJ: Italy sought to protect the interests of its domestic cereal starch industry. The application for interim measures was dismissed on the ground that Italy had not established the imminence of damage. No objection of admissibility was raised on account of the fact that the alleged damage was not imminent for the Italian State as such. See, to the same effect, (Order of the President of July 16, 1993), Case C–296/93R *France v. Commission* [1993] E.C.R. I–4181, ECJ; (Order of the President of July 16, 1993), Case C–307/93R *Ireland v. Commission* [1993] E.C.R. I–4191, ECJ.

[7] (Order of the President of June 29, 1993), Case C–280/93R *Germany v. Council* [1993] E.C.R. I–3667 at I–3677, para. 27, ECJ.

[8] (Order of the President of September 24, 1996), Joined Cases C–239 and C–240/96R *United Kingdom v. Commission* [1996] E.C.R. I–4475 at I–4492, para. 66, ECJ.

[9] (Order of the President of June 15, 1987), Case 142/87R *Belgium v. Commission* [1987] E.C.R. 2589 at 2597, paras 23–24, ECJ; (Order of the President of May 8, 1991), Case C–356/90R *Belgium v. Commission* [1991] E.C.R. I–2423 at I–2429, para. 23, ECJ.

[10] Pastor and Van Ginderachter (cited in n. 16 above), at 600.

[11] (Order of the President of July 13, 1977), Case 61/77RII *Commission v. Ireland* [1977] E.C.R. 1411 at 1413, para. 14, ECJ; (Order of the President of October 25, 1985), Case 293/85R *Commission v. Belgium* [1985] E.C.R. 3521, ECJ.

[12] (Order of June 7, 1985), Case 154/85R *Commission v. Italy* [1985] E.C.R. 1753 at 1758, para. 19, ECJ.

[13] In staff cases, the interests of the service are weighed against the applicant's interests. See, for instance, (Order of the President of July 11, 1988), Case 176/88R *Hanning v. European Parliament* [1988] E.C.R. 3915 at 3919, para. 14, ECJ.

[14] (Order of the President of January 16, 1975), Case 3/75R *Johnson & Firth Brown v. Commission* [1975] E.C.R. 1, ECJ; (Order of the President of May 22, 1978), Case 92/78R *Simmenthal v. Commission* [1978] E.C.R. 1129 at 1137, para. 18, ECJ; (Order of the

public interest.[15] The exercise of weighing those interests against each other may sometimes result in interim measures different from those sought being imposed.[16] This exercise provides yet another illustration of the cautious approach taken by judges hearing applications for interim relief. Since they conduct only a "marginal review" of the application in the main proceedings, it is not certain that the applicant will win his or her case and therefore not unreasonable to have regard to the possible impact of the interim measures sought on others' interests.

13–030 The interest of the opposite party or of a third party sometimes weighs so heavily in the balance that interim measures are not granted even though there has been a manifest infringement of Community law. Thus, the President of the Court of Justice considered that the interests of the inhabitants of Dundalk in having sound water supplies as soon as possible outweighed the Commission's interest in having the relevant Community rules applied to the grant of a public contract for the construction of a water main to carry water from the river to the treatment plant. Notwithstanding the manifest infringement of Community law and the urgency of the interim measures sought, the Commission's application for the suspension of the award of any construction contract until judgment had been given in the main proceedings was rejected.[17]

13–031 An interest originating in an omission or shortcoming on the part of a party in principle carries little weight.[18] It does not prevent the Judge hearing the application for interim relief nevertheless from recognising the parallel interest of third parties and allowing the balance to be tilted in favour of the party which showed negligence in that way. In *Commission v. Belgium*[19] Belgium invoked its interest in the speedy replacement of a very old bus fleet as a defence against an application from the Commission for suspension, by way of interim measure, of the implementation of contracts for the supply of new buses. The President found that Belgium (more specifically the Walloon regional transport company) had been guilty of a gross failure to replace the bus fleet in due time, but nevertheless caused

President of June 13, 1989), Case 56/89R *Publishers Association v. Commission* [1989] E.C.R. 1693 at 1701, para. 35, ECJ; (Order of the President of July 6, 1993), Case T–12/93R *CCE Vittel and CE Pierval v. Commission* [1993] E.C.R. II–785 at II–792—793, paras 19–20, CFI. The balance of interests may, of course, also be used to reinforce other arguments on the basis of which the application for interim measures is rejected, see (Order of the President of September 26, 1997), Case T–183/97R *Micheli and Others v. Commission* [1997] E.C.R. II–1473 at II–1501—1502, para. 75, CFI.

[15] (Order of the President of December 15, 1992), Case T–96/92R *CCE de la Société des Grandes Sources and Others v. Commission* [1992] E.C.R. II–2579 at II–2594, para. 39, CFI.

[16] (Order of the President of January 16, 1975), Case 3/75R *Johnson & Firth Brown v. Commission* [1975] E.C.R. 1 at 6, para. 7, ECJ; (Order of the President of June 16, 1992), Joined Cases T–24 and T–28/92R *Langnese-Iglo and Schöller Lebensmittel v. Commission* [1992] E.C.R. II–1839, CFI; (Order of the President of 16 July 1992), Case T–29/92R *SPO v. Commission* [1992] E.C.R. II–2161, CFI.

[17] (Order of the President of March 13, 1987), Case 45/87R *Commission v. Ireland* [1987] E.C.R. 1369 at 1378, para. 33, ECJ.

[18] (Order of the President of September 27, 1988), Case 194/88R *Commission v. Italy* [1988] E.C.R. 5647 at 5653, para. 16, ECJ.

[19] (Order of the President of April 22, 1994), Case C–87/94R *Commission v. Belgium* [1994] E.C.R. I–1395 at I–1406—1407, paras 39–42, ECJ.

the balance of interests to tip in Belgium's favour on the ground that the dilapidated state of the vehicles constituted a danger to the safety of staff and customers. The decision of the judge hearing the application for interim relief could not perpetuate that situation.

IV. Consequences

The decision on the application takes the form of a reasoned order. It is served on the parties[20] and is enforceable.[21] The interim measure lapses when final judgment is delivered or on the date fixed by the order.[22] On application by a party, the order may at any time be varied or cancelled on account of a change in circumstances.[23] Rejection of an application for an interim measure does not bar the party who made it from making a further application on the basis of new facts. The judge hearing the application for interim relief will then consider whether the new facts justify the grant of the measures sought.[24] **13–032**

In general, the costs in proceedings for interim measures are reserved for the decision on the substance. Usually, costs follow the event in the main proceedings, even if the successful party did not obtain the interim relief which it sought. Unless one of the parties raises the issue of the distribution of costs as between the proceedings for interim relief and the main proceedings (in which case the Court of Justice or the Court of First Instance, as the case may be, will have to rule thereon), the order to pay the costs covers both the costs of the proceedings for interim measures and of the main proceedings.[25] **13–033**

An appeal will lie to the Court of Justice against interim orders of the Court of First Instance within two months of their notification. Appeals are dealt with by way of summary procedure.[26] **13–034**

---

[20] ECJ Rules of Procedure, Art. 86(1); CFI Rules of Procedure, Art. 107(1).

[21] Enforcement of the order may be made conditional on the applicant's lodging security, of an amount and nature to be fixed in the light of the circumstances: ECJ Rules of Procedure, Art. 86(2); CFI Rules of Procedure, Art. 107(2). See also para. 13–003, above. In *R v. Secretary of State for Transport, ex p. Factortame Ltd* [1997] Eu.L.R. 475, at 523G, the English Divisional Court stated that an order of the Court of Justice is an order "which is expressed in mandatory terms and which takes immediate effect. Under Community law, the Order of the President has the same force and direct effect as any other order of the court or provision of Community law. It must immediately be complied with by the party to which it is addressed . . . and failure to do so is a breach of Community law".

[22] ECJ Rules of Procedure, Art. 86(3); CFI Rules of Procedure, Art. 107(3).

[23] ECJ Rules of Procedure, Art. 87; CFI Rules of Procedure, Art. 108.

[24] ECJ Rules of Procedure, Art. 88; CFI Rules of Procedure, Art. 109. See (Order of the President of July 10, 1979), Case 51/79RII *Buttner v. Commission* [1979] E.C.R. 2387 at 2389, para. 1, ECJ; (Order of the President of December 11, 1996), Case T–235/95RII, not published in the E.C.R., para. 27, CFI.

[25] (Order of October 11, 1990), Case T–50/89 *Sparr v. Commission* [1990] E.C.R. II–539 at II–542, para. 9, CFI.

[26] E.C. Statute, Art. 50, paras 2, 3.

CHAPTER 14

UNLIMITED JURISDICTION OF THE COURT OF JUSTICE AND THE COURT OF FIRST INSTANCE IN RESPECT OF ACTIONS RELATING TO SANCTIONS

I. GENERAL

Regulations adopted by the Council pursuant to the provisions of the E.C. Treaty may give the Court of Justice and the Court of First Instance unlimited jurisdiction with regard to sanctions provided for in such regulations.[1] **14–001**

In the case of the ECSC Treaty, fines may be imposed under the third paragraph of Article 47, the sixth paragraph of Article 54, Article 58(4), Article 59(7), Article 64, Article 65(5) and Article 66(6). The Court has "unlimited jurisdiction" in appeals against pecuniary sanctions and penalty payments imposed under the ECSC Treaty (Article 36, second paragraph).

As far as the EAEC Treaty is concerned, the Commission is empowered to impose sanctions by virtue of Article 83. Article 144(b) confers on the

---

[1] E.C. Treaty, Art. 229 (*ex Art. 172*). The relevant regulations are as follows:

(a) Regulation No. 11 of June 27, 1960 concerning the abolition of discrimination in transport rates and conditions, in implementation of Article 79 *[now Article 75]* (3) of the Treaty establishing the European Economic Community ([1959–1962] O.J. Spec. Ed. 60, Art. 25);

(b) Regulation No. 17 of February 6, 1962: First Regulation implementing Articles 85 and 86 *[now Articles 81 and 82]* of the Treaty ([1959–1962] O.J. Spec. Ed. 87, Art. 17);

(c) Regulation (EEC) No. 1017/68 of the Council of July 19, 1968 applying rules of competition to transport by rail, road and inland waterway ([1968] (I) O.J. Spec. Ed. 302, Art. 24);

(d) Council Regulation (EEC) No. 4056/86 of December 22, 1986 laying down detailed rules for the application of Articles 85 and 86 *[now Articles 81 and 82]* of the Treaty to maritime transport ([1986] O.J. L378/4, Art. 21);

(e) Council Regulation (EEC) No. 3975/87 of December 14, 1987 laying down the procedure for the application of the rules on competition to undertakings in the air transport sector ([1987] (O.J. L374/1, Art. 14);

(f) Council Regulation (EEC) No 4064/89 of December 21, 1989 on the control of concentrations between undertakings ([1989] O.J. L395/1, Art. 16).

See also Council Regulation No. 2532/98 of November 23, 1998 concerning the powers of the European Central Bank to impose sanctions: this regulation confers unlimited jurisdiction on the Court of Justice over the review of final decisions whereby a sanction is imposed ([1998] O.J. L318/4, Art. 5).

Court of Justice and the Court of First Instance unlimited jurisdiction in proceedings instituted against such sanctions.[2]

14–002 Sometimes an action for annulment is too narrow to be used in order to contest an act imposing a fine. This is because, in annulment proceedings, the Court has jurisdiction only to review the legality of the act in the light of pleas raised in the application or by the Court of its own motion. If the act is found to be unlawful, it may only be annulled entirely or in part. In the event that the act is partly annulled, the sanction imposed may become unreasonable having regard to the breach of Community law remaining extant. Moreover, a "lawful" act may possibly impose a sanction not consonant with what is considered to be just for reasons peculiar to the person on whom the penalty is imposed or relating to the particular circumstances of the case which may not be taken into account in the judicial review of the legality of the act.

14–003 The precise scope of the Court's "unlimited jurisdiction"[3] in actions brought against sanctions has not yet been definitively determined.

There is no dispute that "unlimited jurisdiction" enlarges the Court's powers in two ways. First, it enables the Court to determine the individual or "subjective" rights of the parties to the proceedings, which means that it is no longer confined to inquiring into the objective legality of the contested act. In this way, the Court may take into account matters to which it would not be entitled to have regard in straightforward judicial review proceedings of the legality of the contested act.[4] Secondly, where the Court has unlimited jurisdiction, it has a more extensive arsenal of sanctions than in proceedings in which only the legality of the contested act is in issue.

Opinions differ, however, as to how far unlimited jurisdiction extends. The broad view of unlimited jurisdiction regards it as an "autonomous" procedure under which the Court may amend or cancel sanctions even though the measure imposing them is not tainted by any illegality. On this view, unlimited jurisdiction denotes a procedure in which the contested measure is tested more extensively. It is claimed, on the other hand, that unlimited jurisdiction embraces all the sanctions which are available to the Court in other procedures. Thus, where the Court has unlimited jurisdic-

[2] The EAEC Treaty, Art. 144(a) also confers unlimited jurisdiction on the Court of Justice and the Court of First Instance in proceedings instituted under Art. 12 to have the appropriate terms fixed for the granting by the Commission of licences or sub-licences. In addition, the Court of Justice or the Court of First Instance may have unlimited jurisdiction under an arbitration clause (E.C. Treaty, Art. 238 *(ex Art. 181)*) or a special agreement (E.C. Treaty, Art. 239 *(ex Art. 182)*) or under the Staff Regulations, Art. 91(1), in disputes of a financial character.

[3] French: "*pleine juridiction*"; German "*Verfahren mit unbeschränkter Ermessensnachprüfung*".

[4] Opinion of Advocate General M. Lagrange in Joined Cases 2 and 3/60 *Niederrheinische Bergwerks-Aktiengesellschaft and Unternehmensverband des Aachener Steinkohlenbergbaues v. High Authority* [1961] E.C.R. 133 at 152, ECJ. See also, as regards the full jurisdiction conferred on the Court of Justice in the case of an action for failure to fulfil obligations by the ECSC Treaty, Art. 88, Case 20/59 *Italy v. High Authority* [1960] E.C.R. 325 at 339, ECJ, "unlimited jurisdiction allowing any submission to be made based not only on legality but on any reasons justifying failure to act".

tion, it may annul an act or award damages as well as order any other form of redress.[5]

In contrast, the narrow view of unlimited jurisdiction links it with other proceedings. On this view, unlimited jurisdiction enables the Court to attach to its pronouncement consequences which it could not impose by virtue of its normal jurisdiction in the proceedings in question. Thus, it is argued, where the Court annuls part of the contested act, it may adjust the sanctions imposed if they no longer seem commensurate with the breach of Community law remaining after that partial annulment.

II. Scope of Review

Whichever of the two views of unlimited jurisdiction is preferred, the Court is empowered to review the legality of the sanction imposed by the contested act. On the view that unlimited jurisdiction enables an all-embracing review to be carried out, this review of the legality of the contested act forms part of the Court's unlimited jurisdiction; on the narrower view, the review is part of the proceedings with which unlimited jurisdiction is coupled. In practice, it makes no difference, since in any case the applicant may adduce submissions for the annulment of the contested act which are targeted exclusively against the sanction, alleging, for instance, that the amount of the sanction is such that it is in breach of the principle of equal treatment or proportionality, or that the reasoning for the sanction is insufficient.[6] **14–004**

The most important difference between the broad and the narrow views of unlimited jurisdiction relates to the assessment of the sanction in so far as it is not unlawful. On the broad view, the Court is entitled to assess the reasonableness of the sanction even where the act imposing it is not tainted by any illegality.[7] On the narrow view, the Court is entitled to do this only if the act is tainted by illegality. **14–005**

[5] For a fuller formulation of this view, see *Commentaire Mégret*, at 89–95; Plouvier, "Le contentieux de pleine juridiction devant la Cour de justice des Communautés européennes" (1973) R.M.C. 365–379.

[6] *e.g.* see Case T–9/89 *Hüls v. Commission* [1992] E.C.R. II–499 at II–617—624, CFI; Case T–10/89 *Hoechst v. Commission* [1992] E.C.R. II–629 at II–738—753, CFI; Case T–11/89 *Shell v. Commission* [1992] E.C.R. II–757 at II–891—903, CFI; Case T–12/89 *Solvay v. Commission* [1992] E.C.R. II–907 at II–1007—1017, CFI; Case T–14/89 *Montedipe v. Commission* [1992] E.C.R. II–1155 at II–1259—1272, CFI; Case T–15/89 *Chemie Linz v. Commission* [1992] E.C.R. II–1275 at II–1385—1399, CFI.

[7] Joined Cases 6 and 7/73 *Commercial Solvents v. Commission* [1974] E.C.R. 223 at 257, paras 51–52, ECJ; Case T–13/89 *ICI v. Commission* [1992] E.C.R. II–1021 at II–1150—1151, paras 389–394, CFI; Case T–77/92 *Parker Pen v. Commission* [1994] E.C.R. II–549, CFI. If an undertaking asks the Court of Justice on appeal to vary the amount of a fine imposed by the Commission on the basis of arguments put forward on appeal, without also setting aside the judgment of the Court of First Instance for infringing the law, the Court has no jurisdiction to reconsider this matter. This is because it is not for the Court of Justice, where it is deciding questions of law in the context of an appeal, to substitute, on grounds of fairness, its own appraisal for that of the Court of First Instance adjudicating, in the exercise of its unlimited jurisdiction, on the amount of a fine imposed on an undertaking by reason of its infringement of Community law (Case C–320/92P *Finsider v. Commission* [1994] E.C.R. I–5697 at I–5725, paras 45–46, ECJ).

14–006 The gravity and the duration of the infringement of Community law are the most important criteria which go to determine the amount of the sanction. In addition, consideration has to be given to the particular circumstances of the case and to the context in which the infringement took place.[8]

III. Force of Unlimited Jurisdiction

14–007 Under the E.C. Treaty, the substance of the Court's unlimited jurisdiction is determined by the regulations which provide for such jurisdiction: the Court may cancel, reduce or increase the fine or penalty payment imposed.[9] Even if the applicant has not expressly claimed that the fine should be cancelled or reduced, the Court may do so of its own motion if it can infer such a claim indirectly from another claim.[10] The question arises as to whether an increase in the fine or penalty imposed would not necessarily be *ultra petita*, with the result that the Court could not make such a pronouncement despite the clear wording of the regulations.[11]

[8] Case 41/69 *ACF Chemiefarma v. Commission* [1970] E.C.R. 661 at 701–703, paras 172–189, ECJ; Case 45/69 *Boehringer v. Commission* [1970] E.C.R. 769 at 805–806, paras 53–61, ECJ; Joined Cases 6 and 7/73 *Commercial Solvents v. Commission* [1974] E.C.R. 223 at 260, para. 51, ECJ; Joined Cases 100–103/80 *Musique Diffusion Française v. Commission* [1983] E.C.R. 1825 at 1906, para. 106, ECJ; Case 322/81 *Michelin v. Commission* [1983] E.C.R. 3461 at 3523–3525, paras 106–114, ECJ; Case 183/83 *Krupp v. Commission* [1985] E.C.R. 3609 at 3626, para. 42, ECJ; Case T–12/89 *Solvay v. Commission* [1992] E.C.R. II–907 at II–1009, para. 309, CFI; Case T–14/89 *Montedipe v. Commission* [1992] E.C.R. II–1155 at II–1263—1264, para. 346, CFI; Joined Cases T–39 and T–40/92 *CB and Europay v. Commission* [1994] E.C.R. II–49 at II–99, para. 143, CFI. For an extensive discussion, see Case T–43/92 *Dunlop Slazenger v. Commission* [1994] E.C.R. II–441 at II–500—516, paras 133–179, CFI.

[9] For the references of the relevant provisions, see n. 1, above. The substance of unlimited jurisdiction is not precisely specified in the case of the ECSC and EAEC Treaties. It further appears from the case law that the award of default interest in staff cases under the Staff Regulations, Art. 91(1), 2nd sentence, falls within the unlimited jurisdiction of the Court of First Instance and, where appropriate, the Court of Justice: Case C–90/95P *De Compte v. European Parliament* [1997] E.C.R. I–1999 at I–2023, para, 45, ECJ.

[10] Case 8/56 *ALMA v. High Authority* [1957 and 1958] E.C.R. 95 at 99–100, ECJ; Case T–65/89 *BPB Industries and British Gypsum v. Commission* [1993] E.C.R. II–389 at II–444, para. 162, CFI.

[11] *Commentaire Mégret*, at 95.

CHAPTER 15

APPEALS

I. SUBJECT-MATTER

A. GENERAL

The fact that an appeal is possible against judicial decisions means that they have to be scrupulously reasoned. This enhances the legitimacy of judicial decisions and the quality of legal protection.[1] 15–001

The establishment of the Court of First Instance and the introduction of the procedure of appeals to the Court of Justice against decisions of that Court constitute the beginnings of a system of two-tier legal protection. Under Article 113(1) of the ECJ Rules of Procedure, an appeal may seek to set aside, in whole or in part, the decision of the Court of First Instance or request the same form of order, in whole or in part, as that sought at first instance.[2] 15–002

B. APPEALS ARE CONFINED TO POINTS OF LAW

Appeals are confined to points of law,[3] irrespective of the type of decision of the Court of First Instance against which they are brought.[4] The Court's jurisdiction to hear appeals is confined to reviewing the legality of decisions of the Court of First Instance in order to remedy errors of law and hence guarantee the necessary coherence of the Community legal order.[5] This avoids the Court of Justice having to inquire into findings of fact already made by the Court of First Instance, which satisfies the dual aim of lightening the workload of the Court of Justice and improving the legal 15–003

---

[1] *Cf.* Waelbroeck, "Le transfert des recours directs au Tribunal de première instance des Communautés européennes—vers une meilleure protection judiciaire des justiciables?", in *La réforme du système juridictionnel communautaire*, Brussels, Editions de l'Université de Bruxelles, 1994, pp. 87–97.

[2] A new form of order may not be sought.

[3] E.C. Treaty, Art. 225 (*ex Art. 168a*) (1); E.C. Statute, Art. 51. See also Case C–136/92P *Commission v. Brazzelli Lualdi and Others* [1994] E.C.R. I–1981 at I–2024, para. 29, ECJ.

[4] (Order of the President of July 11, 1996), Case C–148/96P(R) *Goldstein v. Commission* [1996] E.C.R. I–3883 at I–3897, para. 22, ECJ. Consequently, an appeal against an interim order or an order dismissing an application to intervene may be based only on the pleas listed in the E.C. Statute, Art. 51: (Order of the President of July 19, 1995), Case C–149/95P(R) *Commission v. Atlantic Container Line and Others* [1995] E.C.R. I–2165 at I–2177, paras 17–18, ECJ.

[5] Opinion of Advocate General G. Tesauro in ECJ, Case C–132/90P *Schwedler v. European Parliament* [1991] E.C.R. I–5745 at I–5757, ECJ.

protection of individuals in direct actions. It is also a means of ensuring uniform interpretation of Community law.[6]

15–004 The question arises as to the dividing line between "points of law" in relation to the interpretation and application of Community law and questions of fact which come solely within the purview of the Court of First Instance.[7]

The fact that appeals are confined to points of law does not preclude the Court of Justice from reviewing the legal categorisation of facts found by the Court of First Instance.[8] This is because infringements of Community law do not always occur in the form of a wrong interpretation of the Community rule which has been applied or not applied, but also in that of a wrong categorisation of a given situation of fact, as a result of which the rule at issue is wrongly applied—or, conversely, not applied—in a particular case.[9] In this way, Advocate General Jacobs regards the identification of the relevant product market for the purpose of determining whether a given undertaking is in a dominant position within the meaning of Article 82 (*ex Article 86*) of the E.C. Treaty as a conclusion of law rather than a pure finding of fact. He takes the view that the Court of Justice is entitled to examine whether the Court of First Instance took account of all the relevant factors. If relevant factors were not taken into consideration, the Court of First Instance will have erred in law by basing its conclusions on insufficient reasoning.[10] At the same time, the Advocate General enters a caveat against regarding manifest errors of fact, in some circumstances, as amounting to errors of law. The Court of Justice could intervene only if it appeared from the judgment of the Court of First Instance that that Court had wrongly applied Community law by applying the wrong test in finding the facts or by basing its legal conclusions on insufficient reasoning. It is sufficient for the Court of Justice to review the reasoning set out in the judgment and the appeal court does not look behind it at questions of fact

[6] Council Decision 88/591, Preamble, 5th recital.

[7] Honorat, "Plaider un pourvoi devant la Cour de justice", in Christianos (ed.), *Evolution récente du droit judiciaire communautaire*, Maastricht, European Institute of Public Administration, 1994, I, 21 at 28–34; Sonelli, "Appeals on Points of Law in the Community System—A Review" (1998) C.M.L.Rev. 871–900.

[8] (Order of July 11, 1996), Case C–325/94P *An Taisce and WWF UK v. Commission* [1996] E.C.R. I–3727 at I–3739—3740, paras 28, 30, ECJ; (Order of September 17, 1996), Case C–19/95P *San Marco v. Commission* [1996] E.C.R. I–4435 at I–4447, para. 39, ECJ; Case C–278/95P *Siemens v. Commission* [1997] E.C.R. I–2507 at I–2542—2543, para. 44, ECJ.

[9] Opinion of Advocate General W. Van Gerven in Case C–145/90P *Costacurta v. Commission* [1991] E.C.R. I–5449 at I–5459, ECJ; Case C–132/90P *Schwedler v. European Parliament* [1991] E.C.R. I–5745 at I–5767—5770, paras 13–25, ECJ; Case C–255/90P *Burban v. European Parliament* [1992] E.C.R. I–2253 at I–2270, para. 5, ECJ; Case C–322/93P *Peugeot v. Commission* [1994] E.C.R. I–2727 at I–2735, para. 34, ECJ; (Order of January 21, 1997), Case C–156/96P *Williams v. Court of Auditors* [1997] E.C.R. I–239 at I–253, para. 27, ECJ. See also Mongin, "Les pourvois devant la Cour: un premier bilan", in *Tendances actuelles et évolution de la jurisprudence de la Cour de justice des Communautés européennes*, Maastricht, European Institute of Public Administration, 1993, 231 at 235–237.

[10] Opinion of Advocate General F.G. Jacobs in Case C–53/92P *Hilti AG v. Commission* [1994] E.C.R. I–667 at I–680, point 28, ECJ.

sensu stricto.[11] The Court of Justice has held in this connection that "the appraisal by the Court of First Instance of the evidence put before it does not constitute (save where the clear sense of that evidence has been distorted) a point of law which is subject, as such, to review by the Court of Justice".[12] This apparently means that manifest errors made by the Court of First Instance in reading the documentary evidence adduced may be adjudged by the Court of Justice to be shortcomings in the reasoning. In contrast, the actual appraisal of the documentary evidence is to be regarded as final.[13]

On appeal the Court of Justice is not empowered to substitute, on **15–005**
grounds of fairness, its own assessment for that of the Court of First Instance exercising its unlimited jurisdiction to rule on the amount of fines imposed on undertakings for infringements of Community law.[14] The only review which the Court of Justice may conduct in this connection consists of considering whether the Court of First Instance responded to a sufficient legal standard to all the arguments raised with a view to having the fine abolished or reduced.[15]

---

[11] *ibid.*, at I–687—688, points 46–47. National courts of cassation consider themselves in general to have the power to quash decisions of inferior courts where they disclose an assessment of the facts which does not accord with reality as perceived by a normal observer. Such a manifestly wrong assessment of the facts is regarded as an infringement of the law. Advocate General Jacobs bases his restrictive interpretation of the E.C. Statute, Art. 51, on the aims which it was sought to attain in setting up the Court of First Instance. If the Court of Justice placed itself in a situation in which it would have to carry out a further review of findings of fact, this would subvert the purposes for which the Court of First Instance was established, since jurisdiction—formerly vested in the Court of Justice—was transferred to it to hear and determine certain classes of action which frequently require an examination of complex facts. This allows the Court of Justice to concentrate on its essential task of ensuring uniformity in the interpretation of Community law, whilst allowing sound, effective legal protection within the Community legal order to be retained.

[12] Case C–53/92P *Hilti AG v. Commission* [1994] E.C.R. I–667 at I–707, para. 42, ECJ. But see Case C–32/95P *Commission v. Lisrestal and Others* [1996] E.C.R. I–5373 at I–5399, para. 40, ECJ, in which the Court of Justice held that ". . . the assessment made by the Court of First Instance of the tenor and wording . . ." of letters produced as evidence could be considered on appeal. The Court of Justice cited in support of this view of the scope of its power of review on appeal the judgment in Case C–39/93P *SFEI and Others v. Commission* [1994] E.C.R. I–2681 at I–2710, para. 26, ECJ, in which it held that where the Court of First Instance not only assessed, but also classified, a letter, that qualification could be reviewed on appeal. This is logical, since the qualification of the letter which the Commission sent as a reaction to a complaint under Regulation No. 17 Art. 3(2) was nothing other than a legal classification of a fact in the light of the provisions of Regulation No. 99/63 (now replaced by Regulation No. 2842/98), which determined the applicant's procedural rights. Such a legal classification of a fact is, of course, amenable to review by the Court of Justice on appeal, but in *Lisrestal* no legal classification of facts was involved, only the question whether the Court of First Instance had correctly assessed the evidence adduced, which is an entirely different matter.

[13] *Hilti AG v. Commission*, cited in n. 12, above at I–708, para. 43: "Since [the appellant] challenges the appraisal by the Court of First Instance of certain evidence submitted to it but does not establish, or even, indeed, claim that the Court of First Instance distorted the clear sense of that evidence, its . . . plea is inadmissible and, for that reason, must be rejected."

[14] Case C–310/93P *BPB Industries and British Gypsum v. Commission* [1995] E.C.R. I–865 at I–910, para. 34, ECJ.

[15] Case C–219/95P *Ferriere Nord v. Commission* [1997] E.C.R. I–4411 at I–4440, para. 31, ECJ.

15–006 Appeals must be based on pleas alleging lack of competence of the Court of First Instance, a breach of procedure before it which adversely affects the interests of the appellant, or infringement of Community law by the Court of First Instance.[16] No appeal shall lie regarding only the amount of the costs or the party ordered to pay them.[17]

The person bringing the appeal—the appellant[18]—must clearly state which aspects of the contested decision of the Court of First Instance he is criticising and indicate the contested parts of the judgment, together with the legal arguments supporting those complaints.[19] A complaint which is not explained will be manifestly inadmissible and rejected.[20] Consequently,

---

[16] E.C. Statute, Art. 51, para. 1; Case C–283/90P *Vidrányi v. Commission* [1991] E.C.R. I–4339 at I–4364—4365, paras 11–13, ECJ; Case C–346/90P *F. v. Commission* [1992] E.C.R. I–2691 at I–2709, paras 6–7, ECJ; Case C–53/92P *Hilti AG v. Commission* [1994] E.C.R. I–667 at I–700, para. 10, ECJ; Case C–136/92P *Commission v. Brazzelli Lualdi and Others* [1994] E.C.R. I–1981 at I–2029, para. 48, ECJ. See also Schermers, "The European Court of First Instance" (1988) C.M.L.Rev. 541 at 554–555. As regards in particular the jurisdiction of the Court of Justice to verify whether a breach of procedure adversely affecting the appellant's interests was committed before the Court of First Instance, see (Judgment of December 17, 1998) Case 185/95P *Baustahlgewebe v. Commission*, paras 18–22, ECJ (not yet reported), in which the Court accepted jurisdiction to consider, in an appeal, a plea on the right to legal process within a reasonable period, applicable in the context of judicial proceedings brought against a Commission decision imposing fines on an undertaking for infringement of competition law; after having subsequently found that the principle that proceedings must be disposed of within a reasonable time had been breached by the Court of First Instance (as 32 months had elapsed between the end of the written procedure and the decision to open the oral procedure, and 22 months between the close of the oral procedure and the delivery of judgment), the Court of Justice held that in the absence of any indication that the length of proceedings had affected their outcome in any way, this successful plea could not result in the contested judgment being set aside in its entirety; "for reasons of economy of procedure and in order to ensure an immediate and effective remedy regarding a procedural irregularity of that kind" (para. 48), the Court then held that the plea alleging excessive duration of the proceedings was well founded for the purposes of setting aside the contested judgment in so far as it set the amount of the fine imposed on the appellant at ECU 3 million (*ibid.*), after which it was considered "that a sum of ECU 50 000 constitutes reasonable satisfaction for the excessive duration of the proceedings" (para. 141); consequently, giving final judgment in accordance with Article 54 of the E.C. Statute, the Court of Justice set the fine at ECU 2 950 000 and dismissed the remainder of the appeal (paras 142–143).

[17] E.C. Statute, Art. 51, para. 2. This article also applies if all the other pleas raised by the appellant are rejected: (Order of January 13, 1995), Case C–253/94P *Roujansky* [1995] E.C.R. I–7 at I–12—13, paras 12–14, ECJ; (Order of January 13, 1995), Case C–264/94P *Bonnamy* [1995] E.C.R. I–15 at I–20—21, paras 12–14, ECJ; Case C–396/93P *Henrichs v. Commission* [1995] E.C.R. I–2611 at I–2652, paras 65–66, ECJ; (Order of March 6, 1997), Case C–303/96P *Bernardi v. European Parliament* [1997] E.C.R. I–1239 at I–1257, para. 49, ECJ.

[18] ECJ Rules of Procedure, Art. 112(1)(a).

[19] (Order of April 26, 1993), Case C–244/92P *Kupka-Floridi v. ESC* [1993] E.C.R. I–2041 at I–2045, para. 9, ECJ. The Court of Justice will sometimes particularise the pleas adduced by the appellant (Case C–283/90P *Vidrányi v. Commission* [1991] E.C.R. I–4339 at I–4368, para. 29, ECJ; Case C–255/90P *Burban v. European Parliament* [1992] E.C.R. I–2253 at I–2270, paras 4–5, ECJ; (Order of October 17, 1995), Case C–62/94P *Turner v. Commission* [1995] E.C.R. I–3177 at I–3182, para. 16, ECJ; (Order of March 6, 1997), Case C–303/96P *Bernardi v. European Parliament* [1997] E.C.R. I–1239 at I–1255, paras 37–40, ECJ; Case C–138/95P *Campo Ebro Industrial and Others v. Council* [1997] E.C.R. I–2027 at I–2054, paras 60–61, ECJ.

[20] (Order of December 12, 1996), Case C–49/96P *Progoulis v. Commission* [1996] E.C.R. I–6803 at I–6813, para. 24, ECJ.

it is not enough for the appellant to support a plea by merely referring back to arguments raised in connection with another plea.[21] It is also not permitted in an appeal simply to repeat pleas already raised in the Court of First Instance, since to interpret an appeal in that way would be no more than an attempt to have the case re-tried and no provision is made for retrials by the Court of Justice.[22] Consequently, a plea declared inadmissible by the Court of First Instance cannot be raised afresh by the appellant, although the latter may challenge on specific grounds the lower court's finding that the plea is inadmissible.[23] The appellant must raise arguments in this connection establishing that the Court of First Instance has erred in law.[24]

The limited range of pleas which may be raised on appeal against a decision of the Court of First Instance precludes any change in the subject-matter of the proceedings as compared with the proceedings before the Court of First Instance.[25] Parties are not entitled to seek a new form of order—*i.e.* relating to pleas not raised before the Court of First Instance.[26] The reason for this is that such plea would involve the Court of Justice, not in reviewing the decision of the Court of First Instance, but in carrying out an additional substantive inquiry, thereby changing the subject-matter of the proceedings.[27] Pleas withdrawn by a party in the proceedings before the Court of First Instance are also inadmissible on appeal.[28] This is because the Court's jurisdiction is confined to a review of the findings of law on the pleas argued at first instance.[29] **15–007**

It is not yet clear whether the bar on raising new pleas on appeal and hence on changing the subject-matter of the proceedings should prevent

[21] (Order of February 5, 1997), Case C–51/95P *Unifruit Hellas v. Commission* [1997] E.C.R. I–727 at I–742, para. 33, ECJ.

[22] (Order of April 26, 1993), *Kupka-Floridi v. ESC* [1993] E.C.R. I–2041 at I–2045, para. 10, ECJ; (Order of March 7, 1994), Case C–338/93P *De Hoe v. Commission* [1994] E.C.R. I–819 at I–828—829, paras 17–19, 26, ECJ; (Order of September 26, 1994), Case C–26/94P *X. v. Commission* [1994] E.C.R. I–4379 at I–4385—4386, para. 13, ECJ; (Order of October 17, 1995), Case C–62/95P *Turner v. Commission* [1995] E.C.R. I–3177 at I–3182, para. 17, ECJ; (Order of March 14, 1996), Case C–31/95P *Del Plato v. Commission* [1996] E.C.R. I–1443 at I–1449, para. 20, ECJ.

[23] This may be inferred from, Case C–354/92P *Eppe v. Commission* [1993] E.C.R. I–7027 at I–7049, para. 13, ECJ.

[24] (Order of February 5, 1998), Case C–30/96P *Abello and Others v. Commission* [1998] E.C.R. I–377 at I–395, para. 45, ECJ.

[25] This bar applies both to the appeal itself (ECJ Rules of Procedure, Art. 113(2)) and to the response lodged by the respondent (ECJ Rules of Procedure, Art. 116(2)).

[26] ECJ Rules of Procedure, Arts. 113(1) and 116(1). See also (Order of April 26, 1993), Case C–244/92P *Kupka-Floridi v. ESC* [1993] E.C.R. I–2041 at I–2046—2047, paras 12–20, ECJ; Case C–53/92P *Hilti AG v. Commission* [1994] E.C.R. I–667 at I–709, para. 49, ECJ. *Cf.* Case C–76/93P *Scaramuzza v. Commission* [1994] E.C.R. I–5173 at I–5189—5190, paras 15–19, ECJ; (Order of September 17, 1996), Case C–19/95P *San Marco v. Commission* [1996] E.C.R. I–4435 at I–4450, para. 49, ECJ; (Order of June 11, 1998), Case C–291/97P *H. v. Commission* [1998] E.C.R. I–3577 at I–3599, para. 25, ECJ.

[27] *Cf.* the Opinion of Advocate General C.O. Lenz in, Case C–348/90P *European Parliament v. Virgili-Schettini* [1991] E.C.R. I–5211 at I–5222, ECJ.

[28] Case C–354/92 P *Eppe v. Commission* [1993] E.C.R. I–7027 at I–7049, para. 13, ECJ.

[29] (Order of December 12, 1996), Case C–49/96P *Progoulis v. Commission* [1996] E.C.R. I–6803 at I–6815, para. 32, ECJ; Case C–153/96P *De Rijk v. Commission* [1997] E.C.R. I–2901 at I–2922, para. 18, ECJ.

pleas relating to a matter of public interest (*moyens d'ordre public*) from being raised for the first time on appeal if the Court of First Instance has failed to raise such pleas of its own motion.[30]

15–008 In the response, the respondent may not claim damages for injury allegedly suffered as a result of the bringing of the appeal. As a result of Article 116(1) and (2) of the ECJ Rules of Procedure, such a claim is inadmissible.[31]

15–009 The fact that appeals are confined to points of law means that the Court of First Instance has sole jurisdiction to make findings as to the facts underlying the proceedings at first instance.[32] Parties are not entitled on appeal to raise matters of fact or to offer to adduce evidence of facts[33] which were not found by the Court of First Instance.[34] This is because, if they were so entitled, it would oblige the Court of Justice to make a determination of the facts, which it is not competent to do on appeal.[35] Consequently, the Court of Justice must leave out of account in reviewing the decision of the Court of First Instance any new facts raised.

15–010 A plea which merely takes issue with a factual appraisal made by the Court of First Instance will, of course, be inadmissible.[36] Accordingly, the appraisal of the meaning of the terms of a letter constitutes purely a finding of fact, against which an appeal will not lie.[37] Also the question whether, in an action for damages, the amount of compensation has been sufficiently proven in the application and the reply is exclusively part of the assessment of the facts[38] and cannot be raised on appeal.

---

[30] Lenaerts, "Le Tribunal de premiére instance des Communautés européennes: genèse et premiers pas" (1990) J.T. 409 at 414. *Cf.* the grounds for annulling a measure which the Court of Justice and the Court of First Instance may raise of their own motion (paras 7–092, above) and certain requirements for admissibility which the Court of Justice and the Court of First Instance may inquire into of their own motion, such as whether the time-limits prescribed for bringing certain actions have been complied with.

[31] Case C–35/92P *European Parliament v. Frederiksen* [1993] E.C.R. I–991 at I–1032—1033, paras 33–36, ECJ.

[32] Joliet and Vogel, "Le Tribunal de première instance des Communautés européennes" (1989) R.M.C. 423, at 430. A survey of the points of law which have been considered by the Court of Justice on appeal may be found in Rideau and Picod, "Le pourvoi sur les questions de droit" (1995) R.M.C.U.E. 584 at 594–599.

[33] Case C–396/93P *Henrichs v. Commission* [1995] E.C.R. I–2611 at I–2638—2639, para. 14, ECJ.

[34] (Order of October 17, 1995), Case C–62/94P *Turner v. Commission* [1995] E.C.R. I–3177 at I–3185, para. 25, ECJ; (Judgment of December 10, 1998) Case C–221/97P *Schröder and Others v. Commission*, para 26, ECJ (not yet reported).

[35] Opinion of Advocate General W. Van Gerven in, Case C–137/92P *Commission v. BASF and Others* [1994] E.C.R. I–2555 at I–2565—2566, ECJ; Case C–320/93P *Finsider v. Commission* [1994] E.C.R. I–5697 at I–5724, para. 41, ECJ.

[36] (Order of March 20, 1991), Case C–115/90P *Turner v. Commission* [1991] E.C.R. I–1423 at I–1431, paras 13, 14, ECJ; Case C–283/90P *Vidrányi v. Commission* [1991] E.C.R. I–4339 at I–4364—4365, paras 11–13, ECJ; Case C–132/90P *Schwedler v. European Parliament* [1991] E.C.R. I–5745 at I–5766—5767, paras 9–12, ECJ; Case C–378/90P *Pitrone v. Commission* [1992] E.C.R. I–2375 at I–2396—2397, paras 12–13, ECJ; Case C–346/90P *F. v. Commission* [1992] E.C.R. I–2691 at I–2709, para. 7, ECJ, Case C–326/91P *De Compte v. European Parliament* [1994] E.C.R. I–2091 at I–2148, para. 29, ECJ.

[37] Case C–18/91P *V. v. European Parliament* [1992] E.C.R. I–3997 at I–4013, paras 15–17, ECJ.

[38] Case C–209/94P *Buralux and Others v. Council* [1996] E.C.R. I–615 at I–645, para. 21, ECJ.

The same applies to the appraisal of evidence by the Court of First Instance. Consequently, an appeal brought against decisions of the Court of First Instance concerning the assessment of evidence adduced before it will be inadmissible, unless the Court of First Instance has committed an error of law.[39] Accordingly, an appellant may argue on appeal that evidence was not lawfully obtained or that the Court of First Instance failed to respect the legal rules and general principles relating to the burden of proof or the procedural rules of evidence.[40]

In contrast, the extent of the duty to provide a statement of reasons is a point of law.[41]

In any event, the judgment of the Court of First Instance must be sufficiently reasoned to enable the Court of Justice to review it.[42] The Court of First Instance must have taken account of this requirement also in assessing purely factual matters (for instance, in determining the amount of damage sustained) because the Court of Justice must be in a position to check that the lower court has not breached the law in assessing the facts. **15–011**

C. Against what decisions of the Court of First Instance will an appeal lie?

Under Article 49 of the E.C. Statute of the Court of Justice, an appeal may be brought against final decisions of the Court of First Instance and against decisions of that Court disposing of substantive issues in part only or **15–012**

---

[39] (Order of September 30, 1992), Case C–294/91P *Sebastiani v. European Parliament* [1992] E.C.R. I–4997 at I–5001, para. 13, ECJ; Case C–53/92P *Hilti AG v. Commission* [1994] E.C.R. I–667 at I–707, para. 42, ECJ; Case C–143/95P *Commission v. Socurte and Others* [1997] E.C.R. I–1 at I–23, para. 36, ECJ. See also (Judgment of February 11, 1999) Case C–390/95P *Antillean Rice Mills and Others v. Commission*, para. 29, ECJ (not yet reported): "The Court of First Instance has exclusive jurisdiction to find the facts, save where a substantive inaccuracy in its findings is attributable to the documents submitted to it, and to appraise those facts. That appraisal thus does not, save where the clear sense of the evidence has been distorted, constitue a point of law which is subject, as such, to review by the Court of Justice."); (Judgment of December 17, 1998) Case C–185/95P *Baustahlgewebe v. Commission*, paras 23–25, ECJ (not yet reported).

[40] (Order of January 11, 1996), Case C–89/95P *D. v. Commission* [1996] E.C.R. I–53 at I–62, para. 14, ECJ; (Order of September 17, 1996), Case C–19/95P *San Marco v. Commission* [1997] E.C.R. I–4435 at I–4447, para. 39, ECJ; (Order of October 6, 1997), Case C–55/97P *AIUFFASS and AKT v. Commission* [1997] E.C.R. I–5383 at I–5398, para. 25, ECJ; (Order of October 16, 1997), Case C–140/96P *Dimitriadis v. Court of Auditors* [1997] E.C.R. I–5635 at I–5649—5650, para. 27, ECJ; Case C–401/96P *Somaco v. Commission*, [1998] E.C.R. I–2587 at I–2621, para. 54, ECJ. See also (Judgment of December 10, 1998), Case C–221/97P *Schröder and Others v. Commission*, paras 22–24, ECJ (not yet reported): in reply to the appellants submission that their rights of the defence had been infringed because the Court of First Instance had failed to take account of some statements made at the hearing as well as of some other assertions, the Court of Justice held "that the right to be heard in the context of judicial proceedings does not mean that the court has to incorporate in full in its decision all the submissions put forward by each party. The court, after listening to the submissions of the parties and assessing the evidence, has to decide whether or not to grant the relief sought in the application and give reasons for its decision."

[41] Case C–166/95P *Commission v. Daffix* [1997] E.C.R. I–983, ECJ, and Case C–188/96P *Commission v. V.* [1997] E.C.R. I–6561 at I–6584—6585, para. 24, ECJ.

[42] Case C–259/96P *Council v. De Nil* [1998] E.C.R. I–2915 at I–2945, para. 32, ECJ.

disposing of a procedural issue concerning a plea of lack of competence or inadmissibility.[43]

An appeal will also lie against decisions of the Court of First Instance dismissing an application to intervene.[44] Decisions of the Court of First Instance relating to applications for interim relief may also be the subject of an appeal (E.C. Treaty, Articles 242–243 (*ex Articles 185, 186*)), together with decisions suspending the operation of Council or Commission decisions imposing a financial obligation on natural or legal persons (E.C. Treaty, Article 256 (*ex Article 192*), fourth paragraph).[45]

II. Identity of the Parties

15–013 An appeal may be brought by any party which has been unsuccessful, in whole or in part, in its submissions made before the Court of First Instance,[46] provided that the appeal, if successful, is likely to procure an advantage to the party bringing it.[47] A cross-appeal may therefore be brought only if both parties have been unsuccessful—at least in part—before the Court of First Instance.[48] The Court of Justice may of its own motion raise the objection that a party has no interest in bringing or maintaining an appeal on the ground that an event subsequent to the judgment of the Court of First Instance removes its prejudicial effect as regards the appellant.[49]

As far as concerns interveners who are not Member States or Community institutions, an appeal will lie only if their situation is directly affected by the decision of the Court of First Instance. The interest which an intervener, other than a Member State or a Community institution, must establish in order to be able to bring an appeal is, in principle, the same as it had to establish in order to obtain leave to intervene at first instance

[43] See Case T–60/92 *Noonan v. Commission* [1993] E.C.R. II–911 at II–920, para. 18, CFI, in which the Court of First Instance only declared the application admissible (confirmed on appeal in Case C–448/93P *Commission v. Noonan* [1995] E.C.R. I–2321, ECJ). See also Millett, *The Court of First Instance of the European Communities*, London–Edinburgh, Butterworths, 1990, p. 56; Vaughan and Lasok, *European Court Practice*, p. 245.

[44] E.C. Statute, Art. 50, para. 1. For an application, see (Order of the President of June 17, 1997), Joined Cases C–151 and C–157/97P(I) *National Power and PowerGen* [1997] E.C.R. I–3491, ECJ.

[45] E.C. Statute, Art. 50, para. 2. See (Order of the President of May 5, 1994), Case C–97/94P–R *Schulz v. Commission* [1994] E.C.R. I–1701, E.C.J.

[46] E.C. Statute, Art. 49, para. 2.

[47] Case C–19/93P *Rendo and Others v. Commission* [1995] E.C.R. I–3319 at I–3353, para. 13, ECJ.

[48] Cross appeals are possible under the ECJ Rules of Procedure, Art. 116(1). An intervener before the Court of First Instance, being regarded as a party before that court, has the right to submit a response under the ECJ Rules of Procedure, Article 115, and must, in the absence of any express limitation, be able to raise pleas relating to any point of law on which the contested judgment is based; he may therefore plead before the Court of Justice that the application was inadmissible, despite the fact that the party it supported before the Court of First Instance has not raised such a plea in its response to the appeal and raised it only in its submissions at first instance: (Judgment of February 11, 1999) Case C–390/95P *Antillean Rice Mills and Others v. Commission*, paras 20–23, ECJ (not yet reported).

[49] *Rendo and Others v. Commission* (cited in n. 47, above), at I–3353, para. 23.

(E.C. Statute, Article 37, second paragraph), but the Court of Justice has, in the decision of the Court of First Instance, a more concrete basis for testing that interest than the Court of First Instance has when appraising the interest of a would-be intervener before any decision on the substance has been taken. It is therefore quite possible that the intervener at first instance will be refused leave to appeal.[50]

In contrast, institutions and Member States may invariably appeal, even if the decision of the Court of First Instance does not affect them directly and if they did not intervene in the proceedings at first instance, with the exception, in the latter case, of staff cases.[51]

Persons who have been refused leave to intervene may appeal against that decision of the Court of First Instance.[52]

III. Time-limits

An appeal must be lodged within two months of the notification of the decision appealed against.[53] **15–014**

Appeals against decisions of the Court of First Instance refusing leave to intervene must be brought within two weeks of the notification of the decision dismissing the application.[54]

Cross-appeals must be brought within two months of service on the respondent of notice of appeal[55]—that is to say, within the time-limit for lodging the response.[56]

IV. Consequences

Appeals do not have suspensory effect, but the parties are entitled under Articles 242 and 243 (*ex Articles 185 and 186*) of the E.C. Treaty to apply for suspension of the operation of the decision of the Court of First Instance and for interim measures.[57] If, however, the contested decision of **15–015**

---

[50] Lasok, *The European Court of Justice: Practice and Procedure*, London, Butterworths, 1994, p. 473.

[51] E.C. Statute, Art. 49, para. 3. See, by way of example, the appeal brought by France against the judgment in Case T–70/94 *Comafrica and Dole Fresh Fruit Europe v. Commission* [1996] E.C.R. II–1741, CFI, which led to its annulment: (Judgment of January 21, 1999) Case C–73/97P (not yet reported).

[52] E.C. Statute, Art. 50, para. 1.

[53] E.C. Statute, Art. 49, para. 1.

[54] E.C. Statute, Art. 50, para. 1.

[55] ECJ, Case C–136/92P *Commission v. Brazzelli Lualdi and Others* [1994] E.C.R. I–1981 at I–2034—2035, paras 70–73, ECJ.

[56] ECJ Rules of Procedure, Art. 115(1). See also paras 24–003—24–004.

[57] E.C. Statute, Art. 53, para. 1. For examples, see (Order of the President of November 27, 1990), Case C–242/90P–R *Commission v. Albani and Others* [1990] E.C.R. I–4329 at I–4332, para. 3, ECJ; (Order of the President of January 31, 1991), Case C–345/90P–R *European Parliament v. Hanning* [1991] E.C.R. I–231 at I–237, paras 24–26, ECJ; (Order of the President of April 3, 1992), Case C–35/92P–R *European Parliament v. Frederiksen* [1992] E.C.R. I–2399 at I–2404, paras 17–18, ECJ; (Order of the President of July 6, 1995), Case C–166/95P–R *Commission v. Daffix* [1995] E.C.R. I–1955 at I–1963, para. 17, ECJ; (Order of the President of September 15, 1995), Case C–254/95P-R *European Parliament v.*

the Court of First Instance declares a regulation invalid, the decision takes effect only as from the date of expiry of the period for lodging an appeal or, if an appeal is brought within that period, as from the date of the dismissal of the appeal.[58]

15–016 If the appeal is unfounded, it will be dismissed. In the event that the reasoning of the contested decision of the Court of First Instance contains an infringement of Community law, but its operative part is nevertheless lawful, the appeal will likewise be dismissed. In that event, the Court of Justice sets out the "correct" grounds in its judgment, but does not set aside the judgment of the Court of First Instance (substitution of grounds).[59] The Court of Justice may also find that the operative part of the judgment of the Court of First Instance is correct in law and dismiss the appeal on a legal ground different from the ground or grounds put forward by the Court of First Instance, without pronouncing on the "legality" of the grounds of the lower court's judgment. In such case, the pleas put forward on appeal will not be considered.[60] Furthermore, a plea directed against a superabundant ground contained in a decision of the Court of First Instance will be nugatory and cannot affect the legality of the decision.[61]

15–017 An appeal will be well founded if at least one of the appellant's pleas succeeds. In that event, the Court of Justice will set aside the contested decision. The decision may be set aside in its entirety or only in part. A decision may be set aside in part, not only if the contested decision determines a number of claims made in a single action—the decision on one claim being quashed, for example, and the appeal dismissed as regards

---

Innamorati [1995] E.C.R. I–2707 at I–2716—2717, paras 14–19, ECJ. An application for suspension of the operation of the decision of the Court of First Instance against which an appeal has been brought must be made to the Court of Justice: (Order of the President of November 22, 1991), Case T–77/91R *Hochbaum v. Commission* [1991] E.C.R. II–1285 at II–1291, paras 21–22, CFI.

[58] E.C. Statute, Art. 53, para. 2. Under the E.C. Treaty, Arts. 242 and 243 (*ex Arts. 185 and 186*), a party may also request the Court of Justice to suspend the operation of the regulation declared void or to grant any other interim measures.

[59] Case C–30/91P *Lestelle v. Commission* [1992] E.C.R. I–3755 at I–3786, para. 28, ECJ; Case C–36/92P *SEP v. Commission* [1994] E.C.R. I–1911 at I–1941, para. 33, ECJ; Case C–320/92P *Finsider v. Commission* [1994] E.C.R. I–5697 at I–5723, para. 37, ECJ. Where, in contrast, a fresh appraisal of the facts of the case is required by reason of the adoption of other legal grounds, the Court of Justice may carry out that appraisal only after setting aside the decision of the Court of First Instance. It then gives final judgment on the ground that the state of the proceedings permits it to do so. In this way, the Court of Justice may set aside a judgment of the Court of First Instance and then produce an operative part identical to that set out in the judgment at first instance after making its own assessment of the law and the facts. See Case C–298/93P *Klinke v. Court of Justice* [1994] E.C.R. I–3009, ECJ, in which the Court of Justice set aside a decision of the Court of First Instance and then set out an identical operative part.

[60] (Order of December 3, 1992), Case C–32/92P *Moat v. Commission* [1992] E.C.R. I–6379 at I–6384, para. 11, ECJ; Case C–480/93P *Zunis Holding and Others v. Commission* [1996] E.C.R. I–1 at I–29, paras 15–16, ECJ.

[61] Case C–35/92P *European Parliament v. Frederiksen* [1993] E.C.R. I–991 at I–1032, para. 31, ECJ; Case C–244/91P *Pincherle v. Commission* [1993] E.C.R. I–6965 at I–7004, para. 31, ECJ; (Order of March 25, 1996), Case C–137/95P *SPO and Others v. Commission* [1996] E.C.R. I–1611 at I–1625—1626, para. 47, ECJ; Case C–264/95P *Commission v. UIC* [1997] E.C.R. I–1287 at I–1326, para. 48, ECJ; Case C–395/95P *Geotronics v. Commission* [1997] E.C.R. I–2271 at I–2298—2299, para. 23, ECJ.

the others—,[62] but apparently also if the decision of the Court of First Instance relates only to a single claim. In that case, the Court of Justice will confine itself to quashing one or more grounds of the decision.[63]

In the event that it sets aside a decision of the lower court, the Court of Justice may itself give final judgment in the matter if the state of the proceedings so permits (but is not obliged to do so) or else refer the case back to the Court of First Instance for judgment.[64] **15–018**

The subject-matter of the proceedings concluded by the Court of Justice or the Court of First Instance after a judgment setting a decision aside depends on various factors. It appears from the wording of the first paragraph of Article 54 of the E.C. Statute and Article 119 of the CFI Rules of Procedure that the judgment setting aside the decision of the first-instance court does not extend to the written and/or oral procedure which preceded that decision. What is annulled is therefore determined in the first place by the form of order sought and the pleas put forward by the parties in the pleadings which they originally lodged with the Court of First Instance. Consequently, the judgment setting aside the original decision does not enable them to seek a new form of order or to raise new pleas and to have completely new proceedings determined by the Court of First Instance or the Court of Justice, as the case may be, except where a new plea is based on a new fact within the meaning of Article 48(2) of the CFI Rules of Procedure and Article 42(2) of the ECJ Rules of Procedure. In the second place, regard must be had to the extent to which the judgment of the Court of Justice annulled the decision of the lower court. This can be determined from close consideration of the judgment on appeal. It is clear from earlier case law that in order to comply with a judgment and to implement it fully, regard must be had not only to the operative part but also to the grounds which led to the judgment and constitute its essential basis, in so far as they are necessary to determine the exact meaning of what is stated in the operative part.[65] Depending on the reasoning of the judgment of the Court of Justice, the assessment made by the Court of First Instance of all the pleas submitted may be rejected or the Court of Justice may reject the assessment of one or more pleas and accept the remainder of the lower court's reasoning.[66] Thirdly, the content of the decision of the

[62] Case C–18/91P *V. v. European Parliament* [1992] E.C.R. I–3997, ECJ; Case C–19/93P *Rendo and Others v. Commission* [1995] E.C.R. I–3319, ECJ.

[63] Case C–294/95P *Ojha v. Commission* [1996] E.C.R. I–5863 at I–5919, para. 62, ECJ. See also the Opinion of Advocate General P. Léger in that case, at I–5896—5897, points 178–191.

[64] E.C. Statute, Art. 54, para. 1. For examples, see Case C–404/92P *X.* v. *Commission* [1994] E.C.R. I–4737 at I–4791—4792, para. 25, ECJ; Case C–254/95P *European Parliament v. Innamorati* [1996] E.C.R. I–3423, ECJ; Case C–188/96P *V.* v. *Commission* [1997] E.C.R. I–6561 at I–6587, paras 32, 33, ECJ. *Cf.* Mongin (cited in n. 9, above), at 238. The E.C. Statute Art. 54, para. 1, is also applicable to appeals brought under the E.C. Statute, Art. 50, para. 2: (Order of the President of January 29, 1997), Case C–393/96P(R) *Antonissen v. Council and Commission* [1997] E.C.R. I–441 at I–458, para. 45, ECJ.

[65] Joined Cases 97, 193, 99 and 215/86 *Asteris v. Commission* [1988] E.C.R. 2181 at 2208, para. 27, ECJ.

[66] For an example, see Case T–16/91RV *Rendo and Others v. Commission* [1996] E.C.R. II–1827 at II–1838—1839, para. 28, CFI.

Court of First Instance which is set aside influences the way in which the case is further dealt with.

Where the Court of First Instance dismisses an application, having considered all the pleas raised, and the Court of Justice then sets aside the decision on account of an error of law in assessing one of the pleas, it will be unlikely that in order to wind up the case the Court of Justice or the Court of First Instance will pronounce (again) on the assessment of the pleas that the decision on appeal leaves unaffected. The proceedings will be confined in that event to a re-examination of the plea which the Court of First Instance wrongly rejected, having regard to the determination made by the Court of Justice of the point of law at issue.[67] Where, in contrast, the Court of First Instance grants the application—for instance, in the case of an action for annulment of an act of an institution—on the basis of a plea without considering the other pleas raised and the Court of Justice sets aside its decision on appeal, it would appear that, in order to wind up the case, not only the plea which wrongly succeeded will have to be re-examined, but consideration will also have to be given to those pleas which the Court of First Instance did not examine in its original decision,[68] although it is possible that the case may be able to be decided by upholding only one of the pleas raised.

The Court of Justice will give final judgment in the matter where it finds that all the appellant's claims can be rejected because the Community act in issue was lawfully adopted.[69] Advocate General Jacobs argues that, where the Court of Justice gives final judgment in a matter, a respondent ought to be entitled, in his response, to raise an issue which was raised against the contested Community act before, but not addressed by the Court of First Instance because it granted his claims on other grounds. The Advocate General bases that view on the fact that the Court of Justice has the entire case-file at its disposal[70] and on the fact that Articles 115 and 116 of the ECJ Rules of Procedure do not preclude such a course of action. He further maintains that this would serve the interest of procedural economy.[71] As a corollary, Mr Jacobs suggests that when the Court of First Instance gives judgment on one ground in favour of an applicant, it should make the necessary findings of fact relevant to any other grounds on which the applicant has relied and on which, in the event of an appeal, he might seek to rely as respondent.[72]

---

[67] See the Opinion of Advocate General P. Léger in Case C–294/95P *Ojha v. Commission* [1996] E.C.R. I–5863 at I–5896—5897, points 184–189, ECJ.

[68] Case T–43/89RV *Gill v. Commission* [1993] E.C.R. II–303, CFI.

[69] Case C–345/90P *European Parliament v. Hanning* [1992] E.C.R. I–949 at I–989—990, paras 35–38, ECJ.

[70] ECJ Rules of Procedure, Art. 111(2).

[71] If such issues could not be taken into account, it would invariably be necessary to refer the case back to the Court of First Instance in order to avoid the risk of injustice. That would result in further proceedings, additional costs and possibly a further appeal.

[72] Opinion of Advocate General F.G. Jacobs in Case C–185/90P *Commission v. Gill* [1991] E.C.R. I–4779 at I–4803—4804, ECJ (nevertheless, after quashing the contested judgment, the Court referred the case back to the Court of First Instance for final judgment). It may

The Court of Justice will refer the case back to the Court of First Instance for final judgment where the case has not been completely decided (for example where a damages claim remains outstanding following the judgment on appeal) and additional findings of fact are needed or a fresh look has to be taken at those already made.[73] Where a case is referred back to the Court of First Instance, that Court is bound by the decision of the Court of Justice on points of law.[74]

Where an appeal brought by a Member State or a Community institution which did not intervene in the proceedings before the Court of First Instance is well founded, the Court of Justice may, if it considers it necessary, state which of the effects of the decision of the Court of First Instance which has been set aside are to be considered definitive in respect of the other parties to the litigation.[75]

be seen from Joined Cases T–371/94 and T–394/94 *British Airways and Others v. Commission* [1998] E.C.R. II–2405, CFI, that the Court of First Instance sometimes adopts this approach.

73 Case C–68/91 P *Moritz v. Commission* [1992] E.C.R. I–6849 at I–6893, paras 41–42, ECJ.

74 E.C. Statute, Art. 54, para. 2. For examples, see Case T–43/89RV *Gill v. Commission* [1993] E.C.R. II–303, CFI; Case T–20/89RV *Moritz v. Commission* [1993] E.C.R. II–1423, CFI.

75 E.C. Statute, Art. 54, para. 3.

CHAPTER 16

PROCEEDINGS BROUGHT BY OFFICIALS AND OTHER SERVANTS OF THE COMMUNITIES (STAFF CASES)

I. SUBJECT-MATTER

A. GENERAL

The relationship between the Community and its servants is governed by the "Staff Regulations of officials of the European Communities" and the "Conditions of employment of other servants of the European Communities".[1] Every Community act regarding staff policy must comply with the provisions of the Staff Regulations or Conditions of Employment. The Court of First Instance has jurisdiction in disputes between the Community and its staff within the limits and under the conditions set down in the Staff Regulations or Conditions of Employment.[2] The jurisdiction of the Court of First Instance is delineated in Article 91(1) of the Staff Regulations. It has jurisdiction in any dispute between the Communities and any person to whom the Staff Regulations apply regarding the legality of an act adversely affecting such a person either because the appointing authority has taken a decision or because it has not adopted a measure which it was under a duty to adopt under the Staff Regulations. In the case of disputes of a financial nature, the Court of First Instance has unlimited jurisdiction.[3] 16–001

B. AGAINST WHAT MEASURES WILL AN ACTION LIE?

An action will lie only against an act adversely affecting the person concerned. The expression "act having adverse effect" has two aspects: 16–002

[1] The Conditions of Employment indicate the provisions of the Staff Regulations which apply to categories of Community staff other than officials (temporary staff, auxiliary staff, local staff, special advisers). These staff members are engaged by contract.

[2] E.C. Treaty, Art. 236 (*ex Art. 179*) in conjunction with Art. 225 (*ex Art. 168a*) and the CFI Decision, Art. 3(1)(a).

[3] This chapter deals only with the basic features of staff cases. More detailed discussions can be found in *Commentaire Mégret*, at 335–371; Dubouis, "Fonctionnaires et agents des Communautés européennes" (1965) R.T.D.E. 666–686; (1966) R.T.D.E. 511–522; (1969) R.T.D.E. 648–664; (1970) R.T.D.E. 120–144; (1972) R.T.D.E. 376–394; (1975) R.T.D.E. 280–307; (1978) R.T.D.E. 469–515; (1981) R.T.D.E. 710–763; (1983) R.T.D.E. 86–146; (1990) R.T.D.E. 127–169; (1994) R.T.D.E. 237–276; and Rogalla, *Dienstrecht der Europäischen Gemeinschaften*, Cologne/Berlin/Bonn/Munich, Carl Heymanns Verlag KG, 1992.

(1) the act must have legal effects as far the applicant is concerned; and

(2) those legal effects must be unfavourable to the staff member, with the result that he or she can establish a personal interest in a judgment granting his or her claims.

1. What measures constitute acts having adverse effect?

16–003 An act having adverse effect is one which directly affects the applicant's legal position.[4] This concept is very similar to the expression "binding act" which has been discussed in connection with actions for annulment.[5]

16–004 Where an applicant challenges a "measure of a general nature" (Staff Regulations, Article 90(2), first indent), the application will be admissible only in so far as he or she shows that the act adversely affects him or her.[6] This means that the measure of a general nature must directly affect his or her legal position.[7] If this is not the case, no action will lie against the measure in question, but subsequently an objection of illegality may be raised against it if that measure is used as the basis for an act adversely affecting the applicant.[8]

16–005 Some authorities argue that it may be inferred from the wording of Articles 90 and 91 of the Staff Regulations that a decision will be capable of having adverse effect only if it is taken by the appointing authority.[9] Frequently, decisions of the appointing authority are prepared by a lower-ranking official or in an advisory body. Such preparatory measures are not acts having adverse effect, because they do not affect the applicant's legal position. In some cases, however, acts not performed by the appointing authority actually do have adverse effect. One example is the finding by an invalidity committee that a staff member is not suffering from invalidity, which is an act having adverse effect on the person concerned because it is

---

[4] Case 26/63 *Pistoj v. Commission* [1964] E.C.R. 341 at 352; ECJ; Case 32/68 *Graselli v. Commission* [1969] E.C.R. 505 at 511, para. 4, ECJ.

[5] See para. 7–007, above. For further details see *Commentaire Mégret*, at 335–353; Van Raepenbusch, "Le contentieux de la fonction publique européenne", in *Tendances actuelles et évolution de la jurisprudence de la Cour de justice des Communautés européennes*, Maastricht, European Institute of Public Administration, 1993, 95 at 111–115.

[6] See also Case 125/87 *Brown v. Court of Justice* [1988] E.C.R. 1619 at 1634, para. 17, ECJ.

[7] See, *inter alia*, Case 78/63 *Huber v. Commission* [1964] E.C.R. 367 at 375, ECJ; Case T–135/89 *Pfloeschner v. Commission* [1990] E.C.R. II–153 at II–158, para. 11, CFI; (Order of July 4, 1991), Case T–47/90 *Herremans v. Commission* [1991] E.C.R. II–467 at II–474—475, para. 22, CFI. In so far as the conditions set out in a notice of vacancy exclude a person from applying for the post in question, that person will be adversely affected by the notice. See, by way of example, Case 79/74 *Küster v. European Parliament* [1975] E.C.R. 725 at 730, para. 6, ECJ; Case 25/77 *De Roubaix v. Commission* [1978] E.C.R. 1081 at 1088, para. 8, ECJ.

[8] See, *e.g.* Case T–47/91 *Auzat v. Commission* [1992] E.C.R. II–2536 at II–2544, para. 11, CFI.

[9] See Van Raepenbusch (cited in n. 5, above), at 115. The appointing authority differs depending upon the level of the official or staff member in the hierarchy (Staff Regulations, Art. 2).

the act which actually terminates the invalidity procedure.[10] Another is a selection board's decision, taken in the course of a recruitment competition, to eliminate the applicant from the further stages of the competition.[11]

2. The requirement for an interest

Applicants are entitled to challenge a decision which has implications for their legal position only in so far as that decision adversely affects that legal position. In other words, there must be an advantage for the applicant personally in a judgment granting his or her claims. Accordingly, an applicant has no interest in the annulment of an appointment to a post to which he or she personally is ineligible for appointment.[12] **16–006**

The applicant is entitled only to adduce grievances which affect him or her personally. He or she may not bring an action in the interests of the law or of the institutions.[13] Furthermore, the applicant's interest must be legitimate, present and vested.[14] **16–007**

In addition, the applicant may only make submissions which genuinely serve his or her interest.[15] A plea criticising a defect in the contested act will therefore be inadmissible if the defect was incapable of disadvantaging the applicant.[16] **16–008**

II. Identity of the Parties

A. Applicants

Any person whose relationship with the Community is determined by the Staff Regulations or the Conditions of Employment may bring a dispute concerning the application of the Staff Regulations or the Conditions of Employment before the Court of First Instance.[17] Only "local staff"—staff engaged according to local practice for manual or service duties and paid out of the budget item "general appropriations"—must, under Article 81 of the Conditions of Employment, bring any dispute between them and the institution where they are employed before the competent court in accordance with the laws in force at the place where they perform their duties. **16–009**

---

[10] Case T–54/89 *V. v. European Parliament* [1990] E.C.R. II–659 at II–674—675, para. 45, ECJ; Case C–18/91P *V. v. European Parliament* [1992] E.C.R. I–3997 at I–4015, para. 26, ECJ.

[11] Case T–37/93 *Stagakis v. European Parliament* [1994] E.C.R.–S.C. I–A–137 at I–A–138–139 (English abstract), CFI.

[12] See, *inter alia*, Case T–20/89 *Moritz v. Commission* [1990] E.C.R. II–769 at II–775, para. 16, CFI; Case T–51/90 *Moretti v. Commission* [1992] E.C.R. II–487 at II–494, para. 22, CFI.

[13] Case 85/82 *Schloh v. Council* [1983] E.C.R. 2105 at 2123, para. 14, ECJ; Case T–163/89 *Sebastiani v. European Parliament* [1991] E.C.R. II–715 at II–723, para. 24, CFI.

[14] Case 17/78 *Deshormes v. Commission* [1979] E.C.R. 189 at 197, para. 9, ECJ; (Order of December 14, 1989), Case T–119/89 *Teisonnière v. Commission* [1990] E.C.R. II–7 at II–14, para. 19, CFI.

[15] Case 90/74 *Deboeck v. Commission* [1975] E.C.R. 1123 at 1133, para. 12, ECJ.

[16] *ibid.*, at 1133–1134, paras 13–16. The plea must also be able to be inferred from the content of the complaint (para. 16–018, below).

[17] Staff Regulations, Art. 91(1); Conditions of Employment, Art. 46 (temporary staff), Art. 73 (auxiliaries) and Art. 83 (special advisers).

Persons taking part in recruitment procedures are also among those deriving rights under the Staff Regulations or the Conditions of Employment,[18] together with the legal successors of persons whose relationship with the Community was governed by the Staff Regulations or the Conditions of Employment.[19]

16–010 Members of staff of Community bodies and agencies with legal personality may also bring actions in the Court of First Instance where it appears from the regulation establishing the relevant body or agency that its staff are in a legal position equivalent to that of servants of Community institutions.[20]

16–011 Trade unions and staff associations of employees of the Community which have legal personality are not entitled to bring proceedings pursuant to Article 236 (*ex Article 179*) of the E.C. Treaty because the procedure for complaint and appeal established by Articles 90 and 91 of the Staff Regulations is designed to deal exclusively with individual disputes.[21] Consequently, they must satisfy the requirements of the fourth paragraph of Article 230 (*ex Article 173*) of the E.C. Treaty in order to bring an action for annulment and of Article 235 (*ex Article 178*) and the second paragraph of Article 288 (*ex Article 215*) of that Treaty in order to bring an action for damages. In addition, they may intervene in support of the form of order sought by a party in proceedings instituted under Article 236 of the E.C. Treaty.[22]

B. Defendants

16–012 Actions are brought against the institution from which the act at issue emanated.[23]

16–013 A staff member employed by a body or agency with legal personality in its own right has to bring his or her claim against that body or agency, not against a Community institution.

---

[18] Case 23/64 *Vandevyvere v. European Parliament* [1965] E.C.R. 157 at 163–164, ECJ.

[19] Case 18/70 *Duraffour v. Council* [1971] E.C.R. 515, ECJ; Case 24/71 *Meinhardt v. Commission* [1972] E.C.R. 269 at 275–276, para. 2, ECJ; Case T–65/92 *Arauxo-Dumay v. Commission* [1993] E.C.R. II–597, CFI.

[20] Case 110/75 *Mills v. EIB* [1976] E.C.R. 955 at 968, para. 14, ECJ.

[21] Case 175/73 *Union Syndicale, Massa and Kortner v. Council* [1974] E.C.R. 917 at 926, para. 19, ECJ; Case 18/74 *Syndicat Général du Personnel des Organismes Européens v. Commission* [1974] E.C.R. 933 at 945, para. 15, ECJ; Joined Cases 193 and 194/87 *Maurissen and European Public Service Union v. Court of Auditors* [1989] E.C.R. 1045 at 1075, para. 29, ECJ; (Order of December 4, 1991), Case T–78/91 *Moat and TAO v. Commission* [1991] E.C.R. II–1387 at II–1392, para. 7, CFI.

[22] In accordance with the E.C. Statute, Art. 37, paras 2–3. See, Case T–84/91 *Meskens v. European Parliament* [1992] E.C.R. II–1565 at II–1568, para. 9, CFI: trade-union organisations are widely allowed to intervene in staff cases where the decision is likely to affect a collective interest.

[23] Case 18/63 *Wollast (née Schmitz) v. EEC* [1964] E.C.R. 85 at 96, ECJ. *Cf.* Case T–177/94 *Altmann and Others v. Commission* [1994] E.C.R.–S.C. II–969 at II–978—979 paras 32–45, CFI (action held inadmissible in so far as it was brought against JET, a joint undertaking within the meaning of the EAEC Treaty, Arts. 46, 47, 49 and the JET Council).

III. Special Characteristics

A. The requirement for a pre-litigation procedure

1. Course and time-limits

Under Article 91(2) of the Staff Regulations, an appeal to the Court of First Instance will lie only if the applicant has previously submitted a complaint within the prescribed period to the appointing authority about the act allegedly adversely affecting him or her, and the complaint has been rejected by express or implied decision.[24] The aim of this pre-litigation procedure is to enable the dispute to be settled amicably. Consequently, the complaint must put the appointing authority in a position to know in sufficient detail the applicant's criticisms of the contested act.[25] **16–014**

The question whether the pre-litigation procedure was lawfully conducted may be inquired into by the Court of First Instance of its own motion in considering whether the application made to it is admissible.[26] In this way the Court will examine whether the time-limits prescribed by Articles 90 and 91 of the Staff Regulations were complied with in the course of the pre-litigation procedure and whether the complaint and the application to the Court are consistent with each other.[27]

If a person to whom the Staff Regulations apply seeks to challenge an omission to take a decision relating to him or her, he or she must first submit a request to the appointing authority pursuant to Article 90(1) of the Staff Regulations for the decision in question to be taken.[28] The **16–015**

---

[24] However, there is no obligation to submit a prior complaint against a decision of a selection board for a competition since the appointing authority has no power to annul or vary such a decision (see, *inter alia*, Case 44/71 *Marcato v. Commission* [1972] E.C.R. 427 at 433, paras 4–9, ECJ). If the applicant nevertheless submits a prior complaint against such a decision, it cannot be objected that his application is inadmissible for being out of time. An action against an act which is connected to another act against which the applicant lodged a complaint is admissible, even though the applicant did not submit a prior complaint in respect of the related act (Case 806/79 *Gerin v. Commission* [1980] E.C.R. 3515 at 3524, ECJ).

[25] See, *inter alia*, Case 58/75 *Sergy v. Commission* [1976] E.C.R. 1139 at 1152, para. 32, ECJ; Case 133/88 *Casto del Amo Martinez v. European Parliament* [1989] E.C.R. 689 at 698, para. 9, ECJ; Case T–57/89 *Alexandrakis v. Commission* [1990] E.C.R. II–143 at II–148, para. 8, CFI.

[26] *Alexandrakis v. Commission* (cited in n. 25, above) para. 8.

[27] *e.g.* relating to time-limits, see (Order of July 9, 1991), Case T–48/91 *Minic v. Court of Auditors* [1991] E.C.R. II–479, CFI; as for whether the complaint and the application are consistent with each other, see *Alexandrakis v. Commission* (cited in n. 25, above).

[28] If he or she submits a "complaint" at the same time and then brings an action before the Court of First Instance when it is rejected, that action will be inadmissible for infringing the Staff Regulations, Art. 90(1), (2), see (Order of February 25, 1992), Case T–64/91 *Marcato v. Commission* [1992] E.C.R. II–243 at II–254—258, paras 31–46, CFI. If a person covered by the Staff Regulations wishes to bring an action for damages and the damage is caused by a decision adversely affecting him or her, he or she must submit a complaint pursuant to Art. 90(2). If, in contrast, the damage originated in an administrative act which cannot be characterised as an act having adverse effect, the pre-litigation procedure must commence with a request, under Art. 90(1), for compensation, which, if rejected, will have to be followed by a complaint against the rejection of the request: Case T–391/94 *Baiwir v.*

appointing authority then has four months, starting from the date on which the request was made, to notify the person concerned of its reasoned decision. If at the end of that period no reply to the request has been received, this will be deemed to constitute an implied decision rejecting the request. A complaint may be submitted against such a decision, just as in the case of a decision whose content is unfavourable to the person concerned.[29] The complaint must be submitted to the appointing authority within three months. When time starts to run depends on the type of measure against which the complaint is brought.[30] The appointing authority then has four months from the date on which the complaint was lodged to notify its reasoned decision to the person concerned. If at the end of that period no reply to the complaint has been received, this will be deemed to constitute a decision rejecting the complaint. An action may be brought in the Court of First Instance against such a decision, just as in the case of an express rejection of a complaint.[31] This will only be the case, however, if an action will lie against the act in respect of which the complaint was submitted. The express or implied rejection of a complaint is in fact only confirmation of the "act" (express or implied) about which the person concerned complained and is, *per se*, not a challengeable act.[32]

2. Formal requirements

16–016 Requests for decisions and complaints are not subject to any requirement as to form.[33] Article 90(3) of the Staff Regulations provides that requests and complaints must be submitted through the staff member's immediate

---

Commission [1996] E.C.R.–S.C. II–787 at II–801—802, paras 45–48, CFI (English abstract at I–A–269); Case T–500/93 *Y. v. Court of Justice* [1996] E.C.R.–S.C. II–977, CFI (English abstract at I–A–355). If, however, there is a close link between an action for annulment and a claim for compensation, the compensation claim will be admissible as ancillary to the action for annulment and does not have to be preceded by a request to the appointing authority to make good the alleged damage, followed by a complaint directed against the implied or express rejection of that complaint: Case T–27/90 *Latham v. Commission* [1991] E.C.R. II–35, CFI; Case T–44/93 *Saby v. Commission* [1995] E.C.R.–S.C. II–541 at II–551—552, para. 31, CFI (English abstract at I–A–175); Case T–140/94 *Gutiérrez de Quijano y Llorens v. European Parliament* [1996] E.C.R.–S.C. II–689 at II–709—710, para. 54, CFI (English abstract at I–A–241).

[29] If the appointing authority has already taken a decision adversely affecting the official concerned, that official may no longer commence the pre-litigation procedure by submitting a request for a decision under the Staff Regulations, Art. 90(1), but must directly submit a complaint pursuant to Art. 90(2): Case T–113/95 *Mancini v. Commission* [1996] E.C.R.–S.C. II–543 at II–550—551, para. 28, CFI (English abstract at I–A–239).

[30] Staff Regulations, Art. 90(2) determines when time starts running in each case. Failure to comply with the time-limit for submitting a complaint will inevitably result in a subsequent action being declared inadmissible: (Order of July 14, 1993), Case T–55/92 *Knijff v. Court of Auditors* [1993] E.C.R. II–823, CFI.

[31] Staff Regulations, Art. 90(2), subpara. 2, and Art. 91.

[32] Joined Cases 33 and 75/79 *Kuhner v. Commission* [1980] E.C.R. 1677 at 1693–1694, para. 9, ECJ; (Order of June 16, 1988), Case 371/87 *Progoulis v. Commission* [1988] E.C.R. 3081 at 3088, para. 17, ECJ; (Order of June 7, 1991), Case T–14/91 *Weyrich v. Commission* [1991] E.C.R. II–235 at II–259—260, para. 43, CFI; Case T–4/93 *André v. Commission* [1994] E.C.R.–S.C. II–471 at II–477, para. 21, CFI (English abstract at I–A–145).

[33] Case 54/77 *Herpels v. Commission* [1978] E.C.R. 585 at 601, para. 47, ECJ; Case T–506/93 *Moat v. Commission* [1995] E.C.R.–S.C. II–147 at II–153, para. 18, CFI; Case T–192/94

superior (*par la voie hiérarchique*), except where it concerns that person, in which case it may be submitted to the authority next above. The institutions themselves may lay down procedures for the submission and processing of requests and complaints.[34]

3. Effects

If the pre-litigation procedure does not bring the dispute to an end, an action ("appeal") will lie to the Court of First Instance.[35] The action must be brought within three months. Time starts running on the date of notification of the decision taken in response to the complaint or, in the case of an implied decision rejecting the complaint, on the date of expiry of the period of four months after the complaint was lodged.[36] **16–017**

The prior complaint defines the subject-matter of the action to a negative extent only. The action may not extend the purpose or the subject-matter of the complaint, but may curtail them. Consequently, the subject-matter of the action is defined solely by the application, provided that it remains within the limits laid down by the complaint.[37] Generally, the complaint will not be drawn up by a lawyer and will be very informal, since it aims at achieving an amicable resolution of the dispute.[38] Consequently, it is sufficient if the pleas set out in the application emerge implicitly from the complaint[39] or are closely linked thereto if they do not appear as such in the **16–018**

Maurissen v. Court of Auditors [1996] E.C.R.–S.C. II–1229 at II–1237, para. 31, CFI (English abstract at I–A-425).

34 *Commentaire Mégret*, at 322.

35 Under of the Staff Regulations, Art. 91(4), an applicant may bring an action before the Court of First Instance without awaiting the reply from the appointing authority, provided that he or she applies for interim measures at the same time. The proceedings in the principal action are then suspended until such time as the appointing authority has responded to the complaint.

36 Art. 91(3) provides as follows: where a complaint is rejected by express decision after being rejected by implied decision but before the period for lodging an appeal to the Court of First Instance has expired, time for bringing court proceedings starts to run afresh. That provision may not be invoked to the detriment of an applicant where the latter has already brought an action and the defendant institution seeks to remedy, by means of a late, reasoned rejection of the complaint, the fact that the act adversely affecting the applicant entirely lacked any statement of reasons, see Case T–52/90 *Volger v. European Parliament* [1992] E.C.R. II–121 at II–134—139, paras 31–42, CFI, upheld by Case C–115/92P *European Parliament v. Volger* [1993] E.C.R. I–6549 at I–6588, paras 22–24, ECJ. Where an express decision rejecting a complaint is taken after the period for lodging an appeal has run out, time does not start running afresh; although the express decision makes it clear why the complaint was rejected, it constitutes merely confirmation of the implied decision rejecting the complaint: (Order of June 25, 1998), Case C–312/97P *Fichtner v. Commission* [1998] E.C.R. I–4135 at I–4143, paras 16–17, ECJ, dismissing an appeal against (Order of July 9, 1997), Case T–63/96 *Fichtner v. Commission* [1997] E.C.R. II–563, CFI (English abstract at A–I–189).

37 Case T–134/89 *Hettrich and Others v. Commission* [1990] E.C.R. II–565 at II–572, para. 16, CFI,

38 However, the complaint may be lodged by a lawyer acting on behalf of his client, see Case T–139/89 *Virgili-Schettini v. European Parliament* [1990] E.C.R. II–535, CFI.

39 Case 184/80 *Van Zaanen v. Court of Auditors* [1981] E.C.R. 1951 at 1963–1964, para. 13, ECJ.

complaint.[40] Provided that the subject-matter and the grounds of the complaint are not altered, the application and the pleas adduced in support of it will be admissible.[41] The test is whether an open-minded assessment of the complaint carried out by the appointing authority would have enabled it to know the heads of complaint set out in the application to the Court in order to reach an amicable settlement of the dispute. If the heads of complaint, from the point of view of their subject-matter and purpose, remain the same in the complaint and the application, the application will be admissible, even if those heads of complaint are given a more legal character in pleas and arguments which were not raised as such in the complaint.[42]

Furthermore, according to the case law, a claim for compensation for damage arising out of the contested act may be made even if no mention was made of it in the complaint. This flexible approach is attributable to the close link between such a claim and the complaint made against the contested act.[43]

B. Priority of an action brought under Article 236 *(ex Article 179)* of the E.C. Treaty

16–019 Any dispute arising out of the employment relationship between a person and the Community must if necessary be brought before the Court in accordance with the conditions prescribed by Article 236 of the E.C. Treaty and Articles 90 and 91 of the Staff Regulations. No other judicial procedure may be used for this purpose.[44] The subject-matter of the application determines whether it has to be regarded as a "staff case". Accordingly, an action brought by members of an official's family pursuant

[40] See, *inter alia*, Case 133/88 *Casto del Amo Martinez v. European Parliament* [1989] E.C.R. 689 at 699, para. 10, ECJ; Case T–57/89 *Alexandrakis v. Commission* [1990] E.C.R. II–143 at II–148—149, para. 9, CFI; Case T–2/90 *Ferreira de Freitas v. Commission* [1991] E.C.R. II–103 at II–116, para. 41, CFI.

[41] Joined Cases 75 and 117/82 *Razzouk and Beydoun v. Commission* [1984] E.C.R. 1509 at 1528, para 9, ECJ.

[42] For a case in which this condition was not satisfied, at least as regards one of the pleas raised, see Case T–4/92 *Vardakas v. Commission* [1993] E.C.R. II–357 at II–363—364, paras 16, 17, CFI. See also Case T–588/93 *G. v. Commission* [1994] E.C.R.–S.C. II–875 at II–882—884, paras 27–30, CFI (English abstract at I–A–277); Case T–361/94 *Weir v. Commission* [1996] E.C.R.–S.C. II–381 at II–391, para. 32, CFI (English abstract at I–A–121).

[43] Case 224/87 *Koutchoumoff v. Commission* [1989] E.C.R., 99, ECJ; Case 126/87 *Del Plato v. Commission* [1987] E.C.R. 643, ECJ; Case T–44/93 *Saby v. Commission* [1995] E.C.R.–S.C. II–541 at II–550, para. 28, CFI (English abstract at A–I–175).

[44] Case 9/75 *Meyer-Burckhardt v. Commission* [1975] E.C.R. 1171 at 1181, para. 7, ECJ; (Order of 11 July 1996), Case T–30/96 *Gomes de Sá Pereira v. Council* [1996] E.C.R. II–785 at II–793—794, paras 24–26, CFI. Even if the legality of a recruitment procedure initiated by a Community institution may depend on whether certain acts of the national authorities, to which that institution has turned, are themselves lawful (where, for instance, the Community institution asks the Member State concerned to present suitable candidates for appointment as members of the temporary staff), it is for the person aggrieved to exercise, within the time-limits laid down by the Staff Regulations, the remedies provided for in the Staff Regulations, even if only as a precautionary measure: Case C–246/95 *Coen v. Belgian State* [1997] E.C.R. I–403 at I–424, para. 22, ECJ.

to Articles 235 and 288 (*ex Articles 178 and 215*) of the E.C. Treaty for compensation for damage suffered by them personally as a result of effects of "the conduct of an institution" on the career of the official in question will be inadmissible on the ground that the official himself was "in a position to avail himself of the opportunities afforded by the Treaty to challenge any decision of the institution concerned".[45]

IV. Consequences

A judgment or order of the Court of First Instance in a staff case has the same legal force as its decisions in other types of cases. **16–020**

Depending upon the purpose and outcome of the proceedings, the Court of First Instance may dismiss the application, annul the contested act, award damages—together, in a proper case, with default interest—and, in disputes of a financial nature, impose such measures as it may grant in the exercise of its unlimited jurisdiction. However, the Court of First Instance may not substitute itself for the institution party to the proceedings; at the most, it may provide "guidance" as to the measures to be taken in order to comply with its judgment.[46] At the same time, it must make sure that the scope of the operative part of its judgment emerges clearly from the grounds in conjunction with which it must be read. This is a corollary of the obligation weighing on the Court of First Instance to state reasons for its decisions.[47] **16–021**

Article 88 of the CFI Rules of Procedure provides that in proceedings between the Communities and their servants, the institutions are to bear their own costs, irrespective of the outcome. The applicant, however, may be ordered to pay the institution's costs which he or she unreasonably or vexatiously caused it to incur.[48] **16–022**

[45] (Order of May 7, 1980), Joined Cases 114–117/79 *Fournier v. Commission* [1980] E.C.R. 1529 at 1531, ECJ. See also (Order of June 14, 1995), Joined Cases T–462, T–464 and T–470/93 *Lenz v. Commission*, not reported in the E.C.R., paras 55–59, CFI.

[46] Case 225/82 *Verzyck v. Commission* [1983] E.C.R. 1991 at 2005–2006, paras 19–20, ECJ; Case T–37/89 *Hanning v. European Parliament* [1990] E.C.R. II–463 at II–488—489, para. 79, CFI; Case T–588/93 *G. v. Commission* [1994] E.C.R.–S.C. II–875 at II–882, para. 26, CFI. *Cf.* Case T–73/89 *Barbi v. Commission* [1990] E.C.R. II–619 at II–630, para. 38, CFI.

[47] Opinion of Advocate General W. Van Gerven in Case C–242/90P *Commission v. Albani and Others* [1993] E.C.R. I–3839 at I–3861—3862, ECJ.

[48] For costs in appeals against decisions of the Court of First Instance in staff cases, see Rules of Procedure, Art. 122, para. 2: if the official (or the person treated as an official) unsuccessfully appeals, he or she will in principle have to pay the respondent institution's costs. *e.g.* see (Order of March 20, 1991), Case C–115/90P *Turner v. Commission* [1991] E.C.R. I–1423 at I–1431, para. 15, ECJ; Case C–283/90P *Vidrányi v. Commission* [1991] E.C.R. I–4339 at I–4369, para. 34, ECJ.

CHAPTER 17

JURISDICTION OF THE COURT OF JUSTICE AND THE COURT OF FIRST INSTANCE TO GIVE JUDGMENT PURSUANT TO AN ARBITRATION CLAUSE OR A SPECIAL AGREEMENT

I. ARTICLE 238 (*EX ARTICLE 181*) OF THE E.C. TREATY

A. SUBJECT-MATTER

1. General

Under Article 282 (*ex Article 211*) of the E.C. Treaty, the Community, which has legal personality,[1] enjoys the most extensive legal capacity accorded to legal persons under national law. The Community's participation in legal transactions may give rise to disputes having to be decided judicially. Article 238 of the E.C. Treaty authorises the Community and parties contracting with it to confer jurisdiction over such disputes on the Court of Justice pursuant to an arbitration clause contained in a contract governed by private or public law concluded by or on behalf of the Community.[2] In the absence of such a clause, the national courts have jurisdiction under national law to settle any disputes.[3] **17–001**

There are a number of grounds which may prompt the conclusion of an arbitration clause. The Court of Justice and the Court of First Instance constitute the meeting place of a number of legal cultures, as a result of which they may be regarded as suitable *fora* for determining a dispute **17–002**

[1] E.C. Treaty, Art. 281 (*ex Art. 210*).

[2] See also ECSC Treaty, Art. 42, and EAEC Treaty, Art. 153.

[3] E.C. Treaty, Art. 240 (*ex Art. 183*). In the absence of an arbitration clause, the Court of Justice lacks jurisdiction to rule on any liability in contract where one of the parties brings an action for non-contractual liability under the E.C. Treaty, Art. 235 (*ex Art. 178*). In that event, the fact that the parties have brought their dispute before the Court cannot be regarded as an expression of their intention to confer on the Court jurisdiction over disputes arising out of an agreement: (Order of July 18, 1997), Case T–180/95 *Nutria v. Commission* [1997] E.C.R. II–1317 at II–1329, paras 37–40, CFI. Moreover, a party cannot unilaterally circumvent the division of jurisdiction between the Court of Justice and the national courts by causing the Community institution concerned to reject its request for compensation and then describing that rejection as a decision within the meaning of the E.C. Treaty, Art. 230 (*ex Art. 173*); (Order of July 18, 1997), Case T–44/96 *Oleifici Italiani v. Commission* [1997] E.C.R. II–1331 at II–1345, para. 44, CFI; (Order of October 3, 1997), Case T–186/96 *Mutual Aid Administration Services v. Commission* [1997] E.C.R. II–1633 at II–1646, para. 44, CFI.

relating to an international contract. What is more, an arbitration clause is a means of avoiding a national court's adjudicating on a dispute in which important Community interests are at stake. The Community may also want to bring any disputes before its natural court under a procedure with which it is familiar.[4]

2. What contracts are concerned?

17–003 As has already been noted, the Court of Justice may have jurisdiction to give judgment pursuant to an arbitration clause "contained in a contract concluded by or on behalf of the Community, whether that contract be governed by public or private law". Decided cases have not yet made it clear what is meant by a public-law contract in this context. What may be meant is agreements concluded by the Community with Member States, with third countries or with international organisations (whether or not in the form of a convention) and administrative agreements concluded with individuals.[5] Private-law contracts comprise all contracts into which the Community enters as a party to normal legal transactions.

17–004 The stipulation that the contracts may be concluded "on behalf of the Community" undoubtedly means that entities which are not institutions or bodies of the Community may nevertheless include an arbitration clause in a contract concluded by them on behalf of the Community.[6]

3. Nature and extent of the Court's jurisdiction pursuant to an arbitration clause

17–005 The expression "arbitration clause" employed in Article 238 (*ex Article 181*) of the E.C. Treaty is misleading. Where the Court of Justice (or the Court of First Instance) gives judgment pursuant to an "arbitration clause", it acts, not as an arbitrator, but as a court giving judgments which may be directly enforced.

17–006 The arbitration clause may or may not give the Court of Justice exclusive jurisdiction. If the clause confers an exclusive right on the Court to hear and determine disputes, courts in Member States must decline jurisdiction by reason of the primacy of Community law (*i.e.* compliance with the arbitration clause concluded pursuant to Article 238 (*ex Article 181*) of the E.C. Treaty). If a number of courts, including the Court of Justice, are entitled to determine disputes under the arbitration clause, a problem of *lis alibi pendens* may arise. No specific rules exist for resolving this problem.

17–007 The extent of the Court's jurisdiction emerges from the arbitration clause itself.[7] Because that jurisdiction is conferred by derogation from the

[4] Kremlis, "De quelques clauses d'élection de for et de droit applicable stipulées dans des contrats de droit privé conclus par les Communautés européennes dans le cadre de leurs activités d'emprunt et de prêt" (1986) Diritto comunitario e degli scambi internazionali 777 at 782–783.

[5] For further details, see Bleckmann, "Die öffentlichrechtlichen Verträge der EWG" (1978) N.J.W. 464–467.

[6] *Cf. Commentaire Mégret*, at 377.

[7] See, *e.g.* Case 1/56 *Bourgaux v. Common Assembly* [1954 to 1956] E.C.R. 361 at 367, ECJ.

ordinary rules of law, it must be construed very narrowly.[8] Only claims and pleas arising from the contract containing the arbitration clause or directly connected therewith may be entertained.[9] Consequently, a claim based on the other party's having been unduly enriched inevitably falls outside the scope of the contractual relations between the parties. This means that the Court has no jurisdiction to entertain such a claim pursuant to an arbitration clause.[10] In contrast, counterclaims made by the defendant which are directly based on the contract are admissible.[11]

B. Identity of the parties

Any party bound by the contract embodying the arbitration clause has the right to bring a dispute before the Community Court.[12] In the case of a contract concluded between the Community and a natural or legal person, disputes may be brought before either the Court of Justice or the Court of First Instance depending on whether the applicant is the Community or the individual. The Court of Justice has jurisdiction if the Community initiates the proceedings; the Court of First Instance if they are brought by the individual. This split jurisdiction has the result that a private party which is a defendant in proceedings brought before the Court of Justice by the Community pursuant to an arbitration clause has only one chance of putting over its defence, whereas if the Community is the defendant in proceedings brought by a natural or legal person, it may have a second chance, if it loses, by appealing against the decision of the Court of First Instance. This lack of symmetry in contracting parties' position as litigants is somewhat anomalous.[13] **17–008**

C. Special characteristics

1. Requirements relating to validity

The validity of the arbitration clause is adjudged exclusively on the basis of Article 238 (*ex Article 181*) of the E.C. Treaty and Article 38(6) of the ECJ **17–009**

---

[8] Case C–114/94 *IDE v. Commission* [1997] E.C.R. I–803 at I–866, para. 82, ECJ.

[9] Case 426/85 *Commission v. Zoubek* [1986] E.C.R. 4057 at 4069, para. 11, ECJ. It is possible that the Court would take cognizance of a cluster of contracts concluded by the parties on the basis of an arbitration clause contained in only one (or some) of the contracts. In *Porta v. Commission*, the applicant had concluded contracts, each for a term of one year, over a number of years with the director of the Community's research centre in Ispra to teach at the centre's school. Initially, the contract was only oral, but subsequently it was reduced to writing, whereupon an arbitration clause was added. The Court of Justice held that that arbitration clause entitled it to have regard to all the contracts entered into between Mrs Porta and the Commission, see Case 109/81 *Porta v. Commission* [1982] E.C.R. 2469 at 2480, para. 10, ECJ.

[10] Case C–330/88 *Grifoni v. EAEC* [1991] E.C.R. I–1045 at I–1067, para. 20, ECJ.

[11] *IDE v. Commission* (cited in n. 8 above) paras 82–83.

[12] There is nothing to prevent a party to a contract from assigning his or her rights to a successor. For an example, see Case C–209/90 *Commission v. Feilhauer* [1992] E.C.R. I–2613 at I–2641, para. 5, ECJ.

[13] CFI Decision, Art. 3(1)(c). The further transfer of jurisdiction to the Court of First Instance proposed by the Court of Justice on December 14, 1998, would lead to jurisdiction being vested in all cases in the Court of First Instance; this is in order to put an end to the observed anomaly in the present system, see para. 1–026, n. 84, above.

Rules of Procedure,[14] under which the application must be accompanied by a copy of the arbitration clause. The Court pays no regard to special requirements laid down by the national law applicable to the contract.[15] For the same reason, a court or an administrative authority in a Member State cannot refuse to give effect to the judgment of the Court of Justice or the Court of First Instance, as the case may be, on the ground that the Court's jurisdiction is based on an arbitration clause which is invalid under national law.

2. Applicable law

17–010 The Court respects the parties' choice of applicable law, whether express or implied.[16] In the absence of such a choice, the Rome Convention of June 19, 1980, on the law applicable to contractual obligations is the only possible source of inspiration, apart from the general private international law of the Member States.

3. Procedure before the Court

17–011 The procedure ordinarily applied to direct actions is used for the determination of disputes under an arbitration clause.

D. Consequences

17–012 A judgment given by the Court of Justice or the Court of First Instance pursuant to Article 238 (*ex Article 181*) of the E.C. Treaty is enforceable under Articles 244 and 256 (*ex Articles 187 and 192*) of that Treaty in the same way as any other judgment.

II. Article 239 (*ex Article 182*) of the E.C. Treaty

17–013 Article 239 of the E.C. Treaty allows Member States to conclude a special agreement to refer any dispute between them relating to the subject-matter of the Treaty to the Court of Justice. To date, the Member States have not availed themselves of this facility.

17–014 In the light of Article 292 (*ex Article 219*) of the E.C. Treaty, which puts Member States under an obligation not to submit a dispute concerning the interpretation or application of that Treaty to any method of settlement other than those provided for therein, Article 239 (*ex Article 182*) is not an optional provision. Once a dispute arises relating to "the interpretation or application" of the Treaty which the Member States have no other way of

---

[14] For the present, the CFI Rules of Procedure contain no provision specifically dealing with applications pursuant to the E.C. Treaty, Art. 238 (*ex Art. 181*) hence the provisions of the ECJ Rules of Procedure are applied *mutatis mutandis*.

[15] Case 23/76 *Pellegrini v. Commission* [1976] E.C.R. 1807 at 1818, paras 8–10, ECJ; Case C–209/90 *Commission v. Feilhauer* [1992] E.C.R. I–2613 at I–2642, paras 12–14, ECJ; Case C–299/93 *Bauer v. Commission* [1995] E.C.R. I–839 at I–858, para. 11, ECJ (EAEC Treaty, Art. 153, applied in the same way).

[16] Case 318/81 *Commission v. CO.DE.MI* [1985] E.C.R. 3693 at 3712, paras 18–22, ECJ; Case 220/85 *Fadex v. Commission* [1986] E.C.R. 3387 at 3399, para. 10, ECJ; *Commission v. Feilhauer*, (cited in n. 15, above) at I–2640, para 3, and at I–2643, para. 16.

bringing before the Court of Justice, Article 292 obliges them to conclude a special agreement within the meaning of Article 239 which confers jurisdiction on the Court to resolve the dispute.[17]

[17] *Commentaire Mégret*, at 381.

Chapter 18

JURISDICTION OF THE COMMUNITY COURT OVER DISPUTES RELATING TO INTELLECTUAL PROPERTY RIGHTS

I. Subject-Matter

The Community created Community intellectual property rights by two regulations adopted on the basis of Article 308 (*ex Article 235*) of the E.C. Treaty. The Community trade mark was introduced by Council Regulation No. 40/94 of December 20, 1993.[1] Community plant variety rights were introduced by Council Regulation No. 2100/94 of July 27, 1994, as amended by Council Regulation No. 2506/95 of October 25, 1995.[2] **18–001**

These intellectual property rights are conferred by Community bodies especially set up for the purpose. Community trade marks are granted by the Office for Harmonisation in the Internal Market (Trade Marks and Designs), whilst Community plant variety rights are conferred by the Community Plant Variety Office. The two Offices may also declare intellectual property rights falling within their jurisdiction null and void or cancel them and take decisions on observations or objections submitted by third parties.

Each of those regulations introduces a specific system of legal protection which safeguards the rights of parties affected by the Offices' decisions and takes account of the specific characteristics of intellectual property rights. One or more boards of appeal have been set up at the two Offices to which appeals may be brought against the decisions of other authorities of the **18–002**

---

[1] [1994] O.J. L11 1.

[2] [1994] O.J. L227 1; [1995] O.J. L258 3. The amendment relates to the original regulation, Art. 73, which governs the system of actions brought in the Court of Justice against decisions of the boards of appeal. According to the Regulation No. 2506/95, Preamble, Recital 3, the amendment is intended to "ensure coherence of the system of appeal procedures to the Community jurisdiction in the different fields of industrial and commercial property". To this end, Regulation No. 2506/95 aligns the rules on actions which may be brought against decisions of the Community Plant Variety Office or its boards of appeal with those provided for by Regulation No. 40/94 on the Community trade mark (Art. 63 of the latter regulation is essentially identical to the new of Regulation No. 2100/94, Art. 73, as amended by Regulation No. 2506/95).

relevant Office.[3] An appeal may be brought before the Court of Justice against decisions of a board of appeal.[4]

Article 63 of Regulation No. 40/94 and the new Article 73 of Regulation No. 2100/94 provide that an action may be brought in the Court of First Instance to annul or alter a contested decision. This constitutes a special form of action for annulment whereby the Court has, in addition to the power to annul a decision of a board of appeal, a form of unlimited jurisdiction to alter the board's decision and replace it with its own.

II. Identity of the Parties

A. The defendant

18–003 As has already been mentioned, an appeal will lie to the Court of First Instance against decisions of the Offices' boards of appeal. Nevertheless, the boards of appeal of these Community agencies are not the defendants in proceedings before the Court, rather the Offices themselves. It should be noted in this connection that although the members of the boards of appeal are independent and not bound by any instructions, they constitute an integral part of the relevant Office and hence a decision of a board of appeal is ascribed to the Office to which it belongs in the course of proceedings before the Court.[5]

---

[3] Under Regulation No. 40/94, Art. 57, an appeal will lie from decisions of the examiners (Art. 126 empowers the examiners to take decisions in relation to an application for registration of a Community trade mark (covered by, *inter alia*, Arts 36, 37, 38 and 66)), the Opposition Divisions (under Art. 127 those divisions are responsible for taking decisions on an opposition to an application to register a Community trade mark), the Administration of Trade Marks and Legal Division (responsible for decisions outwith the competence of an examiner, an opposition division or a cancellation division (Article 128)) and the cancellation divisions (responsible for taking decisions in relation to an application for the revocation or declaration of invalidity of a Community trade mark (Art. 129)).

Under Regulation No. 2100/94, Art. 67, appeals will lie against a declaration that a Community plant variety right is null and void (Art. 20), the cancellation of such a right (Art. 21), decisions concerning objections lodged against the grant of such a right (Art. 59), the refusal of applications for a right (Art. 62), the grant of a Community plant variety right (Art. 62), the approval and amendment of a variety denomination (Arts 63 and 66), decisions concerning the fees payable under Art. 83 and costs under Art. 85, the registration and deregistration of particulars in the registers under Art. 87 and public inspection under Art. 88. The Office may grant compulsory exploitation rights under Art. 29 and may in certain circumstances grant exploitation rights to a person not being the holder of the relevant plant variety right under Art. 100(2). Decisions under Art. 29 and 100(2) may also be challenged before the boards of appeal or be the subject of a direct appeal to the Court of First Instance under Art. 74(1).

[4] According to Regulation No. 40/94, Preamble, Recital 13, the Court of First Instance is to exercise at first instance the jurisdiction conferred on the Court of Justice by the Regulation. The same is provided in Regulation No. 2506/95, Preamble, Recital 4 (see n. 2, above) as regards appeals brought against the Community Plant Variety Office. Consequently, from this point on reference will be made to the Court of First Instance where the two regulations speak of the Court of Justice.

[5] See CFI Rules of Procedure, Art. 130(1) under which "[s]ubject to the special provisions of this Title the provisions of these Rules of Procedure shall apply to proceedings brought against the Office for Harmonization in the Internal Market (Trade Marks and Designs) and against the Community Plant Variety Office" and Art. 133(2), which provides that the application initiating the proceedings is to be served on the Office "as defendant".

B. The applicant

18–004 Article 63(4) of Regulation No. 40/94 and the new Article 73(4) of Regulation No. 2100/94 provide that an action may be brought by any party to proceedings before the board of appeal adversely affected by its decision.[6] The other parties to the proceedings before the board of appeal may participate, as interveners, in the proceedings before the Court of First Instance and have the same procedural rights as the main parties.[7] As a result, they may apply for a form of order and put forward pleas in law independently of those applied for and put forward by the main parties.

III. Special Characteristics

A. Pleas in law

18–005 In an action for annulment or alteration brought under Regulation No. 40/94 (Article 63(2)) or Regulation No. 2100/94 (new Article 73(2)), an action may be brought on grounds of lack of competence, infringement of an essential procedural requirement, infringement of the Treaty, of the relevant regulation or of any rule of law relating to their application or misuse of power. These grounds approximate to the pleas which may be raised in an action for annulment brought under Article 230 (*ex Article 173*) of the E.C. Treaty.[8]

B. Time-limits

18–006 Under both regulations an action has to be brought within two months of the date of notification of the decision of the board of appeal (Regulation No. 40/94, Article 63(5); Regulation No. 2100/94, as amended, Article 73(5)).

IV. Consequences

18–007 If the Court of First Instance upholds the claim, it may annul or alter the decision of the board of appeal. Annulment has the same characteristics as a declaration of nullity made pursuant to Article 230 (*ex Article 173*) of the E.C. Treaty. If the Court alters the board's decision, the Court's decision replaces that of the board. In either case, the Office is required to take the necessary steps under Article 63(6) of Regulation No. 40/94 or the new Article 73(6) of Regulation No. 2100/94, as the case may be, to comply with the Court's judgment.

If the appeal is dismissed, the board's decision stands.

An appeal will lie against the decision of the Court of First Instance to the Court of Justice.[9]

---

6 The identity of parties to proceedings before a board of appeal depends on the type of decision against which an appeal has been brought before the board. Regulation No. 40/94, Art. 58, provides that any party to proceedings adversely affected by a decision may appeal to a board. Any other parties to the proceedings are parties to the appeal by operation of law.

7 CFI Rules of Procedure, Art. 134(1) and (2). See para. 22–099, below.

8 See paras 7–091 *et seq.*, above.

9 See paras, 15–001 *et seq.*, above.

CHAPTER 19

JURISDICTION OF THE COURT OF JUSTICE UNDER CONVENTIONS CONCLUDED BY THE MEMBER STATES

I. SUBJECT-MATTER

A. GENERAL

19–001 Both the E.C. Treaty and the E.U. Treaty expressly empower the Member States to conclude agreements with each other in certain areas. In the resulting conventions or in protocols annexed thereto, additional jurisdiction is often conferred on the Court of Justice. That jurisdiction is generally a special power to give preliminary rulings not based on Article 234 (*ex Article 177*) of the E.C. Treaty. Conventions which the Member States have concluded in the area of co-operation in the field of justice and home affairs (*i.e.* the original "third pillar" of the Union) often provide for direct recourse to be made to the Court in order to resolve disputes relating to the application or interpretation of the relevant convention which arise as between Member States or one or more Member States and the Commission.

B. WHAT CONVENTIONS ARE INVOLVED?

19–002 Article 293 (*ex Article 220*) of the E.C. Treaty requires Member States, as far as is necessary, to enter into negotiations with each other with a view to removing barriers in certain areas to the sound functioning of the common market. It was pursuant to that provision that the Convention of September 27, 1968 on Jurisdiction and the Enforcement of Judgments in Civil and Commercial Matters came about ("the Brussels Convention").[1] Since the

[1] On September 16, 1988 the Member States of the Community concluded with the member countries of the European Free Trade Association (EFTA) the Lugano Convention on Jurisdiction and the Enforcement of Judgments in Civil and Commercial Matters, which contains rules on jurisdiction and enforcement similar to those of the Brussels Convention ([1988] O.J. L319/9). However, the Court of Justice has no power to interpret that Convention. Yet the contracting parties did sign a Protocol setting up an information-exchange system providing for the centralisation of judgments of the Court of Justice and courts of last instance in the contracting parties with a view to uniform interpretation. See Jung, "The Brussels and Lugano Conventions: The European Court's Jurisdiction; its Procedures and Methods" (1992) Civil Justice Quarterly 38–51; Tebbens, Kennedy, Kohler (eds), *Civil Jurisdiction and Judgments in Europe*, London, Butterworths, 1992.

Brussels Convention contributes towards the attainment of the common market, it is essential that, just like Community law in the narrow sense,[2] it is applied uniformly in the Member States. To that end, the Protocol of June 3, 1971 confers on the Court of Justice jurisdiction to interpret the Brussels Convention by preliminary ruling at the request of certain national courts.[3]

Furthermore, the Member States have concluded the Convention of June 19–0
19, 1980 on the Law Applicable to Contractual Obligations ("the Rome Convention"), even though this subject is not specifically mentioned in Article 293 (*ex Article 220*) of the E.C. Treaty. Yet it does link up with the aims underlying that provision of the Treaty. It is most probably for that reason that the First Protocol of December 19, 1988 confers on the Court of Justice jurisdiction to interpret the Rome Convention by preliminary ruling at the request of certain national courts.[4]

Even before the Treaty of Amsterdam entered into effect, the Member 19–0
States concluded conventions under the first and third sub-subparagraphs of Article K.3(2)(c) of the E.U. Treaty which conferred on the Court of Justice, in some cases by separate protocols, jurisdiction not based on Article 234 (*ex Article 177*) of the E.C. Treaty to interpret them and sometimes to rule on disputes between Member States or between one or more Member States and the Commission regarding their application and interpretation in a direct action brought by a Member State or the Commission.[5]

---

[2] The Court of Justice has observed that the Brussels Convention was concluded on the basis of the EEC Treaty, Art. 220 (*now Article 293*) 4th indent, whose purpose is to facilitate the working of the common market through the adoption of rules of jurisdiction and through the elimination, as far as possible, of difficulties concerning the enforcement of judgments in the territory of the contracting states. It is for these reasons that the provisions of the Brussels Convention, and also the national provisions to which the Convention refers are linked to the E.C. Treaty: Case C–398/92 *Mund & Fester* [1994] E.C.R. I–467 at I–478, paras 11, 12, ECJ.

[3] Protocol on the interpretation by the Court of Justice of the Convention of September 27, 1968 on Jurisdiction and the Enforcement of Judgments in Civil and Commercial Matters, which entered into force on September 1, 1975. The original Protocol has been adjusted each time new Member States have acceded to the Community (a consolidated version of the Brussels Convention and the Protocol is to be found in [1998] O.J. C27/1–33, which lists the publication references of the successive official versions of the Convention and the Protocol). The Protocol may be found in the Civil Jurisdiction and Judgments Act 1982, Sched. 2.

[4] The First Protocol has not yet entered into effect. For a consolidated version of the Rome Convention and the First Protocol (incorporating all changes consequential upon the accession of new Member States), see [1998] O.J. C27/34–49.

[5] The following conventions have been concluded pursuant to the former E.U. Treaty, Art. K.3(2)(c):

- Convention on Simplified Extradition Procedures between the Member States of the European Union, drawn up by Council Act of March 10, 1995 ([1995] O.J. C78/1; no jurisdiction conferred on the Court of Justice);
- Convention Relating to Extradition between the Member States of the European Union, drawn up by Council Act of September 27, 1996 ([1996] O.J. C313/11). This Convention does not confer jurisdiction on the Court of Justice, but in a declaration appended to the Convention on the follow-up thereto the Council states that it will consider, one year after the entry into force of the Convention, whether jurisdiction should be given to the Court of Justice;
- Convention on the Establishment of a European Police Office (Europol Convention),

II. Survey of the Court's Powers

A. Jurisdiction to give preliminary rulings

-005 Different rules govern the jurisdiction to give preliminary rulings on the interpretation of these conventions and protocols. The differences have to do with limiting the number of courts which are entitled to make references to the Court of Justice.

-006 Under the Protocols annexed to the Brussels and Rome Conventions, only a limited number of courts are entitled to make a reference to the Court of Justice for a preliminary ruling. Only those mentioned in Article 2(1) of the Protocol of June 3, 1971 and in Article 2(a) of the First Protocol of December 19, 1988—for the United Kingdom, the House of Lords and, for Ireland, the Supreme Court—and appellate courts may request a

---

drawn up by Council Act of July 26, 1995 ([1995] O.J. C361/1; as far as dispute settlement is concerned, see the Declaration, Art. 40, made by all the Member States with the exception of the United Kingdom, [1995] O.J. C316/32). By Council Act of July 23, 1996 drawn up on the basis of the former E.U. Treaty, Art. K.3, a Protocol was added on the interpretation, by way of preliminary rulings, by the Court of Justice of the European Communities of the Convention on the Establishment of a European Police Office ([1996] O.J. C299/1). It was signed on July 24, 1996. By Council Act of June 19, 1997, a protocol was drawn up on the privileges and immunities of Europol, the members of its organs, the deputy directors and employees of Europol pursuant to the former E.U. Treaty Art. K.3, and Article 41(3) of the Europol Convention ([1997] O.J. C221 1; for dispute settlement, see Art. 13). The Europol Convention entered into force on October 1, 1998;

- Convention on the Use of Information Technology for Customs Purposes, drawn up by Council Act of July 26, 1995 ([1995] O.J. C316/33; for the powers of the Court of Justice, see Art. 27). By Council Act of November 29, 1996, a Protocol, drawn up on the basis of the former E.U. Treaty, Art. K.3, was annexed to the Convention on the Interpretation, by way of preliminary rulings, by the Court of Justice of the European Communities of the Convention on the Use of Information Technology for Customs Purposes ([1997] O.J. C151/15);
- Convention on the Protection of the European Communities' Financial Interests, drawn up by Council Act of July 26, 1995 ([1995] O.J. C316/48; for the jurisdiction of the Court of Justice, see Art. 8). By Council Act of September 27, 1996, a First Protocol was adopted to that convention ([1996] O.J. C313/1; for the jurisdiction of the Court of Justice, see Art. 8). Subsequently, by Council Act of November, 29, 1996, a Protocol was drawn up, on the basis of the former E.U. Treaty, Art. K.3, on the interpretation by way of preliminary rulings, by the Court of Justice of the European Communities of the Convention on the Protection of the European Communities' Financial Interests (Under Art. 2(1) the Court's powers extend to interpreting both the Convention and the First Protocol) ([1997] O.J. C151/1). By Council Act of June 19, 1997, a Second Protocol was annexed to the Convention ([1997] O.J. C221/11; for the jurisdiction of the Court of Justice, see Arts. 13, 14 and 15);
- Convention on the Fight against Corruption Involving Officials of the European Communities or Officials of Member States of the European Union, drawn up by Council Act of May 26, 1997 ([1997] O.J. C195/1; for the jurisdiction of the Court of Justice, see Art. 12);
- Convention on the Service in the Member States of the European Union of Judicial and Extrajudicial Documents in Civil or Commercial Matters, drawn up by Council Act of May 26, 1997 ([1997] O.J. C261/1; for the interpretative jurisdiction of the Court of Justice, see Art. 17). Also by Council Act of May 26, 1997, a Protocol was drawn up on the interpretation, by the Court of Justice of the European Communities of the Convention on the Service in the Member States of the European Union of Judicial and Extrajudicial Documents in Civil or Commercial matters ([1997] O.J. C261/17, including explanatory reports at 26 and 38);

ruling.[6] A similar restriction is contained in Article 2(1)(a) (the "highest courts"—the House of Lords in the United Kingdom; the Supreme Court in the case of Ireland) and Article 2(1)(b) (courts sitting in an appellate capacity) of the Protocol of May 26, 1997 (service of judicial and extrajudicial documents in civil or commercial matters) and Article 2(2)(a) (the "highest courts"—the Judicial Committee of the House of Lords in the United Kingdom; the Supreme Court in the case of Ireland) and Article 2(2)(b) (courts sitting in an appellate capacity) of the Protocol of May 28, 1998 (jurisdiction and the recognition and enforcement of judgments in matrimonial matters). This restriction was introduced out of concern lest too many questions might be referred in all sorts of private-law disputes. In addition, it was thought that no more heed should be given to differences of interpretation of these Conventions by inferior courts in applying them than was paid to differences as between decided cases of lower courts in a given Member State. Lastly, there was a concern that the Court of Justice should only be required to give preliminary rulings where it was "fully informed", so as to allow stable case law to develop.[7]

Article 2(1) of the Protocol of May 28, 1998 is novel, in comparison with **19–**
the 1971, 1988 and 1997 Protocols in that it allows each Member State to restrict by declaration the courts empowered to make references for preliminary rulings to the highest courts. The reason for this is that judgments on matters covered by the Convention (divorce, legal separation, marriage annulment, parental responsibility for children of a marriage) need to be given as promptly as possible in order not to prejudice the interests of individuals.[8]

A court which, under Article 37 of the Brussels Convention, has to **19–**
decide on an appeal against a decision authorising enforcement of a judicial decision given in another Member State,[9] may under Article 2(3) of the

---

— Convention on Mutual Assistance and Co-operation between Customs Administrations, drawn up by Council Act of December 18, 1997 ([1998] O.J. C24/1; with an explanatory report in [1998] O.J. C189/1; for the jurisdiction of the Court of Justice, see Art. 26);

— Convention on Jurisdiction and the Recognition and Enforcement of Judgments in Matrimonial Matters, drawn up by Council Act of May 28, 1998 ([1998] O.J. C221/1; for the interpretative jurisdiction of the Court of Justice, see Art. 45). A Protocol on the interpretation, by the Court of Justice of the European Communities of the Convention on Jurisdiction and the Recognition and Enforcement of Judgments in Matrimonial Matters was appended to this Convention by Council Act of the same date ([1998] O.J. C221/19, with explanatory reports at 27 and 65);

— Convention on Driving Disqualifications, drawn up by Council Act of June 17, 1998 ([1998] O.J. C216/1; for the jurisdiction of the Court of Justice, see Art. 14).

[6] (Order of November 9, 1983), Case 80/83 *Habourdin v. Italocremona* [1983] E.C.R. 3639, ECJ; (Order of March 18, 1984), Case 56/84 *Von Gallera v. Maître* [1984] E.C.R. 1769, ECJ.

[7] See the Jenard Report (O.J. 1979 C 59, p. 68). But see Ras, "Een nieuwe taak voor het Hof van Justitie E.G." (1975) N.J.B. 1117 at 1180.

[8] Explanatory report ([1998] O.J. C221/4, 66, point 4).

[9] Brussels Convention, Art. 37, sets out the courts in which an appeal may be brought against a decision authorising enforcement of a judgment given in another Member State (in the United Kingdom, the High Court and the magistrates' court (in the case of a maintenance judgment)). The court granting an enforcement order does so in the absence of the person against whom enforcement is sought (Brussels Convention, Art. 34).

Protocol of June 3, 1971 also refer questions to the Court of Justice for a preliminary ruling. A court which, pursuant to Article 40 of the Brussels Convention, has to give judgment on an appeal against a refusal to grant an application for enforcement may make a reference for a preliminary ruling under the general provision contained in Article 2(2) of the Protocol of June 3, 1971.[10]

-009 The aforementioned four Protocols also provide that the "competent authority of a Contracting State" may request the Court of Justice to give a ruling on a question of interpretation of the relevant Convention if judgments given by courts of that state conflict with the interpretation given either by the Court of Justice or in a judgment of one of the courts of a contracting state which is entitled to make references for preliminary rulings.[11] The procurators-general of the courts of cassation of the contracting states constitute a competent authority, but the contracting states may designate any other authority.[12] This means of obtaining a ruling from the Court of Justice after final judgment has been given is inspired by the appeal in cassation in the interests of the law. It affords an opportunity of limiting the effects of an anomalous application of the Convention by means of an interpretation from the Court of Justice which is binding for the future.[13] To date, no "competent authority" has referred such a question.

-010 The highest courts mentioned in Article 2(1) of the Protocol of June 3, 1971, Article 2(1)(a) of the Protocol of May 26, 1997 and Article 3(1) of the Protocol of May 28, 1998 are under an obligation to seek a ruling on interpretation where they consider that a decision on the question is necessary to enable them to give judgment.[14] The latter requirement refers to their assessment of the relevance of possible preliminary questions which all courts must carry out in any event, as under Article 234 (*ex Article 177*) of the E.C. Treaty.[15]

[10] Case 178/83 *Firma P. v. Firma K.* [1984] E.C.R. 3033. ECJ.

[11] Protocol of June 3, 1971, Art. 4; First Protocol of December 19, 1988, Art. 3; Protocol of May 26, 1997, Art. 4; Protocol of May 28, 1998, Art. 6.

[12] Protocol of June 3, 1971, Art. 4(3); First Protocol of December 19, 1988, Art. 3(3); Protocol of May 26, 1997, Art. 4(3); Protocol of May 28, 1998, Art. 6(3).

[13] The interpretation given by the Court of Justice following such a request does not affect the judgments which give rise to the request for interpretation (Protocol of June 3, 1971, Art. 4(2); First Protocol of December 19, 1988, Art. 3(2); Protocol of May 26, 1997, Art. 4(2); Protocol of May 28, 1998, Art. 6(2)).

[14] See Protocol of June 3, 1971, Art. 3(1); Protocol of May 26, 1997, Art. 3(1); and Protocol of May 28, 1998, Art. 4(1). The only Protocol not to put the highest courts under an obligation to request a preliminary ruling is that of December 19, 1988. For a discussion of what is meant by "necessary" in this context, see Vlas, "The Protocol on Interpretation of the EEC Convention on Jurisdiction and Enforcement of Judgments: Over Ten Years in Legal Practice (1975–1985)" (1986) N.I.L.R. 84–98. *Cf.* Case 148/84 *Deutsche Genossenschaftsbank v. Brasserie du Pêcheur* [1985] E.C.R. 1981 at 1990, para. 9, ECJ.

[15] See para. 2–028, above.

Member States have to accept the Court's jurisdiction to give preliminary rulings pursuant to other Conventions[16] and Protocols[17] drawn up on the basis of the former Article K.3 of the E.U. Treaty[18] by means of a declaration, either that any national court or tribunal against whose decisions there is no judicial remedy under national law may make a reference for a preliminary ruling if the court or tribunal in question considers it to be necessary in order to give judgment or that any national court or tribunal may request a preliminary ruling.[19] Courts or tribunals 19–0

---

[16] Convention of May 26, 1997, Art. 12(3)(5), on the fight against corruption involving officials of the European Communities or officials of Member States of the European Union; Convention of December 18, 1997, Art. 26(3)–(8), on mutual assistance and co-operation between customs administrations (Art. 26(8) limits the Court's jurisdiction in precisely the same way as the E.U. Treaty, Art. 35 (*ex Art. K.7*) (5) see para. 20–002, below): the Court "shall not have jurisdiction to check the validity or proportionality of operations carried out by competent law enforcement agencies under this Convention nor to rule on the exercise of responsibilities which devolve upon Member States for maintaining law and order and for safeguarding internal security"); Convention of June 17, 1998 on Driving Disqualifications, Art. 14(2)–(4).

[17] Protocol of July 24, 1996 (Europol); Protocol of November, 29, 1996 (use of information technology for customs purposes); Protocol of November 29, 1996 (protection of the Communities' financial interests), the applicability of which was extended by the Second Protocol of June 19, 1997, Art. 13(2).

[18] See para. 19–004, above.

[19] The following Member States have declared in respect of the Protocol indicated that only national courts or tribunals against whose decisions there is no judicial remedy under national law may make a reference for a preliminary ruling (for the O.J. references of the Protocols, see n. 5, above):

- Protocol of July 24, 1996 (Europol): France and Ireland;
- Protocol of November 29, 1996 (use of information technology for customs purposes): Ireland and Portugal;
- Protocol of November 29, 1996 (protection of financial interests): France, Ireland and Portugal (a Member State may declare that a declaration made under the Protocol of November 29, 1996 does not apply to the Second Protocol of June 19, 1997; see the Second Protocol, Art. 13(3)).

The following Member States have declared that any national court or tribunal may seek a preliminary ruling from the Court of Justice (for the O.J. references of the Protocols, see n. 5, above):

- Protocol of July 24, 1996 (Europol): Austria, Belgium, Finland, Germany, Greece, Italy, Luxembourg, the Netherlands, Portugal and Sweden (as far as Sweden is concerned, see [1997] O.J. C100/1). In addition, Austria, Belgium, Germany, Greece, Italy, Luxembourg, the Netherlands and Portugal reserved the right to make provision in their national law to the effect that, where a question relating to the interpretation of the Convention or the Protocol is raised in a case pending before a national court or tribunal against whose decision there is no judicial remedy under national law, that court or tribunal will be required to refer the matter to the Court of Justice.
- Protocol of November 29, 1996 (use of information technology for customs purposes): Austria, Finland, France, Germany, Greece, the Netherlands and Sweden. In addition, Austria, Germany, Greece and the Netherlands reserved the right to make provision in their national law to the effect that, where a question relating to the interpretation of the Convention or the Protocol is raised in a case pending before a national court or tribunal against whose decision there is no judicial remedy under national law, that court or tribunal will be required to refer the matter to the Court of Justice.
- Protocol of November 29, 1996 (protection of financial interests): Austria, Finland, Germany, Greece, the Netherlands and Sweden (a Member State may declare that a declaration made under the Protocol of November 29, 1996 does not apply to the Second Protocol of June 19, 1997; see Second Protocol, Art. 13(3)). In addition, Austria, Germany, Greece and the Netherlands reserved the right to make provision in

which may request a preliminary ruling are not obliged to do so, even if they consider such a ruling to be necessary in order to give judgment.

B. Direct actions

-012 In the first place, a direct action under these Conventions may be brought in the Court of Justice in the event of a dispute between Member States on the "interpretation or application" of the Convention in question.

In an initial stage, such disputes are to be discussed by the Council with the aim of finding a settlement. If the dispute is not settled within six months, one of the parties may submit it to the Court of Justice.[20]

-013 In the second place, the Commission or one or more Member States may bring a dispute between that institution and one of more Member States on the "application" of a Convention directly before the Court of Justice if it cannot be settled through negotiation.[21]

-014 Lastly, Article 14 of the Second Protocol to the Convention on the Protection of the European Communities' Financial Interests declares the second paragraph of Article 288 (*ex Article 215*) and Article 235 (*ex Article 178*) of the E.C. Treaty to be applicable.

Article 15 of that Protocol gives the Court of First Instance (and, on appeal, the Court of Justice) jurisdiction in proceedings instituted by any natural or legal person for annulment of a decision of the Commission which is addressed to that person or of direct and individual concern to that person, or for interim measures, on the ground of infringement of Article 8

their national law to the effect that, where a question relating to the interpretation of the Convention or the First Protocol is raised in a case pending before a national court or tribunal against whose decision there is no judicial remedy under national law, that court or tribunal will be required to refer the matter to the Court of Justice.

20 Article 27(1) of the Convention on the Use of Information Technology for Customs Purposes, Art. 27(1); Convention on the Protection of the European Communities' Financial Interests, Art. 8(1); (see also First Protocol, Art. 8(1), and Second Protocol, Art. 13(1)); Convention on the Fight against Corruption Involving Officials of the European Communities or Officials of Member States of the European Union, Art. 12(1); Convention on Mutual Assistance and Co-operation between Customs Administrations, Art. 26(1); Convention on Driving Disqualifications, Art. 14(1). Europol Convention, Art. 40(2) (see n. 5, above) provides that if such disputes are not settled within six months, the Member States party to the dispute are to decide, by agreement amongst themselves, the modalities according to which they are to be settled. It appears from a declaration annexed to the Convention, on Art. 40(2) that all the Member States, with the exception of the United Kingdom, agree that in such cases they will systematically submit the dispute to the Court of Justice. For the question of the involvement or non-involvement of the Court of Justice, see Curtin and Pouw, "Samenwerking op het gebied van justitie en binnenlandse zaken in de Europese Unie: pre-Maastricht-nostalgie?" (1995) S.E.W. 579 at 591–596.

21 Convention on the Use of Information Technology for Customs Purposes, Art. 27(2); Convention on the Protection of the European Communities' Financial Interests, Art. 8(2) (see also First Protocol, Art. 8(2), and Second Protocol, Art. 13(2)); Convention on the Fight against Corruption Involving Officials of the European Communities or Officials of Member States of the European Union, Art. 12(2) (this Article restricts the bringing of disputes directly before the Court of Justice to a few Articles of the Convention and then only in so far as they concern a question of Community law or the Communities' financial interests or involve members or officials of Community institutions or bodies set up in accordance with the Treaties establishing the European Communities); Convention on Mutual Assistance and Co-operation Between Customs Administrations, Art. 26(2); Convention on Driving Disqualifications, Art. 14(1).

of the Protocol (infringement of the duty to provide a level of protection of personal data equivalent to that set out in Directive 95/46) or any rule adopted pursuant thereto or misuse of powers in connection with the exchange of information between the Member States and the Commission in connection with combating fraud, active and passive corruption and money laundering.[22]

III. Procedure before the Court

The Statute and the Rules of Procedure of the Court of Justice are applicable in so far as the relevant Convention or Protocol do not provide otherwise.[23] Consequently, the procedure applicable to requests for preliminary rulings generally applies. 19–

It is as yet unclear what procedure will apply to proceedings for resolving disputes between Member States or between Member States and the Commission on the interpretation and application of a number of Conventions concluded pursuant to the former Article K.3(2)(c) of the E.U. Treaty. In the absence of any specific provisions in the Rules of Procedure, the most likely procedure is that employed for direct actions and also employed for cases brought pursuant to an arbitration clause under Article 238 (*ex Article 181*) of the E.C. Treaty. 19–

IV. Consequences

Judgments given by the Court of Justice pursuant to the Conventions and Protocols discussed above have the same consequences as preliminary rulings generally.[24] 19–

Judgments given in direct actions probably have the same effects as judgments given pursuant to an arbitration clause. 19–

[22] Second Protocol, Art. 7(2).

[23] Protocol of June 3, 1971, Art. 5; Second Protocol, Art. 1(1), conferring on the Court of Justice of the European Communities certain powers to interpret the Convention on the Law Applicable to Contractual Obligations, opened for signature in Rome on June, 19, 1980 ([1989] O.J. L48/18); Protocol of July 24, 1996, Art. 3; two Protocols of November 29, 1996, Art. 3; Protocol of May 26, 1997, Art. 5; Protocol of May 28, 1998, Arts. 5, 7; Convention on the Fight against Corruption Involving Officials of the European Communities or Officials of Member States of the European Union, Art. 12(6); Convention on Mutual Assistance and Co-operation between Customs Administrations, Art. 26(6), (7); Convention on Driving Disqualifications, Art. 14(4).

[24] See paras. 6–031 *et seq.*, above.

CHAPTER 20

JURISDICTION OF THE COURT OF JUSTICE WITH REGARD TO POLICE AND JUDICIAL CO-OPERATION IN CRIMINAL MATTERS

Since the entry into force of the Treaty of Amsterdam, the jurisdiction of the Court of Justice extends further than the enforcement of Community law and protection against acts or failures to act of the institutions and Member States contrary to—superior—Community law. The Court now has appreciable competence in the spheres of police and judicial co-operation in criminal matters (the "third pillar", Title VI of the E.U. Treaty)[1] and closer co-operation,[2] upon which Member States so wishing may embark within the field of application of the third pillar under Article 40 (*ex Article K. 12*) of the E.U. Treaty on the conditions set forth in Articles 43 and 44 (*ex Articles K. 15 and K. 16*) of that Treaty. In pursuing such closer co-operation, Member States may make use of the institutions, procedures and mechanisms laid down in the E.U. and E.C. Treaties. **20–001**

The Court's jurisdiction in the field of police and judicial co-operation in criminal matters is provided for in Article 35 (*ex Article K. 7*) of the E.U. Treaty. It may be subdivided into three heads. **20–002**

Under Article 35(1), the Court is empowered to give preliminary rulings on the validity and interpretation of framework decisions and decisions (for these acts, see Article 34 (*ex Article K. 6*) (2)(b) and (c)), on the interpretation of Conventions established under Title VI and on the validity and interpretation of measures implementing them (for such measures, see Article 34(2)(d)).

That jurisdiction has to be expressly accepted by Member States by declaration.[3] In such declaration, the Member State may elect to allow either any court or tribunal against whose decisions there is no judicial

[1] E.U. Treaty, Art. 46 (*ex Art. L*) (b). See also 4–001, above.

[2] E.U. Treaty, Title VII (*ex Title VIa*).

[3] E.U. Treaty, Art. 35 (*ex Art. K. 7*) (2). However, irrespective as to whether a Member State has or has not accepted the Court's jurisdiction under Art. 35(1), it may submit statements of case or written observations to the Court in cases arising under that provision (see E.U. Treaty, Art. 35(4)).

remedy under national law[4] or any court or tribunal to request a preliminary ruling from the Court.[5]

Under Article 35 (*ex Article K. 7*) (5) of the E.U. Treaty, however, the Court of Justice has no jurisdiction to review the "validity or proportionality of operations carried out by the police or other law enforcement services of a Member State or the exercise of the responsibilities incumbent upon Member States with regard to the maintenance of law and order and the safeguarding of internal security".

In addition to that specific power to give preliminary rulings, the Court has jurisdiction in direct actions brought under Article 35 (*ex Article K. 7*) (6) of the E.U. Treaty to review the legality of framework decisions and decisions. This procedure resembles in some respects the action for annulment provided for in Article 230 (*ex Article 173*) of the E.C. Treaty,[6] except that an action may be brought only by a Member State or the Commission and not by any other institution or natural or legal persons. The pleas which may be raised are lack of competence, infringement of an essential procedural requirement, infringement of the E.U. Treaty or of any rule of law relating to its application and misuse of powers. An action must be brought within two months of publication of the measure challenged.

Lastly, under Article 35 (*ex Article K. 7*) (7) of the E.U. Treaty, the Court of Justice has jurisdiction to rule on any dispute between Member States regarding the interpretation or the application of acts adopted under Article 34 (*ex Article K. 6*) (2) whenever such dispute cannot be settled by the Council within six months of its being referred to that institution by one of its members. This procedure bears a resemblance to the action which a Member State may bring before the Court against another Member State under Article 227 (*ex Article 170*) of the E.C. Treaty for failure to fulfil an obligation.[7]

Article 35(7) also confers jurisdiction on the Court of Justice to "rule on any dispute between Member States and the Commission regarding the interpretation or the application of conventions established under Article 34 (*ex Article K.6*) (2)(d)" of the E.U. Treaty. This procedure resembles the action for failure to fulfil obligations which the Commission may bring against a Member State under Article 226 (*ex Article 169*) of the E.C. Treaty.[8]

---

[4] E.U. Treaty, Art. 35(3)(a).

[5] E.U. Treaty, Article 35(3)(b). Austria, Belgium, Germany, Greece and Luxembourg accepted the Court's jurisdiction on these terms when they signed the Treaty.

Austria, Belgium, Germany and Luxembourg further declared that they reserved the right to make provision in their national law to the effect that, where a question relating to the validity or interpretation of an act referred to in the E.U. Treaty, Art. 35(1) is raised in a case pending before a national court or tribunal against whose decisions there is no remedy under national law, that court or tribunal will be required to refer the matter to the Court of Justice.

The Netherlands declared that it accepted the Court's jurisdiction in principle, but was considering on what terms it would do so.

[6] See paras 7–001 *et seq.*, above.

[7] See para. 5–027, above.

[8] See paras 5–022 *et seq.*, above

The jurisdiction of the Court of Justice in regard to closer co-operation between Member States wishing to engage in it within the area of the third pillar is dealt with in Article 40 (*ex Article K. 12*) (4) of the E.U. Treaty. **20–003**

The mechanism of legal protection provided for in Article 35 (*ex Article K.7*) of the E.C. Treaty as outlined above applies in full to such closer co-operation by virtue of the first subparagraph of Article 40 (*ex Article K. 12*) (4), which provides that the provisions of Articles 29 to 41 (*ex Articles K. 1 to K. 13*), including therefore Article 35, are to apply to closer co-operation.

Under the second subparagraph of Article 40 (*ex Article K. 12*) (4) of the E.U. Treaty, however, the Court of Justice has all its powers under the E.C. Treaty in order to enforce the conditions which have to be respected in order to achieve the closer co-operation as laid down in Article 40(1) to (3), which also refer to the obligation to comply with Articles 43 and 44 (*ex Articles K. 15 and K. 16*).[9]

Article 46 (*ex Article L*) (d) of the E.U. Treaty likewise provides that, in so far as the Court of Justice has jurisdiction under the E.U. Treaty, actions of the institutions may be reviewed in the light of the fundamental rights referred to in Article 6 (*ex Article F*) (2) of the E.U. Treaty. **20–004**

[9] Within the sphere of application of the E.C. Treaty, Member States have a similar possibility to establish closer co-operation under the E.C. Treaty, Art. 11 (*ex Art. 5a*). However, it was unnecessary to make specific reference to judicial protection in connection with that closer co-operation, since, as part of Community law, Art. 11 may be judicially enforced.

Part V
PROCEDURE BEFORE THE COURT OF JUSTICE AND THE COURT OF FIRST INSTANCE

CHAPTER 21

INTRODUCTION

The different types of jurisdiction of the Court of Justice and the Court of First Instance give rise to three sorts of procedures: the procedure in the case of direct actions, which is followed where an applicant brings a case before the Court of Justice or the Court of First Instance against a named defendant (irrespective of the type of case); the procedure in the case of a reference for a preliminary ruling, and lastly the procedure in the case of an appeal against a decision of the Court of First Instance. **21–001**

The procedure is governed by the ECSC, E.C. and EAEC Statutes of the Court of Justice, whose provisions have the same legal force as Treaty articles, even though, ever since the Single European Act entered into force on July 1, 1987, the procedural rules contained therein may be amended by the Council, acting unanimously at the request of the Court of Justice and after consulting the Commission and the European Parliament.[1] The rules set out in the Statutes are expanded upon in the Rules of Procedure of the Court of Justice and the Court of First Instance, which are adopted by the Court of Justice and the Court of First Instance in agreement with the Court of Justice, respectively, and approved by the Council by unanimous vote.[2] On top of this, there are also the Supplementary Rules[3] and the Instructions to the Registrar.[4]

---

[1] ECSC Treaty, Art. 45, para. 2; E.C. Treaty, Art. 245 (*ex Article 188*), para. 2; EAEC Treaty, Art. 160, para. 2. This Part refers in principle only to the E.C. Statute.

[2] Court of Justice: see ECSC Statute, Art. 55; E.C. Treaty, Art. 245 (*ex Article 188*), para. 3; EAEC Treaty, Art. 160, para. 3. Court of First Instance: see ECSC Treaty, Art. 32d(4); E.C. Treaty, Art. 225 (*ex Art. 168a*)(4); EAEC Treaty, Art. 140a(4). See also the Rules of Procedure of June 19, 1991 (Court of Justice), [1991] O.J. L176/7, codified version in [1999] O.J. C65/1, and of May 2, 1991 (Court of First Instance), [1991] O.J. L136/1, and L317/34 (corrigenda), as amended by [1999] O.J. L135/92, and Christianos and Picod, "Les modifications récentes du règlement de procédure de la Cour de justice des Communautés européennes" (1991) Rec. Dalloz, Chronique 273–282; Hubeau, "Changements des règles de procédure devant les juridictions communautaires de Luxembourg" (1991) C.D.E. 499–529; Poilvache, "Le règlement de procédure de la Cour de justice des Communautés européennes après les modifications du 15 mai 1991" (1991) J.T. 337–340. For a brief article on the working methods of the Court of Justice which is well worth reading, see Edward, "How the Court of Justice Works" (1995) E.L.Rev. 539–558.

[4] Done at Luxembourg on December 4, 1974 ([1974] O.J. L350/33), last amended on October 3, 1986 ([1986] O.J. C286/4). The CFI Instructions to the Registrar were done at Luxembourg on March 3, 1994 ([1994] O.J. L78/32).

Chapter 22

PROCEDURE IN THE CASE OF DIRECT ACTIONS

The procedure in the case of direct actions consists of two parts, the written procedure and the oral procedure.[1] The case closes with a judicial decision (judgment or order), unless the parties discontinue the proceedings, the applicant withdraws its claims or the Court of Justice or the Court of First Instance, as the case may be, decides that there is no need to proceed to judgment. Judgments of either court may be contested by means of exceptional review procedures. Furthermore, appeals may be brought against decisions of the Court of First Instance.[2] Lastly, parties may apply to the Court of Justice or the Court of First Instance for interpretation of a judgment, rectification of clerical mistakes or rectification of an omission to give a decision. **22–001**

I. The Written Procedure

The purpose of the written procedure is to define the subject-matter of the action and to put before the Court of Justice or the Court of First Instance all the claims of the parties.[3] **22–002**

A. The application

1. Lodging an application

A case is brought before the Court of Justice or the Court of First Instance by addressing an application to the Registrar.[4] **22–003**

The application may be handed in to the registry or sent by post. An application may not be lodged by fax because the registry does not then receive the original.[5] The original, accompanied by all annexes referred to **22–004**

---

[1] E.C. Statute, Art. 18.

[2] See para. 15–012, above.

[3] Advice for lawyers and agents regarding the written procedure before the Court of First Instance drawn up by the Registrar pursuant to the Instructions to the Registrar of March 3, 1994, Art. 18(2) ([1994] O.J. C120/16).

[4] E.C. Statute, Art. 19, para. 1.

[5] (Order of May 15, 1991), Case C–122/90 *Emsland-Stärke v. Commission*, ECJ (not reported in the E.C.R.).

therein, must be lodged together with five copies for the Court and a copy for every other party to the proceedings. Copies must be certified by the party lodging them (in this case the applicant).[6]

22–005 The original of the application must be signed by the agent or lawyer representing the applicant.[7] If it is not so signed, it will not be registered by the Registrar[8] and will be returned to the applicant.[9] The obligation for individuals to have each pleading signed by a lawyer is designed to ensure that what is submitted to the Court of Justice or the Court of First Instance consists of only legal opinions and explanations of fact which are considered by a lawyer to be fit to be put forward.[10] A pleading which was drafted by the party himself and merely formally signed by his lawyer may be regarded, in the light of all the circumstances, as being an inadmissible pleading.[11]

22–006 The application must be dated, but for the purposes of the reckoning of time-limits for taking steps in proceedings, only the date of lodgment at the registry is taken into account (*i.e.* the date on which the application arrives at the registry).[12]

2. Content

22–007 The identity of the parties, the subject-matter of the proceedings and the pleas in law adduced are determined by the application.[13] In the course of the procedure, the application may not, or only exceptionally, be modified in these respects.

22–008 The application must state—

— the name and address of the applicant;

---

[6] ECJ Rules of Procedure, Art. 37(1); CFI Rules of Procedure, Art. 43(1).

[7] E.C. Statute, Art. 17, para. 2. See also ECJ Rules of Procedure, Art. 37(1); CFI Rules of Procedure, Art. 43(1). See also para. 22–185, below.

[8] ECJ Rules of Procedure, Art. 16, and the CFI Rules of Procedure, Art. 24, require the respective Registrars to keep a register in which all pleadings and supporting documents have to be entered.

[9] Joined Cases 220 and 221/78 *ALA and ALFER v. Commission* [1979] E.C.R. 1693 at 1697, paras 3–5, ECJ; (Order of November 29, 1993), Case T–56/92 *Koelman v. Commission* [1993] E.C.R. II–1267 at II–1270, para. 1, CFI.

[10] This suggestion was put forward by Advocate General K. Roemer in Case 108/63 *Merlini v. High Authority* [1965] E.C.R. 1 at 16, ECJ.

[11] Judgment in *Merlini v. High Authority* (cited in n. 10, above), at 9. The Court of Justice seems to have gone further than its Advocate General, who considered the merely formal signature of a pleading by a lawyer only as "negligence by the lawyer in his conduct of the proceedings" which might perhaps be considered incompatible with the dignity of the Court (ECJ Rules of Procedure, Art. 35(1); CFI Rules of Procedure, Art. 41(1)). All the same, this precedent should be approached with some caution given that the Court of Justice held that the pleading drafted by the applicant itself, which the lawyer had signed and lodged as the reply, should not only be rejected as being in breach of the ECSC Statute, Art. 20, and the ECJ Rules of Procedure, Art. 37, but also because it "rais[ed] fresh submissions and arguments" (*ibid.*).

[12] ECJ Rules of Procedure, Art. 37(3); CFI Rules of Procedure, Art. 43(3).

[13] ECJ Rules of Procedure, Art. 37, and the CFI Rules of Procedure, Art. 43, set out general conditions with which every pleading must comply. For the Court of First Instance's *desiderata* as to the structure and layout of the application, see *Advice for lawyers and agents* (cited in n. 3, above).

— the designation of the party against whom the application is made;

— the subject-matter of the proceedings and a summary of the pleas in law on which the application is based;

— the form of order sought by the applicant;

— where appropriate, the nature of any evidence offered in support.[14]

(1) Name and address of the applicant

This requirement raises few problems. Nevertheless, the Court of First Instance was once faced with the question whether the applicant's details could be altered at the request of the defendant. The latter contended that the partnership which had brought the action had no capacity to bring proceedings and moved that the Court should designate the two sole partners as applicants. The Court joined the partners as applicants after finding that they had signed the authority of the lawyer acting in the case.[15] **22–009**

An application may be lodged on behalf of several parties,[16] provided that it has the same subject-matter and raises the same pleas in law as regards each of them.[17] An applicant's successors are entitled to continue proceedings started by the deceased.[18] A legal person resulting from the merger of legal persons who have brought proceedings before the Court of First Instance—or an appeal before the Court of Justice—may continue the proceedings where that person has acquired the rights and obligations of the original applicants/appellants.[19]

The applicant should have an address for service in Luxembourg at which all pleadings may be served. To this end, the application must state the name of the person who is authorised and has expressed willingness to accept all service.[20] **22–010**

If these requirements are not satisfied, all service on the applicant for the purpose of the proceedings will be effected by registered letter addressed to the agent or lawyer of the party. Service is then deemed to be duly effected by the lodging of the registered letter at the post office in Luxembourg.[21] Any procedural time-limits applicable start to run as from the said deemed service, which means that the entire risk of delay in the post is borne by the

---

14 ECJ Rules of Procedure, Art. 38(1); CFI Rules of Procedure, Art. 44(1).

15 (Order of March 30, 1994), Case T–482/93 *Martin Weber v. Commission*, para. 4, CFI (not reported in the E.C.R.). See also Case T–174/95 *Svenska Journalistförbundet v. Council* [1998] E.C.R. II–2289 at II–2304—2306, paras 33–44, CFI.

16 The unintentional omission of the name of one of the applicants can be subsequently remedied if the defendant does not object: see Case 21/58 *Felten und Guilleaume Carlswerk Eisen- und Stahl A.G. and Another v. High Authority* [1959] E.C.R. 99 at 101, ECJ.

17 Case 13/57 *Wirtschaftsvereinigung Eisen- und Stahlindustrie and Others v. High Authority* [1957 and 1958] E.C.R. 265 at 277, ECJ.

18 Case 92/82 *Gutmann v. Commission* [1983] E.C.R. 3127, ECJ.

19 Case 294/83 *Les Verts v. European Parliament* [1986] E.C.R. 1339 at 1363, paras 15–18, ECJ.

20 ECJ Rules of Procedure, Art. 38(2), subpara. 1; CFI Rules of Procedure, Art. 44(2), subpara. 1.

21 ECJ Rules of Procedure, Art. 38(2), subpara. 2; CFI Rules of Procedure, Art. 44(2), subpara. 2.

applicant in the event that he has neglected to provide a more reliable address for service in Luxembourg. In this context, it would even be hard to argue that a postal strike constitutes *force majeure*.

The former, stricter sanction of holding the application to be inadmissible has been replaced by this rule.[22]

(2) Designation of the party against whom the application is made

22–011 The requirement that the application state the name of the party against whom it is made is satisfied if it is sufficiently clear from the application as a whole against whom the action is being brought. The omission of the defendant's name by an oversight does not necessarily mean that the application is inadmissible, provided that the rights of the defence are not impaired.[23] It is sufficient for the judgment to designate the defendant correctly.[24] The defendant's identity may also emerge from the contested act. However, it is not possible to extend the application to include a defendant who is not designated in the application and whose identity does not emerge therefrom.[25]

22–012 Actions relating to disputes between "the Community" and its servants[26] must be brought against the institution in which the applicant is or was employed, in which his or her predecessor was employed or where he or she took part in a recruitment procedure.[27] As regards the non-contractual liability of "the Community",[28] actions for damages must be brought against the institution whose conduct gave rise to the alleged liability.[29]

(3) Subject-matter of the proceedings and summary of the pleas in law on which the application is based

22–013 The application must state the subject-matter of the proceedings. This means that both its purpose and, where appropriate, the act against which the proceedings are brought must be specified. In addition, the application must contain a summary of the pleas in fact and law on which the application is based.

---

[22] (Order of January 29, 1986), Case 297/84 *Sahinler v. Commission* [1986] E.C.R. 443, ECJ.

[23] (Order of July 3, 1986), Case 85/86 *Commission v. Board of Governors of the EIB* [1986] E.C.R. 2215, ECJ (the application, which stated that the defendant was the "European Investment Bank" instead of the "Board of Governors of the European Investment Bank", was declared admissible on the ground that it appeared from that pleading that the action brought under the E[E]C Treaty, Art. 180 (*now Art. 237*) (b), was directed against the EIB's Board of Governors).

[24] Opinion of Advocate General G. Reischl in Case 44/76 *Eier-Kontor v. Council and Commission* [1977] E.C.R. 393 at 413, ECJ.

[25] (Order of November 10, 1977), Case 90/77 *Hellmut Stimming KG v. Commission* [1977] E.C.R. 2113, ECJ.

[26] E.C. Treaty, Art. 236 (*ex Art. 179*).

[27] See, *e.g.* Case 18/63 *Wallast (neé Schmitz) v. EEC* [1964] E.C.R. 85 at 96, ECJ; Case 27/63 *Raponi v. Commission* [1964] E.C.R. 129 at 135–136, ECJ; Joined Cases 79 and 82/63 *Reynier and Another v. Commission* [1964] E.C.R. 259 at 265, ECJ; Case T–497/93 *Hogan v. Court of Justice* [1995] E.C.R. II–703 at II–714, para. 31, CFI. See also para. 16–012 *et seq*, above.

[28] E.C. Treaty, Art. 288 (*ex Art. 215*), para. 2.

[29] See para. 11–012, above.

22–014 The Court of Justice and the Court of First Instance require the subject-matter of the proceedings and the pleas raised to be stated clearly and precisely in order that the defendant may prepare its defence and the Court give judgment without having to have further particulars.[30] In order to secure legal certainty and the sound administration of justice, the essential facts and law on which the application is based must be set out—at least summarily—in the text of the application itself in a coherent and comprehensible manner.[31] If the application fails to provide details of the underlying facts and circumstances, it will be inadmissible on the ground that the Court is unable to rule on it.[32] The text of the application may be further elucidated by references to passages in documents appended to it, but a general reference to such documents cannot constitute a statement of the essential facts and law on which the action is based.[33] However, information may not be provided at the hearing in order to fill gaps in the application.[34] The degree of precision required of an application varies from case to case.[35] The Court of Justice and the Court of First Instance may not go so far in specifying the subject-matter of the application as to impair the rights of the defence or of interested third parties.[36]

22–015 The Court is bound by the subject-matter of the case as stated in the application.[37] A dispute between the applicant and the defendant about the demarcation of the subject-matter of the litigation will not have any bearing on the admissibility of the application so long as the Court is able to define the subject-matter of the action precisely on the basis of the application.[38]

30 Case 281/82 *Unifrex v. Council and Commission* [1984] E.C.R. 1969 at 1983, para. 15, ECJ; Case T–21/90 *Generlich v. Commission* [1991] E.C.R. II–1323 at II–1335—1336, paras 31, 32, CFI; (Order of April 28, 1993), Case T–85/92 *De Hoe v. Commission* [1993] E.C.R. II–523 at II–531—532, para. 20, CFI; upheld by (Order of March 7, 1994), Case C–338/93P *De Hoe v. Commission*, [1994] E.C.R. I–819 at I–830, para. 29, ECJ; (Order of November 29, 1993), Case T–56/92 *Koelman* v. *Commission* [1993] E.C.R. II–1267 at II–1276, para. 21, CFI; Case T–575/93 *Koelman v. Commission* [1996] E.C.R. II–1 at II–16, para. 33, CFI; Case T–84/96 *Cipeke v. Commission* [1997] E.C.R. II–2081 at II–2090, paras 30, 31, CFI. For an action for damages, see (Order of May 14, 1998), Case T–262/97 *Goldstein v. Commission* [1998] E.C.R. II–2175 at II–2185—2188, paras 19–30, CFI.

31 (Order of March 26, 1992), Case T–35/92TO2 *Buggenhout and Others*, paras 16–17, CFI (not reported in the E.C.R.).

32 Case C–52/90 *Commission v. Denmark* [1992] E.C.R. I–2187 at I–2213—2214, paras 17–18, ECJ.

33 (Order of November 29, 1993), Case T–56/92 *Koelman v. Commission* [1993] E.C.R. II–1267 at II–1276, para. 21, CFI; Case T–84/96 *Cipeke v. Commission* [1997] E.C.R. II–2081 at II–2091, paras 33–34, CFI.

34 Case T–195/95 *Guérin Automobiles v. Commission* [1997] E.C.R. II–679 at II–690, para. 26, CFI.

35 See *Commentaire Mégret*, at 422. For an example, see Case T–20/94 *Hartmann v. Council and Commission* [1997] E.C.R. II–595 at II–608, para. 37, CFI.

36 Case 30/68 *Lacroix v. Commission* [1970] E.C.R. 301 at 310–311, paras 21–28, ECJ.

37 Case 232/78 *Commission v. France* [1979] E.C.R. 2729 at 2737, para. 3, ECJ.

38 Case 168/78 *Commission v. France* [1980] E.C.R. 347 at 364–365, paras 17–25, ECJ; Case 270/83 *Commission v. France* [1986] E.C.R. 273, at 300–301, ECJ; (Order of June 19, 1995), Case T–107/94 *Kik v. Council and Commission* [1995] E.C.R. II–1717 at II–1729, para. 29, CFI.

22–016 As far as concerns the requirement for a summary of the pleas in law on which the application is based, it must be possible to identify from the text of the application what the applicant's specific complaints are and the legal and factual particulars on which they are based.[39] The resulting exposition must enable the defendant to protect its interests and the Court to carry out judicial review.

It is also unnecessary for express reference to be made to the provision of Community law which has allegedly been breached or for a legal categorisation to be given to the pleas raised in the application,[40] provided that the pleas emerge sufficiently clearly therefrom.[41] Even an error in citing the provision of Community law on which a plea is based will not cause that plea to be inadmissible.

A mere enumeration of pleas does not suffice. The application must set out the facts and reasoning on which each plea is based.[42] A reference to pleas raised in another case, even if the two cases are linked, does not constitute a sufficient statement of the pleas in law on which the application is based.[43] Such a reference, however, will not render the application

---

[39] Case 111/63 *Lemmerz-Werke GmbH v. High Authority* [1965] E.C.R. 677 at 696, ECJ; Joined Cases 26 and 86/79 *Forges de Thy-Marcinelle and Monceau v. Commission* [1980] E.C.R. 1083 at 1092, para. 4, ECJ; Case C–347/88 *Commission v. Greece* [1990] E.C.R. I–4747 at I–4786, para. 28, ECJ; Case C–52/90 *Commission v. Denmark* [1992] E.C.R. I–2187 at I–2213—2214, para. 17, ECJ; (Order of April 28, 1993), Case T–85/92 *De Hoe v. Commission* [1993] E.C.R. II–523 at II–532, para. 22, CFI; (Order of March 28, 1994), Case T–515/93 *B. v. Commission* [1994] E.C.R.–S.C. II–379 at II–383, para. 12, CFI.

[40] Joined Cases 19 and 21/60, 2 and 3/61 *Société Fives Lille Cail and Others v. High Authority* [1961] E.C.R. 281 at 295, ECJ; Case T–35/93 *Cucchiara and Others v. Commission* [1994] E.C.R.–S.C. II–413 at II–422—423, paras 26, 27, CFI (English abstract at I–A–126).

[41] Joined Cases 7/56 and 3–7/57 *Algera and Others v. Common Assembly* [1957 and 1958] E.C.R. 39 at 64–65, ECJ; Joined Cases 2–10/63 *San Michele and Others v. High Authority* [1963] E.C.R. 327 at 341, ECJ; Case 62/65 *Serio v. Commission* [1966] E.C.R. 561 at 568, ECJ (it must be sufficiently clear from the application as a whole what legal principles the applicant considers have been breached); Case T–18/90 *Jongen v. Commission* [1991] E.C.R. II–187 at II–195, para. 13, CFI. But see Case T–224/95 *Tremblay and Others v. Commission* [1997] E.C.R. II–2215 at II–2244—2245, paras 79–82, CFI, in which the Court of First Instance held that the claim that the defendant had "infringed the Treaty", which was only briefly enlarged upon in general terms in the application, did not enable it to determine the subject-matter of the proceedings sufficiently precisely and so did not enable the Commission effectively to defend itself.

[42] Joined Cases 19 and 21/60, 2 and 3/61 *Société Fives Lille Cail and Others v. High Authority* [1961] E.C.R. 281 at 295, ECJ; Case C–52/90 *Commission v. Denmark* [1992] E.C.R. I–2187 at I–2214, para. 18, ECJ. An application by which an action for damages is brought must contain the following particulars: the evidence from which the conduct alleged against the institution can be identified, the reasons for which the applicant considers that there is a causal link between the conduct and the damage it claims to have suffered, and the nature and extent of that damage: Case T–64/89 *Automec v. Commission* [1990] E.C.R. II–367 at II–390, para. 73, CFI; Case T–167/94 *Nölle v. Council and Commission* [1995] E.C.R. II–2589 at II–2604, para. 32, CFI; Case T–38/96 *Guérin Automobiles v. Commission* [1997] E.C.R. II–1223 at II–1236, para. 42, CFI.

[43] Case 9/55 *Société des Charbonnages de Beeringen and Others v. High Authority* [1954 to 1956] E.C.R. 311 at 325, ECJ; Joined Cases 19 and 65/63 *Satya Prakash v. Commission* [1965] E.C.R. 533 at 546, ECJ. But see Case T–37/91 *ICI v. Commission* [1995] E.C.R. II–1901 at II–1921—1922, para. 47, CFI, in which the Court of First Instance accepted a reference made in one case to another on account of the specific circumstances; namely a close link existed between two cases which had not been joined (the parties, the agents and the

inadmissible if, leaving aside that reference, the application contains all the necessary particulars.[44]

New pleas—that is to say, pleas not raised in the application—may not be introduced in the course of the proceedings unless they are based on matters of law or of fact which come to light in the course of the proceedings.[45] Given the absence of express, unequivocal rules on the matter, a new plea does not have to be submitted immediately, or within a particular period, after the matters of fact or law to which it refers come to light, in order to avoid being time-barred.[46] **22–017**

This does not mean to say, however, that pleas adduced in the application may not subsequently be enlarged upon.[47] Even pleas only raised impliedly may be extended in this way.[48] Accordingly, the applicant is entitled to raise additional arguments in the reply in support of pleas raised in the application.[49] This means that the Court will often have to make a subtle distinction between a new plea and a new argument.[50] In addition, the applicant may clarify in the reply the factual basis on which its pleas are based.[51] Obviously, however, the applicant may "clarify" only pleas which have already been raised in the application. **22–018**

---

lawyers were the same, the actions had been brought before the Court on the same day, the cases had been assigned to the same chamber and the same Judge-Rapporteur and the contested decisions related to aspects of competition on the same market).

44 Case 4/69 *Lütticke v. Commission* [1971] E.C.R. 325 at 335–336, paras 2–4, ECJ.

45 ECJ Rules of Procedure, Art. 42(2); CFI Rules of Procedure, Art. 48(2). For instances in which a new plea was not admitted, see Case 11/81 *Dürbeck v. Commission* [1982] E.C.R. 1251 at 1266, paras 13–15, ECJ; Case 108/81 *Amylum v. Council* [1982] E.C.R. 3107 at 3135–3136, paras 23–26, ECJ; Case 59/83 *Biovilac v. EEC* [1984] E.C.R. 4057 at 4080, paras 24–25, ECJ; Case 5/85 *AKZO Chemie v. Commission* [1986] E.C.R. 2585 at 2610–2611, paras 13–17, ECJ; Joined Cases 279–280, 285 and 286/84 *Rau v. Commission* [1987] E.C.R. 1069 at 1126, para. 38, ECJ; Case T–521/93 *Atlanta and Others v. Commission* [1996] E.C.R. II–1707 at II–1723—1724, paras 39, 40, CFI. For cases in which a new plea was admitted, see Case 14/81 *Alpha Steel Ltd v. Commission* [1982] E.C.R. 749 at 763, para. 8, CFI; Case T–43/89RV *Gill v. Commission* [1993] E.C.R. II–303 at II–319—320, paras 47–49, CFI; Case T–22/92 *Weißenfels v. European Parliament* [1993] E.C.R. II–1095 at II–1108, paras 33–35, CFI; Case T–109/92 *Lacruz Bassols v. Court of Justice* [1994] E.C.R.–S.C. II–105 at II–128, para. 67, CFI (English abstract at I–A–31 at I–A–35); Case T–508/93 *Mancini v. Commission* [1994] E.C.R.–S.C. II–761 at II–770, paras 33, 34, CFI (English abstract at I–A–239); Case T–32/91 *Solvay v. Commission* [1995] E.C.R. II–1825 at II–1839—1841, paras 35–42, CFI. It is also possible for only part of a new plea to be declared admissible: Case T–19/95 *Adia Interim v. Commission* [1996] E.C.R. II–321 at II–333, paras 22–24, CFI.

46 *Solvay v. Commission* (cited in n. 45, above), at II–1840, para. 40.

47 Joined Cases 9 and 12/60 *Vloeberghs v. High Authority* [1961] E.C.R. 197 at 215, ECJ; Case 18/60 *Worms v. High Authority* [1962] E.C.R. 195 at 203, ECJ.

48 Case 306/81 *Verros v. European Parliament* [1983] E.C.R. 1755 at 1764, paras 9, 10, ECJ; Case T–37/89 *Hanning v. European Parliament* [1990] E.C.R. II–463 at II–477—478, para. 38, CFI; Case T–216/95 *Moles García Ortúzar v. Commission* [1997] E.C.R.–S.C. II–1083 at II–1105–1106, para. 87, CFI (English abstract at I–A–403); Case T–217/95 *Passera v. Commission* [1997] E.C.R.–S.C. II–1109 at II–1132, para. 87, CFI (English abstract at I–A–413).

49 Case 2/54 *Italy v. High Authority* [1954 to 1956] E.C.R. 37 at 51, ECJ.

50 For a somewhat sceptical view (expressed already in the very early days of the Community), see Wijckerheld Bisdom, "Enige bijzonderheden over de rechtsgang van het Hof van Justitie van de Europese Gemeenschappen", in *Individuele rechtsbescherming in de Europese Gemeenschappen*, Deventer, Antwerp, Kluwer, 1964, at 61.

51 Case 74/74 *CNTA v. Commission* [1975] E.C.R. 533 at 544, para. 4, ECJ; Case T–21/90 *Generlich v. Commission* [1991] E.C.R. II–1323 at II–1335—1336, para. 32, CFI; Case T–

(4) Form of order sought by the applicant

22–019 The form of order sought (also referred to as "conclusions" or "claims") sets out the decision which the applicant is claiming that the Court should give.[52] It generally takes the form of the operative part of a judgment or order. However, the Court may also infer that a particular form of order is sought from the wording of the application.[53]

The form of order sought must be unequivocal so that the Court is spared from either giving judgment *ultra petita* or from failing to give judgment on one of the heads of the form of order sought. This also protects the rights of the defence.[54] A head of claim set out in the form of order sought which is unclear will be regarded as inadmissible.[55] Since the form of order sought flows from the subject-matter of the proceedings and the pleas in law which have to be summarised in the application, it may not be amended in the course of the proceedings.[56] The applicant is not even entitled to amend the form of order sought where new matters of law or fact have come to light in the course of the proceedings, allowing it to introduce new pleas in law. Accordingly, it cannot alter the nature of the proceedings by amending the form of order sought.[57]

22–020 In the exceptional circumstance where the institution concerned replaces the contested act by an act which does not essentially diverge from it, the applicant may adjust its form of order sought accordingly. It would not be in the interests of the proper administration of justice or of the requirements of procedural economy to oblige the applicant to make a fresh application to the Court against the new act. This is because the actual subject-matter of the proceedings is not changed.[58] It is also possible for the applicant to amend the form of order sought in this way where a contested implied decision is replaced by an express decision with the same content.[59] However, the act against which the original application was brought must be an act against which an action would lie. If that is not so and the original

---

109/92 *Lacruz Bassols v. Court of Justice* [1994] E.C.R.–S.C. II–105 at II–128, para. 67, CFI (English abstract at I–A–30, at I–A–35); Case T–35/93 *Cucchiara and Others v. Commission* [1994] E.C.R.–S.C. II–413 at II–422—424, paras 26–29, CFI (English abstract at I–A–127, at I–A–130).

[52] Case 55/64 *Lens v. Court of Justice* [1965] E.C.R. 837 at 841, ECJ.

[53] Case 8/56 *ALMA v. High Authority* [1957 and 1958] E.C.R. 95 at 99–100, ECJ; Case 80/63 *Degreef v. Commission* [1964] E.C.R. 391 at 408, ECJ; (Order of February 7, 1994), Case C–388/93 *PIA HiFi v. Commission* [1994] E.C.R. I–387 at I–391, para. 10, ECJ.

[54] Joined Cases 46 and 47/59 *Meroni & Co. v. High Authority* [1962] E.C.R. 411 at 419, ECJ.

[55] Case 188/73 *Grassi v. Council* [1974] E.C.R. 1099 at 1107, paras 5–9, ECJ.

[56] Case 232/78 *Commission v. France* [1979] E.C.R. 2729 at 2736–2737, paras 2–4, ECJ; Case 124/81 *Commission v. United Kingdom* [1983] E.C.R. 203 at 232–233, paras 5–7, ECJ; Case T–398/94 *Kahn Scheepvaart v. Commission* [1996] E.C.R. II–477 at II–485, para. 20, CFI.

[57] Case 125/78 *Gema v. Commission* [1979] E.C.R. 3173 at 3191, para. 26, ECJ; Case T–28/90 *Asia Motor France and Others v. Commission* [1992] E.C.R. II–2285 at II–2302—2303, paras 43–44, CFI.

[58] Case 14/81 *Alpha Steel Ltd v. Commission* [1982] E.C.R. 749 at 763, para. 8, ECJ; Joined Cases 351 and 360/85 *Fabrique de Fer de Charleroi v. Commission* [1987] E.C.R. 3639 at 3672, paras 8–11, ECJ.

[59] Case 103/85 *Stahlwerke Peine-Salzgitter AG v. Commission* [1988] E.C.R. 4131 at 4149, paras 11–12, ECJ.

act is replaced by a challengeable act, the form of order sought may not be amended because that would change the subject-matter of the proceedings contrary to Article 19 of the E.C. Statute of the Court of Justice.[60]

(5) Supporting evidence

The applicant must adduce evidence in support of its pleas. If it fails to do so, the pleas will be summarily rejected.[61] In principle, the application must set out the necessary evidence. If evidence is offered in the course of the proceedings, reasons must be given for the delay in tendering it.[62] **22–021**

(6) Accompanying documents

Sometimes documents must accompany the application in order for the action to be validly brought. **22–022**

The lawyer assisting or representing the applicant must lodge at the registry a certificate that he is entitled to practise before a court of a Member State.[63] He or she must provide evidence of the authority conferred on him or her by the client.[64] **22–023**

If the annulment of an act is sought, the application must be accompanied by the contested act.[65] If the application is for failure to act, documentary evidence must be provided of the date on which the relevant institution was requested to act.[66] **22–024**

If the applicant is a legal person governed by private law, the application must be accompanied by proof of its "existence in law". Such proof consists of the instrument or instruments constituting or regulating that legal person or a recent extract from the register of companies, firms or associations or any other proof.[67] The fact that the legal person is governed by private law is determined by the law of its country of origin. At the same time, the applicant must adduce proof that the authority granted to its lawyer has been properly conferred on him or her by someone authorised for the purpose.[68] **22–025**

An application bringing a dispute relating to intellectual property before the Court of First Instance,[69] in the form of an action against the Office for Harmonisation in the Internal Market (Trade Marks and Designs) or **22–026**

---

60 Case T–64/89 *Automec v. Commission* [1990] E.C.R. II–367 at II–389, paras 68–69, CFI.

61 Case 235/82 *Ferriere San Carlo v. Commission* [1983] E.C.R. 3949 at 3968, paras 21–22, ECJ.

62 ECJ Rules of Procedure, Art. 42(1); CFI Rules of Procedure, Art. 48(1).

63 ECJ Rules of Procedure, Art. 38(3); CFI Rules of Procedure, Art. 44(3). A university teacher who, albeit not a practitioner, has rights of audience in his or her Member State is deemed to be a "lawyer" for this purpose.

64 See paras 22–185, 22–186, below.

65 E.C. Statute, Art. 19, para. 2; ECJ Rules of Procedure, Art. 38(4); CFI Rules of Procedure, Art. 44(4).

66 *ibid.*

67 ECJ Rules of Procedure, Art. 38(5)(a); CFI Rules of Procedure, Art. 44(5)(a).

68 ECJ Rules of Procedure, Art. 38(5)(b); CFI Rules of Procedure, Art. 44(5)(b).

69 Council Regulation No. 40/94 of December 20, 1993 on the Community trade mark, Art. 63 ([1994] O.J. L11/1); Council Regulation No. 2100/94 of July 27, 1994 on Community plant variety rights, Art. 73 (as amended) ([1994] L227/1). See Chap. 18, above.

against the Community Plant Variety Office, must also contain the names of all the parties to the proceedings before the board of appeal and the addresses which they had given for the purposes of the notifications to be effected in the course of the proceedings before the board of appeal.[70] In addition, the contested decision has to be appended to the application and the date on which the applicant was notified of it must be indicated.[71]

3. Consequences

22–027 The lodging of the application at the registry causes the case to become pending before the Court of Justice or the Court of First Instance, as the case may be. The Registrar enters the case in the register and gives it a serial number reflecting the order in which it was lodged. The case numbers of the Court of Justice are preceded by the letter "C", those of the Court of First Instance by the letter "T" (for the French "Tribunal").

22–028 The Registrar[72] serves the application on the defendant[73] by dispatch of a copy by registered post with a form for acknowledgement of receipt or by personal delivery against a receipt[74] and, in disputes relating to intellectual property, on the relevant Office and on all parties to the proceedings before the board of appeal, after determining the language of the case in accordance with Article 131(1) of the CFI Rules of Procedure.[75] The Registrar ensures that notice is given in the *Official Journal of the European Communities* of the date of registration of the application initiating proceedings, the names and addresses of the parties, the subject-matter of the proceedings, the form of order sought by the applicant and a summary of the pleas in law and of the main supporting arguments.[76] The purpose of the notice in the C series of the *Official Journal* is to put Community institutions, Member States and natural and legal persons on notice of the proceedings, giving them the opportunity of intervening. Where the Council or the Commission is not a party to the case, the Registrar sends it copies of the application and of the defence, without the annexes thereto, to enable it to assess whether the inapplicability of one of its acts is being invoked under the third paragraph of Article 36 of the ECSC Treaty, Article 241 (*ex Article 184*) of the E.C. Treaty or Article 156 of the EAEC Treaty.[77]

22–029 If the application does not comply with certain requirements or if the requisite accompanying documents are not appended to it, the Registrar prescribes a reasonable period within which the applicant is to comply with requirements either by putting the application in order or by producing any

[70] CFI Rules of Procedure, Art. 132(1), subpara. 1.
[71] CFI Rules of Procedure, Art. 132(1), subpara. 2.
[72] ECJ Rules of Procedure, Art. 17(1); CFI Rules of Procedure, Art. 25(1).
[73] ECJ Rules of Procedure, Art. 39; CFI Rules of Procedure, Art. 45.
[74] ECJ Rules of Procedure, Art. 79; CFI Rules of Procedure, Art. 100.
[75] CFI Rules of Procedure, Art. 133(1).
[76] ECJ Rules of Procedure, Art. 16(6); CFI Rules of Procedure, Art. 24(6).
[77] ECJ Rules of Procedure, Art. 16(7); CFI Rules of Procedure, Art. 24(7).

documents missing.[78] If the applicant fails to comply with the Registrar's directions, the Court of Justice or the Court of First Instance, as the case may be, decides whether this renders the application formally inadmissible.[79]

Service of the application on the defendant will be effected as soon as the application has been put in order or the Court has declared it admissible, notwithstanding the failure to observe the formal requirements in question.[80]

B. The defence

1. Lodging the defence

(1) General

The defendant has one month following service upon it of the application in which to lodge a defence.[81] The President of the Court of Justice or the Court of First Instance, as the case may be, may extend this time-limit on a reasoned application by the defendant, which must be lodged before the original time-limit runs out.[82] **22–030**

As a pleading, the defence is subject to the same formal requirements as the application initiating the proceedings.[83] **22–031**

In disputes relating to intellectual property rights, the Office, as defendant, and interveners within the meaning of Article 134(1) of the CFI Rules of Procedure, may submit responses to the application within a period of two months from the service of the application.[84] Since, in such disputes, interveners may apply for a form of order and put forward pleas in law not applied for or put forward by the main parties, the other parties to the proceedings may, within two weeks of service of the responses, submit replies or rejoinders, in response to the form of order sought and pleas in law put forward by an intervener for the first time. The President may extend the time-limit.[85] **22–032**

(2) Judgments by default and applications to set them aside

If, despite the fact that the originating application was duly served on the defendant, the latter fails to lodge a defence in the proper form within the time prescribed, the applicant may apply for the form of order sought to be **22–033**

---

78 ECJ Rules of Procedure, Art. 38(7); CFI Rules of Procedure, Art. 44(6). The requirements in question are simply those set out in the ECJ Rules of Procedure, Art. 38(3)–(6), and in the CFI Rules of Procedure, Art. 44(3)–(6) (see paras 22–022—22–026, above). See also CFI Rules of Procedure, Art. 132(2).

79 *ibid.*; (Order of July 10, 1984), Case 289/83 *GAARM v. Commission* [1984] E.C.R. 2789, ECJ; (Order of February 8, 1993), Case T–101/92 *Stagakis v. European Parliament* [1993] E.C.R. II–63, CFI; (Order of June 22, 1995), Case T–101/95 *Zedelmaier v. Council and Commission*, CFI (not reported in the E.C.R.).

80 ECJ Rules of Procedure, Art. 39; CFI Rules of Procedure, Art. 45.

81 ECJ Rules of Procedure, Art. 40(1); CFI Rules of Procedure, Art. 46(1).

82 ECJ Rules of Procedure, Art. 40(2); CFI Rules of Procedure, Art. 46(3).

83 See paras 22–003—22–006, above.

84 CFI Rules of Procedure, Art. 135(1).

85 CFI Rules of Procedure, Art. 135(3).

granted. If the Court of Justice or the Court of First Instance, as the case may be, agrees, it will give judgment by default.[86]

The application is served on the defendant.[87] No special formal requirements apply, although the application must comply with the general requirements laid down for pleadings.[88]

Before giving judgment by default, the Court, after hearing the Advocate General, considers whether the application initiating proceedings is admissible, whether the appropriate formalities have been complied with, and whether the application appears well founded.[89]

The Court of Justice or the Court of First Instance, as the case may be, may decide to open the oral procedure relating to the application to grant the applicant's claims. The Court of Justice and the Court of First Instance may order a preparatory inquiry.[90]

A judgment by default is enforceable, although the Court of Justice or the Court of First Instance, as the case may be, may grant a stay of execution until the Court has given its decision on any application to set it aside, or it may make execution subject to the provision of security. In the latter case, the security will be released if no application to set the default judgment aside is made or if such an application fails.[91]

22–034 Application to set aside a judgment by default must be made within one month of service of the judgment. It must be made in the form prescribed for applications initiating proceedings.[92] After the application has been served, the President prescribes a period within which the other party may submit written observations.[93] After a possible preparatory inquiry, the oral procedure takes place. Lastly, the Court gives judgment. No application may be made to have that judgment set aside.[94]

22–035 If an application to set aside a default judgment is rejected, the default judgment remains in place.[95] Conversely, if the application is successful, the judgment setting aside the judgment by default takes its place.

---

[86] ECJ Rules of Procedure, Art. 94(1), subpara. 1; CFI Rules of Procedure, Art. 122(1), subpara. 1. See Case T–42/89 *W. Graf Yorck von Wartenburg v. European Parliament* [1990] E.C.R. II–31, CFI; Case T–85/94 *Branco v. Commission* [1995] E.C.R. II–45 at II–53—54, para. 19, CFI; Case C–274/93 *Commission v. Luxembourg* [1996] E.C.R. I–2019 at I–2039, para. 9, ECJ. For disputes relating to intellectual property rights, see CFI Rules of Procedure, Art. 134(4).

[87] ECJ Rules of Procedure, Art. 94(1), subpara. 2; CFI Rules of Procedure, Art. 122(1), subpara. 2.

[88] ECJ Rules of Procedure, Art. 37; CFI Rules of Procedure, Art. 43.

[89] ECJ Rules of Procedure, Art. 94(2); CFI Rules of Procedure, Art. 122(2). There is no requirement for the Court of First Instance to hear an advocate general; a judge is designated to act as advocate general only where the Court of First Instance sits in plenary session or otherwise so decides: CFI Rules of Procedure, Arts 17–19.

[90] ECJ Rules of Procedure, Art. 94(2); CFI Rules of Procedure, Art. 122(2).

[91] ECJ Rules of Procedure, Art. 94(3); CFI Rules of Procedure, Art. 122(3).

[92] ECJ Rules of Procedure, Art. 94(4); CFI Rules of Procedure, Art. 122(4). See also paras 22–003—22–008, above.

[93] ECJ Rules of Procedure, Art. 94(5); CFI Rules of Procedure, Art. 122(5).

[94] ECJ Rules of Procedure, Art. 94(6), subpara. 1; CFI Rules of Procedure, Art. 122(6).

[95] Case T–42/89 OPPO *European Parliament v. W. Graf Yorck von Wartenburg* [1990] E.C.R. II–299, CFI; Case T–85/94 (122) *Commission v. Branco* [1995] E.C.R. II–2993, CFI.

2. Content

The defence contains — 22–036

- — the name and address of the defendant;
- — the arguments of fact and law relied on;
- — the form of order sought by the defendant;
- — the nature of any evidence offered by him.[96]

(1) Name and address of the defendant

The defence is subject to the same requirements as the application, for instance as regards the address for service, assistance or representation by a lawyer and proof of the existence in law of a legal person governed by private law.[97] 22–037

(2) Arguments of fact and law relied on

The arguments of fact and law relied on must be clearly set out in the defence.[98] The defendant is limited to pleas set out in the defence. In subsequent pleadings, the defendant may introduce new pleas in law only if they are based on matters of law or of fact which come to light in the course of the proceedings.[99] Consequently, "new pleas" have the same standing for both the applicant and the defendant.[1] in order to secure observance of the principle *audi alteram partem*. If the defendant could keep its defence pleas undisclosed until it lodged the rejoinder or, *a fortiori*, until the hearing, the applicant would lose any chance of making a "reply" and of preparing its counter-arguments for the hearing, which would jeopardise proper debate, with both parties putting forward pleas and counter-pleas. 22–038

The defence has to take issue only with pleas raised by the applicant. A counter-claim may be made provided that it is related to the applicant's claim.[2]

---

[96] ECJ Rules of Procedure, Art. 40(1), subpara. 1; CFI Rules of Procedure, Art. 46(1), subpara. 1.

[97] ECJ Rules of Procedure, Art. 40(1), subpara. 2; CFI Rules of Procedure, Art. 46(1), subpara. 2. See also paras 22–009—22–010, above. The defendant may be a person governed by private law where a Community institution asserts a claim against such a person pursuant to an arbitration clause within the meaning of the E.C. Treaty, Art. 238 (*ex Art. 181*) (see Chap 17, above).

[98] Vaughan and Lasok, *European Court Practice*, p. 96.

[99] ECJ Rules of Procedure, Art. 42(2); CFI Rules of Procedure, Art. 48(2). See Case C–136/92P *Commission v. Brazzelli and Others* [1994] E.C.R. I–1981 at I–2031, para. 58, ECJ; Case T–81/97 *Regione Toscana v. Commission* [1998] E.C.R. II–2889 at II–2901, para. 41, CFI.

[1] The German version of the provisions cited accordingly refers to "*Angriffs- und Verteidigungsmittel*".

[2] Case 250/78 *DEKA v. EEC* [1983] E.C.R. 421, ECJ: in this case, the Commission sought to set off against compensation which the Community had to pay the applicant a claim which had been assigned to the Commission for repayment of an amount which had been wrongly paid to the applicant by way of export refunds and monetary compensatory amounts for exports of maize gritz. As a "defence plea", the claim for repayment of the amounts wrongly paid was apparently admissible.

(3) Form of order sought by the defendant

22–039 Generally, the form of order sought by the defendant will claim that the application and the claims set out therein should be dismissed and the applicant ordered to pay the costs. The claim for a costs order is very important, since both the Court of Justice and the Court of First Instance will order the unsuccessful party to pay the costs only "if they have been applied for in the successful party's pleadings".[3] This means that the defendant, too, should not omit to ask the Court to make a costs order against the applicant in case—as it naturally hopes—it is successful in its defence on the substance.[4]

(4) Any evidence offered in support

22–040 At the first possible opportunity, *i.e.* in the defence, the defendant should tender any supporting evidence. If, subsequently, the defendant offers further evidence in the rejoinder or at the hearing, it must give reasons for the delay in tendering it.[5] In this respect, too, the positions of the defendant and the applicant are parallel. Once again, it is the quality of debate before the Court which necessitates each party putting forward supporting evidence at a time when the other can still effectively put forward a counter-argument.

(5) Accompanying documents

22–041 Just as in the case of the application, documents may have to be submitted with the defence.[6]

3. The objection of inadmissibility

22–042 Instead of lodging a defence, the defendant can apply to the Court of Justice or the Court of First Instance (within the time prescribed for lodging a defence) for a decision on an objection of inadmissibility without a ruling on the substance of the case.[7] In that event, the President prescribes a period within which the opposite party may lodge a document containing a statement of the form of order sought by that party and its pleas in law. When it receives the objection and the response to it, the Court decides at an administrative meeting, on a proposal from the Judge-Rapporteur and after hearing the Advocate General, whether to decide on the application for a decision on the preliminary objection or to reserve its decision for final judgment.[8]

22–043 If the Court decides to reserve its decision, the President prescribes new time-limits for the further steps in the proceedings (in practice, this means

[3] ECJ Rules of Procedure, Art. 69(2), subpara. 1; CFI Rules of Procedure, Art. 87(2), subpara. 1.
[4] See also para. 22–118, below.
[5] ECJ Rules of Procedure, Art. 42(1); CFI Rules of Procedure, Art. 48(1).
[6] See paras 22–022—22–026, above.
[7] ECJ Rules of Procedure, Art. 91(1); CFI Rules of Procedure, Art. 114(1).
[8] ECJ Rules of Procedure, Art. 91(2), (3) and (4), subpara. 1; CFI Rules of Procedure, Art. 114(2), (3) and (4), subpara. 1.

that the defendant is given a new time-limit for lodging the defence and hence for the resumption of the written procedure on the substance).

If the Court decides to rule on the objection of inadmissibility, it is dealt with orally, in principle, and a date is fixed for a hearing, unless the Court of Justice or the Court of First Instance, as the case may be, decides differently. If the action is clearly inadmissible, there is a tendency to uphold the objection without holding a hearing. In such a case, the Court, after hearing the Advocate General, declares the action inadmissible by reasoned order.[9] **22–044**

If, after a hearing, a judgment is given refusing the application on the preliminary objection and declaring the action admissible, the President prescribes new time-limits for the further steps in the proceedings.[10] **22–045**

In addition, the Court of Justice and the Court of First Instance may consider at any time of their own motion whether there exists any absolute bar to proceeding with an action.[11] **22–046**

In addition, under Article 111 of the CFI Rules of Procedure, the Court of First Instance may decide by reasoned order that the application is manifestly inadmissible or manifestly lacking any foundation in law without taking further steps in the proceedings.[12] It is not clear whether the defendant can raise an objection by which it calls on the Court to take this step.[13] **22–047**

C. The reply and the rejoinder

After the defence has been lodged, the applicant may supplement its application by lodging a reply within a time-limit prescribed by the President of the Court. The defendant may then lodge a rejoinder on the same terms.[14] Either party may apply to the President for an extension of **22–048**

---

[9] ECJ Rules of Procedure, Art. 92(1); CFI Rules of Procedure, Art. 111. For examples, see (Orders of September 26, 1994), Case 216/83 *Les Verts v. Commission and Council* [1984] E.C.R. 3325, ECJ; Case 296/83 *Les Verts v. European Parliament* [1984] E.C.R. 3335, ECJ; Case 297/83 *Les Verts v. Council* [1984] E.C.R. 3339; (Order of November 26, 1993), Case T–460/93 *Tête and Others v. EIB* [1993] E.C.R. II–1257, CFI; (Order of December 14, 1993), Case T–29/93 *Calvo Alonso-Cortés v. Commission* [1993] E.C.R. II–1389, CFI; (Order of July 20, 1994), Case T–45/93 *Branco v. Court of Auditors* [1994] E.C.R.–S.C. II–641 at II–646, para. 21, CFI (English abstract at I–A–197).

[10] ECJ Rules of Procedure, Art. 91(4), subpara. 2; CFI Rules of Procedure, Art. 114(4), subpara. 2.

[11] ECJ Rules of Procedure, Art. 92(2); CFI Rules of Procedure, Art. 113.

[12] The words "or manifestly lacking any foundation in law" were used in the CFI Rules of Procedure, Art. 111, in order to make it clear that the Court of First Instance cannot deal with a case under that provision where the outcome of the proceedings depends on an assessment of the facts.

[13] CFI Rules of Procedure, Art. 114(1), does not seem to afford any basis for the defendant's doing so since it expressly provides that the Court is to rule on an application made in this way which does not "go to the substance of the case". Of course, the defendant may claim at any time in its defence that the application is manifestly inadmissible and ask the Court to rule on that claim without taking further steps in the written procedure. For examples, see (Order of December 10, 1997), Case T–134/96 *Smets v. Commission* [1997] E.C.R. II–2333 at II–2341, para. 16, CFI; (Order of April 29, 1998), Case T–267/94 *British Coal Corporation v. Commission* [1998] E.C.R. II–705 at II–713—714, paras 22–26, CFI.

[14] ECJ Rules of Procedure, Art. 41(1), (2); CFI Rules of Procedure, Art. 47(1), (2).

time. The parties are not obliged to lodge a reply and a rejoinder. If a party allows the relevant period to expire without lodging such a pleading or if it waives its right to do so, the proceedings continue.[15]

22–049 No specific formal requirements are laid down for replies and rejoinders, although they do have to comply with the general requirements which pleadings have to satisfy.[16]

22–050 The reply and the rejoinder afford each party an opportunity to supplement the application and the defence, respectively, in the light of its opponent's observations. They may contain supplementary arguments supporting or clarifying the pleas raised by the parties. As already noted, if these pleadings offer further evidence, reasons must be given for the delay in tendering it.[17]

22–051 As has also already been observed, neither the reply nor the rejoinder may raise new pleas, unless they are based on matters of law or of fact which have come to light in the course of the proceedings.[18] This will not be the case where, although the party raising the new plea was not previously aware of a matter of fact on which the new substantive plea is based, it could have known of it at the time when the application or the defence, as the case may be, was lodged.[19] If, in contrast, a matter of fact is mentioned for the first time in the defence, the applicant is entitled to raise a plea based thereon in the reply.[20] Lastly, new claims made in the reply or the rejoinder are inadmissible.[21]

22–052 In disputes relating to intellectual property rights, parties may submit replies and rejoinders only if the President, on a reasoned application made within two weeks of service of responses or replies, considers such further pleading necessary and allows it in order to enable the party concerned to put forward its point of view.[22]

22–053 Parties may not make improper use of procedural documents to which they have access in the course of the proceedings. They may use such documents only for the purpose of pursuing their own case. If a party uses some of the procedural documents of other parties for other purposes, such as for provoking public criticism of the other parties' arguments as a result of the disclosure of the documents in question, it infringes a general principle of the due administration of justice according to which parties

---

[15] ECJ Rules of Procedure, Art. 44(1), subpara. 3; CFI Rules of Procedure, Art. 52(2), subpara. 2.

[16] ECJ Rules of Procedure, Art. 37; CFI Rules of Procedure, Art. 43.

[17] ECJ Rules of Procedure, Art. 42(1); CFI Rules of Procedure, Art. 48(1). For a case in which the Court of Justice held, on appeal, that the Court of First Instance was right in considering that the offers of evidence submitted in the reply were out of time and in refusing them on the ground that the appellant had not given reasons for the delay in submitting them, see (Judgment of December 17, 1998) Case C–185/95P *Baustahlgewebe v. Commission*, paras 69–75, ECJ (not yet reported).

[18] ECJ Rules of Procedure, Art. 42(2); CFI Rules of Procedure, Art. 48(2).

[19] Case 110/81 *Roquette Frères v. Council* [1982] E.C.R. 3159 at 3185, para. 31, ECJ.

[20] Joined Cases 12 and 29/64 *Ley v. Commission* [1965] E.C.R. 107 at 118–119, ECJ.

[21] Case T–22/92 *Weißenfels v. European Parliament* [1993] E.C.R. II–1095 at II–1106, para. 27, CFI; Case T–146/95 *Bernardi v. European Parliament* [1996] E.C.R. II–769 at II–782, para. 31, CFI.

[22] CFI Rules of Procedure, Art. 135(2).

have the right to defend their interests free of external influences and particularly from influences on the part of the public. Such an abuse of process may be penalised in the order for costs.[23]

D. THE PRELIMINARY REPORT

After the rejoinder has been lodged or the parties have refrained from lodging a reply or a rejoinder, the written procedure is at an end and the President fixes the date on which the Judge-Rapporteur is to present his preliminary report to the Court of Justice or the Court of First Instance, as the case may be.[24] The preliminary report is not published. It is intended for the administrative meeting of the Court of Justice (the judges, the advocates general and the Registrar) or for the competent chamber of the Court of First Instance (the judges and the Registrar). Where necessary, it proposes measures of organisation of procedure[25] or measures of inquiry.[26] In an appropriate case, the report will discuss the desirability of referring the relevant case to a chamber of the Court of Justice or to the Court of First Instance sitting in plenary session or to a chamber consisting of a different number of judges.[27] The Court of Justice and the Court of First Instance decide on the Judge-Rapporteur's proposals, after hearing the Advocate General.[28] They may decide to open the oral proceedings without proceeding to measures of organisation of procedure or measures of inquiry. If so, the President fixes the opening date.[29] If not, the measures of organisation of procedure or inquiry decided upon have to have been completed before the President fixes the date for the opening of the oral procedure.[30] After the inquiry, the Court of Justice or the Court of First Instance, as the case may be, may prescribe a time-limit within which the parties are to submit written observations. The oral procedure follows after that time-limit has expired. In addition, during the oral procedure measures of organisation of procedure or measures of inquiry may still be prescribed.[31] **22–054**

[23] Case T–174/95 *Svenska Journalistförbundet v. Council* [1998] E.C.R. II–2289 at II–2330, paras 135–139, where the applicant published the Council's defence on the Internet, requesting the public to inform the Council of their comments.

[24] ECJ Rules of Procedure, Art. 44(1); CFI Rules of Procedure, Art. 52(1).

[25] See CFI Rules of Procedure, Art. 64 (see para. 22–069, below).

[26] ECJ Rules of Procedure, Arts. 45–46; CFI Rules of Procedure, Arts. 65–67 (paras 22–070—22–079, below).

[27] See paras 1–008—1–010, 1–021, above.

[28] This is invariably the case for the Court of Justice, only exceptionally for the Court of First Instance where a judge is designated to act as advocate general (CFI Rules of Procedure, Arts 17–19).

[29] ECJ Rules of Procedure, Art. 44(2), subpara. 2; CFI Rules of Procedure, Art. 53.

[30] ECJ Rules of Procedure, Art. 54; CFI Rules of Procedure, Art. 54.

[31] For an example, see Joined Cases T–79, T–84—86, T–89, T–91—92, T–94, T–96, T–98, T–102 and T–104/89 *BASF and Others v. Commission* [1992] E.C.R. II–315 at II–333, para. 25, CFI.

II. The Oral Procedure

A. Opening of the oral procedure

22–055 The President fixes the date for the opening of the oral procedure,[32] after any measures of organisation of procedure or measures of inquiry have been carried out. The Court of Justice and the Court of First Instance take cognizance of cases brought before them in order, depending on when the inquiry was completed. If the preparatory inquiries in several cases are completed simultaneously, the order in which they are dealt with is determined by the dates of entry in the register of the initiating applications.[33] In special circumstances, the President may order that a case be given priority over others.[34] He or she may do so of his or her own motion, although parties may request him or her to do so. Furthermore, the President may in special circumstances, after hearing the parties and the Advocate General, either on his or her own initiative or at the request of one of the parties, defer a case to be dealt with at a later date. On a joint application by the parties the President may directly order that a case be deferred.[35]

22–056 Under Article 44a of the ECJ Rules of Procedure, the Court of Justice may decide a case without an oral procedure. It does so acting on a report from the Judge-Rapporteur after hearing the Advocate General and with the express consent of the parties.[36] There is no equivalent Article in the CFI Rules of Procedure. The Court of Justice will make use of this possibility where the pleas and arguments of the parties, together with the evidence of the facts relied on, have emerged sufficiently during the written procedure and a hearing cannot make any further contribution.

B. Course of the oral procedure

22–057 The proceedings are opened and directed by the President.[37] In principle, they are open to the public, unless the Court of Justice or the Court of First Instance decides, of its own motion or on application by the parties, otherwise for serious reasons.[38] The formal commencement of the oral procedure is marked in theory by the reading of the report for the hearing by the Judge-Rapporteur.[39] In practice, however, the report is no longer read out, unless one of the parties makes a request to this effect, but sent to the parties a few days before the sitting. At the beginning of the sitting, the

---

[32] ECJ Rules of Procedure, Art. 54; CFI Rules of Procedure, Arts. 53–54.
[33] ECJ Rules of Procedure, Art. 55(1); CFI Rules of Procedure, Art. 55(1).
[34] ECJ Rules of Procedure, Art. 55(2), subpara. 1; CFI Rules of Procedure, Art. 55(2), subpara. 1.
[35] ECJ Rules of Procedure, Art. 55(2), subpara. 2; CFI Rules of Procedure, Art. 55(2), subpara. 2.
[36] Tacit acquiescence does not suffice. The fact that a party does not respond to an invitation from the Court of Justice does not give it free rein not to hold a hearing.
[37] ECJ Rules of Procedure, Art. 56(1); CFI Rules of Procedure, Art. 56.
[38] E.C. Statute, Art. 28. Some proceedings must be held *in camera* (see E.C. Treaty, Art. 298 (*ex Art. 225*)).
[39] E.C. Statute, Art. 18, para. 4.

President mentions that the report has been sent out and invites comments. After any comments have been heard, the report is deemed to have been read.

The report for the hearing sets out the facts, an outline of the procedure up to the date of the hearing and a summary of the forms of order sought and of the parties' pleas and arguments. The judgment of the Court of Justice or of the Court of First Instance will be largely based on the report for the hearing and so it is important for the parties that its contents are accurate.[40] Since January 1, 1994, the report for the hearing is no longer printed in the European Court Reports except in special cases. **22–058**

Oral argument is then heard from the parties and any interveners.[41] Each party may address the Court of Justice for 30 minutes or for 15 minutes in a case heard by a chamber of three judges. Before the Court of First Instance, speaking time is generally restricted to 15 minutes. This time may be extended by parties' making a reasoned application to the registry at least 14 days before the hearing. Oral argument is intended to clarify the pleas and arguments raised during the written procedure, of which the judges are already apprised, and to touch on certain aspects of them. In pleading before the Court, the parties may not raise any new pleas unless they are based on matters of law or of fact which have come to light in the course of the proceedings.[42] In contrast, new evidence may be presented at the hearing, although an explanation must be given as to why it was not tendered during the written procedure.[43] **22–059**

After the parties have presented their oral arguments, the President, the Judges and the Advocate General may put questions to the agents, advisers or lawyers of the parties.[44] This affords an opportunity to elucidate any aspects of the case-file remaining unclear and may result in measures of inquiry being repeated or expanded, this being ordered by the Court of Justice or the Court of First Instance after hearing the Advocate General. **22–060**

The oral stage of the procedure is closed by the President after the Advocate General has presented his opinion. The Advocate General reads out his proposal for the operative part, generally a few weeks after the hearing. In the case of the Court of First Instance, where an Advocate General has not been designated in a case, the President declares the oral procedure closed at the end of the hearing.[45] The President also declares the oral proceedings closed where an Advocate General has been designated in a case and he or she delivers his or her opinion in writing by lodging it at the registry.[46] **22–061**

---

[40] Schermers and Waelbroeck, *Judicial Protection*, p. 850.

[41] See paras 22–089—22–104, below.

[42] ECJ Rules of Procedure, Art. 42(2); CFI Rules of Procedure, Art. 48(2).

[43] ECJ Rules of Procedure, Art. 42(1); CFI Rules of Procedure, Art. 48(1).

[44] ECJ Rules of Procedure, Art. 57; CFI Rules of Procedure, Art. 58.

[45] CFI Rules of Procedure, Art. 60.

[46] CFI Rules of Procedure, Art. 61.

C. Reopening of the oral procedure

22–062 The Court of Justice or the Court of First Instance may, after hearing the Advocate General, order the reopening of the oral procedure.[47] It will do so if an apparently determinative matter only becomes apparent after the oral procedure has been closed. If the procedure is reopened, the parties may make further written submissions, additional measures of inquiry may be ordered and, following further oral argument, the Advocate General may deliver a supplementary opinion.[48]

22–063 In refusing to reopen the oral procedure after the judgment in the *PVC* cases,[49] the Court of First Instance equated the circumstances in which a request to that effect might be granted with the conditions which have to be met in order to obtain revision of a judgment. The oral procedure would be reopened only if the applicant or the defendant adduced a fact or reasonable evidence of a fact of which neither it nor the Court could have been aware at the time of the hearing and which possibly had a decisive bearing on the case. Consequently, the deliberations will be only upset for serious reasons in the same way as the authority of a judgment as *res judicata* may be revised only very exceptionally.[50]

22–064 In addition, a party may apply to have the oral procedure reopened if it was not present when it was originally held. Such an application will be granted if the party in question proves that its absence was due to *force majeure*, which, according to settled case law, means abnormal difficulties, independent of the will of the party concerned and apparently inevitable, even if all due care is taken.[51] If the person providing the address for service in Luxembourg for the absent party forgets to forward the summons to attend the hearing, this does not constitute a sufficient ground for ordering the oral procedure to be reopened.[52]

---

[47] ECJ Rules of Procedure, Art. 61; CFI Rules of Procedure, Art. 62. The Court of Justice may reopen the oral procedure before the Advocate General has delivered his or her opinion, see Case 56/77 *Agence Européenne d'Intérims SA v. Commission* [1978] E.C.R. 2215 at 2230, ECJ.

[48] For examples, see Case 383/85 *Commission v. Belgium* [1989] E.C.R. 3069 at 3077–3078, ECJ; Case C–2/90 *Commission v. Belgium* [1992] E.C.R. I–4431, ECJ.

[49] Case T–9/89 *Hüls v. Commission* [1992] E.C.R. II–499 at II–625—627, paras 382–385, CFI; Case T–10/89 *Hoechst v. Commission* [1992] E.C.R. II–629 at II–753—755, paras 372–375, CFI; Case T–11/89 *Shell v. Commission* [1992] E.C.R. II–757 at II–904, paras 372–374, CFI; Case T–12/89 *Solvay v. Commission* [1992] E.C.R. II–907 at II–1017—1018, paras 345–347, CFI; Case T–13/89 *ICI v. Commission* [1992] E.C.R. II–1021 at II–1153, paras 399–401, CFI; Case T–14/89 *Montedipe v. Commission* [1992] E.C.R. II–1155 at II–1273, paras 389–391, CFI; Case T–15/89 *Chemie Linz v. Commission* [1992] E.C.R. II–1275 at II–1400—1401, paras 393–395, CFI. See also Case 77/70 *Prelle v. Commission* [1971] E.C.R. 561 at 566, para. 7, ECJ; Case C–415/93 *Bosman* [1995] E.C.R. I–4921 at I–5057, para. 53, ECJ. See also the refusal of the Court of Justice to reopen the oral procedure after a request from a party which found itself in disagreement with the opinion of the Advocate-General (Judgment of January 21, 1999) Case C–73/97P *France v. Comafrica and Dole Fresh Fruit Europe*, paras 12–15, ECJ (not yet reported).

[50] See paras 22–141—22–146, below.

[51] Case T–12/90 *Bayer v. Commission* [1991] E.C.R. II–219 at II–232, para. 44, CFI.

[52] Case T–235/94 *Galtieri v. European Parliament* [1996] E.C.R.–S.C. II–129 at II–134, para. 17, CFI (English abstract at A–I–43).

III. Measures of Organisation of Procedure and Measures of Inquiry

A. Burden of proof on the parties and role played by the court in fact-finding

Fact-finding is the outcome of a complex interplay between the parties and between the parties and the Court. **22–065**

The classic apportionment of the burden of proof, whereby each party proves the facts on which its claim or defence is based, applies also in Community law.[53] The Court may adjust this by means of presumptions designed to mitigate the substantive inequality between the parties in terms of their ability to prove the necessary facts.[54] For this reason too, a party not having to discharge the burden of proof may nevertheless be obliged to release information to which only it has access, in order to enable its opponent to provide the necessary evidence.[55] **22–066**

The Court may further play an active role in fact-finding.[56] This involvement in fact-finding originates in the mission of the Court of Justice and the Court of First Instance of ensuring that the law is observed.[57] They may do so only if the facts on which the application of the law is based accord with reality. At the same time, the decisions of the Court of Justice and the Court of First Instance often affect the general interest alongside the individual interest of the parties concerned.[58] The potential ramifications of their decisions may prompt the Court of Justice and the Court of First Instance to prescribe measures of inquiry. Lastly, sometimes the facts and the law are so closely intertwined that it is difficult to make a hard and fast distinction between fact-finding and making determinations of law.[59] The allocation of duties as between the Court and the parties which is encapsulated in the maxim *da mihi factum, dabo tibi jus* cannot be unqualifiedly applied. Moreover, the jurisdiction transferred from the Court of Justice to the Court of First Instance was primarily to hear and determine cases requiring a thorough investigation of complex facts, the aim being to relieve the Court of Justice of the time-consuming task of making findings of fact. For its part, the Court of First Instance incorpor-

---

[53] For a more extensive discussion, see Lasok, *The European Court of Justice: Practice and Procedure*, London, Butterworths, 1994, pp. 344–363.

[54] Case 10/55 *Mirossevich v. High Authority* [1954 to 1956] E.C.R. 333 at 343–344, ECJ.

[55] Case 45/64 *Commission v. Italy* [1965] E.C.R. 857 at 867, ECJ. Pursuant to the E.C. Treaty, Art. 10 (*ex Art. 5*), Member States are under a duty to provide the Commission with the information necessary in order for it to monitor whether Community law is being complied with. If a Member State fails to comply with that duty, this in itself is enough to justify proceedings under Art. 226 (*ex Art. 169*). In the course of such proceedings, the Court of Justice may put questions to Member States and order measures of inquiry, see Case 96/81 *Commission v. Netherlands* [1982] E.C.R. 1791, ECJ, and Case 97/81 *Commission v. Netherlands* [1982] E.C.R. 1819, ECJ.

[56] See para. 22–067, below.

[57] E.C. Treaty, Art. 220 (*ex Art. 164*) .

[58] Lasok (cited in n. 53, above), p. 199.

[59] Lenaerts, "Le Tribunal de première instance des Communautés européennes: genèse et premiers pas" (1990) J.T. 409 at 413.

ated in its Rules of Procedure provisions specifically designed to facilitate greater interaction between the Court and the parties with a view to this task. What is involved is the so-called "measures of organisation of procedure" (Article 64). The Court of First Instance makes avid use of such measures, acting in a more inquisitorial manner than the Court of Justice formerly did.[60]

22–067 The fact that the Court has the power to order measures of organisation of procedure and measures of inquiry to be carried out does not release the parties from their obligation to prove their assertions. This is because the judicial contribution to fact-finding is only optional and complementary. Evidence offered in support by the parties[61] must make out a plausible case for their allegations and so constitute at least prima facie evidence. It is only if the evidence satisfies those conditions that the Court will decide, in an appropriate case, to investigate the allegations further by means of measures of organisation of procedure or measures of inquiry.[62] Whether the Court does so decide will be largely determined by the context of the proceedings. In this way, the Court's decision to take particular measures will be influenced by the fact that one party has difficulty, by comparison with its opponent, in obtaining evidence or by the fact that the parties agree on the existence of certain facts.

22–068 Community law does not lay down any specific rules on the use of evidence. All means of proof are admissible, except for evidence obtained improperly.[63]

B. Measures of organisation of procedure

22–069 Article 64 of the CFI Rules of Procedure enables the Court of First Instance to prescribe measures in order to ensure that "cases are prepared for hearing, procedures carried out and disputes resolved under the best possible conditions". Although such measures do not form part of an inquiry prescribed by the Court, they may nevertheless assist in finding the facts of the case.[64]

The measures include putting questions to the parties, inviting them to make written or oral submissions on certain aspects of the proceedings, asking them or third parties for information or particulars, asking for

[60] Vesterdorf, "The Court of First Instance of the European Communities after Two Full Years in Operation" (1992) C.M.L.Rev. 897 at 912–915.

[61] ECJ Rules of Procedure, Art. 38(1); CFI Rules of Procedure, Art. 44(1) as regards the application; ECJ Rules of Procedure, Art. 40(1); CFI Rules of Procedure, Art. 46(1) as regards the defence; ECJ Rules of Procedure, Art. 93(5); CFI Rules of Procedure, Art. 115(4) as regards statements in intervention.

[62] For an example, see (Order of November 21, 1996), Case T–53/96 *Syndicat des Producteurs de Viande Bovine and Others v. Commission* [1996] E.C.R. II–1579 at II–1590, para. 26, CFI. For an extensive discussion, see Brealey, "The Burden of Proof before the European Court" (1985) E.L.Rev. 250–262.

[63] Joined Cases 197–200, 243, 245 and 247/80 *Ludwigshafener Walzmühle v. Council and Commission* [1981] E.C.R. 3211 at 3245, para. 16, ECJ.

[64] For a list of the specific purposes of measures of organisation of procedure, see the CFI Rules of Procedure, Art. 64(2). Note that they include "to facilitate the amicable settlement of proceedings".

documents or any papers relating to the case to be produced, and summoning the parties' agents or the parties in person to meetings.[65]

Measures of organisation of procedure are relatively informal. They do not have the compelling nature of measures of inquiry and—unlike such measures—are not prescribed by order, but notified to the parties by letter from the Registrar. Any party may, at any stage of the procedure, propose the adoption or modification of measures of organisation of procedure. If so, the other parties must be heard before any measures are prescribed. Where the procedural circumstances so require, the Registrar has to inform the parties of the measures envisaged by the Court of First Instance and to give them an opportunity to submit comments orally or in writing.[66] The Judge-Rapporteur may be given the task of putting the measures into effect.[67] The Court of First Instance makes frequent use of this type of measure in order to streamline somewhat the processing of large or complex case-files.[68] The Court of First Instance may, without infringing Article 48(2) of its Rules of Procedure, base its judgment or order on matters which came to its knowledge from replies to questions put to the parties as measures of organisation of procedure on which the parties had the opportunity to state their views in the course of the proceedings.[69]

C. Measures of inquiry

Such measures of inquiry as the Court of Justice or the Court of First Instance should deem necessary are prescribed by order. The order sets out the facts to be established. Before prescribing such measures, the Court hears the Advocate General and, where it proposes to hear oral testimony, commission an expert's report or inspect a place or a thing, the parties as well.[70] The order is served on the parties. The Court of Justice or the Court of First Instance, as the case may be, may entrust the undertaking of the inquiry to the Judge-Rapporteur.[71] During the inquiry, evidence may be submitted in rebuttal and further evidence may be adduced.[72] The parties may be present at measures of inquiry.[73] **22–070**

The following measures of inquiry may be adopted: personal appearance of the parties; a request for information and production of documents; oral testimony; the commissioning of an expert's report, and an inspection of a place or a thing.[74] **22–071**

[65] CFI Rules of Procedure, Art. 64(3). For an example, see Barents, *Procedures*, p. 314.

[66] CFI Rules of Procedure, Art. 64(4).

[67] CFI Rules of Procedure, Art. 64(5).

[68] Biancarelli, "Le règlement de procédure du Tribunal de première instance des Communautés européennes: le perfectionnement dans la continuité" (1991) R.T.D.E. 543– 564. For an example, see Case T–68, T–77 and T–78/89 *SIV and Others v. Commission* [1992] E.C.R. II–1403 at II–1427—1430, paras 40–51, CFI.

[69] Case C–259/96P *Council v. De Nil and Impens* [1998] E.C.R. I–2915 at I–2945, para. 31, ECJ.

[70] ECJ Rules of Procedure, Art. 45(1); CFI Rules of Procedure, Art. 66(1).

[71] ECJ Rules of Procedure, Art. 45(3); CFI Rules of Procedure, Art. 67(1).

[72] ECJ Rules of Procedure, Art. 45(4); CFI Rules of Procedure, Art. 66(2).

[73] ECJ Rules of Procedure, Art. 46(3); CFI Rules of Procedure, Art. 67(2).

[74] ECJ Rules of Procedure, Art. 45(2); CFI Rules of Procedure, Art. 65.

1. Personal appearance of the parties

22–072 The Court of Justice and the Court of First Instance may summon parties to appear personally in order to provide explanations about the case or answer questions.[75] Unlike experts and witnesses, they are not heard under oath.[76] A party who does not comply with a summons from the Court of Justice or the Court of First Instance may not be fined, unlike a witness. As in the case of any hearing, minutes are kept, in which the appearance of parties is recorded. The President and the Registrar sign the minutes.[77]

2. Requests for information and production of documents

22–073 The Court of Justice and the Court of First Instance have the power to require parties—and even Member States and Community institutions not parties to the proceedings—to produce all documents and to supply all information which the Court considers desirable.[78] The Court of Justice and the Court of First Instance may only request the production of documents which are relevant, having regard to the subject-matter of the proceedings.[79] Formal note is taken of any refusal.[80]

That a document produced is allegedly confidential[81] puts the Court under a duty to exercise care in putting it into *inter partes* proceedings. It may do so, after carefully weighing the interests at stake, only where the document is genuinely necessary in order for it to decide the case.[82] There is no formal sanction for a refusal to provide information or to produce documents, but it may affect the outcome of the case.[83]

3. Oral testimony and experts' reports

22–074 Occasionally, the Court of Justice or the Court of First Instance may, either of its own motion or on an application by a party, order that certain facts be proved by witnesses.[84] The Court's order sets out the facts about which the witness is to be examined.[85] Witnesses give their main evidence, after which the President, the Judges, the Advocate General and, subject to the control

---

[75] It is not because parties may "plead" only through their representatives (E.C. Statute, Art. 29) that they themselves may not even address the Court in an inquiry based on the appearance of the parties. For an example, see (Order of December 6, 1989), Case T–59/89 *W. Graf Yorck von Wartenburg v. European Parliament*, CFI (not reported in the E.C.R.).

[76] E.C. Statute, Art. 25.

[77] ECJ Rules of Procedure, Art. 53(1); CFI Rules of Procedure, Art. 76(1).

[78] E.C. Statute, Art. 21. For an example, see Case T–2/90 *Ferreira de Freitas v. Commission* [1991] E.C.R. II–103 at II–109—110, paras 20–21, CFI.

[79] (Order of November 18, 1997), Case T–367/94 *British Coal v. Commission* [1997] E.C.R. II–2103 at II–2110, para. 24, CFI.

[80] E.C. Statute, Art. 21.

[81] A document may be confidential on grounds, for instance, of state security (E.C. Treaty, Art. 296 (*ex Art. 223*) (1)(a)) or professional or business secrecy.

[82] For an extensive discussion, see *Commentaire Mégret*, at 437–438; Vaughan and Lasok, *European Court Practice*, pp. 130–133.

[83] See, *e.g.* Case 155/78 *M. v. Commission* [1980] E.C.R. 1797 at 1811–1812, paras 20–21, ECJ.

[84] ECJ Rules of Procedure, Art. 47(1); CFI Rules of Procedure, Art. 68(1).

[85] For the full content of such an order, see the ECJ Rules of Procedure, Art. 47(2), and the CFI Rules of Procedure, Art. 68(2).

of the President, the parties' representatives may put questions to them.[86] The hearing may be in open court or, on application, *in camera*.[87] After giving his or her main evidence, the witness takes the oath, although he or she may be released from this requirement.[88] The Registrar takes minutes in which the evidence is reproduced. The minutes are checked by the witness and signed by him or her, the President or the Judge-Rapporteur responsible for conducting the examination of the witness and the Registrar. On penalty of a fine, a witness who has been duly summoned must attend the hearing, give evidence and take the oath.[89] Proceedings for perjury are taken at the instance of the Court in the competent court of the Member State concerned.[90] Member States are obliged to treat any violation of an oath by witnesses as if the offence had been committed before one of its courts with jurisdiction in civil proceedings.[91]

The Court of Justice and the Court of First Instance may also order that an expert's report be obtained.[92] The order appointing the expert defines his or her task and sets a time-limit within which the report is to be made.[93] After making his or her report, the expert is sworn in,[94] unless exempted from taking an oath. The provisions on oaths apply. The Court may order that the expert be examined.[95] **22–075**

Witnesses and experts are entitled to reimbursement of their travel and subsistence expenses.[96] In addition, witnesses are entitled to compensation for loss of income, experts to fees.[97] **22–076**

Parties may object to a witness or an expert on the ground that he or she is not a competent or a proper person to act as such or for any other reason.[98] An objection to a witness or an expert must be raised within two weeks after service of the order summoning the witness or appointing the expert; the statement of objection must set out the grounds of objection and indicate the nature of any evidence offered.[99] The Court of Justice or the Court of First Instance, as the case may be, decides on the objection. **22–077**

---

86 ECJ Rules of Procedure, Art. 47(4); CFI Rules of Procedure, Art. 68(4).

87 E.C. Statute, Art. 28.

88 ECJ Rules of Procedure, Art. 47(5); CFI Rules of Procedure, Art. 68(5). The CFI Rules of Procedure, Art. 71, provides that witnesses may take the oath in a manner laid down by their national law (para. 2) or by solemn affirmation equivalent to an oath as well as, or instead of, taking an oath, where this is provided for by the national law (para. 3, subpara. 1).

89 ECJ Rules of Procedure, Art. 48; CFI Rules of Procedure, Art. 69.

90 E.C. Statute, Art. 27; Supplementary Rules, Arts. 6, 7.

91 *ibid.*

92 Olivier, "L'expertise devant les juridictions communautaires" (1994) Gazette du Palais 2–6; For examples, see Joined Cases C–89, C–104, C–114, C–116–117 and C–125–129/85 *Åhlström Osakeyhtiö v. Commission* [1993] E.C.R. I–1307 at I–1592, paras 31, 32, ECJ; Case T–169/89 *Frederiksen v. European Parliament* [1991] E.C.R. II–1403 at II–1421—1425, paras 38–48, CFI; Case T–90/95 *Gill v. Commission* [1997] E.C.R.–S.C. II–1231, CFI.

93 ECJ Rules of Procedure, Art. 49(1); CFI Rules of Procedure, Art. 70(1).

94 ECJ Rules of Procedure, Art. 49(6); CFI Rules of Procedure, Art. 70(6).

95 ECJ Rules of Procedure, Art. 49(5); CFI Rules of Procedure, Art. 70(5).

96 ECJ Rules of Procedure, Art. 51(1); CFI Rules of Procedure, Art. 74(1).

97 ECJ Rules of Procedure, Art. 51(2); CFI Rules of Procedure, Art. 74(2).

98 ECJ Rules of Procedure, Art. 50(1); CFI Rules of Procedure, Art. 73(1).

99 ECJ Rules of Procedure, Art. 50(2); CFI Rules of Procedure, Art. 73(2).

22–078 In order to obtain a statement from witnesses or experts who cannot appear before the Court of Justice or the Court of First Instance, letters rogatory may be issued for the purpose of having them examined.[1] The competent national authority obtains the statements and sends the resulting documents to the Registrar of the Court of Justice or the Court of First Instance, as appropriate.

4. Inspections of the place or thing in question

22–079 To date, the Court of Justice has only undertaken two inspections of a place.[2] The Rules of Procedure contain no specific provisions on the conduct of a visit.

IV. Joinder of Cases

22–080 The President of the Court of Justice or of the Court of First Instance[3] may, at any time after hearing the parties and the Advocate General (if an advocate general has been assigned), order that two or more cases concerning the same subject-matter be joined, on account of the connection between them, for the purposes of the written or oral procedure or of the final judgment.[4] The President may refer the decision to the Court of Justice or the Court of First Instance, as the case may be.

22–081 Cases will be regarded as sufficiently connected, *inter alia*, where they contest the same act[5] using the same submissions[6] or where the same parties are involved in different proceedings based on similar facts.[7]

22–082 Although, in theory, there is no reason why a reference for a preliminary ruling should not be joined with a direct action, it is improbable given the differences in the respective procedures.[8]

22–083 Cases are joined in order to facilitate the processing of cases by avoiding unnecessary repetition of procedural acts. Joinder has sometimes been

---

[1] E.C. Statute, Art. 26; ECJ Rules of Procedure, Art. 52; Supplementary Rules, Arts. 1–3.

[2] Case 14/59 *Société des Fonderies de Pont-à-Mousson v. High Authority* [1959] E.C.R. 215 at 224, ECJ; Joined Cases 42 and 49/59 *SNUPAT v. High Authority* [1961] E.C.R. 53, ECJ.

[3] This power was conferred on the President in order to speed up proceedings, see Christianos and Picod (cited in para. 21–001, n. 2, above), at 278–282.

[4] ECJ Rules of Procedure, Art. 43; CFI Rules of Procedure, Art. 50.

[5] Joined Cases 19 and 20/74 *Kali und Salz and Kali-Chemie v. Commission* [1975] E.C.R. 499 at 517, para. 2, ECJ ("where the two applications seek the same relief"); Case T–1/89 *Rhône-Poulenc v. Commission* [1991] E.C.R. II–867 at II–1046, para. 232, CFI.

[6] Joined Cases 112, 144 and 145/73 *Campogrande and Others v. Commission* [1974] E.C.R. 957 at 974, para. 5, ECJ.

[7] Joined Cases 7 and 9/54 *Groupement des Industries Sidérurgiques Luxembourgeoises v. High Authority* [1954 to 1956] E.C.R. 175, ECJ.

[8] Schermers and Waelbroeck, *Judicial Protection*, p. 836, cite two cases, which were not joined, yet in which the Court of Justice had regard in deciding one case to arguments put forward in the other. The Court observed that the parties' rights had been respected since all the parties to the case had submitted observations in the other. See Case 61/77 *Commission v. Ireland* [1978] E.C.R. 417 at 441–442, paras 19–22, ECJ, and Case 88/77 *Minister for Fisheries v. Schonenberg* [1978] E.C.R. 473 at 490–491, paras 10–13, ECJ. For another example, see Case C–204/90 *Bachmann v. Belgium* [1992] E.C.R. I–249, ECJ; Case 300/90 *Commission v. Belgium* [1992] E.C.R. I–305, ECJ; Case T–27/89 *Latham v. Commission* [1991] E.C.R. II–35, CFI; Case T–63/89 *Latham v. Commission* [1991] E.C.R. II–19, CFI.

justified on the ground that it avoids conflicting interpretations of judgments.[9]

In principle, joinder has no effects on the parties' legal position. It does not preclude separate examination of the cases in the judgment.[10] Furthermore, it is possible for one of the cases to be declared inadmissible after joinder. The arguments put forward in the case declared inadmissible may be taken into account in determining the second or other cases joined.[11] 22–084

The President may at any time disjoin cases.[12] 22–085

V. Preliminary Issues

A party may always make an application to the Court of Justice or the Court of First Instance, as the case may be, under Article 91 of the ECJ Rules of Procedure or Article 114 of the CFI Rules of Procedure, for a decision on a preliminary objection or other preliminary plea which relates to the course of the proceedings but does not go to the substance of the case. This possibility is frequently used by the defence in order to raise an objection of inadmissibility or of want of jurisdiction,[13] but any other application may also be made,[14] such as a request by a party for measures of inquiry[15] or for documents to be excluded from the proceedings[16] or to be treated as confidential[17]; a request that the Court declare that there is no need to proceed to judgment[18]; or a request to remedy alleged procedural defects.[19] 22–086

The application must be made by separate document and state the pleas of fact and law relied on, together with the form of order sought. Any supporting documents must be annexed to it.[20] As soon as the application 22–087

---

[9] Joined Cases 36–38 and 40/59 *Präsident Ruhrkohlen-Verkaufsgesellschaft mbH, Geitling Ruhrkohlen-Verkaufsgesellschaft mbH and Others v. High Authority* [1960] E.C.R. 423 at 438, ECJ.

[10] Joined Cases 7 and 9/54 *Groupement des Industries Sidérurgiques Luxembourgeoises v. High Authority* [1954 to 1956] E.C.R. 175 at 188, ECJ.

[11] Joined Cases 26 and 86/79 *Forges de Thy-Marcinelle et Monceau v. Commission* [1980] E.C.R. 1083 at 1092, para. 4, ECJ.

[12] ECJ Rules of Procedure, Art. 43; CFI Rules of Procedure, Art. 50. For an example, see Case 261/78 *Interquell Stärke-Chemie v. EEC* [1982] E.C.R. 3271 at 3279, para. 4, ECJ.

[13] See paras 22–042—22–047, above.

[14] See Louterman and Febvre, "Les incidents de procédure au sens de l'article 91 du Règlement de procédure de la Cour de justice des Communautés européennes" (1989) Gazette du Palais (doctrine) 276 *et seq.*

[15] See, *e.g.* (Order of June 2, 1960), Joined Cases 33, 46 and 47/59 *Compagnie des Hauts Fournaux de Chasse and Others v. High Authority*, ECJ (not reported in the E.C.R.); (Order of June 20, 1960), Joined Cases 24 and 34/58 *Chambre Syndicale de la Sidérurgie de l'Est de la France v. High Authority*, ECJ (not reported in the E.C.R.).

[16] (Order of March 10, 1966), Case 28/65 *Fonzi v. Commission* [1966] E.C.R. 506, ECJ.

[17] See, *e.g.* (Order of March 20, 1985), Case 260/84 *Minebea v. Council*, ECJ (not reported in the E.C.R.); (Order of April 4, 1990), Case T–30/89 *Hilti v. Commission* [1990] E.C.R. II–163, CFI; (Order of November 15, 1990), Joined Cases T–1–T–4 and T–6–T–15/89 *Rhône-Poulenc and Others v. Commission* [1990] E.C.R. II–637, CFI.

[18] See para. 22–170, below.

[19] (Order of December 14, 1992), Case T–47/92 *Lenz v. Commission* [1992] E.C.R. II–2523, CFI.

[20] ECJ Rules of Procedure, Art. 91(1); CFI Rules of Procedure, Art. 114(1).

has been lodged, the President prescribes a period during which the opposite party may lodge a document containing its pleas and the form of order sought.[21] The remainder of the proceedings is oral, unless the Court of Justice or the Court of First Instance, as the case may be, decides to reach its determination on the basis of the documents submitted by the parties. The Court will decide on the application by order or reserve its decision for the final judgment.[22]

22–088 Furthermore, the Court of Justice and the Court of First Instance may at any time, of its own motion, consider whether there exists any absolute bar to proceeding with an action or declare, after hearing the parties, that the action has become devoid of purpose and that there is no need to adjudicate on it.[23]

VI. Intervention

A. Aim and manner of intervention

22–089 The outcome of proceedings before one of the two Courts may affect both Community institutions and natural or legal persons even though they are not parties. Intervention allows them to join voluntarily in the proceedings on the side of one of the parties. This enables the Court to take their interests into account in deciding the case.

22–090 Intervention does not constitute a means for third parties to enter the proceedings by the back door as parties thereto. In the first place, interveners' submissions must be limited to supporting the submissions of one of the parties.[24] Consequently, an intervener may raise only pleas and arguments which serve to support the submissions of the party on whose side it has intervened.[25] An intervener is at liberty to put forward its own pleas and arguments. Indeed if it were not able to do so, intervention would serve no purpose as the intervener would have to confine itself to repeating the arguments put forward by the party which it supported.[26] Furthermore, it is not bound to discuss the whole of the argument underlying the application.[27] An intervener is not entitled to raise an objection of

[21] ECJ Rules of Procedure, Art. 91(2); CFI Rules of Procedure, Art. 114(2).

[22] ECJ Rules of Procedure, Art. 91(4); CFI Rules of Procedure, Art. 114(4).

[23] ECJ Rules of Procedure, Art. 92(2); CFI Rules of Procedure, Art. 113.

[24] E.C. Statute, Art. 37, para. 4. See paras 22–019—22–020, 22–039, above.

[25] Case C–155/91 *Commission v. Council* [1993] E.C.R. I–939 at I–969—970, paras 22–25, ECJ. A party which intervenes on appeal and was not a party to the proceedings before the Court of First Instance cannot therefore claim that the annulment pronounced by that court in the contested judgment should apply equally to it: Case C–245/95P *Commission v. NTN and Koyo Seiko* [1998] E.C.R. I–401 at I–434, para. 24, ECJ.

[26] Case 30/59 *De Gezamenlijke Steenkolenmijnen in Limburg v. High Authority* [1961] E.C.R. 1 at 18, ECJ; Case T–459/93 *Siemens v. Commission* [1995] E.C.R. II–1675 at II–1687—1688, paras 21–23, CFI.

[27] Case C–156/93 *European Parliament v. Commission* [1995] E.C.R. I–2019, ECJ; Case T–459/93 *Siemens v. Commission* [1995] E.C.R. II–1675 at I–1687—1688, paras 21–23, CFI.

inadmissibility not raised by the defendant[28]; the reason for this is that submissions in an application to intervene must be limited to supporting the submissions of one of the parties[29] and that the intervener must accept the case as it finds it at the time of its intervention.[30] This means that the intervener is bound by any acts which have already been carried out in the course of the proceedings and that new arguments adduced by it are admissible only in so far as they do not alter the framework of the dispute as defined by the applicant.[31]

B. Substantive requirements

Community institutions and Member States are entitled to intervene in cases before the Court of Justice or the Court of First Instance. The same right is "open to any other person establishing an interest in the result of any case submitted to the Court".[32] The term "case" refers only to contentious procedures before the Court of Justice or the Court of First Instance, designed to settle a dispute. Consequently, an application by a natural or legal person to intervene—pursuant to Article 37 of the E.C. Statute—in order to submit written observations in a preliminary ruling procedure pending before the Court of Justice will be inadmissible.[33] **22–091**

[28] Case C–313/90 *CIRFS and Others v. Commission* [1993] E.C.R. I–1125 at I–1183, paras 19–22, ECJ; Case C–225/91 *Matra v. Commission* [1993] E.C.R. I–3203 at I–3254, paras 11, 12, ECJ. *Cf.* Joined Cases 42 and 49/59 *SNUPAT v. High Authority* [1961] E.C.R. 53 at 75, ECJ (where an objection of inadmissibility not raised by the defendant was allowed to be raised on the ground that it sought the rejection of the form of order sought by the applicant). The broad wording employed in that judgment was qualified in Joined Cases C–305/86 and C–160/87 *Neotype Techmashexport v. Commission and Council* [1990] E.C.R. I–2945 at I–2998, para. 18, ECJ. The Court of Justice left it undecided whether an intervener is entitled to raise a plea of inadmissibility not raised by the party it is supporting, because it held that the objection was one based on public policy which the Court could raise of its own motion. The Court held that the objection *was to be* raised of its own motion under the ECJ Rules of Procedure, Art. 92, even though, according to the wording of that Article, the Court only *may* at any time of its own motion consider whether there exists any absolute bar to proceeding with a case (*i.e.* an objection based on public policy). In both the *CIRFS* and the *Matra* cases, the Court refused to entertain the possibility that the intervener could raise an objection of inadmissibility, but then considered the plea of its own motion on the ground that it involved public policy considerations. See also Case T–266/94 *Skibsværftsforeningen and Others v. Commission* [1996] E.C.R. II–1399 at II–1417, paras 38, 39, CFI; Case T–19/92 *Leclerc v. Commission* [1996] E.C.R. II–1851 at II–1878, paras 50–51, CFI; Case T–174/95 *Svenska Journalistförbundet v. Council* [1998] E.C.R. II–2289 at II–2315, paras 77–78, CFI.

[29] E.C. Statute, Art. 37, para. 4.

[30] ECJ Rules of Procedure, Art. 93(4); CFI Rules of Procedure, Art. 116(3).

[31] Joined Cases T–447/93, T–448/93 and T–449/93 *AITEC and Others v. Commission* [1995] E.C.R. II–1971 at II–2015, para. 122, CFI (the intervener stepped outside the framework of the dispute by contesting that a measure constituted state aid within the meaning of the E.C. Treaty, Art. 92 (*now Art. 87*), whereas the applicant had not questioned its nature as state aid); Case T–247/94 *British Steel v. Commission* [1997] E.C.R. II–1887 at II–1921, paras 70–73, CFI (an argument based on the EEA Agreement raised by the intervener was held to be inadmissible because the applicant had not alleged that the Agreement had been breached. Consequently, the argument fell outside the framework of the dispute.)

[32] E.C. Statute, Art. 37; ECSC Statute, Art. 34, refers to "natural or legal persons establishing an interest in the result of any case".

[33] (Order of the President of February 26, 1996), Case C–181/95 *Biogen v. Smithkline Beecham Biologicals* [1996] E.C.R. I–717 at I–720—721, para. 4, ECJ.

22–092 The expression "any other person" covers both natural and legal persons. Entities not formally having legal personality may be given leave to intervene if they have the ability, however circumscribed, to undertake autonomous action and to assume liability. This is because those characteristics constitute the basis for legal personality.[34] Consequently, a body which takes decisions which have legal effects only within the institution of which it constitutes a part has no autonomy *vis-à-vis* third parties and hence does not possess characteristics such as to entitle it to intervene.[35]

22–093 Community institutions and Member States are privileged interveners and do not have to establish an interest in the outcome of the case.[36]

22–094 Any other person must make out a reasonable case for its having an interest in the result of a case brought before the Court of Justice or the Court of First Instance.[37]

Such an interest will exist if the intervener's legal position or economic situation[38] might actually be directly affected by the operative part of the decision to be taken by the Court of Justice or the Court of First Instance.[39] In addition, the interest must be safeguarded by the form of order sought by the party in support of whom the intervener seeks to join in the

---

[34] (Order of December 11, 1973), Joined Cases 41, 43–48, 50, 111, 113 and 114/73 *Générale Sucrière v. Commission* [1973] E.C.R. 1465 at 1468, para. 3, ECJ.

[35] See, in connection with the staff committee of the European Parliament, (Order of November 14, 1963), Case 15/63 *Lassalle v. European Parliament* [1964] E.C.R. 31 at 36, and the Opinion of Advocate General M. Lagrange, at 52–57, ECJ.

[36] Case 138/79 *Roquette Frères v. Council* [1980] E.C.R. 3333 at 3358, paras 17–21, ECJ; Case 139/79 *Maizena v. Council* [1980] E.C.R. 3393 at 3420–3421, paras 17–21, ECJ: if the institutions' right to intervene were to be restricted it would adversely affect their institutional position. Under ECSC Treaty, Art. 34, only natural and legal persons establishing an interest in the result of a case are entitled to intervene. In contrast, Member States are always entitled to intervene in proceedings involving a dispute between other Member States (ECSC Statute, Art. 41).

[37] E.C. Statute, Art. 37, para. 2.

[38] (Order of May 29, 1997), Case T–89/96 *British Steel v. Commission* [1997] E.C.R. II–835 at II–842—843, paras 20, 21, CFI.

[39] (Order of October 4, 1979), Case 40/79 *Mrs P. v. Commission* [1979] E.C.R. 3299, ECJ. See also (Order of March 26, 1992), Case T–35/89TO1 *Zubizarreta and Others v. Albani and Others* [1992] E.C.R. II–1599 at II–1610–1612, paras 32–35, CFI, in which an application seeking to initiate third-party proceedings was dismissed as inadmissible because the applicants could have intervened. By the same token, an undertaking which is the subject of a complaint made to the Commission for infringing the E.C. Treaty, Art. 82 (*ex Art. 86*), has an interest to intervene in proceedings for failure to act (Art. 232 (*ex Art. 175*)) brought by the person who made the complaint against the Commission for failing to take any action. This is because the intervener has an interest in the complaint not causing the Commission to take binding measures against it and therefore in the Court of Justice or the Court of First Instance not declaring the Commission's failure to act contrary to Community law: (Order of May 13, 1993), Case T–74/92 *Ladbroke Racing v. Commission* [1993] E.C.R. II–535 at II–538—539, paras 8–9, CFI. Conversely, an undertaking which has lodged a complaint which has resulted in the Commission's initiating a procedure and adopting a decision finding an infringement of competition law has an interest in the outcome of proceedings brought against the Commission by undertakings to which the decision is addressed. It therefore may intervene in support of the Commission: (Order of November 28, 1991), Case T–35/91 *Eurosport v. Commission* [1991] E.C.R. II–1359 at II–1361, paras 1–6, CFI.

proceedings.[40] It is not sufficient for the intervener to be in a similar situation to one of the parties to the proceedings and for it to maintain on that ground that it has an indirect interest in the grounds of the decision to be given by the Court of Justice or the Court of First Instance.[41] A person's interest in one of the pleas raised by a party to the proceedings succeeding or failing is insufficient if the operative part of the decision to be taken by the Court has no bearing on that party's legal position or economic situation.[42] In the context of an action for damages, it is therefore difficult for a person in a similar situation to the applicant to show that he or she has a "direct and continuing" interest. Since the form of order sought by the applicant in such an action is directed only towards obtaining compensation for the damage sustained by it, a would-be intervener does not have a direct interest in the outcome of the application, but at the most an indirect interest in a judgment whose grounds might influence the manner in which the defendant institution(s) would deal with the intervener's own situation. Such an interest is insufficient.[43]

A natural or legal person to whom a decision is addressed has an interest in intervening in annulment proceedings brought by another addressee of the decision.[44] In contrast, a natural or legal person wishing to intervene in proceedings for the annulment of an act addressed only to one or a small number of persons does not have a direct interest in the annulment of that act even if that person is affected by a similar act.[45]

Associations have the right to intervene if the outcome of the proceed- **22–095**
ings is liable to affect the collective interest defended by the association in question.[46] Thus, an association of undertakings which did not participate in

[40] (Order of November 25, 1964), Case 111/63 *Lemmerz-Werke GmbH v. High Authority* [1965] E.C.R. 716 at 717–718, ECJ; (Order of April 12, 1978), Joined Cases 116, 124 and 143/77 *Amylum v. Council and Commission* [1978] E.C.R. 893 at 895, para. 7, ECJ.

[41] See, however, (Order of July 15, 1981), Case 45/81 *Moksel v. Commission*, (unreported); (Order of December 8, 1993), Case T–87/92 *Kruidvat v. Commission* [1993] E.C.R. II–1375 at II–1379—1380, paras 12–13, CFI.

[42] (Order of the President of June 17, 1997), Joined Cases C–151 and C–157/97 P(I) *National Power and PowerGen* [1997] E.C.R. I–3491 at I–3511, para. 57, ECJ.

[43] (Order of the President of July 17, 1995), Case T–517/93 *Van Parijs v. Council and Commission*, paras 8–13, CFI (not reported in the E.C.R.); (Order of March 7, 1997), Case T–184/95 *Dorsch Consult v. Council and Commission* [1997] E.C.R. II–351 at II–358—360, paras 15–21, CFI. But see (Order of March 20,1985), Case 253/84 *GAEC de la Ségaude v. Council and Commission*, ECJ (not reported in the E.C.R.).

[44] (Order of February 14, 1996), Case C–245/95P *Commission v. NTN Corporation* [1996] E.C.R. I–559 at I–565, para. 9, ECJ; (Order of November 28, 1991), Case T–35/91 *Eurosport v. Commission* [1991] E.C.R. II–1359 at II–1363, para. 15, CFI: such person may intervene in support of the applicant. His interest is not defeated by the fact that he himself did not bring an action to annul the decision. But he may only act as intervener, *i.e.* only support the form of order sought by the applicant.

[45] (Order of June 15, 1993), Joined Cases T–97 and T–111/92 *Rijnoudt and Hocken v. Commission* [1993] E.C.R. II–587, CFI; (Order of December 8, 1993), Case T–87/92 *Kruidvat v. Commission* [1993] E.C.R. II–1375 at II–1379—1380, paras 12, 13, CFI; (Order of September 18, 1995), Case T–375/94 *European Passenger Services v. Commission*, paras 20–26, CFI (not reported in the E.C.R.); (Order of March 20, 1998), Case T–191/96 *CAS Succhi di Frutta v. Commission* [1998] E.C.R. II–573 at II–584, paras 31, 32, CFI.

[46] (Order of October 24, 1962), Case 16/82 *Confédération Nationale des Producteurs de Fruits et*

the prior administrative procedure before the Commission for the application of the competition rules may be given leave to intervene only if:

(1) it represents an appreciable number of the undertakings active in the sector concerned;
(2) its objects include that of protecting its members' interests;
(3) the case may raise questions of principle affecting the functioning of the sector concerned; and
(4) the interests of its members may therefore be affected to an appreciable extent by the forthcoming judgment.[47]

Unlike in the case of individuals applying to intervene, associations therefore do not have to show that their own legal position or economic situation is likely to be affected by the outcome of the case. An association will be regarded as having an interest in intervening if it coincides with that of its members in a context in which the association's intervention will enable the Court of Justice or the Court of First Instance better to assess the background to the case. This somewhat more flexible approach with regard to the interest required to be established by an association wishing to intervene makes up to some extent for the strict approach taken to applications by individuals for leave to intervene.

22–096 Finally, individuals are not entitled to intervene in cases between Member States, between Community institutions or between Member States and Community institutions.[48]

C. Formal requirements

22–097 An application to intervene must be made within three months of publication in the *Official Journal of the European Communities* of the notice "of the date of registration of an application initiating proceedings, the names and addresses of the parties, the subject-matter of the proceedings, the form of order sought by the applicant and a summary of the pleas in law and of the main supporting arguments".[49]

Légumes v. Council [1962] E.C.R. 487 at 488–489, ECJ; (Order of December 11, 1973), Joined Cases 41, 43–48, 50, 111, 113 and 114/73 *Générale Sucrière v. Commission* [1973] E.C.R. 1465 at 1469, paras 7–9, ECJ; (Order of December 8, 1993), Case T–87/92 *Kruidvat v. Commission* [1993] E.C.R. II–1363 at I–1366, para. 10, CFI; (Order of December 8, 1993), Case T–87/92 *Kruidvat v. Commission* [1993] E.C.R. II–1369 at II–1373, paras 12–14, CFI; (Order of March 18, 1997), Case T–135/96 *UEAPME v. Council* [1997] E.C.R. II–373 at II–378, para. 9, CFI.

[47] (Order of December 8, 1993), Case T–87/92 *Kruidvat v. Commission* [1993] E.C.R. II–1375 at II–1380, para. 14, CFI; (Order of May 28, 1997), Case T–120/96 *Lilly Industries v. Commission*, para. 24, CFI (not reported in the E.C.R.).

[48] E.C. Statute, Art. 37, para. 2. For an example, see (Order of the President of February 26, 1996), Case C–181/95 *Biogen v. Smithkline Beecham Biologicals* [1996] E.C.R. I–717, ECJ.

[49] ECJ Rules of Procedure, Art. 93(1); CFI Rules of Procedure, Art. 115(1). See also ECJ Rules of Procedure, Art. 16(6); CFI Rules of Procedure, Art. 24(6). If the party seeking to intervene applies as a result of unforeseeable circumstances or *force majeure* after the three-month period has expired, it may be granted leave pursuant to the E.C. Statute, Art. 42, para. 2. For an example, see (Order of March 22, 1994), Joined Cases T–244 and T–486/93 *TWD Textilwerke Deggendorf GmbH v. Commission*, paras 1–21, CFI (not reported in the E.C.R.).

States party to the Agreement on the European Economic Area (EEA), not being Member States of the European Union, and the EFTA Surveillance Authority may intervene in cases before the Court of Justice or the Court of First Instance where one of the fields of application of that Agreement is concerned. Just as in the case of natural or legal persons wishing to intervene, those states or the Surveillance Authority have to show that they have an interest in the outcome of the proceedings before the Court and may not intervene in proceedings between Member States, between Community institutions or between Member States and Community institutions.[50] 22–098

Finally, it should be noted that in the case of disputes concerning intellectual property rights in which a decision of the Office for Harmonisation in the Internal Market (Trade Marks and Designs) or of the Community Plant Variety Office is brought before the Court of First Instance,[51] special rules on intervention apply as regards parties other than the applicant or the defendant Office who were involved in the proceedings before the relevant board of appeal. Such parties may take part as interveners in the proceedings before the Court of First Instance.[52] They have the same procedural rights as the main parties.[53] In addition, they may, unlike "ordinary" interveners, apply for a form of order and put forward pleas in law independently of those applied for and put forward by the main parties.[54] 22–099

Applications to intervene have to comply with the general requirements applicable to pleadings.[55] Each application has to contain a description of the case, a description of the parties, the intervener's name and address, the intervener's address for service in Luxembourg, the form of order sought in support of which the intervener is applying for leave to intervene and, except in the case of applications made by Member States or Community institutions, a statement of reasons establishing the intervener's interest in the result of the case.[56] An application may not be made by fax.[57] 22–100

Applications to intervene may be made in any official language of the Community. It is only after leave to intervene has been granted that the intervener is obliged to use the language of the case.[58] Member States, however, are always entitled to use their official language.[59] 22–101

---

50 E.C. Statute, Art. 37, para. 3. See also Case T–115/94 *Opel Austria v. Council* [1997] E.C.R. II–39 at II–51, para. 29, and at II–85, para. 138, CFI; Joined Cases T–371/94 and T–394/94 *British Airways and Others v. Commission* [1998] E.C.R. II–2405 at II–2424, para. 27, CFI.

51 See Chap. 18, above.

52 CFI Rules of Procedure, Art. 134(1).

53 CFI Rules of Procedure, Art. 134(2), subpara. 1.

54 CFI Rules of Procedure, Art. 134(1), subpara. 2. See also Barents, *Procedures*, p. 257.

55 See ECJ Rules of Procedure, Art. 37; CFI Rules of Procedure, Art. 43.

56 ECJ Rules of Procedure, Art. 93(1); CFI Rules of Procedure, Art. 115(2).

57 (Order of May 14, 1996), Case T–194/95 intv II *Area Cova v. Council* [1996] E.C.R. II–343 at II–349, para. 4, CFI.

58 See para. 22–173, below.

59 ECJ Rules of Procedure, Art. 29(3), subpara. 4; CFI Rules of Procedure, Art. 35(3), subpara. 4.

22–102 The application to intervene is served on the parties, who are given the opportunity to submit written or oral observations. The President decides on the application by order. He or she may refer the application to the Court of Justice or the Court of First Instance, as the case may be, which then decides by order.[60] If the application is rejected, the order will be reasoned.[61]

22–103 If leave is granted to intervene, the President prescribes a period within which the intervener may submit a statement in intervention. That statement sets out the form of order sought by the intervener, the pleas and arguments on which it relies and, where appropriate, the nature of any evidence offered.[62]

The intervener receives a copy of every document served on the parties. However, in its observations on the application for leave to intervene, a party may ask the Court of Justice or the Court of First Instance, depending on the court in which the case has been brought, to treat particular documents as confidential and not to send copies of them to the intervener.[63] If a request to that effect is not granted, the party concerned may ask for particular documents simply to be withdrawn from the case-file, but such a request will not necessarily be granted.[64]

22–104 Parties may reply to the statement in intervention. The President prescribes a time-limit for making such a reply.[65]

---

[60] ECJ Rules of Procedure, Art. 93(2), subpara. 3; CFI Rules of Procedure, Art. 116(1), subpara. 3. For examples, see (Order of April 8, 1981), Joined Cases 197–200, 243, 245 and 247/80 *Ludwigshafener Walzmühle v. Council and Commission* [1981] E.C.R. 1041, ECJ; (Order of November 28, 1991), Case T–35/91 *Eurosport v. Commission* [1991] E.C.R. II–1359, CFI.

[61] This is specifically prescribed by the CFI Rules of Procedure, Art. 116(1) subpara. 3, since an appeal may lie against the order (see para. 15–012, above). In fact, all decisions concerning applications to intervene are reasoned.

[62] ECJ Rules of Procedure, Art. 93(5); CFI Rules of Procedure, Art. 116(4).

[63] ECJ Rules of Procedure, Art. 93(3); CFI Rules of Procedure, Art. 116(2). In the case of each procedural document for which confidential treatment is requested, the Court of Justice or the Court of First Instance, as the case may be, has to balance the applicant's legitimate concern in maintaining confidentiality against the intervener's equally legitimate concern to have the necessary information for the purpose of being fully in a position to assert its rights and to state its case before the Court: (Order of April 4, 1990), Case T–30/89 *Hilti v. Commission* [1990] E.C.R. II–163 at II–168, para. 11, CFI; (Order of May 29, 1997), Case T–89/96 *British Steel v. Commission* [1997] E.C.R. II–835 at II–843, para. 23, CFI. If documents in the case-file contain confidential information about natural or legal persons who are not parties to the proceedings, those persons are entitled in principle to see the confidential nature of that information protected, unless they have business relations with the intervener or the information is known to third parties; (Order of March 19, 1996), Case T–24/93 *CMBT and Others v. Commission*, para. 7, CFI (not reported in the E.C.R.). In proceedings for interim measures, it is enough that the information for which confidential treatment is sought falls prima facie within the area of business secrecy. See (Order of the President of May 13, 1993), Case T–24/93 R *CMBT v. Commission* [1993] E.C.R. II–543 at II–548, para. 17, CFI.

[64] (Order of March 28, 1979), Case 30/78 *Distillers Company v. Commission*, ECJ, referred to in the report for the hearing in Case 30/78 *Distillers Company v. Commission* [1980] E.C.R. 2229 at 2237.

[65] ECJ Rules of Procedure, Art. 93(6); CFI Rules of Procedure, Art. 116(5).

VII. The Closure of Proceedings

A. The judgment

1. Meaning of the term and how it comes about

The decision of the Court of Justice or of the Court of First Instance which brings the proceedings to an end takes the form of a judgment. Occasionally, however, a judgment is given which determines only some of the issues. Examples are a judgment merely declaring the action admissible[66] or one finding the Community liable but not making any determination of the amount of damages to be paid.[67] **22–105**

The Court of Justice and the Court of First Instance alike deliberate in closed session.[68] Only those judges who were present at the oral proceedings may take part in the deliberations.[69] They are not assisted by interpreters—French is the working language of both Courts and is used in the deliberations—or by other members of staff. The deliberations take place on the basis of a draft judgment drawn up by the Judge-Rapporteur. The judgment ultimately arrived at reflects the views of at least the majority of the judges who took part in the deliberations and may certainly not be regarded as the decision of the Judge-Rapporteur. Every judge taking part in the deliberations is to state his or her opinion and the reasons for it.[70] Pains are taken to reach a consensus among the judges. If a consensus cannot be reached, the decision is taken by a majority vote.[71] It is for this reason that an uneven number of judges always take part in the deliberations: it prevents a tied vote. Where, by reason of a judge being absent or prevented from attending, there is an even number of judges, the most junior judge (where there is equal seniority in office, the younger) is to abstain from taking part in the deliberations unless he or she is the Judge-Rapporteur. In that case, the judge immediately senior to him or her is to abstain from taking part in the deliberations.[72] The judges cast their votes in reverse order to the order of precedence established by their seniority.[73] The aim is that the judgment of judges with less seniority should not be swayed by the view taken by more experienced colleagues.[74] **22–106**

---

66 Case C–70/88 *European Parliament v. Council* [1990] E.C.R. I–2041, at I–2074—2075, operative part, ECJ.
67 Case C–152/99 *Sofrimport v. Commission* [1990] E.C.R. I–2477 at I–2512—2513, operative part, ECJ.
68 ECJ Rules of Procedure, Art. 27(1); CFI Rules of Procedure, Art. 33(1).
69 ECJ Rules of Procedure, Art. 27(2); CFI Rules of Procedure, Art. 33(2).
70 ECJ Rules of Procedure, Art. 27(3); CFI Rules of Procedure, Art. 33(3).
71 ECJ Rules of Procedure, Art. 27(5); CFI Rules of Procedure, Art. 33(5).
72 CFI Rules of Procedure, Art. 32(1). For an example, see Joined Cases T–70 and T–71/92 *Florimex and VGB v. Commission* [1997] E.C.R. II–693 at II–719, para. 60, CFI.
73 ECJ Rules of Procedure, Art. 27(5); CFI Rules of Procedure, Art. 33(5).
74 Schermers and Waelbroeck, *Judicial Protection*, p. 856.

2. Content and formal requirements

22–107 Judgments of the Court of Justice and the Court of First Instance consist of three parts: the introductory part, the grounds for the decision and the operative part.[75]

There are no dissenting opinions as there are, for instance, in the House of Lords, the European Court of Human Rights or the International Court of Justice. Even the judges who voted against the decision ultimately adopted sign the judgment.

22–108 The judgment is given in the language of the case.[76] The judgment in that language is the only authentic version, even though it and the versions published in the other official languages of the Community in the *European Court Reports* are translated from the French.

22–109 The judgment is delivered in open court, the parties being given notice to attend to hear it.[77] The original of the judgment, signed by the President, by the judges who took part in the deliberations and by the Registrar, is sealed and deposited at the registry, the parties being served with certified copies.[78]

3. Legal force

22–110 A judgment of the Court of Justice is binding from the date of its delivery.[79] A judgment of the Court of First Instance also has binding force from the date of delivery, unless it annuls a regulation. In that case, the judgment takes effect only as from the date of the expiry of the period for bringing an appeal or, if an appeal is lodged within that period, as from the date of dismissal of the appeal.[80] Apart from this, bringing an appeal has no suspensory effect.[81]

22–111 The fact that the judgment is binding means that anyone to whom it applies is bound to take the necessary steps to comply with it. That obligation stems from the Treaty Articles which specify the effects of

---

[75] ECJ Rules of Procedure, Art. 63; CFI Rules of Procedure, Art. 81. For further details, see Vaughan and Lasok, *European Court Practice*, pp. 163 *et seq.*

[76] ECJ Rules of Procedure, Art. 29(3), subpara. 1; CFI Rules of Procedure, Art. 35(3), subpara. 1.

[77] ECJ Rules of Procedure, Art. 64(1); CFI Rules of Procedure, Art. 82(1). No provision of the CFI Rules of Procedure or of the E.C. Statute of the Court of Justice provides that the judgments of the Court of First Instance must be delivered within a specified period after the oral procedure: see (Judgment of December 17, 1998) Case C–185/95P *Baustahlgewebe v. Commission*, paras 52–53, ECJ (not yet reported). The same holds true, of course, for the Court of Justice itself.

[78] ECJ Rules of Procedure, Art. 64(2); CFI Rules of Procedure, Art. 82(2).

[79] ECJ Rules of Procedure, Art. 65.

[80] CFI Rules of Procedure, Art. 83; E.C. Statute, Art. 53, para. 2. To date, the Court of First Instance has annulled two regulations: Joined Cases T–163/94 and T–165/94 *NTN Corporation and Koyo Seiko v. Council* [1995] E.C.R. II–1381, CFI, and Case T–115/94 *Opel Austria v. Council* [1997] E.C.R. II–39, CFI.

[81] See para. 15–015, above.

judgments.[82] On a more general level, it also arises because of the function performed by judicial pronouncements.[83]

Judgments imposing a pecuniary obligation on natural or legal persons are enforceable *per se*.[84] They have an order for enforcement appended to them by the competent national authority without any review as to their substance[85] and are enforced in accordance with domestic law, if necessary with the co-operation of the competent judicial and other authorities. 22–112

4. Costs

The order for costs is contained in the final judgment or order which closes the proceedings.[86] 22–113

(1) What costs are recoverable?

Proceedings before the Court of Justice or the Court of First Instance are free of charge. Exceptionally, a party may be ordered to refund avoidable costs which it has caused the Court of Justice or the Court of First Instance to incur, or to pay for excessive copying or translation work carried out at the party's request.[87] 22–114

Recoverable costs are sums payable to witnesses and experts and expenses necessarily incurred by the parties for the purposes of the proceedings, in particular the travel and subsistence expenses and the remuneration of agents, advisers or lawyers.[88] 22–115

The costs must have been caused by bringing the proceedings before the Court of Justice or the Court of First Instance. This means that costs incurred during the pre-litigation stage of a staff case or during the

---

[82] See, *inter alia*, E.C. Treaty, Arts. 228, 233, 244 and 256 (*ex Arts. 171, 176, 187 and 192*); Schockweiler, "L'exécution des arrêts de la Cour", in *Du droit international au droit de l'intégration—Liber amicorum Pierre Pescatore*, Baden-Baden, Nomos, 1987, at 613–635; Toth, "The Authority of Judgments of the European Court of Justice: Binding Force and Legal Effects" (1984) Y.E.L. 1 at 44–68. Díez-Hochleitner, "Le traité de Maastricht et l'inexécution des arrêts de la Cour de justice par les Etats membres" (1994) R.M.U.E. 111–139.

[83] Toth (cited in n. 82, above), at 1.

[84] E.C. Treaty, Art. 244 (*ex Art. 187*), under which Art. 256 (*ex Art. 192*) applies to judgments of the Court of Justice and the Court of First Instance.

[85] In the United Kingdom, application to append to a judgment the order for enforcement is made to the Secretary of State. The person concerned then applies to the High Court in England or Wales or in Northern Ireland or the Court of Session in Scotland for the judgment to be registered, and that court must register the judgment forthwith (European Communities (Enforcement of Community Judgments) Order 1972, S.I. 1972 No 1590, art. 3(1); see also European Communities Act, s.3(3)). Once registered, the judgment has for all purposes of execution, the same force and effect as if it had been a judgment or order given by the High Court or Court of Session on the date of registration; proceedings may be taken on it and any sum payable under it carries interest as if it had been such a judgment or order (*ibid*., art. 4).

[86] ECJ Rules of Procedure, Art. 69(1); CFI Rules of Procedure, Art. 87(1). For a general discussion, see Klinke, "Introduction au régime des dépens et à celui de l'assistance judiciaire gratuite", in Christianos (ed.), *Evolution récente du droit judiciaire communautaire*, Maastricht, European Institute of Public Administration, 1994, I, 137.

[87] ECJ Rules of Procedure, Art. 72; CFI Rules of Procedure, Art. 90.

[88] ECJ Rules of Procedure, Art. 73; CFI Rules of Procedure, Art. 91.

administrative investigation into a purported infringement of competition law are not recoverable, since they are not related to the judicial proceedings.[89] In contrast, all costs incurred for the purposes of the judicial proceedings, including the costs of any interlocutory proceedings, are recoverable.

The salary of officials who represent a Community institution before the Court of Justice or the Court of First Instance does not constitute recoverable costs since a salary is in law paid, not as a fee for representing the institution, but for the purposes of fulfilling an obligation imposed on the institution concerned by the Staff Regulations. However, the travel and subsistence expenses of such officials are recoverable, just like the fee payable to a practitioner assisting the institution.

22–116 The party concerned may bring a dispute about the amount of recoverable costs before the chamber dealing with the case. The chamber decides by order against which no appeal will lie, after hearing the opposite party.[90] Such an application for the taxation of costs is admissible only if it genuinely relates to a dispute about the amount of recoverable costs. An application for an order for costs to be reviewed does not constitute a dispute about the amount of recoverable costs.[91] If the dispute relates to the amount of a lawyer's fees, the Court of Justice or the Court of First Instance, as the case may be, does not rule on whether the fees were appropriate, but only on the extent to which they are recoverable.[92] In so doing, it takes account of the subject-matter and the character of the proceedings,[93] the importance of the dispute from the point of view of Community law, the volume of work involved for the lawyer and the economic importance of the case for the parties concerned.[94] In general, the fees for one lawyer will be accepted as being recoverable costs, but in complex cases the fees of more than one lawyer will be recoverable within

[89] (Order of October 21, 1970), Case 75/69 *Hake v. Commission* [1970] E.C.R. 901 at 902–903, para. 1, ECJ; (Order of November 30, 1994), Case C–294/90 DEP *British Aerospace v. Commission* [1994] E.C.R. I–5423 at I–5428, para. 12, ECJ. See, however, Fiebig, "The Indemnification of Costs in Proceedings before the European Courts" (1997) C.M.L.Rev. 89 at 116–118, who argues that non-recoverable costs connected with the administrative procedure before the Commission may be included in the claim in an action for damages.

[90] ECJ Rules of Procedure, Art. 74(1), in the Court of Justice, the Advocate General is also heard; CFI Rules of Procedure, Art. 92(1).

[91] (Order of 15 July 1993), Joined Cases T–33 and T–74/89 DEPE *Blackman v. European Parliament* [1993] E.C.R. II–837 at II–840, paras 5–6, CFI.

[92] (Order of November 28, 1996), Case T–447/93 (92) *AITEC v. Commission* [1996] E.C.R. II–1631 at II–1638—1639, para. 19, CFI.

[93] Whether a case raises questions already raised in other cases may have a bearing on this: see (Order of July 11, 1995), Cases T–23/90 (92) and T–9/92 (92) *Peugeot v. Commission* [1995] E.C.R. II–2057 at II–2069, para. 30, CFI; (Order of December 13, 1995), Case T–139/95 (92) *Engelking v. Council and Commission*, para. 14, CFI (not reported in the E.C.R.).

[94] (Order of October 21, 1970), Case 75/69 *Hake v. Commission* [1970] E.C.R. 901 at 903, para. 2, ECJ; (Order of November 26, 1985), Case 318/82 *Leeuwarder Papierwarenfabriek v. Commission* [1985] E.C.R. 3727, ECJ; (Order of February 25, 1992), Joined Cases T–18 and T–24/89 *Tagaras v. Court of Justice* [1992] E.C.R. II–153 at II–157, para. 13, CFI; (Order of June 9, 1993), Case T–78/89 DEPE *PPG Industries Glass SpA v. Commission* [1993] E.C.R. II–573 at II–583, para. 36, CFI; (Order of July 15, 1993), Case T–84/91 DEPE *Meskens v. European Parliament* [1993] E.C.R. II–757, CFI.

reasonable limits.[95] The Community Court does not take account of national scales of lawyers' fees.[96]

22–117 As the right to recover costs has its basis in the order of Court of Justice or the Court of First Instance fixing the amount recoverable, interest thereon is payable only from the date of that order.[97]

(2) Who has to pay the costs?

22–118 In principle, the Court of Justice or the Court of First Instance orders the unsuccessful party to pay the costs if they have been applied for in the successful party's pleadings.[98] It is possible to apply for costs for the first time at the stage of the oral procedure.[99]

22–119 An order may be made that the costs be shared or that the parties bear their own costs where each party succeeds on some and fails on other heads or where the Court so decides on specific grounds.[1]

22–120 The successful party may be ordered to pay costs which the Court considers it to have unreasonably or vexatiously caused the other party to bear.[2]

---

[95] (Order of November 8, 1996), Case T–120/89 (92) *Stahlwerke Peine-Salzgitter v. Commission* [1996] E.C.R. II–1547 at II–1556—1557, para. 31, CFI; (Order of November 28, 1996), Case T–447/93 (92) *AITEC v. Commission* [1996] E.C.R. II–1631 at II–1639—1640, para. 23, CFI.

[96] (Order of January 20, 1995), Case T–124/93 *Werner v. Commission* [1995] E.C.R. II–91 at II–98—99, para. 10, CFI; (Order of June 5, 1996), Case T–228/94 (92) *Rusp v. Council and Commission*, para. 11, CFI (not reported in the E.C.R.).

[97] (Order of April 18, 1975), Case 6/72 *Europemballage and Continental Can v. Commission* [1975] E.C.R. 495 at 497, para. 5, ECJ; (Order of June 9, 1993), Case T–78/89 DEPE *PPG Industries Glass SpA v. Commission* [1993] E.C.R. II–573 at II–580—581 paras 25–29, CFI.

[98] ECJ Rules of Procedure, Art. 69(2); CFI Rules of Procedure, Art. 87(2). See Joined Cases 23–24 and 52/63 *Henricot v. High Authority* [1963] E.C.R. 217 at 225, ECJ; Joined Cases 188–190/80 *France, Italy and United Kingdom v. Commission* [1982] E.C.R. 2545 at 2582, para. 39, ECJ. But see Joined Cases 40–48, 50, 54–56, 111, 113 and 114/73 *Suiker Unie and Others v. Commission* [1975] E.C.R. 1663 at 2024, para. 627, ECJ.

[99] Case 113/77 *NTN Toyo Bearing Company v. Council* [1979] E.C.R. 1185 at 1274, Opinion of Advocate General J.-P. Warner, who took the view that omission by a party to ask for costs under the ECJ Rules of Procedure, Art. 69(2), does not debar the Court from awarding them under Art. 69(1); Case T–64/89 *Automec v. Commission* [1990] E.C.R. II–367 at II–391—392, para. 79, CFI; Case T–13/92 *Moat v. Commission* [1993] E.C.R. II–287 at II–301, para. 50, CFI. See, however, Case 298/83 *CICCE v. Commission* [1985] E.C.R. 1105 at 1125, para. 32, ECJ, where costs were claimed in the rejoinder and this was considered to be too late and therefore the claim was inadmissible. This shows a tolerance of the Community Court *vis-à-vis* private parties. In the judgment in *CICCE*, the private party lost its case and would therefore have had to pay the costs. In *Moat* the individual was successful and his claim was not regarded as having been made too late.

[1] Rules of Procedure, Art. 69(3), subpara. 1; CFI Rules of Procedure, Art. 87(3), subpara. 1. For examples, see *Commentaire Mégret*, at 458; Case T–38/96 *Guérin Automobiles v. Commission* [1997] E.C.R. II–1223 at II–1237—1238, paras 48–50, CFI.

[2] ECJ Rules of Procedure, Art. 69(3), subpara. 2; CFI Rules of Procedure, Art. 87(3), subpara. 2. For examples, see Joined Cases 35/62 and 16/63 *Leroy v. High Authority* [1963] E.C.R. 197 at 208, ECJ; Joined Cases 23–24 and 52/63 *Henricot v. High Authority* [1963] E.C.R. 217, at 225, ECJ, Case 148/79 *Korter v. Council* [1981] E.C.R. 615 at 629, paras 19–20, ECJ; Case 263/81 *List v. Commission* [1983] E.C.R. 103 at 118, paras 30–31, ECJ.

22–121 In proceedings between the Communities and their servants, the institutions bear their own costs in any event,[3] unless they were caused unreasonably or vexatiously.[4]

22–122 As interveners, Member States, institutions, EEA States and the EFTA Supervisory Authority bear their own costs.[5] Other interveners may also be ordered to bear their own costs, even if they intervened in support of the successful party.[6] Generally, however, an intervener which intervened in support of the successful party will recover its costs from the unsuccessful party.[7] An intervener which supported the form of order sought by the unsuccessful party may be ordered to pay the costs together with that party. In particular, the Court of Justice and the Court of First Instance may allow the successful party to recover the costs it incurred as a result of the intervention of the intervener.[8]

22–123 If a party discontinues or withdraws from proceedings,[9] that party will be ordered to pay the costs if they have been applied for in the other party's observations on the discontinuance or withdrawal. However, the party discontinuing or withdrawing from proceedings may apply for an order for costs against the other party if this appears justified by that party's conduct. Where the parties have come to an agreement on costs, the decision on costs will be in accordance with that agreement. If costs are not claimed, the parties bear their own costs.[10]

22–124 Where a case does not proceed to judgment, the costs are in the discretion of the Court.[11]

[3] ECJ Rules of Procedure, Art. 70; CFI Rules of Procedure, Art. 88.

[4] For an example, see (Order of December 15, 1995), Case T–131/95 *Progoulis v. Commission* [1995] E.C.R.–S.C. II–907 at II–919—920, paras 52–55, CFI (English abstract at A–I–297).

[5] ECJ Rules of Procedure, Art. 69(4), subparas 1, 2; CFI Rules of Procedure, Art. 87(4), subparas 1, 2.

[6] ECJ Rules of Procedure, Art. 69(4), subpara. 3; CFI Rules of Procedure, Art. 87(4), subpara. 3.

[7] Case T–2/93 *Air France v. Commission* [1994] E.C.R. II–323 at II–359, para. 106, CFI.

[8] See, *e.g.* the 1979 ball bearing cases: Case 113/77 *NTN Toyo Bearing Company v. Council* [1979] E.C.R. 1185 at 1211, para. 31, ECJ; Case 118/77 *ISO v. Council* [1979] E.C.R. 1277 at 1300, para. 62, ECJ; Case 119/77 *Nippon Seiko v. Council and Commission* [1979] E.C.R. 1303 at 1334, para. 38, ECJ; Case 120/77 *Koyo Seiko v. Council and Commission* [1979] E.C.R. 1337 at 1360, para. 63, ECJ; Case 121/77 *Nachi Fujikoshi v. Council* [1979] E.C.R. 1363 at 1385, para. 29, ECJ.

[9] See paras 22–168, 22–169, below.

[10] ECJ Rules of Procedure, Art. 69(5); CFI Rules of Procedure, Art. 87(5). For examples, see (Order of October 16, 1995), Case T–561/93 *Tiercé Ladbroke v. Commission* [1995] E.C.R. II–2755, CFI; (Order of October 22, 1996), Case T–19/96 *Carvel and Guardian Newspapers v. Council* [1996] E.C.R. II–1519, CFI.

[11] ECJ Rules of Procedure, Art. 69(6); CFI Rules of Procedure, Art. 87(6). For an example, see Case T–56/92 *Koelman v. Commission* [1993] E.C.R. II–1267 at II–1278, paras 29–32, CFI.

5. Legal aid

A party who is wholly or in part unable to meet the costs of the proceedings may at any time apply for legal aid.[12] The application, which need not be made through a lawyer,[13] has to be accompanied by evidence of the applicant's need of assistance, in particular by a document from the competent authority under national law certifying his or her lack of means.[14] **22–125**

An application for legal aid may be made prior to proceedings which the applicant wishes to commence. If such an application is made, it must briefly state the subject of the proceedings.[15] **22–126**

In the Court of Justice, the chamber to which the Judge-Rapporteur designated by the President belongs decides, after considering the written observations of the opposite party and after hearing the Advocate General, whether legal aid should be granted in full or in part or whether it should be refused. It considers, *inter alia*, whether the application lodged or to be lodged is not manifestly inadmissible. The chamber gives its order without giving reasons and it is not amenable to appeal.[16] If circumstances alter during the proceedings, the chamber may at any time, either of its own motion or on application, withdraw legal aid.[17] In the Court of First Instance, the President decides whether legal aid should be granted.[18] **22–127**

If legal aid is granted, the cashier of the Court of Justice/Court of First Instance advances the necessary funds. An order granting legal aid may specify an amount to be paid to the lawyer appointed to act for the person concerned or fix a limit which the lawyer's fees and disbursements may not, in principle, exceed.[19] Subsequently the Court may recover these costs from the opposite party if a costs order is made against it.[20] **22–128**

The principal reason why legal aid must be available is that individuals must invariably be represented before the Court of Justice or the Court First Instance by a lawyer. In the event that they were unable to pay **22–129**

---

[12] For a more extensive discussion, see Kennedy, "Paying the Piper: Legal Aid in Proceedings Before the Court of Justice" (1988) C.M.L.Rev. 559–591. A party to proceedings in England and Wales who is legally aided is entitled to have the legal aid order extended to cover the proceedings before the Court of Justice: *R. v. Malborough Street Magistrates, ex p. Bouchereau* [1977] 1 W.L.R. 414.

[13] Application may be made without the assistance of a lawyer not only before proceedings have been brought, but also after the application has been lodged by a lawyer: (Order of February 19, 1997), Case T–157/96AJ *Affatato v. Commission* [1997] E.C.R. II–155, CFI.

[14] ECJ Rules of Procedure, Art. 76(1) and (2), subpara. 2; CFI Rules of Procedure, Art. 94(1) and (2), subpara. 2.

[15] ECJ Rules of Procedure, Art. 76(2), subpara. 1; CFI Rules of Procedure, Art. 94(2), subpara. 1. If such an application is made during the period prescribed for bringing an action before the Court of Justice/Court of First Instance, this prevents time from running until the date on which the order ruling on the application for legal aid is served on the applicant: (Order of January 14, 1993), Case T–92/92 *AJ Lallemand-Zeller v. Commission* [1993] E.C.R. II–31 at II–33, CFI.

[16] ECJ Rules of Procedure, Art. 76(3); CFI Rules of Procedure, Art. 94(2), subparas 3, 4.

[17] ECJ Rules of Procedure, Art. 76(4); CFI Rules of Procedure, Art. 96.

[18] CFI Rules of Procedure, Art. 94(2), subpara. 3.

[19] CFI Rules of Procedure, Art. 95(4).

[20] ECJ Rules of Procedure, Art. 76(5); CFI Rules of Procedure, Art. 97.

lawyer's fees, they would have no access to the Community Court if no-one were prepared to pay the costs of legal representation. This is why the budget of the Court of Justice contains an item covering legal aid.

6. Exceptional review procedures

(1) Third-party proceedings

(a) *Subject-matter*

22–130 Judgments may be prejudicial to the rights of third parties. Notwithstanding the force of *res judicata*, third parties are therefore entitled in exceptional circumstances to contest such judgments.

(b) *Substantive requirements and time-limits*

22–131 Third-party proceedings may be brought by Member States, Community institutions and natural or legal persons "to contest a judgment rendered without their being heard, where the judgment is prejudicial to their rights".[21]

Consequently, an application to bring third-party proceedings on the part of an intervener will be inadmissible. Third-party proceedings instituted by interested third parties who did not have good reasons for failing to intervene in the original proceedings will also be inadmissible.[22] The notice published in the *Official Journal of the European Communities* setting out the subject-matter of the proceedings, the form of order sought and the pleas in law and main supporting arguments[23] is specifically intended to enable third parties to intervene in proceedings whose outcome may be prejudicial to their rights. Only careful third parties who were unable to suspect on the basis of that notice that their rights might be affected can claim that they were not put on notice. An application to bring third-party proceedings by such a party will therefore be admissible.[24] The duty of care is assessed in the light of the circumstances of the case and with due concern not to detract unnecessarily from the authority as *res judicata* of the contested judgment in the interests of legal certainty. The hurdle is therefore set very high. Accordingly, a decision on the part of an interested third party not to intervene in the original proceedings does not satisfy the duty of care where that decision was based on the party's own assessment of the probable outcome of the case based on the information as to the facts and law known at the time when the action was started. This is because further facts may emerge in the course of the proceedings to influence the outcome of the dispute. Moreover, the Court may depart from settled case law.[25]

---

[21] E.C. Statute, Art. 39.

[22] Joined Cases 42 and 49/59 Third-party proceedings *Breedband v. Société des Aciéries du Temple and Others* [1962] E.C.R. 145, ECJ.

[23] ECJ Rules of Procedure, Art. 16(6); CFI Rules of Procedure, Art. 24(6).

[24] Joined Cases 9 and 12/60 Third-party proceedings *Belgium v. Vloeberghs and High Authority* [1962] E.C.R. 171 at 182, ECJ.

[25] (Order of March 25, 1992), Case T–35/89TO1 *Zubizarreta and Others v. Albani* [1992] E.C.R. II–1599 at II–1611—1612, paras 33–35, CFI.

Third-party proceedings may be brought only by parties who could—at least in theory—have taken part in the main proceedings. Since natural or legal persons are not entitled to intervene in proceedings brought under Articles 226–227 (*ex Articles 169–170*) of the E.C. Treaty, they may not bring third-party proceedings against a judgment closing such proceedings.[26] **22–132**

The contested judgment must be prejudicial to the *rights* of the third party. It is not enough that the third party has a legitimate interest to protect.[27] The prejudice to the third party's rights must ensue from the operative part or the grounds[28] of the judgment itself.[29] The alleged prejudice may be material or non-material.[30] **22–133**

Third-party proceedings must be brought within two months of publication of the contested judgment in the *Official Journal of the European Communities*.[31] **22–134**

Where an appeal before the Court of Justice and an application initiating third-party proceedings before the Court of First Instance contest the same judgment of the latter court, the Court of First Instance may, after hearing the parties, stay proceedings until the Court of Justice has delivered its judgment.[32] However, the Court of Justice may defer hearing the appeal until such time as the Court of First Instance has dealt with the application for third-party proceedings.[33] **22–135**

(c) *Formal requirements*

The application initiating third-party proceedings must comply with the general requirements applicable to pleadings and with the specific requirements relating to applications.[34] In addition, the application must specify the contested judgment, state how the judgment is prejudicial to the rights **22–136**

---

26 (Order of the President of December 6, 1989), Case C–147/86TO1 *POIFXG and Others v. Greece and Commission* [1989] E.C.R. 4103, ECJ; (Order of the President of December 6, 1989), Case C–147/86TO2 *PALSO and Others v. Greece and Commission* [1989] E.C.R. 4111, ECJ; (Order of the President of December 6, 1989), Case C–147/86TO3 *PSIITENSM v. Greece and Commission* [1989] E.C.R. 4119, ECJ.

27 ECJ Rules of Procedure, Art. 97(1)(b); CFI Rules of Procedure, Art. 123(1)(b); (Order of September 22, 1987), Case 292/84TO *Bolognese and Others v. Scharf and Commission* [1987] E.C.R. 3563 at 3567, para. 7, ECJ.

28 Joined Cases 9 and 12/60 Third-party proceedings *Belgium v. Vloeberghs and High Authority* [1962] E.C.R. 171 at 183–184, ECJ.

29 See *Commentaire Mégret*, at 465, where it is pointed out that an individual may bring third-party proceedings against a judgment annulling a regulation, since the alleged prejudice then ensues from the judgment, but not against a judgment rejecting an application for the annulment of a regulation, since in that case the alleged prejudice results from the regulation and not from the judgment.

30 Joined Cases 9 and 12/60 Third-party proceedings *Belgium v. Vloeberghs and High Authority* [1962] E.C.R. 171 at 183–184, and the Opinion of Advocate General K. Roemer, at 190, ECJ.

31 ECJ Rules of Procedure, Art. 97(1), subpara. 3; CFI Rules of Procedure, Art. 123(1), subpara. 3.

32 CFI Rules of Procedure, Art. 123(4).

33 It would do so pursuant to the E.C. Statute, Art. 47.

34 ECJ Rules of Procedure, Arts. 37 and 38; CFI Rules of Procedure, Arts. 43 and 44.

of the third party and indicate the reasons for which the third party was unable to take part in the original case.[35]

22–137 The application is addressed to all the parties to the original case. If the contested judgment is varied, the variation may be relied upon against all the parties to the original proceedings since they were summoned to the third-party proceedings.

(d) *Consequences*

22–138 In so far as the third-party proceedings are successful, the contested judgment will be varied.

22–139 The original of the judgment in the third-party proceedings is annexed to the original of the contested judgment. A note of the judgment in the third-party proceedings is made in the margin of the original judgment.[36]

(2) Revision

22–140 Revision affords an opportunity of varying a judgment after a "new fact" has come to light.[37]

(a) *Substantive requirements and time-limits*

22–141 Under the first paragraph of Article 41 of the E.C. Statute of the Court of Justice, an application for revision of a judgment of the Court of Justice or of the Court of First Instance may be made on discovery of a fact which is of such a nature as to be a decisive factor and which, when the judgment was given, was unknown to the Court and to the party claiming the revision.[38] Consequently, revision is not a form of appeal, but an exceptional review procedure that allows an applicant to call in question the authority of *res judicata* attaching to a final judgment on the basis of the findings of fact relied upon by the Court. In order for revision proceedings to be admissible, a number of conditions have to be satisfied:

(1) matters of a factual nature which existed prior to the judgment must have been discovered;

(2) those matters must have been unknown at that time to the Court which delivered the judgment as well as to the party applying for revision; and

---

[35] ECJ Rules of Procedure, Art. 97(1); CFI Rules of Procedure, Art. 123(1).

[36] ECJ Rules of Procedure, Art. 97(3); CFI Rules of Procedure, Art. 123(3).

[37] E.C. Statute, Art. 41. It is not possible, however, to seek revision of a preliminary ruling since there are no parties to the proceedings and Arts. 38 to 41 relating to exceptional pleas are not applicable: (Order of April 28, 1998), Case C–116/96Rev *Reisebüro Binder* [1998] E.C.R. I–1889 at I–1893—1894, paras 6–9, ECJ.

[38] The Court of Justice has extended this provision of the Statute to cover orders producing the same effects as a judgment (Joined Cases C–199/94P and C–200/94P–Rev. *Inpesca v. Commission* [1998] E.C.R. I–831 at I–839, para. 16, ECJ).

(3) the matters must be such that, if the Court had been able to take them into consideration, they might have led it to a different determination of the proceedings.[39]

The late discovery of the new fact must not be attributable to the applicant for revision. Accordingly, where the applicant was aware of the existence of a given report but not of its content at the time of the original proceedings, the report in question did not constitute a new fact.[40] This was because the party's failure to ask for the content of the report to be communicated to it or to apply to the Court for measures of inquiry was part of the reason why the applicant was not apprised of the content of the report before judgment was delivered. The Court of Justice or the Court of First Instance, as the case may be, must also not have been aware of the allegedly "new" fact at the time when judgment was delivered. Accordingly, the Court is aware of the content of a document produced before the end of the oral procedure even though it was not drawn up in the language of the case but in another official language of the Community. There is an irrebuttable presumption that the Court of Justice and the Court of First Instance master all the official languages, and hence they may have cognizance of such a document.[41] **22–142**

As has been mentioned, the fact on which the application for revision is based must have already occurred at the time when judgment was given.[42] The fact must have been in existence—yet unknown—at that time.[43] For that reason, subsequent case law of the Court of Justice or the Court of First Instance cannot be regarded as a new fact for the purposes of Article 41 of the E.C. Statute of the Court of Justice.[44] **22–143**

---

[39] (Order of February 25, 1992), Case C–185/90P-Rev. *Gill v. Commission* [1992] E.C.R. I–993 at I–999, paras 11, 12, ECJ. In that case, the application for revision of a judgment given by the Court of Justice on appeal setting aside a judgment of the Court of First Instance was held to be manifestly inadmissible. In its judgment on appeal, the Court of Justice had given a decision on points of law only and did not adopt a view on the facts as found by the Court of First Instance. Moreover, the Court of Justice had referred the case back to the Court of First Instance and hence the new fact could have been raised before that court. See also (Order of March 26, 1992), Case T–4/89Rev. *BASF v. Commission* [1992] E.C.R. II–1591 at II–1595—1596, paras 8–9, CFI. Naturally, an application for revision which makes no mention of any new fact will be inadmissible, see Case C–295/90Rev. *Council v. European Parliament* [1992] E.C.R. I–5299, ECJ. See also Case 13/69 *Van Eick v. Commission* [1970] E.C.R. 3 at 13, para. 33, ECJ; Case C–130/91Rev *ISAE/VP and Interdata v. Commission* [1995] E.C.R. I–407, ECJ; Case T–8/89Rev. *DSM v. Commission* [1992] E.C.R. II–2399 at II–2405, para. 14, CFI; Case T–14/89Rev. *Montecatini v. Commission* [1992] E.C.R. II–2409 at I–2413, para. 10, CFI.

[40] Case 56/70Rev. *Mandelli v. Commission* [1971] E.C.R. 1, ECJ.

[41] Case 1/60 *FERAM v. High Authority* [1960] E.C.R. 165 at 169–170, ECJ.

[42] Case C–130/91REVII *ISAE/VP and Interdata v. Commission* [1996] E.C.R. I–65 at I–70, ECJ.

[43] Case 116/78Rev. *Bellintani v. Commission* [1980] E.C.R. 23 at 26–27, para. 2, ECJ.

[44] Case C–403/85Rev. *Ferrandi v. Commission* [1991] E.C.R. I–1215 at I–1220, para. 13, ECJ; (Order of March 26, 1992), Case T–4/89Rev. *BASF v. Commission* [1992] E.C.R. II–1591 at II–1596, para. 12, ECJ. *Cf.* Case 56/75 *Elz v. Commission* [1977] E.C.R. 1617 at 1621, para. 7, ECJ, where the Court of Justice held with regard to a judgment of a national court that "[t]he mere fact that the judgment of the Tribunal was subsequent to the judgment of the

22–144 Lastly, the fact must be of such a nature as to be a decisive factor for the outcome of the case.[45] The new fact must potentially form the basis for amending the operative part of the contested judgment. A new fact which is relevant only to an additional ground, but cannot shake the judgment itself, does not satisfy that requirement.[46]

22–145 The application for revision must contest the determination made in the judgment, not the order for costs or any measures taken in order to give effect to the judgment.[47]

22–146 An application for revision of a judgment must be made within three months of the date on which the facts on which the application is based came to the applicant's knowledge.[48] No application for revision may be made after the lapse of 10 years from the date of the judgment.[49]

(b) *Formal requirements*

22–147 The application must be made against all parties to the case in which the contested judgment was given.[50]

22–148 An application for revision must comply with the general requirements for pleadings and the specific requirements for applications.[51] In addition, it must specify the judgment contested, indicate the points on which the judgment is contested, set out the facts on which the application is based, and indicate the nature of the evidence to show that there are facts justifying revision of the judgment, and that the applicable time-limit has been observed.

22–149 Without prejudice to its decision on the substance, the Court of Justice or the Court of First Instance decides on the admissibility of the application after hearing the Advocate General and having regard to the written observations of the parties.[52] If the application is admissible, normal proceedings, resulting in delivery of a judgment, ensue.[53]

Court [of Justice] cannot of itself prevent the first-mentioned judgment from being considered as the discovery of a new fact". However, the national court's judgment merely confirmed earlier judgments of a lower court which were known to the Court of Justice and to the parties, and "drew the foreseeable legal consequences from that confirmation". As a result, the national court's judgment was not a "new fact" and the application for revision was declared inadmissible.

[45] Case 28/64 Rev. *Müller v. Council* [1967] E.C.R. 141 at 144, ECJ; Case 37/71Rev. *Jamet v. Commission* [1973] E.C.R. 295 at 298–299, para. 3, ECJ; Case 107/79Rev. *Schuerer v. Commission* [1983] E.C.R. 3805, ECJ; Case 285/81Rev. I and II *Geist v. Commission* [1984] E.C.R. 1789, ECJ; Case 267/80Rev. *Riseria Modenese v. Council, Commission and Birra Peroni* [1985] E.C.R. 3499 at 3504, para. 12, ECJ; Case C–119/94PRev *Coussios v. Commission*, (not reported in the E.C.R.).

[46] Case 40/71 *Richez-Parise v. Commission* [1972] E.C.R. 73 at 80, para. 21, ECJ; (Order of July 1, 1994), Case T–106/89Rev. *Norsk Hydro A/S v. Commission* [1994] E.C.R. II–419 at II–428, para. 14, CFI.

[47] Case 235/82Rev. *Ferriere San Carlo v. Commission* [1986] E.C.R. 1799 at 1802, para. 9, ECJ.

[48] ECJ Rules of Procedure, Art. 98; CFI Rules of Procedure, Art. 125.

[49] E.C. Statute, Art. 41, para. 3.

[50] ECJ Rules of Procedure, Art. 99(2); CFI Rules of Procedure, Art. 126(2).

[51] ECJ Rules of Procedure, Arts. 37 and 38; CFI Rules of Procedure, Arts. 43 and 44.

[52] ECJ Rules of Procedure, Art. 100(1); CFI Rules of Procedure, Art. 127(2).

[53] ECJ Rules of Procedure, Art. 100(2); CFI Rules of Procedure, Art. 127(3).

The original of the revising judgment is annexed to the original of the judgment revised. A note of the revising judgment is made in the margin of the original of the judgment revised.[54] 22–150

7. Procedural measures after giving of judgment: the interpretation of judgments, rectification of clerical errors or of the omission to give a decision

(1) The interpretation of judgments

22–151 If the meaning or scope of a judgment is in doubt, application may be made to the Court of Justice or the Court of First Instance, as the case may be, to construe it.[55]

22–152 An application for interpretation of a judgment must seek only to resolve an obscurity or ambiguity relating to the determination made in the judgment. Questions concerning the implications of the judgment for other disputes or the content of measures needed in order to give effect to it or points not decided by the judgment do not constitute questions of interpretation for this purpose and hence are inadmissible.[56] Such questions, however, might form the subject-matter of new proceedings.

(a) *Who can bring an application for interpretation?*

22–153 An application for interpretation of a judgment may be made by any party to the proceedings.[57] An intervener in the original proceedings may make an application, irrespective as to the stance taken by the party in whose support it intervened.[58]

22–154 In the case of parallel proceedings, based on the same complaints, in which judgment is given in one or more cases by reference to a judgment in an initial case, all parties involved are entitled to apply for an interpretation of that judgment, even if they were not parties to those particular proceedings.[59] In contrast, an application for interpretation of a judgment which is concerned merely to define the consequences of an earlier judgment constitutes an application to interpret that initial judgment and so only parties to those proceedings are entitled to bring an application for interpretation.[60]

---

[54] ECJ Rules of Procedure, Art. 100(3); CFI Rules of Procedure, Art. 127(4).

[55] E.C. Statute, Art. 40.

[56] Case 70/63A *High Authority v. Collotti and Others* [1965] E.C.R. 275 at 279, ECJ; Case 110/63A *Willame v. Commission* [1966] E.C.R. 287 at 292, ECJ; (Order of September 29,1983), Case 9/81–Interpretation *Court of Auditors v. Williams* [1983] E.C.R. 2859, ECJ; (Order of September 29,1983), Case 206/81A *Alvarez v. European Parliament* [1983] E.C.R. 2865 at 2871, para. 8, ECJ; (Order of December 11, 1986), Case 25/86 *Suss v. Commission* [1986] E.C.R. 3929 at 3932, para. 9, ECJ; (Order of April 20,1988), Joined Cases 146 and 431/85–Interpretation *Maindiaux and Others v. ESC* [1988] E.C.R. 2003 at 2006, para. 6, ECJ; (Order of July 14, 1993), Case T–22/91INT *Inès Raiola-Denti and Others v. Council* [1993] E.C.R. II–817 at II–820, para. 6, CFI.

[57] E.C. Statute, Art. 40.

[58] (Order of April 20, 1988), Joined Cases 146 and 431/85–Interpretation *Maindiaux and Others v. ESC* [1988] E.C.R. 2003 at 2005, para. 4, ECJ.

[59] Case 5/55 *Assider v. High Authority* [1954 to 1956] E.C.R. 135 at 141–142, ECJ.

[60] Case 24/66bis *Getreidehandel v. Commission* [1973] E.C.R. 1599 at 1602–1603, para. 3, ECJ.

22–155 A Community institution, which establishes an interest in having a judgment interpreted, may bring an application for interpretation even if it was not a party to the proceedings which culminated in the judgment whose interpretation is sought.[61]

(b) *Substantive and formal requirements*

22–156 In order for there to be a doubt as to the meaning or scope of a judgment within the meaning of Article 40 of the E.C. Statute, it is sufficient that parties give differing meanings to it.[62]

22–157 The doubt must relate to an issue determined by the judgment. It must therefore attach to the operative part or to one of the grounds determining it. An application for interpretation may not be made to the Court of Justice or the Court of First Instance for interpretation of an ancillary matter which supplements or explains those basic grounds.[63]

22–158 Lastly, there must be a real obscurity or ambiguity in the judgment.[64] The applicant must expressly identify that obscurity or ambiguity.

22–159 The application for interpretation must comply with the general requirements for pleadings and with the specific requirements for applications.[65] It must also specify the judgment in question and the passages of which interpretation is sought.[66]

22–160 The application must be made against all the parties to the case in which the original judgment was given.[67]

22–161 No time-limit is prescribed for bringing an application for interpretation.

(c) *Procedure before the Court and judgment*

22–162 The Court of Justice or the Court of First Instance, as the case may be, gives its decision in the form of a judgment after having given the parties an opportunity to submit their observations and after hearing the Advocate General.[68]

22–163 The original of the interpreting judgment is annexed to the original of the judgment interpreted and a note of the interpreting judgment is made in the margin of the judgment interpreted. The interpreting judgment is binding not only on all parties to the proceedings in which the interpreted

---

[61] E.C. Statute, Art. 40.

[62] Case 5/55 *Assider v. High Authority* [1954 to 1956] E.C.R. 135 at 142, ECJ.

[63] *ibid.*, at 142.

[64] Observations of Advocate General P. VerLoren van Themaat in (Order of September 29, 1983), Case 206/81A *Alvarez v. European Parliament* [1983] E.C.R. 2865 at 2876, ECJ; (Order of July 14, 1993), Case T–22/91INT *Inès Raiola-Denti and Others v. Council* [1993] E.C.R. II–817 at II–820—821, paras 7–10, CFI.

[65] ECJ Rules of Procedure, Arts. 37 and 38; CFI Rules of Procedure, Arts. 43 and 44.

[66] ECJ Rules of Procedure, Art. 102(1); CFI Rules of Procedure, Art. 129(1).

[67] ECJ Rules of Procedure, Art. 102(1), subpara. 2; CFI Rules of Procedure, Art. 129(1), subpara. 2.

[68] ECJ Rules of Procedure, Art. 102(2); CFI Rules of Procedure, Art. 129(2). Of course, if the application for interpretation is manifestly inadmissible, the Court may dismiss it by order (ECJ Rules of Procedure, Art. 92(1); CFI Rules of Procedure, Art. 111). For an example see (Order of July 14, 1993), Case T–22/91INT *Inès Raiola-Denti and Others v. Council* [1993] E.C.R. II–817, CFI.

judgment was given, but also on parties to proceedings in which a judgment was given containing a passage exactly similar to the passage interpreted.[69]

(2) Rectification of clerical errors

Clerical mistakes, errors in calculation and obvious slips in the judgment may be rectified by the Court of Justice or the Court of First Instance by order setting out the rectified text.[70] **22–164**

The Court may take this step of its own motion or on application by a party (including an intervener) within two weeks after delivery of the judgment. **22–165**

The parties are entitled to lodge prior written observations. **22–166**

The Court of Justice or the Court of First Instance takes its decision in closed session after hearing the Advocate General.

The original of the rectification order is annexed to the original of the rectified judgment and a note of the order is made in the margin of the rectified judgment.

(3) Rectification in the event of an omission to give a decision

If the Court of Justice or the Court of First Instance should omit to give a decision on a specific head of claim or on costs, the omission can be rectified on application by any party.[71] The application must be lodged within one month after service of the judgment in question; it is served on the opposite party; and the President prescribes a period within which that party may lodge written observations. After that, the Court decides both on the admissibility and on the substance of the application after hearing the Advocate General.[72] **22–167**

B. Discontinuance

If, before the Court of Justice or the Court of First Instance has given its decision, the parties notify the Court in question that they have reached a settlement of their dispute and that they have abandoned their claims, the President orders the case to be removed from the register and gives a decision as to the costs.[73] **22–168**

---

69 Joined Cases 41, 43 and 44/73–Interpretation *Générale Sucrière v. Commission* [1977] E.C.R. 445 at 464, para. 29, ECJ.

70 ECJ Rules of Procedure, Art. 66; CFI Rules of Procedure, Art. 84. For an example, see (Order of September 15, 1995), Joined Cases T–466, T–469, T–473, T–474 and T–477/93 *O'Dwyer and Others v. Council*, CFI (not reported in the E.C.R.).

71 ECJ Rules of Procedure, Art. 67; CFI Rules of Procedure, Art. 85.

72 For an example, see (Order of October 11, 1990), Case T–50/89 *Sparr v. Commission* [1990] E.C.R. II–539, CFI.

73 ECJ Rules of Procedure, Art. 77, para. 1; CFI Rules of Procedure, Art. 98, para. 1. Those provisions do not apply to proceedings under the ECSC Treaty, Arts. 33 and 35, E.C. Treaty, Arts. 230 and 232 (*ex Arts. 173 and 175*) or the EAEC Treaty, Arts. 146 and 148. The decision on costs is taken in accordance with the ECJ Rules of Procedure, Art. 69(5), or the CFI Rules of Procedure, Art. 87(5), as the case may be.

22–169 The applicant may also discontinue proceedings without the agreement of the opposite party.[74] It does so by informing the Court of Justice or the Court of First Instance, as the case may be, in writing. In this case, too, the President orders the case to be removed from the register and decides as to the costs.[75]

C. No need to proceed to judgment

22–170 The Court of Justice or the Court of First Instance, as the case may be, may decide that there is no need to proceed to judgment on the ground that there is no purpose to the proceedings.[76] If the Court makes a finding to this effect, this closes the proceedings.[77]

VIII. General Remarks

A. Use of languages

22–171 The case may be conducted in any of the following twelve languages: Danish, Dutch, English, Finnish, French, German, Greek, Irish, Italian, Portuguese, Spanish and Swedish.[78] In principle, the applicant chooses the language of the case. However, where the defendant is a Member State or a natural or legal person having the nationality of a Member State,[79] the language of the case will be the official language of that state; where the state has more than one official language, the applicant may choose between them. Exceptionally, the President of the Court of Justice or the Court of First Instance may authorise another Community language to be used for all or part of the proceedings at the joint request of the parties. If, at the request of one of the parties and after the opposite party and the Advocate General have been heard, the President of the Court of Justice or of the Court of First Instance wishes to give such authorisation but all the parties do not agree, he or she must refer the request to the Court of

[74] ECJ Rules of Procedure, Art. 78; CFI Rules of Procedure, Art. 99. The defendant cannot object to the other party's discontinuing the proceedings: see (Order of the President of March 19, 1996), Case C–120/94 *Commission v. Greece* [1996] E.C.R. I–1513, ECJ.

[75] Again, the decision on costs is taken in accordance with the ECJ Rules of Procedure, Art. 69(5), or the CFI Rules of Procedure, Art. 87(5), as the case may be.

[76] This is borne out indirectly by the ECJ Rules of Procedure, Art. 69(6), and the CFI Rules of Procedure, Art. 87(6).

[77] *e.g.* see Case 377/87 *European Parliament v. Council* [1988] E.C.R. 4017 at 4048–4049, paras 10–12, ECJ; Case T–140/89 *Della Pietra v. Commission* [1990] E.C.R. II–717, CFI.

[78] ECJ Rules of Procedure, Art. 29(1); CFI Rules of Procedure, Art. 35(1). For a more extensive discussion, see Barents, *Procedures*, pp. 258–264. Although the Welsh Courts Act 1942 provides that the Welsh language may be used in any court in Wales and the Welsh Language Act 1967 that in any legal proceedings in Wales or Monmouthshire, the Welsh language may be spoken by any person who desires to use it, the ECJ Rules of Procedure, Art. 29(1), and the CFI Rules of Procedure, Art. 35(1), do not allow for the use of Welsh as the language of a case. But note that witnesses and experts may use a language not capable of being a language of the case, ECJ Rules of Procedure, Art. 29(4); CFI Rules of Procedure, Art. 35(4); see para. 22–174, below.

[79] This may occur where a Community institution brings proceedings against a natural or legal person pursuant to an arbitration clause within the meaning of the E.C. Treaty, Art. 238 (*ex Art. 181*).

Justice or the Court of First Instance, as the case may be.[80] A request for leave to derogate from the rule on the use of the language of the case must be accompanied by a detailed and specific statement of reasons, *a fortiori* where the request is made by the applicant, who has to justify a departure from the initial choice made by itself.[81] Institutions may not make such a request.

The language of the case in proceedings relating to intellectual property rights is determined in accordance with a special procedure laid down in Article 131(2) of the CFI Rules of Procedure on account of the fact that the disputes concerned involve individuals. The language of the case is the language, chosen from amongst the official languages, in which the application is drafted where the applicant was the only party to the proceedings before the board of appeal or if no other party objects. If, within a period following lodgment of the application determined by the Registrar, the parties agree to use an official language other than the one used in the application, that language will become the language of the case. However, if a party objects to the language used in the application being the language of the case and the parties cannot agree on the choice of language, the language in which the application for registration in question was filed at the Office becomes the language of the case, unless the President or the Court of First Instance, on the matter being referred to it, finds that the use of that language would not enable all parties to the proceedings before the board of appeal to follow the proceedings and defend their interests. In that case, the President or the Court may designate another official language as the language of the case after receipt of a reasoned request by any party and after hearing the other parties. **22–172**

The language of the case is used "in the written and oral pleadings of the parties and in supporting documents, and also in the minutes and decisions of the Court". The language of the case remains the same in any appeal proceedings. Any supporting documents expressed in another language must be accompanied by a translation into the language of the case.[82] This means that, if an intervener is not a Member State,[83] it must in principle produce a translation in the language of the case of all documents and annexes which it produces.[84] If, however, lengthy documents are involved, extracts may be submitted, unless the Court of Justice or the Court of First Instance, as the case may be, calls for a complete or fuller translation of its own motion or at the request of a party.[85] Generally, a request to use a **22–173**

[80] ECJ Rules of Procedure, Art. 29(2); CFI Rules of Procedure, Art. 35(2).

[81] (Order of May 13, 1993), Case T–74/92 *Ladbroke Racing v. Commission* [1993] E.C.R. II–535 at II–539, para. 14, CFI; (Order of January 24, 1997), Case T–121/95 *EFMA v. Council* [1997] E.C.R. II–87 at II–93, para. 10, CFI.

[82] ECJ Rules of Procedure, Art. 29(3), subpara. 1; CFI Rules of Procedure, Art. 35(3), subpara. 1.

[83] See para. 22–176, below.

[84] CFI Rules of Procedure, Art. 35(3), subpara. 2. For an example, see (Order of June 26, 1996), Case T–11/95 *BP Chemicals v. Commission* [1996] E.C.R. II–599, CFI.

[85] ECJ Rules of Procedure, Art. 29(3), subpara. 3; CFI Rules of Procedure, Art. 35(3), subpara. 3.

language other than the language of the case during the oral procedure will be granted.[86]

22–174 A witness or expert who is unable adequately to express himself or herself in the language of the case, may use another language, even a language not included among the list of possible languages which may be used before the Court. The Registrar arranges for translation into the language of the case.[87]

22–175 The President, the Judges and the Advocate General are entitled to use a language other than the language of the case, in particular in conducting oral proceedings, in putting questions and, as far as the Advocate General is concerned, in delivering his or her opinion. Here, too, the Registrar is responsible for arranging for translation into the language of the case.[88]

22–176 A Member State intervening in a case is entitled to use its official language (or one of its official languages at its election) both during the written procedure and at the hearing. Here again, it is the Registrar who has to arrange for translation into the language of the case.[89] EEA States, not being Member States of the European Union, may be authorised by the Registrar to use an official language other than the language of the case where they intervene in proceedings pending before the Court of Justice or the Court of First Instance or take part in preliminary ruling proceedings.[90]

B. Calculation of time-limits

22–177 The procedural time-limits prescribed by the ECSC Treaty, the E.C. Treaty, the EAEC Treaty, the ECSC, E.C. and EAEC Statutes of the Court of Justice and the Rules of Procedure of the Court of Justice and the Court of First Instance are reckoned in a uniform manner.

22–178 As far as the day from which time starts running (*dies a quo*) is concerned, the following is important. Time-limits calculated from the moment at which an event occurs or an action takes place start to run on the day after the event occurs or the action takes place.[91] This principle is further specified as regards actions for annulment:

> "Where the period of time allowed for commencing proceedings against a measure adopted by an institution runs from the publication of that measure, that period shall be calculated . . . from the end of the

[86] (Order of June 12, 1995), Case T–371/94 *British Airways and Others v. Commission*, para. 13, CFI (not reported in the E.C.R.) and (Order of June 12, 1995), Case T–394/94 *British Midland Airways v. Commission*, para. 13, CFI (not reported in the E.C.R.); (Order of August 16, 1995), Case T–290/94 *Kaysersberg v. Commission* [1995] E.C.R. II–2247 at II–2252, para. 8, CFI; (Order of November 17, 1995), Case T–330/94 *Salt Union v. Commission* [1995] E.C.R. II–2881 at II–2890—2891, paras 25–28, CFI. However, see also n. 81, above, and the associated passage of the main body of the text.

[87] ECJ Rules of Procedure, Art. 29(4); CFI Rules of Procedure, Art. 35(4).

[88] ECJ Rules of Procedure, Art. 29(5); CFI Rules of Procedure, Art. 35(5).

[89] ECJ Rules of Procedure, Art. 29(3), subpara. 4; CFI Rules of Procedure, Art. 35(3), subpara. 4.

[90] ECJ Rules of Procedure, Art. 29(3), subpara. 5; CFI Rules of Procedure, Art. 35(3) subpara. 5.

[91] ECJ Rules of Procedure, Art. 80(1)(a); CFI Rules of Procedure, Art. 101(1)(a).

14th day after publication thereof in the *Official Journal of the European Communities*".[92]

As far as the *running* and *duration* of the period are concerned, it should first be noted that Saturdays, Sundays, official holidays and judicial vacations count towards the period.[93] In addition, *all* procedural time-limits are subject to extensions on account of distance, which are determined by the Court of Justice and published in the *Official Journal of the European Communities*.[94] These extensions also apply to the Court of First Instance.[95] The idea behind this is that, even though procedural documents are validly served at the parties' address for service in Luxembourg, an extension of time is necessary for parties who reside or are established a long way away so as to give all the parties the same time in which to prepare for their participation in the proceedings before the Court. The extension on account of distance is not to be regarded as separate from the procedural time-limit but merely as a prolongation of it.[96] **22–179**

The extensions on account of distance established by the Court of Justice are as follows[97]: for parties habitually resident in Belgium: two days; for Germany, "the European territory of the French Republic and the European territory of the Kingdom of the Netherlands", six days; for "the European territory of the Kingdom of Denmark", Austria, Finland, Greece, Ireland, Italy, Portugal (with the exception of the Azores and Madeira), Spain, Sweden and the United Kingdom, 10 days; for other European countries and territories, two weeks; for the autonomous regions of the Azores and Madeira, three weeks; for other countries, departments and territories, one month. The extensions on account of distance also apply to Community institutions. They qualify for the extension on account of distance applicable to the country in which they are established.[98] It is

92 ECJ Rules of Procedure, Art. 81(1); CFI Rules of Procedure, Art. 102(1). The *Official Journal of the European Communities* is normally available on the day of issue. In that case, time would start running on the 15th day following the day of issue of the *Official Journal* publishing the contested act. If the *Official Journal* is not available on the date appearing on the issue, the period will start running 15 days after the day on which the *Official Journal* was actually published: see Case 98/78 *Racke v. Hauptzollamt Mainz* [1979] E.C.R. 69 at 84, para. 15, ECJ. See also para. 7–126, above.

93 ECJ Rules of Procedure, Art. 80(1)(d) and (e); CFI Rules of Procedure, Art. 101(1)(d) and (e).

94 ECJ Rules of Procedure, Art. 81(2).

95 CFI Rules of Procedure, Art. 101(2).

96 (Order of November 20, 1997), Case T–85/97 *Horeca-Wallonie v. Commission* [1997] E.C.R. II–2113 at II–2122, para. 26, CFI. Consequently, the last day of the time-limit is the day on which the procedural time-limit, together with the time on account of distance, runs out. This is important in order to determine whether the time-limit may be extended because the last day is a Saturday, a Sunday or an official holiday (see para. 22–180, below). In the *Horeca-Wallonie* case, the applicant argued that the procedural time-limit, the "last" day of which fell on Easter Monday—an official holiday—had to be extended, after which time on account of distance started to run. The Court of First Instance rejected this argument.

97 [1991] O.J. L176/32.

98 Case C–137/92P *Commission v. BASF and Others* [1994] E.C.R. I–2555 at I–2644—2645, paras 40–41, ECJ; Case C–245/95P *Commission v. NTN Corporation and Koyo Seiko* [1998] E.C.R. I–401 at I–433—434, paras 19–23, ECJ.

irrelevant that some departments of the institution concerned are located in another country.

22–180 As far as the day on which time stops running (*dies ad quem*) is concerned, two aspects must be borne in mind. First, there is the rule that if the period would otherwise end on a Saturday, Sunday or an official holiday, it is extended until the end of the first following working day.[99]

Secondly, the last day of the period is determined as follows:

> "A period expressed in weeks, months or in years shall end with the expiry of whichever day in the last week, month or year is the same day of the week, or falls on the same date as *the day during which the event or action from which the period is to be calculated occurred or took place*. If, in a period expressed in months or in years, the day on which it should expire does not occur in the last month, the period shall end with the expiry of the last day of that month; where a period is expressed in months and days, it shall first be reckoned in months, then in days."[1]

It should be noted that the key day for determining the last day of a period is the actual day corresponding to the one on which the event or action occurred which caused time to start running, and not the day after, even though that is the day on which time actually started to run.[2] Although this may appear contradictory, it is in fact quite logical, as the following example shows: if the period for bringing an action for annulment starts running as a result of notification of the contested act on April 3, then the two months within which the action must be brought run from April 4, at 0 hours (*i.e.* the *dies a* quo, being the day after notification) to June 3, at midnight (*i.e.* the *dies ad quem*, that it to say, the day which falls on the same date as "the day during which the event or action from which the period is to be calculated occurred or took place", namely the date of notification). Thus the period amounts to precisely two months.

22–181 Let us take a further example to illustrate the rules set out above: a Commission decision is notified to an undertaking established in the Netherlands on October 19, 1992. The usual two-month time-limit ends at midnight on December 19, 1992, but is extended by six days on account of distance, *i.e.* to midnight on December 25, 1992, an official holiday, which produces a further extension to the first working day, *i.e.* midnight on Monday December 28, 1992.

---

[99] ECJ Rules of Procedure, Art. 80(2), subpara. 1; CFI Rules of Procedure, Art. 101(2), subpara. 1.

[1] ECJ Rules of Procedure, Art. 80(1)(b) and (c); CFI Rules of Procedure, Art. 101(1)(b) and (c) (emphasis supplied). These provisions on the *dies ad quem* codify the rule in *Misset* which used to be applied alongside the ECJ Rules of Procedure, Arts. 80–82 (which have now been amended using that very form of words). See Case 152/85 *Rudolf Misset v. Council* [1987] E.C.R. 223 at 236–237, para. 8, ECJ; Joined Cases 281, 283–285 and 287/85 *Germany, France, Netherlands, Denmark and United Kingdom v. Commission* [1987] E.C.R. 3203 at 3249, paras 5–7, ECJ.

[2] See para. 22–178, above.

Documents may be handed in at the entrance of the Court of Justice and the Court of First Instance at any time of the day or night; the security guard will note the exact time of receipt and this will be decisive evidence. 22–182

Lastly, it should be mentioned that the expiry of a time-limit cannot be pleaded if the other party proves the existence of unforeseen circumstances or *force majeure*.[3] This exceptional rule is applicable to any procedural time-limit, but both the Court of Justice and the Court of First Instance take an extremely strict view. The typical case of a clerical error made by the representative of one of the parties is not enough to bring the rule into play. In circumstances such as a post strike which objectively would have taken a careful party by surprise (the strike breaks out suddenly and lasts three weeks, as a result of which the document dispatched in plenty of time arrives a day too late at the registry) may suffice. But to rely on this rule remains a great—and hence unwarranted—risk.[4] 22–183

C. Representation of the parties

Community institutions, Member States and EEA States which are not Member States of the Union are represented by an agent, who has to lodge an authority with the registry of the Court of Justice or the Court of First Instance, as the case may be. An agent may be assisted by an adviser or by a lawyer entitled to practise before a court of a Member State.[5] 22–184

All other parties must be represented by a lawyer entitled to practise before a court of a Member State or of an EEA State not being a Member State of the European Union or by a university teacher who is a national of a Member State whose law accords him or her a right of audience (that is to say, as a university teacher and not as, say, a member of the Bar), even if the applicant is a lawyer with rights of audience before a national court or tribunal.[6] The lawyer must lodge a certificate that he or she is entitled to practise before a court of a Member State or of a non-E.U. EEA State and an authority from the party which he or she represents.[7] 22–185

If the applicant is a legal person governed by private law, the lawyer must ensure that the application contains proof that the authority granted to him or her has been properly conferred on him or her by someone authorised for the purpose.[8] 22–186

[3] E.C. Statute, Art. 42.

[4] See (Order of May 7, 1998), Case C–239/97 *Ireland v. Commission* [1998] E.C.R. I–2655, ECJ, in which the fact that a courier service had not been able to deliver the application to the registry on time because of technical difficulties was not considered to constitute *force majeure*, particularly since the applicant had waited until the day before time was due to run out (including time on account of distance) before sending the application from Ireland.

[5] E.C. Statute, Art. 17.

[6] (Order of December 5, 1996), Case C–174/96P *Lopes v. Court of Justice* [1996] E.C.R. I–6401 at I–6406, para. 10, ECJ, and Case C–175/96P [1996] E.C.R. I–6409 at I–6414, para. 10, ECJ.

[7] ECJ Rules of Procedure, Art. 38(3); CFI Rules of Procedure, Art. 44(3). See also paras 22–023, 22–041, above.

[8] ECJ Rules of Procedure, Art. 38(5); CFI Rules of Procedure, Art. 44(5).

22–187 If necessary, the authority and proof in question may be furnished within a "reasonable time" to be prescribed by the Registrar. The sanction for failing to produce them within the time prescribed is that the Court of Justice or the Court of First Instance will decide, after hearing the Advocate General (only in the case of the Court of Justice), whether non-compliance renders the application formally inadmissible.[9] The same conditions apply to the defence.[10]

[9] ECJ Rules of Procedure, Art. 38(7); CFI Rules of Procedure, Art. 44(6).
[10] ECJ Rules of Procedure, Art. 40(1), subpara. 2; CFI Rules of Procedure, Art. 46(1), subpara. 2.

CHAPTER 23

PROCEDURE IN THE CASE OF A REFERENCE FOR A PRELIMINARY RULING

A request for a preliminary ruling is sent by the national court to the Court of Justice. No formal requirements apply at European level.[1] It is important only that the request actually reaches the Court so that it can be registered at the registry. This is when the case receives its serial number. **23–001**

Notice is given of the request for a preliminary ruling in the *Official Journal of the European Communities*.[2]

The registry requests the national court to lodge the whole of the case-file in order that the Court of Justice may be better placed to give a useful answer.[3]

The national court sets out its request in an order for reference. This is immediately translated into the other official languages of the Community. The Registrar of the Court of Justice notifies it to the parties to the main proceedings (*i.e.* to all "parties" to the case, including any interveners), the Member States (a copy of the original order for reference and a translation in an official language of the Member State in question) and the Commission.[4] Notice is given by registered letter with a form for acknowledgment of receipt, addressed to the lawyers of the parties to the main proceedings or, if the parties are not represented, to their personal address as set out in the order for reference. Notice is given to the Member States by registered letter with a form for acknowledgment of receipt, addressed to the Ministry of Foreign Affairs (with a copy to the Permanent Representation in Brussels). There is in fact no form of address for service whatsoever in Luxembourg in the case of references for preliminary rulings. **23–002**

---

1 However, in 1977 the Court of Justice published a Note for Guidance on References by National Courts for Preliminary Rules (1997) C.M.L.Rev. 1319–1322 (reproduced in *Brealey and Hoskins, Remedies in EC Law*, London, Sweet and Maxwell, 1998 (2nd ed.), Appendix H. In England and Wales, Rules of the Supreme Court, RSC, Ord. 114, governs the procedure as regards references from the High Court and the Court of Appeal and CCR, Ord. 19, r. 11, references from the county court. See also the Crown Court Rules 1982 (S.I. 1989 No. 1109), r. 29. No formal requirements apply to references from magistrates' courts and tribunals in England and Wales. For details, see *ibid*, pp. 229–232.

2 By analogy with ECJ Rules of Procedure, Art. 16(6).

3 See paras 2–018—2–025, above.

4 E.C. Statute, Art. 20, para. 1. *Cf.* the ECJ Rules of Procedure, Art. 103(3), subpara. 1, in conjunction with the ECSC Treaty, Art. 41.

23–003 The Registrar of the Court of Justice further notifies the order for reference to the Council or the European Central Bank "if the act the validity or interpretation of which is in dispute originates from one of them" and to the European Parliament and the Council "if the act the validity or interpretation of which is in dispute was adopted jointly by those two institutions".[5] In exceptional cases, the order for reference is also notified to the European Parliament if the Court of Justice wishes to obtain information from it (for example if the preliminary question has a bearing on the Parliament's prerogatives).[6] The Registrar also notifies the order for reference to the states, other than Member States, which are parties to the EEA Agreement and to the EFTA Surveillance Authority.

23–004 The Member States are notified by service of a copy of the original version of the decisions of national courts and tribunals, accompanied by a translation in the official language of the recipient Member State.[7] States party to the EEA Agreement which are not Member States and the EFTA Surveillance Authority receive a copy of the original version and a translation into the official language of their choice.[8]

23–005 The parties to the main proceedings, the Member States, the Commission and, where appropriate, the European Parliament, the Council and the European Central Bank are entitled to submit statements of case or observations within two months of notification of the order for reference.[9] States party to the EEA Agreement which are not Member States and the EFTA Surveillance Authority may likewise submit statements of case or observations within two months if the national court's decision concerns one of the fields of application of the EEA Agreement.[10] This period is calculated in the same way as for direct actions, including time on account of distance.[11] Time starts to run as from notification, which is determined from the form for acknowledgment of receipt attached to the registered letter sent by the Court. The two-month period may be extended only in the event of "unforeseeable circumstances or *force majeure*" within the meaning of Article 42 of the E.C. Statute of the Court of Justice.

23–006 The written procedure consists solely of this opportunity to submit observations to the Court. The observations received are sent to all those to whom the order for reference was notified. There is no "reply" as between the parties, the Member States, the Commission and the Council should they disagree with each other's views. This follows from the fact that the preliminary ruling procedure is not, formally speaking, a dispute between "parties".

23–007 After the written observations have been submitted or none have been received within the prescribed period, the Judge-Rapporteur draws up the

---

[5] E.C. Statute, Art. 20.

[6] Such a request for information is based on the E.C. Statute, Art. 21. For an example, see Case 20/85 *Roviello v. Landesversicherungsanstalt Schwaben* [1988] E.C.R. 2805, ECJ.

[7] ECJ Rules of Procedure, Art. 104(1), subpara. 1.

[8] ECJ Rules of Procedure, Art. 104(1), subpara. 2.

[9] E.C. Statute, Art. 20, para. 2.

[10] E.C. Statute, Art. 20 para. 3.

[11] See paras 22–177—22–183, above.

"preliminary report" for submission to the administrative meeting of the Court. From that point onwards, the procedure—from the oral procedure to delivery of judgment by the Court of Justice—is the same as in the case of direct actions.

Nevertheless, some aspects warrant specific attention. **23–008**

A preliminary reference may—depending on its degree of difficulty—be **23–009**
assigned to a three- or seven-judge chamber, unless a Member State, the Commission or the Council (where the latter is involved in the proceedings) requests that the case be decided in plenary session.[12]

The Court of Justice also allows parties who have not exercised their **23–010**
right to submit written observations to take part in the hearing. This signifies in fact that a failure to make use of the time-limit for submitting written observations does not mean that there is no right to state one's case orally and answer any questions put by the Court.

This is important since generally the so-called non-contentious nature of **23–011**
preliminary-ruling proceedings appears to be no more than a fiction. That will, for instance, be the case where a Member State submits written observations or a statement of case contending that a part of its national law is compatible with Community law[13] or where a party to the main proceedings seeks implementation of an agreement whilst the other party claims that the agreement is contrary to Community law.[14]

Even if written observations are lodged by all involved, the oral procedure affords a full opportunity for explanations and counter-argument to be presented.

The Court of Justice may dispense with a hearing if no-one who has the **23–012**
right to submit written observations objects.[15]

In principle, the Court of Justice will not prescribe measures of inquiry, **23–013**
since it is for the national court to make the findings of fact in relation to the main proceedings and to draw the necessary conclusions for the purposes of reaching its decision.[16] Neither may the Court of Justice verify the facts placed before it.[17]

As far as representation of the parties to the main proceedings and their **23–014**
attendance at the Court are concerned, the Court has regard to the rules applicable to the court hearing the main case. Consequently, parties do not have to be represented by a lawyer (unlike the position in the case of a direct action[18]) where a party may validly be otherwise represented before the national court (for example by a representative of a representative trade

[12] ECJ Rules of Procedure, Art. 95(2), subpara. 2. See also E.C. Treaty, Art. 221 (*ex Art. 165*), para. 3.

[13] See, *e.g.* Case 26/62 *Van Gend & Loos v. Nederlandse Administratie der Belastingen* [1963] E.C.R. 1, ECJ; Case 293/83 *Gravier v. City of Liège* [1985] E.C.R. 593, ECJ.

[14] See, *e.g.* Case 261/81 *Rau v. De Smedt* [1982] E.C.R. 3961, ECJ.

[15] ECJ Rules of Procedure, Art. 104(4). For an example, see Case C–17/92 *Federación de Distribuidores Cinematográficos v. Spain* [1993] E.C.R. I–2239, ECJ.

[16] Case 17/81 *Pabst & Richarz v. Hauptzollamt Oldenburg* [1982] E.C.R. 1331 at 1346, para. 12, ECJ. See *supra.* paras 6–026, 10–017, above.

[17] Case 104/77 *Oehlschläger v. Hauptzollamt Emmerich* [1978] E.C.R. 791 at 797, para. 4, ECJ. See paras 6–026, 10–017, above.

[18] See paras 22–185—22–187, above.

union in employment disputes in some jurisdictions) or where a party is entitled to plead as a litigant in person.[19]

23–015 The question of the costs incurred by the parties to the main proceedings on account of the reference for a preliminary ruling—in practice, lawyers' fees and expenses, since the actual procedure before the Court of Justice is free of charge—is a matter for the national court.[20] The Court of Justice merely adverts to this in its judgment. In addition, in special circumstances the Court of Justice may "grant, by way of legal aid, assistance for the purpose of facilitating the representation or attendance of a party", which operates in practice in the same way as the grant of legal aid in the context of a direct action.[21] The costs incurred by Member States and Community institutions as a result of their intervention in preliminary-ruling proceedings are not recoverable.[22]

23–016 The language of the case is the language of the court which made the reference for a preliminary ruling. Written observations must be drawn up and the parties have to plead in that language, subject to the proviso that Member States may use their official language or one of their official languages.[23] The use of languages by the President, Judges and the Advocate General is dealt with in the same way as in the case of direct actions.[24]

23–017 No appeal will lie from parties to the main proceedings, Member States or Community institutions against a preliminary ruling, since it is only for national courts and tribunals to decide whether to make a reference and, if so, what its subject-matter should be.[25] Consequently, they decide whether they have received sufficient clarification from the preliminary ruling and

---

[19] For an example, see Case 293/93 *Houtwipper* [1994] E.C.R. I–4249, ECJ.

[20] ECJ Rules of Procedure, Art. 104(5), subpara. 1. The ECJ Rules of Procedure, Arts. 69–75, are concerned with costs of contentious proceedings brought before the Court of Justice. In view of the essential difference between contentious proceedings and proceedings under the E.C. Treaty, Art. 234 (*ex Art. 177*), which are only a step in the proceedings before the national court, those provisions do not cover the recovery of costs and the recoverability of expenses incurred in the main proceedings in connection with a reference for a preliminary ruling. The applicable national provisions must be applied to determine how the costs are to be allocated in such a case: Case 62/72 *Bollmann v. Hauptzollamt Hamburg-Waltershof* [1973] E.C.R. 269 at 275–276, paras 5–6, ECJ. In *R v. Intervention Board for Agricultural Produce, ex p. Fish Producers' Organisation Ltd* [1993] 1 C.M.L.R. 707, the Court of Appeal held that the normal English rule that costs follow the event applies to preliminary ruling procedures. Costs which under national procedural rules have to be borne by a successful party to the main proceedings may not be the subject of a claim for damages brought against the Community, even though the judgment in the main proceedings was based on a declaration made in a preliminary ruling that an act of a Community institution was invalid. This is because to hold the Community liable in damages on this head would place in question the existence and exercise of the exclusive jurisdiction which national courts enjoy in the matter of the costs of the reference for a preliminary ruling under the ECJ Rules of Procedure, Art. 104(5), para. 1: Case T–167/94 *Nölle v. Council and Commission* [1995] E.C.R. II–2589 at II–2606—2607, paras 37–39, CFI.

[21] ECJ Rules of Procedure, Art. 104(5), subpara. 2. See also paras 22–125—22–129, above.

[22] Mortelmans, "Observations in the Cases governed by Article 177 *[now Article 234]* of the EEC Treaty: Procedure and Practice" (1979) C.M.L.Rev. 557 at 568.

[23] ECJ Rules of Procedure, Art. 29(2), last subpara.

[24] See para. 22–175, above.

[25] (Order of May 16, 1968), Case 13/67 *Becher v. Hauptzollamt München-Landsbergerstraße* [1968] E.C.R. 196 at 197, ECJ.

whether they consider it necessary to make a further reference to the Court of Justice.[26] The parties to the main proceedings may urge the national court to make an additional reference, but they have no right to apply to the Court of Justice directly.

Special features of the procedure followed in preliminary ruling proceedings brought before the Court of Justice pursuant to Article 1 of Protocol 34 to the EEA Agreement are prescribed in Article 123b of the ECJ Rules of Procedure. **23–018**

[26] *ibid* See also (Order of October 18, 1979), Case 40/70 *Sirena v. Eda* [1979] E.C.R. 3169, ECJ; (Order of March 5, 1986), Case 69/85 *Wünsche v. Germany* [1986] E.C.R. 947, ECJ; (Order of April 28, 1998), Case C–116/96 Rev. *Reisebüro Binder* [1998] E.C.R. I–1889 at I–1893—1894, paras 6–9, ECJ.

CHAPTER 24

PROCEDURE IN THE CASE OF AN APPEAL AGAINST A DECISION OF THE COURT OF FIRST INSTANCE

The procedure before the Court of Justice in the case of an appeal brought against a decision of the Court of First Instance consists of a written and an oral part. The language of the case is the language of the decision against which the appeal is brought.[1] **24–001**

The written part of the proceedings is limited in principle to two documents, the appeal and the response. **24–002**

The appeal must be lodged at the registry of the Court of Justice or of the Court of First Instance.[2] It has to comply with the requirements generally applying to applications.[3] It sets out the applicant's name and address, the names of the other parties to the proceedings before the Court of First Instance, the pleas in law and legal arguments relied on, and the form of order sought by the appellant.[4] The decision appealed against must be attached to the appeal and the appeal must state the date on which the decision appealed against was notified to the appellant.[5] If the appeal complies with those requirements, it will be served on all the parties to the proceedings before the Court of First Instance.[6] **24–003**

---

1 ECJ Rules of Procedure, Art. 110.

2 ECJ Rules of Procedure, Art. 111(1).

3 ECJ Rules of Procedure, Art. 112(1), subpara. 2, which refers to ECJ Rules of Procedure, Arts. 37 and 38(2) and (3). A clerical error in an application, for instance an incorrect reference to a provision of the E.C. Statute as constituting the basis for an appeal, which has no incidence on the subsequent course of the proceedings, is not a ground for finding the appeal inadmissible: (Order of the President of July 19, 1995), Case C–149/95P(R) *Commission v. Atlantic Container Line and Others* [1995] E.C.R. I–2165 at I–2176, para 14, ECJ.

4 ECJ Rules of Procedure, Art. 112(1), subpara. 1. If the Court of Justice finds that the appeal was lodged within the prescribed period starting from the date on which the Court of First Instance gave judgment, failure to mention the date on which the judgment was notified in the appeal does not make the appeal inadmissible: Case C–91/95P *Tremblay and Others v. Commission* [1996] E.C.R. I–5547 at I–5572, paras 10–11, ECJ.

5 ECJ Rules of Procedure, Art. 112(2).

6 ECJ Rules of Procedure, Art. 114. Interveners before the Court of First Instance are regarded as parties before that court. It follows that they may lodge a response pursuant to the ECJ Rules of Procedure, Article 115(1), without having to make a fresh application to intervene before the Court of Justice. Furthermore, as regards the pleas they may raise, there is no distinction between the parties who are entitled to lodge a response, since they are subject in the same way to the requirements of the ECJ Rules of Procedure, Articles 115 and 116: (Judgment of February 11, 1999) Case C–390/95P *Antillean Rice Mills and Others v. Commission*, paras 17–24, ECJ (not yet reported).

24–004 Within a period of two months after service of the appeal, which may not be extended, any of those parties may lodge a response, which has to be broken down into the same heads as an appeal.[7]

24–005 Leave is required from the President of the Court of Justice to submit a reply, a rejoinder or any other pleading. An application to that effect must be made within seven days of service of the response or the reply, as the case may be.[8]

24–006 In addition, where an appeal is, in whole or in part, clearly inadmissible or clearly unfounded, the Court of Justice may at any time, acting on a report from the Judge-Rapporteur and after hearing the Advocate General, by reasoned order dismiss the appeal in whole or in part.[9]

24–007 Lastly, at the end of the written part of the procedure, the Court may, acting on a report from the Judge-Rapporteur and after hearing the Advocate General and the parties, decide to dispense with the oral part of the procedure unless one of the parties objects on the ground that the written procedure did not enable it fully to defend its point of view. If the Court gives judgment without a hearing, the Advocate General delivers his or her Opinion in open court at a date determined by the President. The Judge-Rapporteur has to make a recommendation in his or her preliminary report as to whether the appeal may be dealt with without a hearing.[10]

24–008 A series of provisions of the Rules of Procedure is stated to be applicable to the procedure before the Court of Justice on appeals from the Court of First Instance.[11] The provisions relate to the bar on introducing new pleas in the course of the proceedings (Article 42(2)), the joinder of cases (Article 43), the Judge-Rapporteur's preliminary report (Article 44), the oral procedure (Articles 55 to 62), judgments (Articles 63 to 68), costs (Articles 69 to 75; see also Article 122), legal aid (Article 76), discontinuance (Articles 77 and 78), service (Article 79), time-limits (Articles 80, 81 and 82), stays of proceedings (Article 82a), interim measures (Articles 83 to 90), intervention (Article 93; see also Article 123), assignment of cases to Chambers (Article 95), third-party proceedings (Article 97), revision (Articles 98, 99 and 100) and interpretation of judgments (Article 102). As a result, the rules applicable to these matters are the same as for direct actions.[12]

---

[7] ECJ Rules of Procedure, Art. 115(2): the name and address of the party lodging the response, the date on which notice of appeal was served on it, the pleas in law and legal arguments relied on and the form of order sought. Art. 38(2) and (3) concerning the address for service and practising certificates also applies.

[8] ECJ Rules of Procedure, Art. 117(1).

[9] ECJ Rules of Procedure, Art. 119(1). For examples, see (Order of February 27, 1991), Case C–126/90P *Bocos Viciano v. Commission* [1991] E.C.R. I–781, ECJ; (Order of March 20, 1991), Case C–115/90P *Turner v. Commission* [1991] E.C.R. I–1423, ECJ; (Order of January 24, 1994), Case C–275/93P *Boessen v. ESC* [1994] E.C.R. I–159, ECJ.

[10] E.C. Statute, Art. 52; ECJ Rules of Procedure, Arts. 120 and 121. For an example, see Case C–354/92P *Eppe v. Commission* [1993] E.C.R. I–7027 at I–7034, ECJ. For the consequences of applying the ECJ Rules of Procedure, Art. 120, see (Judgment of January 21, 1999) Case C–73/97P *France v. Comafrica and Dole Fresh Fruit Europe*, para. 14, ECJ (not yet reported).

[11] ECJ Rules of Procedure, Art. 118.

[12] For the matters concerned, see Chap. 22, above.

The procedure followed where the Court of Justice sets aside a judgment or an order of the Court of First Instance and refers the case back to that Court is set forth in Articles 117 to 121 of the CFI Rules of Procedure. **24–009**

Where the written procedure before the Court of First Instance has been completed when the judgment referring the case back to it is delivered, the course of the procedure is as follows: **24–010**

(1) Within two months from the service upon him or her of the judgment of the Court of Justice the applicant may lodge a statement of written observations.

(2) In the month following the communication to him or her of that statement, the defendant may lodge a statement of written observations. The time allowed to the defendant for lodging it may in no case be less than two months from the service upon him or her of the judgment of the Court of Justice.

(3) In the month following the simultaneous communication to the intervener of the observations of the applicant and the defendant, the intervener may lodge a statement of written observations. The time allowed to the intervener for lodging it may in no case be less than two months from the service upon him or her of the judgment of the Court of Justice.

Where the written procedure before the Court of First Instance has not been completed when the judgment referring the case back to the Court of First Instance was delivered, it is to be resumed, at the stage which it had reached, by means of measures of organisation of procedure adopted by the Court of First Instance.

The Court of First Instance decides on the costs relating to the proceedings instituted before it and to the proceedings on the appeal before the Court of Justice.[13] **24–011**

[13] CFI Rules of Procedure, Art. 121.

APPENDICES

Appendix 1

E.C. Statute of the Court of Justice

Article 1

The Court established by Article 4 of this Treaty shall be constituted and shall function in accordance with the provisions of this Treaty and of this Statute. **A1–001**

Title I

Judges and Advocates-General

Article 2

Before taking up his duties each Judge shall, in open court, take an oath to perform his duties impartially and conscientiously and to preserve the secrecy of the deliberations of the Court.

Article 3

The Judges shall be immune from legal proceedings. After they have ceased to hold office, they shall continue to enjoy immunity in respect of acts performed by them in their official capacity, including words spoken or written.

The Court, sitting in plenary session, may waive the immunity.

Where immunity has been waived and criminal proceedings are instituted against a Judge, he shall be tried, in any of the Member States, only by the Court competent to judge the members of the highest national judiciary.

Article 4

The Judges may not hold any political or administrative office.

They may not engage in any occupation, whether gainful or not, unless exemption is exceptionally granted by the Council.

When taking up their duties, they shall give a solemn undertaking that, both during and after their term of office, they will respect the obligations arising therefrom, in particular the duty to behave with integrity and discretion as regards the acceptance, after they have ceased to hold office, of certain appointments or benefits.

Any doubt on this point shall be settled by decision of the Court.

Article 5

Apart from normal replacement, or death, the duties of a Judge shall end when he resigns.

Where a Judge resigns, his letter of resignation shall be addressed to the President of the Court for transmission to the President of the Council. Upon this notification a vacancy shall arise on the bench.

Save where Article 6 applies, a Judge shall continue to hold office until his successor takes up his duties.

Article 6

A Judge may be deprived of his office or of his right to a pension or other benefits in its stead only if, in the unanimous opinion of the Judges and Advocates-General of the Court, he no longer fulfils the requisite conditions or meets the obligations arising from his office. The Judge concerned shall not take part in any such deliberations.

The Registrar of the Court shall communicate the decision of the Court to the President of the European Parliament and to the President of the Commission and shall notify it to the President of the Council.

In the case of a decision depriving a Judge of his office, a vacancy shall arise on the bench upon this latter notification.

Article 7

A Judge who is to replace a member of the Court whose term of office has not expired shall be appointed for the remainder of his predecessor's term.

Article 8

The provisions of Articles 2 to 7 shall apply to the Advocates-General.

TITLE II

Organisation

Article 9

The Registrar shall take an oath before the Court to perform his duties impartially and conscientiously and to preserve the secrecy of the deliberations of the Court.

Article 10

The Court shall arrange for replacement of the Registrar on occasions when he is prevented from attending the Court.

Article 11

Officials and other servants shall be attached to the Court to enable it to function. They shall be responsible to the Registrar under the authority of the President.

Article 12

On a proposal from the Court, the Council may, acting unanimously, provide for the appointment of Assistant Rapporteurs and lay down the rules governing their service. The Assistant Rapporteurs may be required, under conditions laid down in the Rules of Procedure, to participate in preparatory inquiries in cases pending before the Court and to cooperate with the Judge who acts as Rapporteur.

The Assistant Rapporteurs shall be chosen from persons whose independence is beyond doubt and who possess the necessary legal qualifications; they shall be appointed by the Council. They shall take an oath before the Court to perform their duties impartially and conscientiously and to preserve the secrecy of the deliberations of the Court.

Article 13

The Judges, the Advocates-General and the Registrar shall be required to reside at the place where the Court has its seat.

Article 14

The Court shall remain permanently in session. The duration of the judicial vacations shall be determined by the Court with due regard to the needs of its business.

Article 15

Decisions of the Court shall be valid only when an uneven number of its members is sitting in the deliberations. Decisions of the full Court shall be valid if nine members are sitting. Decisions of the Chambers consisting of three or five Judges shall be valid only if three Judges are sitting. Decisions of the Chambers consisting of seven Judges shall be valid only if five Judges are sitting. In the event of one of the Judges of a Chamber being prevented from attending, a Judge of another Chamber may be called upon to sit in accordance with conditions laid down in the Rules of Procedure.

Article 16

No Judge or Advocate-General may take part in the disposal of any case in which he has previously taken part as agent or adviser or has acted for one of the parties, or in which he has been called upon to pronounce as a Member of a court or tribunal, of a commission of inquiry or in any other capacity.

If, for some special reason, any Judge or Advocate-General considers that he should not take part in the judgment or examination of a particular case, he shall so inform the President. If, for some special reason, the President considers that any Judge or Advocate-General should not sit or make submissions in a particular case, he shall notify him accordingly.

Any difficulty arising as to the application of this Article shall be settled by decision of the Court.

A party may not apply for a change in the composition of the Court or of one of its Chambers on the grounds of either the nationality of a Judge or the absence from the Court or from the Chamber of a Judge of the nationality of that party.

TITLE III

Procedure

Article 17

The States and the institutions of the Community shall be represented before the Court by an agent appointed for each case; the agent may be assisted by an adviser or by a lawyer.

The States, other than the Member States, which are parties to the Agreement on the European Economic Area, and also the EFTA Surveillance Authority referred to in that Agreement, shall be represented in the same manner.

Other parties must be represented by a lawyer.

Only a lawyer authorised to practise before a court of a Member State or of another State which is a party to the Agreement on the European Economic Area may represent or assist a party before the Court.

Such agents, advisers and lawyers shall, when they appear before the Court, enjoy the rights and immunities necessary to the independent exercise of their duties, under conditions laid down in the Rules of Procedure.

As regards such advisers and lawyers who appear before it, the Court shall have the powers normally accorded to courts of law, under conditions laid down in the Rules of Procedure.

University teachers being nationals of a Member State whose law accords them a right of audience shall have the same rights before the Court as are accorded by this Article to lawyers.

Article 18

The procedure before the Court shall consist of two parts: written and oral.

The written procedure shall consist of the communication to the parties and to the institutions of the Community whose decisions are in dispute, of applications, statements of case, defences and observations, and of replies, if any, as well as of all papers and documents in support or of certified copies of them.

Communications shall be made by the Registrar in the order and within the time laid down in the rules of procedure.

The oral procedure shall consist of the reading of the report presented by a Judge acting as Rapporteur, the hearing by the Court of agents, advisers and lawyers and of the submissions of the Advocate-General, as well as the hearing, if any, of witnesses and experts.

Article 19

A case shall be brought before the Court by a written application addressed to the Registrar. The application shall contain the applicant's name and permanent address and the description of the signatory, the name of the party or names of the parties against whom the application is made, the subject-matter of the dispute, the form of order sought and a brief statement of the pleas in law on which the application is based.

The application shall be accompanied, where appropriate, by the measure the annulment of which is sought or, in the circumstances referred to in Article 175 of this Treaty, by documentary evidence of the date on which an institution was, in accordance with that Article, requested to act. If the documents are not submitted with the application, the Registrar shall ask the party concerned to produce them within a reasonable period, but in that event the rights of the party shall not lapse even if such documents are produced after the time-limit for bringing proceedings.

Article 20

In the cases governed by Article 234 (ex Article 177) of this Treaty the decision of the court or tribunal of a Member State which suspends its proceedings and refers a case to the Court shall be notified to the Court by the court or tribunal concerned. The decision shall then be notified by the Registrar of the Court to the parties, to the Member States and to the Commission, and also to the Council or to the European Central Bank if the act the validity or interpretation of which is in dispute originates from one of them, and to the European Parliament and the Council if the act the validity or interpretation of which is in dispute was adopted jointly by those two institutions.

Within two months of this notification, the parties, the Member States, the Commission and, where appropriate, the European Parliament, the Council and the European Central Bank, shall be entitled to submit statements of case or written observations to the Court.

The decision of the aforesaid court or tribunal shall, moreover, be notified by the Registrar of the Court to the States, other than the Member States, which are parties to the Agreement on the European Economic Area and also to the EFTA Surveillance Authority referred to in that Agreement which may, within two months of notification, submit statements of case or written observations to the Court.

Article 21

The Court may require the parties to produce all documents and to supply all information which the Court considers desirable. Formal note shall be taken of any refusal.

The Court may also require the Member States and institutions not being parties to the case to supply all information which the Court considers necessary for the proceedings.

Article 22

The Court may at any time entrust any individual, body, authority, committee or other organisation it chooses with the task of giving an expert opinion.

Article 23

Witnesses may be heard under conditions laid down in the Rules of Procedure.

Article 24

With respect to defaulting witnesses the Court shall have the powers generally granted to courts and tribunals and may impose pecuniary penalties under conditions laid down in the Rules of Procedure.

Article 25

Witnesses and experts may be heard on oath taken in the form laid down in the Rules of Procedure or in the manner laid down by the law of the country of the witness or expert.

Article 26

The Court may order that a witness or expert be heard by the judicial authority of his place of permanent residence.

The order shall be sent for implementation to the competent judicial authority under conditions laid down in the Rules of Procedure. The documents drawn up in compliance with the letters rogatory shall be returned to the Court under the same conditions.

The Court shall defray the expenses, without prejudice to the right to charge them, where appropriate, to the parties.

Article 27

A Member State shall treat any violation of an oath by a witness or expert in the same manner as if the offence had been committed before one of its courts with jurisdiction in civil proceedings. At the instance of the Court, the Member State concerned shall prosecute the offender before its competent court.

Article 28

The hearing in court shall be public, unless the Court, of its own motion or on application by the parties, decides otherwise for serious reasons.

Article 29

During the hearings the Court may examine the experts, the witnesses and the parties themselves. The latter, however, may address the Court only through their representatives.

Article 30

Minutes shall be made of each hearing and signed by the President and the Registrar.

Article 31

The case list shall be established by the President.

Article 32

The deliberations of the Court shall be and shall remain secret.

Article 33

Judgments shall state the reasons on which they are based. They shall contain the names of the Judges who took part in the deliberations.

Article 34

Judgments shall be signed by the President and the Registrar. They shall be read in open court.

Article 35

The Court shall adjudicate upon costs.

Article 36

The President of the Court may, by way of summary procedure, which may, in so far as necessary, differ from some of the rules contained in this Statute and which shall be laid down in the Rules of Procedure, adjudicate upon applications to suspend execution, as provided for in Article 242 (ex Article 185) of this Treaty, or to prescribe interim measures in pursuance of Article 243 (ex Article 186) or to suspend enforcement in accordance with the last paragraph of Article 256 (ex Article 192).

Should the President be prevented from attending, his place shall be taken by another Judge under conditions laid down in the Rules of Procedure.

The ruling of the President or of the Judge replacing him shall be provisional and shall in no way prejudice the decision of the Court on the substance of the case.

Article 37

Member States and institutions of the Community may intervene in cases before the Court.

The same right shall be open to any other person establishing an interest in the result of any case submitted to the Court, save in cases between Member States, between institutions of the Community or between Member States and institutions of the Community.

Without prejudice to the preceding paragraph, the States, other than the Member States, which are parties to the Agreement on the European Economic Area, and also the EFTA Surveillance Authority referred to in that Agreement, may intervene in cases before the Court where one of the fields of application of that Agreement is concerned.

An application to intervene shall be limited to supporting the form of order sought by one of the parties.

Article 38

Where the defending party, after having been duly summoned, fails to file written submissions in defence, judgment shall be given against that party by default. An objection may be lodged against the judgment within one month of it being notified. The objection shall not have the effect of staying enforcement of the judgment by default unless the Court decides otherwise.

Article 39

Member States, institutions of the Community and any other natural or legal persons may, in cases and under conditions to be determined by the Rules of Procedure, institute third-party proceedings to contest a judgment rendered without their being heard, where the judgment is prejudicial to their rights.

Article 40

If the meaning or scope of a judgment is in doubt, the Court shall construe it on application by any party or any institution of the Community establishing an interest therein.

Article 41

An application for revision of a judgment may be made to the Court only on discovery of a fact which is of such a nature as to be a decisive factor, and which, when the judgment was given, was unknown to the Court and to the party claiming the revision.

The revision shall be opened by a judgment of the Court expressly, recording the existence of a new fact, recognising that it is of such a character as to lay the case open to revision and declaring the application admissible on this ground.

No application for revision may be made after the lapse of 10 years from the date of the judgment.

Article 42

Periods of grace based on considerations of distance shall be determined by the Rules of Procedure.

No right shall be prejudiced in consequence of the expiry of a time-limit if the party concerned proves the existence of unforeseeable circumstances or of force majeure.

Article 43

Proceedings against the Community in matters arising from non-contractual liability shall be barred after a period of five years from the occurrence of the event giving rise thereto. The period of limitation shall be interrupted if proceedings are instituted before the Court or if prior to such proceedings an application is made by the aggrieved party to the relevant institution of the Community. In the latter event the proceedings must be instituted within the period of two months provided for in Article 230 (ex Article 173); the provisions of the second paragraph of Article 232 (ex Article 175) shall apply where appropriate.

Title IV

The Court of First Instance of the European Communities

Article 44

Articles 2 to 8 and 13 to 16 of this Statute shall apply to the Court of First Instance and its members. The oath referred to in Article 2 shall be taken before the Court of Justice and the decisions referred to in Articles 3, 4 and 6 shall be adopted by that Court after hearing the Court of First Instance.

Article 45

The Court of First Instance shall appoint its Registrar and lay down the rules governing his service. Articles 9, 10 and 13 of this Statute shall apply to the Registrar of the Court of First Instance *mutatis mutandis*.

The President of the Court of Justice and the President of the Court of First Instance shall determine, by common accord, the conditions under which officials and other servants attached to the Court of Justice shall render their services to the Court of First Instance to enable it to function. Certain officials or other servants shall be responsible to the Registrar of the Court of First Instance under the authority of the President of the Court of First Instance.

Article 46

The procedure before the Court of First Instance shall be governed by Title III of this Statute, with the exception of Article 20.

Such further and more detailed provisions as may be necessary shall be laid down in the Rules of Procedure established in accordance with Article 225 (ex Article 168a)(4) of the Treaty. The Rules of Procedure may derogate from the fourth paragraph of Article 37 and from Article 38 of this Statute in order to take account of the specific features of litigation in the field of intellectual property.

Notwithstanding the fourth paragraph of Article 18 of this Statute, the Advocate-General may make his reasoned submissions in writing.

Article 47

Where an application or other procedural document addressed to the Court of First Instance is lodged by mistake with the Registrar of the Court of Justice it shall be transmitted immediately by that Registrar to the Registrar of the Court of First Instance; likewise, where an application or other procedural document addressed to the Court of Justice is lodged by mistake with the Registrar of the Court of First Instance, it shall be transmitted immediately by that Registrar to the Registrar of the Court of Justice.

Where the Court of First Instance finds that it does not have jurisdiction to hear and determine an action in respect of which the Court of Justice has jurisdiction, it shall refer that action to the Court of Justice; likewise, where the Court of Justice finds that an action falls within the jurisdiction of the Court of First Instance, it shall refer that action to the Court of First Instance, whereupon that Court may not decline jurisdiction.

Where the Court of Justice and the Court of First Instance are seised of cases in which the same relief is sought, the same issue of interpretation is raised or the validity of the same act is called in question, the Court of First Instance may, after hearing the parties, stay the proceedings before it until such time as the Court of Justice shall have delivered judgment. Where applications are made for the same act to be declared void, the Court of First Instance may also decline jurisdiction in order that the Court of Justice may rule on such applications. In the cases referred to in this subparagraph, the Court of Justice may also decide to stay the proceedings before it; in that event, the proceedings before the Court of First Instance shall continue.

Article 48

Final decisions of the Court of First Instance, decisions disposing of the substantive issues in part only or disposing of a procedural issue concerning a plea of lack of competence or inadmissibility, shall be notified by the Registrar of the Court of First Instance to all parties as well as all Member States and the Community institutions even if they did not intervene in the case before the Court of First Instance.

Article 49

An appeal may be brought before the Court of Justice, within two months of the notification of the decision appealed against, against final decisions of the Court of First Instance and decisions of that Court disposing of the substantive issues in part only or disposing of a procedural issue concerning a plea of lack of competence or inadmissibility.

Such an appeal may be brought by any party which has been unsuccessful, in whole or in part, in its submissions. However, interveners other than the Member States and the Community institutions may bring such an appeal only where the decision of the Court of First Instance directly affects them.

With the exception of cases relating to disputes between the Community and its servants, an appeal may also be brought by Member States and Community institutions which did not intervene in the proceedings before the Court of First Instance. Such Member States and institutions shall be in the same position as Member States or institutions which intervened at first instance.

Article 50

Any person whose application to intervene has been dismissed by the Court of First Instance may appeal to the Court of Justice within two weeks of the notification of the decision dismissing the application.

The parties to the proceedings may appeal to the Court of Justice against any decision of the Court of First Instance made pursuant to Article 242 or 243 (ex Article 185 or 186) or the fourth paragraph of Article 256 (ex Article 192) of this Treaty within two months from their notification.

The appeal referred to in the first two paragraphs of this Article shall be heard and determined under the procedure referred to in Article 36 of this Statute.

Article 51

An appeal to the Court of Justice shall be limited to points of law. It shall lie on the grounds of lack of competence of the Court of First Instance, a breach of procedure before it which adversely affects the interests of the appellant as well as the infringement of Community law by the Court of First Instance.

No appeal shall lie regarding only the amount of the costs or the party ordered to pay them.

Article 52

Where an appeal is brought against a decision of the Court of First Instance, the procedure before the Court of Justice shall consist of a written part and an oral part. In accordance with conditions laid down in the Rules of Procedure the Court of Justice, having heard the Advocate-General and the parties, may dispense with the oral procedure.

Article 53

Without prejudice to Articles 242 and 243 (ex Articles 185 and 186) of this Treaty, an appeal shall not have suspensory effect.

By way of derogation from Article 244 (ex Article 187) of this Treaty, decisions of the Court of First Instance declaring a regulation to be void shall take effect only as from the date of expiry of the period referred to in the first paragraph of Article 49 of this Statute or, if an appeal shall have been brought within that period, as from the date of dismissal of the appeal, without prejudice, however, to the right of a party to apply to the Court of Justice, pursuant to Articles 242 and 243 (ex Articles 185 and 186) of this Treaty, for the suspension of the effects of the regulation which has been declared void or for the prescription of any other interim measure.

Article 54

If the appeal is well founded, the Court of Justice shall quash the decision of the Court of First Instance. It may itself give final judgment in the matter, where the state of the proceedings so permits, or refer the case back to the Court of First Instance for judgment.

Where a case is referred back to the Court of First Instance, that Court shall be bound by the decision of the Court of Justice on points of law.

When an appeal brought by a Member State or a Community institution, which did not intervene in the proceedings before the Court of First Instance, is well founded the Court of Justice may, if it considers this necessary, state which of the effects of the decision of the Court of First Instance which has been quashed shall be considered as definitive in respect of the parties to the litigation.

Article 55

The Rules of Procedure of the Court provided for in Article 245 (ex Article 188) of this Treaty shall contain, apart from the provisions contemplated by this Statute, any other provisions necessary for applying and, where required, supplementing it.

Article 56

The Council may, acting unanimously, make such further adjustments to the provisions of this Statute as may be required by reason of measures taken by the Council in accordance with the last paragraph of Article 221 (ex Article 165) of this Treaty.

Article 57

(text not reproduced)

Appendix 2

Rules of Procedure of the Court of Justice of the European Communities

Interpretation **A2–001**

Article 1

In these Rules:

'EC Treaty' means the Treaty establishing the European Community;

'EC Statute' means the Protocol on the Statute of the Court of Justice of the European Community;

'ECSC Treaty' means the Treaty establishing the European Coal and Steel Community;

'ECSC Statute' means the Protocol on the Statute of the Court of Justice of the European Coal and Steel Community;

'EAEC Treaty' means the Treaty establishing the European Atomic Energy Community;

'EAEC Statute' means the Protocol on the Statute of the Court of Justice of the European Atomic Energy Community;

'EEA Agreement' means the Agreement on the European Economic Area.

For the purposes of these Rules:

— 'institutions' means the institutions of the Communities and bodies which are established by the Treaties, or by an act adopted in implementation thereof, and which may be parties before the Court,
— 'EFTA Surveillance Authority' means the surveillance authority referred to in the EEA Agreement.

Title I

Organisation of the Court

Chapter 1
Judges and Advocates-General

Article 2

The term of office of a Judge shall begin on the date laid down in his instrument of appointment. In the absence of any provisions regarding the date, the term shall begin on the date of the instrument.

Article 3

1. Before taking up his duties, a Judge shall at the first public sitting of the Court which he attends after his appointment take the following oath:

'I swear that I will perform my duties impartially and conscientiously; I swear that I will preserve the secrecy of the deliberations of the Court'.

2. Immediately after taking the oath, a Judge shall sign a declaration by which he solemnly undertakes that, both during and after his term of office, he will respect the obligations arising therefrom, and in particular the duty to behave with integrity

and discretion as regards the acceptance, after he has ceased to hold office, of certain appointments and benefits.

Article 4

When the Court is called upon to decide whether a Judge no longer fulfils the requisite conditions or no longer meets the obligations arising from his office, the President shall invite the Judge concerned to make representations to the Court, in closed session and in the absence of the Registrar.

Article 5

Articles 2, 3 and 4 of these Rules shall apply in a corresponding manner to Advocates-General.

Article 6

Judges and Advocates-General shall rank equally in precedence according to their seniority in office.
Where there is equal seniority in office, precedence shall be determined by age.
Retiring Judges and Advocates-General who are reappointed shall retain their former precedence.

Chapter 2
Presidency of the Court and Constitution of the Chambers

Article 7

1. The Judges shall, immediately after the partial replacement provided for in Article 223 (ex Article 167) of the EC Treaty, Article 32b of the ECSC Treaty and Article 139 of the EAEC Treaty, elect one of their number as President of the Court for a term of three years.
2. If the office of the President of the Court falls vacant before the normal date of expiry thereof, the Court shall elect a successor for the remainder of the term.
3. The elections provided for in this Article shall be by secret ballot. If a Judge obtains an absolute majority he shall be elected. If no Judge obtains an absolute majority, a second ballot shall be held and the Judge obtaining the most votes shall be elected. Where two or more Judges obtain an equal number of votes the oldest of them shall be deemed elected.

Article 8

The President shall direct the judicial business and the administration of the Court; he shall preside at hearings and deliberations.

Article 9

1. The Court shall set up Chambers in accordance with the provisions of the second paragraph of Article 221 (ex Article 165) of the EC Treaty, the second paragraph of Article 32 of the ECSC Treaty and the second paragraph of Article 137 of the EAEC Treaty and shall decide which Judges shall be attached to them.
The composition of the Chambers shall be published in the Official Journal of the European Communities.
2. As soon as an application initiating proceedings has been lodged, the President shall assign the case to one of the Chambers for any preparatory inquiries and shall designate a Judge from that Chamber to act as Rapporteur.

3. The Court shall lay down criteria by which, as a rule, cases are to be assigned to Chambers.
4. These Rules shall apply to proceedings before the Chambers.
In cases assigned to a Chamber the powers of the President of the Court shall be exercised by the President of the Chamber.

Article 10

1. The Court shall appoint for a period of one year the Presidents of the Chambers and the First Advocate-General.
The provisions of Article 7(2) and (3) shall apply.
Appointments made in pursuance of this paragraph shall be published in the Official Journal of the European Communities.
2. The First Advocate-General shall assign each case to an Advocate-General as soon as the Judge-Rapporteur has been designated by the President. He shall take the necessary steps if an Advocate-General is absent or prevented from acting.

Article 11

When the President of the Court is absent or prevented from attending or when the office of President is vacant, the functions of President shall be exercised by a President of a Chamber according to the order of precedence laid down in Article 6 of these Rules.
If the President of the Court and the President of the Chambers are all prevented from attending at the same time, or their posts are vacant at the same time, the functions of President shall be exercised by one of the other Judges according to the order of precedence laid down in Article 6 of these Rules.

Chapter 3
Registry

SECTION 1—THE REGISTRAR AND ASSISTANT REGISTRARS

Article 12

1. The Court shall appoint the Registrar. Two weeks before the date fixed for making the appointment, the President shall inform the Members of the Court of the applications which have been made for the post.
2. An application shall be accompanied by full details of the candidate's age, nationality, university degrees, knowledge of any languages, present and past occupations and experience, if any, in judicial and international fields.
3. The appointment shall be made following the procedure laid down in Article 7(3) of these Rules.
4. The Registrar shall be appointed for a term of six years. He may be reappointed.
5. The Registrar shall take the oath in accordance with Article 3 of these Rules.
6. The Registrar may be deprived of his office only if he no longer fulfils the requisite conditions or no longer meets the obligations arising from his office; the Court shall take its decision after giving the Registrar an opportunity to make representations.
7. If the office of Registrar falls vacant before the normal date of expiry of the term thereof, the Court shall appoint a new Registrar for a term of six years.

Article 13

The Court may, following the procedure laid down in respect of the Registrar, appoint one or more Assistant Registrars to assist the Registrar and to take his place in so far as the Instructions to the Registrar referred to in Article 15 of these Rules allow.

Article 14

Where the Registrar and the Assistant Registrars are absent or prevented from attending or their posts are vacant, the President shall designate an official to carry out temporarily the duties of Registrar.

Article 15

Instructions to the Registrar shall be adopted by the Court acting on a proposal from the President.

Article 16

1. There shall be kept in the Registry, under the control of the Registrar, a register initialled by the President, in which all pleadings and supporting documents shall be entered in the order in which they are lodged.
2. When a document has been registered, the Registrar shall make a note to that effect on the original and, if a party so requests, on any copy submitted for the purpose.
3. Entries in the register and the notes provided for in the preceding paragraph shall be authentic.
4. Rules for keeping the register shall be prescribed by the Instructions to the Registrar referred to in Article 15 of these Rules.
5. Persons having an interest may consult the register at the Registry and may obtain copies or extracts on payment of a charge on a scale fixed by the Court on a proposal from the Registrar.
The parties to a case may on payment of the appropriate charge also obtain copies of pleadings and authenticated copies of judgments and orders.
6. Notice shall be given in the Official Journal of the European Communities of the date of registration of an application initiating proceedings, the names and addresses of the parties, the subject-matter of the proceedings, the form of order sought by the applicant and a summary of the pleas in law and of the main supporting arguments.
7. Where the Council or the Commission is not a party to a case, the Court shall send to it copies of the application and of the defence, without the annexes thereto, to enable it to assess whether the inapplicability of one of its acts is being invoked under Article 241 (ex Article 184) of the EC Treaty, the third paragraph of Article 36 of the ECSC Treaty or Article 156 of the EAEC Treaty.

Article 17

1. The Registrar shall be responsible, under the authority of the President, for the acceptance, transmission and custody of documents and for effecting service as provided for by these Rules.
2. The Registrar shall assist the Court, the Chambers, the President and the Judges in all their official functions.

Article 18

The Registrar shall have custody of the seals. He shall be responsible for the records and be in charge of the publications of the Court.

Article 19

Subject to Articles 4 and 27 of these Rules, the Registrar shall attend the sittings of the Court and of the Chambers.

SECTION 2—OTHER DEPARTMENTS

Article 20

1. The officials and other servants of the Court shall be appointed in accordance with the provisions of the Staff Regulations.
2. Before taking up his duties, an official shall take the following oath before the President, in the presence of the Registrar:
'I swear that I will perform loyally, discreetly and conscientiously the duties assigned to me by the Court of Justice of the European Communities'.

Article 21

The organisation of the departments of the Court shall be laid down, and may be modified, by the Court on a proposal from the Registrar.

Article 22

The Court shall set up a translating service staffed by experts with adequate legal training and a thorough knowledge of several official languages of the Court.

Article 23

The Registrar shall be responsible, under the authority of the President, for the administration of the Court, its financial management and its accounts; he shall be assisted in this by an administrator.

CHAPTER 4
ASSISTANT RAPPORTEURS

Article 24

1. Where the Court is of the opinion that the consideration of and preparatory inquiries in cases before it so require, it shall, pursuant to Article 12 of the EC Statute, Article 16 of the ECSC Statute and Article 12 of the EAEC Statute, propose the appointment of Assistant Rapporteurs.
2. Assistant Rapporteurs shall in particular:
   — assist the President in connection with applications for the adoption of interim measures
   — assist the Judge-Rapporteurs in their work.
3. In the performance of their duties the Assistant Rapporteurs shall be responsible to the President of the Court, the President of a Chamber or a Judge-Rapporteur, as the case may be.
4. Before taking up his duties, an Assistant Rapporteur shall take before the Court the oath set out in Article 3 of these Rules.

CHAPTER 5
THE WORKING OF THE COURT

Article 25

1. The dates and times of the sittings of the Court shall be fixed by the President.
2. The dates and times of the sittings of the Chambers shall be fixed by their respective Presidents.

3. The Court and the Chambers may choose to hold one or more sittings in a place other than that in which the Court has its seat.

Article 26

1. Where, by reason of a Judge being absent or prevented from attending, there is an even number of Judges, the most junior Judge within the meaning of Article 6 of these Rules shall abstain from taking part in the deliberations unless he is the Judge-Rapporteur. In that case the Judge immediately senior to him shall abstain from taking part in the deliberations.
2. If after the Court has been convened it is found that the quorum of seven Judges referred to in Article 15 of the EC Statute, Article 18 of the ECSC Statute and Article 15 of the EAEC Statute has not been attained, the President shall adjourn the sitting until there is a quorum.
3. If in any Chamber the quorum of three Judges referred to in Article 15 of the EC Statute, Article 18 of the ECSC Statute and Article 15 of the EAEC Statute has not been attained, the President of that Chamber shall so inform the President of the Court who shall designate another Judge to complete the Chamber.

Article 27

1. The Court and Chambers shall deliberate in closed session.
2. Only those Judges who were present at the oral proceedings and the Assistant Rapporteur, if any, entrusted with the consideration of the case may take part in the deliberations.
3. Every Judge taking part in the deliberations shall state his opinion and the reasons for it.
4. Any Judge may require that any questions be formulated in the language of his choice and communicated in writing to the Court or Chamber before being put to the vote.
5. The conclusions reached by the majority of the Judges after final discussion shall determine the decision of the Court. Votes shall be cast in reverse order to the order of precedence laid down in Article 6 of these Rules.
6. Differences of view on the substance, wording or order of questions, or on the interpretation of the voting shall be settled by decision of the Court or Chamber.
7. Where the deliberations of the Court concern questions of its own administration, the Advocates-General shall take part and have a vote. The Registrar shall be present, unless the Court decides to the contrary.
8. Where the Court sits without the Registrar being present it shall, if necessary, instruct the most junior Judge within the meaning of Article 6 of these Rules to draw up minutes. The minutes shall be signed by that Judge and by the President.

Article 28

1. Subject to any special decision of the Court, its vacations shall be as follows:
   — from 18 December to 10 January,
   — from the Sunday before Easter to the second Sunday after Easter,
   — from 15 July to 15 September.

During the vacations, the functions of President shall be exercised at the place where the Court has its seat either by the President himself, keeping in touch with the Registrar, or by a President of Chamber or other Judge invited by the President to take his place.
2. In a case of urgency, the President may convene the Judges and the Advocates-General during the vacations.
3. The Court shall observe the official holidays of the place where it has its seat.
4. The Court may, in proper circumstances, grant leave of absence to any Judge or Advocate-General.

CHAPTER 6
LANGUAGES

Article 29

1. The language of a case shall be Danish, Dutch, English, Finnish, French, German, Greek, Irish, Italian, Portuguese, Spanish or Swedish.
2. The language of a case shall be chosen by the applicant, except that:

(a) where the defendant is a Member State or a natural or legal person having the nationality of a Member State, the language of the case shall be the official language of that State; where that State has more than one official language, the applicant may choose between them;

(b) at the joint request of the parties the use of another of the languages mentioned in paragraph 1 for all or part of the proceedings may be authorised;

(c) at the request of one of the parties, and after the opposite party and the Advocate-General have been heard, the use of another of the languages mentioned in paragraph 1 as the language of the case for all or part of the proceedings may be authorised by way of derogation from subparagraphs (a) and (b); such a request may not be submitted by an institution of the European Communities.

In cases to which Article 103 of these Rules applies, the language of the case shall be the language of the national court or tribunal which refers the matter to the Court. At the duly substantiated request of one of the parties to the main proceedings, and after the opposite party and the Advocate-General have been heard, the use of another of the languages mentioned in paragraph 1 may be authorised for the oral procedure.

Requests as above may be decided on by the President; the latter may and, where he wishes to accede to a request without the agreement of all the parties, must refer the request to the Court.

3. The language of the case shall in particular be used in the written and oral pleadings of the parties and in supporting documents, and also in the minutes and decisions of the Court.

Any supporting documents expressed in another language must be accompanied by a translation into the language of the case.

In the case of lengthy documents, translations may be confined to extracts. However, the Court or Chamber may, of its own motion or at the request of a party, at any time call for a complete or fuller translation.

Notwithstanding the foregoing provisions, a Member State shall be entitled to use its official language when intervening in a case before the Court or when taking part in any reference of a kind mentioned in Article 103. This provision shall apply both to written statements and to oral addresses. The Registrar shall cause any such statement or address to be translated into the language of the case.

The States, other than the Member States, which are parties to the EEA Agreement, and also the EFTA Surveillance Authority, may be authorised to use one of the languages mentioned in paragraph 1, other than the language of the case, when they intervene in a case before the Court or participate in preliminary ruling proceedings envisaged by Article 20 of the EC Statute. This provision shall apply both to written statements and oral addresses. The Registrar shall cause any such statement or address to be translated into the language of the case.

4. Where a witness or expert states that he is unable adequately to express himself in one of the languages referred to in paragraph (1) of this Article, the Court or

Chamber may authorise him to give his evidence in another language. The Registrar shall arrange for translation into the language of the case.
5. The President of the Court and the Presidents of Chambers in conducting oral proceedings, the Judge-Rapporteur both in his preliminary report and in his report for the hearing, Judges and Advocates-General in putting questions and Advocates-General in delivering their opinions may use one of the languages referred to in paragraph 1 of this Article other than the language of the case. The Registrar shall arrange for translation into the language of the case.

Article 30

1. The Registrar shall, at the request of any Judge, of the Advocate-General or of a party, arrange for anything said or written in the course of the proceedings before the Court or a Chamber to be translated into the languages he chooses from those referred to in Article 29(1).
2. Publications of the Court shall be issued in the languages referred to in Article 1 of Council Regulation No 1.

Article 31

The texts of documents drawn up in the language of the case or in any other language authorised by the Court pursuant to Article 29 of these Rules shall be authentic.

Chapter 7
Rights and Obligations of Agents, Advisers and Lawyers

Article 32

1. Agents, advisers and lawyers appearing before the Court or before any judicial authority to which the Court has addressed letters rogatory, shall enjoy immunity in respect of words spoken or written by them concerning the case or the parties.
2. Agents, advisers and lawyers shall enjoy the following further privileges and facilities:

(a) papers and documents relating to the proceedings shall be exempt from both search and seizure; in the event of a dispute the customs officials or police may seal those papers and documents; they shall then be immediately forwarded to the Court for inspection in the presence of the Registrar and of the person concerned;

(b) agents, advisers and lawyers shall be entitled to such allocation of foreign currency as may be necessary for the performance of their duties;

(c) agents, advisers and lawyers shall be entitled to travel in the course of duty without hindrance.

Article 33

In order to qualify for the privileges, immunities and facilities specified in Article 32, persons entitled to them shall furnish proof of their status as follows:

(a) agents shall produce an official document issued by the party for whom they act, and shall forward without delay a copy thereof to the Registrar;

(b) advisers and lawyers shall produce a certificate signed by the Registrar. The validity of this certificate shall be limited to a specified period, which may be extended or curtailed according to the length of the proceedings.

Article 34

The privileges, immunities and facilities specified in Article 32 of these Rules are granted exclusively in the interests of the proper conduct of proceedings.

The Court may waive the immunity where it considers that the proper conduct of proceedings will not be hindered thereby.

Article 35

1. Any adviser or lawyer whose conduct towards the Court, a Chamber, a Judge, an Advocate-General or the Registrar is incompatible with the dignity of the Court, or who uses his rights for purposes other than those for which they were granted, may at any time be excluded from the proceedings by an order of the Court or Chamber, after the Advocate-General has been heard; the person concerned shall be given an opportunity to defend himself.

The order shall have immediate effect.

2. Where an adviser or lawyer is excluded from the proceedings, the proceedings shall be suspended for a period fixed by the President in order to allow the party concerned to appoint another adviser or lawyer.

3. Decisions taken under this Article may be rescinded.

Article 36

The provisions of this Chapter shall apply to university teachers who have a right of audience before the Court in accordance with Article 17 of the EC Statute, Article 20 of the ECSC Statute and Article 17 of the EAEC Statute.

Title II

Procedure

Chapter 1
Written Procedure

Article 37

1. The original of every pleading must be signed by the party's agent or lawyer.

The original, accompanied by all annexes referred to therein, shall be lodged together with five copies for the Court and a copy for every other party to the proceedings. Copies shall be certified by the party lodging them.

2. Institutions shall in addition produce, within time-limits laid down by the Court, translations of all pleadings into the other languages provided for by Article 1 of Council Regulation No 1. The second subparagraph of paragraph 1 of this Article shall apply.

3. All pleadings shall bear a date. In the reckoning of time-limits for taking steps in proceedings, only the date of lodgment at the Registry shall be taken into account.

4. To every pleading there shall be annexed a file containing the documents relied on in support of it, together with a schedule listing them.

5. Where in view of the length of a document only extracts from it are annexed to the pleading, the whole document or a full copy of it shall be lodged at the Registry.

Article 38

1. An application of the kind referred to in Article 19 of the EC Statute, Article 22 of the ECSC Statute and Article 19 of the EAEC Statute shall state:

(a) the name and address of the applicant;
(b) the designation of the party against whom the application is made;
(c) the subject-matter of the proceedings and a summary of the pleas in law on which the application is based;
(d) the form of order sought by the applicant;
(e) where appropriate, the nature of any evidence offered in support.

2. For the purpose of the proceedings, the application shall state an address for service in the place where the Court has its seat and the name of the person who is authorised and has expressed willingness to accept service.

If the application does not comply with these requirements, all service on the party concerned for the purpose of the proceedings shall be effected, for so long as the defect has not been cured, by registered letter addressed to the agent or lawyer of that party. By way of derogation from Article 79, service shall then be deemed to be duly effected by the lodging of the registered letter at the post office of the place where the Court has its seat.

3. The lawyer acting for a party must lodge at the Registry a certificate that he is authorised to practise before a court of a Member State or of another State which is a party to the EEA Agreement.

4. The application shall be accompanied, where appropriate, by the documents specified in the second paragraph of Article 19 of the EC Statute, the second paragraph of Article 22 of the ECSC Statute and the second paragraph of Article 19 of the EAEC Statute.

5. An application made by a legal person governed by private law shall be accompanied by:

(a) the instrument or instruments constituting or regulating that legal person or a recent extract from the register of companies, firms or associations or any other proof of its existence in law;
(b) proof that the authority granted to the applicant's lawyer has been properly conferred on him by someone authorised for the purpose.

6. An application submitted under Articles 238 and 239 (ex Articles 181 and 182) of the EC Treaty, Articles 42 and 89 of the ECSC Treaty and Articles 153 and 154 of the EAEC Treaty shall be accompanied by a copy of the arbitration clause contained in the contract governed by private or public law entered into by the Communities or on their behalf, or, as the case may be, by a copy of the special agreement concluded between the Member States concerned.

7. If an application does not comply with the requirements set out in paragraphs 3 to 6 of this Article, the Registrar shall prescribe a reasonable period within which the applicant is to comply with them whether by putting the application itself in order or by producing any of the abovementioned documents. If the applicant fails to put the application in order or to produce the required documents within the time prescribed, the Court shall, after hearing the Advocate-General, decide whether the non-compliance with these conditions renders the application formally inadmissible.

Article 39

The application shall be served on the defendant. In a case where Article 38(7) applies, service shall be effected as soon as the application has been put in order or the Court has declared it admissible notwithstanding the failure to observe the formal requirements set out in that Article.

Article 40

1. Within one month after service on him of the application, the defendant shall lodge a defence, stating:

(a) the name and address of the defendant;

(b) the arguments of fact and law relied on;

(c) the form of order sought by the defendant;

(d) the nature of any evidence offered by him.

The provisions of Article 38(2) to (5) of these Rules shall apply to the defence.

2. The time-limit laid down in paragraph 1 of this Article may be extended by the President on a reasoned application by the defendant.

Article 41

1. The application initiating the proceedings and the defence may be supplemented by a reply from the applicant and by a rejoinder from the defendant.
2. The President shall fix the time-limits within which these pleadings are to be lodged.

Article 42

1. In reply or rejoinder a party may offer further evidence. The party must, however, give reasons for the delay in offering it.
2. No new plea in law may be introduced in the course of proceedings unless it is based on matters of law or of fact which come to light in the course of the procedure.

If in the course of the procedure one of the parties puts forward a new plea in law which is so based, the President may, even after the expiry of the normal procedural time-limits, acting on a report of the Judge-Rapporteur and after hearing the Advocate-General, allow the other party time to answer on that plea.

The decision on the admissibility of the plea shall be reserved for the final judgment.

Article 43

The Court may, at any time, after hearing the parties and the Advocate-General, if the assignment referred to in Article 10(2) has taken place, order that two or more cases concerning the same subject-matter shall, on account of the connection between them, be joined for the purposes of the written or oral procedure or of the final judgment. The cases may subsequently be disjoined. The President may refer these matters to the Court.

Article 44

1. After the rejoinder provided for in Article 41(1) of these Rules has been lodged, the President shall fix a date on which the Judge-Rapporteur is to present his preliminary report to the Court. The report shall contain recommendations as to whether a preparatory inquiry or any other preparatory step should be undertaken and whether the case should be referred to the Chamber to which it has been assigned under Article 9(2).

The Court shall decide, after hearing the Advocate-General, what action to take upon the recommendations of the Judge-Rapporteur.

The same procedure shall apply:

(a) where no reply or no rejoinder has been lodged within the time-limit fixed in accordance with Article 41(2) of these Rules;

(b) where the party concerned waives his right to lodge a reply or rejoinder.

2. Where the Court orders a preparatory inquiry and does not undertake it itself, it shall assign the inquiry to the Chamber.
Where the Court decides to open the oral procedure without an inquiry, the President shall fix the opening date.

Article 44a

Without prejudice to any special provisions laid down in these Rules, and except in the specific cases in which, after the pleadings referred to in Article 40(1) and, as the case may be, in Article 41(1) have been lodged, the Court, acting on a report from the Judge-Rapporteur, after hearing the Advocate-General and with the express consent of the parties, decides otherwise, the procedure before the Court shall also include an oral part.

CHAPTER 2
PREPARATORY INQUIRIES

SECTION 1—MEASURES OF INQUIRY

Article 45

1. The Court, after hearing the Advocate-General, shall prescribe the measures of inquiry that it considers appropriate by means of an order setting out the facts to be proved. Before the Court decides on the measures of inquiry referred to in paragraph 2(c), (d) and (e) the parties shall be heard.
The order shall be served on the parties.
2. Without prejudice to Articles 21 and 22 of the EC Statute, Articles 24 and 25 of the ECSC Statute and Articles 22 and 23 of the EAEC Statute, the following measures of inquiry may be adopted:

(a) the personal appearance of the parties;
(b) a request for information and production of documents;
(c) oral testimony;
(d) the commissioning of an expert's report;
(e) an inspection of the place or thing in question.

3. The measures of inquiry which the Court has ordered may be conducted by the Court itself, or be assigned to the Judge-Rapporteur.
The Advocate-General shall take part in the measures of inquiry.
4. Evidence may be submitted in rebuttal and previous evidence may be amplified.

Article 46

1. A Chamber to which a preparatory inquiry has been assigned may exercise the powers vested in the Court by Articles 45 and 47 to 53 of these Rules; the powers vested in the President of the Court may be exercised by the President of the Chamber.
2. Articles 56 and 57 of these Rules shall apply to proceedings before the Chamber.
3. The parties shall be entitled to attend the measures of inquiry.

SECTION 2—THE SUMMONING AND EXAMINATION OF WITNESSES AND EXPERTS

Article 47

1. The Court may, either of its own motion or on application by a party, and after hearing the Advocate-General, order that certain facts be proved by witnesses. The order of the Court shall set out the facts to be established.

The Court may summon a witness of its own motion or on application by a party or at the instance of the Advocate-General.

An application by a party for the examination of a witness shall state precisely about what facts and for what reasons the witness should be examined.

2. The witness shall be summoned by an order of the Court containing the following information:

(a) the surname, forenames, description and address of the witness;

(b) an indication of the facts about which the witness is to be examined;

(c) where appropriate, particulars of the arrangements made by the Court for reimbursement of expenses incurred by the witness, and of the penalties which may be imposed on defaulting witnesses.

The order shall be served on the parties and the witnesses.

3. The Court may make the summoning of a witness for whose examination a party has applied conditional upon the deposit with the cashier of the Court of a sum sufficient to cover the taxed costs thereof; the Court shall fix the amount of the payment.

The cashier shall advance the funds necessary in connection with the examination of any witness summoned by the Court of its own motion.

4. After the identity of the witness has been established, the President shall inform him that he will be required to vouch the truth of his evidence in the manner laid down in these Rules.

The witness shall give his evidence to the Court, the parties having been given notice to attend. After the witness has given his main evidence the President may, at the request of a party or of his own motion, put questions to him.

The other Judges and the Advocate-General may do likewise.

Subject to the control of the President, questions may be put to witnesses by the representatives of the parties.

5. After giving his evidence, the witness shall take the following oath:

'I swear that I have spoken the truth, the whole truth and nothing but the truth.'

The Court may, after hearing the parties, exempt a witness from taking the oath.

6. The Registrar shall draw up minutes in which the evidence of each witness is reproduced.

The minutes shall be signed by the President or by the Judge-Rapporteur responsible for conducting the examination of the witness, and by the Registrar. Before the minutes are thus signed, witnesses must be given an opportunity to check the content of the minutes and to sign them.

The minutes shall constitute an official record.

Article 48

1. Witnesses who have been duly summoned shall obey the summons and attend for examination.

2. If a witness who has been duly summoned fails to appear before the Court, the Court may impose upon him a pecuniary penalty not exceeding euro 5 000 and may order that a further summons be served on the witness at his own expense.

The same penalty may be imposed upon a witness who, without good reason, refuses to give evidence or to take the oath or where appropriate to make a solemn affirmation equivalent thereto.

3. If the witness proffers a valid excuse to the Court, the pecuniary penalty imposed on him may be cancelled. The pecuniary penalty imposed may be reduced at the request of the witness where he establishes that it is disproportionate to his income.

4. Penalties imposed and other measures ordered under this Article shall be enforced in accordance with Articles 244 and 256 (ex Articles 187 and 192) of the EC Treaty, Articles 44 and 92 of the ECSC Treaty and Articles 159 and 164 of the EAEC Treaty.

Article 49

1. The Court may order that an expert's report be obtained. The order appointing the expert shall define his task and set a time-limit within which he is to make his report.
2. The expert shall receive a copy of the order, together with all the documents necessary for carrying out his task. He shall be under the supervision of the Judge-Rapporteur, who may be present during his investigation and who shall be kept informed of his progress in carrying out his task.

The Court may request the parties or one of them to lodge security for the costs of the expert's report.
3. At the request of the expert, the Court may order the examination of witnesses. Their examination shall be carried out in accordance with Article 47 of these Rules.
4. The expert may give his opinion only on points which have been expressly referred to him.
5. After the expert has made his report, the Court may order that he be examined, the parties having been given notice to attend.

Subject to the control of the President, questions may be put to the expert by the representatives of the parties.
6. After making his report, the expert shall take the following oath before the Court:

'I swear that I have conscientiously and impartially carried out my task.'

The Court may, after hearing the parties, exempt the expert from taking the oath.

Article 50

1. If one of the parties objects to a witness or to an expert on the ground that he is not a competent or proper person to act as witness or expert or for any other reason, or if a witness or expert refuses to give evidence, to take the oath or to make a solemn affirmation equivalent thereto, the matter shall be resolved by the Court.
2. An objection to a witness or to an expert shall be raised within two weeks after service of the order summoning the witness or appointing the expert; the statement of objection must set out the grounds of objection and indicate the nature of any evidence offered.

Article 51

1. Witnesses and experts shall be entitled to reimbursement of their travel and subsistence expenses. The cashier of the Court may make a payment to them towards these expenses in advance.
2. Witnesses shall be entitled to compensation for loss of earnings, and experts to fees for their services. The cashier of the Court shall pay witnesses and experts their compensation or fees after they have carried out their respective duties or tasks.

Article 52

The Court may, on application by a party or of its own motion, issue letters rogatory for the examination of witnesses or experts, as provided for in the supplementary rules mentioned in Article 125 of these Rules.

Article 53

1. The Registrar shall draw up minutes of every hearing. The minutes shall be signed by the President and by the Registrar and shall constitute an official record.
2. The parties may inspect the minutes and any expert's report at the Registry and obtain copies at their own expense.

SECTION 3—CLOSURE OF THE PREPARATORY INQUIRY

Article 54

Unless the Court prescribes a period within which the parties may lodge written observations, the President shall fix the date for the opening of the oral procedure after the preparatory inquiry has been completed.
Where a period had been prescribed for the lodging of written observations, the President shall fix the date for the opening of the oral procedure after that period has expired.

Chapter 3
Oral Procedure

Article 55

1. Subject to the priority of decisions provided for in Article 85 of these Rules, the Court shall deal with the cases before it in the order in which the preparatory inquiries in them have been completed. Where the preparatory inquiries in several cases are completed simultaneously, the order in which they are to be dealt with shall be determined by the dates of entry in the register of the applications initiating them respectively.
2. The President may in special circumstances order that a case be given priority over others.

The President may in special circumstances, after hearing the parties and the Advocate-General, either on his own initiative or at the request of one of the parties, defer a case to be dealt with at a later date. On a joint application by the parties the President may order that a case be deferred.

Article 56

1. The proceedings shall be opened and directed by the President, who shall be responsible for the proper conduct of the hearing.
2. The oral proceedings in cases heard in camera shall not be published.

Article 57

The President may in the course of the hearing put questions to the agents, advisers or lawyers of the parties.
The other Judges and the Advocate-General may do likewise.

Article 58

A party may address the Court only through his agent, adviser or lawyer.

Article 59

1. The Advocate-General shall deliver his opinion orally at the end of the oral procedure.
2. After the Advocate-General has delivered his opinion, the President shall declare the oral procedure closed.

Article 60

The Court may at any time, in accordance with Article 45(1), after hearing the Advocate-General, order any measure of inquiry to be taken or that a previous inquiry be repeated or expanded. The Court may direct the Chamber or the Judge-Rapporteur to carry out the measures so ordered.

Article 61

The Court may after hearing the Advocate-General order the reopening of the oral procedure.

Article 62

1. The Registrar shall draw up minutes of every hearing. The minutes shall be signed by the President and by the Registrar and shall constitute an official record.
2. The parties may inspect the minutes at the Registry and obtain copies at their own expense.

CHAPTER 4
JUDGMENTS

Article 63

— The judgment shall contain:
— a statement that it is the judgment of the Court,
— the date of its delivery,
— the names of the President and of the Judges taking part in it,
— the name of the Advocate-General,
— the name of the Registrar,
— the description of the parties,
— the names of the agents, advisers and lawyers of the parties,
— a statement of the forms of order sought by the parties,
— a statement that the Advocate-General has been heard,
— a summary of the facts,
— the grounds for the decision,
— the operative part of the judgment, including the decision as to costs.

Article 64

1. The judgment shall be delivered in open court; the parties shall be given notice to attend to hear it.
2. The original of the judgment, signed by the President, by the Judges who took part in the deliberations and by the Registrar, shall be sealed and deposited at the Registry; the parties shall be served with certified copies of the judgment.
3. The Registrar shall record on the original of the judgment the date on which it was delivered.

Article 65

The judgment shall be binding from the date of its delivery.

Article 66

1. Without prejudice to the provisions relating to the interpretation of judgments the Court may, of its own motion or on application by a party made within two weeks after the delivery of a judgment, rectify clerical mistakes, errors in calculation and obvious slips in it.
2. The parties, whom the Registrar shall duly notify, may lodge written observations within a period prescribed by the President.

3. The Court shall take its decision in closed session after hearing the Advocate-General.
4. The original of the rectification order shall be annexed to the original of the rectified judgment. A note of this order shall be made in the margin of the original of the rectified judgment.

Article 67

If the Court should omit to give a decision on a specific head of claim or on costs, any party may within a month after service of the judgment apply to the Court to supplement its judgment.

The application shall be served on the opposite party and the President shall prescribe a period within which that party may lodge written observations.

After these observations have been lodged, the Court shall, after hearing the Advocate-General, decide both on the admissibility and on the substance of the application.

Article 68

The Registrar shall arrange for the publication of reports of cases before the Court.

Chapter 5
Costs

Article 69

1. A decision as to costs shall be given in the final judgment or in the order which closes the proceedings.
2. The unsuccessful party shall be ordered to pay the costs if they have been applied for in the successful party's pleadings.

Where there are several unsuccessful parties the Court shall decide how the costs are to be shared.
3. Where each party succeeds on some and fails on other heads, or where the circumstances are exceptional, the Court may order that the costs be shared or that the parties bear their own costs.

The Court may order a party, even if successful, to pay costs which the Court considers that party to have unreasonably or vexatiously caused the opposite party to incur.
4. The Member States and institutions which intervene in the proceedings shall bear their own costs.

The States, other than the Member States, which are parties to the EEA Agreement, and also the EFTA Surveillance Authority, shall bear their own costs if they intervene in the proceedings.

The Court may order an intervener other than those mentioned in the preceding subparagraphs to bear his own costs.
5. A party who discontinues or withdraws from proceedings shall be ordered to pay the costs if they have been applied for in the other party's observations on the discontinuance. However, upon application by the party who discontinues or withdraws from proceedings, the costs shall be borne by the other party if this appears justified by the conduct of that party.

Where the parties have come to an agreement on costs, the decision as to costs shall be in accordance with that agreement.

If costs are not claimed, the parties shall bear their own costs.
6. Where a case does not proceed to judgment the costs shall be in the discretion of the Court.

Article 70

Without prejudice to the second subparagraph of Article 69(3) of these Rules, in proceedings between the Communities and their servants the institutions shall bear their own costs.

Article 71

Costs necessarily incurred by a party in enforcing a judgment or order of the Court shall be refunded by the opposite party on the scale in force in the State where the enforcement takes place.

Article 72

Proceedings before the Court shall be free of charge, except that:

(a) where a party has caused the Court to incur avoidable costs the Court may, after hearing the Advocate-General, order that party to refund them;

(b) where copying or translation work is carried out at the request of a party, the cost shall, in so far as the Registrar considers it excessive, be paid for by that party on the scale of charges referred to in Article 16(5) of these Rules.

Article 73

Without prejudice to the preceding Article, the following shall be regarded as recoverable costs:

(a) sums payable to witnesses and experts under Article 51 of these Rules;

(b) expenses necessarily incurred by the parties for the purpose of the proceedings, in particular the travel and subsistence expenses and the remuneration of agents, advisers or lawyers.

Article 74

1. If there is a dispute concerning the costs to be recovered, the Chamber to which the case has been assigned shall, on application by the party concerned and after hearing the opposite party and the Advocate-General, make an order, from which no appeal shall lie.
2. The parties may, for the purposes of enforcement, apply for an authenticated copy of the order.

Article 75

1. Sums due from the cashier of the Court shall be paid in the currency of the country where the Court has its seat.
At the request of the person entitled to any sum, it shall be paid in the currency of the country where the expenses to be refunded were incurred or where the steps in respect of which payment is due were taken.
2. Other debtors shall make payment in the currency of their country of origin.
3. Conversions of currency shall be made at the official rates of exchange ruling on the day of payment in the country where the Court has its seat.

Chapter 6
Legal Aid

Article 76

1. A party who is wholly or in part unable to meet the costs of the proceedings may at any time apply for legal aid.

The application shall be accompanied by evidence of the applicant's need of assistance, and in particular by a document from the competent authority certifying his lack of means.

2. If the application is made prior to proceedings which the applicant wishes to commence, it shall briefly state the subject of such proceedings.

The application need not be made through a lawyer.

3. The President shall designate a Judge to act as Rapporteur. The Chamber to which the latter belongs shall, after considering the written observations of the opposite party and after hearing the Advocate-General, decide whether legal aid should be granted in full or in part, or whether it should be refused. The Chamber shall consider whether there is manifestly no cause of action.

The Chamber shall make an order without giving reasons, and no appeal shall lie therefrom.

4. The Chamber may at any time, either of its own motion or on application, withdraw legal aid if the circumstances which led to its being granted alter during the proceedings.

5. Where legal aid is granted, the cashier of the Court shall advance the funds necessary to meet the expenses.

In its decision as to costs the Court may order the payment to the cashier of the Court of the whole or any part of amounts advanced as legal aid.

The Registrar shall take steps to obtain the recovery of these sums from the party ordered to pay them.

Chapter 7
Discontinuance

Article 77

If, before the Court has given its decision, the parties reach a settlement of their dispute and intimate to the Court the abandonment of their claims, the President shall order the case to be removed from the register and shall give a decision as to costs in accordance with Article 69(5), having regard to any proposals made by the parties on the matter.

This provision shall not apply to proceedings under Articles 230 and 232 (ex Articles 173 and 175) of the EC Treaty, Articles 33 and 35 of the ECSC Treaty and Articles 146 and 148 of the EAEC Treaty.

Article 78

If the applicant informs the Court in writing that he wishes to discontinue the proceedings, the President shall order the case to be removed from the register and shall give a decision as to costs in accordance with Article 69(5).

Chapter 8
Service

Article 79

Where these Rules require that a document be served on a person, the Registrar shall ensure that service is effected at that person's address for service either by the dispatch of a copy of the document by registered post with a form for acknowledgement of receipt or by personal delivery of the copy against a receipt.

The Registrar shall prepare and certify the copies of documents to be served, save where the parties themselves supply the copies in accordance with Article 37(1) of these Rules.

CHAPTER 9
TIME-LIMITS

Article 80

1. Any period of time prescribed by the EC, ECSC and EAEC Treaties, the Statutes of the Court or these Rules for the taking of any procedural step shall be reckoned as follows:

(a) where a period expressed in days, weeks, months or years is to be calculated from the moment at which an event occurs or an action takes place, the day during which that event occurs or that action takes place shall not be counted as falling within the period in question;

(b) a period expressed in weeks, months or in years shall end with the expiry of whichever day in the last week, month or year is the same day of the week, or falls on the same date, as the day during which the event or action from which the period is to be calculated occurred or took place. If,
in a period expressed in months or in years, the day on which it should expire does not occur in the last month, the period shall end with the expiry of the last day of that month;

(c) where a period is expressed in months and days, it shall first be reckoned in whole months, then in days;

(d) periods shall include official holidays, Sundays and Saturdays;

(e) periods shall not be suspended during the judicial vacations.

2. If the period would otherwise end on a Saturday, Sunday or an official holiday, it shall be extended until the end of the first following working day.

A list of official holidays drawn up by the Court shall be published in the *Official Journal of the European Communities*.

Article 81

1. Where the period of time allowed for initiating proceedings against a measure adopted by an institution runs from the publication of that measure, that period shall be calculated, for the pruposes of Article 80(1)(a), from the end of the 14th day after publication thereof in the *Official Journal of the European Communities*.
2. The extensions, on account of distance, of prescribed time-limits shall be provided for in a decision of the Court which shall be published in the *Official Journal of the European Communities*.

Article 82

Any time-limit prescribed pursuant to these Rules may be extended by whoever prescribed it.

The President and the Presidents of Chambers may delegate to the Registrar power of signature for the purpose of fixing time-limits which, pursuant to these Rules, it falls to them to prescribe or of extending such time-limits.

CHAPTER 10
STAY OF PROCEEDINGS

Article 82a

1. The proceedings may be stayed:

(a) in the circumstances specified in the third paragraph of Article 47 of the EC Statute, the third paragraph of Article 47 of the ECSC Statute and the third paragraph of Article 48 of the EAEC Statute, by order of the Court or of the Chamber to which the case has been assigned, made after hearing the Advocate-General;

(b) in all other cases, by decision of the President adopted after hearing the Advocate-General and, save in the case of references for a preliminary ruling as referred to in Article 103, the parties.

The proceedings may be resumed by order or decision, following the same procedure.

The orders or decisions referred to in this paragraph shall be served on the parties.

2. The stay of proceedings shall take effect on the date indicated in the order or decision of stay or, in the absence of such indication, on the date of that order or decision.

While proceedings are stayed time shall cease to run for the purposes of prescribed time-limits for all parties.

3. Where the order or decision of stay does not fix the length of stay, it shall end on the date indicated in the order or decision of resumption or, in the absence of such indication, on the date of the order or decision of resumption.

From the date of resumption time shall begin to run afresh for the purposes of the time-limits.

Title III

Special Forms of Procedure

Chapter 1

Suspension of Operation or Enforcement and Other Interim Measures

Article 83

1. An application to suspend the operation of any measure adopted by an institution, made pursuant to Article 242 (ex Article 185) of the EC Treaty, the second paragraph of Article 39 of the ECSC Treaty and Article 157 of the EAEC Treaty, shall be admissible only if the applicant is challenging that measure in proceedings before the Court.

An application for the adoption of any other interim measure referred to in Article 243 (ex Article 186) of the EC Treaty the third paragraph of Article 39 of the ECSC Treaty and Article 158 of the EAEC Treaty, shall be admissible only if it is made by a party to a case before the Court and relates to that case.

2. An application of a kind referred to in paragraph 1 of this Article shall state the subject-matter of the proceedings, the circumstances giving rise to urgency and the pleas of fact and law establishing a prima facie case for the interim measures applied for.

3. The application shall be made by a separate document and in accordance with the provisions of Articles 37 and 38 of these Rules.

Article 84

1. The application shall be served on the opposite party, and the President shall prescribe a short period within which that party may submit written or oral observations.

2. The President may order a preparatory inquiry.

The President may grant the application even before the observations of the opposite party have been submitted. This decision may be varied or cancelled even without any application being made by any party.

Article 85

The President shall either decide on the application himself or refer it to the Court.

If the President is absent or prevented from attending, Article 11 of these Rules shall apply.

Where the application is referred to it, the Court shall postpone all other cases, and shall give a decision after hearing the Advocate-General. Article 84 shall apply.

Article 86

1. The decision on the application shall take the form of a reasoned order, from which no appeal shall lie. The order shall be served on the parties forthwith.
2. The enforcement of the order may be made conditional on the lodging by the applicant of security, of an amount and nature to be fixed in the light of the circumstances.
3. Unless the order fixes the date on which the interim measure is to lapse, the measure shall lapse when final judgment is delivered.
4. The order shall have only an interim effect, and shall be without prejudice to the decision of the Court on the substance of the case.

Article 87

On application by a party, the order may at any time be varied or cancelled on account of a change in circumstances.

Article 88

Rejection of an application for an interim measure shall not bar the party who made it from making a further application on the basis of new facts.

Article 89

The provisions of this Chapter shall apply to applications to suspend the enforcement of a decision of the Court or of any measure adopted by another institution, submitted pursuant to Articles 244 and 256 (ex Articles 187 and 192) of the EC Treaty, Articles 44 and 92 of the ECSC Treaty and Articles 159 and 164 of the EAEC Treaty.

The order granting the application shall fix, where appropriate, a date on which interim measure is to lapse.

Article 90

1. An application of a kind referred to in the third and fourth paragraphs of Article 81 of the EAEC Treaty shall contain:

(a) the names and addresses of the persons or undertakings to be inspected;

(b) an indication of what is to be inspected and of the purpose of the inspection.

2. The President shall give his decision in the form of an order. Article 86 of these Rules shall apply.

If the President is absent or prevented from attending, Article 11 of these Rules shall apply.

Chapter 2
Preliminary Issues

Article 91

1. A party applying to the Court for a decision on a preliminary objection or other preliminary plea not going to the substance of the case shall make the application by a separate document.

The application must state the pleas of fact and law relied on and the form of order sought by the applicant; any supporting documents must be annexed to it.

2. As soon as the application has been lodged, the President shall prescribe a period within which the opposite party may lodge a document containing a statement of the form of order sought by that party and its pleas in law.

3. Unless the Court decides otherwise, the remainder of the proceedings shall be oral.

4. The Court shall, after hearing the Advocate-General, decide on the application or reserve its decision for the final judgment.

If the Court refuses the application or reserves its decision, the President shall prescribe new time-limits for the further steps in the proceedings.

Article 92

1. Where it is clear that the Court has no jurisdiction to take cognisance of an action or where the action is manifestly inadmissible, the Court may, by reasoned order, after hearing the Advocate-General and without taking further steps in the proceedings, give a decision on the action.

2. The Court may at any time of its own motion consider whether there exists any absolute bar to proceeding with a case or declare, after hearing the parties, that the action has become devoid of purpose and that there is no need to adjudicate on it; it shall give its decision in accordance with Article 91(3) and (4) of these Rules.

Chapter 3
Intervention

Article 93

1. An application to intervene must be made within three months of the publication of the notice referred to in Article 16(6) of these Rules.

The application shall contain:

(a) the description of the case;

(b) the description of the parties;

(c) the name and address of the intervener;

(d) the intervener's address for service at the place where the Court has its seat;

(e) the form of order sought, by one or more of the parties, in support of which the intervener is applying for leave to intervene;

(f) a statement of the circumstances establishing the right to intervene, where the application is submitted pursuant to the second or third paragraph of Article 37 of the EC Statute, Article 34 of the ECSC Statute or the second paragraph of Article 38 of the EAEC Statute.

The intervener shall be represented in accordance with Article 17 of the EC Statute, Article 20 of the ECSC Statute and Article 17 of the EAEC Statute.

Articles 37 and 38 of these Rules shall apply.
2. The application shall be served on the parties.
The President shall give the parties an opportunity to submit their written or oral observations before deciding on the application.
The President shall decide on the application by order or shall refer the application to the Court.
3. If the President allows the intervention, the intervener shall receive a copy of every document served on the parties. The President may, however, on application by one of the parties, omit secret or confidential documents.
4. The intervener must accept the case as he finds it at the time of his intervention.
5. The President shall prescribe a period within which the intervener may submit a statement in intervention.
The statement in intervention shall contain:

(a) a statement of the form of order sought by the intervener in support of or opposing, in whole or in part, the form of order sought by one of the parties;

(b) the pleas in law and arguments relied on by the intervener;

(c) where appropriate, the nature of any evidence offered.

6. After the statement in intervention has been lodged, the President shall, where necessary, prescribe a time-limit within which the parties may reply to that statement.

Chapter 4
Judgments by Default and Applications to Set Them Aside

Article 94

1. If a defendant on whom an application initiating proceedings has been duly served fails to lodge a defence to the application in the proper form within the time prescribed, the applicant may apply for judgment by default.
The application shall be served on the defendant. The Court may decide to open the oral procedure on the application.
2. Before giving judgment by default the Court shall, after hearing the Advocate-General, consider whether the application initiating proceedings is admissible, whether the appropriate formalities have been complied with, and whether the application appears well founded. The Court may order a preparatory inquiry.
3. A judgment by default shall be enforceable. The Court may, however, grant a stay of execution until the Court has given its decision on any application under paragraph 4 to set aside the judgment, or it may make execution subject to the provision of security of an amount and nature to be fixed in the light of the circumstances; this security shall be released if no such application is made or if the application fails.
4. Application may be made to set aside a judgment by default.
The application to set aside the judgment must be made within one month from the date of service of the judgment and must be lodged in the form prescribed by Articles 37 and 38 of these Rules.
5. After the application has been served, the President shall prescribe a period within which the other party may submit his written observations.
The proceedings shall be conducted in accordance with Article 44 et seq. of these Rules.
6. The Court shall decide by way of a judgment which may not be set aside. The original of this judgment shall be annexed to the original of the judgment by default. A note of the judgment on the application to set aside shall be made in the margin of the original of the judgment by default.

Chapter 5
Cases Assigned to Chambers

Article 95

1. The Court may assign any case brought before it to a Chamber in so far as the difficulty or importance of the case or particular cicumstances are not such as to require that the Court decide it in plenary session.
2. The decision so to assign a case shall be taken by the Court at the end of the written procedure upon consideration of the preliminary report presented by the Judge-Rapporteur and after the Advocate-General has been heard.

However, a case may not be so assigned if a Member State or an institution of the Communities, being a party to the proceedings, has requested that the case be decided in plenary session. In this subparagraph the expression 'party to the proceedings' means any Member State or any institution which is a party to or an intervener in the proceedings or which has submitted written observations in any reference of a kind mentioned in Article 103 of these Rules.

The request referred to in the preceding subparagraph may not be made in proceedings between the Communities and their servants.
3. A Chamber may at any stage refer a case back to the Court.

Article 96

(repealed)

Chapter 6
Exceptional Review Procedures

SECTION 1—THIRD-PARTY PROCEEDINGS

Article 97

1. Articles 37 and 38 of these Rules shall apply to an application initiating third-party proceedings. In addition such an application shall:

(a) specify the judgment contested;
(b) state how that judgment is prejudicial to the rights of the third party;
(c) indicate the reasons for which the third party was unable to take part in the original case.

The application must be made against all the parties to the original case.

Where the judgment has been published in the *Official Journal of the European Communities*, the application must be lodged within two months of the publication.
2. The Court may, on application by the third party, order a stay of execution of the judgment. The provisions of Title III, Chapter I, of these Rules shall apply.
3. The contested judgment shall be varied on the points on which the submissions of the third party are upheld.

The original of the judgment in the third-party proceedings shall be annexed to the original of the contested judgment. A note of the judgment in the third-party proceedings shall be made in the margin of the original of the contested judgment.

SECTION 2—REVISION

Article 98

An application for revision of a judgment shall be made within three months of the date on which the facts on which the application is based came to the applicant's knowledge.

Article 99

1. Articles 37 and 38 of these Rules shall apply to an application for revision. In addition such an application shall:

(a) specify the judgment contested;

(b) indicate the points on which the judgment is contested;

(c) set out the facts on which the application is based;

(d) indicate the nature of the evidence to show that there are facts justifying revision of the judgment, and that the time-limit laid down in Article 98 has been observed.

2. The application must be made against all parties to the case in which the contested judgment was given.

Article 100

1. Without prejudice to its decision on the substance, the Court, in closed session, shall, after hearing the Advocate-General and having regard to the written observations of the parties, give in the form of a judgment its decision on the admissibility of the application.
2. If the Court finds the application admissible, it shall proceed to consider the substance of the application and shall give its decision in the form of a judgment in accordance with these Rules.
3. The original of the revising judgment shall be annexed to the original of the judgment revised. A note of the revising judgment shall be made in the margin of the original of the judgment revised.

Chapter 7
Appeals Against Decisions of the Arbitration Committee

Article 101

1. An application initiating an appeal under the second paragraph of Article 18 of the EAEC Treaty shall state:

(a) the name and address of the applicant;

(b) the description of the signatory;

(c) a reference to the arbitration committee's decision against which the appeal is made;

(d) the description of the parties;

(e) a summary of the facts;

(f) the pleas in law of and the form of order sought by the applicant.

2. Articles 37(3) and (4) and 38(2), (3) and (5) of these Rules shall apply.
A certified copy of the contested decision shall be annexed to the application.
3. As soon as the application has been lodged, the Registrar of the Court shall request the arbitration committee registry to transmit to the Court the papers in the case.
4. Articles 39, 40 and 55 et seq. of these Rules shall apply to these proceedings.
5. The Court shall give its decision in the form of a judgment. Where the Court sets aside the decision of the arbitration committee it may refer the case back to the committee.

CHAPTER 8
INTERPRETATION OF JUDGMENTS

Article 102

1. An application for interpretation of a judgment shall be made in accordance with Articles 37 and 38 of these Rules. In addition it shall specify:

(a) the judgment in question;

(b) the passages of which interpretation is sought.

The application must be made against all the parties to the case in which the judgment was given.
2. The Court shall give its decision in the form of a judgment after having given the parties an opportunity to submit their observations and after hearing the Advocate-General.
The original of the interpreting judgment shall be annexed to the original of the judgment interpreted. A note of the interpreting judgment shall be made in the margin of the original of the judgment interpreted.

CHAPTER 9
PRELIMINARY RULINGS AND OTHER REFERENCES FOR INTERPRETATION

Article 103

1. In cases governed by Article 20 of the EC Statute and Article 21 of the EAEC Statute, the procedure shall be governed by the provisions of these Rules, subject to adaptations necessitated by the nature of the reference for a preliminary ruling.
2. The provisions of paragraph 1 shall apply to the references for a preliminary ruling provided for in the Protocol concerning the interpretation by the Court of Justice of the Convention of 29 February 1968 on the mutual recognition of companies and legal persons and the Protocol concerning the interpretation by the Court of Justice of the Convention of 27 September 1968 on jurisdiction and the enforcement of judgments in civil and commercial matters, signed at Luxembourg on 3 June 1971, and to the references provided for by Article 4 of the latter Protocol.
The provisions of paragraph 1 shall apply also to references for interpretation provided for by other existing or future agreements.
3. In cases provided for in Article 41 of the ECSC Treaty, the text of the decision to refer the matter shall be served on the parties in the case, the Member States, the Commission and the Council.
These parties, States and institutions may, within two months from the date of such service, lodge written statements of case or written observations.
The provisions of paragraph 1 shall apply.

Article 104

1. The decisions of national courts or tribunals referred to in Article 103 shall be communicated to the Member States in the original version, accompanied by a translation into the official language of the State to which they are addressed.
In the cases governed by Article 20 of the EC Statute, the decisions of national courts or tribunals shall be notified to the States, other than the Member States, which are parties to the EEA Agreement, and also to the EFTA Surveillance Authority, in the original version, accompanied by a translation into one of the

languages mentioned in Article 29(1), to be chosen by the addressee of the notification.

2. As regards the representation and attendance of the parties to the main proceedings in the preliminary ruling procedure the Court shall take account of the rules of procedure of the national court or tribunal which made the reference.

3. Where a question referred to the Court for a preliminary ruling is manifestly identical to a question on which the Court has already ruled, the Court may, after informing the court or tribunal which referred the question to it, hearing any observations submitted by the persons referred to in Article 20 of the EC Statute, Article 21 of the EAEC Statute and Article 103(3) of these Rules and hearing the Advocate-General, give its decision by reasoned order in which reference is made to its previous judgment.

4. Without prejudice to paragraph 3 of this Article, the procedure before the Court in the case of a reference for a preliminary ruling shall also include an oral part. However, after the statements of case or written observations referred to in Article 20 of the EC Statute, Article 21 of the EAEC Statute and Article 103(3) of these Rules have been submitted, the Court, acting on a report from the Judge-Rapporteur, after informing the persons who under the aforementioned provisions are entitled to submit such statements or observations, may, after hearing the Advocate-General, decide otherwise, provided that none of those persons has asked to present oral argument.

5. It shall be for the national court or tribunal to decide as to the costs of the reference.

In special circumstances the Court may grant, by way of legal aid, assistance for the purpose of facilitating the representation or attendance of a party.

Chapter 10
Special Procedures Under Articles 103 to 105 of the EAEC Treaty

Article 105

1. Four certified copies shall be lodged of an application under the third paragraph of Article 103 of the EAEC Treaty. The Commission shall be served with a copy.

2. The application shall be accompanied by the draft of the agreement or contract in question, by the observations of the Commission addressed to the State concerned and by all other supporting documents.

The Commission shall submit its observations to the Court within a period of 10 days, which may be extended by the President after the State concerned has been heard.

A certified copy of the observations shall be served on that State.

3. As soon as the application has been lodged the President shall designate a Judge to act as Rapporteur. The First Advocate-General shall assign the case to an Advocate-General as soon as the Judge-Rapporteur has been designated.

4. The decision shall be taken in closed session after the Advocate-General has been heard.

The agents and advisers of the State concerned and of the Commission shall be heard if they so request.

Article 106

1. In cases provided for in the last paragraph of Article 104 and the last paragraph of Article 105 of the EAEC Treaty, the provisions of Article 37 et seq. of these Rules shall apply.

2. The application shall be served on the State to which the respondent person or undertaking belongs.

CHAPTER 11
OPINIONS

Article 107

1. A request by the Council for an Opinion pursuant to Article 300 (ex Article 228) of the EC Treaty shall be served on the Commission and on the European Parliament. Such a request by the Commission shall be served on the Council, on the European Parliament and on the Member States. Such a request by a Member State shall be served on the Council, on the Commission, on the European Parliament and the other Member States.

The President shall prescribe a period within which the institutions and Member States which have been served with a request may submit their written observations.

2. The Opinion may deal not only with the question whether the envisaged agreement is compatible which the provisions of the EC Treaty but also with the question whether the Community or any Community institution has the power to enter into that agreement.

Article 108

1. As soon as the request for an Opinion has been lodged, the President shall designate a Judge to act as Rapporteur.
2. The Court sitting in closed session shall, after hearing the Advocates-General, deliver a reasoned Opinion.
3. The Opinion, signed by the President, by the Judges who took part in the deliberations and by the Registrar, shall be served on the Council, the Commission, the European Parliament and the Member States.

Article 109

Requests for the Opinion of the Court under the fourth paragraph of Article 95 of the ECSC Treaty shall be submitted jointly by the Commission and the Council.

The Opinion shall be delivered in accordance with the provisions of the preceding Article. It shall be communicated to the Commission, the Council and the European Parliament.

TITLE IV
Appeals Against Decisions of the Court of First Instance

Article 110

Without prejudice to the arrangements laid down in Article 29(2)(b) and (c) and the fourth subparagraph of Article 29(3) of these Rules, in appeals against decisions of the Court of First Instance as referred to in Articles 49 and 50 of the EC Statute, Articles 49 and 50 of the ECSC Statute and Articles 50 and 51 of the EAEC Statute, the language of the case shall be the language of the decision of the Court of First Instance against which the appeal is brought.

Article 111

1. An appeal shall be brought by lodging an application at the Registry of the Court of Justice or of the Court of First Instance.
2. The Registry of the Court of First Instance shall immediately transmit to the Registry of the Court of Justice the papers in the case at first instance and, where necessary, the appeal.

Article 112

1. An appeal shall contain:

(a) the name and address of the appellant;

(b) the names of the other parties to the proceedings before the Court of First Instance;

(c) the pleas in law and legal arguments relied on;

(d) the form or order sought by the appellant.
Article 37 and Article 38(2) and (3) of these Rules shall apply to appeals.
2. The decision of the Court of First Instance appealed against shall be attached to the appeal. The appeal shall state the date on which the decision appealed against was notified to the appellant.
3. If an appeal does not comply with Article 38(3) or with paragraph 2 of this Article, Article 38(7) of these Rules shall apply.

Article 113

1. An appeal may seek:
— to set aside, in whole or in part, the decision of the Court of First Instance;
— the same form of order, in whole or in part, as that sought at first instance
and shall not seek a different form of order.
2. The subject-matter of the proceedings before the Court of First Instance may not be changed in the appeal.

Article 114

Notice of the appeal shall be served on all the parties to the proceedings before the Court of First Instance. Article 39 of these Rules shall apply.

Article 115

1. Any party to the proceedings before the Court of First Instance may lodge a response within two months after service on him of notice of the appeal. The time-limit for lodging a response shall not be extended.
2. A response shall contain:

(a) the name and address of the party lodging it;

(b) the date on which notice of the appeal was served on him;

(c) the pleas in law and legal arguments relied on;

(d) the form of order sought by the respondent.

Article 38(2) and (3) of these Rules shall apply.

Article 116

1. A response may seek:
— to dismiss, in whole or in part, the appeal or to set aside, in whole or in part, the decision of the Court of First Instance;
— the same form of order, in whole or in part, as that sought at first instance and shall not seek a different form of order.
2. The subject-matter of the proceedings before the Court of First Instance may not be changed in the response.

Article 117

1. The appeal and the response may be supplemented by a reply and a rejoinder or any other pleading, where the President, on application made within seven days of service of the response or of the reply, considers such further pleading necessary and expressly allows it in order to enable the party concerned to put forward its point of view or in order to provide a basis for the decision on the appeal.
2. Where the response seeks to set aside, in whole or in part, the decision of the Court of First Instance on a plea in law which was not raised in the appeal, the appellant or any other party may submit a reply on that plea alone within two months of the service of the response in question. Paragraph 1 shall apply to any further pleading following such a reply.
3. Where the President allows the lodging of a reply and a rejoinder, or any other pleading, he shall prescribe the period within which they are to be submitted.

Article 118

Subject to the following provisions, Articles 42(2), 43, 44, 55 to 90, 93, 95 to 100 and 102 of these Rules shall apply to the procedure before the Court of Justice on appeal from a decision of the Court of First Instance.

Article 119

Where the appeal is, in whole or in part, clearly inadmissible or clearly unfounded, the Court may at any time, acting on a report from the Judge-Rapporteur and after hearing the Advocate-General, by reasoned order dismiss the appeal in whole or in part.

Article 120

After the submission of pleadings as provided for in Article 115(1) and, if any, Article 117(1) and (2) of these Rules, the Court may, acting on a report from the Judge-Rapporteur and after hearing the Advocate-General and the parties, decide to dispense with the oral part of the procedure unless one of the parties objects on the ground that the written procedure did not enable him fully to defend his point of view.

Article 121

The report referred to in Article 44(1) shall be presented to the Court after the pleadings provided for in Article 115(1) and Article 117(1) and (2) of these Rules have been lodged. The report shall contain, in addition to the recommendations provided for in Article 44(1), a recommendation as to whether Article 120 of these Rules should be applied. Where no such pleadings are lodged, the same procedure shall apply after the expiry of the period prescribed for lodging them.

Article 122

Where the appeal is unfounded or where the appeal is well founded and the Court itself gives final judgment in the case, the Court shall make a decision as to costs.

In proceedings between the Communities and their servants:

— Article 70 of these Rules shall apply only to appeals brought by institutions;
— by way of derogation from Article 69(2) of these Rules, the Court may, in appeals brought by officials or other servants of an institution, order the parties to share the costs where equity so requires.

If the appeal is withdrawn Article 69(5) shall apply.

When an appeal brought by a Member State or an institution which did not intervene in the proceedings before the Court of First Instance is well founded, the Court of Justice may order that the parties share the costs or that the successful appellant pay the costs which the appeal has caused an unsuccessful party to incur.

Article 123

An application to intervene made to the Court in appeal proceedings shall be lodged before the expiry of a period of one month running from the publication referred to in Article 16(6).

TITLE V

Procedures Provided for by the EEA Agreement

Article 123a

1. In the case governed by Article 111(3) of the EEA Agreement, the matter shall be brought before the Court by a request submitted by the Contracting Parties to the dispute. The request shall be served on the other Contracting Parties, on the Commission, on the EFTA Surveillance Authority and, where appropriate, on the other persons to whom a reference for a preliminary ruling raising the same question of interpretation of Community legislation would be notified.

The President shall prescribe a period within which the Contracting Parties and the other persons on whom the request has been served may submit written observations.

The request shall be made in one of the languages mentioned in Article 29(1). Paragraphs 3 and 5 of that Article shall apply. The provisions of Article 104(1) shall apply *mutatis mutandis*.

2. As soon as the request referred to in paragraph 1 of this Article has been submitted, the President shall appoint a Judge-Rapporteur. The First Advocate-General shall, immediately afterwards, assign the request to an Advocate-General.

The Court shall, after hearing the Advocate-General, give a reasoned decision on the request in closed session.

3. The decision of the Court, signed by the President, by the Judges who took part in the deliberations and by the Registrar, shall be served on the Contracting Parties and on the other persons referred to in paragraph 1.

Article 123b

In the case governed by Article 1 of Protocol 34 to the EEA Agreement, the request of a court or tribunal of an EFTA State shall be served on the parties to the case, on the Contracting Parties, on the Commission, on the EFTA Surveillance Authority and, where appropriate, on the other persons to whom a reference for a preliminary ruling raising the same question of interpretation of Community legislation would be notified.

If the request is not submitted in one of the languages mentioned in Article 29(1), it shall be accompanied by a translation into one of those languages.

Within two months of this notification, the parties to the case, the Contracting Parties and the other persons referred to in the first paragraph shall be entitled to submit statements of case or written observations.

The procedure shall be govered by the provisions of these Rules, subject to the adaptations called for by the nature of the request.

MISCELLANEOUS PROVISIONS

Article 124

1. The President shall instruct any person who is required to take an oath before the Court, as witness or expert, to tell the truth or to carry out his task

conscientiously and impartially, as the case may be, and shall warn him of the criminal liability provided for in his national law in the event of any breach of this duty.

2. The witness shall take the oath either in accordance with the first subparagraph of Article 47(5) of these Rules or in the manner laid down by his national law.

Where his national law provides the opportunity to make, in judicial proceedings, a solemn affirmation equivalent to an oath as well as or instead of taking an oath, the witness may make such an affirmation under the conditions and in the form prescribed in his national law.

Where his national law provides neither for taking an oath nor for making a solemn affirmation, the procedure described in paragraph 1 shall be followed.

3. Paragraph 2 shall apply *mutatis mutandis* to experts, a reference to the first subparagraph of Article 49(6) replacing in this case the reference to the first subparagraph of Article 47(5) of these Rules.

Article 125

Subject to the provisions of Article 245 (ex Article 188) of the EC Treaty and Article 160 of the EAEC Treaty and after consultation with the Governments concerned, the Court shall adopt supplementary rules concerning its practice in relation to:

(a) letters rogatory;

(b) applications for legal aid;

(c) reports of perjury by witnesses or experts, delivered pursuant to Article 27 of the EC Statute and Article 28 of the ECSC and EAEC Statutes.

Article 126

These Rules replace the Rules of Procedure of the Court of Justice of the European Communities adopted on 4 December 1974 (*Official Journal of the European Communities* No L 350 of 28 December 1974, p. 1), as last amended on 15 May 1991.

Article 127

These Rules, which are authentic in the languages mentioned in Article 29(1) of these Rules, shall be published in the *Official Journal of the European Communities* and shall enter into force on the first day of the second month following their publication.

Annex I

Decision on Official Holidays

THE COURT OF JUSTICE OF THE EUROPEAN COMMUNITIES,

having regard to Article 80(2) of the Rules of Procedure, which requires the Court to draw up a list of official holidays;

DECIDES:

Article 1

For the purposes of Article 80(2) of the Rules of Procedure the following shall be official holidays:

— New Year's Day;

— Easter Monday;

— 1 May;
— Ascension Day;
— Whit Monday;
— 23 June;
— 24 June, where 23 June is a Sunday;
— 15 August;
— 1 November;
— 25 December;
— 26 December.

The official holidays referred to in the first paragraph hereof shall be those observed at the place where the Court of Justice has its seat.

Article 2

Article 80(2) of the Rules of Procedure shall apply only to the official holidays mentioned in Article 1 of this Decision.

Article 3

This Decision, which shall constitute Annex I to the Rules of Procedure, shall enter into force on the same day as those Rules.

It shall be published in the *Official Journal of the European Communities*.

ANNEX II

Decision on Extension of Time-Limits on Account of Distance

THE COURT OF JUSTICE OF THE EUROPEAN COMMUNITIES,

having regard to Article 81(2) of the Rules of Procedure relating to the extension, on account of distance, of prescribed time limits;

DECIDES:

Article 1

In order to take account of distance, procedural time-limits for all parties save those habitually resident in the Grand Duchy of Luxembourg shall be extended as follows:

— for the Kingdom of Belgium: two days,
— for the Federal Republic of Germany, the European territory of the French Republic and the European territory of the Kingdom of the Netherlands: six days,
— for the European territory of the Kingdom of Denmark, for the Kingdom of Spain, for Ireland, for the Hellenic Republic, for the Italian Republic, for the Portuguese Republic (with the exception of the Azores and Madeira), for the Republic of Austria, for the Republic of Finland, for the Republic of Sweden and for the United Kingdom: 10 days,
— for other European countries and territories: two weeks,
— for the autonomous regions of the Azores and Madeira of the Portuguese Republic: three weeks,
— for other countries, departments and territories: one month.

Article 2

This Decision, which shall constitute Annex II to the Rules of Procedure, shall enter into force on the same day as those Rules.

It shall be published in the *Official Journal of the European Communities*.

Supplementary Rules

Chapter I
Letters Rogatory

Article 1

Letters rogatory shall be issued in the form of an order which shall contain the names, forenames, description and address of the witness or expert, set out the facts on which the witness or expert is to be examined, name the parties, their agents, lawyers or advisers, indicate their addresses for service and briefly describe the subject-matter of the proceedings.

Notice of the order shall be served on the parties by the Registrar.

Article 2

The Registrar shall send the order to the competent authority named in Annex I of the Member State in whose territory the witness or expert is to be examined. Where necessary, the order shall be accompanied by a translation into the official languages of the Member State to which it is addressed.

The authority named pursuant to the first paragraph shall pass on the order to the judicial authority which is competent according to its national law.

The competent judicial authority shall give effect to the letters rogatory in accordance with its national law. After implementation the competent judicial authority shall transmit to the authority named pursuant to the first paragraph the order embodying the letters rogatory, any documents arising from the implementation and a detailed statement of costs. These documents shall be sent to the Registrar of the Court.

The Registrar shall be responsible for the translation of the documents into the language of the case.

Article 3

The Court shall defray the expenses occasioned by the letters rogatory without prejudice to the right to charge them, where appropriate, to the parties.

Chapter II
Legal Aid

Article 4

The Court, by any order by which it decides that a person is entitled to receive legal aid, shall order that a lawyer be appointed to act for him.

If the person does not indicate his choice of lawyer, or if the Court considers that his choice is unacceptable, the Registrar shall send a copy of the order and of the application for legal aid to the authority named in Annex II, being the competent authority of the State concerned.

The Court, in the light of the suggestions made by that authority, shall of its own motion appoint a lawyer to act for the person concerned.

Article 5

The Court shall advance the funds necessary to meet expenses.

It shall adjudicate on the lawyer's disbursements and fees; the President may, on application by the lawyer, order that he receive an advance.

Chapter III
Reports of Perjury by a Witness or Expert

Article 6

The Court, after hearing the Advocate-General, may decide to report to the competent authority referred to in Annex III of the Member State whose courts have penal jurisdiction in any case of perjury on the part of a witness or expert before the Court, account being taken of the provisions of Article 124 of the Rules of Procedure.

Article 7

The Registrar shall be responsible for communicating the decision of the Court. The decision shall set out the facts and circumstances on which the report is based.

Final Provisions

Article 8

These Supplementary Rules replace the Supplementary Rules of 9 March 1962 (OJ No 34 of 5.5.1962, p. 1113/62).

Article 9

These Rules, which shall be authentic in the languages referred to in Article 29(1) of the Rules of Procedure, shall be published in the *Official Journal of the European Communities*.

These Rules shall enter into force on the date of their publication.

Annex I
List Referred to in the First Paragraph of article 2

Belgium
The Minister for Justice

Denmark
The Minister for Justice

Germany
The Federal Minister for Justice

Greece
The Minister for Justice

Spain
The Minister for Justice

France
The Minister for Justice

Ireland
The Minister for Justice

Italy
The Minister for Justice

Luxembourg
The Minister for Justice

Netherlands
The Minister for Justice

Austria
The Federal Minister for Justice

Portugal
The Minister for Justice

Finland
The Ministry of Justice

Sweden
The Ministry of Justice

United Kingdom
The Secretary of State

Annex II

List Referred to in the Second Paragraph of article 4

Belgium
The Minister for Justice

Denmark
The Minister for Justice

Germany
Bundesrechtsanwaltskammer

Greece
The Minister for Justice

Spain
The Minister for Justice

France
The Minister for Justice

Ireland
The Minister for Justice

Italy
The Minister for Justice

Luxembourg
The Minister for Justice

Netherlands
Algemene Raad van de Nederlandse Orde van Advocaten

Austria
The Federal Minister for Justice

Portugal
The Minister for Justice

Finland
The Ministry of Justice

Sweden
Sveriges Advokatsamfund

United Kingdom
The Law Society, London (for applicants resident in England or Wales)
The Law Society of Scotland, Edinburgh (for applicants resident in Scotland)
The Incorporated Law Society of Northern Ireland, Belfast (for applicants resident in Northern Ireland)

ANNEX III
LIST REFERRED TO IN ARTICLE 6

Belgium
The Minister for Justice

Denmark
The Minister for Justice

Germany
The Federal Minister for Justice

Greece
The Minister for Justice

Spain
The Minister for Justice

France
The Minister for Justice

Ireland
The Attorney-General

Italy
The Minister for Justice

Luxembourg
The Minister for Justice

Netherlands
The Minister for Justice

Austria
The Federal Minister for Justice

Portugal
The Minister for Justice

Finland
The Ministry of Justice

Sweden
Riksåklagaren

United Kingdom
Her Majesty's Attorney-General, for witnesses or experts resident in England or Wales
Her Majesty's Advocate, for witnesses or experts resident in Scotland
Her Majesty's Attorney-General, for witnesses or experts resident in Northern Ireland

Appendix 3

Rules of Procedure of the Court of First Instance of the European Communities

Interpretation

Article 1

In these Rules: A3–001

— 'EC Treaty' means the Treaty establishing the European Community,
— 'EC Statute' means the Protocol on the Statute of the Court of Justice of the European Community,
— 'ECSC Treaty' means the Treaty establishing the European Coal and Steel Community,
— 'ECSC Statute' means the Protocol on the Statute of the Court of Justice of the European Coal and Steel Community
— 'EAEC Treaty' means the Treaty establishing the European Atomic Energy Community (Euratom);
— 'EAEC Statute' means the Protocol on the Statute of the Court of Justice of the European Atomic Energy Community.
— 'EEA Agreement' means the Agreement on the European Economic Area.

For the purposes of these Rules:

— 'institutions' means the institutions of the Communities and bodies which are established by the Treaties, or by an act adopted in implementation thereof, and which may be parties before the Court of First Instance.
— 'EFTA Surveillance Authority' means the surveillance authority referred to in the EEA Agreement.

Title 1

Organisation of the Court of First Instance

Chapter 1

President and Members of the Court of First Instance

Article 2

1. Every Member of the Court of First Instance shall, as a rule, perform the function of Judge.

Members of the Court of First Instance are hereinafter referred to as 'Judges'.

2. Every Judge, with the exception of the President, may, in the circumstances specified in Articles 17 to 19, perform the function of Advocate-General in a particular case.

References to the Advocate-General in these Rules shall apply only where a Judge has been designated as Advocate-General.

Article 3

The term of office of a Judge shall begin on the date laid down in his instrument of appointment. In the absence of any provision regarding the date, the term shall begin on the date of the instrument.

Article 4

1. Before taking up his duties, a Judge shall take the following oath before the Court of Justice of the European Communities:

'I swear that I will perform my duties impartially and conscientiously; I swear that I will preserve the secrecy of the deliberations of the Court.'

2. Immediately after taking the oath, a Judge shall sign a declaration by which he solemnly undertakes that, both during and after his term of office, he will respect the obligations arising therefrom, and in particular the duty to behave with integrity and discretion as regards the acceptance, after he has ceased to hold office, of certain appointments and benefits.

Article 5

When the Court of Justice is called upon to decide, after consulting the Court of First Instance, whether a Judge of the Court of First Instance no longer fulfils the requisite conditions or no longer meets the obligations arising from his office, the President of the Court of First Instance shall invite the Judge concerned to make representations to the Court of First Instance, in closed session and in the absence of the Registrar.

The Court of First Instance shall state the reasons for its opinion.

An opinion to the effect that a Judge of the Court of First Instance no longer fulfils the requisite conditions or no longer meets the obligations arising from his office must receive the votes of at least seven Judges of the Court of First Instance. In that event, particulars of the voting shall be communicated to the Court of Justice.

Voting shall be by secret ballot; the Judge concerned shall not take part in the deliberations.

Article 6

With the exception of the President of the Court of First Instance and of the Presidents of the Chambers, the Judges shall rank equally in precedence according to their seniority in office.

Where there is equal seniority in office, precedence shall be determined by age.

Retiring Judges who are reappointed shall retain their former precedence.

Article 7

1. The Judges shall, immediately after the partial replacement provided for in Article 225 (ex Article 168a) of the EC Treaty, Article 32d of the ECSC Treaty and Article 140a of the EAEC Treaty, elect one of their number as President of the Court of First Instance for a term of three years.

2. If the office of President of the Court of First Instance falls vacant before the normal date of expiry thereof, the Court of First Instance shall elect a successor for the remainder of the term.

3. The elections provided for in this Article shall be by secret ballot. If a Judge obtains an absolute majority he shall be elected. If no Judge obtains an absolute majority, a second ballot shall be held and the Judge obtaining the most votes shall be elected. Where two or more Judges obtain an equal number of votes the oldest of them shall be deemed elected.

Article 8

The President of the Court of First Instance shall direct the judicial business and the administration of the Court of First Instance. He shall preside at plenary sittings and deliberations.

Article 9

When the President of the Court of First Instance is absent or prevented from attending or when the office of President is vacant, the functions of President shall be exercised by a President of a Chamber according to the order of precedence laid down in Article 6.

If the President of the Court of First Instance and the Presidents of the Chambers are all prevented from attending at the same time, or their posts are vacant at the same time, the functions of President shall be exercised by one of the other Judges according to the order of precedence laid down in Article 6.

CHAPTER 2

CONSTITUTION OF THE CHAMBERS AND DESIGNATION OF JUDGE-RAPPORTEURS AND ADVOCATES-GENERAL

Article 10

1. The Court of First Instance shall set up Chambers composed of three or five Judges and shall decide which Judges shall be attached to them.
2. The composition of the Chambers shall be published in the *Official Journal of the European Communities*.

Article 11

1. Cases before the Court of First Instance shall be heard by Chambers composed in accordance with Article 10.

Cases may be heard by the Court of First Instance sitting in plenary session under the conditions laid down in Articles 14, 51, 106, 118, 124, 127 and 129.

Cases may be heard by a single Judge where they are delegated to him under the conditions specified in Articles 14 and 51 or assigned to him pursuant to Article 124, Article 127(1) or Article 129(2).

2. In cases coming before a Chamber, the term 'Court of First Instance' in these Rules shall designate that Chamber. In cases delegated or assigned to a single Judge the term "Court of First Instance" used in these Rules shall also designate that Judge.

Article 12

1. The Court of First Instance shall lay down criteria by which cases are to be allocated among the Chambers.

The decision shall be published in the *Official Journal of the European Communities*.

Article 13

1. As soon as the application initiating proceedings has been lodged, the President of the Court of First Instance shall assign the case to one of the Chambers.
2. The President of the Chamber shall propose to the President of the Court of First Instance, in respect of each case assigned to the Chamber, the designation of a Judge to act as Rapporteur; the President of the Court of First Instance shall decide on the proposal.

Article 14

1. Whenever the legal difficulty or the importance of the case or special circumstances so justify, a case may be referred to the Court of First Instance sitting in plenary session or to a Chamber composed of a different number of Judges.

2. (1) The following cases, assigned to a Chamber composed of three Judges, may be heard and determined by the Judge-Rapporteur sitting as a single Judge where, having regard to the lack of difficulty of the questions of law or fact raised, to the limited importance of the case and to the absence of other special circumstances, they are suitable for being so heard and determined and have been delegated under the conditions laid down in Article 51:

(a) cases brought pursuant to Article 236 (ex Article 179) of the E.C. Treaty or Article 152 of the EAEC Treaty;

(b) cases brought pursuant to the fourth paragraph of Article 230 (ex Article 173), the third paragraph of Article 232 (ex Article 175) and Article 235 (ex Article 178) of the E.C. Treaty, to the second paragraph of Article 33, Article 35 and the first and second paragraphs of Article 40 of the ECSC Treaty and to the fourth paragraph of Article 146, the third paragraph of Article 148 and Article 151 of the EAEC Treaty that raise only questions already clarified by established case-law or that form part of a series of cases in which the same relief is sought and of which one has already been finally decided;

(c) cases brought pursuant to Article 238 (ex Article 181) of the E.C. Treaty, Article 42 of the ECSC Treaty and Article 153 of the EAEC Treaty.

(2) Delegation to a single Judge shall not be possible:

(a) in cases which raise issues as to the legality of an act of general application;

(b) in cases concerning the implementation of the rules:

— on competition and on control of concentrations,

— relating to aid granted by States,

— relating to measures to protect trade,

— relating to the common organisation of the agricultural markets, with the exception of cases that form part of a series of cases in which the same relief is sought and where one of those cases has already been finally decided;

(c) in the cases referred to in Article 130(1).

(3) The single Judge shall refer the case back to the Chamber if he finds that the conditions justifying delegation of the case are no longer satisfied.

3. The decisions to refer or to delegate a case which are provided for in paragraphs (1) and (2) shall be taken under the conditions laid down in Article 51.

Article 15

The Court of First Instance shall appoint for a period of one year the Presidents of the Chambers.

The provisions of Article 7(2) and (3) shall apply.

The appointments made in pursuance of this Article shall be published in the *Official Journal of the European Communities*.

Article 16

In cases coming before a Chamber the powers of the President shall be exercised by the President of the Chamber.

In cases assigned or delegated to a single Judge the powers of the President, with the exception of those referred to in Articles 105 and 106, shall be exercised by that Judge.

Article 17

When the Court of First Instance sits in plenary session, it shall be assisted by an Advocate-General designated by the President of the Court of First Instance.

Article 18

A Chamber of the Court of First Instance may be assisted by an Advocate-General if it is considered that the legal difficulty or the factual complexity of the case so requires.

Article 19

The decision to designate an Advocate-General in a particular case shall be taken by the Court of First Instance sitting in plenary session at the request of the Chamber before which the case comes.

The President of the Court of First Instance shall designate the Judge called upon to perform the function of Advocate-General in that case.

Chapter 3

Registry

SECTION 1 — THE REGISTRAR

Article 20

1. The Court of First Instance shall appoint the Registrar.

Two weeks before the date fixed for making the appointment, the President of the Court of First Instance shall inform the Judges of the applications which have been submitted for the post.

2. An application shall be accompanied by full details of the candidate's age, nationality, university degrees, knowledge of any languages, present and past occupations and experience, if any, in judicial and international fields.
3. The appointment shall be made following the procedure laid down in Article 7(3).
4. The Registrar shall be appointed for a term of six years. He may be reappointed.
5. Before he takes up his duties the Registrar shall take the oath before the Court of First Instance in accordance with Article 4.
6. The Registrar may be deprived of his office only if he no longer fulfils the requisite conditions or no longer meets the obligations arising from his office; the Court of First Instance shall take its decision after giving the Registrar an opportunity to make representations.
7. If the office of Registrar falls vacant before the usual date of expiry of the term thereof, the Court of First Instance shall appoint a new Registrar for a term of six years.

Article 21

The Court of First Instance may, following the procedure laid down in respect of the Registrar, appoint one or more Assistant Registrars to assist the Registrar and to take his place in so far as the Instructions to the Registrar referred to in Article 23 allow.

Article 22

Where the Registrar is absent or prevented from attending and, if necessary, where the Assistant Registrar is absent or so prevented, or where their posts are vacant, the President of the Court of First Instance shall designate an official or servant to carry out the duties of Registrar.

Article 23

Instructions to the Registrar shall be adopted by the Court of First Instance acting on a proposal from the President of the Court of First Instance.

Article 24

1.There shall be kept in the Registry, under the control of the Registrar, a register initialled by the President of the Court of First Instance, in which all pleadings and supporting documents shall be entered in the order in which they are lodged.
2. When a document has been registered, the Registrar shall make a note to that effect on the original and, if a party so requests, on any copy submitted for the purpose.
3. Entries in the register and the notes provided for in the preceding paragraph shall be authentic.
4. Rules for keeping the register shall be prescribed by the Instructions to the Registrar referred to in Article 23.
5. Persons having an interest may consult the register at the Registry and may obtain copies or extracts on payment of a charge on a scale fixed by the Court of First Instance on a proposal from the Registrar.

The parties to a case may on payment of the appropriate charge also obtain copies of pleadings and authenticated copies of orders and judgments.

6. Notice shall be given in the *Official Journal of the European Communities* of the date of registration of an application initiating proceedings, the names and addresses of the parties, the subject-matter of the proceedings, the form of order sought by the applicant and a summary of the pleas in law and of the main supporting arguments.
7. Where the Council or the Commission is not a party to a case, the Court of First Instance shall send to it copies of the application and of the defence, without the annexes thereto, to enable it to assess whether the inapplicability of one of its acts is being invoked under Article 241 (ex Article 184) of the EC Treaty, the third paragraph of Article 36 of the ECSC Treaty or Article 156 of the EAEC Treaty.

Article 25

1. The Registrar shall be responsible, under the authority of the President, for the acceptance, transmission and custody of documents and for effecting service as provided for by these Rules.
2. The Registrar shall assist the Court of First Instance, the President and the Judges in all their official functions.

Article 26

The Registrar shall have custody of the seals. He shall be responsible for the records and be in charge of the publications of the Court of First Instance.

Article 27

Subject to Articles 5 and 33, the Registrar shall attend the sittings of the Court of First Instance.

SECTION 2 — OTHER DEPARTMENTS

Article 28

The officials and other servants whose task is to assist directly the President, the Judges and the Registrar shall be appointed in accordance with the Staff Regulations. They shall be responsible to the Registrar, under the authority of the President of the Court of First Instance.

Article 29

The officials and other servants referred to in Article 28 shall take the oath provided for in Article 20(2) of the Rules of Procedure of the Court of Justice before the President of the Court of First Instance in the presence of the Registrar.

Article 30

The Registrar shall be responsible, under the authority of the President of the Court of First Instance, for the administration of the Court of First Instance, its financial management and its accounts; he shall be assisted in this by the departments of the Court of Justice.

CHAPTER 4

THE WORKING OF THE COURT OF FIRST INSTANCE

Article 31

1. The dates and times of the sittings of the Court of First Instance shall be fixed by the President.
2. The Court of First Instance may choose to hold one or more sittings in a place other than that in which the Court of First Instance has its seat.

Article 32

1. Where, by reason of a Judge being absent or prevented from attending, there is an even number of Judges, the most junior Judge within the meaning of Article 6 shall abstain from taking part in the deliberations unless he is the Judge-Rapporteur. In this case, the Judge immediately senior to him shall abstain from taking part in the deliberations.

Where, following the designation of an Advocate-General pursuant to Article 17, there is an even number of Judges in the Court of First Instance sitting in plenary session, the President of the Court shall designate, before the hearing and in accordance with a rota established in advance by the Court of First Instance and published in the *Official Journal of the European Communities*, the Judge who will not take part in the judgment of the case.
2. If after the Court of First Instance has been convened in plenary session, it is found that the quorum of nine Judges has not been attained, the President of the Court of First Instance shall adjourn the sitting until there is a quorum.
3. If in any Chamber the quorum of three Judges has not been attained, the President of that Chamber shall so inform the President of the Court of First Instance who shall designate another Judge to complete the Chamber.
4. If in any Chamber of three or five Judges the number of Judges assigned to that Chamber is higher than three or five respectively, the President of the Chamber shall decide which of the Judges will be called upon to take part in the judgment of the case.

5. If the single Judge to whom the case has been delegated or assigned is absent or prevented from attending, the President of the Court of First Instance shall designate another Judge to replace that Judge.

Article 33

1. The Court of First Instance shall deliberate in closed session.
2. Only those Judges who were present at the oral proceedings may take part in the deliberations.
3. Every Judge taking part in the deliberations shall state his opinion and the reasons for it.
4. Any Judge may require that any question be formulated in the language of his choice and communicated in writing to the other Judges before being put to the vote.
5. The conclusions reached by the majority of the Judges after final discussion shall determine the decision of the Court of First Instance. Votes shall be cast in reverse order to the order of precedence laid down in Article 6.
6. Differences of view on the substance, wording or order of questions, or on the interpretation of a vote shall be settled by decision of the Court of First Instance.
7. Where the deliberations of the Court of First Instance concern questions of its own administration, the Registrar shall be present, unless the Court of First Instance decides to the contrary.
8. Where the Court of First Instance sits without the Registrar being present it shall, if necessary, instruct the most junior Judge within the meaning of Article 6 to draw up minutes. The minutes shall be signed by this Judge and by the President.

Article 34

1. Subject to any special decision of the Court of First Instance, its vacations shall be as follows:
 — from 18 December to 10 January,
 — from the Sunday before Easter to the second Sunday after Easter,
 — from 15 July to 15 September.

During the vacations, the functions of President shall be exercised at the place where the Court of First Instance has its seat either by the President himself, keeping in touch with the Registrar, or by a President of Chamber or other Judge invited by the President to take his place.
2. In a case of urgency, the President may convene the Judges during the vacations.
3. The Court of First Instance shall observe the official holidays of the place where it has its seat.
4. The Court of First Instance may, in proper circumstances, grant leave of absence to any Judge.

Chapter 5

Languages

Article 35

1. The language of a case shall be Danish, Dutch, English, Finnish, French, German, Greek, Irish, Italian, Portuguese, Spanish or Swedish.
2. The language of the case shall be chosen by the applicant, except that:
 (a) at the joint request of the parties, the use of another of the languages mentioned in paragraph 1 for all or part of the proceedings may be authorised;

(b) at the request of one of the parties, and after the opposite party and the Advocate-General have been heard, the use of another of the languages mentioned in paragraph 1 as the language of the case for all or part of the proceedings may be authorised by way of derogation from subparagraph (a); such a request may not be submitted by an institution.

Requests as above may be decided on by the President; the latter may and, where he proposes to accede to a request without the agreement of all the parties, must refer the request to the Court of First Instance.

3. The language of the case shall be used in the written and oral pleadings of the parties and in supporting documents, and also in the minutes and decisions of the Court of First Instance.

Any supporting documents expressed in another language must be accompanied by a translation into the language of the case.

In the case of lengthy documents, translations may be confined to extracts. However, the Court of First Instance may, of its own motion or at the request of a party, at any time call for a complete or fuller translation.

Notwithstanding the foregoing provisions, a Member State shall be entitled to use its official language when intervening in a case before the Court of First Instance. This provision shall apply both to written statements and to oral addresses. The Registrar shall cause any such statement or address to be translated into the language of the case.

The States, other than the Member States, which are parties to the EEA Agreement, and also the EFTA Surveillance Authority, may be authorised to use one of the languages mentioned in paragraph 1, other than the language of the case, when they intervene in a case before the Court of First Instance. This provision shall apply both to written statements and oral addresses. The Registrar shall cause any such statement or address to be translated into the language of the case.

4. Where a witness or expert states that he is unable adequately to express himself in one of the languages referred to in paragraph 1 of this Article, the Court of First Instance may authorise him to give his evidence in another language. The Registrar shall arrange for translation into the language of the case.

5. The President in conducting oral proceedings, the Judge-Rapporteur both in his preliminary report and in his report for the hearing, Judges and the Advocate-General in putting questions and the Advocate-General in delivering his opinion may use one of the languages referred to in paragraph 1 of this Article other than the language of the case. The Registrar shall arrange for translation into the language of the case.

Article 36

1. The Registrar shall, at the request of any Judge, of the Advocate-General or of a party, arrange for anything said or written in the course of the proceedings before the Court of First Instance to be translated into the languages he chooses from those referred to in Article 35(1).

2. Publications of the Court of First Instance shall be issued in the languages referred to in Article 1 of Council Regulation No 1.

Article 37

The texts of documents drawn up in the language of the case or in any other language authorised by the Court of First Instance pursuant to Article 35 shall be authentic.

Chapter 6

Rights and Obligations of Agents, Advisers and Lawyers

Article 38

1. Agents, advisers and lawyers, appearing before the Court of First Instance or before any judicial authority to which it has addressed letters rogatory, shall enjoy

immunity in respect of words spoken or written by them concerning the case or the parties.

2. Agents, advisers and lawyers shall enjoy the following further privileges and facilities:

(a) papers and documents relating to the proceedings shall be exempt from both search and seizure; in the event of a dispute the customs officials or police may seal those papers and documents; they shall then be immediately forwarded to the Court of First Instance for inspection in the presence of the Registrar and of the person concerned;
(b) agents, advisers and lawyers shall be entitled to such allocation of foreign currency as may be necessary for the performance of their duties;
(c) agents, advisers and lawyers shall be entitled to travel in the course of duty without hindrance.

Article 39

In order to qualify for the privileges, immunities and facilities specified in Article 38, persons entitled to them shall furnish proof of their status as follows:

(a) agents shall produce an official document issued by the party for whom they act and shall forward without delay a copy thereof to the Registrar;
(b) advisers and lawyers shall produce a certificate signed by the Registrar. The validity of this certificate shall be limited to a specified period, which may be extended or curtailed according to the length of the proceedings.

Article 40

The privileges, immunities and facilities specified in Article 38 are granted exclusively in the interests of the proper conduct of proceedings.

The Court of First Instance may waive the immunity where it considers that the proper conduct of proceedings will not be hindered thereby.

Article 41

1. Any adviser or lawyer whose conduct towards the Court of First Instance, the President, a Judge or the Registrar is incompatible with the dignity of the Court of First Instance, or who uses his rights for purposes other than those for which they were granted, may at any time be excluded from the proceedings by an order of the Court of First Instance; the person concerned shall be given an opportunity to defend himself.

The order shall have immediate effect.

2. Where an adviser or lawyer is excluded from the proceedings, the proceedings shall be suspended for a period fixed by the President in order to allow the party concerned to appoint another adviser or lawyer.

3. Decisions taken under this Article may be rescinded.

Article 42

The provisions of this Chapter shall apply to university teachers who have a right of audience before the Court of First Instance in accordance with Article 17 of the EC Statute, Article 20 of the ECSC Statute and Article 17 of the EAEC Statute.

Title 2

Procedure

Chapter 1

Written Procedure

Article 43

1. The original of every pleading must be signed by the party's agent or lawyer.

The original, accompanied by all annexes referred to therein, shall be lodged together with five copies for the Court of First Instance and a copy for every other party to the proceedings. Copies shall be certified by the party lodging them.
2. Institutions shall in addition produce, within time-limits laid down by the Court of First Instance, translations of all pleadings into the other languages provided for by Article 1 of Council Regulation No 1. The second subparagraph of paragraph 1 of this Article shall apply.
3. All pleadings shall bear a date. In the reckoning of time-limits for taking steps in proceedings only the date of lodgment at the Registry shall be taken into account.
4. To every pleading there shall be annexed a file containing the documents relied on in support of it, together with a schedule listing them.
5. Where in view of the length of a document only extracts from it are annexed to the pleading, the whole document or a full copy of it shall be lodged at the Registry.

Article 44

1. An application of the kind referred to in Article 19 of the EC Statute, Article 22 of the ECSC Statute and Article 19 of the EAEC Statute shall state:
(a) the name and address of the applicant;
(b) the designation of the party against whom the application is made;
(c) the subject-matter of the proceedings and a summary of the pleas in law on which the application is based;
(d) the form of order sought by the applicant;
(e) where appropriate, the nature of any evidence offered in support.

2. For the purposes of the proceedings, the application shall state an address for service in the place where the Court of First Instance has its seat and the name of the person who is authorised and has expressed willingness to accept service.

If the application does not comply with these requirements, all service on the party concerned for the purposes of the proceedings shall be effected, for so long as the defect has not been cured, by registered letter addressed to the agent or lawyer of that party. By way of derogation from Article 100, service shall then be deemed to have been duly effected by the lodging of the registered letter at the post office of the place where the Court of First Instance has its seat.
3. The lawyer acting for a party must lodge at the Registry a certificate that he is authorised to practise before a Court of a Member State or of another State which is a party to the EEA Agreement.
4. The application shall be accompanied, where appropriate, by the documents specified in the second paragraph of Article 19 of the EC Statute, in the second paragraph of Article 22 of the ECSC Statute and in the second paragraph of Article 19 of the EAEC Statute.
5. An application made by a legal person governed by private law shall be accompanied by:
(a) the instrument or instruments constituting and regulating that legal person or a recent extract from the register of companies, firms or associations or any other proof of its existence in law;
(b) proof that the authority granted to the applicant's lawyer has been properly conferred on him by someone authorised for the purpose.

5a. An application submitted under Article 238 (ex Article 181) of the EC Treaty, Article 42 of the ECSC Treaty or Article 153 of the EAEC Treaty pursuant to an aribitration clause contained in a contract governed by public or private law, entered into by the Community or on its behalf, shall be accompanied by a copy of the contract which contains that clause.
6. If an application does not comply with the requirements set out in paragraphs 3 to 5 of this Article, the Registrar shall prescribe a reasonable period within which

the applicant is to comply with them whether by putting the application itself in order or by producing any of the above-mentioned documents. If the applicant fails to put the application in order or to produce the required documents within the time prescribed, the Court of First Instance shall decide whether the non-compliance with these conditions renders the application formally inadmissible.

Article 45

The application shall be served on the defendant. In a case where Article 44(6) applies, service shall be effected as soon as the application has been put in order or the Court of First Instance has declared it admissible notwithstanding the failure to observe the formal requirements set out in that Article.

Article 46

1. Within one month after service on him of the application, the defendant shall lodge a defence, stating:
   (a) the name and address of the defendant;
   (b) the arguments of fact and law relied on;
   (c) the form of order sought by the defendant;
   (d) the nature of any evidence offered by him.

The provisions of Article 44(2) to (5) shall apply to the defence.
2. In proceedings between the Communities and their servants the defence shall be accompanied by the complaint within the meaning of Article 90(2) of the Staff Regulations of Officials and by the decision rejecting the complaint together with the dates on which the complaint was submitted and the decision notified.
3. The time-limit laid down in paragraph 1 of this Article may be extended by the President on a reasoned application by the defendant.

Article 47

1. The application initiating the proceedings and the defence may be supplemented by a reply from the applicant and by a rejoinder from the defendant.
2. The President shall fix the time-limits within which these pleadings are to be lodged.

Article 48

1. In reply or rejoinder a party may offer further evidence. The party must, however, give reasons for the delay in offering it.
2. No new plea in law may be introduced in the course of proceedings unless it is based on matters of law or of fact which come to light in the course of the procedure.

If in the course of the procedure one of the parties puts forward a new plea in law which is so based, the President may, even after the expiry of the normal procedural time-limits, acting on a report of the Judge-Rapporteur and after hearing the Advocate-General, allow the other party time to answer on that plea.

Consideration of the admissibility of the plea shall be reserved for the final judgment.

Article 49

At any stage of the proceedings the Court of First Instance may, after hearing the Advocate-General, prescribe any measure of organisation of procedure or any measure of inquiry referred to in Articles 64 and 65 or order that a previous inquiry be repeated or expanded.

Article 50

The President may, at any time, after hearing the parties and the Advocate-General, order that two or more cases concerning the same subject-matter shall, on account of the connection between them, be joined for the purposes of the written or oral procedure or of the final judgment. The cases may subsequently be disjoined. The President may refer these matters to the Court of First Instance.

Article 51

1. In the cases specified in Article 14(1), and at any stage in the proceedings, the Chamber hearing the case may, either on its own initiative or at the request of one of the parties, propose to the Court of First Instance sitting in plenary session that the case be referred to the Court of First Instance sitting in plenary session or to a Chamber composed of a different number of Judges. The Court of First Instance sitting in plenary session shall, after hearing the parties and the Advocate-General, decide whether or not to refer a case.

The case shall be maintained before or referred to a Chamber composed of five Judges where a Member State or an institution of the European Communities which is a party to the proceedings so requests.

2. The decision to delegate a case to a single Judge in the situations set out in Article 14(2) shall be taken, after the parties have been heard, unanimously by the Chamber composed of three Judges before which the case is pending.

Where a Member State or an institution of the European Communities which is a party to the proceedings objects to the case being heard by a single Judge the case shall be maintained before or referred to the Chamber to which the Judge-Rapporteur belongs.

Article 52

1. Without prejudice to the application of Article 49, the President shall, after the rejoinder has been lodged, fix a date on which the Judge-Rapporteur is to present his preliminary report to the Court of First Instance. The report shall contain recommendations as to whether measures of organisation of procedure or measures of inquiry should be undertaken and whether the case should be referred to the Court of First Instance sitting in plenary session or to a Chamber composed of a different number of Judges.

2. The Court of First Instance shall decide, after hearing the Advocate-General, what action to take upon the recommendations of the Judge-Rapporteur.

The same procedure shall apply:

(a) where no reply or no rejoinder has been lodged within the time-limit fixed in accordance with Article 47(2);

(b) where the party concerned waives his right to lodge a reply or rejoinder.

Article 53

Where the Court of First Instance decides to open the oral procedure without undertaking measures of organisation of procedure or ordering a preparatory inquiry, the President of the Court of First Instance shall fix the opening date.

Article 54

Without prejudice to any measures of organisation of procedure or measures of inquiry which may be arranged at the stage of the oral procedure, where, during the written procedure, measures of organisation of procedure or measures of inquiry have been instituted and completed, the President shall fix the date for the opening of the oral procedure.

Chapter 2

Oral Procedure

Article 55

1. Subject to the priority of decisions provided for in Article 106, the Court of First Instance shall deal with the cases before it in the order in which the preparatory inquiries in them have been completed. Where the preparatory inquiries in several cases are completed simultaneously, the order in which they are to be dealt with shall be determined by the dates of entry in the register of the applications initiating them respectively.
2. The President may in special circumstances order that a case be given priority over others.

The President may in special circumstances, after hearing the parties and the Advocate-General, either on his own initiative or at the request of one of the parties, defer a case to be dealt with at a later date. On a joint application by the parties the President may order that a case be deferred.

Article 56

The proceedings shall be opened and directed by the President, who shall be responsible for the proper conduct of the hearing.

Article 57

The oral proceedings in cases heard in camera shall not be published.

Article 58

The President may in the course of the hearing put questions to the agents, advisers or lawyers of the parties.

The other Judges and the Advocate-General may do likewise.

Article 59

A party may address the Court of First Instance only through his agent, adviser or lawyer.

Article 60

Where an Advocate-General has not been designated in a case, the President shall declare the oral procedure closed at the end of the hearing.

Article 61

1. Where the Advocate-General delivers his opinion in writing, he shall lodge it at the Registry, which shall communicate it to the parties.
2. After the delivery, orally or in writing, of the opinion of the Advocate-General the President shall declare the oral procedure closed.

Article 62

The Court of First Instance may, after hearing the Advocate-General, order the reopening of the oral procedure.

Article 63

1. The Registrar shall draw up minutes of every hearing. The minutes shall be signed by the President and by the Registrar and shall constitute an official record.

2. The parties may inspect the minutes at the Registry and obtain copies at their own expense.

CHAPTER 3

MEASURES OF ORGANISATION OF PROCEDURE AND MEASURES OF INQUIRY

SECTION 1 — MEASURES OF ORGANISATION OF PROCEDURE

Article 64

1. The purpose of measures of organisation of procedure shall be to ensure that cases are prepared for hearing, procedures carried out and disputes resolved under the best possible conditions. They shall be prescribed by the Court of First Instance, after hearing the Advocate-General.
2. Measures of organisation of procedure shall, in particular, have as their purpose:
   (a) to ensure efficient conduct of the written and oral procedure and to facilitate the taking of evidence;
   (b) to determine the points on which the parties must present further argument or which call for measures of inquiry;
   (c) to clarify the forms of order sought by the parties, their pleas in law and arguments and the points at issue between them;
   (d) to facilitate the amicable settlement of proceedings.
3. Measures of organisation of procedure may, in particular, consist of:
   (a) putting questions to the parties;
   (b) inviting the parties to make written or oral submissions on certain aspects of the proceedings;
   (c) asking the parties or third parties for information or particulars;
   (d) asking for documents or any papers relating to the case to be produced;
   (e) summoning the parties' agents or the parties in person to meetings.
4. Each party may, at any stage of the procedure, propose the adoption or modification of measures of organisation of procedure. In that case, the other parties shall be heard before those measures are prescribed.

Where the procedural circumstances so require, the Registrar shall inform the parties of the measures envisaged by the Court of First Instance and shall give them an opportunity to submit comments orally or in writing.
5. If the Court of First Instance sitting in plenary session decides to prescribe measures of organisation of procedure and does not undertake such measures itself, it shall entrust the task of so doing to the Chamber to which the case was originally assigned or to the Judge-Rapporteur.

If a Chamber prescribes measures of organisation of procedure and does not undertake such measures itself, it shall entrust the task to the Judge-Rapporteur.

The Advocate-General shall take part in measures of organisation of procedure.

SECTION 2 — MEASURES OF INQUIRY

Article 65

Without prejudice to Articles 21 and 22 of the EC Statute, Articles 24 and 25 of the ECSC Statute and Articles 22 and 23 of the EAEC Statute, the following measures of inquiry may be adopted:
   (a) the personal appearance of the parties;
   (b) a request for information and production of documents;
   (c) oral testimony;

(d) the commissioning of an expert's report;
(e) an inspection of the place or thing in question.

Article 66

1. The Court of First Instance, after hearing the Advocate-General, shall prescribe the measures of inquiry that it considers appropriate by means of an order setting out the facts to be proved. Before the Court of First Instance decides on the measures of inquiry referred to in Article 65(c), (d) and (e) the parties shall be heard.

The order shall be served on the parties.

2. Evidence may be submitted in rebuttal and previous evidence may be amplified.

Article 67

1. Where the Court of First Instance sitting in plenary session orders a preparatory inquiry and does not undertake such an inquiry itself, it shall entrust the task of so doing to the Chamber to which the case was originally assigned or to the Judge-Rapporteur.

Where a Chamber orders a preparatory inquiry and does not undertake such an inquiry itself, it shall entrust the task of so doing to the Judge-Rapporteur.

The Advocate-General shall take part in the measures of inquiry.

2. The parties may be present at the measures of inquiry.

SECTION 3 — THE SUMMONING AND EXAMINATION OF WITNESSES AND EXPERTS

Article 68

1. The Court of First Instance may, either of its own motion or on application by a party, and after hearing the Advocate-General and the parties, order that certain facts be proved by witnesses. The order shall set out the facts to be established.

The Court of First Instance may summon a witness of its own motion or on application by a party or at the instance of the Advocate-General.

An application by a party for the examination of a witness shall state precisely about what facts and for what reasons the witness should be examined.

2. The witness shall be summoned by an order containing the following information:

(a) the surname, forenames, description and address of the witness;
(b) an indication of the facts about which the witness is to be examined;
(c) where appropriate, particulars of the arrangements made by the Court of First Instance for reimbursement of expenses incurred by the witness, and of the penalties which may be imposed on defaulting witnesses.

The order shall be served on the parties and the witnesses.

3. The Court of First Instance may make the summoning of a witness for whose examination a party has applied conditional upon the deposit with the cashier of the Court of First Instance of a sum sufficient to cover the taxed costs thereof; the Court of First Instance shall fix the amount of the payment.

The cashier of the Court of First Instance shall advance the funds necessary in connection with the examination of any witness summoned by the Court of First Instance of its own motion.

4. After the identity of the witness has been established, the President shall inform him that he will be required to vouch the truth of his evidence in the manner laid down in paragraph 5 of this Article and in Article 71.

The witness shall give his evidence to the Court of First Instance, the parties having been given notice to attend. After the witness has given his main evidence the President may, at the request of a party or of his own motion, put questions to him.

The other Judges and the Advocate-General may do likewise.

Subject to the control of the President, questions may be put to witnesses by the representatives of the parties.

5. Subject to the provisions of Article 71, the witness shall, after giving his evidence, take the following oath:

'I swear that I have spoken the truth, the whole truth and nothing but the truth.'

The Court of First Instance may, after hearing the parties, exempt a witness from taking the oath.

6. The Registrar shall draw up minutes in which the evidence of each witness is reproduced.

The minutes shall be signed by the President or by the Judge-Rapporteur responsible for conducting the examination of the witness, and by the Registrar. Before the minutes are thus signed, witnesses must be given an opportunity to check the content of the minutes and to sign them.

The minutes shall constitute an official record.

Article 69

1. Witnesses who have been duly summoned shall obey the summons and attend for examination.

2. If a witness who has been duly summoned fails to appear before the Court of First Instance, the latter may impose upon him a pecuniary penalty not exceeding euro 5 000 and may order that a further summons be served on the witness at his own expense.

The same penalty may be imposed upon a witness who, without good reason, refuses to give evidence or to take the oath or where appropriate to make a solemn affirmation equivalent thereto.

3. If the witness proffers a valid excuse to the Court of First Instance, the pecuniary penalty imposed on him may be cancelled. The pecuniary penalty imposed may be reduced at the request of the witness where he establishes that it is disproportionate to his income.

4. Penalties imposed and other measures ordered under this Article shall be enforced in accordance with Articles 244 and 256 (ex Articles 187 and 192) of the EC Treaty, Articles 44 and 92 of the ECSC Treaty and Articles 159 and 164 of the EAEC Treaty.

Article 70

1. The Court of First Instance may order that an expert's report be obtained. The order appointing the expert shall define his task and set a time-limit within which he is to make his report.

2. The expert shall receive a copy of the order, together with all the documents necessary for carrying out his task. He shall be under the supervision of the Judge-Rapporteur, who may be present during his investigation and who shall be kept informed of his progress in carrying out his task.

The Court of First Instance may request the parties or one of them to lodge security for the costs of the expert's report.

3. At the request of the expert, the Court of First Instance may order the examination of witnesses. Their examination shall be carried out in accordance with Article 68.

4. The expert may give his opinion only on points which have been expressly referred to him.

5. After the expert has made his report, the Court of First Instance may order that he be examined, the parties having been given notice to attend.

Subject to the control of the President, questions may be put to the expert by the representatives of the parties.

6. Subject to the provisions of Article 71, the expert shall, after making his report, take the following oath before the Court of First Instance:

'I swear that I have conscientiously and impartially carried out my task.'

The Court of First Instance may, after hearing the parties, exempt the expert from taking the oath.

Article 71

1. The President shall instruct any person who is required to take an oath before the Court of First Instance, as witness or expert, to tell the truth or to carry out his task conscientiously and impartially, as the case may be, and shall warn him of the criminal liability provided for in his national law in the event of any breach of this duty.

2. Witnesses and experts shall take the oath either in accordance with the first subparagraph of Article 68(5) and the first subparagraph of Article 70(6) or in the manner laid down by their national law.

3. Where the national law provides the opportunity to make, in judicial proceedings, a solemn affirmation equivalent to an oath as well as or instead of taking an oath, the witnesses and experts may make such an affirmation under the conditions and in the form prescribed in their national law.

Where their national law provides neither for taking an oath nor for making a solemn affirmation, the procedure described in the first paragraph of this Article shall be followed.

Article 72

1. The Court of First Instance may, after hearing the Advocate-General, decide to report to the competent authority referred to in Annex III to the Rules supplementing the Rules of Procedure of the Court of Justice of the Member State whose courts have penal jurisdiction in any case of perjury on the part of a witness or expert before the Court of First Instance, account being taken of the provisions of Article 71.

2. The Registrar shall be responsible for communicating the decision of the Court of First Instance. The decision shall set out the facts and circumstances on which the report is based.

Article 73

1. If one of the parties objects to a witness or to an expert on the ground that he is not a competent or proper person to act as witness or expert or for any other reason, or if a witness or expert refuses to give evidence, to take the oath or to make a solemn affirmation equivalent thereto, the matter shall be resolved by the Court of First Instance.

2. An objection to a witness or to an expert shall be raised within two weeks after service of the order summoning the witness or appointing the expert; the statement of objection must set out the grounds of objection and indicate the nature of any evidence offered.

Article 74

1. Witnesses and experts shall be entitled to reimbursement of their travel and subsistence expenses. The cashier of the Court of First Instance may make a payment to them towards these expenses in advance.

2. Witnesses shall be entitled to compensation for loss of earnings, and experts to fees for their services. The cashier of the Court of First Instance shall pay witnesses and experts their compensation or fees after they have carried out their respective duties or tasks.

Article 75

1. The Court of First Instance may, on application by a party or of its own motion, issue letters rogatory for the examination of witnesses or experts.
2. Letters rogatory shall be issued in the form of an order which shall contain the name, forenames, description and address of the witness or expert, set out the facts on which the witness or expert is to be examined, name the parties, their agents, lawyers or advisers, indicate their addresses for service and briefly describe the subject-matter of the proceedings.

Notice of the order shall be served on the parties by the Registrar.

3. The Registrar shall send the order to the competent authority named in Annex I to the Rules supplementing the Rules of Procedure of the Court of Justice of the Member State in whose territory the witness or expert is to be examined. Where necessary, the order shall be accompanied by a translation into the official language or languages of the Member State to which it is addressed.

The authority named pursuant to the first subparagraph shall pass on the order to the judicial authority which is competent according to its national law.

The competent judicial authority shall give effect to the letters rogatory in accordance with its national law. After implementation the competent judicial authority shall transmit to the authority named pursuant to the first subparagraph the order embodying the letters rogatory, any documents arising from the implementation and a detailed statement of costs. These documents shall be sent to the Registrar.

The Registrar shall be responsible for the translation of the documents into the language of the case.

4. The Court of First Instance shall defray the expenses occasioned by the letters rogatory without prejudice to the right to charge them, where appropriate, to the parties.

Article 76

1. The Registrar shall draw up minutes of every hearing. The minutes shall be signed by the President and by the Registrar and shall constitute an official record.
2. The parties may inspect the minutes and any expert's report at the Registry and obtain copies at their own expense.

Chapter 4

Stay of Proceedings and Declining of Jurisdiction by the Court of First Instance

Article 77

Without prejudice to Article 123(4), Article 128 and Article 129(4), proceedings may be stayed:

(a) in the circumstances specified in the third paragraph of Article 47 of the EC Statute, the third paragraph of Article 47 of the ECSC Statute and the third paragraph of Article 48 of the EAEC Statute;

(b) where an appeal is brought before the Court of Justice against a decision of the Court of First Instance disposing of the substantive issues in part only, disposing of a procedural issue concerning a plea of lack of competence or inadmissibility or dismissing an application to intervene;

(c) at the joint request of the parties.

Article 78

The decision to stay the proceedings shall be made by order of the President after hearing the parties and the Advocate-General; the President may refer the matter to the Court of First Instance. A decision ordering that the proceedings be resumed shall be adopted in accordance with the same procedure. The orders referred to in this Article shall be served on the parties.

Article 79

1. The stay of proceedings shall take effect on the date indicated in the order of stay or, in the absence of such an indication, on the date of that order.

While proceedings are stayed time shall, except for the purposes of the time-limit prescribed in Article 115(1) for an application to intervene, cease to run for the purposes of prescribed time-limits for all parties.

2. Where the order of stay does not fix the length of the stay, it shall end on the date indicated in the order of resumption or, in the absence of such indication, on the date of the order of resumption.

From the date of resumption time shall begin to run afresh for the purposes of the time-limits.

Article 80

Decisions declining jurisdiction in the circumstances specified in the third paragraph of Article 47 of the EC Statute, the third paragraph of Article 47 of the ECSC Statute and the third paragraph of Article 48 of the EAEC Statute shall be made by the Court of First Instance by way of an order which shall be served on the parties.

CHAPTER 5

JUDGMENTS

Article 81

The judgment shall contain:

- a statement that it is the judgment of the Court of First Instance,
- the date of its delivery,
- the names of the President and of the Judges taking part in it,
- the name of the Advocate-General, if designated,
- the name of the Registrar,
- the description of the parties,
- the names of the agents, advisers and lawyers of the parties,
- a statement of the forms of order sought by the parties,
- a statement, where appropriate, that the Advocate-General delivered his opinion,
- a summary of the facts,
- the grounds for the decision,
- the operative part of the judgment, including the decision as to costs.

Article 82

1. The judgment shall be delivered in open court; the parties shall be given notice to attend to hear it.
2. The original of the judgment, signed by the President, by the Judges who took part in the deliberations and by the Registrar, shall be sealed and deposited at the Registry; the parties shall be served with certified copies of the judgment.
3. The Registrar shall record on the original of the judgment the date on which it was delivered.

Article 83

Subject to the provisions of the second paragraph of Article 53 of the EC Statute, the second paragraph of Article 53 of the ECSC Statute and the second paragraph of Article 54 of the EAEC Statute, the judgment shall be binding from the date of its delivery.

Article 84

1. Without prejudice to the provisions relating to the interpretation of judgments, the Court of First Instance may, of its own motion or on application by a party made within two weeks after the delivery of a judgment, rectify clerical mistakes, errors in calculation and obvious slips in it.
2. The parties, whom the Registrar shall duly notify, may lodge written observations within a period prescribed by the President.
3. The Court of First Instance shall take its decision in closed session.
4. The original of the rectification order shall be annexed to the original of the rectified judgment. A note of this order shall be made in the margin of the original of the rectified judgment.

Article 85

If the Court of First Instance should omit to give a decision on costs, any party may within a month after service of the judgment apply to the Court of First Instance to supplement its judgment.

The application shall be served on the opposite party and the President shall prescribe a period within which that party may lodge written observations.

After these observations have been lodged, the Court of First Instance shall decide both on the admissibility and on the substance of the application.

Article 86

The Registrar shall arrange for the publication of cases before the Court of First Instance.

CHAPTER 6

COSTS

Article 87

1. A decision as to costs shall be given in the final judgment or in the order which closes the proceedings.
2. The unsuccessful party shall be ordered to pay the costs if they have been applied for in the successful party's pleadings.

Where there are several unsuccessful parties the Court of First Instance shall decide how the costs are to be shared.

3. Where each party succeeds on some and fails on other heads, or where the circumstances are exceptional, the Court of First Instance may order that the costs be shared or that each party bear its own costs.

The Court of First Instance may order a party, even if successful, to pay costs which it considers that party to have unreasonably or vexatiously caused the opposite party to incur.

4. The Member States and institutions which intervened in the proceedings shall bear their own costs.

The States, other than the Member States, which are parties to the EEA Agreement, and also the EFTA Surveillance Authority, shall bear their own costs if they intervene in the proceedings.

The Court of First Instance may order an intervener other than those mentioned in the preceding subparagraph to bear his own costs.

5. A party who discontinues or withdraws from proceedings shall be ordered to pay the costs if they have been applied for in the observations of the other party on the discontinuance. However, upon application by the party who discontinues or withdraws from proceedings, the costs shall be borne by the other party if this appears justified by the conduct of that party.

Where the parties have come to an agreement on costs, the decision as to costs shall be in accordance with that agreement.

If costs are not claimed in the written pleadings, the parties shall bear their own costs.

6. Where a case does not proceed to judgment, the costs shall be in the discretion of the Court of First Instance.

Article 88

Without prejudice to the second subparagraph of Article 87(3), in proceedings between the Communities and their servants the institutions shall bear their own costs.

Article 89

Costs necessarily incurred by a party in enforcing a judgment or order of the Court of First Instance shall be refunded by the opposite party on the scale in force in the State where the enforcement takes place.

Article 90

Proceedings before the Court of First Instance shall be free of charge, except that:

(a) where a party has caused the Court of First Instance to incur avoidable costs, the Court of First Instance may order that party to refund them;

(b) where copying or translation work is carried out at the request of a party, the cost shall, in so far as the Registrar considers it excessive, be paid for by that party on the scale of charges referred to in Article 24(5).

Article 91

Without prejudice to the preceding Article, the following shall be regarded as recoverable costs:

(a) sums payable to witnesses and experts under Article 74;

(b) expenses necessarily incurred by the parties for the purpose of the proceedings, in particular the travel and subsistence expenses and the remuneration of agents, advisers or lawyers.

Article 92

1. If there is a dispute concerning the costs to be recovered, the Court of First Instance hearing the case shall, on application by the party concerned and after hearing the opposite party, make an order, from which no appeal shall lie.

2. The parties may, for the purposes of enforcement, apply for an authenticated copy of the order.

Article 93

1. Sums due from the cashier of the Court of First Instance shall be paid in the currency of the country where the Court of First Instance has its seat.

At the request of the person entitled to any sum, it shall be paid in the currency of the country where the expenses to be refunded were incurred or where the steps in respect of which payment is due were taken.

2. Other debtors shall make payment in the currency of their country of origin.
3. Conversions of currency shall be made at the official rates of exchange ruling on the day of payment in the country where the Court of First Instance has its seat.

Chapter 7

Legal Aid

Article 94

1. A party who is wholly or in part unable to meet the costs of the proceedings may at any time apply for legal aid.

The application shall be accompanied by evidence of the applicant's need of assistance, and in particular by a document from the competent authority certifying his lack of means.

2. If the application is made prior to proceedings which the applicant wishes to commence, it shall briefly state the subject of such proceedings.

The application need not be made through a lawyer.

The President shall, after considering the written observations of the opposite party, decide whether legal aid should be granted in full or in part, or whether it should be refused. He shall consider whether there is manifestly no cause of action. He may refer the matter to the Court of First Instance.

The decision shall be taken by way of an order without giving reasons, and no appeal shall lie therefrom.

Article 95

1. The Court of First Instance, by any order by which it decides that a person is entitled to receive legal aid, shall order that a lawyer be appointed to act for him.
2. If the person does not indicate his choice of lawyer, or if the Court of First Instance considers that his choice is unacceptable, the Registrar shall send a copy of the order and of the application for legal aid to the authority named in Annex II to the Rules supplementing the Rules of Procedure of the Court of Justice, being the competent authority of the State concerned.
3. The Court of First Instance, in the light of the suggestions made by that authority, shall of its own motion appoint a lawyer to act for the person concerned.
4. An order granting legal aid may specify an amount to be paid to the lawyer appointed to act for the person concerned or fix a limit which the lawyer's disbursements and fees may not, in principle, exceed.

Article 96

The Court of First Instance may at any time, either of its own motion or on application, withdraw legal aid if the circumstances which led to its being granted alter during the proceedings.

Article 97

1. Where legal aid is granted, the cashier of the Court of First Instance shall advance the funds necessary to meet the expenses.
2. The President, who may refer the matter to the Court of First Instance, shall adjudicate on the lawyer's disbursements and fees; he may, on application by the lawyer, order that he receive an advance.
3. In its decision as to costs the Court of First Instance may order the payment to the cashier of the Court of First Instance of the whole or any part of amounts advanced as legal aid.

The Registrar shall take steps to obtain the recovery of these sums from the party ordered to pay them.

Chapter 8

Discontinuance

Article 98

If, before the Court of First Instance has given its decision, the parties reach a settlement of their dispute and intimate to the Court of First Instance the abandonment of their claims, the President shall order the case to be removed from the register and shall give a decision as to costs in accordance with Article 87(5) having regard to any proposals made by the parties on the matter.

This provision shall not apply to proceedings under Articles 230 and 232 (ex Articles 173 and 175) of the EC Treaty, Articles 33 and 35 of the ECSC Treaty and Articles 146 and 148 of the EAEC Treaty.

Article 99

If the applicant informs the Court of First Instance in writing that he wishes to discontinue the proceedings, the President shall order the case to be removed from the register and shall give a decision as to costs in accordance with Article 87(5).

Chapter 9

Service

Article 100

Where these Rules require that a document be served on a person, the Registrar shall ensure that service is effected at that person's address for service either by the dispatch of a copy of the document by registered post with a form for acknowledgement of receipt or by personal delivery of the copy against a receipt.

The Registrar shall prepare and certify the copies of documents to be served, save where the parties themselves supply the copies in accordance with Article 43(1).

Chapter 10

Time-Limits

Article 101

1. Any period of time prescribed by the EC, ECSC and EAEC Treaties, the Statutes of the Court of Justice or these Rules for the taking of any procedural step shall be reckoned as follows:

(a) Where a period expressed in days, weeks, months or years is to be calculated from the moment at which an event occurs or an action takes place, the day during which that event occurs or that action takes place shall not be counted as falling within the period in question;

(b) A period expressed in weeks, months or in years shall end with the expiry of whichever day in the last week, month or year is the same day of the week, or falls on the same date, as the day during which the event or action from which the period is to be calculated occurred or took place. If, in a period expressed in months or in years, the day on which it should expire does not occur in the last month, the period shall end with the expiry of the last day of that month;

(c) Where a period is expressed in months and days, it shall first be reckoned in whole months, then in days;
(d) Periods shall include official holidays, Sundays and Saturdays;
(e) Periods shall not be suspended during the judicial vacations.

2. If the period would otherwise end on a Saturday, Sunday or official holiday, it shall be extended until the end of the first following working day.

The list of official holidays drawn up by the Court of Justice and published in the *Official Journal of the European Communities* shall apply to the Court of First Instance.

Article 102

1. Where the period of time allowed for commencing proceedings against a measure adopted by an institution runs from the publication of that measure, that period shall be calculated, for the purposes of Article 101(1), from the end of the 14th day after publication thereof in the *Official Journal of the European Communities*.
2. The extensions, on account of distance, of prescribed time-limits provided for in a decision of the Court of Justice and published in the *Official Journal of the European Communities* shall apply to the Court of First Instance.

Article 103

1. Any time-limit prescribed pursuant to these Rules may be extended by whoever prescribed it.
2. The President may delegate power of signature to the Registrar for the purpose of fixing time-limits which, pursuant to these Rules, it falls to the President to prescribe, or of extending such time-limits.

Title 3

Special Forms of Procedure

Chapter 1

Suspension of Operation or Enforcement and Other Interim Measures

Article 104

1. An application to suspend the operation of any measure adopted by an institution, made pursuant to the second paragraph of Article 242 (ex Article 185) of the EC Treaty, the second paragraph of Article 39 of the ECSC Treaty and Article 157 of the EAEC Treaty, shall be admissible only if the applicant is challenging that measure in proceedings before the Court of First Instance.

An application for the adoption of any other interim measure referred to in the third paragraph of Article 243 (ex Article 186) of the EC Treaty, the third paragraph of Article 39 of the ECSC Treaty and Article 158 of the EAEC Treaty shall be admissible only if it is made by a party to a case before the Court of First Instance and relates to that case.

2. An application of a kind referred to in paragraph 1 of this Article shall state the subject-matter of the proceedings, the circumstances giving rise to urgency and the pleas of fact and law establishing a prima facie case for the interim measures applied for.
3. The application shall be made by a separate document and in accordance with the provisions of Articles 43 and 44.

Article 105

1. The application shall be served on the opposite party, and the President of the Court of First Instance shall prescribe a short period within which that party may submit written or oral observations.

2. The President of the Court of First Instance may order a preparatory inquiry.

The President of the Court of First Instance may grant the application even before the observations of the opposite party have been submitted. This decision may be varied or cancelled even without any application being made by any party.

Article 106

The President of the Court of First Instance shall either decide on the application himself or refer it to the Chamber to which the case has been assigned in the main proceedings or to the Court of First Instance sitting in plenary session if the case has been assigned to it.

If the President of the Court of First Instance is absent or prevented from attending, he shall be replaced by the President or the most senior Judge, within the meaning of Article 6, of the bench of the Court of First Instance to which the case has been assigned.

Where the application is referred to a bench of the Court of First Instance, that bench shall postpone all other cases and shall give a decision. Article 105 shall apply.

Article 107

1. The decision on the application shall take the form of a reasoned order. The order shall be served on the parties forthwith.
2. The enforcement of the order may be made conditional on the lodging by the applicant of security, of an amount and nature to be fixed in the light of the circumstances.
3. Unless the order fixes the date on which the interim measure is to lapse, the measure shall lapse when final judgment is delivered.
4. The order shall have only an interim effect, and shall be without prejudice to the decision on the substance of the case by the Court of First Instance.

Article 108

On application by a party, the order may at any time be varied or cancelled on account of a change in circumstances.

Article 109

Rejection of an application for an interim measure shall not bar the party who made it from making a further application on the basis of new facts.

Article 110

The provisions of this Chapter shall apply to applications to suspend the enforcement of a decision of the Court of First Instance or of any measure adopted by another institution, submitted pursuant to Articles 244 and 256 (ex Articles 187 and 192) of the EC Treaty, Articles 44 and 92 of the ECSC Treaty and Articles 159 and 164 of the EAEC Treaty.

The order granting the application shall fix, where appropriate, a date on which the interim measure is to lapse.

Chapter 2

Preliminary Issues

Article 111

Where it is clear that the Court of First Instance has no jurisdiction to take cognisance of an action or where the action is manifestly inadmissible or manifestly lacking any foundation in law, the Court of First Instance may, by reasoned order, after hearing the Advocate-General and without taking further steps in the proceedings, give a decision on the action.

Article 112

The decision to refer an action to the Court of Justice, pursuant to the second paragraph of Article 47 of the EC Statute, the second paragraph of Article 47 of the ECSC Statute and the second paragraph of Article 48 of the EAEC Statute, shall, in the case of manifest lack of competence, be made by reasoned order and without taking any further steps in the proceedings.

Article 113

The Court of First Instance may at any time, of its own motion, consider whether there exists any absolute bar to proceeding with an action or declare, after hearing the parties, that the action has become devoid of purpose and that there is no need to adjudicate on it; it shall give its decision in accordance with Article 114(3) and (4).

Article 114

1. A party applying to the Court of First Instance for a decision on admissibility, on lack of competence or other preliminary plea not going to the substance of the case shall make the application by a separate document.

The application must contain the pleas of fact and law relied on and the form of order sought by the applicant; any supporting documents must be annexed to it.

2. As soon as the application has been lodged, the President shall prescribe a period within which the opposite party may lodge a document containing a statement of the form of order sought by that party and its pleas in law.

3. Unless the Court of First Instance otherwise decides, the remainder of the proceedings shall be oral.

4. The Court of First Instance shall, after hearing the Advocate-General, decide on the application or reserve its decision for the final judgment. It shall refer the case to the Court of Justice if the case falls within the jurisdiction of that Court.

If the Court of First Instance refuses the application or reserves its decision, the President shall prescribe new time-limits for further steps in the proceedings.

Chapter 3

Intervention

Article 115

1. An application to intervene must be made within three months of the publication of the notice referred to in Article 24(6).

2. The application shall contain:

(a) the description of the case;
(b) the description of the parties;
(c) the name and address of the intervener;
(d) the intervener's address for service at the place where the Court of First Instance has its seat;
(e) the form of order sought, by one or more of the parties, in support of which the intervener is applying for leave to intervene;
(f) a statement of the circumstances establishing the right to intervene, where the application is submitted pursuant to the second or third paragraph of Article 37 of the EC Statute, Article 34 of the ECSC Statute or the second paragraph of Article 38 of the EAEC Statute.

Articles 43 and 44 shall apply.
3. The intervener shall be represented in accordance with Article 17 of the EC Statute, the first and second paragraphs of Article 20 of the ECSC Statute and Article 17 of the EAEC Statute.

Article 116

1. The application shall be served on the parties.
The President shall give the parties an opportunity to submit their written or oral observations before deciding on the application.
The President shall decide on the application by order or shall refer the decision to the Court of First Instance. The order must be reasoned if the application is dismissed.
2. If the President allows the intervention, the intervener shall receive a copy of every document served on the parties. The President may, however, on application by one of the parties, omit secret or confidential documents.
3. The intervener must accept the case as he finds it at the time of his intervention.
4. The President shall prescribe a period within which the intervener may submit a statement in intervention.
The statement in intervention shall contain:
(a) a statement of the form of order sought by the intervener in support of or opposing, in whole or in part, the form of order sought by one of the parties;
(b) the pleas in law and arguments relied on by the intervener;
(c) where appropriate, the nature of any evidence offered.
5. After the statement in intervention has been lodged, the President shall, where necessary, prescribe a time-limit within which the parties may reply to that statement.

Chapter 4

Judgments of the Court of First Instance Delivered After its Decision has Been set Aside and the Case Referred Back to it

Article 117

Where the Court of Justice sets aside a judgment or an order of the Court of First Instance and refers the case back to that Court, the latter shall be seised of the case by the judgment so referring it.

Article 118

1. Where the Court of Justice sets aside a judgment or an order of a Chamber, the President of the Court of First Instance may assign the case to another Chamber composed of the same number of Judges.
2. Where the Court of Justice sets aside a judgment delivered or an order made by the Court of First Instance sitting in plenary session, the case shall be assigned to that Court as so constituted.
2a. Where the Court of Justice sets aside a judgment delivered or an order made by a single Judge, the President of the Court of First Instance shall assign the case to a Chamber composed of three Judges of which that Judge is not a member.
3. In the cases provided for in paragraphs 1, 2 and 2a of this Article, Articles 13(2), 14(1) and 51 shall apply.

Article 119

1. Where the written procedure before the Court of First Instance has been completed when the judgment referring the case back to it is delivered, the course of the procedure shall be as follows:

(a) Within two months from the service upon him of the judgment of the Court of Justice the applicant may lodge a statement of written observations;
(b) In the month following the communication to him of that statement, the defendant may lodge a statement of written observations. The time allowed to the defendant for lodging it may in no case be less than two months from the service upon him of the judgment of the Court of Justice;
(c) In the month following the simultaneous communication to the intervener of the observations of the applicant and the defendant, the intervener may lodge a statement of written observations. The time allowed to the intervener for lodging it may in no case be less than two months from the service upon him of the judgment of the Court of Justice.

2. Where the written procedure before the Court of First Instance had not been completed when the judgment referring the case back to the Court of First Instance was delivered, it shall be resumed, at the stage which it had reached, by means of measures of organisation of procedure adopted by the Court of First Instance.
3. The Court of First Instance may, if the circumstances so justify, allow supplementary statements of written observations to be lodged.

Article 120

The procedure shall be conducted in accordance with the provisions of Title II of these Rules.

Article 121

The Court of First Instance shall decide on the costs relating to the proceedings instituted before it and to the proceedings on the appeal before the Court of Justice.

Chapter 5

Judgments by Default and Applications to set Them Aside

Article 122

1. If a defendant on whom an application initiating proceedings has been duly served fails to lodge a defence to the application in the proper form within the time prescribed, the applicant may apply to the Court of First Instance for judgment by default.

The application shall be served on the defendant. The Court of First Instance may decide to open the oral procedure on the application.
2. Before giving judgment by default the Court of First Instance shall consider whether the application initiating proceedings is admissible, whether the appropriate formalities have been complied with, and whether the application appears well founded. It may order a preparatory inquiry.
3. A judgment by default shall be enforceable. The Court of First Instance may, however, grant a stay of execution until it has given its decision on any application under paragraph 4 of this Article to set aside the judgment, or it may make execution subject to the provision of security of an amount and nature to be fixed in the light of the circumstances; this security shall be released if no such application is made or if the application fails.
4. Application may be made to set aside a judgment by default.
The application to set aside the judgment must be made within one month from the date of service of the judgment and must be lodged in the form prescribed by Articles 43 and 44.
5. After the application has been served, the President shall prescribe a period within which the other party may submit his written observations.

The proceedings shall be conducted in accordance with the provisions of Title II of these Rules.
6. The Court of First Instance shall decide by way of a judgment which may not be set aside. The original of this judgment shall be annexed to the original of the judgment by default. A note of the judgment on the application to set aside shall be made in the margin of the original of the judgment by default.

CHAPTER 6

EXCEPTIONAL REVIEW PROCEDURES

SECTION 1 — THIRD-PARTY PROCEEDINGS

Article 123

1. Articles 43 and 44 shall apply to an application initiating third-party proceedings. In addition such an application shall:
   (a) specify the judgment contested;
   (b) state how that judgment is prejudicial to the rights of the third party;
   (c) indicate the reasons for which the third party was unable to take part in the original case before the Court of First Instance.

The application must be made against all the parties to the original case.

Where the judgment has been published in the *Official Journal of the European Communities*, the application must be lodged within two months of the publication.
2. The Court of First Instance may, on application by the third party, order a stay of execution of the judgment. The provisions of Title III, Chapter 1, shall apply.
3. The contested judgment shall be varied on the points on which the submissions of the third party are upheld.

The original of the judgment in the third-party proceedings shall be annexed to the original of the contested judgment. A note of the judgment in the third-party proceedings shall be made in the margin of the original of the contested judgment.
4. Where an appeal before the Court of Justice and an application initiating third-party proceedings before the Court of First Instance contest the same judgment of the Court of First Instance, the Court of First Instance may, after hearing the parties, stay the proceedings until the Court of Justice has delivered its judgment.

Article 124

The application initiating third-party proceedings shall be assigned to the Chamber which delivered the judgment which is the subject of the application; if the Court of First Instance sitting in plenary session delivered the judgment, the application shall be assigned to it. If the judgment has been delivered by a single Judge, the application initiating third-party proceedings shall be assigned to that Judge.

SECTION 2 — REVISION

Article 125

Without prejudice to the period of ten years prescribed in the third paragraph of Article 41 of the EC Statute, the third paragraph of Article 38 of the ECSC Statute and the third paragraph of Article 42 of the EAEC Statute, an application for revision of a judgment shall be made within three months of the date on which the facts on which the application is based came to the applicant's knowledge.

Article 126

1. Articles 43 and 44 shall apply to an application for revision. In addition such an application shall:

(a) specify the judgment contested;
(b) indicate the points on which the application is based;
(c) set out the facts on which the application is based;
(d) indicate the nature of the evidence to show that there are facts justifying revision of the judgment, and that the time-limits laid down in Article 125 have been observed.

2. The application must be made against all parties to the case in which the contested judgment was given.

Article 127

1. The application for revision shall be assigned to the Chamber which delivered the judgment which is the subject of the application; if the Court of First Instance sitting in plenary session delivered the judgment, the application shall be assigned to it. If the judgment has been delivered by a single Judge, the application for revision shall be assigned to that Judge.
2. Without prejudice to its decision on the substance, the Court of First Instance shall, after hearing the Advocate-General, having regard to the written observations of the parties, give its decision on the admissibility of the application.
3. If the Court of First Instance finds the application admissible, it shall proceed to consider the substance of the application and shall give its decision in the form of a judgment in accordance with these Rules.
4. The original of the revising judgment shall be annexed to the original of the judgment revised. A note of the revising judgment shall be made in the margin of the original of the judgment revised.

Article 128

Where an appeal before the Court of Justice and an application for revision before the Court of First Instance concern the same judgment of the Court of First Instance, the Court of First Instance may, after hearing the parties, stay the proceedings until the Court of Justice has delivered its judgment.

SECTION 3—INTERPRETATION OF JUDGMENTS

Article 129

1. An application for interpretation of a judgment shall be made in accordance with Articles 43 and 44. In addition it shall specify:
(a) the judgment in question;
(b) the passages of which interpretation is sought.

The application must be made against all the parties to the case in which the judgment was given.
2. The application for interpretation shall be assigned to the Chamber which delivered the judgment which is the subject of the application; if the Court of First Instance sitting in plenary session delivered the judgment, the application shall be assigned to it. If the judgment has been delivered by a single Judge, the application for interpretation shall be assigned to that Judge.
3. The Court of First Instance shall give its decision in the form of a judgment after having given the parties an opportunity to submit their observations and after hearing the Advocate-General.

The original of the interpreting judgment shall be annexed to the original of the judgment interpreted. A note of the interpreting judgment shall be made in the margin of the original of the judgment interpreted.
4. Where an appeal before the Court of Justice and an application for interpretation before the Court of First Instance concern the same judgment of the Court of

First Instance, the Court of First Instance may, after hearing the parties, stay the proceedings until the Court of Justice has delivered its judgment.

Title 4

Proceedings Relating to Intellectual Property Rights

Article 130

1. Subject to the special provisions of this Title, the provisions of these Rules of Procedure shall apply to proceedings brought against the Office for Harmonisation in the Internal Market (Trade Marks and Designs) and against the Community Plant Variety Office, (both hereinafter referred to as 'the Office'), and concerning the application of the rules relating to an intellectual property regime.
2. The provisions of this Title shall not apply to actions brought directly against the Office without prior proceedings before a Board of Appeal.

Article 131

1. The application shall be drafted in one of the languages described in Article 35(1), according to the applicant's choice.
2. The language in which the application is drafted shall become the language of the case if the applicant was the only party to the proceedings before the Board of Appeal or if another party to those proceedings does not object to this within a period laid down for that purpose by the Registrar after the application has been lodged.

If, within that period, the parties to the proceedings before the Board of Appeal inform the Registrar of their agreement on the choice, as the language of the case, of one of the languages referred to in Article 35(1), that language shall become the language of the case before the Court of First Instance.

In the event of an objection to the choice of the language of the case made by the applicant within the period referred to above and in the absence of an agreement on the matter between the parties to the proceedings before the Board of Appeal, the language in which the application for registration in question was filed at the Office shall become the language of the case. If, however, on a reasoned request by any party and after hearing the other parties, the President finds that the use of that language would not enable all parties to the proceedings before the Board of Appeal to follow the proceedings and defend their interests and that only the use of another language from among those mentioned in Article 35(1) makes it possible to remedy that situation, he may designate that other language as the language of the case; the President may refer the matter to the Court of First Instance.
3. In the pleadings and other documents addressed to the Court of First Instance and during the oral procedure, the applicant may use the language chosen by him in accordance with paragraph 1 and each of the other parties may use a language chosen by that party from those mentioned in Article 35(1).
4. If, by virtue of paragraph 2, a language other than that in which the application is drafted becomes the language of the case, the Registrar shall cause the application to be translated into the language of the case.

Each party shall be required, within a reasonable period to be prescribed for that purpose by the Registrar, to produce a translation into the language of the case of the pleadings or documents other than the application that are lodged by that party in a language other than the language of the case pursuant to paragraph 3. The party producing the translation, which shall be authentic within the meaning of Article 37, shall certify its accuracy. If the translation is not produced within the period prescribed, the pleading or the procedural document in question shall be removed from the file.

The Registrar shall cause everything said during the oral procedure to be translated into the language of the case and, at the request of any party, into the language used by that party in accordance with paragraph 3.

Article 132

1. Without prejudice to Article 44, the application shall contain the names of all the parties to the proceedings before the Board of Appeal and the addresses which they had given for the purposes of the notifications to be effected in the course of those proceedings.

The contested decision of the Board of Appeal shall be appended to the application. The date on which the applicant was notified of that decision must be indicated.

2. If the application does not comply with paragraph 1, Article 44(6) shall apply.

Article 133

1. The Registrar shall inform the Office and all the parties to the proceedings before the Board of Appeal of the lodging of the application. He shall arrange for service of the application after determining the language of the case in accordance with Article 131(2).

2. The application shall be served on the Office, as defendant, and on the parties to the proceedings before the Board of Appeal other than the applicant. Service shall be effected in the language of the case.

Service of the application on a party to the proceedings before the Board of Appeal shall be effected by registered post with a form of acknowledgment of receipt at the address given by the party concerned for the purposes of the notifications to be effected in the course of the proceedings before the Board of Appeal.

3. Once the application has been served, the Office shall forward to the Court of First Instance the file relating to the proceedings before the Board of Appeal.

Article 134

1. The parties to the proceedings before the Board of Appeal other than the applicant may participate, as interveners, in the proceedings before the Court of First Instance.

2. The interveners referred to in paragraph 1 shall have the same procedural rights as the main parties.

They may support the form of order sought by a main party and they may apply for a form of order and put forward pleas in law independently of those applied for and put forward by the main parties.

3. An intervener, as referred to in paragraph 1, may, in his response lodged in accordance with Article 135(1), seek an order annulling or altering the decision of the Board of Appeal on a point not raised in the application and put forward pleas in law not raised in the application.

Such submissions seeking orders or putting forward pleas in law in the intervener's response shall cease to have effect should the applicant discontinue the proceedings.

4. In derogation from Article 122, the default procedure shall not apply where an intervener, as referred to in paragraph 1 of this Article, has responded to the application in the manner and within the period prescribed.

Article 135

1. The Office and the interveners referred to in Article 134(1) may submit responses to the application within a period of two months from the service of the application.

Article 46 shall apply to the responses.

2. The application and the responses may be supplemented by replies and rejoinders by the parties, including the interveners referred to in Article 134(1), where the President, on a reasoned application made within two weeks of service of the responses or replies, considers such further pleading necessary and allows it in order to enable the party concerned to put forward its point of view.

The President shall prescribe the period within which such pleadings are to be submitted.

3. Without prejudice to the foregoing, in the cases referred to in Article 134(3), the other parties may, within a period of two months of service upon them of the response, submit a pleading confined to responding to the form of order sought and the pleas in law submitted for the first time in the response of an intervener. That period may be extended by the President on a reasoned application from the party concerned.

4. The parties' pleadings may not change the subject-matter of the proceedings before the Board of Appeal.

Article 136

1. Where an action against a decision of a Board of Appeal is successful, the Court of First Instance may order the Office to bear only its own costs.

2. Costs necessarily incurred by the parties for the purposes of the proceedings before the Board of Appeal and costs incurred for the purposes of the production, prescribed by the second subparagraph of Article 131(4), of translations of pleadings or other documents into the language of the case shall be regarded as recoverable costs.

In the event of inaccurate translations being produced, the second subparagraph of Article 87(3) shall apply.

Final Provisions

Article 137

These Rules, which are authentic in the languages mentioned in Article 35(1), shall be published in the *Official Journal of the European Communities*. They shall enter into force on the first day of the second month from the date of their publication.

BIBLIOGRAPHY

Ackermann, T., case note in (1998) C.M.L.Rev. 783–799: 3–010

Adiba Sohrab, J., case note in (1994) C.M.L.Rev. 875–887: 3–013

Alexander, W., "The Temporal Effects of Preliminary Rulings" (1988) Y.E.L. 11–26: 6–039

Arnull, A., "National Courts and the Validity of Community Acts" (1988) E.L.Rev. 125–131: 2–055

Arnull, A., "The Use and Abuse of Article 177 EEC" (1989) M.L.R. 622–639: 2–051

Arnull, A., case note in (1990) E.L.Rev. 321–326: 2–002

Arnull, A., "Challenging EC Anti-dumping Regulations; The Problem of Admissibility" (1992) E.Comp.L.Rev. 73–81: 7–069

Arnull, A., "The Evolution of the Court's Jurisdiction Under Article 177" (1993) E.L.Rev. 129–137: 2–012, 2–014

Arnull, A., "Owning up to Fallibility: Precedent and the Court of Justice" (1993) C.M.L.Rev. 247–266: 6–036

Arnull, A., case note in (1993) C.M.L.Rev. 613–622: 2–025

Arnull, A., case note in (1994) C.M.L.Rev. 377–386: 2–023

Arnull, A., case note in (1996) C.M.L.Rev. 319–335: 7–071

Arnull, A., "Liability for Legislative Acts under Article 215(2) EC", in T. Heukels and A. McDonnell (eds), *The Action for Damages in Community Law*, The Hague, London, Boston, Kluwer Law International, 1997, 129–151: 11–046

Auvret-Finck, J., "Les avis 1/91 et 1/92 relatifs au projet d'accord sur la création de l'Espace économique européen" (1993) C.D.E. 38–59: 12–005

Barav, A., "The Exception of Illegality in Community Law: A Critical Analysis" (1974) C.M.L.Rev. 366–386: 9–001, 9–009

Barav, A., "Considérations sur la specifité du recours en carence en droit communautaire" (1975) R.T.D.E. 53–71: 8–020

Barav, A., "Failure of Member States to Fulfil Their Obligations Under Community Law" (1975) C.M.L.Rev. 369–383: 5–011

Barav, A., "Preliminary Censorship? The Judgment of the European Court in Foglia v. Novello" (1980) E.L.Rev. 443–468: 2–039

Barav, A., "Imbroglio préjudiciel" (1982) R.T.D.E. 431-483: 2–039

Barav, A., "La plénitude de compétence du juge national en sa qualité de juge communautaire in *l'Europe et le Droit—Mélanges en hommage à J. Boulouis*, Paris, Ed. Dalloz, 1991, 1–20: 3–003

Barav, A., "Omnipotent Courts", in D. Curtin and T. Heukels (eds), *Institutional Dynamics of European Integration. Essays in Honour of H.G. Schermers*, Dordrecht, Martinus, Nijhoff, 1994, 265–302: 3–016

Barav, A., "The Effectiveness of Judicial Protection and the Role of the National Courts", in *Judicial Protection of Rights in the Community Legal Order*, Brussels, Bruylant, 1997, 259–296: 3–016

Barents, R., "The Court of Justice and the EEA Agreement: Between Constitutional Values and Political Realities", in J. Stuyck and A. Looijestijn-Clearie (eds), *The European Economic Area EC–EFTA: Institutional Aspects and Financial Services*, Deventer, Kluwer, 1994, 57–71: 12–005

Barents, R., *Procedures en procesvoering voor het Hof van Justitie en het Gerecht van eerste aanleg van de EG*, Deventer, Kluwer, 1996, 525 pp.: 1–004, 13–004, 22–171

Bebr, G., "Judicial Remedy of Private Parties against Normative Acts of the European Communities: The Role of Exception of Illegality" (1966) C.M.L.Rev. 7–31: 9–009

Bebr, G., "Examen en validité au titre de l'article 177 du traité CEE et cohésion juridique de la Communauté" (1975) C.D.E. 379–424: 10–008

Bebr, G., "The Existence of a Genuine Dispute: an Indispensable Precondition for the Jurisdiction of the Court Under Article 177 EEC Treaty" (1980) C.M.L.Rev. 525–537: 2–039

Bebr, G., *Development of Judicial Control of the European Communities*, The Hague, Martinus Nijhoff, 1981, 822 pp.: 10–004

Bebr, G., "Preliminary Rulings of the Court of Justice: Their Authority and Temporal Effect" (1981) C.M.L.Rev. 475–507: 6–039

Bebr, G., "The Rambling Ghost of "Cohn–Bendit": Acte clair and the Court of Justice" (1983) C.M.L.Rev. 439–472: 2–051

Bebr, G., "Direct and Indirect Judicial Control of Community Acts in Practice: the Relation Between Articles 173 and 177 of the EEC Treaty" (1984) Mich.L.Rev. 1229–1249: 6–039

Bebr, G., "Arbitration Tribunals and Article 177 of the EEC Treaty" (1985) C.M.L.Rev. 489–504: 2–011

Bebr, G., "The Reinforcement of the Constitutional Review of Community Acts Under Article 177 EEC Treaty (cases 314/85 and 133 to 136/85)" (1988) C.M.L.Rev., 667–691: 2–004, 2–055

Bebr, G., case note in (1991) C.M.L.Rev. 415–427: 2–002

Bellamy, C.W. and Child, G.D., *The Common Market Law of Competition* (4th ed.), Sweet and Maxwell, 1993, 740–743: 13–002

Bellis, J., "Judicial Review of EEC Anti-dumping and Anti-subsidy Determinations after Fediol: The Emergence of a New Admissibility Test" (1984) C.M.L.Rev. 539–551: 7–068

Bergerès, M.-Ch., "La reformulation des question préjudicielles en interprétation par la Cour de justice des Communautés européennes" (1985) Rec. Dalloz, Chronique 155–162: 2–020

Bergerès, M.-Ch., *Contentieux communautaire*, Paris, Presses Universitaires de France, 1989, 346 pp.: 7–095

Bergerès, M.-Ch., "La CJCE et la pertinence de la question préjudicielle" (1993) Rec. Dalloz, Chronique, 245–247: 2–023

Betlem, G., case note in (1996) C.M.L.Rev. 137–147: 6–022

Biancarelli, J., "Les principes généraux du droit communautaire applicables en matière pénale" (1987) R.S.C.D.P.C. 131–166: 3–020

Biancarelli, J., "La création du Tribunal de première instance des Communautés européennes: un luxe ou une nécessité?" (1990) R.T.D.E. 1–25: 1–026

Biancarelli, J., "Le règlement de procédure du Tribunal de première instance des Communautés européennes: le perfectionnnement dans la continuité" (1991) R.T.D.E. 543–564: 22–069

Biancarelli, J., "Le contrôle de la Cour de justice des Communautés européennes en matière d'aides publiques" (1993) A.J.D.A. 412–436: 5–017, 5–018

Biancarelli, J., "Présentation générale du Tribunal de première instance des Communautés européennes" (1995) R.M.C.U.E. 564–567: 1–026

Bleckmann, A., "Die öffentlichrechtlichen Verträge der EWG" (1978) N.J.W. 464–467: 17–003

Bleckmann, A., "Zur Klagebefugnis für die Individualklage vor dem Europäischen Gerichtshof", in *Festschrift für C.F. Menger—System des verwaltungsgerichtlichen Rechtsschutzes*, Cologne/Berlin/Bonn/Munich, Carl Heymanns Verlag KG, 1985, 871–885: 7–043

Blumann, C., "Régime des aides d'Etat: jurisprudence récente de la Cour de justice (1989–1992)" (1992) R.M.C. 721–739: 5–016

Borchardt, G., "The Award of Interim Measures by the European Court of Justice" (1985) C.M.L.Rev. 203–236: 13–003

Borgsmidt, K., "The Advocate General at the European Court of Justice: A Comparative Study" (1988) E.L.Rev. 106–119: 1–011

Boulouis J. and Darmon, M., *Contentieux communautaire*, Paris, Dalloz, 1997, 467 pp.: 7–117, 13–002

Bradley, K., "Maintaining the Balance: the Role of the Court of Justice in Defining the Institutional Position of the European Parliament" (1987) C.M.L.Rev. 41–64: 7–106

Bradley, K., "The Variable Evolution of the Standing of the European Parliament in Proceedings before the Court of Justice" (1988) Y.E.L. 27–57: 7–032

Brealey, M., "The Burden of Proof before the European Court" (1985) E.L.Rev. 250–262: 22–027

Brealey M. and Hoskins, M., *Remedies in EC Law*, London, Sweet & Maxwell, 1998 (2nd ed.), 3–26, 99–117, 128–148, 154–155, 169–176, 204, 214–224, 227–228, 229–232, 250–254, 271 *et seq.*, 331–332, 345–346, 350–372, 579: 1–004, 2–005, 2–023, 2–047, 2–051, 3–003, 3–007, 3–013, 3–016, 3–023, 5–005, 5–035, 6–013, 7–007, 8–020, 9–001, 11–001, 23–001

Bridge, J., "Procedural Aspects of the Enforcement of European Community Law through the Legal Systems of the Member States" (1984) E.L.Rev. 28–42: 3–002

Bronkhorst, H.J., "The Valid Legislative Act as a Cause of Liability of the Communities", in T. Heukels and A. McDonnell (eds), *The Action for Damages in Community Law*, The Hague, London, Boston, Kluwer Law International, 1997, 153–165: 11–033

Brouwer O., and Carlin, F., "Qualité pour agir dans les procédures anti-dumping après l'arrêt Extramet" (1991) D.P.C.I. 243–267: 7–069

Caranta, R., "Judicial Protection against Member States: a new jus commune takes Shape" (1995) C.M.L.Rev. 703–726: 3–023

Carreau, D., "Droit communautaire et droits nationaux: concurrence ou primauté? La contribution de l'arrêt 'Simmenthal'" (1978) R.T.D.E. 381–418: 3–008

Chevallier, R.-M., and Maidani, D., *Guide pratique. Article 177*, Luxemburg, Office for Official Publications of the European Communities, 1982, 121 pp.: 6–011

Christianos, V., "Le Tribunal de première instance et la nouvelle organisation judiciaire des Communautés européennes", in *Le Tribunal de première instance des Communautés européennes*, Maastricht, European Institute for Public Administration, 1990, 17–50: 1–017

Christianos, V. and Picod, F., "Les modifications récentes du règlement de procédure de la Cour de justice des Communautés européennes" (1991) Rec. Dalloz, Chronique, 273–282: 21–001, 22–080

Christianos, V., "La compétence consultative de la Cour de justice à la lumière du traité sur l'union européenne" (1994) R.M.C.U.E. 37–44: 12–006, 12–013, 12–016

Couzinet, F., "La faute dans le régime de la responsabilité non contractuelle des Communautés européennes" (1986) R.T.D.E. 367–390: 11–034

Curtin, D., "The Decentralised Enforcement of Community Law Rights. Judicial Snakes and Ladders", in *Constitutional Adjudication in European Community and National Law. Essays for the Hon. Mr Justice T.F. O'Higgins*, Dublin, Butterworths (Ireland), 1992, 33–49: 3–003

Cruz Vilaça, J.L., "The Court of First Instance of the European Communities: A Significant Step towards the Consolidation of the European Community as a Community Governed by the Rule of Law" (1990) Y.E.L. 1–56: 1–026

Cruz Vilaça, J.L., "La procédure en référé comme instrument de protection juridictionnelle des particuliers en droit communautaire", in *Scritti in onore di Giuseppe Federico Mancini*, Milan, Giuffrè editore, 1998, II, 257–306: 13–004

Dantonel-Cor, N., "La violation de la norme communautaire et la responsabilité extracontractuelle de l'Etat" (1998) R.T.D.E. 75–91: 3–023

Darmon, M., "Le statut contentieux du Parlement européen", in *L'Europe et le Droit—Mélanges en hommage à J. Boulouis*, Paris, Ed. Dalloz, 1991, 75–96: 7–032

Dashwood, A. and White, R., "Enforcement Actions Under Articles 169 and 170 EEC" (1989) E.L.Rev. 388–413: 5–001, 5–007, 5–033

Bellescize, D. de, "L'article 169 du traité de Rome, et l'efficacité du contrôle communautaire sur les manquements des Etats membres" (1977) R.T.D.E. 173–213: 5–032

Delgrange, X. and Ypersele, P. van, case note in (1997) J.T. 430–434: 2–016

Díez-Hochleitner, J., "Le traité de Maastricht et l'inexécution des arrêts de la Cour de justice par les Etats membres" (1994) R.M.U.E. 111–139: 22–111

Docksey, C., case note in (1995) C.M.L.Rev. 1447–1459: 3–013

Donner, A.M., "Uitlegging en toepassing", in *Miscellanea W.J. Ganshof van der Meersch*, Brussels, Bruylant, 1972, II, 103–126: 6–024

Donner, A.M., "The Constitutional Powers of the Court of Justice of the European Communities" (1974) C.M.L.Rev., 127–140: 1–014

Donner, A.M., "The Court of Justice as a Constitutional Court of the Communities", in *Tussen het echte en het gemaakte*, Zwolle, Tjeenk Willink, 1986, 343–361: 1–014

Dubois, P., "L'exception d'illégalité devant la Cour de justice des Communautés européennes" (1978) C.D.E. 407–439: 9–009, 9–015

Dubouis, L., "Fonctionnaires et agents des Communautés européennes" (1965) R.T.D.E. 666–686; (1966) R.T.D.E. 511–522; (1969) R.T.D.E. 648–

664; (1970) R.T.D.E. 120–144; (1972) R.T.D.E. 376–394; (1975) R.T.D.E. 280–307; (1978) R.T.D.E. 469–515; (1981) R.T.D.E. 710–763; (1983) R.T.D.E. 86–146; (1990) R.T.D.E. 127–169; (1994) R.T.D.E. 237–276: 16–001

Due, O., "A Constitutional Court for the European Communities", in *Constitutional Adjudication in European Community and National Law. Essays for the Hon. Mr. Justice T.F. O'Higgins*, Dublin, Butterworths (Ireland), 1992, 3–10: 1–014

Dumon, F., "La Cour de justice: Questions préjudicielles", in *Les Novelles: Droit des Communautés européennes*, Brussels, Larcier, 1969, 341–366: 6–012

Ebke. W.F., "Les techniques contentieuses d'application du droit des Communautés européennes" (1986) R.T.D.E. 209–230: 5–001

Edward, D.A.O., "How the Court of Justice Works" (1995) E.L.Rev. 539–558: 21–001

Emiliou, N., "State Liability under Community Law: Shedding more Light on the Francovich Principle" (1996) E.L.Rev. 399–411: 3–023

Evans, A.C., "The Enforcement Procedure of Article 169 EEC: Commission Discretion" (1979) E.L.Rev. 442–456: 5–022

European Union/Selected Instruments taken from the Treaties, Book I, Volume I, Luxembourg, Office for Official Publications of the European Communities, 1995, 683–696: 6–004

Ferry, J.E., "Interim Relief under the Rome Treaty—The European Commission's Powers" (1980) E.I.P.R. 330–335: 13–003

Fiebig, A., "The Indemnification of Costs in Proceedings before the European Courts" (1997) C.M.L.Rev. 89–134: 22–115

Fines, F., "Etude de la responsabilité extracontractuelle de la Communauté économique européenne", in *Bibliothéque de droit international*, Vol. 101, Paris, Librairie générale de droit et de jurisprudence, 1990, 501 pp.: 11–001

Fitzpatrick, B. and Szyszczak, E., "Remedies and Effective Judicial Protection in Community Law" (1994) M.L.R. 434–441: 3–023

Flynn, J., "How will Article 100A (4) work? A Comparison with Article 93" (1987) C.M.L.Rev. 689–707: 5–021

Fuss, E.-W., "La responsabilité des Communautés européennes pour le comportement illégal de leurs organes" (1981) R.T.D.E. 1–32: 11–034

Gautron, J.-Cl., "Les compétences du Tribunal de premiére instance" (1995) R.M.C.U.E. 568–575: 1–026

Genevois, B., "Der Conseil d'Etat und das Gemeinschaftsrecht: Antagonismus oder Komplementarität?" (1985) Eu.R. 355–367: 2–051

Gilmour, D., "The Enforcement of Community Law by the Commission in the Context of State Aids: the Relationship Between Article 93 and 169 and the Choice of Remedies" (1981) C.M.L.Rev. 63–77: 5–016

Glaesner, A., "Die Vorlagepflicht unterinstanzlicher Gerichte im Vorabentscheidungsverfahren" (1990) Eu.R. 143–157: 2–004

Goffin, L., "La Cour de justice: Recours en indemnité", in *Les Novelles: Droit des Communautés européennes*, Brussels, Larcier, 1969, 333–339: 11–078

Goffin, L., "Le manquement d'un Etat membre selon la jurisprudence de la Cour de justice des Communautés européennes", in *Mélanges Fernand Dehousse, La construction européenne*, Paris/Brussels, Nathan/Labor, 1979, II, 211–218: 5–022, 5–051, 5–058

Goffin, L., "La recevabilité du recours en indemnité devant la Cour de justice des Communautés européennes" (1981) J.T. 1–5: 11–018

Goffin, L., "De l'incompétence des juridictions nationales pour constater l'invalidité des actes d'institutions communautaires" (1990) C.D.E. 216–226: 2–004

Gormley, L., case note in (1990) C.M.L.Rev. 141–150: 6–029

Gray, C., "Advisory Opinions and the European Court of Justice" (1983) E.L.Rev. 24–39: 12–017

Greaves, R., "Locus Standi under Article 173 EEC when Seeking Annulment of a Regulation" (1986) E.L.Rev. 119–133: 7–043

Greaves, R. "The Nature and Binding Effect of Decisions under Article 189 EC" (1996) E.L.Rev. 3–16: 7–039

Grévisse, F. and Bonichot, J.–Cl., "Les incidences du droit communautaire sur l'organisation et l'exercice de la fonction juridictionnelle dans les Etats membres", in *L'Europe et le Droit—Mélanges en hommage à J. Boulouis*, Paris, Ed. Dalloz, 1991, 297–310: 3–003

Gyselen, L., "La transparence en matière d'aides d'Etat: Les droits des tiers" (1993) C.D.E. 417–444: 7–072

Haardt, W.L., case note in (1966–1967) C.M.L.Rev. 441–444: 2–007

Haguenau, C., "Sanctions pénales destinées à assurer le respect du droit communautaire" (1993) R.M.C. 351–361: 3–020

Harding, C., "The Choice of Court Problem in Cases of Non-Contractual Liability Under EEC Law" (1979) C.M.L.Rev. 389–406: 11–028

Harding, C., "The Private Interest in Challenging Community Action" (1980) E.L.Rev. 354–362: 7–046

Harding, C., "The Impact of Article 177 of the EEC Treaty on the Review of Community Action" (1981) Y.E.L. 93–113: 10–019

Harding, C., "The Review of EEC Regulations and Decisions" (1982) C.M.L.R. 311–323: 7–093

Heidenhain, M., "Zur Klagebefugnis Dritter in der europäischen Fusionskontrolle" (1991) Eu.Z.W. 590–595: 7–071

Hepting, R., "Art. 177 EWGV und die private Schiedsgerichtsbarkeit" (1982) Eu.R. 315–333: 2–011

Hermann-Rodeville, J., "Un exemple de contentieux économique: le recours en indemnité devant la Cour de justice des Communautés européennes" (1986) R.T.D.E. 5–51: 11–031

Heukels, T., "De niet–contractuele aansprakelijkheid van de Gemeenschap ex art. 215, lid 2, EEG: Dynamiek en continuïteit" (1983–1991) (II)" (1992) S.E.W. 317–347: 11–032, 11–036, 11–040

Heukels, T., case note in (1993) C.M.L.Rev. 368–386: 11–049

Heukels, T., case note in (1996) C.M.L.Rev. 337–353: 3–014

Heukels, T. and A. McDonnell, A., "Limitation of the Action for Damages against the Community: Considerations and New Developments", in T. Heukels and McDonnell, (eds), *The Action for Damages in Community Law*, The Hague, London, Boston, Kluwer Law International, 1997, 217–241: 11–077

Honorat, E., "Plaider un pourvoi devant la Cour de justice", in V. Christianos (ed.), *Evolution récente du droit judiciaire communautaire*, Maastricht, European Institute for Public Administration, 1994, I, 21–37: 15–004

Hoskins, M., "Tilting the Balance: Supremacy and National Procedural Rules" (1996) E.L.Rev. 365–377: 98, 3–013

Hubeau, F., La répétition de l'indu en droit communautaire" (1981) R.T.D.E. 442–470: 3–007

Hubeau, F., "Changements des règles de procèdure devant les juridictions communautaires de Luxembourg" (1991) C.D.E. 499–529: 21–001

Hyland, N., "Temporal Limitation of the Effects of Judgments of the Court of Justice—A review of recent case–law" (1995) Ir.J.E.L. 208–233: 10–024

Isaac G., "La modulation par la Cour de justice des Communautés européennes des effets dans le temps de ses arrêts d'invalidité" (1987) C.D.E. 444–470: 10–024

Isaac, G., *Droit communautaire général*, Paris, Masson, 1990, 320 pp.: 6–005

Jacobs, F.G., "Is the Court of Justice of the European Communities a Constitutional Court?", in *Constitutional Adjudication in European Community and National Law. Essays for the Hon. Mr. Justice T.F. O'Higgins*, Dublin, Butterworths (Ireland), 1992, 25–32: 1–014

Jacobs, F.G. "Remedies in National Courts for the Enforcement of Community Rights", in *Liber amicorum Diez de Velasco*, Madrid, Editorial Tecnos, 1993, 969–983: 3–003

Jacqué, J.-P., case note in (1986) R.T.D.E. 500–511: 7–063

Jeantet, Ch. "Originalité de la procédure d'interprétation du traité de Rome" (1966) J.C.P., Doctrine, No 1987: 6–036

Joliet, R., *Le droit institutionnel des Communautés européennes—Le contentieux*, Liège, Faculté de Droit, d'Economie et de Sciences sociales de Liege, 1981, 302 pp.: 2–041, 2–053, 5–001, 6–005, 6–013, 6–036, 7–095, 7–108, 7–135, 9–009, 10–004, 10–017

Joliet R. and Vogel, W., "Le Tribunal de première instance des Communautès européennes" (1989) R.M.C. 423–431: 1–029, 15–009

Joliet, R. "L'article 177 du traité CEE et le renvoi préjudiciel" (1991) Riv.dir.eur. 591–616: 2–057

Joliet, R., Bertrand, V. and Nihoul, P., "Protection juridictionnelle provisoire et droit communautaire" (1992) Riv.dir.eur. 253–284: 3–017, 13–002—13–003, 13–026

Joliet, R., "Coopération entre la Cour de justice des Communautés européennes et les juridictions nationales" (1993) J.T.D.E. 2–8: 3–016

Joris, T., case note in (1993) S.E.W. 698–703: 5–016

Joshua, J., "Balancing the Public Interests: Confidentiality, Trade Secret and Disclosure of Evidence in EC Competition Procedures" (1994) E.Comp.L.Rev. 68–80: 7–109

Jung, H., "Das Gericht erster Instanz der Europäischen Gemeinschaften" (1992) Eu.R 246–264: 1–026

Jung, H., "The Brussels and Lugano Conventions: The European Court's Jurisdiction; its Procedures and Methods" (1992) Civil Justice Quarterly 38–51: 19–002

Kaddous, C., "L'arrêt France c. Commission de 1994 (Accord concurrence) et le contrôle de la 'légalité' des accords externes en vertu de l'art. 173 CE: la difficile réconciliation de l'orthodoxie communautaire avec l'orthodoxie internationale" (1996) C.D.E. 613–633: 10–004

Kakouris, C.N., "Do the Member States possess Judicial Procedural 'Autonomy'?" (1997) C.M.L.Rev. 1389–1412: 3–003

Kapteyn, P.J.G., "The Role of the Court of Justice in the Development of the Community Legal Order", in *Il ruolo del giudice internazionale nell'evoluzione del diritto internazionale e comunitario*, Milan, CEDAM, 1995, 157–173: 1–014

Kapteyn, P.J.G., "Europe's Expectations of its Judges", in R.H.M. Jansen, D.A.G. Koster and R.F.B. Van Zutphen (eds), *European Ambitions of the National Judiciary*, The Hague, London, Boston, Kluwer Law International, 1997, 181–189: 1–002

Karagiannis, S., "L'expression 'accord envisagé' dans l'article 228, §6 du traité CE" (1998) C.D.E. 105–136: 12–010

Kennedy, T., "Paying the Piper: Legal Aid in Proceedings Before the Court of Justice" (1988) C.M.L.Rev. 559–591: 22–125

Kerse, C.S., *EEC Antitrust Procedure* (3rd ed.), London, Sweet & Maxwell, 1994, 474 pp.: 7–019, 13–002

Kerse, C.S., "Procedures in EC Competition Cases: The Oral Hearing" (1994) E.Comp.L.Rev. 40–43: 7–108

Kheitmi, R., "La fonction consultative de la Cour de justice des Communautés européennes" (1967) R.T.D.E. 553–594: 12–017

Kirschner, H. and Klüpfel, K., *Das Gericht erster Instanz der Europäischen Gemeinschaften*, Cologne/Berlin/Bonn/Munich, Carl Heymanns Verlag, 1998, 316 pp.: 1–026

Klinke, U., "Introduction au régime des dépens et à celui de l'assistance judiciaire gratuite", in V. Christianos (ed.), *Evolution récente du droit judiciaire communautaire*, Maastricht, European Institute for Public Administration, 1994, I, 133–164: 22–113

Kornblum, U., "Private Schiedsgerichte und Art. 177 EWGV", in *Jahrbuch für die Praxis der Schiedsgerichtsbarkeit*, Heidelberg, Verlag Recht und Wirtschaf GmbH 1988, 102–110: 2–011

Kovar, R., "La compétence consultative de la Cour de justice et la procédure de conclusion des accords internationaux par la Communauté économique européenne", in *Mélanges offerts à P. Reuter*, Paris, Pedone, 1981, 357–377: 12–001, 12–004, 12–013

Kovar, R., case note in (1987) C.D.E. 300–332: 7–063

Kovar, R., "Cour de justice. Recours préjudiciel en interprétation et en appréciation de validité—Examen de la question préjudicielle par la Cour de justice" (1991) J.C.D.I., vol. 161–26–2, nr. 24: 6–013

Kremlis, G., "De quelques clauses d'élection de for et de droit applicable stipulées dans des contrats de droit privé conclus par les Communautés européennes dans le cadre de leurs activités d'emprunt et de prêt" (1986) Diritto comunitano e degli scambi internazionali 777–793: 17–002

Labayle, H., "La Cour de justice des Communautés et les effets d'une déclaration d'invalidité" (1982) R.T.D.E. 484–510: 10–025

Lagrange, M., "L'action préjudicielle dans le droit interne des Etats membres et en droit communautaire" (1974) R.T.D.E. 268–297: 2–046, 10–009

Langeheine, B., "Judicial Review in the Field of Merger Control" (1992) J.B.L. 121–135: 7–071

Lasok, P., *The European Court of Justice: Practice and Procedure*, London, Butterworths, 1994, 739 pp.: 13–011, 15–013, 22–066

Lauwaars, R.H., *Lawfulness and Legal Force of Community Decisions*, Leiden, Sijthoff, 1973, 355 pp.: 8–006, 9–006, 9–009, 9–015, 9–018

Lauwaars, R.H., "Auxiliary Organs and Agencies in the EEC" (1979) C.M.L.Rev. 365–387: 10–006

Lauwaars, R.H. case note in (1991) S.E.W. 478–480: 3–016

Lenaerts, K., *Le juge et la constitution aux Etats–Unis d'Amérique et dans l'ordre juridique européen*, Brussels, Bruylant, 1988, 817 pp.: 1–014

Lenaerts, K., "Nuclear Border Installations: A Case-Study" (1988) E.L.Rev. 159–187: 5–019

Lenaerts, K., "Le Tribunal de première instance des Communautés européennes: genése et premiers pas" (1990) J.T. 409–415: 1–026, 15–007, 22–066

Lenaerts, K., "The Development of the Judicial Process in the European Community after the Establishment of the Court of First Instance", in *Collected Courses of the Academy of European Law*, Volume I, Book 1, Florence/Dordrecht, European University Institute, Martinus Nijhoff, 1991, 53–113: 1–026

Lenaerts, K., "Some Thoughts about the Interaction between Judges and Politicians" (1992) Y.E.L. 1–34: 1–014

Lenaerts, K., "Rechtsbescherming en rechtsafdwinging: de functies van de rechter in het Europees gemeenschapsrecht" (1992–1993) R.W. 1105–1118: 4–003

Lenaerts, K., "Regulating the Regulatory Process: 'Delegation of Powers' in the European Community" (1993) E.L.Rev. 23–49: 6–015, 7–026, 7–099, 10–006, 11–039

Lenaerts, K., "Form and Substance of the Preliminary Rulings Procedure", in D. Curtin and T. Heukels (eds), *Institutional Dynamics of European Integration. Essays in Honour of H.G. Schermers*, Dordrecht, Martinus Nijhoff, 1994, 355–380: 6–029

Lenaerts K. and Vanhamme, J., "Procedural Rights of Private Parties in the Community Administrative Process" (1997) C.M.L.Rev. 531–569: 7–108

Lenaerts, K., "The Legal Protection of Private Parties under the EC Treaty: a Coherent and Complete System of Judicial Review", in *Scritti in onore di Giuseppe Federico Mancini*, Milan, Giuffrè editore, 1998, II, 591–623: 3–019, 7–064

Lenaerts, K. and Van Nuffel, P., Bray R., (ed.), *Constitutional Law of the European Union*, London, Sweet & Maxwell, 1999, 700 pp.: 1–002, 2–014, 2–051, 4–001, 4–004, 5–005, 5–022, 6–006, 7–026, 7–097, 7–102, 11–043

Lenaerts, K., "Le respect des droits fondamentaux en tant que principe constitutionnel de l'Union européenne", in *Mélanges Michel Waelbroeck*, Brussels, Bruylant, 1998, in the press: 4–001

Mire, P. le, case note in (1994) A.J.D.A. 724–728: 7–006

Lenz, C.O., "Rechtsschutz im Binnenmarkt: Stand und Probleme" (1994) N.J.W. 2063–2067: 4–003

Lipstein, K., "Foglio v. Novello—Some Unexplored Aspects", in *Du droit international au droit de l'intégration—Liber amicorum Pierre Pescatore*, Baden–Baden, Nomos, 1987, 373–385: 2–039

Louis, J.–V. "Le rôle de la Commission dans la procédure en manquement selon la jurisprudence récente de la Cour de justice", in *Du droit international au droit de l'intégration—Liber amicorum Pierre Pescatore*, Baden–Baden, Nomos, 1987, 387–409: 5–054

Louterman, D. and Fébvre, M., "Les incidents de procédure au sens de l'article 91 du Règlement de procédure de la Cour de justice des Communautés européennes" (1989) Gazette du Palais (doctrine) 276–281: 22–086

Lysén, G., "Three Questions on the Non–Contractual Liability of the EEC" (1985) 2 L.I.E.I. 86–120: 11–032—11–033, 11–042

Mahieu, M., "Illégalité et responsabilité en droit communautaire", in *Mélanges Roger O. Dalcq*, Brussels, Larcier, 1994, 388–406: 11–034, 11–047

Mancini, G.F., "Access to Justice: Individual Undertakings and EEC Antitrust Law—Problems and Pitfalls" (1989) Fordham I.L.J. 189–203: 7–071

Mancini, G.F. and Keeling, D., "From CILFIT to ERT: the Constitutional Challenge facing the European Court" (1991) Y.E.L. 1–13: 2–051

Masclet, J.–Cl., "Vers la fin d'une controverse? La Cour de justice tempère l'obligation de renvoi préjudiciel et interprétation faite aux juridictions suprêmes (art. 177), alinea 3, CEE" (1983) R.M.C. 363–373: 2–051

Mathijsen, P., "Nullité et annulabilité des actes des institutions européennes", *Miscellanea W.J. Ganshof van der Meersch*, Brussels, Bruylant, 1972, II, 271–283: 7–006

Mattera, A., "L'ordonnance du 22 avril 1994 sur les 'bus wallons'" (1994) R.M.U.E. 161–171: 13–017

McDonagh, A., "Pour un élargissement des conditions de recevabilité des recours en contrôle de la légalité par des personnes privées en droit communautaire: le cas de l'article 175 du traité CE" (1994) C.D.E. 607–637: 8–014

Mead, Ph., "The Relationship between an Action for Damages and an Action for Annulment: the Return of Plaumann", in T. Heukels and A. McDonnell (eds), *The Action for Damages in Community Law*, The Hague, London, Boston, Kluwer Law International 1997, 243–258: 11–003

Mehdi, R., "Le droit communautaire et les pouvoirs du juge national de l'urgence" (1996) R.T.D.E. 77–100: 3–017

Meij, A.W.H., "Article 215 (2) EC and Local Remedies", in T. Heukels and A. McDonnell (eds), *The Action for Damages in Community Law*, The Hague, London, Boston, Kluwer Law International, 1997, 273–284: 11–020

Mertens de Wilmars, J., "La procédure suivant l'article 177 CEE" (1965) S.E.W. 437–448: 10–009

Mertens de Wilmars, J. and Verougstraete, I., "Proceedings against Member States for Failure to Fulfil their Obligations" (1970) C.M.L.Rev. 385–406: 5–001

Mertens de Wilmars, J., "Het kort geding voor het Hof van Justitie van de Europese Gemeenschappen" (1986) S.E.W. 32–54: 13–005, 13–011

Michel, N., "La protection des droits conférés par l'ordre juridique européen", in P. Tercier, P. Volken and N. Michel (eds), *Aspects du droit européen*, Fribourg, Editions universitaires Fribourg Suisse, 1993, 43–70: 3–003

Millett, T., *The Court of First Instance of the European Communities*, London–Edinburgh, Butterworths, 1990, 144 pp.: 1–026, 15–012

Mischo, J., "Un rôle nouveau pour la Cour de justice?" (1990) R.M.C. 681–686: 1–014

Mischo, J., "The Competence of the Judiciary of the Netherlands Antilles and Aruba to request Preliminary Rulings from the Court of Justice of the European Communities", in *Met het oog op Europa*, Curaçao (1991) Stichting Tijdschrift voor Antilliaans Recht–Justicia 140–145: 2–012

Moitinho de Almeida, J.C., "Le recours en annulation des particuliers (article 173, deuxième alinéa, du traite CE): nouvelles réflexions sur l'expression 'la concernent . . . individuellement' ", *Festschrift für Ulrich Everling*, Baden–Baden, Nomos, 1995, 849–874: 7–052

Moloney, N., case note in (1998) C.M.L.Rev. 731–745: 5–024

Mongin, B., "Les pourvois devant la Cour: Un premier bilan", in *Tendances actuelles et évolution de la jurisprudence de la Cour de justice des Communautés européennes*, Maastricht, European Institute for Public Administration, 1993, 231–242: 15–004, 15–018

Mongin, B., "Le juge national et les mesures provisoires ordonnées en vertu du droit communautaire", in V. Christianos (ed.), *Evolution récente du droit judiciaire communautaire*, Maastricht, European Institute for Public Administration, 1994, 125–131: 3–017

Mortelmans, K.J.M., "Observations in the Cases Governed by Article 177 of the EEC Treaty: Procedure and Practice" (1979) C.M.L.Rev. 557–590: 23–015

Nafilyan, G., "La position des Etats membres et le recours en manquement des article 169 CEE et 141 CEEA" (1977) R.T.D.E. 214–243: 5–001

Neuwahl, N., case note in (1993) C.M.L.Rev. 1185–1195: 12–004

Neuwahl, N., "Article 173 Paragraph 4 EC: Past, Present and Possible Future" (1996) E.L.Rev. 17–31: 7–041

Neville Brown, L., "The First Five Years of the Court of First Instance and Appeals to the Court of Justice: Assessment and Statistics" (1995) C.M.L.Rev. 743–761: 1–026

Nihoul, P., "La recevabilité des recours en annulation introduits par un particulier à l'encontre d'un acte communautaire de portée générale" (1994) R.T.D.E. 171–194: 7–043

Oliver, P., "Le droit communautaire et les voies de recours nationales" (1992) C.D.E. 348–374: 3–003

Oliver, J., "Joint Liability of the Community and the Member States", in T. Heukels and A. McDonnell (eds), *The Action for Damages in Community Law*, The Hague, London, Boston, Kluwer Law International, 1997, 285–310: 11–026—11–027

Oliver, P., case note in (1997) C.M.L.Rev. 635–680: 3–023

Olivier, M., "L'expertise devant les juridictions communautaires" (1994) Gazette du Palais 2–6: 22–075

Pache, E., "Keine Vorlage ohne Anfechtung?" (1994) Eu.Z.W. 615–620: 10–010

Palacio González, J., *El Sistema Judicial Comunitario*, Bilboa, Universidad de Deusto, 1996, 87–94: 1–026

Parkinson, K., "Admissibility of Direct Actions by Natural or Legal Persons in the European Court of Justice: Judicial Distinctions Between Decisions and Regulations" (1989) Texas I.L.J. 433–461: 7–043

Pastor B. and Ginderachter, E. Van., "La procédure en référé" (1989) R.T.D.E. 561–621: 3–017, 13–004, 13–011, 13–014, 13–015, 13–028

Pescatore, P., "Remarques sur la nature juridique des 'décisions des représentants des Etats membres réunis au sein du Conseil'" (1966) S.E.W. 579–586: 5–007

Pescatore, P., "Reconnaissance et contrôle judiclaire des actes du Parlement européen" (1978) R.T.D.E. 581–594: 10–005

Pescatore, M., "Die Gemeinschaftsverträge als Verfassungsrecht—ein Kapitel Verfassungsgeschichte in der Perspektive des europäischen Gerichtshofs, systematisch geordnet", in *Festschrift Kutscher*, Baden–Baden, Nomos, 1981, 319–338: 1–014

Pescatore, P., "Article 177", in *Traité instituant la CEE. Commentaire article par article*, Paris, (1992) Economica Nos 61, 65, 70: 6–026, 6–031, 6–034, 6–038, 10–024

Pfeiffer, T., "Keine Beschwerde gegen EUGH–Vorlagen?" (1994) N.J.W., 1996–2002: 2–027

Piroche, A., "Les mesures provisoires de la Commission des Communautés européennes dans le domaine de la concurrence" (1989) R.T.D.E. 439–469: 13–003

Pisuisse, C.S. case note in (1990) S.E.W. 599–606: 6–029

Plouvier, L., "Le contentieux de pleine juridiction devant la Cour de justice des Communautés européennes" (1973) R.M.C. 365–379: 14–003

Plouvier, L., *Les décisions de la Cour de justice des Communautés européennes et leurs effets juridiques*, Brussels, Bruylant, 1975, 310 pp.: 11–083

Poilvache, F., "Le règlement de procédure de la Cour de justice des Communautés européennes aprés les modifications du 15 mai 1991" (1992) J.T. 337–340: 21–001

Poilvache, F., "Compétence préjudicielle et dispositions nationales inspirées du droit communautaire" (1998) J.T.D.E. 121–125: 6–022

Prechal, S., "Community Law in National Courts: the Lessons from Van Schijndel" (1998) C.M.L.Rev. 681–706: 3–003, 3–014

Ras, H.E., "Een nieuwe taak voor het Hof van Justitie E.G." (1975) N.J.B. 1177–1186: 19–006

Rasmussen, H., "The European Court's Acte Clair Strategy in CILFIT (Or: Acte Clair, of course! But what does it mean?)" (1984) E.L.Rev. 242–259: 2–051

Ress, G., and Ukrow, J., "Direct Actions before the EC Court of Justice. The Case of EEC Anti-dumping Law", in *Adjudication of International Trade Disputes in International and National Economic Law*, Pupil, Volume 7, Fribourg, University Press, 1992, 159–260: 7–066

Rideau J., and Picod, F., *Code de procédures communautaires*, Paris, Litec, 1994, 1075 pp.: 2–053, 5–035, 6–012, 6–017, 6–034

Rideau J. and Picod, F., "Le pourvoi sur les questions de droit" (1995) R.M.C.U.E. 584–601: 15–009

Rinze, J., "The Role of the European Court of Justice as a Federal Constitutional Court" (1993) P.L. 426–443: 1–014

Röben, V., *Die Einwirkung der Rechtsprechung des Europäischen Gerichtshofs auf das Mitgliedstaatliche Verfahren in öffentlichrechtlichen Streitigkeiten*, Berlin, Springer Verlag, 1998, 478 pp.: 3–003

Rodríguez Iglesias, G.C., "Der Gerichtshof der Europäischen Gemeinschaften als Verfassungsgericht" (1992) Eu.R. 225–245: 1–014

Rodríguez Iglesias, G.C. "Zu den Grenzen der verfahrensrechtlichen Autonomie der Mitgliedstaaten bei der Anwendung des Gemeinschaftsrechts" (1997) Eu.Gr.Z. 289–295: 3–003

Rogalla, D., *Dienstrecht der Europäischen Gemeinschaften*, Cologne/Berlin/Bonn/Munich, Carl Heymanns Verlag KG, 1992, 328 pp.: 16–001

Scherer J. and Zuleeg, M., "Verwaltungsgerichtsbarkeit", in M. Schweitzer (ed.), *Europäisches Verwaltungsrecht*, Vienna, Verlag der österreichischen Akademie der Wissenschaften, 1991, 197–240: 1–025

Schermers, H.G., "The European Court of First Instance" (1988) C.M.L.Rev. 541–558: 15–006

Schermers, H.G., case note in (1992) C.M.L.Rev. 133–139: 3–017

Schermers, H.G., and Waelbroeck, D., *Judicial Protection in the European Communities*, Deventer, Kluwer, 1992; 585 pp.: 2–013, 5–058, 7–005, 7–042, 7–043, 7–087, 8–009, 11–036, 22–082, 22–106, 22–112

Schermers H.G. and Swaak, C.P.A., "Official Acts of Community Servants and Article 215 (4) EC", in T. Heukels and A. McDonnell (eds), *The Action for Damages in Community Law*, The Hague, London, Boston, Kluwer Law International, 1997, 167–178: 11–017

Schneider, J.P., "Effektiver Rechtsschutz Privater gegen EG–Richtlinien nach dem Maastricht–Urteil des Bundesverfassungsgerichts" (1994) Archiv des öffentlichen Rechts 294–320: 7–044

Schockweiler, F., "L'exécution des arrêts de la Cour", in *Du droit international au droit de l'intégration—Liber Pierre Pescatore*, Baden–Baden, Nomos, 1987, 613–635: 2–057, 22–111

Schockweiler, F., Wivines G. and Godart, J.M., "Le régime de la responsabilité extra–contractuelle du fait d'actes juridiques dans la Communauté européenne" (1990) R.T.D.E. 27–74: 11–034, 11–037, 11–046

Schockweiler, F., "La notion de détournement de pouvoir en droit communautaire" (1990) A.J.D.A. 435–443: 7–121

Schockweiler, F., "La responsabilité de l'autorité nationale en cas de violation du droit communautaire" (1992) R.T.D.E. 27–50: 5–064

Schockweiler, F., "Die Haftung der EG–Mitgliedstaaten gegenüber dem einzelnen bei Verletzung des Gemeinschaftsrechts" (1993) Eu.R. 107–133: 11–018

Schwartz, I., "Voies d'uniformisation du droit dans la CEE: règlements de la Communauté ou conventions entre les Etats membres" (1978) J.D.I. 751–804: 5–007

Simon D. and Barav, A., "Le droit communautaire et la suspension provisoire des mesures nationales: Les enjeux de l'affaire Factortame" (1990) R.M.C. 591–597: 3–016

Slot, P.J., Procedural Aspects of State Aids: the Guardian of Competition versus the Subsidy Villains?" (1990) C.M.L.Rev. 741–760: 5–014

Slynn, Lord, of Hadley, "What is a European Community Law Judge?" (1993) Cambridge L.J. 234–244: 1–002

Smit and Herzog (now Campbell and Powers), *The Law of the European Community*, New York, Matthew Bender & Co., 1976, 5–321, 5–540–541: 5–022, 9–001

Sonelli, S., "Appeals on points of law in the Community system. A review" (1998) C.M.L.Rev. 871–900: 15–004

Spinks, S.O., note to *Automec v. Commission* (1991) C.M.L.R. 453–462: 7–022

Storm, P.M., case note in (1967) C.D.E. 311-320: 2–007

Storm, P.M., "Quod licet iovi. The Precarious Relationship between the Court of Justice of the European Communities and Arbitration", in *Essays on International and Comparative Law in Honour of Judge Erades*, The Hague, T.M.C. Asser Institute, 1983, 144–177: 2–011

Stuyck, J. and Wytinck, P., case note in (1991) C.M.L.Rev. 205–223: 6–007

Szyszczak, E., "Making Europe more Revelant to its Citizens: Effective Judicial Process" (1996) E.L.Rev. 351–364: 3–003

Szyszczak, E. and Delicostopoulos, J., "Intrusions into National Procedural Autonomy: The French Paradigm" (1997) E.L.Rev. 141–149: 3–014

Szyszczak, S., case note in (1992) C.M.L.Rev. 604–614: 3–013

Tatham, A.F., "Restitution of Charges and Duties levied by the Public Administration in Breach of European Community Law: a Comparative Analysis" (1994) E.L.Rev. 146–168: 11–026

Tebbens, H., Kennedy, T., Kohler, C., (eds) (trans. Bray, R., and Baillie, A.), *Civil jurisdiction and Judgments in Europe*, London, Butterworths, 1993, 408 pp.: 19–002

Temple Lang, J., "Article 5 of the EEC Treaty: the Emergence of Constitutional Principles in the Case Law of the Court of Justice" (1987) Fordham I.L.J. 503–537: 3–021

ter Kuile, B.H., "To Refer or not to Refer: About the Last Paragraph of Article 177 of the EC Treaty", in D. Curtin and T. Heukels (eds), *Institutional Dynamics of European Integration. Essays in Honour of H.G. Schermers*, Dordrecht, Martinus Nijhoff, 1994, II, 381–389: 2–054

Tesauro, G., "La sanction des infractions au droit communautaire" (1992) Riv.dir.eur. 477–509: 3–020

Tesauro, G., "Responsabilité des Etats membres pour violation du droit communautaire" (1996) R.M.U.E. 15–34: 3–023

Thomas, B., "Infractions et manquements des Etats membres au droit communautaire" (1991) R.M.C. 887–892: 5–022

Timmermans, C.W.A., case note in (1987) C.M.L.Rev. 93: 3–017

Timmermans, C.W.A., "Judicial Protection against the Member States: Articles 169 and 177 Revisited", in D. Curtin and T. Heukels (eds), *Institutional Dynamics of European Integration: Essays in Honour of H.G. Schermers*, Dordrecht, Martinus Nojhoff, 1994, 391–407: 5–023

Tizzano, A., "Litiges fictifs et compétence préjudicielle de la Cour de justice européenne" (1981) R.G.D.I.P. 514–528: 2–039

Tomuschat, C., *Die gerichtliche Vorabentscheidung nach den Verträgen über die Europäischen Gemeinschaften*, Berlin/Heidelberg/New York, Springer-Verlag, 1964, 226 pp.: 10–010

Toth, A.G., "The Law as it stands on the Appeal for Failure to Act" (1975) 2 L.I.E.I. 65–93: 8–009

Toth, A.G., "The Authority of Judgments of the European Court of Justice: Binding Force and Legal Effects" (1984) Y.E.L. 1–77: 6–037, 22–111

Toth, A.G., case note in (1990) C.M.L.Rev. 573–587: 3–016

Toth, A.G., "The Concepts of Damage and Causality as Elements of Non-contractual Liability", in T. Heukels and A. McDonnell (eds), *The Action for Damages in Community Law*, The Hague, London, Boston, Kluwer Law International, 1997, 179–198: 11–050, 11–056, 11–059, 11–065

Trabucchi, A., "L'effet erga omnes des décisions préjudicielles rendues par la CJCE" (1974) R.T.D.E. 56–87: 6–036

Tridimas, T., "The Role of the Advocate General in the Development of Community Law: Some Reflections" (1997) C.M.L.Rev. 1349–1387: 1–004

Usher, J., "The Interrelationship of Articles 173, 177 and 184 EEC" (1979) E.L.Rev. 36–39: 9–009

Vandersanden, G., and Barav, A., *Contentieux communautaire*, Brussels, (1977) Bruylant, 722 pp.: 6–012, 6–013, 7–092, 7–095

Vandersanden, G., "Une naissance désirée: le Tribunal de première instance des Communautés européennes" (1988) J.T. 545–548: 1–017

Vandersanden, G., case note in (1989) C.M.L.Rev. 551–561: 7–029

Vandersanden, G. and Dony, M., *La responsabilité des Etats membres en cas de violation du droit communautaire*, Brussels, Bruylant, 1997, 413 pp.: 3–023

van der Woude, M.H., "Le Tribunal de première instance 'Les trois premières années' " (1992) R.M.U.E. 113–157: 1–026

van der Woude, M.H., "Liability for Administrative Acts under Article 215(2) E.C.", in T. Heukels and McDonnell (eds), *The Action for Damages in Community Law*, The Hague, London, Boston, Kluwer Law International, 1997, 109–128: 11–036

van Gerven, W., "De niet-contractuele aansprakelijkheid van de Gemeenschap wegens normatieve handelingen" (1976) S.E.W. 2–28: 11–042

van Gerven, W., "Non-Contractual Liability of Member States, Community Institutions and Individuals for Breaches of Community Law with a View to a Common Law for Europe" (1994) *Maastricht Journal of European and Comparative Law* 6–40: 11–033, 11–055

van, Gerven, W., "Bridging the Gap between Community and National Laws: towards a Principle of Homogeneity in the Field of Legal Remedies?" (1995) C.M.L.Rev. 679–702: 3–003

van Gerven, W., "Bridging the Unbridgeable: Community and National Tort Laws after Francovich and Brasserie" (1996) I.C.L.Q. 507–544: 3–023

Van Ginderachter, E., "Recevabilité des recours en matière de dumping" (1987) C.D.E. 623–666: 7–069

Van Ginderachter, E., "Le Tribunal de première instance des Communautés européennes. Un nouveau–né prodige?" (1989) C.D.E. 63–105: 1–026

Van Ginderachter, E., "Le référé en droit communautaire" (1993) Rev.dr.ULB 113–145: 13–002

Van Raepenbusch, S., "Le contentieux de la fonction publique européenne", in *Tendances actuelles et évolution de la jurisprudence de la Cour de justice des Communautés européennes*, Maastricht, European Institute for Public Administration, 1993, 95–131: 16–003, 16–005

van Rijn, T., *Exceptie van onwettigheid en prejudiciële procedure inzake geldigheid van gemeenschapshandelingen*, Deventer, Kluwer, 1978, 292 pp.: 9–001, 9–005, 9–006, 9–009, 9–015, 9–017—9–018, 10–004

van Rijn, T., case note in (1980) C.D.E. 190–205: 9–009

Vaughan, D. and Lasok, P., *Butterworths European Court Practice*, London, Butterworths, 1993, 581 pp.: 15–012, 22–038, 22–073, 22–107

Vesterdorf, B., "The Court of First Instance of the European Communities after Two Full Years of Operation" (1992) C.M.L.Rev. 897–915: 1–026, 22–066

Vlas, P., "The Protocol on Interpretation of the EEC Convention on Jurisdiction and Enforcement of Judgments: Over Ten Years in Legal Practice (1975–1985)" (1986) N.I.L.R. 84–98: 19–010

von Heydebrand und der Lasa, H.C., "Die Nichtigkeitsklage von Unternehmen aus Drittländern vor dem EuGH gegen 'Verordnungen' im Bereich des Antidumpingsrechts" (1985) N.J.W. 1257–1259: 7–043

Waelbroeck, D., "Le principe de la non–rétroactivité en droit communautaire à la lumière des arrêts 'isoglucose' " (1983) R.T.D.E. 363–392: 10–025

Waelbroeck, D., "Le transfert des recours directs au Tribunal de première instance des Communautés européennes—vers une meilleure protection judiciaire des justiciables?", in *La réforme du système juridictionnel communautaire*, Brussels, Editions de l'Université de Bruxelles, 1994, 87–97: 15–001

Waelbroeck, D. and Verheyden, A.-M., "Les conditions de recevabilité des recours en annulation des particuliers contre les actes normatifs communautaires" (1995) C.D.E. 399–441: 7–041

Waelbroeck, D. and Fosselard, D., case note in (1996) C.M.L.Rev. 811–829: 7–060

Waelbroeck, M., Waelbroeck, D. and Vandersanden, G., La Cour de Justice, in M. Waelbroeck, J.-V. Louis, D. Vignes, J.-L. Dewost, G.

Vandersanden, *Commentaire Megret*, Vol. 10, Brussels, Editions de l'Université de Bruxelles, 1993, 666 pp.: 5–001, 5–040, 6–012, 6–016, 9–006, 9–008, 10–004—10–005, 10–010, 13–003, 13–005, 13–011, 13–026, 14–003, 14–007, 16–001, 16–003, 16–016, 17–004, 17–014, 22–014, 22–073, 22–119, 22–133

Waelbroeck, M. and Waelbroeck, D., *Répertoire de droit communautaire*,
key words: Exception d'illégalité, Paris, (1994/2), Ed. Dalloz: 398
key words: Carence (recours en), 1994/1: 387
key words: Responsabilité (de la Communauté), 1994/3: 11–005

Wainwright, R., "Article 186 EEC: Interim Measures and Member States" (1977) E.L.Rev. 349–354: 13–005

Walsh, D., "The Appeal of an Article 177 EEC Referral" (1993) M.L.R. 881–886: 2–027

Ward, A., "Government Liability in the United Kingdom for Breach of Individual Rights in European Community Law" (1990) 1 Anglo-Am.L.R. 35: 3–003

Watson, P., case note in (1987) C.M.L.Rev. 89–97: 3–017

Wegener, B., "Keine Klagebefugnis für Greenpeace und 18 andere. Anmerkung zu EuGH, Rs C–321/95 P (Greenpeace)" (1998) Zeitschrift für Umweltrecht 131–135: 7–052

Weiler, J., "The Court of Justice on Trial. Review Essay of Hjalte Rasmussen: On Law and Policy in the European Court of Justice" (1987) C.M.L.Rev. 555–589: 1–014

Weib, W., "Die Einschränkung der zeitlichen Wirkungen von Vorabentscheidungen nach Art. 177 EGV" (1995) EuR. 377–397: 10–024

Wijckerheld Bisdom, C.R.C., "Enige bijzonderheden over de rechtsgang van het Hof van Justitie van de Europese Gemeenschappen", in *Individuele rechtsbescherming in de Europese Gemeenschappen*, Deventer, Antwerp, Kluwer, 1964, 59–73: 22–018

Wils, W., "Concurrent Liability of the Community and a Member State" (1992) E.L.Rev. 191–206: 11–018

Winter, J.A., "Supervision of State Aid: Article 93 in the Court of Justice" (1993) C.M.L.Rev. 311–329: 5–014

Wooldridge, F., "Disguised Contributions in Kind; the European Court Refuses a Preliminary Ruling on Hypothetical Questions" (1993) 2 L.I.E.I. 69–81: 2–023

Zuleeg, M., "Der Beitrag des Strafrechts zur europäischen Integration" (1992) J.Z. 761–769: 3–020

INDEX

(All references are to paragraph number)